MONKS, MARTYRS, SOLDIERS AND SARACENS

Philip Mayerson

MONKS, MARTYRS, SOLDIERS AND SARACENS

Papers on the Near East in Late Antiquity
(1962–1993)

Published by
The Israel Exploration Society
in association with
New York University
Jerusalem 1994

ISBN 965-221-025-0

TABLE OF CONTENTS

List of plates   ix

Introduction   1

1 "Agricultural Evidence in the Colt Papyri" (The Ancient Agricultural
Regime of Nessana and the Central Negev). *Excavations at Nessana*, Vol.
I, H. D. Colt, ed. London, 1962, pp. 224–269.   21

2 "The Desert of Southern Palestine According to Byzantine Sources". *Proceedings of the American Philosophical Society* 107, No. 2 (1963), pp.
160–172.   40

3 "The First Muslim Attacks on Southern Palestine (A.D. 633–634)". *Transactions and Proceedings of the American Philological Association* 95 (1964),
pp. 155–199.   53

4 "The Issue of the Teleilat el-'Anab". *Bulletin of the American Schools of Oriental Research* 178 (1965), p. 69.   99

5 "A Note on Demography and Land Use in the Ancient Negeb". *Bulletin of
the American Schools of Oriental Research* 185 (1967), pp. 39–43.   100

6 "Observations on the 'Nilus' *Narrationes*: Evidence for an Unknown Christian Sect?". *Journal of the American Research Center in Egypt* 12 (1975), pp.
51–74.   105

7 "An Inscription in the Monastery of St. Catherine and the Martyr Tradition
in Sinai". *Dumbarton Oaks Papers* 30 (1976), pp. 375–379.   129

8 "Procopius or Eutychius on the Construction of the Monastery at Mount
Sinai: Which is the More Reliable Source". *Bulletin of the American Schools
of Oriental Research* 230 (1978), pp. 33–38.   134

9 "Anti-Black Sentiment in the *Vitae Patrum*". *Harvard Theological Review*
79 (1979), pp. 304–311.   140

10 "The Ammonius Narrative: Bedouin and Blemmye Attacks in Sinai". *The
Bible World, Essays in Honor of Cyrus H. Gordon*, G. Rendsburg, et. al. eds.
New York, 1980, pp. 133–148.   148

11 "Mauia, Queen of the Saracens — A Cautionary Note". *Israel Exploration
Journal* 30 (1980), pp. 123–131.   164

12 "The Clysma–Phara–Haila Road on the Peutinger Table". *Coins, Culture,
and History in the Ancient World, Numismatic and Other Studies in Honor
of Bluma L. Trell*. Detroit, 1981, pp. 167–176.   173

13 "The Pilgrim Routes to Mount Sinai and the Armenians". *Israel Exploration Journal* 32 (1982), pp. 44–57. 183

14 "The City of Elusa in the Literary Sources of the Fourth–Sixth Centuries". *Israel Exploration Journal* 33 (1983), pp. 247–253. 197

15 "P. Oxy. 3574: 'Eleutheropolis of the New Arabia'". *Zeitschrift für Papyrologie und Epigraphik* 53 (1983), pp. 251–258. 204

16 "Codex Sinaiticus: An Historical Observation". *Biblical Archaeologist* (1983), pp. 54–56. 212

17 "Antiochus Monachus' Homily on Dreams: An Historical Note". *Journal of Jewish Studies* 35 (1984), pp. 51–56. 216

18 "Wheat in the Roman World: An Addendum". *Classical Quarterly* 34 (1984), pp. 243–245. 222

19 "'Palaestina' vs. 'Arabia' in the Byzantine Sources". *Zeitschrift für Papyrologie und Epigraphik* 56 (1984), pp. 223–230. 224

20 "Urbanization in *Palaestina Tertia*: Pilgrims and Paradoxes". Originally published in Hebrew in *Cathedra* 45 (1987), pp. 19–40. 232

21 "The Wine and Vineyards of Gaza in the Byzantine Period". *Bulletin of the American Schools of Oriental Research* 257 (1985), pp. 75–80. 250

22 "Nea Arabia (P. Oxy. 3574): An Addendum to *ZPE* 53". *Zeitschrift für Papyrologie und Epigraphik* 64 (1986), pp. 139–148. 256

23 "The Beersheba Edict". *Zeitschrift für Papyrologie und Epigraphik* 64 (1986), pp. 141–148. 259

24 "Choricius of Gaza on the Watersupply System of Caesarea". *Israel Exploration Journal* 36 (1986), pp. 269–272. 267

25 "The Saracens and the *Limes*". *Bulletin of the American Schools of Oriental Research* 262 (1986), pp. 35–47. 271

26 "Libanius and the Administration of Palestine". *Zeitschrift für Papyrologie und Epigraphik* 69 (1987), pp. 251–260. 284

27 "Justinian's Novel 103 and the Reorganization of Palestine". *Bulletin of the American Schools of Oriental Research* 269 (1988), pp. 65–71. 294

28 "A Note on the Roman *Limes*: 'Inner' versus 'Outer'". *Israel Exploration Journal* 38 (1988), pp. 181–183. 301

29 "*P. Ness.* 58 and Two *Vaticinia*: *ex Eventu* in Hebrew". *Zeitschrift für Papyrologie und Epigraphik* 77 (1989), pp. 283–286. 304

30 "The Meaning of the Word *Limes* (λίμιτον) in the Papyri". *Zeitschrift für Papyrologie und Epigraphik* 77 (1989), pp. 287–291. 308

31 "Saracens and Romans: Micro–Macro Relationships". Bulletin of the American Schools of Oriental Research 274 (1989), pp. 71–79.   313

32 "The Word Saracen (Σαρακηνός) in the Papyri". *Zeitschrift für Papyrologie und Epigraphik* 79 (1989), pp. 283–287.   322

33 "Towards a Comparative Study of a Frontier". *Israel Exploration Journal* 40 (1990), pp. 267–279.   327

34 "The Words τονάχιον and γονάχιον in the Egyptian Papyri". *Zeitschrift für Papyrologie und Epigraphik* 83 (1990), pp. 241–242.   340

35 "The Use of the Term *Phylarchos* in the Roman–Byzantine East". *Zeitschrift für Papyrologie und Epigraphik* 88 (1991), pp. 291–295.   342

36 "The Gaza 'Wine' Jar (*Gazition*) and the 'Lost' Ashkelon Jar (*Askalônion*)". *Israel Exploration Journal* 42 (1992), pp. 76–80.   347

37 "The Island of Iotabê — A Reprise". *Bulletin of the American Schools of Oriental Research* 287 (1992).   352

38 The Meaning and Etymology of the Word μαν(ν)ούθιον. "*Studies in the Archaeology and History of Ancient Israel in Honor of Moshe Dothan*", H. Heltzer, A. Segal and D. Kaufman (eds.), Haifa University, 1993, pp. 195–197.   356

39 A Confusion of Indias: Asian India and African India in the Byzantine Sources. *Journal of the American Oriental Society*, 113 (1993), pp. 169–174.   361

40 "The Use of Ascalon Wine in the Medical Writers of the Fourth to the Seventh Centuries". *Israel Exploration Journal* 43 (1993), pp. 169–173.   367

LIST OF PLATES

Pl. 1. The Monastery of St. Catherine in Sinai (cover photo).

Pl. 2. Nessana (formerly Auja el-Hafir): Aerial view of excavated fort and churches on the acropolis.   **4**

Pl. 3. Nessana: Architect's rendering of the Martyrium, North Church, fort and South Church.   **4**

Pl. 4. Nessana: Architect's rendering of fort and North Church complex.   **5**

Pl. 5. Nessana: Recently excavated church east of the acropolis.   **5**

Pl. 6. A papyrus document from Nessana, *P. Ness.* 82, recording amounts of wheat, barley and vetch (?) sown and reaped.   **39**

Pl. 7. Avdat (ancient Eboda/Oboda): Aerial view of the site, fort and churches within the military installation.   **98**

Pl. 8. Avdat: The acropolis with fort, North Church, South Church and monastic buildings (?).   **98**

Pl. 9. The fortified monastery built by Justinian in Sinai, now known as the Monastery of St. Catherine.   **133**

Pl. 10. Shifta (ancient Sobata): Aerial view of the excavated town. Note reservoir and church near the center of the town.   **246**

Pl. 11. The South Church of Shifta.   **247**

Pl. 12. The Central Church of Shifta.   **247**

Pl. 13. The North Church of Shifta.   **248**

Pl. 14. Ruheiba/Raheiba (ancient name unknown): Aerial view of the town. Note the excavated church in the upper left of photograph.   **248**

Pl. 15. Kurnub (ancient Mampsis): Aerial view of the excavated town with its two churches. Note the building outside its walls (caravanserai?).   **249**

Pl. 16. Khalasa (ancient Elousa): Aerial view of the town, former administrative center of *Palaestina Tertia*, now robbed of most of its stone and covered with sand.   **249**

Pl. 17. The "Beersheba" inscription.   **258**

Pl. 18. The Monastery of St. George (Choziba) in the Wadi Qelt.   **359**

Pl. 19. The Monastery of Mar Saba in the Wadi Kidron.   **360**

Pl. 20. The excavated Monastery of Euthymius (Khan el-Ahmar) in the plain of Adumim.   **360**

*To Miriam and Clare
and Joy*

INTRODUCTION

Between the covers of this volume are papers covering a variety of topics pertaining to the subject matter printed on the title page. These forty papers cover a period of some forty years of work, and, since they are mostly concerned with Palestine and Sinai, I take the number to be a good omen, even though factitious. Be that as it may, the reader will find that many papers are adversarial or rebuttals of positions taken by other scholars. They range from a few pages to what the late Herbert Youtie, a distinguished papyrologist, called "scriptiunculae". Other papers are lengthier, and address problems from a different point of view, or present a synthesis of material recently come to light and in need of investigation.

The papers are printed in the order in which they were published. To alleviate the inconvenience of this arrangement for the reader, I have provided abstracts of the forty papers following a short historical sketch. The rationale for this somewhat prosaic arrangement is the active process by which these papers came to be written over a period of four decades: ideas come to mind, questions arise, and new material comes to light demanding further investigation and consequent publication. Let me give an illustration. Most scholars have accepted as a given that Palaestina Salutaris (= Tertia) was organized ca. 358, usually citing Brünnow and Domaszewski, who themselves cite earlier scholars. I used that date myself, but after working on *P. Oxy.* 3574 (Papers Nos. 15 and 22), I began to question it. I looked into the primary source material, mostly Libanius, and found the basis for ca. 358 wanting. More substantial evidence was found in works of Jerome and others, making it more than highly plausible that the province was organized ca. 390 (Papers Nos. 19 and 26). As for one thing leading to another, my pursuit of the Saracens led me from Palestine and Sinai to Jordan, Egypt, Syria, Mesopotamia, South Arabia and Ethiopia, and to an island in the Red Sea.

My attention was directed to Late Antiquity[1] in the Near East — generally not a field of interest for a classicist — by a chance find in the Negev of Southern Palestine. An archaeological expedition led by H. D. Colt, between the years 1935 and 1937, at a remote site called Auja el-Hafir near the Sinai border, chanced upon a

---

1 I use the words "Late Antiquity" to indicate historical events, conditions and artifacts in the Near East from the time of Constantine the Great to that of the Umayyad caliphs. Although many of my papers use the conventional term "Byzantine" to encompass this period, there has been a tendency of late, especially among archaeologists, to use terms such as "Late Roman" or "Byzantine–Early Arab" to cover the same period of time.

1

cache of papyrological documents that had been preserved by the collapse of a wattle-roof over a storeroom. The documents were turned over to New York University, where, under the direction of C. J. Kraemer, three volumes were submitted for publication under the title of *Excavations at Nessana* (the name of the site was revealed in the papyri). Volume I contained the archaeological report; Volume II consisted of literary material, sacred and secular; and Volume III contained the non-literary papyri, comprising 180 major and minor documents dating from the beginning of the sixth to the end of the seventh century A.D., from the reign of Anastasius (491–518) well into the time of the Umayyad caliphs.

It is evident from the material uncovered at Nessana (churches, martyrium, inscriptions, papyri and agricultural installations) that monasticism and the organized church provided the energy and vitality for settled life in the southern desert of Palestine. The same may be said of Nessana's sister communities in the Negev highlands.

In the fourth century A.D., a new phase of settlement began in the Negev highlands, after a hiatus of several centuries of Nabataean control. The region renewed itself following the acceptance of Christianity as the official religion of the Roman state and the rise of anchorite and of monastic movements inspired by the charisma of such holy men as Saints Antony and Pachomius in Egypt and Hilarion in Palestine. Sites formerly occupied by Nabataeans, or populated by their remnants, were repopulated to an extent far beyond that of the Nabataeans or their predecessors during the Iron Age. In place of the trading communities of the Nabataeans came eremites, monastic orders and the church. At a focal point on the Sinai Peninsula, a somewhat similar development took place. At Mount Sinai — often called "the Holy Mountain" — where, according to tradition, Moses conversed with God and received the Law, solitaries and their cells abounded in the region surrounding the site. A church took root at the foot of the mountain and gradually extended its influence to the oasis of Pharan, where it was believed that the Israelite tribes fought and defeated the Amalekites.

The movement into the traditional deserts of the Hebrew Bible brought the population into touch and conflict with an equally traditional denizen, the Bedouin, known at that time by the Greek-speaking people as Saracens or Ishmaelites. This nomadic population earned its livelihood in great measure by trading and raiding. For the raiding Saracen, the unguarded monastic community was a target of opportunity; the eremite even more so. The Saracen also provided, for a fee, a number of services for isolated communities: he was a guide through the wilderness, he transported provisions and supplies, and carried messages between distant outposts. There were peaceful Saracens and outlaw Saracens; they could be one and the same, depending upon conditions of security and relationships with local and imperial authorities. The pious monks — the "saints" of popular belief — who were unfortunate enough to be victims of marauding Saracens — earned their martyrdom "through a baptism of blood".

Since life on the frontiers of the empire was hazardous, the imperial government was compelled — and vigorously petitioned by ecclesiastics and townsmen — to provide protection in the form of mobile (para)military forces, and, in more remote places, fortifications. Nessana, for example, situated at a crossroads and at the entrance to the Sinai wilderness, had a fortress to serve mostly as a place of refuge in the event of a Saracen attack in large numbers. A camel corps was also based at the town, presumably to protect not only the community, but also merchants on their way to ports on the Mediterranean and the Red Sea, although the Nessana documents do not reflect caravan trade of the kind that had been carried on by the Nabataeans. In this region, pilgrimage in large measure took the place of caravan trade, and the military unit undoubtedly helped to protect the hundreds of pilgrims as they made their way to and from the celebrated religious site at Mount Sinai.

Pilgrims came from all parts of the Roman world to visit biblical sites, to witness the spiritual discipline of the monks, to pray at the tombs of the martyrs who had fallen through imperial persecution and by Saracen weapons, and to touch — or purchase — their relics. The cult of saints and martyrs, along with imperial and private largess to the church and monastic orders, spurred the economy. The settled population grew exponentially. The deserts of the Near East, to adapt a phrase from Athanasius, the biographer of St. Antony, became cities, at least in those areas where Rome and Persia were not engaged in their century-long struggle. As for the highland region of the Central Negev, it too had undergone a transformation. Hamlets became villages; villages became towns. Churches and chapels were constructed in numbers that exceeded the spiritual needs of the local population. Large numbers of farmsteads and terraced farmlands existed at a considerable distance from settled communities, apparently safe, if not from banditry of individuals, at least from tribal attacks. The region became open country.

The beginning of the end came with two major defeats for Rome: one by the Persians in 614 and the other by the Arabs in 636. Under the Umayyad caliphs, Muslims and Christians lived side by side, but as the Islamic conquest swept over more favorable lands, and with an Abbasid caliphate hostile to Christianity, the deserts resumed their ancient character. By the ninth century, the bedouin once more ruled the desert. The thriving communities of the Negev highlands were abandoned along with their churches, reliquaries, monasteries and monastic cells. Only a few pockets of their former life survived, as, for example, the Monastery at Saint Catherine at the foot of Mount Sinai.

A number of observations in this brief historical sketch have their origin in the finds of the Colt Archaeological Expedition, the richest of which were the Nessana documents, the first major collection of papyri to be uncovered in Palestine. It was the non-literary documents that caught my eye, particularly the significant number concerned with agriculture. To witness active agricultural activity in an arid region, lacking perennial sources of water, and with an average rainfall of 85 mm. (less than 4 inches) — means far insufficient for raising the crops of wheat and barley mentioned in the papyri — was, to say the least, most unusual. I undertook an investigation of this phenomenon, first in the form of a Ph.D. dissertation, and then, with a grant from the Rockefeller Foundation, through an archaeological survey of the Central Negev in 1956–57. The outcome of the Sinai War in 1956 made it possible for me to work alone, without need of a military escort. It also enabled me to make a survey of North Sinai, particularly the area around Ain Qudeirat (Kadeis Barnea).

Pl. 2. Nessana (formerly Auja el-Hafir): Aerial view of excavated fort and churches on the acropolis.

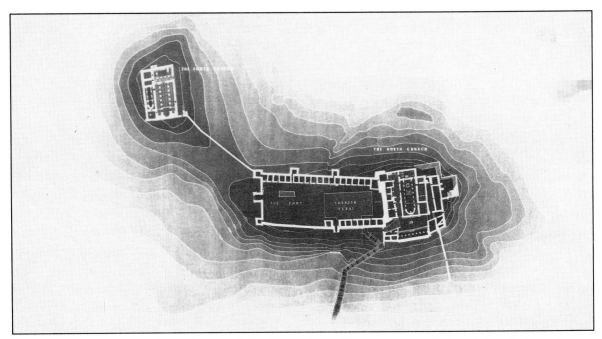

Pl. 3. Nessana: Architect's rendering of the Martyrium, North Church, fort and South Church.

4

Pl. 4. Nessana: Architect's rendering of fort and North Church complex.

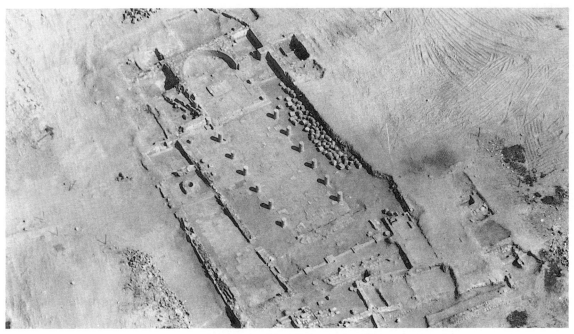

Pl. 5. Nessana: Recently excavated church east of the acropolis.

Paper No. 1   My survey, the first detailed one of its kind, focused upon the floodwater systems which enabled the inhabitants to augment a meager supply of rainfall in order to produce crops of wheat and barley. My report also included such aspects of the physical environment of the Central Negev as topography, soils, climate (rainfall and dewfall), water resources and floodwater. Since a unique document, *P. Colt* 82 (= *P. Ness.* 82), provides information on the number of *modii* of wheat and barley sown and the amount reaped, I visited a number of Bedouin tribes of the Negev, and, with the aid of an interpreter, inquired into the amounts they sowed and the yield they obtained in good, average and poor years. (These semi-nomadic tribes repaired some of the ancient floodwater systems and sowed crops of wheat and barley. They also had small gardens of fruit trees and vines.) The results of my survey were first published as a monograph under the auspices of the British School of Archaeology in Jerusalem: *The Ancient Agricultural Regime of Nessana and the Central Negeb*. It was then included in Volume I of the final publication of the Colt Expeditiion. I publish here a segment of that report analyzing the agricultural evidence in the Colt papyri (Paper No. 1).

Papers Nos. 4, 5 and 18   In time, other scholars, notably botanists and geographers, began an investigation of the agricultural installations, and offered conclusions at variance with mine. These papers are responses to their theories, which did not take into account either ancient or modern agricultural practices, or the Colt (= Nessana) papyri.

Paper No. 21   After having put aside this specialization, which has its limitations, I returned to it some twenty years later upon reading of a survey and excavation of exceptionally large wine-presses in the Central Negev. I put together the archaeological material with the literary evidence of the period and produced a paper on "The Wine and Vineyards of Gaza in the Byzantine Period", which adds substance to the position I took in my original report and in Paper No. 5.

Papers Nos. 36 and 40   Paper No. 21 led, in the curious way in which scholarship works, to two quasi-agricultural articles, Papers Nos. 36 and 40: "The Gaza 'Wine' Jar (*Gazition*) and the 'Lost' Ashkelon Jar (*Askalônion*)" and "The Use of Ascalon Wine in the Medical Writers of the Fourth to the Seventh Centuries". Through documentary evidence from Greek and Coptic papyri, and from Stephanus of Byzantium and Leontius Neapolitanus, Paper No. 36 makes known particulars concerning a storage-jar bearing the name of the city Ascalon. Paper No. 40 finds the wine of Ascalon, in contrast to that of Gaza, barely mentioned in the literary sources, but prominently cited by Byzantine medical writers, particularly by Alexander of Tralles. It was a special quality of Ascalon wine that made it more useful to medical practitioners than other wines.

The survey and analysis of the documents and installations relating to agriculture were followed by five papers on the literary evidence for the history of Southern Palestine and Sinai. Most of this material, which came from the hands of the monks and the reports of pilgrims, has been long known, but was viewed with suspicion by historians or cast aside as being fictitious. The Nessana finds, however, provided the stimulus to review and reassess the evidence and to investigate its relationship with what was then known of Nessana and other towns of the Central Negev.

Paper No. 2   The first sortie into this field, Paper No. 2, probed the Byzantine sources for the desert of Southern Palestine and Sinai. One neglected work was the *Narrationes*, attributed to a certain Nilus, considered by critics to be either a piece of fiction or unreliable as evidence for human and animal sacrifice. There is no question that the writer of the *Narrationes* was an eremite who lived at Mount Sinai when monasticism began to flourish, sometime at the end of the fourth or the early part of the fifth century. He witnessed a Saracen raid that resulted in the deaths of a number of monks and the abduction of his son. Events within the narrative take place at Pharan, Mount Sinai and other sites in Sinai and the Negev as far north as Elusa, the administrative center for Southern Palestine west of the 'Arabah. This material was integrated with the Nessana papyri, the itinerary of the Piacenza pilgrim, and observations from the field, which contribute to the history of Southern Palestine and Sinai between the fifth and seventh centuries.

Paper No. 3   This was followed in Paper No. 3 by a detailed analysis of the various accounts of the first Muslim attacks on Southern Palestine in 633/34. Earlier historians had not satisfactorily explained why Southern Palestine was the choice of Muslims for their first attacks. The evidence of Theophanes and Nicephorus was examined from a narrower perspective, particularly with reference to local history and topographical considerations. The capitulation of Aila to Muhammad was a key strategic move since it opened the way into Southern Palestine. After reviewing the defensive arrangements — or the lack thereof — in the Negev and Sinai, it became apparent that Southern Palestine lacked any formidable defenses, and that Abu-Bakr led his forces from Arabia through Aila and swept unchallenged through Sinai — possibly attacking Pharan on the way — to the district of Gaza, where he was met by a hastily dispatched force from Caesarea.

Paper No. 6   In the process of working on the Byzantine sources for the deserts of Southern Palestine and Sinai (Paper No. 2), it struck me that the Nilus *Narrationes* was a most unusual, if not unique, report on eremitic life at Mount Sinai at an early stage of its development. Delving more deeply into this memoire, as I believe it was, both as to its critics and its content, I devoted an entire paper to the narrative (Paper No. 6). Unlike other patristic writings, the *Narrationes* is free of Christology, of Trinitarianism, of

7

diabolism and of miracles. There are no direct quotations from the New Testament and no use of the word *abba* for the more revered inhabitants of the desert. The narrative cites or alludes to the Scriptures in one form or another thirty-two times. Of these, only two have echoes of the New Testament; the remaining citations and allusions are from the Old Testament. The life described is closer to philosophical asceticism than to Christian monasticism. It was also apparent that the writer of the narrative was a highly educated man, who was trained in the florid rhetorical style of the period. Paper No. 6 also contains translations of many passages considered significant for an understanding of the text in its time and place.

Paper No. 10

A companion piece, so to speak, of Nilus' *Narrationes* is the Ammonius narrative "concerning the holy fathers killed by barbarians on the mountain of Sinai and at Raithou" (Paper No. 10). It too has been rejected by modern scholars as having no historical value. Unlike the Nilus narrative, however, it is not all of one piece and may represent a conflation of two distinct accounts. The Mount Sinai episode is a straightforward account written in the first person singular by a pilgrim who witnessed a Saracen attack at Mount Sinai and its environs that resulted in the death of forty monks. The raid on Raithou on the west coast of Sinai is reported by a Bedouin and a monk who fled and sought safety at Mount Sinai. The attack on Raithou was carried out by Blemmyes who made an amphibious landing and killed a large number of the hermit residents before being wiped out by a band of archers from Pharan. Paper No. 10 attempts to sort out the historical from the fabricated.

Paper No. 8

If the four previous papers add a dimension of verisimilitude to the history of Sinai, Paper No. 8 seeks to discredit the historicity of Procopius' account in *de Aed.* 5.8. of the events which led Justinian to order the construction of a fortified structure and church at Mount Sinai. Even though the historian was a contemporary of the emperor and a recorder of his achievements, almost everything Procopius has to say about Sinai does not jibe with the facts. The central issue is his statement that "the emperor built a very strong fortress and established there a considerable garrison of troops, in order that the barbarian Saracens might not be able from that region...make inroads with complete secrecy into the lands of Palestine proper". On this major point, evidence is provided to show that a military post at Mount Sinai by its very geographical position could not have prevented hostile Bedouin from infiltrating to the north if they had an inclination to do so. A more reliable source of information for the construction of the church and fortified structure is Eutychius who lived some 400 years after Procopius. According to Eutychius, the monks at Mount Sinai complained to the emperor about the misdemeanors and felonies of the "Ishmaelite Arabs" and petitioned him for protection. Justinian ordered his legate to build a monastery, in effect the fortified structure that still stands today at the foot of Mount Sinai.

There are two papers that deal specifically with the Monastery of St. Catherine at Sinai:

Paper No. 7

Paper No. 7 treats an inscription in the South Chapel of the monastery and the martyr tradition in Sinai. A recent editor of the inscription has translated the Greek *d dekados* as "four times ten" or "forty". Although he had no epigraphic analogue or parallel for the translation, he was led to the number by the association with the forty martyrs of the Ammonius narrative. My paper holds that the number should not be taken as "four times ten", or "forty", but as "the fourteenth" (i.e., four-teenth). The number refers synecdochically to the 14th of January, which, according to the martyr tradition of Sinai — and recorded both in the Nilus and Ammonius narratives — commemorates the Bedouin raid that resulted in the death of a number of monks and solitaries in and around Mount Sinai. It was a red-letter day at the monastery in Sinai, and on modern calendars of the Greek Orthodox church. The 14th of January also commemorates "Fathers Killed in Sinai and Raithou".

Paper No. 16

Paper No. 16 concerns a report of a recent find of a number of fragments of the famous Codex Sinaiticus within the walls of the Monastery of St. Catherine. The report claims that the so-called "biblical uncial" script and the Codex Sinaiticus written in that script, both dated to the fourth century, originated in Sinai and "possibly were produced at the same monastery". The reliability of these statements is more than highly doubtful. The monastic community at Mount Sinai, such as it was in the fourth century, was small and scattered. Life itself was a struggle to provide the means of keeping body and soul together and to survive the periodic attacks of marauding Saracens. Conditions were not such that would stimulate the creation of a style of script and facilitate the production of codices on vellum of the size and quality of the Sinaiticus.

Paper No. 17

Tangentially related to Mount Sinai in Paper No. 17 is a homily on dreams, as told by the seventh-century monk Antiochus. It is the story of a monk on Mount Sinai who was deceived by diabolical visions and dreams regarding his Christian faith. He left the Holy Mountain and "went to Palestine, to Noara and Livias, the headquarters of the Jews". He embraced Judaism, had himself circumsized, and took a wife, and became known as a second Abraham. For his having converted to the religion of the hateful Jews and for vilifying his former belief, he died a painful death. However, the mention of Noara and Livias as centers of Jewish life is a legitimate piece of evidence for the history of the period. Although both places are known to us — one more so than the other — the fact that they were "headquarters of the Jews" is not. The background of both sites is explicated in Paper No. 17.

Two papers touch on the historical geography of Sinai:

Paper No. 12   Paper No. 12 examines one section of the well-known Peutinger Table, the Clysma–Phara–Haila road, and comes to the conclusion that the route was not a major, or correctly stated, line of communication for the fourth century or later. The stated mileage between Clysma and Phara(n) is reasonably accurate, but that between Pharan and Aila cannot be rationalized. It appears evident that the cartographer had no detailed information on the routes through Sinai, unlike other sections of the map, and that he could only give a schematic notion of the region in terms of distances and intervening stations.

Paper No. 13   Paper No. 13 refutes the position that the accepted pilgrim route from Jerusalem to Mount Sinai was along the coast of the Mediterranean to Pelusium and to Clysma, and then proceeded through the wadis of western Sinai to Pharan and Mount Sinai. This position was brought into question by the large number of Armenian inscriptions in Wadi Haggag (Wadi of the Pilgrims) on the eastern side of the peninsula. Several itineraries of the sixth century, especially the Theodosian one, coupled with the importance of Aila as a way station en route to Mount Sinai, indicate that the popular pilgrim route went along the eastern side of Sinai before turning westward. To this has been added the experience of an archaeologist who trekked back and forth over the routes to Mount Sinai, where he lived for almost a decade.

Paper No. 9   Somewhat further afield is Paper No. 9 on anti-black sentiment in the *Vitae Patrum*, a rebuttal of the view that to early Christians color was inconsequential. To support this thesis a number of episodes from the *Vitae Patrum* are cited concerning a certain black monk called Abba Moses. Although these episodes fall under the rubric of humility, they are patent examples of prejudicial treatment and humiliation of a monk because of his color. Other blacks cited in the *Vitae Patrum* are demons and devils representing such evil forces as fornication, lust, arrogance, pride, disobedience and distracting thoughts.

Paper No. 14   Turning from the wilderness to the habitable regions of Palaestina Tertia, Paper No. 14 attempts to give a fuller account of the history of the city of Elusa, an administrative center for the province. Encyclopedias and dictionaries give a "bare-bones" account of this important site, generally focusing upon a statement in Jerome's life of Palestine's proto-monk Hilarion that the town was half civilized. An investigation of the sources of the fourth to the sixth centuries proves otherwise. Elusa was quite civilized, as we learn from the letters of Libanius and Procopius of Gaza. Zenobius, the teacher of Libanius, came from Elusa, and rose to become the sophist of the city of Antioch. Equally known as a rhetor of distinction was Zenobius' cousin.

Libanius mentions the city in his correspondence and orations more than any other in Palestine and Arabia. The letters of Procopius of Gaza to a former resident of Elusa, who traveled back forth from Egypt to Elusa, provides unusual data on the physical environment (drought and encroaching sand dunes) of the region.

Paper No. 20 On a broader scale, Paper No. 20 takes up the development of urbanization in Palaestina Tertia and the causes for the phenomenon. At the same time a paradox is observed: the development takes place in the western section of the province, in the Central Negev highlands, where water supplies are very limited, whereas the region east of the Wadi 'Arabah does not have a comparable development, despite good supplies of water and the existence of a major highway (the *Via Nova Traiana*) running through the province to commercial centers. As indicated in the above historical sketch, monasticism and pilgrimage associated with the veneration of saints and martyrs provided the impetus for this development. However, monks and pilgrims, or their guides, used roads, and their choice of roads had to do not only with security, but also with the physical character of the land through which they ran. In the marginal areas that comprised Palaestina Tertia, the availability of arable soil and topographical features that encouraged the efficient use of runoff were necessary factors to support a growing population. The six major sites in the Central Negev are described with respect to their geographical setting, their estimated populations, and the number of churches excavated (11) or sighted (9). The relationship of the communities at Mount Sinai and Pharan with the towns of the Central Negev is examined in light of the literary sources and papyrological documents. What remains unexplained is why the one site on the road to Mount Sinai, or near it, that is rich in water and arable land, Kadesh Barnea, had no comparable development. Paper No. 20 was translated into Hebrew when the press to which it was submitted changed its format. The original text of the article is provided here in place of the Hebrew.

The appearance of the words "Eleutheropolis of Nea Arabia" in an Egyptian papyrus, *P. Oxy.* 3574, has generated six papers concerned with the reorganization, or the several reorganizations, of the province of Palestine between the years 314–318 and ca. 536.

Paper No. 15 Paper No. 15 is a reaction to a published statement that Nea Arabia was the name of an Egyptian province and that Eleutheropolis was an unknown site within that province. Holding that Eleutheropolis was the well-known city of Palestine, the paper brings historical and archaeological evidence to support the position that sometime during the reign of Diocletian, a province similar to that of Idumaea was carved out of Palestine and out of part of Palestinian Arabia Petraea (i.e., the Negev), and that Eleutheropolis, the former capital of Idumaea, was designated as its administrative center. The Edomite tradition was strong enough in the region for the name Nea Arabia to be given to the newly created province.

Paper No. 22

Paper No. 22 is a response to an objection raised in connection with the foregoing, in which a statement was made that Idumaea had been inhabited by Edomite Arabs. The writer held that the Edomites were not Arabs and that no province of the Roman or Byzantine empire received its name without reference to local traditions of nomenclature of peoples or places. However, with citations from Stephanus of Byzantium, who in turn cites the third or fourth century geographer Uranius, that the Idumaeans were of Arab stock, and with one from Jerome on the geographical extent of the Idumaean region ("...Eleutheropolis all the way to Petra and Aila is the possession of Esau"), Paper No. 22 all the more makes Southern Palestine, and not Egypt, the reasonable choice for the location of Nea Arabia and the city of Eleutheropolis.

Paper No. 19

The appearance of *P. Oxy.* 3574 opened up a Pandora's box with regard to several assumptions that have been made concerning the provincial organization of what was formerly part of Provincia Arabia. The central issue raised by the surfacing of Nea Arabia in *P. Oxy.* 3574 is whether we know anything about the reorganization of the province of Palestine during the first eight or nine decades of the fourth century. Not only is there a question of precisely when and what part of the southern portion of the province of Arabia was incorporated into Palestine, but also whether Palaestina Salutaris (later Tertia) was organized ca. 358, a date that is consistently cited for that event. Paper No. 19 analyzes the Byzantine sources on the question and comes to the conclusion that the province of Palestine experienced a number of territorial and administrative changes during the first eight or nine decades of the fourth century. However, it is the compelling remark of Jerome and the appearance in the Nessana papyri of a military unit bearing the emperor's name that leads us to conclude that the province of Palaestina Salutaris was organized ca. 390 during the reign of Theodosius I.

Paper No. 26

Paper No. 26 on Libanius and the administration of Palestine follows closely on the heels of the above-mentioned paper. The correspondence of Libanius, vital for the reconstruction of the ambience and the history of the period in which the eminent orator flourished, unfortunately does not provide the kind of firm evidence for which historians have an affection. Scholars working primarily through internal evidence and inference wrote a history of his life and times (Sievers), and gave a chronological basis for his undated correspondence (Seeck). It was Sievers who proposed that 358 was the year in which Palestine was divided into two provinces. Paper No. 26 considers the governors of Palestine who are known solely through

Libanius' correspondence, and more narrowly interprets the letters that were taken as evidence for the division of the province in 358. The paper concludes that the province of Palestine was not split into a Prima and a Secunda (or a Salutaris) in 357/8, and that it remained a single province until ca. 390, when it was divided into three provinces: Prima, Secunda and Salutaris (later Tertia). The most convincing evidence of all — the key, so to speak — appears in Justinian's edict, Novel 103 of 536, which decrees a change in the title and authority of the governor of Palestine. The edict gives a historical precis of the administrative titles of the governor of the province. Palestine was one province when its governor held the title of Proconsul, and when it was divided into three provinces, the three governors were reduced in rank to *ordinarii*. The Theodosian Code confirms the fact that a Proconsul governed a unified Palestine late in the fourth century. Sometime after 363 and before 386 the governor was given the rank of Proconsul. By 390/2, Palestine — probably including a portion of Arabia — was divided into three, and from that time on, but not before, our sources provide numerical modifiers for Palaestina.

Paper No. 27
Paper No. 27 takes up a fuller reading of Justinian's Novel 103 on the reorganization of Palestine (ca. 536). Its bearing on the date of the tripartite division of Palestine ca. 390 has been discussed in the preceding abstract. The body of the edict deals with the reorganization of the province to repair the consequences of civil disorder and economic upheaval caused by the Samaritan revolt of 529. To that end, Justinian upgraded the rank and staff of the governor of Palaestina Prima and gave him the responsibility for the maintenance of public order and the collection of taxes within all three Palestinian provinces. In addition to providing the governor with an armed force, the edict clarified the responsibilities of both the governor and the *dux* with respect to internal affairs within the province. Novel 103 is correlated with evidence from Cyril of Scythopolis, Zosimus, Malalas, Procopius and Choricius of Gaza.

Paper No. 23
An offshoot of Justinian's Novel 103 crops up in Paper No. 23 on the Beersheba edict, four fragmentary inscriptions of the Byzantine period. The fragments contain a variety of elements: a portion of an imperial edict, a schedule of annual assessments placed on towns for certain personnel, including a Vicarius. One fragment lists eighteen towns in trans-Jordanian Palaestina Tertia with sums of *solidi* assigned to them. Paper No. 23 analyzes the magnitude of the obligations placed upon the communities in terms of the purchasing power of the *solidus* as indicated in the Nessana papyri. Judging from the value of the *solidus* in the papyri, the annual assessments indicated in the inscriptions were modest and not excessive. Hence, the view put forward by two scholars that the assessments imposed upon the towns were on behalf of the *annona militaris* does not match the sums of money required to support a body of frontier troops. Paper No. 23 con-

cludes that the assessments were an extraordinary tax placed upon the communities of the three Palestinian provinces following Justinian's reorganization of the power structure as outlined in Novel 103. The creation of a Proconsul of Palestine with civil and military responsibilities required the additional personnel indicated in the inscriptions. The Beersheba edict was issued to provide support for the enlarged *officium* of the Proconsul. On this basis, the edict should be dated to 536 or somewhat later.

There follow a number of papers that are concerned specifically with the Saracens and their relationship with the Romans and the Roman military. Although this topic has been touched upon in connection with events in Sinai and southern Palestine, these papers embrace a wider area of action in the Near East, including Egypt. Arising out of this discussion comes the question of the meaning of the troubling word *limes*: does it mean a line of defensive installations (forts, fortlets, towers) against Saracen movements and attacks, or does it simply mean "frontier" or "frontier district"?

Paper No. 11 Paper No. 11 is a cautionary note on the use of the account of a successful attack against the Romans by Mauia, Queen of the Saracens, during the reign of Valens. The settlement she imposed was that an Arab solitary by the name of Moses be ordained a bishop. The story was first set down by Rufinus in the fifth century. He recounts, in addition to the raid, the confrontation between Moses, an adherent of the Nicean creed, and Lucius, the Arian bishop of Alexandria. The story of Moses and Mauia was elaborated upon by later church historians and then, with other historical fragments, made into whole cloth by some modern historians. The two incidents — Mauia's raid and Moses' ordination — originate in Rufinus. It was out of his personal experience in Alexandria and among the solitaries of the Egyptian desert that he framed not so much a record of historical events, as a powerful anti-Arian statement. Paper No. 11 raises a number of questions concerning the events recorded by subsequent church historians.

Paper No. 25 Roman fortified positions on the eastern frontier, usually designated by the word *limes* (*Limes Palaestinae, Limes Arabicus*), have been the subject of recent investigations. Paper No. 25 looks into the question of whether the *limes* comprised a coordinated system of border garrisons in terms of the evidence from the western sector of Palaestina Tertia; it then applies the conclusion to the eastern sector of the province. As for the Saracens, they were a constant threat both within and beyond the lines of fortified positions. The strategy of the Romans was designed to protect not borders, but the thinly settled populations and lines of communication. The word "frontier" is a more meaningful term than "border" in defining the word *limes* in the provinces of Palestine, Arabia and possibly Syria. "A sufficient force" would be gathered from one or more garrisons to defend against large numbers of attacking Saracens; the *castra* and *castella* on the frontiers also served as a refuge for the settled population in the event of attack. Saracen phylarchs, on the other hand, when not allied with the Romans against their enemies, were employed, or bought off, to keep peace in the uninhabited fringe regions.

Paper No. 35 Paper No. 35 takes issue with the use of the term *phylarchos* in Roman–Byzantine East as an official Roman administrative title. Roman authorities, as is well known, enrolled Arab tribes as *foederati* to keep the peace along the broad frontiers of the eastern provinces and to serve as an auxiliary fighting force in Rome's wars against the Persians and the Goths. Some scholars have perceived a change from the fourth century on in the way in which Rome organized these relationships by giving one tribal chief authority over other tribes: that is, giving him control over other tribal chiefs. For the designated chief, Roman authorities used the term "phylarch" as an official administrative title. Paper No. 35 reviews the evidence for this conclusion and finds it lacking. It is doubtful whether the Roman government on its own authority could place tribes under the leadership of one phylarch without the willingness of the tribal leaders themselves. In the matter of usage, the term "phylarch" has a long history, during which its meaning has changed in accordance with the character of the group of persons under the leadership of an individual. During late antiquity, the term had no precise specific meaning that would limit its use to a particular organized group, a fact that prevented it from becoming an official title in the Roman hierarchy. The word is also found in association with a variety of ethnic tribal groups, including Saracens allied with Persia. Documents from Egypt complicate the matter further: the term was used for liturgical officers of the city of Oxyrhynchos and for the sons of rulers among the Blemmyes and Noubades. A most compelling argument against the use of the word "phylarch" as an official Roman administrative title is that Syriac writers who record the conflict between Rome and Persia, and their Saracen allies, do not employ any term suggesting a translation of Greek *phylarchos*.

Two additional papers are concerned with the word *limes*:

Paper No. 30 Paper No. 30 is concerned with the use of the word in the Egyptian papyri. It is not found earlier than the fourth century, but it appears as late as the early Arab period. There is ambiguity and confusion in translations of the word in Egyptian documents and other sources. One cannot use words meaning "border" where there are no borders in the conventional sense of the term, but only outlying districts of civilization or undefined tracts of land. Confusion is added when *limes* is taken without qualification as a line of military installations. Paper No. 30 suggests that in order to clarify what has become a muddled situation, it would be best to translate *limes* as "frontier" or "frontier district" or their equivalents in other languages. It would help even more if it were possible to be more specific by distinguishing between two different kinds of frontiers: frontiers of settlement and military frontiers. There may also be occasions in which it would be useful to use the term "political frontier", when, for example, describing an uninhabited and unfortified region under the apparent control of a governing power.

Paper No. 28 Paper No. 28, brief though it is, has considerable substance, since it defines with citations the precise geographical orientation for the words "inner" and "outer" when used with the word *limes* in Ammianus Marcellinus, Malalas and Theophanes. The Greek or Latin word "inner" should be taken to mean "further out", "deeper" or "more remote" (from civilization); the word "outer", which is not commonly employed, "closer" or "nearer" (to civilization). Citations from Athanasius and the *Apophthegmata Patrum* make these meanings clear, and help support a reading in Malalas over that of Theophanes.

Paper No. 33 The interpretation of the word *limes* as a frontier or frontier district leads, in Paper No. 33, to an investigation on a broader scale: a comparison of two frontiers of different historical periods. For the purposes of this study, a comparison was undertaken of settlements in the Negev in Iron Age II, the period of the United Monarchy (ca. 1000 B.C.E.) and those of the Byzantine period. Although many scholars consider early biblical narratives quasi-historical, legendary, or contrived, these narratives provide a fairly accurate tableau of ancient nomadic and semi-nomadic lifestyles and attitudes. Investigators have focused their attention upon certain Iron Age structures that they have dubbed "forts" and "fortresses", with the inference that they served a military function. These were viewed as "forerunners of the *limes*" and were taken as part of the building activity of Israelite kings. Paper No. 33, on the basis of evidence from the Byzantine period, takes issue with these conclusions and demonstrates that the frontier of the Negev during these two widely separated periods shared certain characteristics that bear upon one another, and that to discuss one period in isolation from others, especially those that have ample documentary evidence, may lead to faulty conclusions. The use of comparative material provides a reasonable approach to the interpretation of archaeological and documentary evidence and adds a significant dimension to the history of a region.

Paper No. 31 Paper No. 31 examines two contrasting viewpoints, one of an anthropologist and the other of an archaeologist, regarding the relationship of the nomadic population (Saracens) to the settled inhabitants in the late Roman–Byzantine era, based essentially on the interpretation of different kinds of archaeological evidence. Paper No. 31 takes the position that for the era in question, the true temper of the relationship can only be assessed by an analysis of the literary sources, which are particularly rich for that period. The complexities of the relationship are demonstrated in detail: there was both conflict and symbiosis between Roman and Saracen, and a *Pax Romana* never existed between the two. As to the position that the Roman military strategy was to monitor and control the movement of Arab tribes, there is no evidence that it ever did so, or, indeed, that it was designed for that purpose.

Paper No. 32 Paper No. 32 turns once more to the papyri to see how the Saracens were portrayed in the documents of Egypt and Nessana. The word Saracen was employed by the Greek-speaking population to describe two different kinds of Arabs: the nomad and the settled Muslim. As for the nomad, the documents reflect the same aspects found in the literary sources mentioned in Paper No. 31: they raided settlements for prisoners or plunder, or they provided communities with a wide range of services. The Islamic conquest produced another kind of Saracen, a Muslim dedicated to the principles of Islam, which held that nomadic life was incompatible with Islam. To the Greek-speaking population there was no distinction between the two: both nomads and settled Muslims (or any Arabs) were called Saracens.

Paper No. 29 Paper No. 29 reviews *P. Ness.* 58 in light of two false prophecies, written in Hebrew and dated to the eighth/ninth centuries, on the coming of the Arabs to Palestine. The prophecies brought to mind the Nessana papyrus, a post Conquest document concerning a sum of money for "γεωμετρία of the Saracens" and γεωμορία of an Arab tribe. The editor of the document dated the piece to the late seventh century and believed that it represented a receipt for tax on assigned land. However, the false prophecies, in speaking of Ishmaelites "measuring the land with ropes" and "dividing the land for a price", provide parallels for the two Greek terms that are central to an understanding of *P. Ness.* 58. Paper No. 29 assesses these parallels in view of the Umayyad policy of settlement on newly conquered land. Apart from the prophecies, the large numbers of Umayyad inscriptions found throughout the Negev and the archaeological material that is being brought to light further attest to this policy.

Paper No. 34 In pursuing the subject of Saracens in the papyri, the meaning of a word and its variant (γονάχιον, τονάχιον) became the topic of Paper No. 34. The word appears in documents of the early Arab period, and the proposed meaning was given as "prayer rug". Since prayer rugs were not in general use in the early years of Islam, another explanation had to be sought. A citation in Leontius Neapolitanus' life of St. John the Almsgiver and in Athanasius' Latin translation of the life shows the meaning of the word to be that of a cloak or a blanket-like wrap. The word itself is derived from the Semitic and is an orthographic variant of a well-known Greek word.

Paper No. 38

Another word with an obscure etymology crops up some ten times in Cyril of Scythopolis and other recorders of the deeds and miracles of the monks of the Judaean desert. Paper No. 38 treats the meaning and etymology of the Greek word μαν(ν)ούθιον. The meaning of the word offers no difficulty, since the context in which it appears clearly indicates that in the singular form it is a branch or twig that the monks cut or gathered and stored within the monastery as kindling or firewood. As for its etymology, the Greek word is derived from a well-attested Semitic root with the basic meaning of "part" or "portion", to which Greek endings *-ion* and *-ia* were added. It thus acquired the meaning of "part(s)" or "piece(s)" with the ellipsis of "bush(es)".

Paper No. 37

Trailing a wily Persian Saracen by the name of Amorkesos to the island of Iotabē in the Red Sea led to Paper No. 37 and a review of what we know of the island's history. The recorded history of the island of Iotabē spans a brief history of sixty years, during which it changed hands at least four times. Amorkesos took possession of the island in 473 A.D., evicted the Roman tax collectors, and became wealthy by collecting taxes. During the reign of Anastasius (ca. 498) it was recovered by the Romans. By the time of Justinian, the island was in the hands of Jews, as we learn from Procopius. By ca. 534, the *dux* Aratius recovered the island by a military action. Paper No. 37 discounts the view of some scholars that the island served to control shipping. Textual evidence makes it clear that Iotabē served to tax merchandise coming from region(s) known as India and then to tranship it to Roman ports. Iotabē has persistently been identified with the island of Tiran, even though archaeological investigation has ruled out that possibility. The identification of Iotabē with any island, ancient or modern, remains in doubt.

Paper No. 24

Choricius of Gaza. (fl. 530), orator and teacher of rhetoric, composed an eulogy on Stephanus, governor of Palaestina Prima, and the *dux* Aratius, and in so doing has filled in some gaps in the history of Palestine during the reign of Justinian. In his encomium of Stephanus, he has given us the sole literary statement concerning the water supply system of Caesarea, which some scholars have taken as evidence of the governor having repaired the city's aqueduct. Paper No. 24 cites in full Choricius' passage to show that Stephanus did not repair the aqueduct, but rather cleared it of obstacles that prevented the free flow of water from the springs to the public fountains in Caesarea. No doubt these obstacles were caused by the accumulation of debris which, if not cleared periodically, would reduce the flow of water in the tunnels and channels leading from the spring to the public fountains. The action of the governor was purely one of maintenance.

Paper No. 39

Paper No. 39 on the confusion of Indias in the Byzantine sources — Asian India versus Africa India — developed from a question that arose about which India was meant in citations of Red Sea ports that received merchandise from India. My interest was also stimulated by the use of such geographical terms as "inner" and "outer", a subject treated in Paper No. 28. After the fourth century the region and people meant by the terms "India" and "Indians" varied considerably in the Byzantine documents. The knowledge of a geographical India in South Asia was preserved by several writers, notably Ammianus Mercellinus; however, writers such as Rufinus, Gelasius and Socrates had Ethiopia in mind, whereas to Philostorgius, India was South Arabia. A century after these ecclesiastical historians, John Malalas presents us with thirty-six citations of the word "India" and "Indians". Twelve of these are found in descriptions of biblical events and episodes in the life of Alexander the Great. The remaining citations fall within the reign of Justinian and Malalas' own lifetime. From his perspective, Axum in Ethiopia and the inner kingdoms associated with it were Indian, while the Homerites prior to their defeat was not. However, when the Axumites defeated the Homerites, the two regions became one India. Malalas also mentions Saracen Indians as having been sent out to attack Persians on behalf of the Romans.

A final word. It is in the character of historical investigation to challenge, as have many papers in this collection, the assumptions and conclusions of other scholars. Although it is hoped that the positions taken in these forty papers are based on well-founded evidence, they should, in the interest of providing greater historical probability, be subjected to the self-same process.

I wish to take this opportunity to thank my colleagues at several institutions for their generous support, friendship and hospitality: at the Department of Classics of New York University, the Institute of Archaeology of the Hebrew University of Jerusalem, the National Library of the Hebrew University of Jerusalem, the Israel Exploration Society and the Albright Archaeological Institute of the American Schools of Oriental Research. I would also like to extend a special word of thanks and encouragement to those former M.A. and Ph.D. candidates who sought me out and who have elected to make a name for themselves in the field of Late Antiquity. To Tsipi Kuper-Blau, who performed onerous editorial tasks with equanimity, and to Avraham Pladot, who designed the book and improved the quality of the photography, my sincere appreciation. Finally, I owe a profound debt of gratitude to my friend and colleague Joseph Aviram, who was the prime mover of this volume, as well as of many other scholarly publications.

January 1994

Philip Mayerson
New York University

VI. AGRICULTURAL EVIDENCE IN THE COLT PAPYRI

Most of the agricultural evidence, like that found in the Egyptian papyri, has to be gleaned from various legal instruments, accounts, and requisitions (see Appendix II). One document (82), however, has to be singled out, for it seems unparalleled in any of the papyri or treatises that have come down to us. It is an account of amounts of wheat, barley, and *aracus* sown and reaped. So far as I know, it is the only ancient document which gives the exact yield from an amount sown.

From divisions of property (16, 21, 31), a bill of sale (23), a notice to transfer taxes (24), and a cession of land (32), we can determine the organization of the land; from accounts dealing with the disposition of wheat (40, 83), food tax (69), church offerings (80), receipts in kind (81), sales of dates (90, 91), and requisitions of wheat and oil (61–67), we are able to enumerate the major crops and estimate the productivity of the land.* None of the documents gives any evidence of animal husbandry, herds or flocks. We know from 35 and 37, however, that a camel corps was stationed at Nessana, so there is little doubt that camel breeding was one of the local occupations, and that camels were used in agricultural operations such as ploughing, threshing, and hauling (for the use of camels as plough animals in Roman Tripolitania, see Ward-Perkins 1950.21).

Land Organization

The agricultural organization of Nessana, as far as we can see in the papyri, was a relatively simple one. The land was held by free owners; there is no hint of the *colonus*,† of *emphyteusis*, or of any other form of land tenure, but the possibility of tenant farming may be found in 80–83. The sixth-century documents of the soldiers' archive (14–30) clearly indicate that both the military and civilian populations owned land; for in 16, 21, and 24 we find civilian lands bordering those of the soldiers. In 31, the longest papyrus in the collection and dated to the sixth century, soldiers are not even mentioned in the division of a considerable estate of farm lands and buildings.

Civilian farmers and soldiers were free to exchange (23), cede (24, 32), or sell (16) their holdings provided that, it appears, payment of taxes was guaranteed (24, 32). Nor were the soldiers, even early in the sixth century, restricted in their movement; former residents of Nessana lived in Rhinocorura (15), Alexandria (30), and Elusa (29).

There is also evidence in 32, 55, 58, and 59 of collective responsibility—i.e. on the part of the landowners—for the collection of land-taxes (δημόσια) and for other administrative affairs relating to the land. This collective responsibility continued after the Arab conquest; we find requisitions from the Arab governor at Gaza for wheat and oil (60–67) addressed τοῖς Νεστάνων ('to the people of Nessana'), and in 58 (dated about 682–689), a commission of eight men καὶ εἰ

---

* To this evidence must be added the seeds which were discovered with the papyri in Room 8 of the monastery church of SS. Sergius and Bacchus. Since the wattle roof had collapsed soon after—or perhaps before—the abandonment of the site, the papyri, seeds, and miscellaneous debris in Room 8 became a sealed deposit and remained undisturbed until excavated by the Colt Expedition. The specimens were turned over to C. O. Erlanson of the U.S. Department of Agriculture and to G. L. Wittrock of the New York Botanical Garden, who identified and arranged them taxonomically. The list (see Appendix I) is not as revealing as one might expect; most of the seeds are weeds, and those which indicate sown or planted crops provide little more evidence than that found in the papyri. Such fruits as the almond, peach, and walnut, though they could have been grown in the Negeb, might also have been imported.

† Schwabe 1954.48–49 contends that Libanius inherited certain estates in the vicinity of Elusa which were farmed by Jewish *coloni*, and that his oration (47) to Theodosius I in 390 referred to these lands. Their location, however, is uncertain and has been the subject of much debate (see Pack 1935.46–52).

λιπὶ τοῦ χορίου ὑμῶν Νεστάνων ('and others of our district of Nessana') are concerned with γεωμετρία and γεωμορία (cf. **89**.25).*

The land itself—possibly reflecting the original division when *limitanei* were first stationed at Nessana—is classified as seed-land, vineyard, and garden.† The three-fold division is a simple, practical one for an arid region; the meadows, woodlands, osier groves, or the complex system of land classification which Heichelheim 1938.144–145 describes for the more favoured regions of Palestine and Syria, are, of course, not possible under the climatic conditions of the Negeb. Because of the scarcity of water and the uneven topography, land classifications were probably more rigid than in Egypt, say, where garden, vineyard, and seed-land were virtually interchangeable. I believe that areas in the Negeb were allocated to planted and sown crops with careful regard to topography and availability of water.

In accordance with the universal custom, ancient and modern, fields were given names or were identified by their location. In **16**, one field is called *Alon* . . ., and another, *Airegla*; in **23**, *Koreothas*; in **24**, a parcel of seed-land is located in a section known as *Nearer Alagrad*. In **82**, the names *Ragorion*, *Kat*, *Malalkani*, *Alphag*, *Beraein*, *Seram*, and *Malzemarche* are all obviously the names of wadis in the neighbourhood of the village of Birein (or Beraein). Two of the names have survived to this day, Seram and Birein. (Seram is not 4 or 5 miles away as Kraemer 1958.238 states; its outlet is but a short distance from the remains of the Byzantine village of Birein.) In the same way, I would interpret *Abiathalba* (**21**) as being the name of a wadi.

Some indication of the size of a field is given in **24**, a notice to transfer title on 5 *kabiaiai* of seed-land. Kraemer 1958.79 points out in his note to line 5 that the parcel of land measured 0.4 *jugerum*, or approximately 1 dunam (0.1 hectare, about 0.25 acre). Judging from the arrangements of terraces in the wadis (see below p. 235), 5 *kabiaiai* would be about an average size field. It would be an error to think in terms of units much larger than this, for topographical considerations limited cultivation to relatively small patches of land. However, a landowner might have had title to a number of such units in various wadis.

The largest 'farm' indicated in the Nessana documents probably belonged to the church. In his introduction to **82**, Kraemer 1958.238 estimates at 71 acres the amount of land given over to the cultivation of the wheat, barley, and *aracus* mentioned in the account. His estimate,

---

* The similarities between the agricultural organization of Nessana and that indicated in the seventh–eighth century νομος γεωργικός, 'The Farmer's Law', are so striking that it is worthwhile to cite some of Ashburner's observations on the law (1912.70–71): 'The country is divided into χωρία which may be translated as districts. All the landowners within a district are cultivating farmers. . . . Each district forms a unit for fiscal purposes; that is to say, each and all of the farmers of the district are responsible for the taxes of the whole district, and if one farmer fails to pay his due proportion, it has to be made good by others. . . . The whole body of occupying farmers is described as the commoners (οἱ κοινωνοί) or commonalty (ἡ κοινότης) of the district. . . . The lot might contain cornland, vineyard, fig and vegetable gardens, woodland and uncultivated land. The chief products were corn and wine: the olive is never mentioned. Vineyard and gardens were marked off by fences and trenches. . . . A farmer's power of disposition over his lot was apparently limited to dealings with another farmer of the same district. He could exchange his lot with him either for a season or in perpetuity; he might let his lot to him or hire him to cultivate it. But there is no trace of a power of sale to outsiders.' (See also Heitland 1921.462–464.)

† The word 'garden', a translation of the Greek κῆπος, is often misleading. In the West, 'garden' generally means a flower or vegetable garden. In the East, however, the word has more the meaning of 'orchard' in which vegetables may be grown (see especially Homer, *Od.* 7.129; 24.247–248). It is this common misconception, I believe, that has led Ashburner 1912.71 to interpret κῆπος in 'The Farmer's Law' as 'vegetable garden'. (Cf. *Ecclesiastes* 2.5–6: 'I made me gardens and orchards and I planted trees in them of all kinds of fruit'; see also Liddell-Scott; Smith's *Dictionary of the bible* and other biblical encyclopaedias under 'Gardens'.)

however, is based on the assumption that 5 *modii* of wheat and barley were sown to the *jugerum* (about 13 kilos per dunam), which would be suitable for Italy but not for the semi-arid Negeb. The likelihood, based on Bedouin practices (see below p. 228) and the unit of measurement indicated in **24**, is that only half that amount, or 2.5 *modii*, was sown to the *jugerum* (about 7 kilos per dunam). The amount of land under cultivation in various wadis (omitting the small patch of *aracus*) should, then, approximate 135 acres or 540 dunams. Very curiously this works out to 1 *modius* per 5 *kabiaiai* (or 1 dunam) of land, and it is quite possible that this was the unit of land measurement at Nessana much as the dunam is used in Palestine.

Crops

When Baradez 1949.199–201 undertook to judge what crops were cultivated by the Romans on the Sahara frontier, he had to admit that it involved considerable conjecture. After ruling out the date-palm because it is particularly extravagant in its water requirements, he attributed to the Romans the cultivation of the olive and cereals such as wheat, barley, and sorghum. We, however, are in a far better position than Baradez, since the Nessana papyri provide us with substantial evidence of the cultivation of wheat, barley, grapes, olives, figs, and dates. The immediate impression one receives from the papyri is that wheat (σῖτος) is the important cereal crop; only two documents (**81**, **82**) mention barley at all.* The account of grain yield, **82**, is most informative, for it shows that five times as much wheat was sown as barley (450 *modii* of wheat as against 90 of barley). In **81**, an account of receipts in hand, there are only two entries for barley (42½ *modii*); the other six are for wheat (115½ *modii*). The remaining documents (**40**, **60–67**, **69**, **80**, **83**) speak only of wheat.

Grain yields in the neighbourhood of Nessana, as we learn from **82**, appear surprisingly high for a region with less than 100 mm. of rainfall. Excerpting that portion of the account which shows completed entries for the amount of wheat sown and reaped, we have these statistics:

Place	Modii Sown	Modii Reaped	Yield (-fold)
Ragorion to Kat	40	270	6.75
Malalkani	40	288	7.20
Alphag	180	1225	6.80

For barley, **82** records the following:

Place	Modii Sown	Modii Reaped	Yield (-fold)
Alphag	50	402	8.0
Birein (Beraein)	40	350	8.7

* Modern cultivation in the Negeb is just the reverse of that portrayed in the Nessana papyri. Epstein 1939.71 points out that in Bedouin agriculture barley accounts for about 80 per cent of the total crop sown; it is only in the west and north of the district—where there is approximately 200 mm. of precipitation—that wheat is sown (see also Lowe 1944.31–32).

It is surprising to find that barley played an inferior role to wheat, in view of the fact that barley is more drought resistant and gives higher yields. Jasny 1944.14–15 believes that scholars have overemphasized the importance of wheat in classical antiquity; in Syria, Palestine, and other Mediterranean countries he states that wheat was 'definitely second, and frequently a very poor second to barley'. Citing Spain, he believes that its dry climate 'makes it probable that barley was the principal grain crop of that country over the whole classical period and possibly for a long time afterwards'. (See also Heichelheim 1938.129; Jardé 1925.124–125.) The evidence in the Nessana documents contradicts this view, for in spite of the region's aridity wheat predominated over barley. In any event, we may regard the Nessanites' preference for wheat flour as some indication of their high standard of living.

We can safely say that the yield of wheat at Nessana during the ninth indiction in the seventh century A.D. was 7-fold; of barley, 8-fold and more. These figures compare favourably, indeed very favourably, with those given in ancient and mediaeval documents for regions having a far greater rainfall thàn the Negeb.* The question arises, however, whether the yields in **82** represent an average year or an unusually productive one occasioned by a heavy rainfall. As a basis for comparison, I questioned Bedouin farmers, particularly those who had farmed the Central Negeb, on the amount of wheat and barley sown per dunam (0.1 hectare, about 0.25 acre) and the amount reaped.† The following figures represent a collation of the information gathered at various localities (cf. yields given by Lowe 1944.31–32).

WHEAT

Sown (kilos per dunam)	Yield (kilos)		Yield (-fold)
	Exceptional	100	14–20
5–7	Good	50–70	7–14
	Satisfactory	30–50	4–10
	Poor	0–20	0–4

BARLEY

Sown (kilos per dunam)	Yield (kilos)		Yield (-fold)
	Exceptional	200	29–33
6–7	Good	70–80	10–15
	Satisfactory	40–60	6–10
	Poor	0–20	0–3

We can reasonably assume that the 7- and 8-fold yields indicated in **82** represent not an exceptional, but rather a satisfactory-to-good year. Also, it is reasonable to assume that yields in some years were far higher, possibly as high as 10- or 20-fold, and in other years, lower.‡ The explanation of such relatively good returns in a marginal area like Nessana lies in the character of the irrigation practices (i.e. irrigation by flood water) which was forced upon the inhabitants

* Wheat: Palestine, 5-fold (Heichelheim 1938.128–129); Egypt, 4.5- to 10-fold (Johnson 1936.59); Italy, 10- to 15-fold (Varro 1.44.1); Italy, 4-fold (Columella 3.3.4); Sicily, 8- to 10-fold (Cicero 2-*Verr.* 47.112). I have omitted the obviously exaggerated yields given by Herodotus 1.193; Theophrastus *H.P.* 8.7.4; Strabo 7.4.6, 15.3.11; Varro 1.44.2, and Pliny 18.94–95 (see Jardé 1925.34–35).

In mediaeval England, yields of 4- or 5-fold were considered normal; 8- to 10-fold were maximum returns (Percival 1921.416). In thirteenth-century Palestine, Prawer 1951.151 estimates the wheat yield to be about the same as that obtained by the modern fellah, 3.5- to 8-fold.

Roman and Greek documents are silent on the yield expected from a crop of barley. For Roman Egypt, Johnson 1936.59 estimates a 7- to 12-fold return; Scramuzza 1937.269 for Sicily, 8 *medimni* per *jugerum* minimum (8-fold).

† While a considerable amount of caution must be exercised in accepting Bedouin figures, I found them acceptably conservative and consistent on the amount sown; somewhat over-optimistic on what was considered a good yield. Bedouin practices are, I believe, far more reliable for comparative purposes than those of the modern Israeli farmer, who uses modern equipment and fertilizers, and generally restricts his planting to flat lands having an average rainfall of 200 mm. or more. (He plants 10–12 kilos per dunam and considers 200 kilos per dunam as a good yield, 60 as a poor one.) The Bedouin farmer, on the other hand, cultivates more modestly, planting less seed than the modern farmer, and, more important, is experienced in wadi-cultivation.

‡ In **83**, an account of wheat stored on three threshing floors, Kraemer 1958.242 finds a relationship between seed and crop that would indicate a yield of 5.6-fold for the son of al-Ubayy and 3.7-fold for George son of Hanun. If the interpretation is correct (i.e. if the seed wheat set aside from the crop represents the amount sown in the previous year) there is then evidence of a year (684/5?) for which the yield may be considered satisfactory-to-poor. However, it is not certain that the farmers set aside an amount of seed wheat equal to that sown the previous year. Individual farmers may have increased or decreased their acreage from one year to the next. Thus there is some doubt that this type of evidence is useful in establishing crop yields.

by topographical and climatic influences. Flood water, variable as it is from year to year, provides not only the moisture needed to maturate the seed,* but also the fertilizing silt which automatically renews the soil after every flood. In areas where precipitation exceeds 200 mm., farmers rely solely on direct rainfall, and unless crops are rotated and fertilizers applied, intensive cultivation of the soil will exhaust it to the point where yields, regardless of the availability of water, will be no more than several times the amount sown.

It is also possible to estimate roughly the total yearly wheat production at Nessana during the seventh century. P.Colt **69** informs us that the total amount of wheat that Nessana contributed in kind for one year (680/1?) for the military supply tax was 1180 *modii* (about 8700 kilos, or 290 U.S. bushels). According to the *entagia* (**61–63**), requisitions for a six-month period in the year 675 totalled 502 *modii*, approximately the same amount indicated in **69**. In other words, the Arab governor taxed the inhabitants of Nessana about 300 bushels of wheat per year. If this amount represented 10 per cent. of the total yearly wheat production, Nessana produced some 3000 bushels of wheat per year. However, in **82** it should be noted that one wadi alone, *Alphag*, was able to produce 1225 *modii*, or more than 300 bushels. Arab tax demands, therefore, appear to have been quite modest, probably less than 10 per cent. If Arab demands represented 5 per cent., the total yearly wheat production would have been in the neighbourhood of 6000 bushels, a rather reasonable figure. To take this one step further: by adopting Jardé's estimate (1925.135) of 5 *medimni* (about 220 kilos, or 7.5 bushels) as the amount of wheat consumed by an average Athenian per year, 6000 bushels would have provided rations for 800 people. By way of comparison, Bedouins of the tribe cultivating land near Tell el Milh have told me that they receive a monthly government allotment of 11 kilos of wheat per person, or 132 kilos per year. At this rate, 6000 bushels of wheat would provide for over 1300 people. Since the Nessanites undoubtedly lived under more stringent conditions than the classical Greeks and somewhat better than the Bedouins, I estimate that 6000 bushels would have fed some 1000 inhabitants. (Cf. Kraemer 1958.31 who, on the basis of a register of payers of poll-tax, estimates the population of Nessana to have been not more than 1500.)

P.Colt **82** also records, in addition to wheat and barley, the sowing of 30 *modii* of ἄρακος and a yield of 97 *modii*. But, unlike the cereals, no place name is given for the area in which it was grown, possibly indicating that it was planted in small patches, as the Bedouins plant their tobacco, and in several areas.† It is quite evident, however, that *aracus* was not an important crop at Nessana: of the three crops listed in **82**, *aracus* represents only 5.3 per cent. of the total amount sown, while barley represents 15.8, and wheat 78.9.

---

* According to Myers 1944.28, water is the major limiting factor in crop production in dry land areas. Experiments at an Israeli settlement in the Negeb show how true this can be, even when the soil is carefully prepared (Weitz 1950.35). The following figures show maximum wheat yields (kilos per dunam) for three successive years in which there was considerable variation in rainfall:

Crop	1943/4 (*132 mm.*)	1944/5 (*242 mm.*)	1945/6 (*167 mm.*)
Wheat	27.5	163	87
Barley	25	167	80

† The precise meaning of *aracus* is not known beyond the fact that it is a legume. Westermann 1922.28, for example, believes that it is alfalfa, but Schnebel 1925.185–187 comes to the conclusion, after examining a number of possibilities, that its meaning beyond that of a legume cannot be determined.

The evidence for grapes, olives, figs, and dates is not as direct as that for cereals. That there were vineyards at Nessana is attested by the papyri (**16**, **31**, **34**, **97**), but the extent of vine cultivation is more clearly shown by archaeological evidence, i.e. the numerous stone heaps surrounding the town-site. (For a detailed discussion of these stone heaps, see below pp. 249–257). Our knowledge of the cultivation of the olive depends almost entirely upon the *entagia* (**60–67**) and an account of food tax (**69**). These documents record tax demands for wheat and oil. In **69**, the Nessanites were taxed a total of 1017 *xestai* of oil (approximately 480 litres, or 130 U.S. gallons), of which 610 were paid in kind. The *entagia* (**61–63**) show that the Arab governor requested 505 *xestai* of oil for a six-month period in the year 675, or a probable total of 1000 *xestai* (125 gal.) for the year.

I have estimated above that requests for grain possibly approximated 5 per cent. of the total yield. If the same percentage applies to oil, the total annual production was about 20,000 *xestai*, or 2500 gallons. Using the estimate of 2.75 gallons per inhabitant made by Scramuzza 1937.272 for Sicily, 2500 gallons would have provided for the needs of 900 inhabitants, a figure which is very close to my calculation based on the estimated wheat crop.*

The evidence for the cultivation of dates rests largely on two long and complex accounts, **90** and **91**, and to a lesser degree on archaeological finds. Kraemer 1958.261–271, who has analysed the contents of these two documents with particular reference to the economy of Nessana, has estimated that in one year over 2500 baskets (*koukia*) were sold to the traders named in the accounts. We may also assume that unless dates were primarily a cash crop additional amounts were grown for local consumption. If it were not for the appearance of these two accounts and the fragments of palm fronds which had been used as a bond in the mud-wattle roof of a room in the North Church complex, one might question whether date-palms had been cultivated on any scale in the neighbourhood of Nessana. Baradez 1949.180, lacking such evidence for the Saharan frontier, comes to the conclusion that the Romans did not attempt the cultivation of the date-palm because it requires a much greater amount of water than wheat does. We can be sure, however, that this was not the case at Nessana, for the Wadi Hafir and its many tributaries receive amounts of water during the winter floods sufficient to irrigate the relatively small areas given over to the cultivation of grains and drought-resistant fruit trees. (In the Hadhramaut, van der Meulen 1932.74 observed that one good flood a year is enough to produce a successful harvest of dates.) Further, an almost perennial supply of ground water can be found at no great depth below the surface of main wadis, and this could have been tapped by shallow wells (*themail*).† It is also important to note that while most ground water (i.e. well water) is con-

---

* A rough calculation of the number of trees involved may serve to give a clearer picture of olive culture in the Negeb. Frank 1933.170–171 estimates that olive trees in ancient Italy produced about 15–20 lb. of oil per tree (1 lb. = about 0.3 litres = 0.08 gal.). Using his lower figure, 20,000 *xestai* of oil could have been produced from some 2000 trees.

† A far more ingenious method was possibly used, one which would have had the date-palms irrigate themselves, as is the modern practice in North Africa and Southern Palestine. It is, therefore, worth while to cite in full the description given by Grasovsky-Weitz 1932.16–17 of this unique method of 'self-irrigation' which, in all probability, is a continuation of a traditional practice in these arid areas: 'Along the sand dunes of the coast in the southern part of the country [Palestine], where the water table is low, the date growers plant their palms in the following manner: Large trenches or holes of large dimensions or sometimes even entire excavations, which means the removal of thousands of cubic metres of soil, are dug in order to reach about half or one metre from the water table. At this depth the large date offshoots are planted and then watered for a number of seasons. Once roots have developed and have

sidered too saline for general irrigation purposes, most of it can be used to irrigate the date-palm (Grasovsky-Weitz 1932.12). In antiquity the adverse effects of salts on plants were well-known (Vergil *Georg.* 2.238–240; Columella 3.1.19; *Geop.* 2.10.8); but it was equally well-known that the date-palm was not affected by salinity (*Geop.* 2.10.8) and even required the addition of salt when none was present (Theophrastus *H.P.* 2.6.2; Palladius 11.12.2; *Geop.* 2.10.9).

The evidence for the cultivation of figs, pomegranates, and almonds is indeed slim, but it would be difficult to think of any settled community in Palestine which would not have grown these dietary staples. Their drought-resistant qualities make them particularly ideal for cultivation in the Negeb. In **32**, a συκαμπελών, or 'fig-vineyard', is mentioned, which I interpret to mean a vineyard in which fig trees were also grown (see below p. 254). As for pomegranates, we only know of their seeds being found in a room of the North Church complex (see Appendix I). Whether these fruits were grown for commercial purposes cannot, of course, be determined, but it is safe to say that they were at least grown for local consumption.

It is significant that Bedouin farmers cultivate all of the fruits mentioned in the Nessana documents, though on a rather small scale. On the flats to the side of the Wadi Hafir, quite close to the ancient site of Nessana, are found two sizable gardens with a large variety of trees: pomegranate, fig, olive, date-palm, almond, and even a species of apple. The space between the trees was given over to vines and barley. In February of 1957, I visited the garden just west of Auja and found two almond trees in full bloom (Pl. XLII.7), an amazing sight amid the surrounding barrenness. If the Bedouin farmer was successful with his almond trees, I have no doubt that the Nessanites also cultivated them.

APPENDIX I

*BOTANICAL SPECIMENS**

Cucurbitaceae

Citrullus colocynthis Schrad. COLOCYNTH OR BITTER APPLE

Fabaceae

Medicago hispida. BUR CLOVER
Medicago hispida Gaertn. BUR CLOVER

Gramineae

Aristida sp.
Avena barbata Brot. SLENDER OAT
Avena fatua L. WILD OAT
Bromus scoparius L. BROME GRASS
Cynodon dactylon (L.) Pers. BERMUDA GRASS
Elymus (prob. *E. Delileanus* Schult)
Festuca brevis (Boiss & Kotsch) Koch.
Hordeum murinum L. MOUSE BARLEY
Hordeum spontaneum Koch.
Hordeum vulgare L. BARLEY
Koeleria phleoides (Vill.) Pers.
Lolium perenne L. PERENNIAL RYE GRASS
Lolium temulentum L. DARNEL
Phalaris minor Retz. CANARY GRASS
Phalaris paradoxa L. CANARY GRASS
Stipa tortillis Desf. NEEDLE GRASS
Trigonella arabica Del.
Triticum aesticum L.

Juglandaceae

Juglans sp. WALNUT

Lauraceae

Laurus nobilis. BAY TREE

Punicaceae

Punica granatum L. POMEGRANATE

Rosaceae

Prunus amygdalus Batsch. ALMOND
Prunus persica. PEACH

Vitaceae

Vitis vinifera. WINE GRAPE

---

* Seeds, leaves, stems, etc., found in a sealed deposit in Room 8 of the North Church complex and identified by C. O. Erlanson, U.S. Department of Agriculture, and G. L. Wittrock, New York Botanical Gardens.

APPENDIX II

SUMMARY OF COLT PAPYRI RELATING TO AGRICULTURE

P.Colt **16**: (July 11, 512) A division of property recording changes in ownership of property jointly held by two soldiers, Zunayn son of Abraham, and John son of Asad, and John's sister. The property—apparently all lying to the east of Nessana—consists of a garden (7,24: κηπίον), a parcel of land 'from the *Abiathalbon*' (14,29), a field (χωρίον) called *Alon* . . . (18), a field called *Airegla* (21), and a vineyard (33). Included in the division are two pieces of property unidentifiable because of lacunae. It is possible that one may be a garden since its northern boundary (13,28) is the κῆπος of Bagdathos. All parcels of land are identified by adjoining property owners. In lieu of his share of the garden, Zunayn accepts 4 *solidi* from the common fund (7–11). He also waives his share of the *Abiathalbon* to John son of Asad for 1½ *solidi* (14–15, 28–32).

21: (June 30, 562) A division of seed-lands (17,34: σπόριμα χωρία), living quarters and tools among the four children of Sergius, a soldier of the camp. The document breaks off after the initial division (30–40) to one of the sons, Elias, who receives for his share in the buildings seven *solidi* less seven carats. From the seed-land (34–37) situated 'in the *Abiathalba*', Elias receives his one-fourth share with all legal rights over it (μετὰ παντὸς αὐτῆς δικαίου). The property is identified by adjoining property owners.

23: (566/7?) A contract in which a civilian acknowledges to a soldier that he has sold the latter his share of a courtyard and bake-oven, and has received in exchange some fields (7: χωρία). The soldier is guaranteed (5–7) that 'there will not fall upon you or your heirs the public taxes due upon the fields [called] *Koreothas*'.

24: (Nov. 26, 569) A notice addressed to the recorder in Elusa to transfer 5 *kabiaiai* of seed-land (5,9: χωρίον σπόριμον) from the paternal estate of two brothers, soldiers of the camp, to another soldier. The land, situated to the south of Nessana, is within village bounds and in a place called *Nearer Alagrad* (6–7,9). It is bounded on three sides by adjoining property owners; on the south, by wasteland (7: χέρση). The land is ceded with all its rights (6,9: μετὰ παντὸς αὐτοῦ δικαίου). If the new owner should become impoverished, the payment of taxes is guaranteed by the ceding party.

31: (VI) A division of farm lands and town buildings among the three sons of Eulais (Victor, Sergius, and Khalaf-Allāh). The papyrus is the longest in the collection, but in its present state, it is only one-third or two-fifths of its original length indicating that the amount of real estate involved must have been considerable. The estate of Eulais contained in the extant text is as follows:
1. *house* (3–9);
2. *house*—obviously a caravanserai—with 96 beds, an upper storey and a vacant lot in front situated near the fort on the hill and the 'Entrance Road' (32–39);
3. *house* with courtyard and vacant lot situated on a public street (39–47);
4. *vineyard* (ἀμπελών) with walls (φραγμοί) designated as east and west boundaries, the north and south boundaries being adjoining property owners (9–13; 47–51);
5. *seed-land* (σπόριμον) located above the vineyard, its boundaries being a wall (φραγμός) on the east, the water channel (ὑδραγόγιον) of Khalaf-Allāh on the west; the north and south boundaries being adjoining property owners (13–19);
6. '*dry garden*' (ξηροκήπιον) located to south of village and bounded on all sides by property owners (19–27); see Kraemer 1958.100–101, note to line 20;
7. '*dry garden*' *thachbisa* (ξηροκήπιον θαχβισα) bounded on the west and north by the water-channel (ὑδραγόγιον) owned by Victor and Sergius, on the south by a wall (φραγμός), and on the east by Victor's property (27–31); see Kraemer 1958.101, note to line 28;
8. parcel of land—classification unknown because of a lacuna—bounded on the west by a wall (φραγμός) and at other points by property owners (51–56).

32: (VI) An acknowledgment by three men, possibly more, that a certain Valens had ceded (8–14) them all his seed-lands (σπόριμα χωρία), half of a 'fig-vineyard' (συκαμπελών) and a share of a water-tank (ὑδρηρὸς λάκκος) located in it. Ceded with the seed-lands were their 'names and bounds' (ὀνομασίαι καὶ γειτνιάσεις); with the 'fig-vineyard' and tank went 'all the rights of entry and exit, and all the other privileges and appurtenances and their use and ownership' (μετὰ παντὸς αὐτῶν δικαίου καὶ εἰσ[ό]δου καὶ ἐξόδου καὶ λυπῶν δικαιωμάτων καὶ χρηστηρείων αὐτῶν πάντων [καὶ] τὴν τούτων νομὴν καὶ δεσποτίαν). A fragment at the bottom of the document (17–19) deals with various rights to water. Two of these are clear; the right of passage and the right to conduct water; the third, undecipherable, should be the right to draw water (μετὰ παντὸς [αὐτῶν δι] καίου καὶ εἰσόδου καὶ [ἐ]ξ[όδου] καὶ ὑδραγωγείων κ[αι .....]τα.ειων).

34: (VI) A fragment of a contract in which property is being transferred or leased. A vineyard is involved with vines furnished with props (2: εὐεντελίᾳ ἀμπέλῳ ἐπὶ χάρακει), and newly set out (9: κατανευθέντος νεοφύτου ἀμπελῶνος).

35: (VI) A levy of 30 camels and 34 dromedaries imposed on the village to supply the needs of army and church.

37: (560–580?) An inventory of camels attached to military unit at Nessana. At least 38 camels are mentioned; the original list probably contained an inventory of some 200 camels.

40: (Early VII) Amounts of wheat (σῖτος) 'for sale' (εἰς πρᾶσιν) or 'for salary' (εἰς τροφία). The amounts preserved 'for sale' are 10, 32, and 21 *modii*; those entered as receipts 'for salary' are 3 and, in more doubtful readings, 5 and 12 *modii*.

58: (Late VII) Receipt issued by a group of Nessanites to Sergius son of George for γεωμετρία τῶν Σαρακηνῶν (8) and γεωμορία (10).

59: (October, 684?) Acknowledgment by a commission of four men that they have received land-tax (δημόσια) and poll-tax payments in full.

60–67: (674–677) *Entagia*: Demand-notes from the Arab governor at Gaza to the people of Nessana for the delivery of ——— σίτου μόδιοι; ——— ἐλαίου ξέσται. The eight documents are summarized as follows:

No.	Date	Period		Amount			
60	Nov. 674	5 months (Nov–March)	70 *mod.* wheat		70 *xes.* oil		
61	Aug. 675	2 „ (June–July)	96 „	„	96 „	„
62	Oct. 675	2 „ (Sept–Oct)	310 „	„	310 „	„
63	Oct. 675	2 „ (Dec–Jan)	96 „	„	96 „	„
64*	Feb. 676	2 „ (Feb–March)	279 „	„	279 „	„
65	676?	? (April–May?)	205 „	„	205 „	„
66	Feb. 677	2 „ —	90 „	„	90 „	„
67	689	(not given)	270 „	„	270 „	„

* Belongs to Sycamazon, not to Nessana.

69: (680/1?) An account of receipts for ρουζικόν (Arabic *rizk*) the food allowance of Arab troops. It is divided into two sections, the former (2–6, totalled in 11) listing amounts paid in kind (*modii* of wheat and *xestai* of oil), the latter (7–10, totalled in 12–13) amounts paid in money. The account is complete and represents Nessana's quota for one year of the military supply tax. Each of the individual entries corresponds to the amount demanded in a single *entagion*.

Translation:

Account of food-tax for the ninth indiction.

462 *mod.* of wheat	231 *xes.* of oil
300 „ „ „	150 „ „ „
8 „ „ „	4 „ „ „
370 „ „ „	185 „ „ „
40 „ „ „	40 „ „ „

Also price of:

170 *mod.* of wheat	170 *xes.* of oil	11⅓ *nomismata*
67 ,, ,, ,,	67 ,, ,, ,,	4½ ,,
124 ,, ,, ,,	124 ,, ,, ,,	8¼ ,,
46 ,, ,, ,,	46 ,, ,, ,,	3¹⁄₁₂ ,,

Totals: 1180 *mod.* of wheat   610 *xes.* of oil
Price of: 407 ,, ,, ,,   407 ,, ,, ,, 27⅛ *nomismata.*

80: (ca. 685) Record of nine donations of wheat made to the church of St. Sergius in sums ranging from two to ten *modii.*

81: (ca. 685) Account of receipts in kind.

Wheat	*Barley*
15 *modii*	12 *modii*
4 ,,	30½ ,,
5⅛ ,,	
20 ,,	
6 ,,	
65 ,,	

82: (VII) Account of grain sown and reaped in the Birein area.

Text

+ γνῶ(σις) [σίτ(ου)] ἥτι ἐσπίραμε(ν) εἰ(ς) τ(ὴν) γῆν Βεραειν.
ἐσπίραμεν ἀπ(ὸ) τοῦ Ρ[.]γοριου εἰ(ς) Κατ σίτ(ου) μ(ό)δ(ια) μ
(καὶ) ἐπ[ο]ίεισα[ν τ]αῦτα μ(ό)δ(ια) μ̄ τὰ σπαρθ(έντα) σίτ(ου) μ(ό)δ(ια) σο
τ[ὸ πρ]ῶ(τον) ἁλόνιον· (καὶ) ἐσπίραμεν εἰς Μαλαλκανι σίτ(ου) μ(ό)δ(ια) μ
5 (καὶ) ἐποίεισαν σ[ίτ(ου)] μ(ό)δ(ια) σπη. τὸ δεύτερ(ον) ἁλόνιου.
(καὶ) ἐ[σπ]ίραμε(ν) εἰς Αλφαγ σίτ(ου) μ(ό)δ(ια) ρπ (καὶ) ἐξέβαλεν σίτ(ου) μ(ό)δ(ια) ασκε
(καὶ) ἐσπ[ί]ρ(αμεν) εἰς [Α]λφαγ κρ(ι)θ(ῶν) μ(ό)δ(ια) ν (καὶ) ἐξέβαλεν κρ(ι)θ(ῶν) μ(ό)δ(ια) υβ
(καὶ) ἐσπίρ(αμεν) εἰς Βεραει[ν] κρ(ι)θ(ῶν) μ(ό)δ(ια) μ (καὶ) ἐ[ξ]έ[β]αλεν κρ(ι)θ(ῶν) μ(ό)δ(ια) τν
(καὶ) ἐσπίρ(αμεν) ἀρ(άκου) μ(ό)δ(ια) λ (καὶ) ἐξέβαλεν ἀρ(άκου) μ(ό)δ(ια) ϙζ
10 (καὶ) ἐσπίρα(μεν) εἰς Σεραμ σίτ(ου) μ(ό)δ(ια) ρ (καὶ) ἐποίεισεν σίτ(ου) μ(ό)δ(ια)
(καὶ) ἐσπίρα(μεν) εἰς Μαλζημαρχε σίτ(ου) μ(ό)δ(ια) ϙ (καὶ)

verso
+ γνῶ(σις) σί(του) ἥτι ἐσπίρ[α]με(ν) εἰ(ς) [. . . . .] σίτ(ου) μ(ό)δ(ια) τ (καὶ)
ἐποίεισεν ὅσα ἐσπίρ(αμεν) [σί]τ(ου) μ(ό)δ(ια) . [. .]ο
(καὶ) ἐσπίρ(αμεν) κρ(ι)θ(ῶν) μ(ό)δ(ια) νε (καὶ) ἐποίεισεν κρ(ι)θ(ῶν) μ(ό)δ(ια)

Summary

Place	*Modii Sown*	*Modii Reaped*	*Remarks*
From Ragorion to Kat	40 wheat	270	On threshing floor #1
Malalkani	40 wheat	288	On threshing floor #2
Alphag	180 wheat	1225	
	50 barley	402	
Berain	40 barley	350	
	30 *aracus*	97	
Seram	100 wheat	unrecorded	
Malzemarche	90 wheat	unrecorded	

83: (684/5?) Account of wheat stored on three threshing floors, thirteenth indiction:

1st threshing floor	33 *modii* of wheat belonging to ———
2nd „ „	45 „ „ „ „ „ ———
3rd „ „	150 „ „ „ „ „ ———
1st „ „	9 „ „ „ „ „ ———
2nd „ „	60 „ „ „ „ „ ———
	14 „ „ seed wheat
	4 „ „ wheat of the *trobelia*
3rd „ „	115 „ „ „ belonging to ———
minus 31	„ „ seed wheat
	4½ „ „ wheat of the *trobelia*

90–91: (VI–VII) Daily record of sales of dates (λόγος πράσεως φοινικίων). **90** contains over two hundred entries and covers a period of 8 months (Oct.–May); **91** is fragmentary, only some fifty entries remaining. Each entry gives the date of sale, name of purchaser, the number of baskets purchased; the rate (the number of baskets per *solidus*), and their condition (καθαρός or ρυπαρός). At the end of each column the total cash received is entered. I cite as examples the first two entries of **90** (3–4) and the total receipts at the end of the first column (36).

Date	Buyer	Amount	Price	Condition
Oct. 17	Timothy son of Rufinus	2 baskets	8 per sol.	unclean
Oct. 17	Julian son of Bias	4 „	7½ „ „	clean

Total: dates 93½ baskets
      10 solidi 39½ carats
      Deduct for cleaning 9⅝ carats
      Balance: 11 solidi 5⅞ carats

94: (VIII) Wax tablet containing scattered lines of an account dealing with *xestai* of oil and *modii* of wheat.

97: (VI) A fragment of a division of property or transfer of ownership. Isolated words relating to farm lands can be read: (22) σπόρ[ι]μα; (30) ἀμπελία; (41) σ]πόριμα; (44) ἀμ]πελών.

105: (VI–VII) Fragment probably of a contract. The word (2) χερσοκοπία, 'the breaking up of χέρσος' into productive land is preserved.

APPENDIX III

PLACE NAMES*

Modern	Ancient		Modern	Ancient
Abda	Eboda		Raheiba	
Abde	Oboda		Ruheiba	?
'Abdeh	Obeda		Ruheibeh	
*Avdat			*Rehovot Hanegev	
*Ovdat				
			Sbeita	Sobata
Auja	Nessana		Sbeitah	
Auja Hafir	Nesana		S'beita	
Hafir el Auja	Nestana		Sbaita	
el-Auja			Esbeita	
el-'Awǧà			es-Sbejta	
el-hafir			Isbeiṭā	
hafir el-'audschā			*Shivta	
*Nitsanah				
			Seram	Seram
Beersheba	Birosaba			
			Wadi Abyed	
Birein	Beraein		Abiad	
*Beerotayim			*Lavan	
Khalasa	Elusa		Asluj	
el-Ḥalaṣa			*Revivim	
el-Chalasa				
*Halutsa			Hafir	
			*Nitsanah	
Kurnub	Mampsis			
Qurnub			Ramliya	
*Mamshit			Ramliyeh	
			*Avdat	

* Under the place names used in the text this appendix gives some of the orthographical variants used by other writers. Names marked with an asterisk are Israeli replacements or equivalents for Arabic place names.

ABBREVIATIONS AND BIBLIOGRAPHY

Abel 1933 = M. Abel, *Géographie de la Palestine*, Vols. I–II. Paris, 1933

Albright 1940 = William F. Albright, *From Stone Age to Christianity*. Baltimore, 1940

Amiran 1954 = Ruth Amiran, 'The Cities of the Negev' (summary), *Israel Exploration Journal*, Vol. IV, No. 1. Jerusalem, 1954

Antoninus Martyr = Antoninus Martyr, 'De Locis Sanctis' in *Itinera Hierosolymitana*, edited by T. Tobler and A. Molinier. Geneva, 1879

Ashbel 1936 = D. Ashbel, 'On the Importance of Dew in Palestine', *Journal of the Palestine Oriental Society*, Vol. XVI. Jerusalem, 1936

Ashbel 1939 = D. Ashbel, 'The Very Exceptional Rainy Season of 1937–38', *Journal of the Palestine Oriental Society*, Vol. XIX. Jerusalem, 1939

Ashbel 1949 = D. Ashbel, 'Frequency and Distribution of Dew in Palestine', *The Geographical Review*, Vol. XXXIX, No. 2. New York, 1949

Ashburner 1912 = Walter Ashburner, 'The Farmer's Law', *The Journal of Hellenic Studies*, Vol. XXXII. London, 1912

Avi-Yonah 1937 = M. Avi-Yonah, 'The Economic Past of the Negeb', *Palestine and Middle East Economic Magazine*, Vol. IX, No. 6. Tel-Aviv, 1937

Avi-Yonah 1937a = M. Avi-Yonah, *The Ancient Water Works of Palestine*. Jerusalem, 1937 (typescript)

Avi-Yonah 1952 = M. Avi-Yonah, 'Ancient Remains in the Negev', *Zion*, Vol. III, No. 2. Jerusalem, 1952

Avi-Yonah 1958 = M. Avi-Yonah, 'The Economics of Byzantine Palestine', *Israel Exploration Journal*, Vol. VIII, No. 1. Jerusalem, 1958

Awad 1953 = Hassan Awad, 'Ground Water and Human Geography: Ways of Life in Desert Regions', *Proceedings of the Ankara Symposium on Arid Zone Hydrology* (UNESCO Arid Zone Programme). Paris, 1953

Baly 1935 = Colin Baly, 'S'baita', *Palestine Exploration Fund Quarterly Statement*, October. London, 1935

Baradez 1949 = Jean Baradez, *Fossatum Africae. Recherches aériennes de l'organization des confins sahariens a l'époque romaine*. Paris, 1949

Bartlett 1879 = S. C. Bartlett, *From Egypt to Palestine*. New York, 1879

Billiard 1913 = Raymond Billiard, *La vigne dans l'antiquité*. Lyon, 1913

Blake 1947 = G. S. Blake and G. M. J. Goldschmidt, *Geology and Water Resources of Palestine*. Jerusalem, 1947

Bonar 1857 = Horatius Bonar, *The Desert of Sinai*. New York, 1857

Bowen 1958 = Richard LeBaron Bowen, Jr., Frank P. Albright, *et al.*, *Archaeological Discoveries in South Arabia*. Baltimore, 1958

Boyko 1955 = H. Boyko, 'Climatic, Ecoclimatic and Hydrological Influences on Vegetation', *Plant Ecology*, *Proceedings of the Montpellier Symposium* (UNESCO). Paris, 1955

Bradford 1949 = John Bradford, 'Buried Landscapes in Southern Italy', *Antiquity*, Vol. XXIII, No. 90. Newbury, Berks., 1949

Bradford 1950 = John Bradford, 'The Apulia Expedition: An Interim Report', *Antiquity*, Vol. XXIV, No. 94. Newbury, Berks., 1950

Brittain 1952 = Robert Brittain, *Let There be Bread*. New York, 1952

Brogan-Smith 1957 = Olwen Brogan and David Smith, 'The Roman Frontier Settlement at Ghirza: An Interim Report', *The Journal of Roman Studies*, Vol. XLVII. London, 1957

Butler 1921 = Howard C. Butler, *Syria. Publications of the Princeton University Archaeological Expedition to Syria in 1904–5*, Division III. Leyden, 1921

Calder 1951 = Ritchie Calder, *Men Against the Desert*. London, 1951

Caponera 1954 = Dante Caponera, *Water Laws in Moslem Countries* (FAO Development Paper No. 43). Rome, 1954

Cato = *M. Porci Catonis De Agri Cultura Liber*, edited by G. Goetz. Leipzig, 1922

Caton-Thompson-Gardner 1939 = G. Caton-Thompson and W. Gardner, 'Climate, Irrigation, and Early Man in the Hadhramaut', *The Geographical Journal*, Vol. XCIII, No. 1. London, 1939

Chaptal 1932 = L. Chaptal, 'La lutte contre la sécheresse', *La Nature*, Vol. LX, Part 2. Paris, 1932

Cicero = *M. Tulli Ciceronis Scripta Quae Manserunt Omnia*, edited by R. Klotz. Leipzig, 1852 (*Caecin. = Pro A. Caecina Oratio; 2-Verr. = In L. Catilinam Oratio Secunda*)

CIL = Corpus Inscriptionum Latinarum, Vols. I–XVI. Berlin, 1836–1936

Cod.Just. = Corpus Juris Civilis: Institutiones, Digesta, Codex Iustinianus, Novellae, edited by P. Krueger, T. Mommsen and W. Kroll, Vols. I–III. Berlin, 1880–1895

Columella = *Lucius Junius Moderatus Columella on Agriculture*, edited and translated by H. B. Ash, E. M. Forster and E. Heffner, Vols. I–III, Loeb Classical Library. London, 1948–1955

Crawford 1954 = O. G. S. Crawford, 'A Century of Air-photography', *Antiquity*, Vol. XXVIII, No. 112. Newbury, Berks., 1954

Crist 1954 = Raymond E. Crist, 'The Mountain Village of Dahr, Lebanon', *Annual Report of the Smithsonian Institution 1953*. Washington, 1954

Demosthenes Or. = *Demosthenis Orationes*, edited by F. Blass, Vols. I–III, 4th edition. Leipzig, 1892–1901

Desert Research Proceedings 1953 = 'Excursion', *Desert Research Proceedings* (Research Council of Israel Special Publication No. 2). Jerusalem, 1953

Despois 1949 = Jean Despois, *L'Afrique du Nord* (Colonies et Empires, Série 4: Géographie de l'union française). Paris, 1949

Digest = see *Cod.Just.*

Diodorus = *Diodori (Siculi) Bibliotheca Historica*, edited by F. Vogel, Vols. I–V. Leipzig, 1888–1906

Duvdevani 1953 = S. Duvdevani, 'Dew Gradients in Relation to Climate, Soil and Topography', *Desert Research Proceedings* (Research Council of Israel Special Publication No. 2). Jerusalem, 1953

Epstein 1939 = Eliahu Epstein, 'Bedouin of the Negeb', *Palestine Exploration Quarterly*, April. London, 1939

Evenari-Koller 1956 = Michael Evenari and Dov Koller, 'Masters of the Desert', *Scientific American*, Vol. CXCIV, No. 4. New York, 1956

Fairchild 1930 = David Fairchild, *Exploring for Plants*. New York, 1930

Fl. Cresconius Corippus *de laud.Just.Aug.* = 'Fl. Cresconius Corippus, De laudibus Justini Augusti Minoris', edited by I. Bekker, *Corpus Scriptorum Historiae Byzantinae*, Vol. XVIII. Bonn, 1836

Frank 1933 = Tenney Frank, 'Rome and Italy of the Republic', *An Economic Survey of Ancient Rome*, Vol. I. Baltimore, 1933

Gauckler 1897–1903 = *Enquête sur les installations hydrauliques romaines en Tunisie*, edited by Paul Gauckler. Tunis, 1897–1903

Geop. = Geoponica, edited by H. Beckh. Leipzig, 1895

Glueck 1951 = Nelson Glueck, 'Explorations in Eastern Palestine, IV', *Annual of the American Schools of Oriental Research*, Vols. XXV–XXVIII in 2 parts. New Haven, 1951

Glueck 1953 = Nelson Glueck, 'Explorations in Western Palestine', *Bulletin of the American Schools of Oriental Research*, No. 131. Baltimore, 1953

Glueck 1955 = Nelson Glueck, 'Further Explorations in the Negeb', *Bulletin of the American Schools of Oriental Research*, No. 137. Baltimore, 1955

Glueck 1957 = Nelson Glueck, 'The Fifth Season of Exploration in the Negeb', *Bulletin of the American Schools of Oriental Research*, No. 145. Baltimore, 1957

Glueck 1958 = Nelson Glueck, 'The Sixth Season of Archaeological Exploration in the Negeb', *Bulletin of the American Schools of Oriental Research*, No. 149. Baltimore, 1958

Glueck 1958a = Nelson Glueck, 'The Seventh Season of Archaeological Exploration in the Negeb', *Bulletin of the American Schools of Oriental Research*, No. 152. Baltimore, 1958

Goodchild 1950 = R. G. Goodchild, 'Roman Tripolitania: Reconnaissance in the Desert Frontier Zone', *The Geographical Journal*, Vol. CXV. London, 1950

Gottman 1942 = Jean Gottman, 'New Facts and Some Reflections on the Sahara', *The Geographical Review*, Vol. XXXII. New York, 1942

Grasovsky-Weitz 1930 = Asaph Grasovsky and Joseph Weitz (or Waitz), 'Fig Growing in Palestine (1930)', *Government of Palestine, Department of Agriculture and Forests. Agricultural Leaflets, Series IV*, No. 28. Jerusalem, 1930

18

Grasovsky-Weitz 1932 = Asaph Grasovsky and Joseph Weitz (or Waitz), 'The Date-Palm in Palestine', *Government of Palestine, Department of Agriculture and Forests. Agricultural Leaflets, Series IV*, No. 29. Jerusalem, 1932

Gregorius Turonensis *Hist.Franc.* = 'Gregorius Turonensis, Historia Francorum' in J. P. Migne, *Patrologiae Cursus Completus ... Series Latina*, Vol. LXXI. Paris, 1844–1864

Guy 1938 = P. L. O. Guy, 'Archaeological Survey of Palestine', *The Quarterly of the Department of Antiquities in Palestine*, Vol. VIII, No. 4. Jerusalem, 1938

Handcock 1922 = P. S. P. Handcock, 'Vines', *Dictionary of the Apostolic Church*, edited by Hastings, Selbie, and Lambert, Vol. II. New York, 1922

Hartley 1944 = B. J. Hartley, 'Dry Farming Methods in the Aden Protectorate', *Middle East Supply Centre Agricultural Report No. 6*. Cairo, 1944

Heichelheim 1938 = F. M. Heichelheim, 'Roman Syria', *An Economic Survey of Ancient Rome*, edited by T. Frank. Baltimore, 1938

Heitland 1921 = W. E. Heitland, *Agricola*. Cambridge, 1921

Herodotus = *Herodoti Historiarum Libri IX*, edited by H. Kahlenberg, Vols. I–II. Leipzig, 1921–1922

Hitier 1925 = Henri Hitier, 'Condensateurs des vapeurs atmosphériques dans l'antiquité', *Comptes rendus des seances de la Société nationale*, Vol. XI. Paris, 1925

Homer *Od.* = *Homeri Opera*, edited by T. W. Allen. Oxford C.T. (*Od.* = *Odyssea*)

Huntington 1911 = Ellsworth Huntington, *Palestine and its Transformation*. Boston, 1911

Isidorus *Orig.* = 'Isidori Hispalensis Episcopi Etymologiarum Libri XX', edited by F. Otto, *Corpus Grammaticorum Latinorum Veterum*, Vol. III. Leipzig, 1883

Isr.Met.Ser. 1952 = 'Climatological Data for the Negev', *State of Israel, Ministry of Transport and Communications, Series A, Meteorological Notes*, No. 4, Jerusalem, 1952

Isr.Met.Ser. 1952a = 'Climatological Normals', *State of Israel, Ministry of Transport and Communications, Series A, Meteorological Notes*, No. 3. Jerusalem, 1952

Jardé 1925 = Auguste Jardé, 'Les céréales dans l'antiquité grecque', *Bibliothéque des écoles françaises d'Athènes et de Rome*, Fasc. 130. Paris, 1925

Jasny 1944 = Naum Jasny, 'The Wheats of Classical Antiquity', *The Johns Hopkins University Studies in Historical and Political Science Series*, Vol. LXII, No. 3. Baltimore, 1944

Johnson 1936 = Allan C. Johnson, 'Roman Egypt to the Reign of Diocletian', *An Economic Survey of Ancient Rome*, edited by T. Frank, Vol. II. Baltimore, 1936

Kallner-Amiran 1950–1 = D. H. Kallner-Amiran, 'Geomorphology of the Negev Highlands', *Israel Exploration Journal*, Vol. I, No. 2. Jerusalem, 1950–1

Kearney 1905 = Thomas H. Kearney, 'Agriculture Without Irrigation in the Sahara Desert', *U.S. Department of Agriculture, Bureau of Plant Industry, Bulletin* No. 86. Washington, 1905

Kearney 1908 = Thomas H. Kearney, 'Dry-Land Olive Culture in Northern Africa', *U.S. Department of Agriculture, Bureau of Plant Industry, Bulletin* No. 125. Washington, 1908

Kedar 1956 = Yehuda Kedar, 'The Problem of the Mounds or "Tuleilat el 'Anab" and their Relation to Ancient Agriculture in the Central Negev', *Bulletin of the Israel Exploration Society*, Vol. XX, No. 1–2 (Hebrew). Jerusalem, 1956

Kedar 1957 = Yehuda Kedar, 'Water and Soil from the Desert: Some Ancient Agricultural Achievements in the Central Negev', *The Geographical Journal*, Vol. CXXIII. London, 1957

Kedar 1957a = Yehuda Kedar, 'Ancient Agriculture at Shivta in the Negev', *Israel Exploration Journal*, Vol. VII, No. 3. Jerusalem, 1957

Keen 1946 = B. A. Keen, *The Agricultural Development of the Middle East*. London, 1946

Kirk 1938 = George E. Kirk, 'Archaeological Exploration in the Southern Desert', *Palestine Exploration Quarterly*, October. London, 1938

Kirk 1941 = George E. Kirk, 'The Negev, or Southern Desert of Palestine', *Palestine Exploration Quarterly*, April. London, 1941

Kraemer 1958 = Casper J. Kraemer, 'Non-Literary Papyri', *Excavations at Nessana*, Vol. III. Princeton, 1958

La Blanchère 1897 = Du Coudray La Blanchère, 'L'amenagement de l'eau et l'installation rurale dans l'Afrique ancienne', *Nouvelles archives des missions scientifiques*, Vol. VII. Paris, 1897

Lewis 1953 = Norman N. Lewis, 'Lebanon—The Mountain and its Terraces', *The Geographical Review*, Vol. XLIII, No. 1. New York, 1953

Liddell-Scott = H. G. Liddell and R. Scott, *A Greek-English Lexicon*, new edition by H. S. Jones. Oxford, 1925–1940

Lowdermilk 1944 = Walter C. Lowdermilk, *Palestine, Land of Promise*. New York, 1944

Lowdermilk 1953 = Walter C. Lowdermilk, 'Floods in Deserts', *Desert Research Proceedings* (Research Council of Israel Special Publication No. 2). Jerusalem, 1953

Lowdermilk 1954 = Walter C. Lowdermilk, 'The Use of Flood-Waters by the Nabataeans and Byzantines' (summary), *Israel Exploration Journal*, Vol. IV, No. 1. Jerusalem, 1954

Lowe 1944 = B. A. Lowe, 'Dry Farming in the Beersheba District of Palestine', *Middle East Supply Centre Agricultural Report No. 6*. Cairo, 1944

Magnus Aurelius Cassiodorus *Var.* = 'Magnus Aurelius Cassiodorus, Variarum Libri XII' in J. P. Migne, *Patrologiae Cursus Completus . . . Series Latina*, Vol. LXIX. Paris, 1844–1864

Marcus Diaconus *Vit.Porph.* = *Marci Diaconi Vita Porphyrii Episcopi Gazensis*, edited by the Societas Philologa Bonnensis. Leipzig, 1895

Masson 1948 = H. Masson, 'Condensations atmosphérique non enregistrables au pluviomètre', *Bulletin de l'institute français d'Afrique noire*, Vol. X. Dakar, 1948

Mayerson 1959 = Philip Mayerson, 'The Ancient Agricultural Remains in the Central Negeb: The *teleilât el-'anab*', *Bulletin of the American Schools of Oriental Research*, No. 153. Baltimore, 1959

Mayerson 1960 = Philip Mayerson, 'The Ancient Agricultural Remains in the Central Negeb: Methodology and Dating Criteria', *Bulletin of the American Schools of Oriental Research*, No. 160. Baltimore, 1960

Meigs 1953 = Peveril Meigs, 'Designs and Use of Homoclimatic Maps; Dry Climates of Israel as Example', *Desert Research Proceedings* (Research Council of Israel Special Publication No. 2). Jerusalem, 1953

Moussly 1951 = Nazim Moussly, *Le problème de l'eau en Syrie*. Lyon, 1951

Musil 1908 = Alois Musil, *Arabia Petraea*, 3 vols. in 4, Vol. I *Moab*; Vol. II (in 2 parts) *Edom*; Vol. III *Ethnologischer Reisebericht*. Vienna, 1907–1908

Musil 1928 = Alois Musil, *Palmyrena*. New York, 1928

Myers 1944 = Harold E. Myers, 'Dry Land Farming Practices', *Middle East Supply Centre Agricultural Report No. 6*. Cairo, 1944

P.Colt = see Kraemer 1958

P.Ryl. = J. de M. Johnson, Victor Martin, *et al.*, *Catalogue of the Greek Papyri in the John Rylands Library, Manchester*, Vols. I–IV. Manchester, 1911–1952

Pack 1935 = Roger A. Pack, *Studies in Libanius and Antiochene Society under Theodosius*. (Place of publication not stated), 1935

Palladius = *Palladii Rutilii Tauri Aemiliani Opus Agriculturae*, edited by J. C. Schmitt. Leipzig, 1898

Palmer 1871 = E. H. Palmer, *The Desert of the Exodus*, Vols. I–II. Cambridge, 1871

Percival 1921 = John Percival, *The Wheat Plant, A Monograph*. London, 1921

Perold 1927 = A. I. Perold, *Treatise on Viticulture*. London, 1927

Plato *Leg.* = *Platonis Opera*, edited by J. Burnet. Oxford C.T. (*Leg.* = *Leges*)

Pliny = *C. Plini Secundi Naturalis Historiae*, edited by C. Mayhoff, 2nd edition, Vols. I–VI. Leipzig, 1892–1909

Poidebard 1934 = A. Poidebard, *La trace de Rome dans le désert de Syrie. Le limes de Trajan à la conquête arabe. Récherches aériennes (1925–1932)*, Texte et Atlas. Paris, 1934

Pomponius Mela = *Pomponii Melae De Situ Orbis Libri Tres*, edited by C. H. Tzschvckio. Leipzig, 1806–1807

Portes-Ruyssen 1886–1889 = Ludovic Portes and F. Ruyssen, *Traité de la vigne et de ses produits*, Vols. I–III. Paris, 1886–1889

Prawer 1951 = J. Prawer, 'On Agriculture under the Crusaders', *Eretz-Israel*, Vol. I (Hebrew). Jerusalem, 1951

Procopius *Anec.* = *Procopii Caesariensis Opera Omnia*, edited by J. Haury, Vols. I–III. Leipzig, 1905–1913 (*Anec.* = Anecdota/Historia Arcana)

Ravikovitch 1953 = S. Ravikovitch, 'The Aeolian Soils of the Northern Negev', *Desert Research Proceedings* (Research Council of Israel Special Publication No. 2). Jerusalem, 1953

Ravikovitch-Pines-Dan 1956 = S. Ravikovitch, F. Pines and Y. Dan, 'Desert Soils of Southern Israel (The Central and Southern Negev)', *Agricultural Research Station, Rehovot, Special Bulletin No. 5.* Rehovot, 1956

Robinson 1856 = Edward Robinson et al., *Biblical Researches in Palestine and in the Adjacent Regions*, Vols. I–III, 2nd edition. London, 1856

Rostovtzeff 1922 = Michael Rostovtzeff, *A Large Estate in Egypt in the Third Century B.C.* (University of Wisconsin Studies in the Social Sciences and History, No. 6.) Madison, 1922

Schlumberger 1951 = Daniel Schlumberger, *La Palmyrène du Nord-Ouest.* Paris, 1951

Schnebel 1925 = Michael Schnebel, *Die Landwirtschaft in hellenistischen Ägypten.* Munich, 1925

Schwabe 1954 = M. Schwabe, 'Jewish Peasants in the Negev in the Talmudic Period' (summary), *Israel Exploration Journal*, Vol. IV, No. 1. Jerusalem, 1954

Scramuzza 1937 = V. M. Scramuzza, 'Roman Sicily', *An Economic Survey of Ancient Rome*, edited by T. Frank, Vol. III. Baltimore, 1937

Shalem 1953 = N. Shalem, 'La stabilité du climat en Palestine', *Desert Research Proceedings* (Research Council of Israel Special Publication No. 2). Jerusalem, 1953

Shaw 1947 = Sydney H. Shaw, *Southern Palestine Geological Map on a Scale of 1/250,000 with Explanatory Notes.* Jerusalem, 1947

Shiftan 1954 = Z. L. Shiftan, 'Underground Water in the Negev' (summary), *Israel Exploration Journal*, Vol. IV, No. 1. Jerusalem, 1954

Sidonius Apollinaris *Carm.* = *C. Sollius Apollinaris Sidonius*, edited by P. Mohr. Leipzig, 1895 (*Carm. = Carmina*)

Soils 1957 = *Soils: The Yearbook of Agriculture 1957.* Washington, 1957

Stark 1852 = Karl B. Stark, *Gaza und die philistäische Küste.* Jena, 1852

Stevens 1941 = Courtenay E. Stevens, 'Agriculture and Rural Life in the Later Roman Empire', *The Cambridge Economic History of Europe*, edited by J. H. Clapham and E. Power, Vol. I. Cambridge, 1941

Stewart 1857 = Robert W. Stewart, *The Tent and the Khan.* Edinburgh, 1857

Strabo = *Strabonis Geographica*, edited by A. Meineke, Vols. I–III. Leipzig, 1915–1925

Tadmor 1958 = N. H. Tadmor, M. Evenari, L. Shanan and D. Hillel, 'The Ancient Desert Agriculture of the Negev', *Ktavim*, Vol. VIII, No. 1–2. Rehovot, 1958

Taubenschlag 1944 = Raphael Taubenschlag, *The Law of Greco-Roman Egypt in the Light of the Papyri.* New York, 1944

Theophrastus *H.P.* = *Theophrasti Eresii Opera Quae Supersunt Omnia*, edited by F. Wimmer, 2 vols. in 1. Leipzig, 1854–1862 (*H.P. = De Historia Plantarum*)

Totius Orbis Descriptio = 'Totius Orbis Descriptio', *Geographi Graeci Minores*, edited by C. Muller, Vol. II. Paris, 1882

Tristram 1873 = H. B. Tristram, *The Land of Moab.* New York, 1873

U.N. Economic Survey 1949 = *Final Report. United Nations Economic Survey Mission for the Middle East*, Part II. New York, 1949

van der Meulen 1932 = D. van der Meulen and H. von Wissman, *Hadhramaut.* Leyden, 1932

van der Meulen 1947 = D. van der Meulen, *Aden to the Hadhramaut.* London, 1947

Varro = *M. Terenti Varronis Rerum Rusticarum Libri Tres*, edited by G. Goetz. Leipzig, 1912

Vergil *Georg.* = *P. Vergili Maronis Eclogae et Georgica*, edited by W. Janell. Leipzig, 1930

Viala-Ravaz 1903 = P. Viala and L. Ravaz, *American Vines (Resistant Stock)*, translated by R. Dubois and E. Twight. San Francisco, 1903

Vitruvius *Arch.* = *Vitruvii De Architectura Libri X*, edited by F. Krohn. Leipzig, 1912

Ward-Perkins 1950 = J. B. Ward-Perkins, 'Gasr es Suq el-Oti: A Desert Settlement in Central Tripolitania', *Archaeology*, Vol. III, No. 1. New York, 1950

Water Measurements 1947 = *Water Measurements Prior to October 1944*, Department of Land Settlement and Water Commissioner, Irrigation Service. Jerusalem, 1947

Weitz 1950 = Joseph Weitz, *The Struggle for the Land.* Tel-Aviv, 1950

Westermann 1922 = W. L. Westermann, 'The "Dry Land" in Ptolemaic and Roman Egypt', *Classical Philology*, Vol. XVII. Chicago, 1922

Wiegand 1920 = Theodor Wiegand, 'Sinai', *Wissenschaftliche Veröffentlichungen des Deutsche-Türkischen Denkmalschutz-Kommandos*. Fasc. I. Berlin, 1920

Woolley-Lawrence 1936 = C. Leonard Woolley and T. C. Lawrence, *The Wilderness of Zin*. New York, 1936 (first published as the *Annual of the Palestine Exploration Fund for 1914–15*)

Worthington 1946 = E. B. Worthington, *Middle East Science*. London, 1946

Zohary 1954 = M. Zohary, 'Notes on Ancient Agriculture in the Central Negev', *Israel Exploration Journal*, Vol. IV, No. 1. Jerusalem, 1954

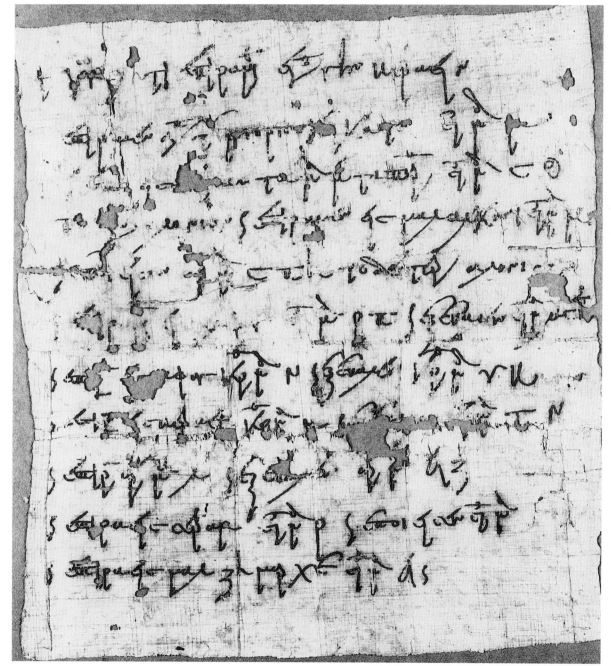

Pl. 6. A papyrus document from Nessana, *P. Ness.* 82, recording amounts of wheat, barley and vetch (?) sown and reaped.

THE DESERT OF SOUTHERN PALESTINE ACCORDING TO
BYZANTINE SOURCES*

PHILIP MAYERSON

Department of Classics, New York University

THE history of the Negeb, obscure as it is, is further darkened by the lack of accounts of travelers who made their way through this *terra incognita,* as it surely must have been even in ancient times. For the post-Biblical period we possess only two such accounts: the *itinerarium* (*ca.* A.D. 570) of Antoninus of Placentia [1] and the *diēgēmata* or *narrationes* of Nilus the Ascetic (*d.* A.D. 430).[2] In both instances the portion of their work dealing specifically with the Negeb is small but, nevertheless, it is of considerable value in adding to and confirming what is known of the region for the Byzantine period.

The lack of this kind of evidence is understandable: merchants or caravaneers, the most frequent travelers of the roads through the Negeb and adjacent regions, rarely kept diaries or put their adventures into writing,[3] and for those intrepid pilgrims who wished to tour the Biblical sites of Sinai, the coastal roads of Palestine and the Sinai Peninsula were easier and, more importantly, safer to travel than the direct route through the Central Negeb and the Tih desert of Sinai. However, safety and accessibility were not—and still are not—the only criteria for the determined tourist; it seems simply that the Biblical sites of the Negeb never held much attraction for the early Christian traveler. Beersheba, for example, appears to have held no interest whatsoever for foreign visitors even though it was accessible and a well-known Old Testament site. But I suspect that it and other places in the Negeb lacked the dramatic qualities and the tangible relics associated with such places as Jerusalem, Hebron, Gaza, or Mount Sinai.

The historicity of Antoninus' journey from Placentia to the Holy Land has not been challenged in recent times and the itinerary has often been cited, particularly with respect to the *loca sancta* of Jerusalem and Mount Sinai. Nilus, however, has not fared as well as Antoninus. Heussi, the chief antagonist of the unity of Nilus the writer of the epistles and Nilus the writer of the *narratio,* considers the narrative to be so riddled with elements of Greek *Romanliteratur* that it has questionable value as history or autobiography:

Sie zeigt in der Komposition des Ganzen und in manchen Einzelheiten der Handlung unverkennbare Verwandtschaft mit der griechischen Romanliteratur. . . . Ein Grund, mich gegen die Verwertung der Narratio als einer guten Geschichtsquelle von autobiographischen Wert zu wenden, war für mich die Beobachtung, dass manch Züge an die Technik an den Inhalt der griechischen Romanliteratur erinnern.[4]

---

* For convenience in citation, I use the following abbreviations in the footnotes:

Enc. Isl.—Encyclopaedia of Islam, ed. M. Th. Houtsma, T. W. Arnold, R. Basset, R. Hartman, Leyden, 1913–1934.

Geyer—*Itinera Hierosolymitana Saeculi* IIII–VIII (*Corpus Scriptorum Ecclesiasticorum Latinorum*), 39, ed. P. Geyer, Vienna, 1898.

Ness I—Excavations at Nessana: excavation report, I, H. Dunscombe Colt *et al.,* London, 1962.

Ness III—Excavations at Nessana: non-literary papyri 3, Casper J. Kraemer, Jr., Princeton, 1958.

P.Colt—See *Ness III.*

PG—Patrologiae cursus completus . . . , series graeca, ed. J.-P Migne.

PL—Patrologiae cursus completus . . . , series latina, ed. J.-P Migne.

Tobler—*Itinera Hierosolymitana et Descriptiones Terrae Sanctae* (*Publications de la Société de l'Orient latin. Série géographique* I–II), ed. T. Tobler and A. Molinier, Geneva, 1879.

[1] Geyer, 159–191, 195–218; Tobler, 91–138. Antoninus is known under a number of names among which are Antoninus Martyr and Antoninus of Placentia or Piacenza. For the sake of simplicity, we shall call him Antoninus. The account, however, was written by a person other than Antoninus (Geyer, xxvi; ch. 1, p. 159), and is, therefore, sometimes referred to as the Anonymous of Placentia.

[2] *PG* LXXIX, cols. 589–693. Nilus is also known by a number of other names or epithets (see art. "Neilus" in *Pauly's Real-Encyclopädie d. class. Altertumswissenschaft,* ed. G. Wissowa, **16** (2): col. 2186, Stuttgart, 1935); we shall simply call him Nilus.

[3] One exception is P.Colt 89, an account of a small trading company. While it is quite fragmentary and, I believe, hardly representative of caravan trade in the Negeb, it is informative for conditions along the north-south route from the Negeb to Mount Sinai. See below, p. 165.

[4] K. Heussi, *Das Nilus problem,* 6–7, Leipzig, 1921. Heussi's position is summed up on pp. 6–10. See also

In dating the narrative, Heussi, finding no anachronism that would date the composition to a later century, places it at the end of the fourth or the beginning of the fifth century A.D.[5]

Père Abel, without entering the controversy of the historicity of the narrative, but tacitly treating it as if it were historical, corrects a toponomical reference in the text, changing "Souka" to "Soubaita" (col. 688). The latter reading had appeared in the critical apparatus of Migne's edition as one of the variants of the Vatican manuscripts collated by Allatius. Abel later supported the correction by an unmistakable reading in the tenth- or eleventh-century manuscript (Code St.-Croix 5, fol. 55 v.) in the library of the Greek Patriarch of Jerusalem.[6]

Finally, Devréesse, in his account of Christianity in the Sinai Peninsula, holds for the most part with Heussi that the *narratio* probably comes from the pen of one of the Sinaitic writers, that it is pure fiction, and that the account was padded with ethnographical and other descriptive material in order to give the tale a semblance of verisimilitude. His position is summed up in these words: "Pour dire toute ma pensée, je crois bien que le P. Abel a tiré du Pseudo-Nil tout ce que l'histoire doit et retenire, c'est-à-dire la mention de Sbaita." [7]

This writer does not wish to enter the controversy of whether the *narratio* is an autobiographical and accurate account of the adventures of Nilus and his son Theodulus or whether the

author of the *narratio* and the author of the epistles is one and the same person. I am willing to accept, for the time being at least, the critical appraisal of Heusii and Devréesse on the historicity of Nilus and his son.[8] But, however fictitious the *narratio* may be, there are elements within the narrative which bear on the history of Sinai and the Negeb for the late fourth and early fifth centuries, elements which cannot be glossed over by assuming that the entire account, with the exception of the word Soubaita, is of no historical value. The very appearance of the name Soubaita makes us prick up our ears, and the accuracy of the writer (which we hope to show below) in his description of travel through the desert and of Soubaita and Elusa, gives us the scent of something more than fiction in the account.

At its worst, we may consider the *narratio* as a kind of historical fiction in which the author has placed his major characters, Nilus and Theodulus, in a setting that is historically true.[9] Regardless of whether or not the writer was a Sinaitic monk other than Nilus himself, the fact is that he was without doubt knowledgeable with respect to the topography and local conditions of Sinai and the Negeb. The incidental information he provides should be as important to us, or at least as acceptable, as that which scholars have accepted for the religious practices of pre-Islamic Arabs.[10]

The author of the narrative, writing at the end of the fourth or the beginning of the fifth century, describes an event which is historically acceptable:

his Untersuchungen zu Nilus dem Asketen, *Texte und Untersuchungen zur Geschichte der altchristlichen Literatur* **42**(2): 123–159, Leipzig, 1917; Nilus der Asket und der überfall der mönche am Sinai, *Neue Jahrbücher für das klassische Altertum* **37**: 107–121, 1916; art. "Neilus" in *Real-Enc.* (note 2). For a brief critique of Heussi's position, see *Analecta Bollandiana* **38**: 421–423, 1920.

[5] *Real-Enc.* (note 2), **16**(2): col. 2186; *Texte u. Untersuch.* (note 4), 154; *Neue Jahrb.* (note 4), 108.

[6] F.–M. Abel, Une mention byzantine de Sbaïta, *Byzantion* **1**: 57, 1924; Note sur Subaïta, *Jour. Palestine Orient. Soc.* **15**: 7–11, 1935. While the manuscripts support a reading of Soubaita or Subaita, the Nessana papyri (P.Colt 75 and 79) give Sobata, Sōbata, or Sōbetōēs. We shall follow the manuscript of the Greek Patriarch in Jerusalem and use Soubaita.

[7] R. Devréesse, Le Christianisme dans la peninsula sinaïtique des origines à l'arrivée des Musulmans, *Revue Biblique* **49**: 222, 1940. To speak of a "school" of writers at Mount Sinai in the late fourth or early fifth century is, in my view, anachronistic. It is doubtful whether we can speak of a "school" at Mount Sinai much before the time of John Climacus (*ca.* 525–600); certainly no school existed long before the time Justinian built the monastery of St. Catherine.

[8] The reader will soon discover that, although I attempt to stand aside in this controversy and consider only the incidental information, I have little doubt as to the historicity of the adventures of a man by the name of Nilus and his son *as their experiences appeared to them.*

[9] The narrative is reminiscent of American films and novels on the adventures of early pioneers in the West. A child is abducted by marauding Indians. The son is sought for unceasingly by the father who endures the worst hardships in tracking down the wandering tribe of Indians, falls into the hands of an unfriendly tribe, and is saved by the sudden appearance of the cavalry at the moment he is to be put to death. Finally, with the aid of a noble Indian chief, the father is reunited with his child. On the other side of the coin, experiences in the wilderness *are* dramatic and very often read like fiction. These adventures are sometimes difficult for scholarly critics to appreciate or evaluate.

[10] E.g., *Encyclopaedia of religion and ethics*, ed. J. Hastings, **1**: 660, 665; **2**: 534; **3**: 174; **6**: 863, New York, 1955. *Cf. Devréesse* (note 7), 220: "la description des mœurs et de la religion des Sarracènes, vraisemblablement copiée ou inspirée d'ailleurs."

a plundering raid by Saracens (i.e., Bedouins) on the monastic settlements in Sinai and the massacre of a number of eremites in the wilderness surrounding Mount Sinai. Whether this was one raid or a series of raids we have no way of knowing, but it is generally accepted that the event took place at the end of the fourth or the beginning of the fifth century, between 373 and 410.[11] In other words, the author of the narrative was not far removed from the events about which he wrote; he may have actually witnessed the raids or heard of them through an eyewitness.

The adventures of Nilus and his son came about as a consequence of one of these Bedouin raids or *razzias* on the monastic settlements scattered about Mount Sinai. Nilus managed to escape but his son, Theodulus, was captured and carried off by the Bedouins. The description of the *razzia* (col. 628) is accurate enough: the Bedouins made a sudden attack, Indian-style, and after accomplishing their primary objective—carrying off the provisions stored up by the monks— they abused and killed the bewildered and helpless monks. Some escaped into surrounding wilderness, but Theodulus and several other young men were carried off into captivity. The Bedouins, if we are to believe the vivid account of one of the captives who succeeded in fleeing (col. 641) and the details filled in later by Theodulus (col. 688), were going to sacrifice the young men to the Morning Star, but since they overslept, the proper time for the ceremony passed.

After the dead had been buried, Nilus returned to Pharan where the council (*boulē*) decided to make representations to a king (i.e., a sheikh) named Ammanes for having violated the terms of his agreement with the town (col. 661), an agreement apparently to safeguard its inhabitants and the neighboring regions against the *razzias* of the tribes under his control.[12] For this pur-

pose two young runners were fitted out for the distant journey to Ammanes' camp. They returned with the sheikh's assurance that the agreement was still in force, that he would indemnify those who had suffered, and that he would punish the renegades. Ammanes was moved to this course of action not by altruism or by an outraged sense of justice but by self-interest: he enjoyed a considerable return from trading with the Pharanites (col. 665) and did not wish to have the arrangement disturbed.

The Nilus narrative gives us a reasonable picture of how isolated communities in the deserts of Sinai and Palestine (*Palaestina Salutaris*, later *Palaestina Tertia*) dealt with the problem of security in the late fourth century. The evidence points to communities, not the imperial government or its agents, making private agreements with Bedouin sheikhs for protection against the incursions of local tribes, a common situation when the central government lacks the strength or interest to provide for the security of isolated towns.[13] The terms of such agreements are, of course, unknown but probably included, as did later agreements, allowances in kind and in money in return for freedom from harassment. It may be reasonable to assume that the towns of the Negeb south of the defensive line indicated in the *Notitia dignitatum* (Menois-Birsama-Beersheba-Malaatha)[14] also had similar protective agreements with local sheikhs, if not with this very Ammanes whose tribes seem to have covered the Negeb as well as Sinai.[15] We

---

[11] Heussi, *Texte u. Untersuch.* (note 4), 147. The account of martyrdom of the Sinai monks by Ammonius, unquestionably a late compilation from various sources (see Devréesse, note 7, p. 219), dates the beginning of the Bedouin uprisings to December 28, 373 (S. L. de Tillemont, *Mémoires pour servir à l'histoire écclesiastique* 7: 574–575, Paris, 1707). In this writer's opinion, there is nothing in the Nilus narrative that would argue against this early date.

[12] On the name of the Bedouin sheikh, see Raymond Weill, La presqu'île du Sinai (*Bibliothéque de l'École des Hautes Études, Sciences historique et philologique*, Fasc. 171), 219–221, Paris, 1908. See also art. "Amān" in *Enc. Isl.* 1 (new ed.), 429. We are struck by the fact that no ecclesiastical authority is involved in these deal-

ings, even though the raids were directed against the monasteries and their inhabitants. Is it possible that these events took place before the establishment of a well-organized episcopal see at Pharan?

[13] See John L. Burckhardt, *Travels in Syria and the Holy Land*, 213, 343, 389, 403, London, 1822, for examples of Syrian towns under Turkish rule paying tribute to Bedouin sheiks for a measure of peace.

[14] *Notitia dignitatum . . . in partibus Orientis et Occidentis,* ed. E. Böcking, 1, ch. 29: 78–80.

[15] Here it is interesting to speculate that the situation described above may predate by a few years the arrangement entered into by Mauvia, "queen of the Saracens" and widow of a Bedouin king (Ammanes?), with the imperial government during the reign of Valentinian and Valens (364–375). In exchange for making a certain holy man, Moses, bishop of Pharan, she agreed to stop raiding the borders of Egypt and Palestine, to convert to Christianity, and to become a loyal and faithful phylarch of the Romans. (Socrates *H.E.* 4, 36, Sozomenus *H.E.* 6, 38, Theodoretus *H.E.* 4, 23; for an example in more recent times of Bedouins led by the widow of a sheikh, see John L. Burckhardt, *Notes on the Bedouins and the Wahabys* 2: 268–269, London, 1831.)

are, in fact, not far removed from the agreement concluded by Mohammed and the bishop (?) of Aila in 631, in which, in return for 300 *solidi,* the city of Aila was given a guarantee of protection against raids by the tribes controlled by Mohammed.[16]

Following the report of the runners that Ammanes was willing to heal the breach of peace, Pharan dispatched envoys to seek out the sheikh and to renew the treaty (col. 665), and, although the Pharanites were the injured party, they went loaded down with gifts, presumably to "sweeten" the task of negotiating or to make part or full payment of the stipulated tribute.[17] Nilus, clinging to the hope that his son was still alive, joined the envoys who were making the long trek through the wilderness to Ammanes' camp.

The journey through the desert took twelve days. On the eighth day, the band of travelers were out of water and suffering from thirst. Those who had some knowledge of the region claimed that there was a spring (*pēgē*) nearby and all members of the party scattered in a frantic search for it. Nilus, slowed down by age and wishing to maintain a shred of his dignity, was left behind by the eagerness of the others, but upon climbing a hill, he stumbled upon the spring which, unfortunately, was surrounded by Bedouins. Easily sighted by the Bedouins, Nilus, in hopes of finding his son a captive in this tribe, gave up without a struggle and submitted to being dragged about in a violent manner. He was saved, however, by the appearance of an armed guard that quickly put the Bedouins to flight. Four days later, the party reached Ammanes' camp where Nilus was told that his son was still alive and that he had been sold as a slave to someone in the city of Elusa. The sheikh generously provided Nilus with two guides to lead him to Elusa. On the way, a trader, who had seen Nilus at the Bedouin encampment and knew of his predicament, assured him that his son was safe at Elusa, that he had been purchased by a Christian priest, and that he was now fulfilling the duties of a sexton (*neōkoros*), the lowest grade in the hierarchy of the church.

This portion of the narrative takes us from Pharan to Ammanes' camp, a journey of twelve

days, eight of which were taken up in reaching the spring, the remaining four in traveling to the Bedouin encampment. Abel, assuming the journey to be a true account, estimates that by covering thirty kilometers a day Nilus and the envoys reached a spring in the neighborhood of Kadeis and that the soldiers who saved Nilus and the Pharanites were stationed close by.[18] Abel admits to some difficulty in pinpointing the exact place of the spring, for if it were in the neighborhood of Kadeis, a four-day journey to the Bedouin encampment would bring them near Gaza or beyond Beersheba. Since the encampment would not likely be so far to the north, Abel suggests that the "spring" may have been one of the wells further south, near Djebel Maqrah, and thus the four-day trip from the "spring" would take them to the neighborhood of Elusa, a more logical emplacement for Ammanes' camp.[19]

In reviewing the journey from Pharan to Ammanes' camp and thence to Elusa, we must note the general vagueness of the writer as to details, particularly topographical and toponymical. Whereas he is very specific in naming the monastic settlements which came under attack by the Bedouins, sites which R. Weill has been fairly successful in identifying,[20] he is pointedly uninformative about the site of the spring and of Ammanes' camp. This lack of information, I believe, is not the result of oversight or of literary style, but of the fact that the region was truly a *terra incognita* to all except, perhaps, the Bedouins. Therefore, the attempt to locate the site of the spring and Ammanes' camp is probably quite futile, although the description of the spring very loosely fits that of Ain Kadeis.[21]

What then can be legitimately extracted from the description of Nilus' journey to the Bedouin sheikh? The narrative describes a journey in a northerly direction from Pharan (Wadi Feiran) through a desert lacking water, resting places, fixed habitations, and even chance meetings with Bedouins. There can be no doubt that Nilus and his party took the little-known and less-traveled north-south route through the desert al-

[16] al-Balādhurī in *The origins of the Islamic state,* trans. P. K. Hitti, **1**: 92, New York, 1916.

[17] *Cf.* J. L. Burckhardt (note 13), 467: "The authority of the Bedouins is now (in 1816) at an end, though their sheikhs receive from the Turkish governors a yearly tribute under the names of presents, clothes, and money."

[18] *Byzantion* (note 6), 53: "La position est trop importante pour n'avoir pas été comme de nos jours surveillée par une station militaire."

[19] *Ibid.,* 57–58.

[20] R. Weill (note 12), 219–221.

[21] *Cf.* Leonard Woolley and T. E. Lawrence, *The Wilderness of Zin,* 70–71, London and New York, 1936: "Ain Kadeis . . . too remote to come to the notice of such Arab guides as live at any distance."

Tih in Central Sinai. Two- or three-days journey from Pharan via the pass at el-Rakimeh, the most logical one to take if departing from Pharan, would lead the party from the mountain ranges of southern Sinai to the limestone plateau of al-Tih, the "Desert of the Banī Isrā'īl." According to Arab geographers, al-Tih was 40 *farsakh* (*ca.* 230 kms.) long and equally broad, had few palm trees and springs, consisted of partly stony and partly sandy soil, and took about six days to traverse.[22]

We can reasonably assume that Nilus and his party had camels carrying a supply of water to cover approximately six days of travel in the desert of al-Tih, and that they had counted on reaching the spring which some members of the party knew about. The name of the spring—and we need not question whether it was a spring or a well—is not given, nor is any other topographical or toponymical information, since the party, traveling without Bedouin guides, had none to give the writer. Al-Tih was simply a desert to traverse as quickly as possible in order to reach one of the springs (Ain el-Qudeirat, Ain Qusaima, Ain Kadeis, Ain Muweilah) in its northern limits, all of which are clustered fairly close together.[23]

The trip from the spring to Ammanes' camp offers some difficulty to Abel who assumes that Nilus and his party traveled in a straight line for four days until they reached their objective. It is on this account that Abel places the "spring" farther to the south at one of the wells of Djebel Maqrah, so that the four-day journey would not take Nilus too far to the north. However, we need not assume that Ammanes' camp was so fixed that the trip was made without some searching here and there for the Bedouin sheikh whose camp could have been anywhere in North Sinai or the Central Negeb.

Confirmation of some of the details of this route may be found in Antoninus' journey through the Tih desert some two hundred years later. Departing from Gaza, Antonius and his companions traveled to Elusa, "a city at the head of the desert which extends to Sinai."[24] Twenty miles from Elusa, he and his party stopped at a hospice from which they began their journey into the "inner" or "greater" desert.[25] With camels carrying water for the party, they walked through the desert for five or six days. Every morning and evening each man received a *sextarius* (a pint) of water.[26] On the eighth day,[27] they arrived "at a place where Moses drew water from the rock" and shortly thereafter at Mount Sinai.

Significantly, after his visit to Mount Sinai, Antoninus did not return by the same route. It was announced at Mount Sinai that the Saracen festival was coming to an end and hence it would not be safe for pilgrims to travel the route by which they had come. Some therefore returned to Jerusalem through Egypt (i.e., by Clysma, Pelusium, and the *via maris*) and some through Arabia (to Aila at the head of the Gulf of Aqaba and thence by roads passing through the Negeb).[28] Between Mount Sinai and Clysma, Antoninus notes the fortified town of Pharan[29] and two *castella* containing hospices.[30] We know from other accounts that the road from Mount Sinai to Egypt and the *via maris* was well provided with way stations, forts, and soldiers.[31]

These then were the two main arteries leading from Mount Sinai to Egypt and Palestine. The road leading from Clysma into Egypt and then to Palestine, the *grande route ordinaire,* was particularly well protected by soldiers who were used

---

[22] See art. "al-Tih" in *Enc.Isl.* 4(2): 763; Guy Le Strange, *Palestine under the Moslems* 29–30, London, 1890; R. Weill (note 12), 119–120; see esp. Maqrizi, trans. U. Bouriant, *Mémoires, Mission archéologique française au Caire* 17: 630–631, Paris, 1900.

[23] For a description of this region, see Woolley and Lawrence (note 21), 70–88.

[24] Geyer, ch. 34, p. 181: "et inde venimus in civitate Elusa in caput heremi, qui vadit ad Sina."

[25] *Ibid.,* ch. 35–36, pp. 182–183. For further discussion on the hospice and the departure into the "inner" desert, see below p. 170.

[26] *Ibid.,* ch. 36, p. 183. It is interesting to note that the Israeli soldier is trained to get along on about the same ration of water: for operations in the desert he is allowed one canteen (quart) of water per day.

[27] Reading *octava die* (*recensio altera,* Geyer, 213) instead of *octava decima die* on p. 183.

[28] *Ibid.,* ch. 39, p. 185: "quia iam se complebant dies festi Saracenorum, praeco exivit: ut, quia non subsisteret per heremo reverti, per quo ingressi sumus, alii per Aegyptum, alii per Arabiam reverterentur in sanctam civitatem." *Cf.* ch. 36, p. 183.

[29] *Ibid.,* ch. 40, pp. 185, 214.

[30] *Ibid.,* ch. 41, p. 187. See also below, p. 170.

[31] Geyer (*Petrus diaconus*), 115: "A Pelusio autem usque ad montem Syna sunt mansiones duodecim." *Ibid.* (*Sanctae Silviae Peregrinatio*), ch. 7, pp. 46–47: "donec pervenirent usque ad mare rubrum, qui locus nunc de castro, quod ibi est, appellatur Clesma . . . Sunt ergo a Clesma, id est a mare rubro, usque ad Arabium civitatem (Thou or Bubastis?) mansiones quattuor per heremo, sic tamen per heremum, ut cata mansiones monasteria sint cum militibus et praepositis, qui nos deducebant semper de castro ad castrum."

to escort pilgrims from one fortified station to the next. The road leading from Mount Sinai to Aila by-passed the Tih desert and, apparently, ran along the eastern coast of the Sinai Peninsula after leaving the mountains to the south. It appears to have been a fairly safe but shorter route which, when the traveler reached Aila, enabled him to use the road from Aila through Elusa to Jerusalem.[32] However, the accounts of both Antoninus and Nilus make it abundantly clear that the road through Central Sinai was not a customary north-south route for travelers to take on their way to or from Mount Sinai. Neither writer mentions a single *mansio, castrum, castellum,* or *xenodochium* in the Tih desert, nor has archaeological exploration produced any evidence to support the existence of a well-traveled road. The Tih desert, waterless and unsafe, provided a route in the sense that one could, although with difficulty, make his way through it. The Nilus account gives us a good description of its hazards; Antoninus was able to travel unscathed because of a Bedouin festival which enjoined trading and raiding during its celebration. When it came time for Antoninus and his party to return to Palestine, the moratorium on trading and raiding was over and the pilgrims wisely chose to take a safer route back to Jerusalem. While security arrangements and accommodations on the two major roads might have changed from Nilus' time to that of Antoninus, on the north-south route through the Tih desert they did not.

Further, had the central route through Sinai assumed some importance during the Byzantine period, we would expect to find some measure of imperial interest in establishing military outposts near the springs of North Sinai or at a point where the north-south and east-west routes crossed, at Qal'at Nakhl for example, the *puteus Soldani* of later writers.[33] Abel believes that the

area near the spring was too important not to have been the site of a Byzantine police post and that soldiers of some such post rescued Nilus from the Bedouins.[34] However, the text (col. 669) is too vague to suggest anything more than "our armed guard," and should be interpreted to mean that the caravan of Pharanites, like any other caravan carrying valuable wares, had its own armed escort.

In 1956 this writer had the opportunity of surveying these northern sites in Sinai and could find no evidence of forts or of urban activity on a scale comparable with that of the Negeb. The Byzantine remains to be found are generally a few scattered villages of some dozen or so houses (rather, huts). Ain el-Qudeirat represents the best spring, and its valley is the most fertile, in the entire region, including the Negeb, yet there is no sign of a Byzantine fort or of a church, the true indices of prosperity and imperial interest. The ancient village cited by Woolley and Lawrence and others [35] is a poor one by Negeb standards, hardly worth the name of village. The same is true of another cluster of huts a short distance away in a tributary of the Wadi Umm Hashim.

How limited an interest the Byzantines had in the Tih desert along the north-south route can be seen in a sixth-seventh century document, P. Colt 89. This so-called caravan account lists the purchases and expenditures made by a small company of traders engaged in petty trading on its way to and from Mount Sinai. The major transaction was the receipt of 270½ *solidi* from a Father Martyrius at the "Holy Mountain" (Mount Sinai), the sum possibly to be transferred for safe-keeping to a larger episcopal city in Palestine. Of interest to us is the fact that the traders had to pay a Bedouin three *solidi,* a not insubstantial sum, for guiding them to the Holy Mountain.[36] Traveling through a true wilder-

---

[32] The Theodosian itinerary (A.D. *ca.* 530) makes this perfectly clear (Geyer, ch. 27, p. 148): "De Hierusalem in Elusath (Elusa) mansiones III, de Elusath in Aila mansiones VII. . . . De Aila usque in monte Syna mansiones VIII, si compendiaria volueris ambulare per heremum, sin autem per Aegyptum, mansiones XXV." The number of stations between Elusa and Aila agrees quite well with the Peutinger map: Elusa, Oboda (Eboda), Lysa, Gypsaria, Rasa (Gerasa), Ad Dianam, Haila (Aila). See Y. Aharoni, The Roman Road to Aila (Elath), *Israel Exploration Jour.* **4**: 9–16, 1954 for a discussion of the map.

[33] The earliest mention of a station at this point was made by Fr. Jacopo of Verona (1335), "Liber peregrinationis Fr. J. de Verona," ed. R. Rohricht, *Revue de l'Orient latin* **3**: 227–228, 1895. From the fourteenth

century on, pilgrims seem to have preferred the Gaza-Qal'at Nakhl-Mount Sinai route to the longer one via Egypt. The way station at Qal'at Nakhl was established primarily for the convenience of Moslem pilgrims en route from Egypt to Mecca, but it also served those traveling south from Gaza to Mount Sinai. On the lack of pre-medieval remains at the site, see Beno Rothenberg, *God's wilderness: discoveries in Sinai,* 67, London, 1961.

[34] *Op. cit.* (note 18), 53.

[35] Woolley and Lawrence (note 21), 80; Rothenberg (note 33), 40.

[36] Note that no transactions were entered in the account between the payment for the Bedouin guide and the receipt of money from Father Martyrius (lines 22–23). The traders apparently conducted no business whatever in the al-Tih desert.

ness, they were in no position to bargain and had to pay a high price for the services of a guide and, presumably, for safe passage. The absence of a similar fee in the rest of the account makes it seem likely that another route was taken back to Palestine. From the whole tenor of the document, the traders do not appear to have been experienced in traveling through this region or in handling animals: a she-ass dies, one camel runs away, and Bedouins steal another. In sum, the document can hardly be cited as evidence of a regular trade route through the al-Tih desert.

To return to the Nilus narrative, upon his arrival at Elusa and his reunion with Theodulus, Nilus was given a first-hand account of his son's adventures following his capture by the Bedouins. The story of how Theodulus, about to be sacrificed to the Morning Star, was saved because the Bedouins overslept may have all the earmarks of an oriental tale or of Bedouins playing a cat-and-mouse game with their captive and is of no particular interest to us here. But what follows that episode is of interest for it takes us out of Bedouin encampments into the settled Negeb.

The Bedouins continued harassing their captive until, as Theodulus relates,

we came near the rest of the inhabited world. Then without my knowing what they had in mind, they entered a town called Soubaita and announced to the inhabitants that I was for sale. Many times idlers approached them but no one offered more than two pieces of gold. Finally, they [the Bedouins] went out and stationed themselves before the gates of the town and, as is their custom, placed a bare sword on my neck and announced to all that they would behead me if someone did not make a [suitable] offer.[37]

---

[37] *PG* LXXIX, col. 688: . . . ἕως ἤλθομεν πλησίον τῆς οἰκουμένης λοιπόν. Τότε γὰρ οὐκ οἶδα τί βουλευσάμενοι εἰσάγουσιν εἰς κώμην καλουμένην Σουκᾶ εἶτα (Συβαῖτα) καὶ τὴν ἐμὴν τοῖς αὐτόθι προαγγέλλουσι πρᾶσιν. Πολλάκις δὲ πρὸς ἑαυτοῖς ἐπιστρέψαντες ἄπρακτοι, οὐδενὸς πλέον δύο χρυσῶν δοῦναι βεβουλημένου, τέλος ἐξαγαγόντες καὶ πρὸ τῆς κώμης στήσαντες, ὡς εἰώθεισαν, γυμνὸν ἐπιτιθέασίν μου τῷ τραχήλῳ τὸ ξίφος, ἢν μηδεὶς ὠνήσαιτο, καρατομήσειν πᾶσιν προλέγοντες εἰθέως.

If we can judge by later prices for slaves in the Negeb, the Bedouins had every right to be outraged at the offer of two pieces of gold (two *solidi*). P.Colt 89 gives as the price for a slave boy 6 *solidi* plus a camel worth 4⅓ *solidi* (total: 10⅓ s.) for a slave girl 3 *s.* plus a camel worth 6⅓ s. (total: 9⅓ s.). In 359 a contract of sale written in Ascalon records the sale of a fourteen-year old girl for 14 s. (Allen C. Johnson and Louis C. West, *Byzantine Egypt: economic studies,* 134, Princeton, 1949). In taking Theodulus outside of the town and threatening to kill him if someone did not come up with a better offer, the Bedouins were saying no more than "I'd rather throw it away than accept that ridiculous price." The

Theodulus pleaded most abjectly for someone to purchase him and, according to Theodulus, someone did take pity on him, purchased him, and brought him to Elusa where, as Nilus had learned earlier (col. 676), he was sold to a priest and was serving as a sexton of the church.

With this portion of the narrative we are brought from Sinai into the Central Negeb, from the desert to the edge of the *oecumene.* That Soubaita is the town that the Bedouins sought out as the market place in which to sell Theodulus is significant: first it confirms, and is itself corroborated by, what is known archaeologically about the sites to the south of Soubaita, and secondly it sheds some light on the history of the Central Negeb in the late fourth or early fifth century.

To the Bedouins then, civilization begins near Soubaita, and Soubaita is a market town for the disposal of booty, much as Gaza was to become after the Central Negeb lost its settled population. About 20 kms. to the west-southwest lay Nessana and about 15 kms. to the southeast Eboda, both within the perimeter of the *oecumene,* but in the fourth century stagnant and lightly populated. Archaeological evidence at Nessana for the third and fourth centuries is so slim that we may question whether an organized community was in existence at the site during this period.[38] With the construction of a fort and the stationing of border militia (*limitanei*) after the first quarter of the fifth century, the imperial government revived the town as a community integrated within the Empire.[39] At Eboda, conditions were, with but minor differences, about the same: activity continued in the "Roman" part of the town site until the end of the third century; after that there is a noticeable gap until the "Byzantine" town was established. The fort at Eboda is dated to the beginning of the sixth century, the churches to the first third of that century.[40] However, at Elusa, about twenty-five kilometers northwest of Soubaita, exploratory

---

taboo on shedding blood within the town is evident in the act of taking Theodulus before the town gates. (*Cf.* the taboo on Christian burials within pagan Gaza, Marcus Diaconus, *Vita Porphyrii,* 23.)

[38] *Ness I,* 16.

[39] See also *Ness III,* 16.

[40] M. Avi-Yonah and A. Negev, A city of the Negeb: excavations in Nabataean, Roman and Byzantine Eboda, *London Illus. News,* 944, Nov. 26, 1960; A. Negev, Avdat: a caravan halt in the Negev, *Archaeology* 14: 125–126, 1961; personal conversations with A. Negev.

sondages in the town middens show that the third- and fourth-century horizons are strongly represented, as we should expect in an administrative center of *Palaestina Salutaris* (*Tertia*).[41] We also know about Elusa from Jerome, writing some thirty years after the organization of the province in 359. He characterizes the city as pagan, worshiping Venus as the Morning Star, and "in many respects half-civilized because of its location."[42] The evidence suggests, therefore, that in the late fourth century Elusa and Soubaita were the two major communities in the Central Negeb,[43] that they lay outside of the effective *limes* of Palestine west of the Wadi Arabah,[44] and that gradually imperial interest and urban activity spread southward toward Nessana and Eboda.

Parallel to, if not in concert with, the urban development of the region is the extension of Christianity into the Negeb. It can hardly be said that in the late fourth century the church had secured a foothold in the region, even in Elusa, the very administrative center of the Negeb. About the middle of the century, Christianity was brought to the Saracens by Hilarion, the celebrated monk whom S. L. de Tillemont calls "perhaps the first apostle among the Saracens."[45] On a visit to a disciple of his in the "desert of Kadeis" he stopped at Elusa whither, according to his biographer Jerome,[46] his fame as a worker of miracles and an exorcist of demons among the Saracens had preceded him. With very little missionary effort on his part, he impressed the inhabitants with his holiness and they importuned him to establish a church—to them more of a hospital or a clinic than a church—in the city.

The enthusiasm of the population for the new faith did not result in wholesale conversion. If we are to judge by conditions in the nearby coastal cities of Gaza and Raphia, Christianity in South Palestine had to struggle for its very existence. In 394, when Porphyry assumed the episcopal seat of Gaza, the Christian population of the great city totaled a mere 127, while villages close to the city were still entirely pagan.[47] Keeping alive the flame of Christianity in Gaza, and presumably in the towns and villages of the Negeb, was possible only by virtue of the organization of the church and the dynamism of such bishops as Porphyry. In 401, however, Porphyry obtained an imperial rescript enabling him to close all pagan temples in Gaza, an action which could be accomplished only with the assistance of imperial troops; once accomplished, however, the burden of the church in gaining converts was considerably lightened.

Conditions in the Negeb were probably much worse than they were in Gaza. But the church had established an episcopal seat at Elusa, the capital of the Negeb, and as we can learn from the Nilus narrative, it was a small island in a sea of paganism. The village of Soubaita to which Theodulus was taken and sold as a slave was entirely pagan. If there had been a Christian community within the town, the writer of the narrative certainly would have had Theodulus directing his pleas, at least in some part, to Christian sensibilities rather than to the mercantile interests of prospective buyers (col. 668). His purchaser, undoubtedly realizing that he had a marketable Christian and that he could turn a quick profit, took him to Elusa and resold him to the bishop, who inducted him into the lowest rank of the clergy and set him to work as a *neōkoros* or sexton.[48] The bishop, however, did not immediately free the boy but bound him to a contract of obligatory service, a *paramonē*, in which, it appears, his manumission was to be deferred until the terms of the *paramonē* had

---

[41] G. E. Kirk, The Negev, or southern desert of Palestine, *Palestine Exploration Quart.*, 61, April 1941.

[42] *Vita Hilarionis* in *PL* XXIII, col. 41: "Colunt autem illam (*sc.* Venerem) ob Luciferum, cujus cultui Saracenorum natio dedita est. Sed et ipsum oppidum ex magna parte semibarbarum est propter loci situm."

[43] Adding support to the reliability of the incidental information provided by the writer of the Nilus narrative is the official name or administrative title of the two communities: Elusa is a *polis* (cols. 673, 676), Soubaita a *kōmē* (col. 688), undoubtedly subordinated to Elusa for administrative purposes. For the many citations of Elusa as a *polis,* see P.Colt 14, 16, 18, *passim.* We have no supporting citations for Soubaita, but its proximity to Elusa and Nessana's designation as a *kōmē* make it very likely that the text gives us the official name of the town, i.e., *kōmē* Soubaita. Note also that when the writer of the narrative mentions Pharan (cols. 589, 660), he does not give its administrative title. Did Pharan in this period lie outside of the borders and have no official status within the Empire?

[44] *Loc. cit.* (note 14). See above, p. 162.

[45] *Op. cit.* (note 11), 567.

[46] *PL* XXIII, col. 41.

[47] Adolph Harnack, *The mission and expansion of Christianity in the first three centuries,* trans. J. Moffatt, 2: 112, New York, 1908; Martin Meyer, *History of the city of Gaza* (*Columbia University Oriental Studies* 5), 64, New York, 1907.

[48] *PG* LXXIX, col. 676: καὶ ὁ παῖς εἴρηται μὲν τελεῖν ἐν τῷ ἱερατικῷ τάγματι, τὰς πρώτας τέως τῶν νεοκόρων (νεωκόρων) ὑπερεσίας πεπιστευμένος.

been met.[49] The bishop, after restoring Nilus and his son to good health, asked them to remain at Elusa,

and so as not to have it appear that he was using coercion by virtue of the price that he paid for the boy and so as not to have it appear that like a slave-owner he was insisting on the *paramonē,* he agreed to abide by our decision. But in this one thing he was adamant: that we assume the sacred yoke [of priesthood] even though we were unwilling.[50]

The bishop of Elusa is portrayed in the Nilus narrative as most eager to build up his congregation and to propagate the faith. This eagerness leads him to purchase the boy Theodulus, to limit his freedom of movement by means of the *paramonē,* and to install him as a sexton in the church. (Was there such a shortage of Christians at Elusa that he had to go to this extreme to obtain a sexton for the church?) And in his desire to gain active workers for the propagation of the faith, he insists upon ordaining Nilus and his son, the latter being only a boy.

Devréesse, however, believes that to speak of a bishop at Elusa at the end of the fourth or the beginning of the fifth century is an anachronism unsupported by historical documentation.[51] True as it may be that evidence, apart from the Nilus narrative, is lacking, its absence does not necessarily make an episcopal seat in Elusa an anachronism. The earliest dated Christian inscription in the Negeb, prior to excavations at 'Auja Hafir (Nessana), is dated to 509 and that oddly enough comes from the remote town of Nessana itself; the earliest at Elusa is 531, at Beersheba 516.[52] Excavations at 'Auja Hafir have uncovered inscriptions which give us an earlier date of 464 and lead to the reasonable assumption that Christianity

was firmly established at this little town in 450.[53] If this is true at Nessana, a *kōmē* subordinated to Elusa, can we not assume that the church had its organization established at Elusa by 400? Whatever inscriptions we have from Elusa have been found by surface exploration, not by excavation. If stone plunderers, who have already stripped Elusa of its stone down to building foundations, have left something for future excavations, we may yet uncover earlier evidence for Christianity —perhaps the name of its first bishop—at the site where it was first introduced into the Negeb.

As for "documents authentiques de l'histoire," which Devréesse claims are lacking, we have a list of bishops who attended various oecumencial councils in the fourth and fifth centuries and the following summary is informative for the Negeb and *Palaestina Salutaris (Tertia):* [54]

Year	Council	City	Bishop
325	Nicaea	Aila	Peter
347	Sardica	Petra	Asterius
359	Seleucia	Petra	Germanus
381	Constantinople	– – –	– – –
431	Ephesus	Elusa	Theodulus (Abdellas)
449	Ephesus	– – –	– – –
451	Chalcedon	Elusa	Aretas
		Aila	Beryllus

If, as the above table illustrates, Aila and Petra were episcopal sees as early as the first half of the fourth century—and what pitifully small congregations they must have had—it is not unlikely that a bishop was established at Elusa shortly after Hilarion's visit and the organization of *Palaestina Salutaris* in 359 with Elusa as an administrative center. Secondly, and more particularly, the records show unequivocally that a bishop of Elusa attended the Council of Epheus in 431. Can we not, in conjunction with the epigraphical evidence cited above, assume that the episcopate existed at Elusa for some years prior to 431, say some thirty to fifty years? Curiously enough the name of the bishop who attended the Council of Ephesus is Theodulus or Abdellas, the latter being merely the Arabic version ('Abd Allāh) of Theodulus. Had not the name been common in the Negeb,[55] we could easily work out a chronology to show that the Theodulus of the Nilus narrative, who was only a boy at the time of the

---

[49] On the nature of the *paramonē,* see W. L. Westermann, the paramone as a general service contract, *Jour. Juristic Papyrology* 2: 9–50, 1948, esp. p. 16; see also P.Colt 56 for a late example of a release from *paramonē.* I wish to thank Prof. H. C. Youtie for reviewing my interpretation and for his helpful suggestions on how the instrument might have been used.

[50] *PG* LXXIX, col. 692: Ὡς δὲ ἂν μὴ δόξαι βίαν προσάγειν ὑπνοίᾳ τῆς ὑπὲρ τοῦ παιδὸς δεδομένης τιμῆς, μηδὲ δεσποτικώτερον ἀπαιτεῖν τὴν παραμονήν, πράττειν ἐπέτρεπε πᾶν τὸ δοκοῦν κατὰ γνώμην, ἐν τούτῳ μόνον τυραννήσας ἡμᾶς τὸ τὸν ζυγὸν ἐπιθεῖναι τὸν ἱερατικὸν μὴ βουλομένοις.

[51] *Op. cit.* (note 7), 222, fn. 1.

[52] A. Alt, *Die griechischen Inschriften der Palaestina Tertia westlich der Araba (Wissenschaftliche Veröffentlichungen des deutsch-türkischen Denkmalschutz-Kommandos,* Heft II), Insc. Nos. 131, 55, 16, Berlin and Leipzig, 1921.

[53] Nessana insc. 35 summarized in *Ness III, 9, 15.*

[54] Taken from Rudolph E. Brünnow and Alfred v. Domaszewski, *Die Provincia Arabia* 3: 334–345, Strassburg, 1909.

[55] See *Ness III,* 333–334, for the frequent occurrence of the name in the Nessana documents.

Bedouin insurrections, had by 431 succeeded his benefactor, the probable first bishop of Elusa, and was in fact the same Theodulus who attended the Council of Ephesus. We need not, however, stretch the evidence this far; we should, nevertheless, have no doubt as to the existence of a bishop at Elusa in the late fourth century.

By the time of Antoninus' journey to Mount Sinai (*ca.* 570) two hundred years later, the church had won its struggle against paganism and Christianity had emerged triumphant in the Negeb. Accompanying this triumph was the stability, public security, and prosperity engendered by imperial interest and encouraged by the steady growth of a settled population. To this same period must be credited the widest application of agricultural techniques which turned desert wastelands into productive farmlands.[56]

Antoninus' itinerary gives no reflection of the richness of the archaeological evidence for the sixth century, and it is only by indirection that Antoninus supplies us with details which fit into the historical mosaic of the region. Why he decided upon the trip to Mount Sinai via the Negeb we shall never know, unless his interest and curiosity were piqued by some travel agent or guide at Gaza, a city which Antoninus eulogizes as "magnificent, delightful; its inhabitants most respectful, friendly in every way, lovers of travelers."[57] But it is clear from the account which follows that pilgrims were offered a certain number of attractions that were designed to work upon the sympathies of the religious and to loosen the purse strings of the gullible.[58] Apart from the income acquired by sensational means, towns and churches profited from housing and feeding pilgrims, churches and monasteries from donations in money or in kind. It was undoubtedly from such pilgrims that Father Martyrius of Mount Sinai accumulated the sum of 270½ *solidi* which he turned over to the company of traders mentioned in P.Colt. 89.[59]

Antoninus and his companion, arriving at Elusa and hearing the bishop relate the tale of an unfortunate girl who became an ascetic in the desert east of the Wadi Arabah, decided upon a side trip to Segor (Zoara) near the Dead Sea. There they found a convent of fifteen or sixteen young girls whom neighboring Christians supplied with food. They had a trained lion that frightened away strangers and, the visitors were told, led the convent's donkey to the pasture. This remarkable lion was offered to Antoninus for the sum of 100 *solidi*. Antoninus, apparently, was not a gullible tourist or simply did not know what he would do with the beast once he had bought it; he chose to decline the offer but sent instead to Jerusalem for three tunics for each girl, vegetables for their larder, and a supply of lamp oil.[60]

Following this episode, the itinerary has the following entry:

Setting out from the city of Elusa we went into the desert. Twenty miles away there is a fort in which there is the hospice of St. George in which travelers have a kind of shelter or hermits their keep. And from there we went into the inner desert. . . .[61]

This brief note is the only contemporary description we possess of the Negeb for the sixth century. In spite of its baldness, it is worth noting that Elusa ("at the head of the desert which extends to Sinai") and the region south of it are described as desert, that twenty Roman miles from Elusa were a fort and a hospice, and that one departed from that point into the "inner" desert.

At a period when cultivation of desert lands was unquestionably at its peak, it may seem rather surprising to have Antoninus describe the region just south of Elusa as desert (*heremum*). But the Negeb, even in the spring and at the height of its prosperity, would have appeared a desert to a European, particularly an Italian. Further, there is evidence that even as early as the third century sand dunes covered part of the cultivable area near Elusa[62] and were probably

---

[56] See Woolley and Lawrence (note 21), 47–48; *Ness III,* 16–17, 23–24; P. Mayerson, The ancient agricultural remains of the Central Negeb: methodology and dating criteria, *Bull. Amer. Schls. Orient. Res.* No. 160: 37, 1960.

[57] Geyer, ch. 33, p. 180: "Gaza autem civitas splendid deliciosa, homines honestissimi omni liberalitate decori, amatores peregrinorum."

[58] For trade in holy relics in Byzantine Palestine, see M. Avi-Yonah, Economics of Byzantine Palestine, *Israel Exploration Jour.* **8**: 45–46, 1958.

[59] See above, p. 165.

[60] Tobler, ch. 34, p. 110. With regard to the number of tunics provided, I read *tunicas ternas* in place of *tunicas tricenas* (Tobler, 110 fn. f, 130). For a less-believable version of this story, see Geyer, 181.

[61] *Ibid.,* ch. 35, p. 182: "Proficiscentes de civitate Elusa, ingressi heremum. Ad XX milia est castrum, in quo est xenodochius sancti Georgi, in quo habent quasi refugium transeuntes vel heremitae stipendia. Ex inde intrantes interiorem heremum. . . ." For minor textual variations, see Tobler, 111, 130.

[62] Kirk (note 41), 59.

encountered for a good distance along the old road which leads from Elusa past Raheiba (Byzantine name unknown) to Nessana. The condition remains unchanged to this day. A truer reflection of how the desert and the sown can exist side by side may be seen in Procopius' letter (spurious) to Jerome: "There will be a time when you will see Elusa again and you will weep at the sand blown by the winds and devastating the vines right down to their roots." [63]

Antoninus reports the presence of a fort (*castrum*) and a hospice (*xenodochium*) of St. George twenty Roman miles (30 kms.) away from Elusa. Abel has already pointed out that, if the description did not apply to 'Auja Hafir (Nessana), it would suit Soubaita since one of its churches was dedicated to St. George. [64] Kraemer, on the assumption that Soubaita was not a *castrum* like Nessana, was inclined to locate the hospice in Nessana even though he found no evidence for such a building either in the inscriptions or in the papyri. [65] However, an examination of the details of the itinerary can make the identification of Nessana and the *castrum* less tenuous.

The distance from Elusa to Nessana, about thirty-two kilometers (a one-day journey), most closely approximates the twenty Roman miles. Judging from P.Colt 72 and 73, two orders from the Arab *symbolos* of Gaza for guides to Mount Sinai, Nessana was the last important station on the central route to Sinai, and it is from a fort that Antoninus and his party leave for the "inner" desert and Mount Sinai. Most important, however, is the archaeological evidence which ties in closely with the itinerary. The Byzantine fort at Nessana, occupying the main ridge of the hill south of the North Church complex, was originally designed for the *numerus* stationed at Nessana but apparently never saw use by the military. The archaeological finds in the fort contained many spindle whorls, fragments of mirrors, quantities of glass, and other objects of household use, but no recognizable military weapons. [66] At the time the fort was built it had seven rooms along its west wall. At a later period, at about the time of the remodeling of the North Church complex and the demobilization of the *numerus,* about

twenty additional rooms were added to the west and east walls. The conclusion of the archaeologists, based upon similarities in the masonry work used in the North Church complex and upon inferential evidence from the papyri, was that the church took over the fort when it was abandoned by the military (*ca.* 600), and converted it into a monastery. [67]

I would suggest, however, that the fort was converted not into a monastery but into the *xenodochium* at which Antoninus stopped in 570. It is quite apparent that the fort had seen very little, if any, use by the military, and even though Kraemer conservatively estimates that by 600 imperial troops were no longer at Nessana, [68] the likelihood is that sometime in Justinian's reign the formal military organization of Nessana was abandoned and the fort became available for other uses. [69] Antoninus speaks of the fort *in which* there is a hospice; i.e., the hospice was within the fort itself. [70] That it was not uncommon to have *xenodochia* within forts is supported by Antoninus' description of two *castella* in Sinai which had no military function yet served as hospices: at Surandala, "there is a small fort . . . having nothing within it except a church and its priest and two hospices for travelers," [71] and at a place where the sons of Israel crossed the [Red] Sea and pitched their camp, there also is "a small fort within which is a hospice." [72] But what makes the hospice at Nessana different from the others mentioned by Antoninus is the arrangement of rooms along the east and west walls of the fort rather than in a separate building within a fortified area. This, perhaps, is the reason that Antoninus speaks of the hospice as "a kind of shelter for travelers."

As for the name of the *xenodochium*, St. George, there need be no compelling reason for it to be associated with the church and monastery of SS. Sergius and Bacchus, often called only St. Sergius, which occupied the North Complex. St.

[63] *Epist.* 150 in *PL* XXII, col. 1224: "Erit enim tempus cum iterum videbis Elusam et flebis arenam dejectam ventis et radice tenus vastantem vites."

[64] *Jour. Palestine Orient. Soc.* (note 6), 10.

[65] *Ness III,* 29.

[66] *Ness I,* 17.

[67] *Ness I,* 17, 52; pls. 62, 66.

[68] *Ness III,* 24.

[69] Procopius, *Anecdota,* 24, 12–14.

[70] *In quo* in most manuscripts; one codex (E. Cod. Vatic. 636 A) has *ubi est.*

[71] Geyer, ch. 41, p. 187: "in quo loco est castellum modicum qui vocatur Surandala, nihil habet intus praeter ecclesiam cum presbytero suo et duo xenodochia propter transeuntes." (*Cf.* Tobler, 132: "Est etiam infra castellum ecclesia cum syndochio propter transeuntes.")

[72] *Ibid.,* ch. 41, p. 187: "et illic similiter castellum modicum, infra se xenodochium."

George was a well-known saint to whom churches were dedicated at Soubaita and Eboda, and it is possible that the hospice in the fort at Nessana was similarly dedicated. We should note, however, that an eleventh-century manuscript has the reading *Sergii* in place of *Georgii*,[73] and to western copyists, who knew St. George far better than St. Sergius, it would have been the easiest of all errors to substitute *Georgii* for *Sergii,* an error that is found in other sections of the itinerary even in collocation with St. Bacchus.[74] Be that as it may, one thing is clear: one could not enter the fort proper from the abutting church and monastery of SS. Sergius and Bacchus even though late construction shows that the church had cut through the north wall of the fort and occupied a small corner (Room 12) of the fortified area.[75] Either the monks did not wish to have their privacy invaded by pilgrims and hermits who occupied their *xenodochium* or the hospice was independent of the church and monastery of SS. Sergius and Bacchus. The evidence strongly suggests that the monastery of St. Sergius sponsored the hospice within the fort and that in Antoninus' time it was known as *xenodochium sancti Sergii.*

The Nessana papyri attest to additional facilities for travelers. P.Colt 31, a division of property, mentions an obvious *khan* or caravansary, the house of Abu Joseph son of Doubab, equipped with ninety-six beds and having an upper story and a vacant lot in front. Another building mentioned in the same document, the house of Abu 'l-Mughira, may also have been a *khan.*[76] From the apparent trade names of the two buildings and from the fact that they were in private hands, it is quite likely that they were used by Arab caravaneers and hence were unsuitable for Christian pilgrims, particularly Europeans. Pilgrims were undoubtedly housed in the *xenodochium* in the fort close to the two main

churches which occupied the hill.[77] The fact that the hospice was shared by hermits and pilgrims may indicate that pilgrims were so few that the converted fort was occupied mainly by hermits. The archaeological finds (spindle whorls, fragments of mirrors, quantities of glass, household objects) would support this view. It is also interesting to note that the house of Abu Joseph son of Doubab, with its ninety-six beds, would provide accommodations for the men (merchants, guides, guards) of one of the smaller caravans which originated in Mecca and traveled to Gaza.[78]

Finally, Antoninus and his companions departed from Nessana and went into the "inner desert and came to a place of which it is said: [He hath turned fertile] land into salt for the wickedness of them that dwell therein."[79] The exact route of Antoninus and his party is, of course, unknown, but soon after leaving Nessana they observed a salt plain (*sebkha*),[80] a common topographical feature of North Sinai and one which stirred the writer to quote a line from Psalm 107. If the party took the well-marked road leading to Birein and Qusaima, it would have passed one such salt plain less than one-day's journey from Nessana, and one-day's journey would have taken it into the al-Tih desert.

The term "inner desert" is used in a technical sense: i.e., a desert region devoid of a settled population and generally inhabited, if at all, by nomads.[81] There is no conflict in calling the

[73] Paris., lat. 12, 77 in Tobler, 111.

[74] The Vatican manuscript (E. cod. Vatic. 636 A in Tobler, p. 134) has the following confusion: "Et inde venimus in civitate Barbarisso, ubi requiescit sanctus Bacchus, frater sancti Giorgii. . . . In ipsa civitate (Sura) passi sunt sanctus Bacchus et sanctus Giorgius, set sanctus Giorgius in civitate Tyra requiescit." See also Geyer, 218.

[75] *Ness I*, pls. 63, 66.

[76] See *Ness III*, 27. P.Colt 79, an account recording contributions to the church and monastery of St. Sergius, mentions a *matronikia,* "women's quarters (?)." We cannot, however, be sure that it served as a hospice, if such it was, for women pilgrims.

[77] Fortresses converted into hospices have historical implications which this writer hopes to detail in another paper. Briefly, the evidence suggests the following: that Procopius' bitter statements (*Anecdota*, 18, 22; 23, 6, 8; 24, 12–14) on Justinian's treatment of the *limitanei* and on the effects of their demobilization, have little or no application to the Negeb or Sinai; that Justinian probably found sufficient protection in continuing arrangements with Bedouin sheikhs (phylarchs), and that the arrangements were effective until Heraculius withdrew imperial support; that the settlements in the Negeb and Sinai were able, with their own resources, to cope with the "barbarian Saracens," and that both regions continued to prosper in the decades following Justinian's death, possibly to a degree of prosperity even greater than it was during Justinian's reign.

[78] See art. "Mecca" in *Enc.Isl.* **3** : 440.

[79] Geyer, ch. 35, p. 182: "Ex inde intrantes interiorem heremum venimus ad loca de quo dicitur: Terra in salsugine a malitia inhabitantium in ea."

[80] See art. "sebkha" in *Enc.Isl.* **4** : 202.

[81] Alois Musil (*Arabia Deserta*, 38, 111, 237, 494, New York, 1927), uses the term in just this sense. The fine distinction which Devréesse (Arabs-Perse et Arabes-Romaines, Lakhmides et Gassanids, *Vivre et penser*, 293, 1942) makes for the inner and outer desert and for the

region between Elusa and Nessana "desert" and that south of Nessana "inner desert": the element which distinguishes the two is settled communities, or in other words the *oecumene*.

In contrast with the Nilus narrative where the border between the "inner desert" and the *oecumene* in the late fourth century was near Soubaita, in Antoninus' itinerary the limit of the inhabited world had extended itself west and south for a considerable distance.   Not only do

inner and outer frontier does not apply to the Negeb and Sinai.

the surface remains show that wadi cultivation extended far to the south of Nessana and Eboda, but P.Colt 82, a seventh-century account of grain yields, shows that the inhabitants of Nessana had large holdings in the wadies near Birein, twelve kilometers south of Nessana.   The extension of the *oecumene* to the south and the west came, unquestionably, as the result of progressive settlement in the region beginning some time in the middle of the fifth century and continuing at least to the time of the Islamic invasions of the seventh century.

The First Muslim Attacks on Southern Palestine
(A.D. 633-634)

PHILIP MAYERSON

NEW YORK UNIVERSITY

I. INTRODUCTION

There is general agreement among scholars of Islam and the late Roman Empire that the Arab traditions (*hadith*) concerning the history of the early Muslim wars of conquest are confused in their chronology and distorted by partisan fabrications, whereas the credentials of the Byzantine chronographers for historical accuracy are more secure and reliable.* Hence, critical scholars like De Goeje, Caetani, and Becker[1] have relied primarily upon the latter in reconstructing the causes and events that resulted in the Muslim conquest of Syria and Palestine. As a result of this lack of balance in the sources, historians have leaned too heavily on the Byzantine writers, evidently in despair of detecting a meaningful pattern in the seemingly "non-objective" design of Arab expansion into Mediterranean territory. As a further consequence, some scholars have indulged in sweeping generalizations, imaginative reconstructions, and oversimplifications that give to the historical canvas a kind of one-dimensional aspect. In particular, no satisfactory explanation has been given for the conditions which made Southern Palestine the choice of the Muslims for their first attacks rather than, say, the southern extension of the former Ghassanid principate in Syria.

* To the American Council of Learned Societies grateful acknowledgement must be made for the Fellowship that made possible this and other work. Acknowledgement must also be made to the Colt Archaeological Institute for generously helping to defray the cost of printing this paper.

[1] M. J. De Goeje, *Mémoire sur la conquête de la Syrie* (*Mémoires d'histoire et de géographie orientales*[2] (Leiden 1886) 1-2; L. Caetani, *Annali dell' Islam* 2 (Milan 1907) 561-69. Most historians follow De Goeje and Caetani for this difficult period. See *inter alios* C. M. Becker, "The Expansion of the Arabs," *Cambridge Mediaeval History* 2 (New York 1923) 339; B. Lewis, *The Arabs in History* (London 1950) 36-37; P. K. Hitti, *History of Syria* (New York 1951) 412; J.-J. Waardenburg, *L'Islam dans le miroir de l'occident* (Paris 1963) 53-54.

In all fairness to these scholars, however, we must keep in mind
that, when the sources were being critically studied in the late
nineteenth and early twentieth centuries, the focus of scholarly
interest was on the Arabian peninsula, Syria, and Transjordan;
very little was known of the archaeology and topography of
Southern Palestine and Sinai.[2]   In recent years, exploration and
excavation, particularly in that part of Southern Palestine known
as the Negeb,[3] have made the region less of a *terra incognita* than
it had been before; and we are offered fresh material with which
to reframe and reinterpret the evidence long known from literary
sources.   Although radical revisions of early Islamic history will
not be forthcoming, the evidence can be made more plausible
historically; and certain generalizations, at least in their application to Southern Palestine, will be stripped of their cogency.

II. THEOPHANES AND NICEPHORUS CONSTANTINOPOLITANUS

The most detailed description of the early Arab invasions
appears in Theophanes' chronography for the years 633–634.[4]
An earlier reference to the Muslims appears in the chronicle for
the year 632.   Theophanes notes the death of Muhammad, the
accession of Abu-Bakr, and then gives a brief biography of the
prophet, including the information that he married the widow
Chadiga (Khadija), who had commercial dealings with Palestine
and Egypt, and that Muhammad learned about Christian and
Jewish doctrines when he came to Palestine on business matters.[5]
The only other previous notice in Theophanes concerning the

[2] Note for example that map No. 23 in the *Cambridge Mediaeval History* (above, note
1) and Hitti's map (above, note 1) 413 show the Wadi ʿAraba curving southwest
into the Sinai peninsula instead of emptying directly into the head of the Gulf of
ʿAqaba.

[3] I.e. the region of Southern Palestine, roughly a right triangle in shape, whose
northern limit is a line extending from Gaza through Beersheba to the southern end
of the Dead Sea; its eastern boundary is the Wadi ʿAraba, and its hypotenuse corresponds to the present international boundary between Israel and Egypt (Sinai) running
from the Gulf of ʿAqaba to the Mediterranean.

[4] *Chronographia*, ed. C. De Boor (Leipzig 1883) 1.335–36; Latin translation by
Athanasius Bibliothecarius, 2.210–11: *Anno mundi* 6123–6124, *anno divinae incarnationis*
623–624, 22nd and 23rd years of the reign of Heraclius, 1st and 2nd of Abu-Bakr,
23rd and 24th years of the episcopate of Sergius at Constantinople, 1st and 2nd of the
episcopate of Modestus at Jerusalem, 13th and 14th of the episcopate of George at
Alexandria.   On the irregularities in Theophanes' dating formulae, see *ibid*. 2.464–
515.

[5] *Chronographia* (above, note 4) 1.332–34, 2.208–9.

Muslims is a brief mention of the three bloody battles of Yarmuk, Gabatha, and Dathesmon (Athesmon), in which the Roman army suffered severe losses at the hands of the "desert Amalec."[6]

For the year 633 Theophanes records a number of events, none of which occurred in that particular year. After noting the civil war in Persia and the great quantities of precious stones sent to Heraclius by the sovereign of India on the occasion of his victory over the Persians, Theophanes recalls certain earlier events: Muhammad was dead (632); he had appointed four emirs to wage war against the Christian Arab tribes (629); the Muslims marched against a town called Moucheôn, in which Theodorus the Vicarius was stationed, and wished to attack the Arabs on the day they were to sacrifice to their idols; learning of this from a member of the Quraish tribe, Theodorus gathered all the soldiers of the desert garrisons, and, knowing the day on which the Muslim forces intended to make their attack, anticipated them in a region called Mothous (Mu'ta) where his forces killed three of the emirs and most of the host; one of the emirs, Khalid, whom they called "the sword of God," escaped. Theophanes then states:

> There were some neighboring tribes who received a modest money allowance from the emperors for guarding the entrances of the desert. At this time a eunuch came to distribute the soldiers' allowance; and when the Arabs came according to custom to receive their pay, the eunuch chased them away, saying, "The emperor scarcely gives money to his soldiers, much less to these dogs." The Arabs were upset, went to their compatriots and showed them the way to the district of Gaza, the entrance of the desert extending toward Sinai, and exceptionally rich.[7]

[6] *Chronographia* (above, note 4) 1.332, 2.208.

[7] *Chronographia* (above, note 4) 1.335–36, 2.210: ἦσαν δέ τινες τῶν πλησίον Ἀράβων λαμβάνοντες παρὰ τῶν βασιλέων ῥόγας μικρὰς πρὸς τὸ φυλάξαι τὰ στόμια τῆς ἐρήμου. ἐν αὐτῷ δὲ τῷ καιρῷ ἦλθέ τις εὐνοῦχος διδῶν τὰς ῥόγας τῶν στρατιωτῶν, καὶ ἐλθόντες οἱ Ἄραβες κατὰ τὸ ἔθος λαβεῖν τὴν ῥόγαν αὐτῶν, ὁ εὐνοῦχος ἀπεδίωξεν αὐτούς, λέγων ὅτι "ὁ δεσπότης μόγις τοῖς στρατιώταις δίδωσι ῥόγας, πόσῳ μᾶλλον τοῖς κυσὶ τούτοις;" θλιβέντες οὖν οἱ Ἄραβες ἀπῆλθον πρὸς τοὺς ὁμοφύλους, καὶ αὐτοὶ ὡδήγησαν αὐτοὺς ἐπὶ τὴν χώραν Γάζης στομίου οὔσης τῆς ἐρήμου κατὰ τὸ Σιναῖον ὄρος πλουσίας σφόδρα.

erant autem quidam Arabum iuxta positorum, qui accipiebant ab imperatoribus rogas pauxillas ad custodiendum stomia heremi. eodem vero tempore venit quidam spado daturus militum rogas. et cum venissent Arabes secundum consuetudinem accepturi rogam suam, eunuchus impulit dicens, quia "dominus vix dat militibus rogas, quanto minus canibus istis." videntes ergo Arabes hoc abierunt ad sui generis viros et ipsi duxerunt eos in regionem Gazae, quae aditus erat heremi contra Sinaeon montem locuples valde.

For the year 634, Theophanes continues the story of the invasion:

> In this year Abu-Bakr sent four commanders—they too having been shown the way, as I said before, by the Arabs—who came and took Heran (*var.* Ran, Eran) and the whole district of Gaza. Then Sergius, scarcely having come from Caesarea of Palestine with a few soldiers, engaged them [the Muslims] in battle and was the first to be killed; his soldiers, numbering three hundred, died with him. And taking many prisoners and much booty, they withdrew with a splendid victory.[7a]

In addition to the references in Theophanes, a brief passage in Nicephorus Constantinopolitanus alludes to a similar but not, as De Goeje and Caetani believe, the same incident. In describing the events of the year 635, Nicephorus relates the barbarous way in which Sergius, who seems to have been the *magister militum* before Theodorus Trithyrius, had been put to death by the Arabs. He brought it upon himself, says Nicephorus,

> because he induced Heraclius not to accede to sending the Saracens their customary allowance of thirty pounds of gold through commercial exchange [*i.e.* in the form of commodities worth thirty pounds of gold] from the Roman government; henceforth they began to inflict outrages on Roman territory.[8]

De Goeje, conflating these two sources, makes the generalization that the Arab tribes of Southern Palestine and of Arabia Petraea

---

[7a] *Chronographia* (above, note 4) 1.336, 2.210–11: Τούτῳ τῷ ἔτει ἔπεμψεν Ἀβουβάχαρος στρατηγοὺς τέσσαρας, οἳ καὶ ὁδηγηθέντες, ὡς προέφην, ὑπὸ τῶν Ἀράβων ἦλθον καὶ ἔλαβον τὴν Ἥραν καὶ πᾶσαν τὴν χώραν Γάζης. μόγις δὲ ἐλθών ποτε ἀπὸ Καισαρείας Παλαιστίνης Σέργιος σὺν στρατιώταις ὀλίγοις καὶ συμβαλὼν πόλεμον κτείνεται πρῶτος σὺν τοῖς στρατιώταις τριακοσίοις οὖσιν. καὶ πολλοὺς αἰχμαλώτους λαβόντες καὶ λάφυρα πολλὰ ὑπέστρεψαν μετὰ λαμπρᾶς νίκης.
Mundi anno VIcxxiiii, divinae incarnationis anno DCxxiiii, anno imperii Heraclii vicesimo tertio cum misisset Abubacharus praetores quattuor, qui ducti fuerant, ut praetuli, ab Arabibus, venerunt atque ceperunt Ran et totam regionem Gazae. tandemque aliquando cum venisset a Caesaria Palaestinae cum militibus paucis, inito bello perimitur primus cum exercitu, qui trecentorum erat virorum, et multis captivis acceptis et exuviis plurimis reversi sunt cum victoria splendida.
[8] *Opuscula historica*, ed. C. De Boor (Leipzig 1880) 23: αἰτίαν δὲ αὐτῷ ἐπῆγον ὡς αὐτὸς παρεσκεύασεν Ἡράκλειον μὴ συγχωρεῖν Σαρακηνοῖς [ἐκ τῆς Ῥωμαίων γῆς ἐκπορεύεσθαι] τὰς συνήθως παρεχομένας αὐτοῖς τριάκοντα χρυσίου λίτρας δι' ἐμπορικῆς ἀμοιβῆς ἐκ τῆς Ῥωμαϊκῆς πολιτείας ἐκπέμπειν· ἐντεῦθέν τε αὐτοὺς ἄρξαι τῇ Ῥωμαίων λυμαίνεσθαι χώρᾳ. I have not translated the clause bracketed by the editor but I shall comment on it below, page 167.

received an annual allowance from the emperor of thirty pounds of gold for guarding the entrances of the desert. Angered at having their subsidy suspended, the Arabs believed themselves relieved of their obligations to the Byzantines and served as guides to the Muslim troops in their invasions of Palestine.[9] De Goeje also advances the view that Heraclius, his treasury empty owing to the war with the Persians, had unwisely suspended the yearly subsidy to the border Arabs as a measure of economy. To this De Goeje adds the observation that the Syrian inhabitants, who were burdened by financial obligations to the state and split by religious differences, gave passive encouragement to the invading Arabs; and when they saw that the Arabs did not pillage or devastate the land, they did not hesitate to show their partiality for the Arabs.[10]

Caetani, with but minor modifications, adopts De Goeje's interpretation of the Byzantine sources and further elaborates on the evidence by assuming that *all* Arabs in the pay of the Byzantines were Christians, and that the eunuch was sent as a special emissary of Heraclius to announce formally to the assembled chiefs of the Arab tribes that the revenues of the empire did not permit the continuation of the usual stipend.[11]

Becker, whose treatment of the early Arab attacks is commended by historians, prudently removes some of the sharp edges from De Goeje's and Caetani's conclusions; but he still retains the

[9] *De Goeje* (above, note 1) 29.

[10] De Goeje (above, note 1) 29–30. He cites the works of A. Müller, G. Weil, and H. Gelzer in support of this generalization, but their observations are mostly inferential and based on theological differences in the large cities of Syria and Egypt. The application of these generalizations to Southern Palestine and Sinai for the early years of Muslim penetration should be considered highly speculative. Caetani (above, note 1) 1115, note 3, attempts to find in the Armenian chronicler, Sebeos, evidence for a discontented population inviting invasion by the Muslims; but Sebeos places the blame on the Jews of Edessa who had been punished by Heraclius for their rebellion, and not, as Caetani would like to see, on the Christian Arabs. See also Caetani's generalization (*ibid.* 1120, note 2c) on the assistance given to the Muslim invaders by the inhabitants out of their hatred for the Byzantine government.

[11] E.g. Caetani (above, note 1) 1112–13: "È detto in Teofane che dopo la infelice spedizione di Muʿtah, nella quale i Musulmani subirono sì gravi perdite, si presentò un eunuco (della corte imperiale) e percorse la provincia di confine della Siria e della Palestina, nel tempo quando secundo l'antica consuetudine si distribuiva agli Arabi cristiani lo stipendio, che solevasi sempre concedere ai capi delle tribù di confine, quale compenso per la difesa della frontiera." *Ibid.* 1114: "L'eunuco di cui parla Teofano, dev'essere stato l'emissario dell'Imperatore per annunziare agli Arabi cristiani che le finanze dell' Impero non consentivano temporaneamente la continuazione degli stipendi soliti."

essence of their inferences that are based largely on Theophanes and Nicephorus.[12]

In reviewing the evidence, I find nothing in Theophanes, Nicephorus, or for that matter in the Arab *hadith*, to support the three major conclusions advanced by De Goeje, Caetani, or Becker: (1) that the Arabs involved were Christians, (2) that Heraclius suspended the yearly subsidies to *all* the border tribes,[13] (3) that the settled inhabitants of Syria and Palestine had given active or passive aid to the Muslims as early as 634. And one major question emerges, one which goes to the heart of the problem: why should the Muslims, who had in their ranks experienced merchants and guides, have to rely on Arabs, particularly Syrian Arabs or Arabs of Central Arabia, to guide them over the well-known and well-marked route to the district of Gaza? Similarly, is it conceivable that the first Caliph, Abu-Bakr, who had lived as a well-to-do merchant in Mecca, or ʿAmr ibn al-ʿAs, who was of Quraishite birth and who, according to Arab tradition, was the leader of the detachment assigned to Southern Palestine, would need the help of disgruntled Arabs to show him the way to Gaza, the established terminus of Meccan caravans?[14]

[12] Becker (above, note 1) 339–40. For an evaluation of Becker, see *inter alios* J. Sauvaget, *Introduction à l'histoire de l'Orient Musulman: Éléments de bibliographie* (Paris 1946) 116.

[13] Caetani (above, note 1) 1114, and Becker (above, note 1) 340 take into account the fact that the Ghassanids fought on the side of the Byzantines against the Muslims, and hence they agree that the northern tribes received different treatment from those of the south. Becker admits that we know very little about the tribes of North Arabia and claims that the defeat of the Muslims at Muʾta shows that they were enemies of Medina. The latter conclusion must be based on the assumption that Theodorus the Vicarius commanded Bedouin mercenaries or that Muhammad's forces were attacking a large number of hostile tribes in the region of Muʾta. In my view, Theodorus carried out a police action, not unlike the one mentioned by Choricius (below, page 181), with troops stationed in various garrisons around Moucheôn (see below, note 30). Lewis (above, note 1) 52 states simply that the sources say nothing about the tribes that lay between Medina and Syria.

[14] Theophanes (above, note 4) 1.333 states that Muhammad himself had come to Palestine, presumably traveling with the caravans owned by his wife. ʿAmr ibn al-ʿAs, the leader of one of the early attacks on Southern Palestine, possibly even the one mentioned by Theophanes, was a member of the Quraish and undoubtedly had traveled often on the Mecca-Gaza route. According to Arab tradition, the tomb of Muhammad's great-grandfather or great-uncle was located in Gaza, "the market for the people of the Hedjaz" (Guy Le Strange, *Palestine under the Moslems* [London 1890] 442). ʿUmar ibn al-Khattab, who later became caliph, lived for a period of time in Gaza and grew rich there. And following Heraclius' victory over the Persians, Arab tradition also tells us that a body of Quraish merchants migrated to Gaza

The answers to these questions, I believe, lie in interpreting Theophanes' statements more restrictively; that is, his information does not refer to a general condition on the southern borders of Syria and Palestine but to a specific region whose inhabitants possessed special knowledge of routes that were unknown or unfamiliar to the Muslims.   While we do not know the source of Theophanes' information, it seems, clearly, that it originated in Palestine, possibly in Gaza or Caesarea, and that the report concerned itself with, as Theophanes says, "the district of Gaza, which was the entrance (*stomion*) of the desert extending towards Mount Sinai."[15]

A key point in this problem is the identification of the site that Theophanes calls "Heran."   The Muslims, he says, "came and took Heran (*var*. Ran or Eran) and the whole district of Gaza."[16] De Goeje does not attempt an identification but frankly admits that he does not know exactly what place or region Theophanes meant by this name.[17]   Caetani suggests that it is possibly an error and a confused reference to the capture of Lakhmiḍ Hira, on the Euphrates, by Khalid ibn al-Walid.[18]

I would suggest, however, that it is not an error and a confused reference, but rather that Heran, Eran, or Ran, is a garbled version of the Greek name of a site in Sinai, namely Pharan (Φαράν), modern Feiran; more likely it is a garbling or a clipped form of the Arabic name of the same site, Fârân Hârûn (Ahrûn).[19] It is true that Theophanes cites Pharan in an earlier reference; but here he is speaking of Theodorus as the "bishop of Pharan," and the title obviously came from Greek ecclesiastical sources.[20]

(M. A. Meyer, *History of the City of Gaza: Columbia University Oriental Studies* 5 [New York 1907] 74).   It is hardly likely that there was any route which the Arabs of the Hedjaz knew better than the one which led to Gaza.

[15] Theophanes, *loc. cit.* (above, note 7).

[16] Theophanes, *loc. cit.* (above, note 7a).   See also the critical apparatus for line 16.

[17] De Goeje (above, note 1) 34.   [18] Caetani (above, note 1) 1143, note 1.

[19] Place names, of course, are particularly subject to corruption in manuscript tradition.   In general, Theophanes' text shows a rather loose handling of Arabic names both in orthography and accentuation.   For the possibility of a clipped form of an Arabic place name in the Nessana papyri, see *PColt* 89 in C. J. Kraemer, *Excavations at Nessana: Non-Literary Papyri* 3 (Princeton 1958) 260.   For the appearance of Pharan in Arab sources, see Le Strange (above, note 14) 44.

[20] Theophanes (above, note 4) 1.330, 2.206.   Theodorus was condemned for monothelitism by the council of Latran (649) and by the sixth oecumenical council of Constantinople (680) (M. Le Quien, *Oriens Christianus* 3 [Paris 1740] 753).   On the meaning of Pharan in his title, see below, page 197.

If, as I believe, Theophanes' source for the early Muslim attacks on Southern Palestine was derived from the Arabic translated into Gréek, it is reasonable to expect that the name of Pharan was garbled in its transmission. The confusion in the various codices and in Athanasius' Latin version leads me to suspect that it was. But even if this is a mistaken assumption, the context very clearly refers to a site in Sinai.[21] Theophanes' statement emphasizes the fact that the district of Gaza was the entrance (*stomion*) of the desert extending towards Mount Sinai and that the Muslims, guided by disgruntled tribesmen, came and took "the site" and the whole district of Gaza. Mount Sinai is in south-central Sinai; the desert associated with it is the Tih wilderness, the "Desert of the Bani Isra'il,"[22] and its extension into the Negeb on the north and to the mountain ranges in the south-central portion of the Sinai peninsula. In other words, the Muslim attack on Palestine came from the south of the Sinai peninsula and worked its way northward to the district of Gaza. The Muslims, therefore, must not have followed the commercial route to Gaza, which bypassed the Sinai peninsula, but rather entered the desert near Aila and then headed south and west into the wilderness of Sinai toward Mount Sinai and, most probably, toward Pharan.

In the Byzantine period we know of three entrances or approaches (*stomia*) to the desert and Mount Sinai: at Gaza (the western), at Elusa and the Central Negeb (the central), and at

[21] A less likely candidate for the site would be the oasis of Gharandel on the road from Pharan to Clysma (Suez). It is called Surandala by Antoninus Placentius (*Itinera Hierosolymitana saeculi IIII–VIII* in *Corpus scriptorum ecclesiasticorum Latinorum* 39, ed. P. Geyer, [Vienna 1898] 187; Arandara by Petrus Diaconus (*ibid.*) 118; Arandoulan by the monk Anastasius (F. Nau, Les **Récits** inédits du moine Anastase," *Revue de l'Institut catholique de Paris* 7 [1902] 116; "Le **Texte** grec des récits du moine Anastase sur les saints pères du Sinai, *Oriens Christianus* 2 [1902] 77). R. Weill, *La presqu'île du Sinai* in *Bibliothèque de l'École des Hautes Études, Sciences historiques et philologiques* fasc. 171 (Paris 1902) 99–103, 203, 232, 266, identifies the Taran of Arab geographers, some of whom associate it with Pharan, with Gharandel. The site, however, appears to have been little more than a fortlet enclosing a church and two hospices and hardly worth the effort of a *razzia*. Antonius Placentius (*loc. cit.*) describes it thus: "modicum castellum . . . nihil habet intus praeter ecclesiam cum presbytero suo et duo xenodochia propter transeuntes."

[22] See art. "al-Tih" in *Encyclopaedia of Islam*, ed. M. Th. Houtsma, *et al.* (Leiden 1913–1934) 4(2).763. According to the description of Arab geographers, al-Tih was 40 *farsakh* (*ca.* 150 miles) long and equally broad, had few palm trees and springs, consisted of partly stony and partly sandy soil, and took about six days to traverse.

Aila and the head of the Gulf of 'Aqaba (the eastern). These *stomia* lay on the roads or tracks leading into the wilderness and were points at which travelers could make arrangements for supplies, caravans, and guides before entering the desert.[23] The route from Gaza to Sinai proceeded along the *via maris* to a point in Egypt from which a road went to Clysma at the head of the Gulf of Suez and then on to Mount Sinai. This was the *grande route ordinaire* for pilgrims en route to the Holy Mountain from Palestine; and at the time of Egeria's pilgrimage in the sixth century, the desert road from Clysma to Egypt was protected by soldiers who escorted pilgrims from one fortified station to the next.[24]

The central route led from Elusa, "at the head of the desert that leads to Sinai," through the Central Negeb to Nessana and then through the heart of the Tih desert to the mountain ranges to the south. This is the most direct route of all, but the least secure.[25] The eastern route from Aila, shorter but perhaps not as safe or as comfortable as the *via maris*, led from Jerusalem (or Gaza) to Elusa in the Central Negeb and then by the trans-Negeb

[23] Cf. Antoninus Placentius' praise of Gaza (*op. cit.* [above, note 21] 180): ". . . magnificent, delightful; its inhabitants most respectful, friendly in every way, lovers of travelers (amatores peregrinorum)." Antoninus, who is known under the names of Antoninus Martyr and Antoninus of Placentia or Piacenza did not, of course, write the *itinerarium* (see Ch. 1, page 157) but since his name is the only one associated with it, I shall, for the sake of convenience and simplicity, use his name as the writer of the account.

[24] See *Sanctae Silviae peregrinatio* in *Corp. script. ecc. Lat.* (above, note 21) 47: "Sunt ergo a Clesma, id est a mare rubro, usque ad Arabiam civitatem [Thou or Bubastis?] mansiones quattuor per heremo, sic tamen per heremum, ut cata mansiones monasteria sint cum militibus et praepositis qui nos deducebant semper de castro ad castrum." The date of the pilgrimage is still debated (see *Itinerarium Egeriae*, ed. O. Prinz [Heidelberg 1960] viii), but I follow A. A. Vasiliev, *Justin the First* (Cambridge 1950) 276, note 30; 364, note 44. Petrus Diaconus (above, note 21) 115, copying an early *itinerarium*, gives the number of way stations from Jerusalem to Mount Sinai as twenty-two; from Pelusium to Mount Sinai as twelve: "Ab Hierusalem autem usque ad montem sanctum Syna sunt mansiones viginti duo . . . A Pelusio autem usque ad montem Syna sunt mansiones duodecim."

[25] Antoninus Placentius (above, note 21) 181–82: "et inde [Gaza] venimus in civitate Elusa in caput heremi, qui vadit ad Sina . . . Proficiscentes de civitate Elusa, ingressi heremum. Ad XX milia est castrum in quo est xenodochius sancti Georgi (Sergii), in quo habent quasi refugium transeuntes vel heremitae stipendia. Exinde intrantes interiorem heremum." On the identification of the castrum as Nessana, see P. Mayerson, "The Desert of Southern Palestine according to Byzantine Sources," *Proceedings of the American Philosophical Society* 107 (April 1963) 170–71; see also Kraemer (above, note 19) 29.

route to Aila. From Aila, the road apparently ran for a short distance along the eastern coast of the Sinai peninsula and then turned southwest toward Mount Sinai and Pharan.[26] St. Jerome speaks of Pharan as being a three-day journey from Aila, indicating the existence of a direct route between the two towns.[27] There were also lesser routes emanating from these *stomia* which, though unrecorded in the Byzantine period, were undoubtedly known by the Bedouins and other inhabitants of the desert. The biblical Way of Shur, for example, running more or less parallel to the *via maris*, avoided the coastal sand dunes and connected with roads leading into Palestine.[28]

To return to Theophanes' description of the events immediately after the defeat of the Muslims at Mu'ta, he states that:

> There were some neighboring [*plêsion*] tribes who received a modest money allowance [*rogas*] from the emperors for guarding the entrances of the desert. At this time [in 633? or right after the defeat at Mu'ta in 629?] a eunuch [*tis eunouchos*] came to distribute the soldiers' allowance; and when the Arabs came according to custom to receive their pay [*roga*], the eunuch

[26] Theodosius, *De situ terrae sanctae* (*ca.* 530) in *Corp. script. ecc. Lat.* (above, note 21) 148: "De Hierusalem in Elusath [Elusa] mansiones III, de Elusath in Aila mansiones VII... De Aila usque in monte Syna mansiones VIII, si compendiaria volueris ambulare per heremum, sin autem per Aegyptum, mansiones XXV." The number of stations between Elusa and Aila agrees quite well with the Peutinger map: Elusa, Oboda (Eboda), Lysa, Gypsaria, Rasa (Gerasa), Ad Dianam, Haila (Aila). For a discussion of these stations, see Y. Aharoni, "The Roman Road to Aila (Elath)," *Israel Exploration Journal* 4 (1954) 9–16. Petrus Diaconus (above, note 21) 115 may have preserved a description of this same route: "Pars Arabiae iungitur Palaestinae, inaccessibile iter habet; nam licet mansionibus quindecim .a... eat (interiaceat?) loca tamen ipsa sine aqua sunt." The number of stations agrees with Theodosius if the writer had in mind the road from Elusa to Aila to Mount Sinai. The inaccessibility of the road and the lack of water should be regarded as an overstatement.

[27] *De situ et nom. Hebr.* in *Patrologia Latina* (J.-P. Migne) 23 Col. 944: "[Pharan] est... trans Arabiam contra australem plagam, et distat ab Aila contra Orientem itinere trium dierum."

[28] See W. F. Albright, "Abram the Caravaneer: A New Interpretation," *Bulletin of the American Schools of Oriental Research* 163 (October 1961) 37–38 for an appreciation of the quality of this road for caravans. Another road might be the Darb el-Haj (the biblical Way of the Wilderness?) which cuts across the northern part of the Tih plateau and is a direct route from Aila to Egypt and to connecting roads to Mount Sinai and Pharan. It is quite possible that Bedouins used this route throughout all periods of history and it may even be the one which Jerome had in mind (above, note 27). However, at an important way station on this road, Qual ᶜat Nakhl, no evidence predating medieval times has been found (see B. Rothenberg, *God's Wilderness: Discoveries in Sinai* [London 1961] 67).

chased them away, saying, "The emperor scarcely gives money [*rogas*] to his soldiers, much less to these dogs." [29]

The statements regarding "neighboring tribes" and "a eunuch" are couched in language so vague as to make it impossible to say whether the Arabs were Syrian (*i.e.* trans-Jordanian), Palestinian, or Sinaitic, or whether the unnamed eunuch was a high ranking emissary and treasurer of Heraclius' court.   Nor is it possible to determine whether these Arabs were paid by the Byzantines to prevent the infiltration of other Arabs from the Arabian peninsula, or, as I believe, were merely the tribes on the roads leading to Mount Sinai who were paid off so that pilgrims could journey in safety to this celebrated Biblical site. These are questions which none of the sources bears upon and can only be answered by conjecture. What is clear, however, is that, after defeating the Persians, Heraclius organized some form of defense in Syria just south of the Dead Sea; and when Muhammad's forces threatened the pagan Arabs in the region of Mu'ta, Theodorus the Vicarius was able to "gather all the soldiers of the desert garrisons" and repulse the Muslim attack. [30] What is also clear is the fact that the southern line of defense in 629 was no longer near Aila, a border point of *Palaestina Tertia* on the Gulf of ʿAqaba, [31] and that Bedouins had relatively free movement from the Arabian peninsula up to the region near the Dead Sea.

The remaining portion of Theophanes' entry for the year 633 and the notice of events for 634 place us on a surer footing:

The Arabs were upset, went to their compatriots [*homophylous*] and showed them the way to the district of Gaza, the entrance of the desert extending towards Sinai, and exceptionally rich.

[29] Theophanes, *loc. cit.* (above, note 7). The use of the technical term *rogas* gives the account an authentic sound even if other elements, particularly the reputed words of the eunuch to the tribesmen, appear fabricated. *Roga* is the word used in a Nessana document, *PColt* 92 dated *ca.* 685, for a cash allowance (Kraemer [above, note 19] 291). With regard to the eunuch, there might be some derogatory implication in the use of the word if we were more knowledgeable of early Islamic attitudes towards eunuchism (see art. "Eunuch" in *Encyclopaedia of Religion and Ethics* 5, ed. J. Hastings [New York 1928], 582, 584.
[30] Theophanes (above, note 4) 1.335: ... ὁ βικάριος ... συνάγει πάντας τοὺς στρατιώτας τῶν παραφυλάκων ... On the use of the word *stratiōtai* to indicate regular troops, see Vasiliev (above, note 25) 243, and Kraemer (above, note 19) 20.
[31] See below, page 169.

For 634:

> In this year Abu-Bakr sent four commanders—they too having
> been shown the way, as I said before, by the Arabs—who came and
> took Heran [Ran or Eran] and the whole district of Gaza.   Then
> Sergius, scarcely having come from Caesarea of Palestine with a
> few soldiers, engaged them [the Muslims] in battle and was the
> first to be killed; his soldiers, numbering three hundred, died with
> him.   And taking many prisoners and much booty, they with-
> drew with a splendid victory.[32]

The area of conflict now becomes sharply defined: we are no
longer in the region east of the Wadi ʿAraba but in Southern
Palestine and the Sinai peninsula.   Theophanes' evidence should
therefore be restricted to this region; whatever conclusions may be
drawn from this evidence must rest on the nature of conditions
(topographical, demographic, political, and military) of the
region itself.

In contrast to Theophanes, the evidence in Nicephorus is far less
informative, far less detailed:

> [Sergius] induced Heraclius not to accede to sending the Saracens
> their customary allowance [*tas synêthôs parechomenas*] of thirty
> pounds of gold through commercial exchange [*i.e.* in the form of
> commodities worth thirty pounds of gold] from the Roman
> government; henceforth they [the Saracens] began to inflict
> outrages on Roman territory.[32a]

As stated above, Caetani believes that the incidents reported by
Theophanes and Nicephorus are one and the same, and, like De
Goeje before him, has taken considerable liberties in interpreting
the text:

> De Goeje in reporting this highly important passage [in Theo-
> phanes] cites another in Nicephorus Constantinopolitanus which
> also alludes to the same event.   The Emperor, it is said, was
> accustomed to pay the Saracen border tribes the sum of thirty
> pounds of gold per year so that they might serve as a check on
> the other Saracens from the interior of Arabia.   However, when
> he suspended the payment of this stipend, the angry Arabs invaded
> Palestine and when they captured the patricius Sergius some-
> what later, they considered him to be the chief supporter of the
> imperial measure and wished to avenge themselves in a cruel and
> barbarous manner.[33]

[32] Theophanes, *loc. cit.* (above, note 7a).   [32a] Nicephorus, *loc. cit.* (above, note 8).
[33] Caetani (above, note 1) 1113.   Cf. De Goeje (above, note 1) 29.

There is no suggestion whatever in Nicephorus that the purpose of the money was to pay the Arabs to act as a check on others coming from the interior of Arabia. On the contrary, there is a strong intimation in the portion of the text bracketed by the editor De Boor that the purpose of the payment was *to induce these Arabs to leave Roman territory*.[34] As for identifying the Sergius mentioned by Theophanes as the leader of the small detachment from Caesarea with the Sergius who was tortured to death by the Saracens, we certainly cannot be sure that they were one and the same person: the name Sergius, like Theodorus, George, and John, was a very common one, and the two Sergii could have been entirely different persons.[35] And lastly, there is no indication in Nicephorus that Muslim or Christian Arabs invaded Palestine proper.

We must conclude that the statements of Theophanes and Nicephorus do not refer to the same incident. At best, the point of similarity between the two is that they reflect a general condition arising from Heraclius' decision to cut down on payments of various kinds to Arab tribes: payments not only to prevent Arabs from infiltrating from the interior of Arabia, but payments also to Arabs within the empire to keep peace along the roads and highways, and payments to other tribes to stay out of the empire. Further, we should not believe that one payment of thirty pounds of gold a year, or its equivalent in commodities, took care of all the Arab tribes on the southern borders of Roman territory.[36] On the contrary, the likelihood is that individual payments were made to a number of Arab tribes and that Theophanes and Nicephorus were reporting separate incidents which arose as a result of cutting off payments to two such groups.

[34] Nicephorus, *loc. cit.* (above, note 8).

[35] See *inter alios* the onomastica in Theophanes (above, note 4) 2.555 ff., and Kraemer (above, note 19) 333–41 for the Nessana papyri. For the difficulties in sorting out men named Sergius, see Caetani (above, note 1) 1137, note 1.

[36] Thirty pounds of gold would have been a nominal sum for protecting the eastern borders of the Roman Empire. The sum, approximately 2200 *solidi*, would have hardly bought 400 camels at the rate of 5–7 *solidi* a camel, the price in Southern Palestine at about this time (see *PColt* 89 in Kraemer [above, note 19] 255–57). E. Stein, *Studien zur Geschichte des byzantinischen Reiches* (Stuttgart 1919) 4, estimates that at the end of Justinian's reign, the Lahkmid ꜤAmr received 100 pounds of gold as part of the Roman policy in keeping peace on the Syro-Mesopotamian border. The 30 pounds of gold mentioned by Nicephorus is insignificant in comparison with the hundreds and thousands of pounds of gold donated to the church in an earlier period (see M. Avi-Yonah, "The Economics of Byzantine Palestine," *Israel Exploration Journal* 8 [1958] 42–45).

We are therefore left with the account of Theophanes as the most reliable Greek source for the initial attacks of the Muslim forces on *Palaestina Tertia*. It remains for us to see whether Theophanes' report dovetails with other evidence of the region, and whether the interpretation that follows is consistent with conditions in the desert of Southern Palestine for the early decades of the seventh century. One *caveat* must be entered, however. We must disengage ourselves from the rather full descriptions that we possess of Arab life in Northern Syria, particularly along the Syro-Mesopotamian *limes*. The political vicissitudes and intrigues of these Arabs (especially those of the Ghassanid and Lahkmid dynasties), their complex relations with the Byzantine emperors and Persian kings, their association and consequent involvement in non-orthodox forms of Christianity, their relations with the wealthy cities of Syria such as Bostra, Damascus, Homs, and Antioch,[37] have very little or no bearing on the life and conditions of the Arabs in the desert of Southern Palestine and Sinai. This region was far removed from the perennial conflict between the Byzantines and the Persians; its faith was solidly Orthodox and not subject to the proselytizing interests of the Monophysites or Nestorians;[38] and its commercial routes, while of some importance, did not attract the hordes of tribes and create the highly developed urban life of the cities mentioned above. Most significantly, our sources do not record one bishop of the Arabs or one bishop of the Arab encampments (*parembolê*) for this region; the area where these bishops were concentrated lay to the north of the Dead Sea and along the Syro-Mesopotamian border.[39]

Throughout recorded history the Sinai peninsula and the Negeb have been primarily transit areas, unsuited by climate and topography for settled habitation except under unusual circumstances. The perennial inhabitants of this marginal region were Bedouins who, in addition to eking out an existence by their flocks and herds, added to their livelihood by trading and raiding:

[37] See e.g. P. Henri Charles, "Le christianisme des Arabes nomades sur le limes," *Bibliothéque de l'École des Hautes Études, Sciences religieuses* 52 (1936) 29 ff; I. Kawar, "Procopius on the Ghassanids," *Journal of the American Oriental Society* 77 (1957) 79–87.

[38] Charles (above, note 37) 96. A. A. Vasiliev, "Notes on Some Episodes Concerning the Relations between the Arabs and the Byzantine Empire from the Fourth to the Sixth Century," *Dumbarton Oaks Papers* Nos. 9–10 (Cambridge 1956) 309–10.

[39] For the distribution of the bishoprics, see Charles' map (above, note 37) 66.

trading whenever the strong arm of authority kept them under control, raiding whenever that control was absent or relaxed. A supplementary source of income was no doubt derived from tribute exacted from the settlements that managed to establish and maintain themselves in this inhospitable area, or from service as guides over the lesser-known routes of the desert. Notices of these activities have largely gone unrecorded; but with the interest of the Roman government in maintaining open lines of communication in and near this region, and with the mounting attraction of Christian ascetics to that part of the desert associated with the Bible, our sources begin to record contact between Bedouins and the settled people of the region.

III. AILA AND MUHAMMAD

A notable move on the part of the Roman government toward the end of the third century or the beginning of the fourth was the stationing of a legion, the *Legio decima Fretensis* in Aila on the Gulf of ʿAqaba.[40] Most scholars attribute this to the reforms of Diocletian[41] but, in any case, the placement of a military unit

[40] R. E. Brünnow and A. v. Domaszewski, *Die Provincia Arabia* 3 (Strassburg 1904–1909) 275; Art. "Legio" in *RE* 12 [1925] 1674.

[41] The attribution of this move to the military reforms of Diocletian does not, in my opinion, pinpoint the specific need for a legion at Aila. If we take a closer look at what was happening along the major trade routes at the end of the third century, the move begins to make more sense. From the first century onwards, the bulk of east–west trade moved through Egyptian ports on the Red Sea or through the Persian Gulf–Euphrates Basin routes to North Syria *via* Palmyra. Towards the close of the third century both Palmyra and Egypt were in a state of upheaval: Palmyra desiring to take advantage of anarchical conditions to carve out a caravan empire for herself; Egypt being beset by the revolt of Firmus—the trader whose ships sailed to India— and by marauding Blemmyes. It was Aurelian, *restitutor Orientis*, who destroyed Palmyra in 273 and brought to an end her role as an *entrepôt* between east and west. In Egypt, the chaos occasioned by Firmus and the Blemmyes must have, in like fashion, caused a disruption in its share of the Red Sea trade. (Trouble in Egypt did not cease with the death of Firmus since Diocletian had similar difficulties with Achilleus, and the Blemmyes continued to be bothersome up to the time of Justinian. See Vasiliev [above, note 24] 288.) In the light of these developments, it seems best to interpret the shift of the *Legio X Fretensis* to Aila as part of the revival of the old South Arabian trade routes which had declined in the years following 106 when Roman emperors adopted a deliberate policy of taking control of east–west trade out of the hands of Arab caravaneers (M. P. Charlesworth, *Trade-Routes and Commerce of the Roman Empire* [Cambridge 1924] 62; Avi-Yonah [above, note 36] 40–41). We may date the shift of the legion as early as Aurelian's reign, possibly about 274, when he reinforced Syria Phoenice and Arabia with two new legions (H. Mattingly, "The Imperial Recovery," *Cambridge Ancient History* 12 [New York 1939] 308–9). With the

as large as a legion at this particular junction of Palestine and the Hedjaz of Arabia unquestionably resulted from the recognition of Aila's strategic position as a border control point at the crossroad of key highways into Syria and Palestine: the *via nova Traiana*, extending northwards to Bostra and Damascus, and the old trans-Negeb roads leading to Gaza (*via* Eboda and Elusa) and Jerusalem (*via* the Wadi ʿAraba, Mampsis and Hebron).[42]   At the beginning of the fifth century, Aila is signalized in the *Notitia dignitatum*[43]–our last reference to the Tenth Legion– as the only city in the three Palestines in which the Romans stationed a legion; the defense of other posts along the *limes Palaestinae* was left to smaller military units.

The main approach to Aila from the north and the east, by the *via nova Traiana* and all later roads, is through the Wadi Ithm (*var.* Jitm, Yutm, Jetoum), a gorge-like pass that descends steeply for several thousand feet from the high plateau region of the northeast to a point in the Wadi ʿAraba a short distance above the ancient town.[44]   Access to this pass was guarded by a number of forts of which one, Praesidium, garrisoned by the *Cohors quarta Phrygum* in the early fifth century, protected the opening to the pass.[45]   The southern approach to Aila was the coastal road from the Hedjaz, a passsage so narrow as to be often flooded by the tides of the Gulf of ʿAqaba.   In the late ninth century, a new road was laid over the ridge of Djebel Umm Nsele in order to make the town more accessible from the south.   Until the opening of the Suez Canal, Aila, or its later counterpart ʿAqaba, was a central point for assembling pilgrims from Syria, Egypt, and North Africa en route to Mecca and for all traffic going to and from the Hedjaz to Egypt across the Sinai peninsula.[46]

beginning of the fourth century, we note a heightened activity in trade and trading communities that increases in tempo as Rome entered into an era of perennial conflict with the aggressive dynasty of the Sassanids.

[42] P. F.-M. Abel, *Géographie de la Palestine* 2 (Paris 1938) map 10; Aharoni, (above, note 24) 9–16; M. Harel, "The Roman Road at the Maʿaleh ʿAqrabbim," *Israel Exploration Journal* 9 (1959) 177–79.

[43] Ed. O. Seeck (Berlin 1876) 73.

[44] Brünnow and v. Domaszewski (above, note 40) 1.471–72; A. Musil, *Arabia Petraea* (Vienna 1907) 2(1).256–64, 2(2).187–89.

[45] Abel (above, note 42) 182.

[46] A. Musil, *The Northern Hegaz* (*American Geographical Society Oriental Studies and Explorations* No. 1 New York 1926) 321–22.   Art. "Aila" in *Enc. Isl.* 1 (above, note 22) 210–11.

Aila was in fact a *stomion*, an entrance to the desert extending to the commercial *entrepôts* of Arabia just as Theophanes' Gaza was an entrance to the desert extending toward Sinai.   With a legion stationed at Aila, tariffs could be collected and commercial transactions conducted peaceably at a point where caravans or ships entered Roman territory.[47]   And since it is axiomatic in these regions that commercial highways are also avenues of invasion from the desert, Aila was also a key outpost for protecting Palestine, and Sinai as well, against an influx of marauding Bedouins from the Hedjaz.[48]

With the strategic importance of Aila in mind, the capitulation of the city to Muhammad in 630 (9 A.H.) assumes an importance far greater than has been heretofore attached to it.   In this year,

[47] See art. "Mecca" in *Enc. Isl.* 3 (above, note 22) 437: "They [the Meccans] obtained from them [states adjoining Arabia] safe conducts and capitulations, permitting free passage of their caravans.   This is what their chronicles call the 'guarantee of Caesar and Chosroes' . . . Commercial transactions were carried through at the frontier towns or in towns specially designated for this purpose.   In Palestine these were the ports of Aila and Ghazza and perhaps also Jerusalem."   Epiphanius, *Haer.*, in *Patrologia Graeca* (J.-P. Migne) 42.29–32, cites Aila as one of the *stomia* on the Red Sea to Roman territory.   For ships originating from the port of Aila, see Vasiliev (above, note 24) 295.

[48] Cf. Y. Aharoni, "The Negeb of Judah," *Israel Exploration Journal* 8 (1958) 35. The strategic importance of Aila (ʿAqaba) has not been overlooked in modern times. During World War I, the successful attack and occupation of the port by Bedouins in July 1917, was designed, according to the organizer of the attack, T. E. Lawrence, to remove the threat to the flanks of the British army along the Beersheba–Gaza line as well as the possibility of an attack on the Suez Canal by way of Sinai.   Once in the hands of the British, an attack was mounted from ʿAqaba on the Turkish army opposing the British on the borders of Palestine.   The Turks did not anticipate an attack from the desert since ʿAqaba was strongly protected by its high hills, which the Turks had fortified, but weakly manned for miles back.   If a landing had been attempted by sea, a small Turkish unit could have held up a much larger force in the passes (T. E. Lawrence, *Seven Pillars of Wisdom* [Oxford 1935] 167–68).   In 1925, the British government, alarmed by the activities of the marauding bands of Wahhabis in the northern districts of the Hedjaz and by the possibility that they might capture the port and become a source of disturbance on the southern borders of Palestine, annexed ʿAqaba to the mandated territory of Transjordan (H. St. J. B. Philby, *Arabia* [New York 1930] 313).   In 1948, following the establishment of the State of Israel, the Israelis were quick to build the city of Eilat on the west shore of the Gulf of ʿAqaba as a counterpoise to the Arab position on the eastern shore, thereby protecting the backdoor to the new state.   In the nineteenth century, there were at least two west–east attacks on Arabia *via* Sinai and ʿAqaba.   In 1811, Tusun Beg led 800 cavalry across Sinai through ʿAqaba to Yenbo for his assault on Medina.   The March took fourteen days (J. B. Glubb, *War in the Desert* [London 1960] 48).   Ibrahim Pasha, in the middle of the century, used a similar route when he attacked the Hedjaz.   For military activity around ʿAqaba during the twelfth century, see art. "Ayla" in *Encyclopaedia of Islam* (new ed.), ed. H. A. R. Gibb *et al.* 1 (Leiden 1960) 784.

Muhammad, having heard a report in Medina that a great Byzantine army composed of "Greeks, ʿÂmila, Lakhm, Judhâm, and others"[49] was advancing into Arabia, led an expedition against the oasis of Tabuk about 300 miles northwest of Medina. Hitti's account of this event is as follows:

> ... Muhammad led in person an expedition against the oasis of Tabûk in northern al-Hijâz, whence he opened negotiations with neighboring settlements which led to their submission. The people were granted security and the right to retain their property and profess their religion on condition that they paid an annual tribute. First among those settlements was Aylah (Aila) at the head of the Gulf of al-ʿAqabah, whose population was Christian. South of it on the gulf stood Maqna with a Jewish population mostly engaged in weaving and fishing. Another was Adhruh, with a population of about a hundred families, which lay between Petra and Maʿân. An hour's journey to the north of Adhruh, on the Roman road from Busra to the Red Sea, lay al-Jarbâ', whose people were also Christians.[50]

We possess two texts of the agreement entered into by Muhammad and the "chief" of Aila, Yuhanna ibn-Ru'bah: one preserved by Ibn-Ishaq, the other by Ibn-Saʿd. Caetani is not sure whether these texts are two different versions of the same document or two distinct documents.[51] It seems clear, to me at least, that the version preserved by Ibn-Saʿd is the letter Muhammad placed in the hands of his envoys and contains the terms of agreement, threats against the city if the terms were not met, and the assurance that the envoys had power to negotiate.[52] The

---

[49] al-Balâdhuri, *The Origins of the Islamic State (Kitâb Futûh al-Buldân)*, trans. P. K. Hitti, in *Columbia University Studies in History, Economics and Public Law* 68 (New York 1916) 92.

[50] Hitti, (above note 1) 410. Cf. his *History of the Arabs* (London and New York 1956) 119 where he speaks of the "Jewish tribes in the oases of Maqna, Adhruh and al-Jarbâ' to the south [of Aila?]." Becker's account (above, note 1) 326 lumps the four settlements together as "small Jewish and Christian settlements" and further on (339–340) he seems to imply—if he is not referring to the "year of declarations"— that these agreements created "friendly relations with at least a few tribes on the southern boundary of Palestine."

[51] Caetani, (above, note 1) 253.

[52] The letter ends with the statement: "Furnish supplies to the people of Maqna so that they may return to their country." It appears that the Jews of Maqna, who dwelt far to the south of Aila near the outlet of the Gulf of ʿAqaba, had migrated to Aila, probably seeking some protection within Roman territory against Muhammad's campaign against Jews following his success against the Meccans in 627. (Hitti

version of Ibn-Ishak contains the text of the final agreement—or an abstract of it since the amount of the tribute (*jizyah*) is not stated—worked out between Yuhanna and Muhammad at Tabuk. Be that as it may, it is clear that the agreement gave the people of the city of Aila, as well as their ships and caravans, the right of protection [against raids] by Muhammad and the tribes under his control. In return, Aila gave the Muslims

> access to water from the wells, when they desire it, nor are they [the people of Aila] to prohibit them from the road, which they desire to travel, whether by land or sea.[53]

> To this al-Baladhuri adds that Yuhanna ibn Ru'bah agreed

> to pay on every [non-Muslim] adult in his land one *dînâr* [*i.e.* one *solidus*] per annum, making it 300 *dînârs* in all.   The Prophet made it a condition on them that they provide with board and lodging whosoever of the Moslems may pass by them.[54]

The interpretation of this important agreement between Muhammad and Aila must be viewed from both sides. For Muhammad, the capitulation of Aila opened the back door to Palestine and Sinai for raids by his tribes.   By terms of the agreement, the narrow passes surrounding Aila lay open to undisturbed passage by his forces; the town itself could provide a rest area and, most importantly, an ample supply of water for a large force of men before it entered the arid wastelands of Palestine and Sinai. That Muhammad had in mind a raid against Palestine is hardly disputable, for in 632 (11 A.H.) he organized a raiding party under the leadership of Usama, the son of one of the commanders who had fallen at Mu'ta. When Muhammad died before the expedition departed, Abu-Bakr, his successor, had Usama execute the orders of the prophet.[55]   According to the tradition communicated by Ibn-Ishak, Usama was to make a *razzia* "on the borders of al-Balqâ' [*i.e.* the region east of the Dead Sea], and the Dârum of Palestine [Southern Palestine]."[56] De Goeje

[above, note 50] 117.   al-Baladhuri [above, note 49] 93–94 details the subsequent agreement between Muhammad and the people of Maqna.)   It also appears that later tradition confused the religion of the frontier town of Aila with that of Maqna; hence we find De Goeje (above, note 1) 9 speaking of the Jewish inhabitants of Aila and Maqna.

[53] Caetani (above, note 1) 254, note 1.
[54] al-Baladhuri (above, note 49) 92.
[55] De Goeje (above, note 1) 20.
[56] De Goeje (above, note 1) 17.

7 + T.P. 95

cites a number of Arabic sources that could support the view that Southern Palestine was the main, if not the sole, objective of this expedition.[57]   The failure or success of this raiding expedition—or expeditions, if there were two—is not known.[58]

In 633, following the wars of the *ridda* (apostasy) and the restoration of the *status quo* in the Arabian peninsula, Abu-Bakr renewed Muhammad's plan and sent an appeal to the tribes of Arabia, "calling them for a 'holy war' and arousing their desire in it and in the obtainable booty from the Greeks."[59]   Once more arrangements were made for the invasion of Syria and Palestine. The detachment under the command of ʿAmr ibn al-ʿAs was instructed by Abu-Bakr "to follow the way of Aila with Palestine for objective."[60]   All this would probably have been in vain had not Muhammad opened up the *stomion* into Palestine and Sinai by his agreement with the people of Aila.

On the Byzantine side, the inhabitants of Aila were on the horns of a dilemma.   Arabs though they were (but Christianized and settled), they could not have had any sympathy for, interest in, or perhaps even knowledge of, the new religion that Muhammad had fostered among the tribes of Arabia.   To them, in the absence of a military force and strong centralized authority in the region, Bedouins meant raids or the payment of tribute or, more likely, both.   And no matter how unbearable the tax burden may have been and whatever religious differences the community may have had with the officially recognized church, it is hardly conceivable that Aila or any border settlement would have welcomed Bedouins as their masters.[61]

At the time of Muhammad's expedition to Tabuk, the *Legio decima Fretensis*, or whatever was left of it, had long been dis-

---

[57] De Goeje (above, note 1) 18–19.   On Dârum, De Goeje states: "Par le Dâroum d'Ibn Ishâk il faut entendre, non pas la forteresse au Sud de Gaza, mais le district de ce nom dans le Sud-Est de la Palestine, dont parlent si souvent Eusèbe et Jérôme et que Yacout mentionne sous la forme syrienne de Dârroumâ."

[58] C. Brockelmann, *The History of the Islamic People*, trans. J. Carmichael and M. Perlmann (New York 1947) 45–46.

[59] al-Baladhuri (above, note 49) 165.   Note that the appeal was sent to the inhabitants of Mecca, Taif, Yemen, and all the Arabs in the Nejd and Hedjaz; no appeal was made to any of the tribes within Roman territory.

[60] al-Baladhuri (above, note 49) 166–67.

[61] The inhabitants certainly would never have agreed with the statement made by John the Lydian (*De magistratibus* 3.70) in Justinian's time that "a foreign invasion seemed less formidable to the tax payers than the arrival of the officials of the treasury."

banded or removed from Aila.   If it did not suffer the fate of other regular border troops during Justinian's reign,[62] it most assuredly did not survive the long Persian war between Heraclius and Chosroes (613–628).   At best, Aila might have had a self-organized police unit, somewhat like the one at Pharan,[63] but it could only have been effective against desultory raids of small bands.   As for fortifications that might have survived the withdrawal or disbandment of the Tenth Legion, they doubtless went the way of similar installations at Nessana and Eboda in the Negeb and Adhruh in Syria: they lost their effectiveness as forts and were converted to other uses.[64]   Hence, in the face of the overwhelming forces that Muhammad had gathered at Tabuk, and in the face of his threats of raids and destruction, Aila could only agree to negotiate with the prophet and attempt to get the best possible terms.   It is also quite likely that the city had on other occasions paid tribute to other tribes that made a show of force in its vicinity; payment and tribute in the form of gifts, money, or both, were the usual procedure when desert settlements wished to survive without the strong hand of governmental authority to support them.[65]

The negotiant for the city of Aila, Yuhanna ibn-Ru'bah (John son of Rubah), is described in Arabic sources as "king" or "chief" of Aila who, when he presented himself to the prophet, carried a cross of gold on his chest.[66]   This "king" or "chief" was unquestionably the bishop of Aila[67] who, in the absence of civil or military authorities, negotiated with Muhammad for the safety

[62] Procopius, *Anecdota* 24.12–14.

[63] Antoninus Placentius (above, note 21) 186.   See below, page 182.

[64] For Nessana and Eboda, see below, pages 185–86.   For Adhruh, Brünnow and v. Domaszewski 1 (above, note 40) 431–63.   Note (pages 431–34) how the area enclosed by the walls of the fort became filled with private dwellings.

[65] We may cite the example of the town of Pharan in the late fourth century making a private agreement with a sheikh named Ammanes for protection against harassment by the tribes under his control (Mayerson [above, note 25] 162).   See J. L. Burckhardt, *Travels in Syria and the Holy Land* (London 1822) 213, 343, 403 for examples of Syrian towns under Turkish rule paying tribute to Bedouin sheikhs for a measure of peace.

[66] Caetani (above, note 1) 253.

[67] See art. "Ayla" in *Enc. Isl.* 1 (note 48) 784.   Kawar (above, note 37) 85–86 calls John of Aila an Arab phylarch of *Palaestina Tertia* and states that he should be included in the list of known phylarchs.   In the absence of supporting documentation, it is difficult to understand why John son of Rubah should be considered an Arab phylarch.

of the city's inhabitants and for the preservation of its commercial interests.   It is well known that, from the fourth century on, the bishop was not only a spiritual leader but also the protector of his flock against gouging officials and the defender of the community against desert raiders and barbarian invaders.[68]   It was, in fact, the church that maintained law and order in regions forgotten or forsaken by the imperial government[69] and, more important, provided the *raison d'être* for the continuation of settled life in the wilderness.   Whatever sense of responsibility these abandoned communities felt for the central government or for their neighboring settlements is, of course, not known; but we can speculate that, like most isolated communities, they fended for themselves without the knowledge of, or regard for, the consequences that might arise as a result of an *ex parte* decision, or whether their actions were in agreement with official policy.[70]   We may speculate further that the people of Aila considered that their bishop had concluded an exceptionally reasonable agreement with the Muslims, and that by the payment of only 300 *solidi* (about four pounds of gold) they were able to escape destruction and at the same time have Muhammad's guarantee of protection.

Aila was neutralized in 630, and the way to Southern Palestine was open; yet Muhammad did not mount an offensive against Roman territory. Perhaps the defeat of his forces at Mu'ta in the previous year convinced him that he was not strong enough for the task.   In 630/1 (A.H. 9), the "year of delegations," tribes from

---

[68] C. H. Coster, "Christianity and the Invasions: Synesius of Cyrene," *Classical Journal* 55 (1960) 291; R. MacMullen, *Soldier and Civilian in the Later Roman Empire* (Cambridge 1963) 139–40.

[69] Cf. Procopius, *Anecdota* 24.12–14: "[Justinian] . . . took away from them [the *limitanei*] the very name of regular troops.   Thereafter . . . the soldiers found themselves obliged to look to the hands of those accustomed to works of piety." (Loeb trans.)   The Nessana documents, although not specifying in all instances the clerical titles of the people involved (cf. *PColt* 75 in Kraemer [above, note 19] 212–14), illustrate how church officers became responsible officials of the town after the border militia unit had been disbanded toward the end of the sixth century.   At Aila, conditions must have been quite the same: the bishop became the political leader of the community and was aided by a group of elders.

[70] Cf. H. A. R. Gibb, "Arab-Byzantine Relations under the Umayyad Caliphate," *Dumbarton Oaks Papers* No. 12 (Cambridge 1958) 222: "The complex of [medieval] society was made up of a mosaic of small communities that lived their own lives, carried on their own affairs and fended for themselves, often in isolation from the other communities, and almost always without much notice being taken of what they were doing or whether it was in agreement with official policy."

the Arabian peninsula offered their allegiance to the prophet and swelled the ranks of his army; still no move was made against the Byzantines.[71]   Sometime in 632 (A.H. 10), Muhammad seemed ready to undertake an expedition against Syria and/or Palestine (under the command of Usama); but the prophet's death and the consequent upheaval caused by the wars of the *ridda* delayed any serious consideration of an attack against the Byzantines.   After Abu-Bakr had unified the peninsular Arabs with the sword of Khalid ibn al-Walid, the time was ripe for a "holy war" and *razzias* against the "Greeks"; hence Abu-Bakr's appeal to the Arabian tribes.   It should be kept in mind, however, that, until the autumn of 633, the sources record only *one* contact between Muslims and Byzantines—possibly two if Usama's expedition reached its objective—and that was at Mu'ta where the Muslims were soundly defeated.   Therefore, it is understandable that Muhammad and Abu-Bakr may have been somewhat hesitant and reluctant to launch a large-scale offensive into Roman territory; the Muslims apparently were not as sure as historians are of the weaknesses of the empire.   It may also explain why the first raids into Southern Palestine did not proceed along well-known roads to the district of Gaza but went into Sinai and then northward into Palestine.

IV. Sinai and the Negeb

It is at this point that the Byzantine and Arab sources on the first Muslim attacks on Southern Palestine converge.   The Saracens of whom Theophanes speaks were, in my opinion, Bedouin tribes of Southern Palestine and Sinai who, angered at the refusal of the imperial government to pay them, turned to their Muslim compatriots and "showed them the way to the district of Gaza, the entrance of the desert extending towards Sinai."   The success of the first raids must be attributed not only to Muhammad's foresight in opening the back door to Palestine, *i.e.* Aila, but also to the fact that Arab tribes had made no real

---

[71] Hitti (above, note 50) 119.   It should also be noted that the Muslims, before and after Muhammad's death, were far more aggressive against Arab tribes in the Arabian peninsula than against those within Roman territory.   Cf. al-Baladhuri (above, note 49) 143–62.

show of strength in this region for over two hundred years and hence defensive installations, many of which in the first instance had never been designed to meet massive attacks, had been allowed to deteriorate.   However, all had not been peaceful prior to 633, for it is possible to show a pattern of raids and incursions in Sinai and Palestine extending back to the fourth century.[72] Toward the end of this century, Byzantine sources record a number of Bedouin raids within the borders of the Roman Empire, but the most successful was one undertaken by the widow of a sheikh, Mavia or Mauvia, who succeeded in defeating the army sent against her by Valens (*ca.* 376).   Peace was established when the Romans acceded to her request to ordain as bishop a Saracen named Moses, who lived as an eremite "on the borders of Egypt and Palestine, and who was preeminent for his faith, piety, and miracles."   As a result, a large number of conversions were said to have been made, including the whole tribe of Sheikh Zokomos; and these Christianized Arabs fought against the Goths, Persians and other Saracens.[73]

This is the last that we hear of anything that might resemble a large-scale movement of Bedouins in Sinai or Southern Palestine before 633.   The likelihood is that considerable numbers of them were siphoned off to serve as auxiliaries in, or allies of, the Roman army, or where absorbed by the border settlements of Palestine and Egypt either as members of militia units (*limitanei*) or as inhabitants of the towns of the Negeb.[74]   But Bedouin raids and harassment continued to be a part of life, not only for the communities in the desert but throughout Palestine, Syria, and

[72] For destruction caused by invading Arab tribes in the second century see A. Negev, "Nabataean Inscriptions from ʿAvdat (Oboda)," *Israel Exploration Journal* 13 (1963) 123–24.

[73] For Mavia, see Socrates, *HE* 4.36; Sozomenus, *HE* 6.38; Theodoretus, *HE* 4.23; Rufinus, *HE* 2.6; Cassiodorus, *Hist. trip.* 9; Theopanes (above, note 4) 1.65–66. The story of Mavia is a favorite among church historians and later chroniclers mainly, of course, because of her conversion to Christianity.   For Zokomos, see Socrates, *HE* 4.36.

[74] Mavia sent an army to help repel the attack of the Goths on Constantinople (Theophanes [above, note 4] 1.65), while Zokomos' tribe was used against the Persians (Sozomenus, *HE* 6.38).   How many of these Bedouins were incorporated into the military units to guard the eastern borders is unknown, but Sozomenus (*ibid.*) tells us that Zokomos' men were also used against the Saracens.   The *Notitia dignitatum* (above, note 43) 59, 68 lists one Saracen unit on the Egyptian border and two in Phoenicia.   Note also the large number of Arabic names in the onomasticon of the Nessana papyri (Kraemer [above, note 19] 333–41, 352–55).

Phoenicia as well.[75] As a defense against these raids, the imperial government strung a line of defensive installations across the northern Negeb: Menois, Birsama, Birosaba, and Moleatha (Malaatha). This line was flanked on either side by military detachments protecting the main lines of communications: *i.e.* the *via maris* to the west and the *via nova Traiana* to the east of the Wadi ʿAraba.[76] Between the east and west legs of this *pi*-shaped figure was a kind of no-man's land that was left largely to the Bedouins and the towns that managed to maintain themselves without the help of military forces.

This was the situation at the beginning of the fifth century, as we learn from the *Notitia dignitatum*; but as urbanization spread throughout the Negeb—unquestionably spurred by the revival of old trade routes as the wars between Byzantium and Persia created dislocations along the Mesopotamian routes—there was a corresponding increase in imperial interest and military activity south of the earlier *limes*. At least two, possibly three, defensive installations were added at strategic points south of the existing line. At Nessana, the crossroads of the way from Aila to Rhinocoroura and the north-south road from the Negeb into Sinai and Egypt, a fort was built and a camel corps was organized shortly after the first quarter of the fifth century.[77] At Eboda, on the

[75] For the years 373–410, see sources cited by Vasiliev (above, note 38) 307–9 and K. Heussi, "Untersuchungen zu Nilus dem Asketen," *Texte und Untersuchungen zur Geschichte der altchristlichen Literatur* 42(2) (Leipzig 1917) 147. For the fifth and sixth centuries, Vasiliev (*ibid.*) 309–15. See also Priscus Panites in *Fragmenta historicorum Graecorum* 4, ed. K. Müller (Paris 1885) 76; Evagrius Scholasticus in *Patrologia Graeca* (J.-P. Migne) 86(2).2846; Choricius Gazeus, *Opera*, ed. R. Foerster and E. Richtsteig (Leipzig 1929) 75. If the church historians give us a fairly accurate picture of conditions in the diocese of the East, Arab raiders could roam and plunder rather freely throughout the countryside, while the cities were safe from their depradations. In all the source material prior to the reign of Heraclius, we have only one mention made of a city, Arbela, in Persian territory, that was taken and looted by Bedouins (Vasiliev [*ibid.*] 309). Such phrases as "all the regions of the east at that time were ravaged by the Saracens" and "a sudden attack of the barbarians runs through the limits of Egypt, Palestine, Phoenicia, and Syria" must be taken with a grain of salt.

[76] Abel (above, note 42) 180–84, map 10; *Notitia dignitatum* (above, note 43) 59, 73–74. With the exception of Malaatha (Moleotha), outposts in the Negeb were manned by cavalry units which could act swiftly against raiding Bedouins. The fairly level loessial terrain on the coastal plain and around the Beersheba plateau was ideal for the use of horses. Note also that while a cohort was stationed at Malaatha, it was backed up by a cavalry unit at Cherumula (Kh. Khermel) to the northeast. To the east of Malaatha and Chermula, the terrain becomes very rough until the steep scarps of the Dead Sea watershed are reached.

[77] Kraemer (above, note 19) 16.

main road from Aila to Gaza at the point not far from where the
road emerges from the steep scarps of the Ramon cirque onto the
hill region of the Central Negeb, a fort was constructed at the beginning of the sixth century.[78]   Similarly at Mampsis, if Woolley
and Lawrence are correct in their description of the site as a
fortified town, the place was chosen as a defensive point that
commanded the junction of roads leading across the northern
Negeb and northwards to Hebron and Jerusalem at the point
where, as at Eboda, the road emerged from the Dead Sea–Wadi
ʿAraba region.[79]   Like most other Byzantine sites in the Negeb,
Nessana, Eboda, and Mampsis had been occupied in earlier
periods, particularly during the time of the Nabataean monarchy,
undoubtedly for the same strategic reasons.

The Sinai peninsula, however, lying as it did to the south of the
commercial routes from Syria and the Hedjaz to the Mediterranean, remained unchanged.   Apart from continued interest
of eremites and pilgrims in sacred sites, particularly in the region
around Mount Sinai, there is no evidence of an increase in
urbanization on a scale comparable with that of the Negeb.   The
sole community worthy of the name was Pharan, one day's
journey from Mount Sinai. For the rest, there were occasional
hamlets in the wilderness, as for example the small aggregation of
houses in and near the Wadi Qudeirat, that managed to survive
without military assistance or defensive installations.[79a]   As the
Roman *oecûmenê* pressed further south in the Negeb during the
fifth and sixth centuries, the home of the Bedouins was more and
more restricted to the unsettled wilderness of the Sinai peninsula.

During two centuries before the occupation of Palestine by the
Persians, the sources indicate that the Bedouins of Southern
Palestine and Sinai posed no serious threat to the security of the
region.   From descriptions of their behavior, they acted more like
petty thieves than enemies of the state, at times themselves needing
protection against attacks by other Bedouin tribes.   We hear

[78] M. Avi-Yonah and A. Negev, "A City of the Negeb: Excavations in Nabataean,
Roman and Byzantine Eboda," *Illustrated London News* (Nov. 26, 1960) 944; A.
Negev, "Avdat: A Caravan Halt in the Negev," *Archaeology* 14 (1961) 125–26;
personal conversations with A. Negev.   See also Mayerson (above, note 25) 166–67.

[79] L. Woolley and T. E. Lawrence, *The Wilderness of Zin* (London and New York
1936) 137–39; Abel (above, note 42) 177; Y. Aharoni, "Tamar and the Roads to
Elath," *Israel Exploration Journal* 13 (1963) 36–38.

[79a] Mayerson (above, note 25) 165.

nothing of Bedouin activities during the fifth century, though we can assume that their behavior was no different from what it was in the succeeding century. During Justinian's reign, Choricius of Gaza eulogizes the governor of Palestine, Stephen, for his forthright action in checking the incursions from Egypt of some Saracens who disturbed the peace and committed injustices against the border cities: "For gathering a sufficient force, you chastised the evil of these people who were deprived in every way of your forgiveness."[80] However, the Bedouins themselves were in need of help when they were attacked by tribes unfriendly to them, as Choricius tells us in his eulogy of Summus:

> The enemy had fallen on those in Egypt who spend their lives in tents, as you know, and when you learned of this, you were enraged and you advanced full of anger; many of those who faced you became your captives and many, formerly prisoners of their compatriots [homophylôn], ceased through your efforts to merit the name of slaves.[81]

These disturbances apparently caused no alarm in Gaza, the richest city in the region, since the city wall had been allowed to deteriorate to such an extent that, according to Choricius, it was a wall in name only, for most of it lay open to those approaching or leaving the city. It was Pheme, the civil head of Gaza, who "declared war even though the enemy was at peace" and saw to it that the inhabitants rebuilt the wall and provided it with a defensive trench.[82]

On the peninsula itself, the monks of Mount Sinai, hearing of Justinian's interest in building monasteries and churches, complained to him that the Ishmaelite Arabs (Bedouins) were plundering their food stores, creating general havoc, entering their cells, and pillaging them of whatever they contained, and, breaking into churches, gulping down the Eucharist. Justinian ordered a fortified monastery to be built for their protection, the now famous monastery of St. Catherine; and in a fortified community nearby, he settled a number of slaves, together with their

---

[80] Choricius, (above, note 75), *Laud. Arat. et Steph.* 57–58, dated 535–536. Note that the method of meeting such an attack was to gather forces, presumably from among the *limitanei* closest to the source of the disturbance, just as Theodorus the Vicarius met the threat at Mu'ta (above, pages 157, 165).

[81] Choricius, (above, note 75), *Laud. Summi* 75, written before 535–540.

[82] Choricius, (above, note 75), *Laud. Marc.* 32, dated 535–548: . . . πολέμους ἐκήρυττε πολεμίων ἡσυχαζόντων.

7*

wives and children, whose duty it was to protect the monastery. Provisions for these and the monks of the monastery were to be supplied by Egypt.[83]

The plea of the monks for protection against the Bedouins—even if we were to discount nothing in their plea as overstatement—contains a description of malfeasances and misdemeanors rather than felonies and homicides. Had there been a massacre on a scale even smaller than the one at the end of the fourth century,[84] the martyrdom of these solitaries would certainly have been a major issue in their indictment of the actions of the Bedouins.[85]

At Pharan, the civil center of Sinai and seat of the bishop, conditions were about the same. Antoninus Placentius, who visited Mount Sinai and Pharan shortly after Justinian's death, tells us that Pharan—he makes no statement concerning the defensive arrangement at Mount Sinai beyond the fact that the monastery was surrounded by walls—was protected by a wall and had a police unit of 80 publicly domiciled men (condomae) who, along with their families, received a food and clothing allowance from Egypt. Each man had a Saracen mare, also fed at public expense, with which he patrolled the desert, protecting the monasteries and hermits against Saracen treachery. But in spite of the police, the Bedouins, says Antoninus,

> were unafraid for when the people go out of the city, they bolt their doors and take their keys with them. And those who remain within, do likewise [i.e. lock their doors] because of Saracen

[83] The most reliable account of the circumstances surrounding the building of the monastery is found in Eutychius' Annales (Patrologia Graeca [J.-P. Migne] 140.1071–72). Eutychius also mentions that Justinian built monasteries at Clysma (Suez) and at Raithou, but that the best fortified was the one at Mount Sinai. Procopius, Aed. 5.8, mentions the same incident; but his account differs substantially from that of Eutychius and, in my opinion, is filled with discrepancies which deserve to be treated more fully. Note, however, that Procopius says that the monks enjoyed "without fear the solitude which is very precious to them" and that "the emperor built a very strong fortress and established there a considerable garrison of troops in order that the barbarian Saracens might not be able from that region, which, as I have said, is uninhabited, to make inroads without complete secrecy into the lands of Palestine proper." (Loeb trans.) Both statements have no foundation in fact.
[84] See Mayerson (above, note 25) 161–62.
[85] A similar case was laid before Emperor Anastasius (491–518) by St. Sabas on behalf of his lavra on the Kedron in the Judaean desert. He asked the emperor for a fort to be built near his monasteries for protection against Saracen raids. The emperor acceded to the demand but, apparently, the imperial order was never carried out (see Vasiliev [above, note 38] 311).

treachery, since when they go out they have nowhere to go save sky and sand.[86]

Antoninus also calls our attention to two *castella* in the wilderness: at Surandala,

> there is a small fort . . . having nothing within it except a church and its priest and two hospices for travelers . . . and at a place where the sons of Israel crossed the [Red] Sea and pitched their camp, there too is a fort within which is a hospice.[87]

Whether these two fortlets at one time housed troops, police units, or were simply fortified monasteries, we do not know; but what is clear is that, by Antoninus' time, small communities deep in the wilderness of Sinai and far removed from any source of military assistance were able to cope with whatever hostile forces may have been present in the region.

To the north, in the Negeb, the archaeological remains of those sites that have escaped the depredations of stone plunderers tell virtually the same story: the towns did not take any extraordinary precautions to protect themselves against an ordered assault; at most, they attempted to protect themselves against small bands of raiders. The towns of Sobata (Sbeita, Shivta), Elusa (Khalasa, Halutsa), Nessana (Auja, Nitsana), Saadi, and Raheiba had nothing that resembled a city wall; their protection seems to have been the continuous lines of houses and garden walls.[88] The town of Sobata had nine entrances, only three of

---

[86] Antoninus, (above, note 21) 184 for Mount Sinai: "monasterium circumdatum muris munitis"; 186 for Pharan: "In ipso loco civitas munita muris de lateribus . . . Octingentas condomas militantes in publico cum uxoribus suis, annonas et vestes de publico accipientes de Aegypto . . . praeter singulis diebus habentes singulas equas Saracenas, qui capitum paleas et hordeum, de publico accipient, discurrentes cum ipsis per heremum pro custodia monasteriorum et heremitarum propter insidias Saracenorum, ante quorum timorem non exagitantur Saraceni. Nam exeuntes de ipsa civitate a foris illi serant et claves tollent secum. Et illi, qui sunt ab intus, similiter faciunt propter insidias Saracenorum, quia nec habent, ubi exeant foris praeter caelum et harenam." Cf. A. Musil, *Palmyrena* (*American Geographical Society Explorations and Studies* No. 4 New York 1928) 36 for a modern analogy: "The settlement was full of Bedouins who entered the houses at will as if they were masters there . . . The five gendarmes stationed in the settlement for its protection were openly laughed at by them."

[87] Antoninus (above, note 21), 187: "in quo loco est castellum modicum qui vocatur Surandala, nihil habet intus praeter ecclesiam cum presbytero suo et duo xenodochia propter transeuntes . . . et illic similiter castellum modicum, infra se xenodochium."

[88] Woolley and Lawrence (above, note 79) 125, 91, 127, 129; H. D. Colt *et alii*, *Excavations at Nessana: Excavation Report* 1 (London 1962) 5.

which were gateways; the remainder were simply the ends of
streets that led into the open country.[89]   At Eboda ('Abda,
Avdat), Mampsis (Kurnub), and Mishrafa, a low wall surrounded
the settlement, all around or only in part as in the case of Eboda.[90]
Woolley and Lawrence, in describing the best of these town walls
at Kurnub, call it

> a poor affair, an obstacle rather than real wall of defense intended
> rather to resist mounted raiders than an ordered assault.[91]

All told, there is a remarkable concinnity between these unwalled
or low-walled settlements and the inability of Bedouins, as
Procopius and Ammianus Marcellinus tell us, to storm a wall or
even to surmount a low barrier.[92]

In the open country there are numerous farmsteads throughout
the Central Negeb and its extension into northern Sinai.[93]   The
farmhouses associated with the remains of terrace walls and other
agricultural installations are generally two, three, or four room
constructions with no suggestion, even where these houses are
situated in remote and isolated wadis, that they were fortified in
any way so as to fend off any attackers.[94]   In the terraced wadis
closer to the town, one often finds small towers, originally two
stories high and not unlike those that still can be seen throughout
the Near East, sufficient to house the farmer as he guarded his
crops from thieves before and after the harvest and to shelter him
during the critical period of winter rains and floods.   By way of
contrast, we find nothing in the Negeb that resembles the fortified
farmhouse, the "gusr," of Tripolitania; in comparison, the Negeb
was open country, free from the danger of mass attack.[95]

[89] Colt (above, note 88) 5.

[90] Woolley and Lawrence (above, note 79) 139, 108, 110.

[91] Woolley and Lawrence (above, note 79) 139.

[92] Procopius, *Hist.* 2.19.12, 2.9.3–4; Ammianus Marcellinus 25.6.8; for the greater
adaptability of Saracens for raiding than for pitched battles, Ammianus Marcellinus
14.4.1–3; 23.3.8; 31.16.5.   Cf. Woolley and Lawrence (above, note 79) 91: "...a
blank dry-stone wall can stop a Beduin raid..."

[93] See P. Mayerson, "The Ancient Agricultural Regime of Nessana and the
Central Negeb," in Colt (above, note 88) 213–15.

[94] Personal observation.   See also Woolley and Lawrence (above, note 79) 50.
For the description of farmhouses of the Israelite period in two isolated areas of the
Negeb, see Y. Aharoni *et alii*, "The Ancient Desert Agriculture of the Negev," *Israel
Exploration Journal* 10 (1960) 24–36; 8 (1958) 231–68.

[95] For Tripolitania, see e.g. J. B. Ward-Perkins, "Gasr es-Suk el-Oti," *Archaeology*
3 (1950) 25–30; further references in MacMullen (above, note 68) 19–22.   J. Maspéro,

In a sense the forts at Nessana and Eboda cited above are an anomaly in that they are the only surviving remains of military fortifications originally designed to withstand a major assault. However, these were undoubtedly planned at Constantinople and constructed on order of the imperial government.[96]   The town defenses, on the other hand, must have been erected by their inhabitants, who knew the habits and limitations of the local Bedouins.   Significantly, the forts at Nessana and Eboda saw little or no military use.   At Nessana, the archaeological finds contained no recognizable military weapons but rather spindle whorls, fragments of mirrors, quantities of glass, and other objects of household use.[97]   Similarly, at Eboda there was no evidence that the fort had ever been put to the use for which it had been originally designed.[98]

As for the Bedouins themselves, we are fortunate to have an eyewitness account of what they were like in the late sixth century, not long before the first Muslim attacks on Sinai and Southern Palestine.   Antoninus Placentius traveled to Mount Sinai *via* the Negeb and the Tih desert.   Setting out from Gaza, Antoninus and his companions went to Elusa, which is described as being "at the head of the desert that leads to Sinai."[99]   Upon hearing the bishop of Elusa relate the tale of an unfortunate girl who had become an ascetic in the desert east of the Wadi ᶜAraba, the pilgrims decided to take a side trip to Segor (Zoara) near the Dead Sea where they found a convent of young girls.   On returning to Elusa, Antoninus and his companions set out for Mount Sinai.   Twenty miles from

Organization militaire de l'Egypte byzantine in *Bibliothèque de l'École des Hautes Études, Sciences historiques et philologiques* fasc. 201 (Paris 1912) 13, makes this comment on Egypt which also holds good for Southern Palestine and Sinai: "Mais qu'étaient ces accidents médiocres et isolés, ces razzias de barbares, dirigées sans plan ni idée de conquête, exécutées par des poignées d'hommes, en comparaison de ce qui se passait sur les autres frontières de l'empire, en Mésopotamie, en Mésie, en Italie, en Afrique? En fait, aucun danger apparent ne menaçait, au VIᵉ siècle, la tranquillité de la vallée du Nil."

[96] Colt (above, note 88) 6.   Cf. Woolley and Lawrence (above, note 79) 49: "The forts there are of Justinian's plan and most probably his work, but only a bureaucratic pedant could have imposed on a desert such incongruous defences, which seem intended rather to complete a theory than to meet a local need."

[97] Colt (above, note 88) 17.

[98] Personal conversations with the excavator, A. Negev.   Mr. Negev believes that the fort with its many gateways was, in the first instance, poorly designed as a defensive installation.

[99] See above, note 25.

Elusa they came to a fort, which has been identified as the fort at
Nessana, from which point they entered the "inner desert." A
short distance south of Nessana, Antoninus observed a salt plain
(*sebkha*) and a few bizarre Aethiopians (Negroes?) of the kind that
he had seen in Jerusalem.[100]

Up to this point, the narrative does not contain a single reference
to Saracens or to any precaution, military or civil, to be taken
against them. By Antoninus' time, the fort at Nessana had lost its
military function and had been converted into a hospice
(*xenodochium*) and a refuge for hermits.[101] It is only when the
travelers are well into the Tih desert that they have their first
experience with Bedouins. Undoubtedly the pilgrims had hired a
guide and an interpreter at Gaza, Elusa, or possibly at Nessana,
the last important station on the central route to Sinai.[102] The
narrative that follows contains a description of the almost timeless
conditions of Bedouin life in the Tih desert: poverty and beggary
on the one hand, trading and banditry on the other. We are even
provided with a demographic statistic—not to be taken any more
seriously than any statistic tendered by a travel guide—that there
were 12,600 Bedouins in the Tih desert. It should be noted,
however, that the Bedouins knew of sources of water in this
supposedly waterless desert,[103] that they were pagans, that for
religious reasons trading and raiding were prohibited, and that at
the end of their festival, the moratorium on raiding came to an
end and the pilgrims were advised to take a safer route back to
Jerusalem:

> We went on foot through the desert for five or six days. Camels
> carried our water of which each of us received a pint in the
> morning and a pint at night. When the water in the skins
> turned bitter, we put sand in to sweeten it. Moreover, families
> of Saracens, or rather their women, came from the desert and sat
> by the wayside, half-clothed, crying and begging for food from
> travelers. Their husbands appeared and brought skins of cold
> water from the inner desert and offered [water to us] and received

[100] Mayerson (above, note 25) 170–71.

[101] Mayerson (above, note 25) 170.

[102] See *PColt* 72 and 73 in Kraemer (above, note 19) 205–8, orders from the Arab
governor at Gaza to a certain George of Nessana to provide guides for travelers to
Mount Sinai.

[103] For the technique of gathering water in the absence of wells and springs, see
Mayerson (above, note 93) 246–49.

bread in return. They also brought bunches of roots, the sweet smell of which was beyond all perfumes. Nothing was sold because they were celebrating their holy days and they considered it anathema [to sell anything]. Now the people who go through this very great desert number 12,600.[104]

And some days later, in the region of Mount Sinai, the pilgrims were privileged to witness the Bedouin ritual connected with their worship of the moon:

On a part of this mountain [Sinai or Choreb] the Saracens have placed their idol, marble and white as snow. There also lives their priest who is dressed in a dalmatic and a linen pallium. When the time of the festival is at hand, at the rising of the moon, the marble begins to change color ⟨before the moon rises⟩ on the day of their festival. Presently, the moon appeared, and when they began to pray, the marble turned black as pitch. At the end of their festival, it returned to its original color. We were all quite amazed at the event... And because the Saracen holidays were now drawing to a close, the announcement was made [at Mount Sinai] not to remain in or to return through the desert by which we had come; some, therefore, returned to the Holy City by way of Egypt, others by way of Arabia [*i.e. via* Aila].[105]

---

[104] Antoninus (above, note 21) 183: Ambulantibus nobis per heremum dies V vel VI cameli nobis aquam portantes, sextarium mane et sextarium sero per hominem accipiebamus. Amarescente aqua illa in utres in felle mittebamus in ea harenam et indulcabatur. Familia autem Saracenorum vel uxores eorum venientes de heremo, ad viam sedentes in lamentatione, et sareca missa ante se petiebant panem a transeuntibus et veniebant viri ipsarum, adducebant utres cum aqua frigida de interiore parte heremi et dabant, et accipiebant sibi panes et adducebant resticulas cum radices, quorum odor suavitatis super omnia aromata, nihil licentes; quia anathema habebant et dies festos suos celebrabant. Populus autem, qui per ipsum maiorem heremum ingrediebatur, numerus duodecim milia sexcenti."

[105] Antoninus (above, note 21) 184–85: "Et in ipso monte in parte montis habent idolum suum positum Saraceni marmoreum, candidum tam quam nix. In quo etiam permanet sacerdos ipsorum indutus dalmatica et pallium lineum. Quando etiam venit tempus festivitatis ipsorum recurrente luna, ⟨antequam egrediatur luna,⟩ ad diem festum ipsorum incipit colorem mutare marmor illa; mox luna introierit, quando coeperint adorare, fit nigra marmor illa tamquam pice. Completo tempore festivitatis revertitur in pristinum colorem, unde omnino mirati sumus... Et quia iam se complebant dies festi Saracenorum, praeco exivit: ut, quia non subsisteret per heremo reverti, per quo ingressi sumus, alii per Aegyptum, alii per Arabiam reverterentur in sanctam civitatem." Although the text is muddled at some points— I have bracketed one clause which seems repetitive and which is omitted in some manuscripts—the meaning is clear enough. For routes from Sinai to Palestine, see above, pages 162–63.

To this we may add the evidence of the Nessana papyri. *PColt* 89, a sixth-seventh century document, lists the purchases and expenditures made by a small company of traders on its way to and from Mount Sinai. Apparently traveling by the same route taken by Antoninus and his companions, the traders paid a Bedouin the substantial sum of three *solidi* to guide them and, presumably, to provide safe passage through the Tih desert to the Holy Mountain. The absence of any mention of a similar fee in the rest of the account makes it appear likely that on their return to Palestine they took one of the western roads. Since they were not traveling under safe conduct, Bedouins stole one of their camels for the return of which the traders had to pay a sum of money. The document also contains the name of the tribe responsible for the theft, the bani al-Udayyid, perhaps the same tribe that led the Muslims "to the district of Gaza, the entrance to the desert extending to Sinai."[106]

If, then, the Bedouins of Southern Palestine were not a serious threat to the security of the empire, it is not at all remarkable, nor reprehensible as Procopius would have it, that Justinian decided to abandon the system of border fortifications and *limitanei*.[107] The move (*ca*. 545) undoubtedly accompanied the changeover in defensive arrangements along the eastern frontiers, particularly along the Syro-Mesopotamian border where the Persians were successfully employing Lakhmid Arabs to raid Roman territory. As a counterpoise to Alamoundaras (Mundhir), the client-king of the Persians, Justinian placed the Ghassanid Arethas "who ruled over the Saracens of Arabia as phylarch . . . in command of as many tribes as possible," and bestowed on him the title of king and patrician.[108] Extending this defensive system to the southern border between Syria and the Arabian peninsula, Justinian appointed another Ghassanid, Abochorabus (Abu-Karib), as phylarch, after having received the Palm Groves (Tabuk?) as a

---

[106] Kraemer (above, note 19) 251–60; Mayerson (above, note 25) 165–66. If the editor of *PColt* 89 is correct in thinking that Emazen may be a clipped form of Syko-mazen, then it is virtually certain that the traders took one of the western roads back to Palestine.

[107] Procopius, *Anecdota* 24.12–14. J. B. Bury, *History of the Later Roman Empire* 2 (London 1923) 358, note 4, places the move after 545 and states that it applied only to the East.

[108] Procopius, *Hist.* 1.17.47–48; Bury (above, note 107) 91.

gift, and the Kindite Kais (Qays), who had given up his patrimony (in the Nejd?) in order to become a phylarch.[109]

The system of employing Arabs to fight Arabs was for Justinian a practical solution to the problem of combating an elusive and slippery foe both within and beyond the borders of the empire. The phylarchate also lent itself to considerable economies, for it was far cheaper to pay relatively small sums of money, in kind or in gifts, to Arab sheikhs to guard or guarantee peace on the borders than to support a static system of forts and a border militia that lacked the mobility of the Bedouins and that over the years had lost its effectiveness as a fighting force.

Justinian's move to disband the border militia is dated to the middle of the sixth century; but we learn from the Nessana documents that the military organization persisted in some form until the end of the century, although it is difficult to say to what degree the men who still carried the name of "most loyal soldier" functioned as a military unit. In any event, the editor of the papyri believes that by 600 A.D. imperial troops were no longer at Nessana.[110]   In my opinion, however, the *formal* abandonment of the military organization should be dated somewhat earlier, since by Antoninus' time (*ca.* 570) the fort had already been converted into a hospice for travelers and a refuge for local hermits; and the two *castella* in Sinai, if not merely fortified churches, had also lost their military complement.[111]

In place of the border militia some form of the phylarchate seems to have been adopted for the unsettled areas of Southern Palestine and Sinai. *PColt* 160, a fragment of an undated letter, has a tantalizing reference to the "new (or newly appointed)

[109] Bury (above, note 107) 325–26. See also Kawar (above, note 37) 79–87 for a comprehensive view of the phylarchate under Justinian. Kawar argues (85–87) that Qays was the phylarch over all *Palestina Tertia,* but it can hardly be likely that he controlled any part of Southern Palestine or Sinai. Kawar rightly acribes to Arethas the job of dealing with the raids of the Lakhmids against Roman territory, and to Abu-Karib the assignment of protecting the southern segment of the Roman frontier with Arabia against raids from the peninsula. However, I would limit the sphere of action of these phylarchs to the regions of the empire outside the *oecûmenê,* i.e. beyond the settled areas.   If I am correct in this view, it is less than accurate to say, as Becker (above, note 1) 339 and others claim, that the Arabs controlled the termini of east–west trade or of the spice routes, although they unquestionably exercised a degree of control over caravans as they passed through their sphere of influence.

[110] Kraemer (above, note 19) 24.

[111] See above, page 186; Mayerson (above, note 25) 169–70.

phylarch," to various foodstuffs, and to the requisition of straw and barley,[112] all of which is reminiscent of the *condomae* stationed at Pharan, who received from Egypt an allowance of food (*annonas*) for their families and straw and barley (*paleas et hordeum*) for their horses.[113]   Such agreements between the government and local sheikhs, of course, were not guarantees of absolute safety for individual travelers through the desert, but rather were designed for the protection of communities against raids by tribes under the control of the phylarch.[114]

However scanty the evidence may be for the defensive realignments in Southern Palestine following the abandonment of the limitanean system, the results in the years shortly after the event are more evident.   In Nessana, a small town on the border of the Tih desert, there is a burst of building activity between the years 601 and 605, which must attest not only to the prosperity but also to a high degree of stability and security in the region.   The epigraphical evidence shows that at least three buildings went up in that time in addition to the remodeling of existing ecclesiastical structures.[115]   The excavator of the site rightly states:

> There can be no doubt that the churches and their appendages were the focal point of this activity but the fact that we have no inscriptional evidence from any secular building should not divert us from considering the possibility of a similar constructional boom taking place in the lower town.[116]

We can reasonably assume that the other towns in the Negeb were equally affluent and confident in the security of the region.

All this changed within a decade.   The waves of Persian conquest under Chosroes II that engulfed Antioch in 611, Jerusalem in 614 and Gaza and Egypt in 618/619, had a devastating effect on the diocese of the Orient.   And while it may be idle to speculate upon the psychological consequences of the Persian successes, there

[112] Kraemer (above, note 19) 323.   Kraemer's comments on the meaning of the word phylarch should be disregarded.

[113] See above, note 86.

[114] For the violation of an agreement between a sheikh and the community of Pharan in the late fourth century, see Mayerson (above, note 25) 162–63.   See also Musil (above, note 86) 182, who records the personal experience of having been attacked and robbed of his possessions by raiding Bedouins under the control of a sheikh to whom the Turkish government paid a monthly salary for suppressing robberies.

[115] For a summary of the evidence, see Kraemer (above, note 19) 28–29.

[116] Colt (above, note 88) 21.

can be no doubt that the pillaging of the most holy city of Jerusalem, the desecration of its sanctuaries, and the massacre of
thousands of its inhabitants, was the single most telling blow to the
security of Christian communities throughout Palestine and to their
faith in the imperial government.   To the Bedouins, on the other
hand, the general consternation caused by the invasions was an
open invitation to cast aside their fear of Roman authority and to
indulge their appetite for raiding.   It was just one week before the
capture of Jerusalem that the Saracens launched a surprise attack
against the Great Lavra on the Kedron—the same monastery on
whose behalf St. Sabas had applied to Emperor Anastasius (491–
518) for the construction of a fort to protect the monks against
Bedouin attacks—and massacred the monks who had not managed
to escape by fleeing beyond the Jordan.[117]

In 619, Sophronius, undeterred by Persian occupation of
Palestine, brought the body of John Moschus from Rome for
burial at Mount Sinai; but when he reached Ascalon, he found
the road to the Holy Mountain blocked "because of the tyrannical
incursions of those who are called Agareni."[118]   Presumably,
Sophronius planned on making his way to Mount Sinai by the route
common to most travelers, the *via maris*; but in Ascalon he obviously
could not secure guides or find a caravan willing to assume the
risks of a journey along roads made unsafe by Bedouin raids.

In the narrative (*diêgêsis*) of the Sinaitic monk Anastasius (*ca.*
650), mention is made of a time past when "the road to Palestine
was in the hands of the barbarians, causing a serious shortage of
oil at the Holy Mountain."[119]   The editor of the text would
attribute the cause to either the Persian or Muslim invasions,[120] but
we need not attribute the disruption to major military movements;
a more likely cause was the general chaos that Bedouins of
Southern Palestine and Sinai created in the region following, or
just prior to, Persian occupation of Palestine.

---

[117] See above, note 85.   A. A. Vasiliev, *History of the Byzantine Empire* (Madison
1954) 195, calls the Persian conquest of Palestine and the pillaging of Jerusalem a
turning point in the history of the province.

[118] *Eulogium* in *Patrologia Latina* (J.-P. Migne) 74.121: Cum autem ille [Sophronius]
Ascalonem appulisset et fieri non posse didicisset ut ad sanctum montem Sina per-
veniret, propter tyrannicas incursiones eorum qui vocantur Agareni . . ."

[119] Nau, *Récits* (above, note 21) 16–17; *Texte* (ibid.) 65.

[120] *Récits* (above, note 21) 17, note 1.   The dates that Nau assigns to both events—
614 for the Persian invasion, 624 for the Muslim—should be disregarded.

By the time Heraclius recovered the city of Jerusalem in 628, the communities of Southern Palestine and Sinai had been left to their own devices for almost half a generation. In the absence of imperial authority in the region—there is no evidence that the Persians filled the vacuum created by the withdrawal of the Byzantines—the towns no doubt returned to the well-tried *modus vivendi* of paying tribute to local Bedouin tribes in return for guarantees against raids. The agreement between Muhammad and the cities of Aila and Adhruh was a sign of the times: town by town, not by collective negotiation by an agent of the imperial government, communities came to terms with those forces that threatened their security.[121]

In the Negeb and Sinai, it seems that it was not so much a matter of simple survival or the fear of mass attack, since defensive installations of the towns were neither changed nor bolstered. With one exception, possibly two, the towns passed peacefully, at least in a physical sense, through the period of Persian occupation to the time of organized government under the Arab caliphs later in the seventh century.[122] The roads, however, were no longer protected by the military, or by the fear of it, nor could agreements between individual communities and Bedouin tribes have any force beyond town limits. It is along the roads that we hear of Bedouin raids and brigandage; we hear nothing of massacres among the religious communities or of the capture of towns.

If my interpretation of Theophanes' evidence is correct, Heraclius, upon recovering Palestine, paid the tribes in Southern Palestine to keep the peace along the roads leading to Mount Sinai; and when payments were discontinued, the Bedouins not only went back to raiding but also appealed to their compatriots

[121] See above, page 172. The silence of the Nessana papyri during this period is ominous (cf. Kraemer [above, note 19] 30). It is only toward the end of the seventh century, after the Arab caliphate had restored law and order in Southern Palestine, that the papyri begin to speak again, not only of taxes and requisitions of supplies, but also of personal matters. Most importantly, two documents dealing with the disposition of Arab troops (*ca.* 685) indicate that soldiers were stationed at this cross-road leading into the heart of the Sinai desert (Kraemer [*ibid.*] 290–304). The requisitions of the Arab governor at Gaza for Nessanites to provide the services of a guide for individuals traveling to Mount Sinai (above, note 102) further illustrate the return to law and order in this region.

[122] C. Baly, "S'baita," *Palestine Exploration Fund Quarterly Statement* (October 1935) 172–73.

in the Hedjaz for additional support.   Theophanes makes it very clear that the nearest military post from which help could be obtained was Caesarea, *over 80 miles from Gaza*, and much further from such towns of the Negeb as Elusa, Sobata, Mampsis, Nessana and Eboda.   In contrast with Heraclius' defensive arrangements east of the Wadi ꜥAraba—where a line was set up just south of the Dead Sea and, when Bedouin forces threatened, Theodorus the Vicarius "gathered all the garrisons of the desert" and repelled the attack—the region west of the ꜥAraba was completely devoid of any military posts from which a commander could "gather a sufficient force of men" as the governor of Palestine had been able to do a century earlier.[123]   When an attack developed in the region of Gaza, a message had to go far north to Caesarea before troops could be sent to assist the beleaguered towns in the south.   It would be remarkable if Sergius and his three hundred men (trained for desert warfare?) had reached the district of Gaza within three to four days after news of the Bedouin attacks became known in Gaza.   It is quite apparent, therefore, that Heraclius had either abandoned any concern for Southern Palestine or, more likely, that he thought that no serious threat to the security of Palestine could develop from that quarter.   What he probably did not know was that Aila had come to terms with the Muslims and that Muslim forces, using Aila as a *stomion*, swelled the number of militant Bedouins in Sinai, thereby setting the stage for the kind of attacks rarely experienced by the communities in the region.

The one clear exception to this relatively peaceful transition from Byzantine to Arab rule is Eboda.   This prominent town on the trans-Negeb road from Aila to Gaza is situated on a high ridge, the crown or "acropolis" of which is occupied largely by a fortress on the eastern portion of the hill and by church buildings to the west.   The eight-towered fortress had two main entrances in the north and south walls, and three secondary entrances on the east and west walls.   The town itself extended in a series of terraces down a spur of the western slope. Excavations on the acropolis have revealed a heavy layer of ashes in the towers of the fort and in the adjoining ecclesiastical buildings.   The gates of the fort facing south and west were blocked with building stones, column

---

[123] Above, page 181.

drums, and other material, indicating to the excavator that a desperate attempt had been made on the part of the inhabitants to defend themselves from attack. Destruction was limited to the area of the acropolis; the town below was untouched. A small chapel situated in the northeast corner of the fort bore no traces of the conflagrations, and hence is assumed to have been built after the firing of the fort and church complex. The destruction is attributed to the Persians in 619–620.[124]

In response to my request for more detailed information supporting the date of destruction of the buildings on the acropolis, Mr. Avram Negev, the excavator, kindly responded and gave his permission to cite his letter. Mr. Negev gives two possibilities: (a) between 614 and the reconquest of Jerusalem by Heraclius, (b) after 636. Mr. Negev maintains that the latter date is untenable since it does not fit well into the general archaeological evidence of the Negeb. The evidence from excavations at Sobata and Nessana shows that the towns continued to flourish during the whole of the seventh and eighth centuries, but that at Eboda there was no evidence to indicate the existence of a settlement at a date later than the middle of the seventh century. "I can see no reason," he writes, "why Avdat [Eboda] should have been destroyed by the same Arabs who tolerated the existence of other cities in the Negev."

As to dating the destruction of the buildings on the acropolis to the years between 614 and 629, Mr. Negev states:

> If the Arab conquest was not the reason for the destruction of Avdat, we must perforce come to the other date, that of the Persian invasions. I must admit that I have found no positive evidence proving the presence of Persians at Avdat. No coins, no typical pottery—nothing. This might, perhaps, indicate that the blow was sudden, quick and not long lasting. The Persians planned the conquest of Egypt but it could not be accomplished by sea because the Byzantine fleet dominated the Mediterranean. The only other way was by land routes, one of which passed near Avdat. Subeita and Auja [Nessana] were then off the main road. It is my belief that the Persian attack must have occurred after 618 [the last dated inscription found at Eboda is 618 when the abbot of the monastery was buried in the

---

[124] Avi-Yonah and Negev (above, note 78) 947; Negev (above, note 78) 129–30. Personal conversations and correspondance with A. Negev. See also Woolley and Lawrence (above, note 79) 109–22.

atrium of the South Church on the acropolis]. After the Persian withdrawal from the Negev, the inhabitants remaining at Avdat built the chapel in the fort to replace the churches which were burnt during the Persian invasion. Other reconstructed buildings were observed here and there. It seems that the bulk of the inhabitants left the city before 636. When the Arabs conquered Avdat, it must already have been a dead city.

I cannot concur, however, with Mr. Negev's *a priori* conclusion that the Persians, on their way to Egypt through the Negeb in 619–620, destroyed the buildings on the acropolis of Eboda. There simply is no evidence that the Persians used any route in their march to Egypt other than the one traversed by most armies, even the Arab army in 640, namely the *via maris*.[125] Nor did the Persians have to resort to any other route since control of the coastal region gave them a stranglehold on the interior. Even if they had marched from the interior of the Negeb to the coast—a most unlikely possibility—or from the coastal plain inland, the inhabitants of Eboda, long without a military force, would have undoubtedly capitulated without a struggle in the face of an approaching Persian army.

In one respect I agree with the excavator: the attack must have been sudden and unexpected. But in my view, the destruction at Eboda cannot be attributed to the Persians or to the post-Yarmuk (636) successes of the Muslims. I would, rather, set the date at 634 or shortly before, say ten or fifteen years, and place the responsibility either on local Bedouin tribes or on one of Abu-Bakr's raiding parties operating in Southern Palestine in 634 in concert with local Bedouins. The latter possibility seems to be the more probable one since in this region Bedouins appear never to have been successful in mounting a mass attack on any of the communities until Abu-Bakr sent a considerable force of men into Southern Palestine.[126] Further, the fact that Eboda was attacked

---

[125] See N. H. Baynes, "The Successors of Justinian," *Cambridge Mediaeval History* 2 (New York 1923) 291: "It was probably in the spring of 619 that the next step was taken in the Persian plan of conquest, when Shahrbarâz invaded Egypt. He advanced by the coast road, capturing Pelusium and spreading havoc among its numerous churches and monasteries."

[126] According to al-Baladhuri (above, note 49) 167, Abu-Bakr placed 3000 men under the command of ʿAmr ibn al-ʿAs and kept sending reinforcements until he had 7500 men. While these figures are unquestionably exaggerated, there can be little doubt that Abu-Bakr poured more fighting men into Southern Palestine and Sinai than had ever been seen there before.

while towns such as Nessana and Sobata escaped is additional support for my belief that raiding parties were at work. Eboda—prosperous, ungarrisoned, and furthest removed from Caesarea—made an excellent target of opportunity for Abu-Bakr's raiders on their way to or from the district of Gaza. And if there is any substance to the Arab tradition that ʿAmr ibn al-ʿAs and his forces withdrew to Ghamr in the Wadi ʿAraba after his initial contact with the Byzantines coming from Casearea,[127] it would seem more than likely that the Muslims had attacked Eboda after their incursions into Sinai and the district of Gaza. Ghamr, two stages from Aila and just off the Wadi ʿAraba road, is easily approached by the northern leg of the road leading from Eboda down the escarpments of the Ramon cirque to the ʿAraba.[128]

Very closely related to the situation at Eboda is the second, but not as clear, exception to the relatively peaceful transition from Byzantine to Arab rule. As stated above,[129] I believe that the Heran, Eran, or Ran of Theophanes is Pharan and that this town was the first to fall before the attacks of Abu-Bakr's raiders in 634. Curiously enough, Pharan, the largest community in the Sinai wilderness and one which had close contact with the monastic settlements in and around Mount Sinai, drops completely from the historical scene at about this time. While an argument *ex silentio* may not be entirely persuasive, it is compelling enough to give us pause.

In the narrative of the Sinaitic monk, Anastasius, written after 650, mention is made of a number of sites virtually unknown in the Sinai peninsula, and even of Aila; but not one mention is made of the city of Pharan.[130] This omission cannot merely be fortuitous since we know that Pharan contained at least two churches and was the seat of the bishop.[131] Weill, in his citation of the evidence for Pharan. comments:

---

[127] De Goeje (above, note 1) 35–36. Cf. Musil (above, note 46) 321.

[128] Caetani (above, note 1) 1124, note 1; 1131. For a description of the road from Eboda to the Wadi ʿAraba, see Aharoni (above, note 26) 13; Harel (above, note 42) 177–78. Although logic would have it that the Muslims attacked Eboda on their way from Gaza, it is also quite possible that the town fell before the Muslims as they headed toward Gaza.

[129] Above, page 161.

[130] See Nau, *Récits* and *Texte* (above, note 21).

[131] See art. "Sinai" in *Dictionnaire d'archéologie chrétienne et de liturgie* 15, ed. F. Gabrol (Paris 1950) 1469.

On entend encore parler, au viie siècle, d'un évêque de Pharan, le célèbre hérèsiarque Théodorus, après quoi la ville de Pharan tombe en oubli et, bien vivante encore aux temps d'Antonin Martyr, périt obscurément sous l'assaut des Saracènes; ce n'est qu'au xve siècle que nous entendrons prononcer à nouveau son nom et qu'on nous décrira ses ruines.[132]

In reality, our last notice of Pharan as a city is given by Antoninus at the end of the sixth century (*ca.* 575).[133] The mention of Theodorus, who was condemned by the Council of Latran (649) and the sixth oecumenical council of Constantinople (680), as bishop of Pharan need not have any reference to the town of Pharan since the name was used—like the bishop of Sinai, the church of Pharan, or the church of Sinai—in a geographical sense and was the title of the prelate overseeing all Christian affairs on the peninsula.[134] By the time of the anonymous account of the conversion of the Christian Bedouins at Mount Sinai, written by a contemporary of the event,[135] the name Pharan was no longer associated with the town in the Wadi Feiran, but with a "fort" (*tou kastrou Pharan*) very close to the monastery of St. Catharine. This fort was probably the *monasterium servorum* (Dir ol Abid) built by Justinian for the slaves who were "to guard and protect the monastery [of St. Catharine]."[136] After the forcible conversion of the descendants of these slaves to Islam in the time of Marwan I (684–685), the monks of Mount Sinai destroyed their homes.[137]

v. Conclusion

We may now venture a reconstruction of the events leading to the year 634 and the first Muslim attacks on Sinai and Palestine. The success of the Persians in Syria and their capture of Jerusalem was the signal for the outbreak of hostilities by Bedouin tribes in *Palaestina Tertia*. So far as we know, these hostilities were restricted to lines of communication; the towns themselves survived, probably by paying tribute to local tribes. When Heraclius

---

[132] Weill (above, note 21) 261.
[133] See above, page 182.
[134] See Weill (above, note 21) 222; above, note 20.
[135] Nau, *Récits* (above, note 21) 7.
[136] Eutychius (above, note 83) 1071.
[137] Eutychius 1072. Nau, *Récits* (above, note 21) 129–30.

recovered Palestine and Syria in 628, he organized a system of defenses in Syria just south of the Dead Sea in the region of Moucheôn and Mu'ta; the limitanean system in the Negeb and along the north-south axis of the Wadi ʿAraba, obsolete and abandoned since the time of Justinian, was not renewed, nor, apparently, deemed vital to the defense of the southern border of the empire.   After the defeat of Muhammad's forces at Mu'ta in 629, the imperial government must have felt even more convinced that no serious threat could arise from the Arabian peninsula, let alone from Palestine or Sinai.

In 630, Muhammad's activities, radiating from Tabuk close to the unprotected borders of the empire, brought Aila, the gateway to Southern Palestine and Sinai, under his control.   The significance of this move has long been underestimated, but there can be little doubt that the pressure Muhammad exerted on strategically located Aila was part of his design to find an outlet for his forces into Palestine and Syria.   By the terms of the agreement between the prophet and the people of Aila, the Muslims gained passage through the narrow passes surrounding the town whose defense by even a small force of men could easily have prevented Muhammad's use of this ingress into Palestine.   In addition, Aila provided the necessary food, water, and a resting place for troops before a military operation through the desert. To the people of Aila, on their own for many years and without knowledge of, or regard for, the consequences of the agreement, it was a simple and inexpensive solution to the problem of surviving in an area surrounded by hostile Bedouins.

The death of Muhammad in 632 and the wars of apostasy delayed any serious consideration of an attack against the Byzantines.   However, an opportunity arose in 633 when the pagan Bedouins of Southern Palestine and Sinai, angered at the refusal of the imperial government to pay them their money allowance, turned to their Muslim kinsmen in the Hedjaz and offered to show them "the way to the district of Gaza, the entrance of the desert extending towards Sinai." Abu-Bakr, who had been privy to Muhammad's plans, saw the chance to execute one phase of the prophet's strategy and hence declared a holy war against the Byzantines.   He ordered a large force of men—Arab tradition gives the number as 3000, later augmented to 7500— under ʿAmr ibn al-ʿAs to take the coast road to Aila.   The direction of the attack on Palestine was not along the well-known and well-marked road from Aila to Gaza; but with the help of Bedouins who knew their way over the lesser-known routes and where to find supplies of water, the attack was to go deep into Sinai and thence northward to the district of Gaza. The advantage of this plan was a surprise maneuver from an unexpected quarter against communities little prepared for, and certainly not expecting, a mass attack.

The most attractive prize for a raiding party in Sinai was Pharan, the largest community in the wilderness. The small monastic communities in the peninsula offered little in the way of booty and seem not to have been molested. The monastery at Mount Sinai, another possible target, was, by virtue of the great walls built by Justinian, impregnable to attacks by raiders.

After an attack on the unsuspecting town of Pharan, or site *x* in Sinai, if I am incorrect in my identification, the raiders worked their way north, probably not by the slow sand-dune covered *via maris* but by an interior route, such as the ancient Shur road, into the district of Gaza [138] Near Gaza they met their first real opposition from the Byzantines. Intelligence of the *razzias* must have reached Gaza, and word was sent to Caesarea, the nearest military post, 80 miles distant, for help. The military commander at Caesarea, apparently not greatly concerned and thinking that he had to deal with the usual kind of raiding band, sent down to the Negeb a small force of 300 men under the command of a certain Sergius. Sergius and his men were easily routed by ʿAmr's superior force. The Muslims then withdrew to Ghamr to await reinforcements from Medina. On the line of withdrawal lay Eboda, another rich prize and ripe for the taking. When the word was spread of an approaching attack, the inhabitants hastily fortified the citadel, but it was to no avail since the town was not in a position to defend itself against a mass attack. The acropolis was put to the torch by the Muslims, who then continued their way on the main road from Eboda down escarpments to the Wadi Araba to the rendezvous point at Ghamr.

[138] Cf. the route taken by Sultan Baybars in the thirteenth century (Woolley and Lawrence [above, note 79] 56–57).

Pl. 7. Avdat (ancient Eboda/Oboda): Aerial view of the site, fort and churches within the military installation.

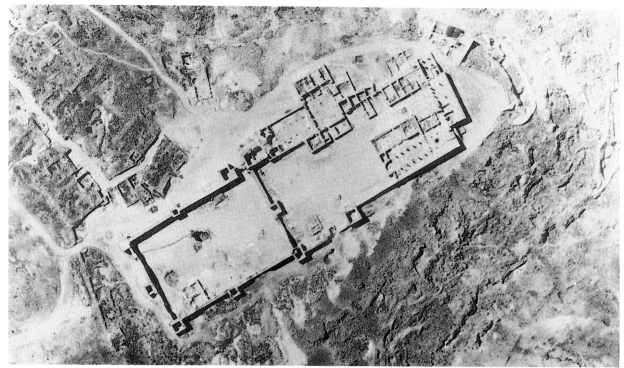

Pl. 8. Avdat: The acropolis with its fort, North Church, South Church and monastic buildings (?).

THE ISSUE OF THE TELEILÂT EL-'ANAB

Philip Mayerson

In a recent number of this BULLETIN [1] Y. Kedar has challenged this writer's view of the origin of the *teleilât el-'anab* as published in 1959. Since 1959, however, I have defended my position on three different occasions [2]; it is regrettable therefore that Dr. Kedar did not take into account this later material. In reply to Dr. Kedar, I submitted an article to the BULLETIN reviewing the problem and touching upon other matters associated with ancient agricultural practices in the Negeb, but the editors did not feel justified in continuing the debate and suggested instead a brief statement.

My last published comment on the stone heaps (*teleilât*) runs as follows: " I am not so wedded to my theory—which I only maintain is more plausible than others—that I would not divorce myself from it if sound and substantive evidence were adduced in support of the efficient runoff (soil-crusting) theory or any other theory." Since making this statement I have not seen any new evidence published that would make me change my mind.

As I have stated before, the issue is not so much the *teleilât* themselves but rather one of methodology. The approach of Dr. Kedar and other Israeli scholars to this problem is largely through experimentation. On the other hand, I have maintained the position that without the support of ancient or modern analogies from regions having similar geo-physical characteristics, experiments cannot prove that the ancient farmer stripped his slopes of their cover in order to increase rates of runoff or erosion; experiments can only prove a theory to be scientifically demonstrable, nothing more. It is on this premise that I find the theories cited by Kedar to be speculative and overly sophisticated. The latest experiment,[3] in which slopes were cleared of stone, raked, tamped, rolled and sprinkled, is yet further removed from ancient—or even modern—practices.

Let me again repeat my willingness to yield my own theory of the *teleilât* to any other that is based on a cogent methodological approach. However, until we agree on valid criteria for judging the evidence, our conclusions must, of necessity, be at variance.

---

[1] BULLETIN, No. 176 (December 1964), pp. 47-49.

[2] BULLETIN, No. 153 (December, 1960), pp. 27-37; *Science*, Vol. 134 (December, 1961), pp. 1751-1752: *ibid.* Vol. 137 (July, 1962), pp. 171-172.

[3] M. Evenari, L. Shanan, N. Tadmor, *Runoff-Farming in the Negev Desert of Israel II* (Rehovot, 1964), pp. 32-34. This report was received while the present article was in progress.

69

A NOTE ON DEMOGRAPHY AND LAND USE IN THE ANCIENT NEGEB

Philip Mayerson

The research program being carried out by a group of Israeli scholars at the ancient sites of Sobata and Eboda in the Central Negeb has produced important data for the appreciation of the region's ecology.[1] This writer has been particularly struck by the rainfall figures that were carefully and systematically recorded at these two sites for the three-year period 1960-1963. Through the kindness of a faculty member of the Department of Biology of the Hebrew University, who supplied figures for the years 1964 and 1965, we are now able to examine moisture conditions for Sobata and Eboda over a five-year period.[2]

	1960/1	1961/2	1962/3	1963/4	1964/5	Aver.
Shivta (Sobata)	102.5 mm	50.6	29.5	143.0	166.0	98.3
Avdat (Eboda)	57.2 mm	51.0	27.7	175.0	161.0	94.2

What interests this writer most are the implications of these figures for the demography of the Central Negeb, given the assumption that there has been no material change in climatic conditions during the last four or five millenia.[3] In the virtual absence of any evidence for the size of the populations that inhabited the prominent remains of settlements in the region, various impressionistic estimates have been made. One of the earliest was made by A. Reifenberg: 80,000 to 100,000 inhabitants during the Byzantine period.[4] Curiously enough these same figures cropped up in a recent newspaper article describing the experimental

---

[1a] M. Evenari, L. Shanan, N. Tadmor, *Runoff-Farming in the Negev Desert of Israel*: Progress Report on the Avdat and Shivta Farm Projects for the years 1958-1962 (Rehovot, 1963).

[b] M. Evenari, L. Shanan, N. Tadmor, *Runoff-Farming in the Negev Desert of Israel* II: Progress Report on the Avdat and Shivta Farm Projects 1962/3 Season (Rehovot, 1964).

[2] The hydrological year of the Negeb generally begins in October, reaches its peak, depending on the area, during the four months from December to March, and drops sharply in April and May; no rain falls from June to December.

[3] For a survey of current views on the problem of climatic change, see P. Mayerson, *The Ancient Agricultural Regime of Nessana and the Central Negeb* (London, 1961), p. 8.

[4] "The Struggle between the 'Desert and the Sown'," *Desert Research Proceedings*: Research Council of Israel Special Publications No. 2 (Jerusalem, 1953), p. 385.

work presently being conducted in the Negeb but the inhabitants are described as "Nabataeans."[5]

Y. Kedar followed with an estimate of the six cities in the Central Negeb (presumably Sobata, Eboda, Nessana, Mampsis, Elusa, Ruheiba) as ranging from between 3,000 and 6,000.[6] In a later article on ancient agriculture in the vincinity of Sobata, Dr. Kedar, on the basis of a count of field systems, the area covered by the remains of the ancient town, and an average annual rainfall figure of 100 mm, made an estimate of the available number of dunams, liters of water per day, and square meters of house space per capita for populations of 20,000, 10,000, and 5,000 at ancient Sobata (presumably Byzantine, but not stated).[7]

In view of the rainfall figures now in hand, we must review the problem of population density in the Central Negeb and raise the question of whether the average annual rainfall can be used as a meaningful statistic. From the figures given above, the average over a five-year period—98.3 for Sobata and 94.2 for Eboda—comes reasonably close to the commonly stated 100 mm annual average rainfall. However, on a year-to-year basis, the situation is quite different. Moisture conditions at Eboda for the three-year period 1960-1963 (57.2, 51.0, and 27.7 mm) were critical; the year 1962/3 was a disaster. At Sobata, 16 km to the northwest of Eboda, the year 1960/1 might be considered average, but the succeeding two years can only be considered a severe drought; the year 1962/3, like that at Eboda, was virtually rainless (29.5 mm).

In a region where there are no springs, few wells (none at Sobata and only one at Eboda, probably late and used in connection with the bathhouse below the town), and where the inhabitants had to rely on water stored in cisterns, a series of years like those between 1960 and 1963 means quite simply that large populations could not have been supported no matter how efficient they might have been in collecting and conserving water.[8] How, indeed, could large settled populations be provided with drinking water, let alone water for animals, crops, and caravans on the trans-Negeb routes, when the rainfall for three years at Sobata totalled 182.6 mm or 7 inches; that at Eboda 135.9 mm or a little more than 5 inches? And what of the periods when the drought continued for more than two or three years, say the proverbial seven?

The answer to these questions must be that populations in the settled areas of the Negeb were conditioned by the availability of water and that they must have fluctuated in proportion to the length of time drought conditions persisted. Add to this the effect of changing political and economic conditions and it will not be difficult to see that we cannot predicate any statistics on the basis of an average annual rainfall, the number of dunams covered by a site, or the number of field systems. We can also come to the conclusion that population estimates for any period of history that range from 10,000 to 20,000 for any one site are

[5] *The New York Times*, December 18, 1966.

[6] "Water and Soil from the Desert: Some Ancient Agricultural Achievements in the Central Negev," *The Geographical Journal* 123 (1957), pp. 180, 182.

[7] "Ancient Agriculture at Shivtah in the Negev," *Israel Exploration Journal* 7 (1957), pp. 184-189.

[8] For a description of cisterns in the Central Negeb, see *op. cit.* (note 3), pp. 36-39.

40

most unrealistic; those from 5,000 to 10,000 highly improbable. The best that can be said is that the populations of these so-called urban sites were modest.

How modest these populations were can be detected from two seventh century A. D. documents from Nessana, 19 km to the west of Sobata and possessing a number of good wells. One document, P. Colt 76, an incomplete register of payers of poll-tax, points to a population of 174 taxable males, representing a possible maximum of 1,500 persons of every age, sex, and class.[9] This writer, in analyzing P. Colt 69, an account recording the amount of wheat that the town of Nessana contributed in one year for the Arab military supply tax (*rizq*), estimated that the total wheat production for the year was capable of feeding 1,000 people.[10] The likelihood is, however, that both calculations are too high, for even if the estimated total wheat production is accurate, a substantial portion of it must have been set aside as a reserve for the lean years.

Even at sites more favorably situated than those of the Central Negeb, populations were small. At Aila, where there is a good supply of water, we hear of only 300 non-Muslim (male) adults when Muhammad came to terms with the city in 630 A. D.[11] At Adhruh, in trans-Jordanian *Palaestina Tertia*, a similar agreement was made with a probable population of 100 taxable adults.[12] Even taking into consideration political and economic conditions on the eve of the Islamic conquest, and the tactics that may have been employed by the towns to conceal their true numbers, the probability is that both Aila and Adhruh had small populations.[13]

The rainfall figures given above also have implications that bear upon the use to which land was put for agricultural purposes, given the security and the expenditure of energy to build the installations necessary to augment an inadequate supply of water from direct rainfall.[14] It is obvious that where rainfall varies in a five-year period from a marginal 175 mm to an exceedingly submarginal 27 mm, the risks of engaging in *extensive* planting of perennials (i. e. orchards and vineyards) are too great, no matter how drought-resistant the varieties planted. Not only do newly set-out trees and vines require supplementary supplies of water to get them started, but under severe drought conditions, additional water must be provided in order to keep plants alive. In the event of a sustained drought, the moisture requirements of perennials can compete seriously with the needs of the inhabitants for

[9] *Excavations at Nessana*, III, ed. C. J. Kraemer (Princeton, 1958), p. 218.

[10] *Op. cit.* (note 3), p. 19. The estimate was based on an arbitrary figure of 5% which was considered reasonable. Note, however, that the Nessanites preferred to pay one-third of the total demand in money rather than in kind. See *op. cit.* (note 9), p. 200.

[11] al-Balâdhuri, *The Origins of the Islamic State* (Kitâb Futûh al-Buldân), trans. P. K. Hitti, in *Columbia University Studies in History, Economics and Public Law* 68 (New York, 1916), p. 92.

[12] *Ibid.* For a description of Adhruh, see R. E. Brünnow and A. v. Domaszewski, *Die Provincia Arabia*, I (Strassburg, 1904), pp. 431-463.

[13] Cf. C. L. Woolley and T. E. Lawrence, *The Wilderness of Zin* (London, 1936), p. 144: ". . . Aila was a very small place at the best of times."

[14] For these installations see *op. cit.* (n. 3), pp. 2, 21-36.

41

drinking water, especially where, as at Sobata, the inhabitants had to depend solely on water stored in cisterns.

The experience at the research farm at the site of ancient Sobata demonstrates this point quite amply. Between the years 1958 and 1962, 140 trees and 84 vines were set out on 5.5 dunams (c. 1.5 acres) of land designed to receive runoff water from surrounding watersheds. Each tree and vine when planted received a number of supplementary irrigations totalling 85-125 liters of water per plant; thereafter the orchard was supposed to be dependent on runoff water for moisture.[15] However, in the severe drought of 1962/3, when runoff was slight, supplementary irrigation totalling 100-300 liters of water had to be given each tree and vine during the months of March and April 1963 in order to insure its survival.[16]

If we were to extend these conditions beyond an experimental plot to much larger acreage, and consider the possibility of the drought continuing for another year or two, we would have some idea of how seriously orchards could compete with the needs of the inhabitants for drinking water. We can also see the possibility of orchards going without supplementary irrigations when a persistent drought put drinking water at a premium.

The cultivation of annuals, on the other hand, provides a greater degree of certainty in terms of food production. Wheat and barley, two staples of ancient man's diet, require moderate amounts of water, and start and complete their growth cycle largely during the rainfall period, a period which is also low in rates of evaporation. Further, grains need only be planted when moisture conditions are right; if they are not, the seed can be saved for a year in which there is ample moisture in the soil. Hence, the culivation of annuals (i. e. field crops) comes at a time when water is available and not in competition with the personal needs of the inhabitants.

The experience at the research farm near the site of ancient Eboda is illuminating. In the 1961/2 season, when only 51 mm of rain fell, seed was sown after one flood of runoff water, estimated at 120 m³, covered the three-fifths of a dunam set aside for an experiment with two varieties of wheat. Although the field received no additional runoff, a good crop was obtained.[17] The following year 1962/3, which was very dry while the scanty rains produced no usable amounts of runoff, field crops were not planted.[18]

Similarly, the ancient farmer in the Negeb must not have engaged in dryland seeding but, like his modern counterpart in South Arabia [19] or the experimental farmer, waited for his land to be moistened to a sufficient depth with runoff water before sowing his field crops; if no runoff came into his fields, he must have left them unsown. But there also must have been years, like those of 1963/4 and 1964/5, when good moisture conditions—good at least for the Negeb—made it possible for

[15] Op. cit. (note 1a), p. 41.
[16] Op. cit. (note 1b), p. 8; for Avdat, see p. 14.
[17] Op. cit. (note 1a), p. 109.
[18] Op. cit. (note 1b), p. 19.
[19] Op. cit. (note 3), p. 21.

42

him to get high yields. During these years he undoubtedly planted as many acres as he possibly could in order to provide himself with a supply of food against the dry, lean ones. It was also during these " good " years that he could replenish his cisterns which not only gave him a reserve of drinking water for him and his animals, but also provided irrigation water for his perennials.

If the above assumptions are correct, the amount of land given over to the cultivation of field crops must have exceeded by far that set aside for orchards and vineyards. There is some confirmation of this in the Nessana documents: wheat and barley were the main items of agricultural production, and " seed lands " are mentioned with greater frequency than orchards or vineyards.[20]

Further, because the availability of water from one year to the next is so variable—variable in terms of little water as against no water— field-crop acreage per person or family in the ancient Negeb must have been considerably higher than in other regions of the Mediterranean basin with greater rates of rainfall. While differences in rates and distribution of rainfall in more favored regions produced varying yields, the ancient farmer in the Negeb had to balance off one year, two years, or more of fallow fields and no production with maximal productivity during the years of adequate rainfall. Hence, the large number of field systems and cisterns that we find in the Negeb correlate not so much to the density of its population, but rather to the need of the inhabitants to compensate for the harsh terms imposed on them by a difficult climate and an equally difficult topography.

[20] For a summary of the Nessana papyri relating to agriculture, see *op. cit.* (note 3), pp. 49-52.

Observations on the 'Nilus' *Narrationes*:
Evidence for an Unknown Christian Sect?

PHILIP MAYERSON

In his last major publication, Professor W. F. Albright raised again the question of the historicity of the *Narrationes* (*diêgêmata*), a fifth–century document attributed in the manuscript tradition to a certain Nilus.[1] Albright's interest in the narrative lay in finding evidence for human sacrifice in the biblical period; and since the *Narrationes*,[2] though considerably post-biblical, tell the story of a young man who had a narrow escape from being sacrificed to the god of the Morning Star by the Bedouins of the Sinai desert, he felt justified in citing the account to support his views. Professor Albright, of course, was well aware that the historicity of the *Narrationes* had been under scholarly attack for the past fifty years and more; and to counter the critics of the narrative he cited this writer's use of it for evidence on local conditions in Sinai and Southern Palestine in the beginning of the fifth century A.D.[3] Encouraged by Professor Albright, although not committed to his views, I have looked further into the *Narrationes*, and I have come to the conclusion that we are in possession of a document that, if not unique, is unusual in many ways. However, anyone reopening the case of the *Narrationes* after it has been closed for so many years may appear as a fool rushing in where angels fear to tread. Among almost all historians of religion and patrologists, and in current encyclopedias and manuals of patrology, the narrative has been condemned as a fabrication, a romance, worthless for ethnography and religion.[4] The first in a series of indictments was published by K. Heussi in 1916. Influenced by E. Rhode, the historian of literature, Heussi discovered many affinities between the narrative and the Greek novel; both contained themes or motifs involving love and adventure, the "odyssey" motif which offers many opportunities for dramatic descriptions, for exaggerations and for the grotesque.[5] Heussi declared the *Narrationes* to be a pure piece of *Romanliteratur*. Heussi's verdict was sustained three decades later by a scholar investigating the ethnography and religious practices of pre-Islamic Arabs. J. Henninger, who gives an exhaustive and invaluable review of the literature on the *Narrationes* prior to 1955, systematically researched the evidence in the narrative for human and animal sacrifice. He found that his conclusions on the ethnographical data confirmed the verdict arrived at by Heussi and other church historians, and *pari passu* his criticism lent weight to their verdict.[6] From virtually all sides then, the *Narrationes* have been declared "guilty" and condemned to be a pariah in the community of historical documents.

I have taken the position—and still maintain it—that there are elements in the *Narrationes* that quite legitimately bear on the history of *Palaestina Salutaris* (*Tertia*) for the late fourth and early fifth centuries; that the author of the narrative, whoever he may have been, because of his knowledge of the topography and local conditions, must have been an inhabitant of Sinai for some period of time; that the description of a plundering raid by Bedouins on the monastic settlements in Sinai and of the massacre of a small number of eremites in the wilderness surrounding

Mount Sinai is reasonably accurate; that the narrative gives us a reasonable picture of how isolated communities in the deserts of Sinai and Palestine dealt with the problem of security. I have also commented that the narrative at its worst may be considered a kind of historical fiction in which the author has placed his major characters in a setting that has historical verisimilitude. On the other side of the coin, experiences in the wilderness *are* dramatic and very often read like fiction, and it is these experiences that scholarly critics find difficult to appreciate or evaluate.[7]

Before any attempt is made to reopen the case of the *Narrationes*, a brief rebuttal must be entered against the methodology employed by Heussi and Henninger, the two prime antagonists to the historicity of the narrative. When the work was assumed to be from the hand of Nilus of Ancyra, the author of numerous letters and several moral and ascetic treatises, the narrative was searched for elements that would bear upon the life and thought of this prolific abbot who was also a follower of St. John Chrysostom. Heussi was quite right in declaring that the *Narrationes* were not written by Nilus of Ancyra—*pace* Albright[8]—but he adduced little evidence from the narrative itself to support his claim; instead he relied heavily on literary themes and motifs and to a lesser degree on seeming inconsistencies. I believe, as I hope to demonstrate, that there is substantial internal evidence for assuring ourselves that the *Narrationes* were not from the hand of the author of the letters and treatises now gathered together in volume seventy-nine of Migne's *Patrologia Graeca* (hereafter *PG* 79). However, separating the narrative from the other work of Nilus is no reason for assuming that it is *Romanliteratur*, especially on the basis of literary themes and motifs. Adventure and love—and the love motif has been stretched considerably in its application to the *Narrationes*[9]—are not necessarily restricted to fiction; they can be found in real life!

As for the ethnographical data contained in the *Narrationes*, they were subject to an intensive cross-examination by Henninger. I do not wish, nor do I feel competent, to dispute his detailed arguments on the validity of the material contained in the narrative. I only wish to draw attention to one significant flaw in his presentation: he did not examine the context in which the bulk of the ethnographical data was given. In fact, had he done so, he might have found additional support for his arguments, which were based largely on the lack of corroboration from other sources on pre-Islamic religious practices. What was the context? *Narratio II* is mostly taken up with the author relating the reasons for his taking leave of his wife and retreating with one of his two sons to the Sinai desert where he could pursue the life of a solitary. After lamenting the massacre of the holy men[10] and the absence of divine providence to prevent it, he ends by saying that it is time for him to describe the superior (or former) life (*proteron bion*)[11] of the holy men and to tell of the life of the savages who attacked them. His predisposition is clearly to contrast two ways of life, that of the Bedouins and that of the eremites. He certainly cannot be expected to be kindly disposed to those whom he has just described as murderers of a number of his compeers. The reader then should be prepared for a prejudiced account regardless of whether the writer had any sure knowledge—which I suspect he did not—of the customs and religious practices of the Bedouins. On the other hand, we should equally be prepared to hear a passionate defense—and we do—of the way of life that he and others like him had adopted.

Narratio III opens with a description of the Bedouin way of life and their barbarous rituals involving human and animal sacrifice, a description which historians of religion have seized upon and which Henninger has taken pains to prove worthless. In *PG* 79 the description takes up only two short columns (612B–613C) of 57 lines. This is followed by a considerably longer and more detailed account of the eremitic way of life, a fervid description not only of how and why it is practiced, but also of its accompanying benefits. In *PG* 79 this takes up 7 columns (613C–625C) of 240 lines!

All the above taken into consideration, it does not necessarily prove that every item of information in columns 612–613 of *Narratio III* is so tainted with prejudice that it is completely worthless. By the same token, however tainted these data may be, it does not necessarily contaminate other information in the narrative which bears upon ancient life in the deserts of Sinai and Southern Palestine. In particular, I refer to those episodes involving the abduction and recovery of the writer's son, Theodoulus. It must be borne in mind that, apart from the question of whether the account is a true one or a piece of fiction, the author was not an historian or an anthropologist. We certainly cannot expect him to evaluate dispassionately and disinterestedly Bedouin customs and rituals, particularly as they are practiced in the wilderness and beyond the control of civil authorities—practices which may involve murder, thievery, sadism, mental and physical torture, cat-and-mouse games played with captives, all of which I believe are described in the narrative.

One more question must be raised before concluding this *exordium*. If Nilus of Ancyra is not the author of the narrative, how did his name become attached to it? The answer, I believe, lies in the character and content of the writings—the letters and various treatises—attributed to Nilus: they are, by and large, concerned with moral and spiritual subjects associated with monastic life. Quasten cites the works collected under his name as an "ascetical corpus."[12] A better description, perhaps, would be a "corpus of philosophical asceticism." It is not surprising, therefore, to find a Christian paraphrase of the *Enchiridion* of Epictetus among the spurious works bearing Nilus's name. Further, it is not an uncommon device to associate the work of an unknown, or of someone in bad odor, with the name of one who has an unassailable reputation—such as Nilus, John Chrysostom or Epiphanius of Salamis—the name providing authority and authenticity to the work. So it is that recent scholarship has discovered several treatises of Evagrius of Pontus, who was suspected of heresy, hiding under the name of Nilus of Ancyra.[13]

One very obvious answer to why the name of Nilus became attached to the *Narrationes* is that the narrative has a good deal to say about "philosophical asceticism," although of a very different kind from that preached by the genuine Nilus. The second reason for the inclusion of the narrative with the other works of Nilus is a letter (*Ep.* 4, 62, cols. 580–581) which in the present collection is immediately followed by the *Narrationes*. The letter has as its purpose to exalt the power of faith and to glorify Nilus's countryman and martyr, Plato of Ancyra in Galatia. The letter tells of a certain old man from Galatia and his son who lived among the ascetics "on a mountain called Sinai where Moses received the law." One day the heathen barbarians made a sudden attack and captured, and bound in chains a number of monks, the son of the old man among them. The old man, who had hidden himself in a cave, was distraught over the loss of his son and prayed to St. Plato to take pity on him. At the same time, the son in captivity prayed to the martyr to have compassion and to perform a miracle. Instantly, Plato appeared before him mounted on a horse. He had another horse with him and urged the young man to mount it. The young man tore off his chains as if they were cobwebs, mounted the horse, and in a flash both soon arrived at the side of the old man. Plato, however, disappeared as father and son were reunited.

F. Degenhart, the exponent of the unity of the works attributed to Nilus, attempts—rather weakly as I see it—to rationalize the discrepancies between the narrative and the letter. He sees the narrative—which, by the way, contains no mention of a miracle or of a St. Plato—as a further elaboration of the details contained in the letter, and that the letter focused in particular on St. Plato, for whom Nilus had a special affection.[14] Heussi, the opponent of the unitarian approach of Degenhart, takes another tack. He recognizes certain affinities between the letter and the narrative as well as their differences. His conclusion with regard to the differences is that the letter describes an attack but not a martyrdom, that the original story of Theodoulus had nothing to do with the martyrdom of the Sinai monks, and that the author of the narrative linked the two stories together. Heussi calls special attention to the fact that the letter says nothing about human sacrifice and that the author borrowed the motif of human sacrifice from Greek romance.[15]

These arguments simply do not hold water. At best they can be nothing more than mere conjectures. One can equally conjecture that the writer of the letter was influenced by the narrative —we have no firm date for the writing of the *Narrationes*—and then adapted it to make his point regarding the power of faith and of St. Plato.

I believe that there is a far simpler explanation of how Nilus's name became attached to the *Narrationes*. Whoever was responsible or collating or copying the manuscripts which now bear the name of Nilus was attracted by the similarities between the letter and the narrative: both had to do with a father and son living as eremites in Sinai, a Bedouin raid, an abduction, and the ultimate recovering of the son. In addition to these similarities there is a strange, clipped opening to the *Narrationes*; the narrative lacks anything of the kind which might be considered an introduction (589A):

> Wandering about after the attack of the barbarians, I came to Pharan. As I listened,
> I heard some speakers praise the life of the solitary. They said many things in their
> own behalf and glorified their way of life. . . .

It appears very likely that, whether by design or by accident, at least several opening sentences or paragraphs of the narrative are lost. If I am correct, and had these lines survived, we might have had some better indications both of the original character and of the author of the *Narrationes*. But be that as it may, by the tenth century the name of Nilus of Ancyra had become firmly attached to the narrative: the synaxaria and menologies of that and later times summarize the adventures of Nilus and Theodoulus in the wilderness of Sinai, and the particulars of these experiences could only have come from the *Narrationes*.[16] Of course, common to these synaxaria and menologies are varying biographical details and varying dates on which to honor St. Nilus and to mark the death of the holy men on Mount Sinai. However, uncommon to these documents is a comment critical of the behavior of Nilus, a criticism which might be shared by a modern reader. The writer of the synaxarion marking the celebration of St. Nilus on 12 November has this to say concerning the reaction of Nilus to the abduction of his son: "He bewailed him more than is fitting, as is shown in the writing which he composed."[17]

By the time of Nicephorus Callistus in the fourteenth century, the *Narrationes* and the other works of Nilus were securely wedded together and remained so until the twentieth century when Heussi raised objection to the legitimacy of the association. Nicephorus eulogizes Nilus for narrating brilliantly and with considerable pathos the martyrdom of the Fathers on Mount Sinai as well as the tragic captivity of his children (*sic*) when "the barbarians, who are called Blemmyes, made an incursion and committed murder on no mean scale."[18] And so, by the vagaries of history and of textual tradition, it happened that Nilus of Ancyra in Galatia, who probably had only the vaguest notion of what life was like in the wilderness of Sinai, became to be known as Nilus Sinaita and the author of the *Narrationes*.

Up to this point we have been speculating on the association of Nilus of Ancyra with the *Narrationes*. There still remains the possibility—if we may speculate further—that a man by the name of Nilus, other than the Nilus of Ancyra, was the author of the narrative. The evidence may hardly be worth citing but it should be noted that in *PG 79* all the treatises, with the exception of the *Narrationes*, identify the writer in one manner or another as St. Nilus; the manuscripts of the narrative, on the other hand, have no prefatory word such as *hagios* or *makarios* before his name, but simply call him "Nilus, the desert solitary." Hence, whoever gathered together the material attributable to Nilus of Ancyra could easily have made the assumption that both Niluses were one and the same. However, it must be admitted once more that we are in the realm of pure speculation and that for the present, and pending further research, the author of the *Narrationes* must be considered anonymous and unknown.[19]

What, then, makes the *Narrationes* unusual or unique? It is, of course, what the narrative has to say and, peculiarly, what it does not say. Ordinarily, arguments *ex silentio* are inadmissible, or at best ineffective instruments of proof. However, when reading material originating from an eremitic community during the climax of the patristic age, there is the normal expectation of finding it suffused with Christian beliefs of the time, be they rational or irrational. This is not the case with the *Narrationes*. There is no Christology, no Trinitarianism, no diabolism or demonism, no miracles, no direct quotations from the New Testament, no use of the word *abba* for the more reverend inhabitants of the desert. All these elements can be found in the letters or treatises of Nilus of Ancyra and in one form or another in the eremitic literature of the period. What is even more remarkable is that the name of "Jesus" or "Christ" does not appear once in the narrative. In a context citing past instances of injustice, Jesus is referred to obliquely as "the suspected king" (609B: *ho hyponouomenos basileus*). The word "Christ" appears in one prepositional phrase (*kata Christon*) as a periphrasis for "Christian." It occurs late in the narrative when a report is brought to the father that his son has been bought by "a priest of the holy Christian mysteries" in Elusa (676A). The word *Christon* appears once more (689A) in a context in which it is a patent error for *chreston*.

One need only glance at Ammonius's *Forty Martyrs of the Sinai Desert*, an account presumably of the same disaster that overtook the eremitic communities on Sinai, to see the difference between the *Narrationes* and the more conventional language of ascetic literature.[20] Ammonius's narrative is replete with Christological apparatus, with martyrs—a word which in our narrative is never applied to the victims of the Bedouin attack—with anecdotes that are reminiscent of, if not borrowed from, the *Apophthegmata Patrum*. His monks are "athletes of Christ," experience miracles, wrestle with the devil and exorcise evil spirits. All this and much more, but nothing of the kind that resembles the *Narrationes*.

Turning aside from expectations and looking at the text itself, it is immediately discernible that the narrative has been composed by a man of some education. The verbal furbelows and embellishments—the rhetorical questions, antitheses, hesitations, long speeches, *exempla* and parallels, extended similes and metaphors—all point to the writer having received formal training in one of the rhetorical schools of his day. The narrative is therefore made up largely of elements of the kind that Cicero (*de part. orat.* 9.32) recommends as producing an effective *narratio*: "Wonder, suspense, and the unexpected, intermixed with emotional disturbance, dialog between persons, grief, anger, fear, joy, desire."[21]

In view of the rhetorical character of the narrative, several observations should be made. The accuracy of the historical moment is naturally obscured, but not necessarily obliterated, by the heavy rhetorical overlay. This is especially the case in the long speeches in which the writer through a form of prosopopeia strives for a particular emotional effect. Hence the reliability of the details contained within these manufactured speeches must be carefully weighed. Further, the writer, either by his schooling or through personal discipline, conspicuously avoids citations from, or allusions to, pagan sources or materials. There is in fact not a single mention of any writer, pagan or Christian; the sole source of *exempla* or parallels is the Scriptures. The narrative cites or alludes to the Scriptures in one form or another some thirty-two times.[22] Of these, two only have echoes of the language of the New Testament; one is a specific reference to the time of Herod and the slaughter of the infants.[23] There is no evidence that the writer had any intimate knowledge of the New Testament. The remaining citations and allusions are from the Old Testament, of which three are direct quotations taken from the Septuagint.[24]

The narrative is written in the first person singular, as if the writer were composing a letter or a memoir concerning his experiences. He sees himself as a philosopher and the disciple of an eremitic sect in Sinai. The picture he gives of himself, however, is certainly not that of a philosopher-hero. It is evident from his actions that he is excessively emotional, ambivalent, unsure of the nature of God's justice, and generally insecure in his philosophical views.[25] The true heroes, at least those who are most consistent in their fortitude and commitment to their ideals, are the writer's son Theodoulus, a Pharanite woman whose son was killed in the Bedouin raid, and an eremite who falls to a Bedouin's sword rather than betray the whereabouts of his fellow eremites.[26]

What is more important than the personalities of the narrative is the description of the Sinaitic sect, and what is extraordinary about it is that its adherents retreated to the wilderness for purely philosophical reasons: namely, to seek tranquillity through solitude and to practice self-denial. While it is true that philosophy and asceticism were virtually synonymous in the fourth century, the general movement from the world to find a higher life in the deserts was done either in the name of Jesus Christ or to escape political or social evils. No such justification is given here. This sect is by far closer in spirit to Epictetus than to Paul; it is concerned almost exclusively with serenity, self-control, knowledge, purity, free will, moral asceticism, vegetarianism and celibacy;[27] it has little to do with the grosser forms of austerities—the branding of the flesh and battling the devil—practiced by the monastics who populated the deserts of Egypt and Syria.

So it is that the writer of the narrative comes across more as a preacher of Stoic-Cynic morality than as a Christian. He espouses philosophy, but not philosophy *kata Christon* or philosophy *pneumatikê* of Nilus of Ancyra.[28] And yet he is a Christian, but what form of Christianity he and his fellow eremites subscribe to is not clear. The writer describes the practice of the eremites coming together in one congregation on the Lord's Day (620C), and that (621A) "they also take part in the divine mysteries (*theia mysteria*) and entertain each other with the exercise of suitable discourses (*logia*), and they encourage each other with ethical advice."[29] And when describing the attack of the Bedouins, which came when the writer and his son "had come down from the sacred mountain to visit the holy men in the place of the [Burning] Bush," the attackers forced them to come out of the church and ordered "the priest of the holy place" to stretch out his neck to their swords (628B).[30] Then, at the very end of the narrative, after the old man and his son have been reunited, the bishop of Elusa presses them to accept "the yoke of priesthood" (692B).[31]

Christian though these eremites may have been, Mount Sinai and its environs obviously had a special meaning for them, more so than it did for other of their co-religionists. The clue—an important one in my opinion—to that special meaning is found at the very end of *Narratio III*, the conclusion to the writer's eulogy on the way of life of the Sinaitic solitaries. The eremites are compared to Moses and Elijah; they imitate their *aretê* and practice their modest and unaffected ways. We are then told (625A-B):

> In this desert, Moses, while avoiding the treachery of the Egyptians and pasturing the flocks of Jethro, observed that wondrous sight of the all-devouring flame....Later, leading his people out [of Egypt], he was, on this mountain, appointed Lawgiver, at that time only of the Jewish, but now of every nation,[32] because of the relationship of nature when grace came to the entire race. For the laws governing his people, placed on a lampstand, shone forth, even though, prior to their once having been made clear, they had been hidden under the bushel of (i.e., obscured by) language.

As for Elijah, the writer of the narrative tells us that he fled from Jezebel to Sinai where "he lived in this cave, dressed in a sheepskin, the ancient dress of his ancestors. And he saw God in a light breeze and heard the voice prophesying what He had decreed. The first and last convincing proof of men's fortitude and perseverance."

There are, admittedly, difficulties in extracting the precise meaning of these statements. Whose nature is being referred to? Is it Moses'? God's? Or some philosophical Physis? Who was the recipient of the grace? Was it the Jews? Or all people, Jews and non-Jews? And was it Christ's coming that spread grace to the entire world? Further, the sentence containing the metaphor of the lampstand and the bushel seems to have been garbled, if not in transmission, then by the writer. And is the metaphor of the lampstand and the bushel an echo of "hiding one's light under a bushel" of Matthew 5.15, Mark 4.21, and Luke 8.16; 11.33? Or was the figure a commonplace one by the fourth century? And what does the writer mean by "the first and last convincing proof of men's fortitude and perseverance"? Does it refer to the activities of both Moses and Elijah, or only to Elijah? And, finally, does the writer mean to exclude Christ whose theophany, according, to Matthew 17.2, was witnessed by Moses and Elijah? However tantalizing these questions may be, it is clear that the place where Moses received the Law, and where Elijah lived and heard "the still small voice" of God, had special meaning for the writer and, presumably, for the eremites he was describing. It was unquestionably the compelling reason for their seeking out Sinai as the place in which, like Moses and Elijah, they might be alone before God and serve him. It is also evident, as the narrative amply demonstrates, that the Old Testament was their primary, if not exclusive, source of instructive literature in which they found their inspiration, *exempla*, and the rationale for their way of life. To take this one step further, there is the reasonable expectation that the eremites had in their possession, and studied, texts of the Old Testament.

As a conclusion to these observations, I would maintain that the narrative is not a romance and is not completely worthless as a historical document. Even if we were to agree that it was a piece of fiction—for what audience? and for what purpose? It certainly is not a romance, its characters not of that genre, its setting no never-never land. The narrative was obviously written by a man who was not a native of Sinai but who lived there for a period of time. If the writer of the narrative composed a piece of fiction, he was at least not creating it in a vacuum, and it must have had some relationship to the time and place in which it was written. To say that it did not would mean that we would have to exclude all works of fiction, even the comedies of Aristophanes, as having no value whatever for historical reconstructions.

The major difficulty in accepting the *Narrationes* is that it has no clear parallel and does not belong to an established genre of literature. Nevertheless, I believe that the narrative contains legitimate evidence for an ascetic sect, somewhat Christianized but to what extent unknown, that maintained itself for a short period of time following the establishment of Christianity in *Palaestina Tertia* in 359. The members of this sect, not having a corporate structure, and scattered about Sinai in huts and caves, were easy targets for periodic Bedouin raids. The sect undoubtedly petered out, or was absorbed by a more organized and more orthodox community that began to develop in the fifth century and ultimately was able to convince the emperor Justinian to build the now famous fortified monastery of St. Catherine. It may be interesting to speculate what chance any isolated monastic community in Sinai—together with its manuscripts and ikons—might have had to survive *razzias* and conquests and enter the twentieth century if it had not been for this massive fortress at the foot of the Mountain of Moses.

In support of the observations made above, the seven episodes which make up the *Narrationes* in *PG* 79 now deserve a closer examination. The following epitome is designed to illustrate more specifically the character of the eremitic sect as it is set forth by the writer of the narrative. It is also designed to illustrate the writer's rhetorical style which, as already stated, provides a better understanding of the narrative and the time in which it was written.[33] And, finally, if these observations and the accompanying summary support the case for the historicity of the *Narrationes*—or at least for a reprieve from the charge that the narrative is pure fiction and without any redeeming value—it is hoped that future investigation will improve the text and will bring out additional evidence, pro and con, to bear on the worth of this unusual and, I believe, unique document.

*****

Narratio I: No sooner has Theodoulus' father, the writer of the narrative, entered Pharan after the Bedouin attack than he hears some people[34] praise the life of the solitary (589A-592A):

> It is full of tranquillity and free from all confusion; through solitude it broadens the condition of the soul that pursues knowledge (*enphilosophousan*) through observation and in this way progresses near the knowledge (*gnôsis*) of the holy things[35] of God, which all wise men from time immemorial agree is the highest desire and the supreme happiness.

When they see the old man's distress, they encourage him to speak. He admits that he has been attracted to their way of life and that he knows how very attractive solitude is. He has admired it so very much that in his overwhelming desire for it, he left behind everything: home, country, relatives, friends, possessions. However, the recent disaster has made it impossible for him to praise this way of life. He cries out (593A): "Oh what foolishness! I am induced to give up mourning for my son and to philosophize (*philosophein*). And yet my thoughts never give me time or allow me to think of anything other than the murder of Theodoulus." The old man continues to lament over the loss of his son. He visualizes the many different ways in which he may have been murdered; he believes that he can hear his agonized cry; he imagines what he would have seen if he had been a witness to his murder. The old man then indulges in a long series of rhetorical questions and exclamations (593B–ff): "Oh my pitiable son! Are you alive or are you dead? Oh the bitter slavery if you escaped death! Oh your tombless tomb if a savage's sword slew you! How am I to lament your slavery? How am I to weep your death?" There follows the imagined suffering and beatings that Theodoulus would have to endure if he were enslaved by the Bedouins.

From slavery, the old man turns to mental images of his son's death (596A): "But if you are dead, where on your body did you bear your wound? From what place did the wellhead of your blood stream forth? How, befouled with gore, did you gasp and perform the dance of death with your wretched feet?... What wild beast has torn your limbs to pieces? What birds took their fill of your flesh?" He continues in this vein, visualizing every possible agony that his son can suffer in dying as well as his own pain in remaining alive to bear the calamity. He is not even able to enjoy the luxury of witnessing his son's last breath or of having the consolation of friends after the funeral. He recalls with regret that Theodoulus has shared with him the hardships of the desert; yet his son emulated Isaac's obedience to the wishes of his father Abraham. The old man's suffering touches his listeners, and they urge him to unburden himself, for, they say (600A), "the soul is relieved of its despondency when it recites its misfortunes; by the narration of its sorrows, the soul, as it were, is emptied of its unhappiness." This statement of psychological insight is supported by two similes: rain relieving the cloud of its gloom and darkness; suppressed suffering is like a suppurating sore that has no means of being drained of its pus.

Narratio II: The old man responds to the invitation to unburden himself, and in addition he gives his reasons for chosing a life of self-denial and solitude in the wilderness. He begins his story in this way (600C–601B):

> My friends, I fathered two sons; one of them I am now lamenting, the other stayed with my wife, resolving that it was sufficient either for the propagation of the race or for serving me in my old age. For I judged it fitting for every rational man not to revel in pleasure excessively nor to abuse the freedom of established custom

(*i.e.*, marriage) to the outrage of nature; but at once to stop ministering to the goal of the Creator for the increase of the race, yet not to minister to the encouragement of the passion which necessitated marriage, so that when a man's potency is later weakened and his desires are naturally quenched by the calm of old age, his attainment of temperance might not be ascribed to the necessity of age but to the choice of what is honorable.[36] For man without experience in war never sets up a trophy, and an athlete cannot boast of victory when the contest has been called off, since no one was wrestling with him and there was no fall. Now it dignifies the contestant in the prime of his youth, when his passions are inflamed and he burns with desire, to rule his longing with reason and strangle the yearning which urges him to marital intercourse, even if it is lawful and bears witness that it was a matter of his own free will. [At that time] some strong desire of those places where I have now been ruined attracted me, and by my reason I was completely uplifted in my solitude, being unable to perceive or regard anything save this. For when the love of something or other grasps the soul, it draws it forcibly away from everything worthy of serious consideration and carries it toward a longing, and the soul neither refuses nor considers toil, trouble, or injury. For everything governed willingly by absolute power is an eager slave to desire and gladly assumes the yoke of submission out of free choice and self-imposed necessity.

The old man relates how he approached his wife, with whom he had a close and intimate bond, with his decision. Though the thought of separation was painful to her, she accepted his decision with philosophical fortitude and even helped him enter his life of solitude with peace of mind. As for the children, one would remain with his mother; the other, Theodoulos, would go with his father into the desert. The old man's account ends with a long metaphor, ostensibly dealing with the hardships of adapting to a new way of life: his wife sent him off with a favorable wind, but a hurricane arose and shattered the ships (the body) but the rich cargo (the spirit) was saved.

The people listening to the old man then raise questions regarding God's justice in connection with the massacre (604D). What, they ask, was the explanation for the death of the holy men who served God blamelessly? "Did the power of Providence do nothing but remain silent during such a tragic event? Not preventing the attack although it could have done so? Not striking blind those who had acquiesced in the action? Not withering those lawless hands which had been lifted against the holy men?" "How often," they continue (604D–605C), "the Scriptures declare that these actions have been taken on behalf of sanctified men." In support of their views, they cite and enlarge upon incidents recorded in the Old Testament: an angel destroying the Assyrian army sent against Hezekiah (2 Kings 19.15ff.; Is. 37.36); Elisha blinding his adversaries (2 Kings 6.18); the man of God withering the hand of idolatrous Jeroboam (1 Kings 13.4); angels blinding the Sodomites who insist on invading Lot's house (Gen. 19.11). How is it then, they ask, that these holy men died without receiving divine help?

To these questions the old man gives a philosopher's answer (608C–609B): "Why must we debate the nature of Providence? And who understands God's judgments well enough in troublesome questions to defend the justice of the Lord's ways? All human reason is not powerful enough for such an inquiry, and when it is overwhelmed by an inability to comprehend, it fails to find a reasonable cause to assign to events." He then proceeds to say that there are many examples in the past of wicked men's schemes being carried out while justice remained silent about retribution and vengeance. The examples are introduced by way of rhetorical questions and paralipsis. He adduces the case of Cain and Abel (Gen. 4.8) and adds a bit of pathos to the account, apparently to tug on the heart strings. He also cites the case of Jezebel ordering the death of Naboth (1 Kings

21.10), and Doeg massacring the priests (1 Samuel 22.18). The latter is supported by a direct quotation from Psalms 79.3. Then, somewhat reminiscent of Hebrews 11.37 but without specific reference to it, the old man says (609A): "How was it that bands of prophets and apostles died, plotted against by evil-doers, cut to pieces, strangled and stoned to death; and not only did they not deserve to die, but they had always been benefactors of their murderers?" The old man closes his citation of examples by "not speaking" of the children who were drowned in Egypt at the order of the Pharaoh (Exod. 1.22) and those killed by Herod (Matt. 2.16) "so that the suspected king might not grow up."[37]

In all the cases cited, the "Judge" remained silent while patiently observing the transgressions of the wicked against his laws. However, he has established a day of judgment and reserves punishment until that time. But this is not the occasion to discuss opinions regarding God's justice. With this statement, the old man concludes his reply to the questions posed by his audience and returns to his personal situation, to his grief and his suffering. He then states that it is time to tell the rest of his story and to describe the life of the holy men in Sinai and to speak about the life of the savages who attacked them. Always the philosopher, he has an explanation for taking this tack (612A–B): The earnest pursuit of knowledge is distressing when it has been silenced, and the failure to acquire the information it desires is oppressive until its desire to gain that knowledge is fulfilled.

Narratio III: The old man begins with a description of the Bedouin way of life. He cites the area they inhabit and the fact that they never engage in manufacture, commerce, or agriculture; the sword is their only principle of life. They maintain themselves by eating the flesh of animals of the desert or by ambushing travelers. But if these are lacking, they eat their camels or they kill members of their own family or clan for food. They live like dogs. They worship the Morning Star and when it rises they sacrifice the best of their spoils to it. They prefer especially to use boys in the prime of their life and they sacrifice them at dawn on a heap of stones.

The mention of the sacrifice of boys causes the old man some distress, and he addresses his audience directly (612D–613A) with an outburst of "Oh my friends!" and then goes on to say how dreadful it is that a boy's attractiveness should be useful for their purpose and the body of a chaste soul should be offered without pity to their abominable deities. After this emotional outburst, the old man returns to describing how, in the absence of boys, the Bedouins rely on a spotless white camel for their sacrifice. The details of the ritual are then laid out: The Bedouins march around the camel three times; one of their sheikhs or priests leads the parade and they sing a hymn to the Morning Star; after the third circle, the leader of the march draws his sword, strikes the jugular vein of the camel and drinks the blood; the others then fall upon the camel and devour every bit of its flesh, entrails, and bones before the rising of the sun. The old man closes his description with a more general statement: the Bedouins shift from place to place and encamp where there is accessible fodder for their flocks and where they find a good supply of water.

Having completed his description of the barbarian Bedouin, the old man turns his attention to a way of life which ostensibly he knows best, the life of the eremite in the Sinai desert (613C):

> Those who pursue the monastic life choose a few places of the desert where somehow or other they take care of their bodily needs within reach of water. Some build huts, while others live in caves and hollows. A few know the nourishment that fire offers, and with diligence some are able to overcome the barrenness of such a desert for the production of food. With a small hoe they work as much of the scarce and poor soil as necessity forces them to do in order to eke out a living however inadequate it may be.[38] Most of them observe a diet of raw vegetables and fruits, and they are content with simple and plain food...so that

they might not devote a great deal of time to the care of the body and be neglectful of a more compelling pursuit. With a pure mind they worship God with sobriety and do not weigh down their reasoning power by overindulging in meat, nor do they flatter and please the stomach with the smell of sauces.

The mention of the delights of the table leads the old man into an excursus on the evils of gluttony in his day (616A–C) and the lengths to which the palate must be served by sight, smell, and taste. He then contrasts this with the eating habits of the eremites (616C–617B):

But their way of life is not like what has been described nor is it passionately eager for a luxurious mode of living. For not only have they set a limit on the quality of their pleasures and mock the excess of need as empty and unprofitable, but from the ways in which they so excel, they also strive zealously for a considerable amount of self-control, nourishing themselves just enough so as not to die against the will of the Creator and lose the rewards of working good deeds in life. On that account, some take food only on the Lord's day and spend the rest of the week abstaining from food. Others cut the time short and prepare a table twice weekly. Still others eat only on one day, earnestly showing by all possible means that they love needing nothing and fasting. They obey the laws of nature and yield only to their bodily needs, coming to such a necessity only when they perceive that the power of life is completely weakened and no longer helpful for the toils having to do with virtue. For within each of them their passion for angelic life is so intense that they wish to demonstrate their needing nothing by being content with little, and they eagerly contend to overcome the weakness of their nature by the excess of their desire.

The old man now turns his attention to other attitudes and practices of the Sinaitic solitaries (617C–620B). Money, he says, has no place among them for they neither buy nor sell. Each one provides the other with whatever is needed. Vegetables, fruits, and bread in short supply are tokens of love, love which is demonstrated not by the size or quality of the gift but by the manner in which it is bestowed. Jealousy and envy are not present. The one who is preeminent in virtue ascribes it to the power of God, not to his own efforts; he is not the one who performs praiseworthy things by himself; he is rather (620A) "an instrument of effective grace." Superiority is sought not in pride and presumption but in "a radiant life." On this account, these men have fled civilized society and live in the desert, showing their good actions to God from whom they hope to be recompensed for their labors. Their good works done for God are not shown to men, for the seeker of human glory is deprived of the true reward which is "eternal and true glory." As for their relationship to one another, the old man says (620C–621C):

They do not live near one another, but keeping themselves mostly shut up in their dwellings, they are separated from one another by a distance of about two and one-half miles (20 stadia) or more. They do so not out of misanthropy nor out of a beast-like nature (for how could those, who are so disposed to one another in the way I have described, be so?), but because they wish to train their character in deep solitude with a view toward what is pleasing to God, and they are eager to commune with the Divinity without distractions. This is either difficult or impossible to do properly in crowds and confusion, with the uproar of besieging neighbors distracting one's reasoning power and conditioning it for pleasurable rather than for useful things, things which should not be acted upon impulsive-ly. ... On the Lord's day they gather together in one congregation[39] on a regular basis, and they come to visit one another every week lest, perversely, complete separation may in time sever their bond of unity. For a while they forget their customary habits, for they are aware that excessive separation roils one's disposition and it unlearns the togetherness and partnership of love acquired by long association. So then, they take part in the divine mysteries and entertain each other with the exercise of suitable discourses, and they encourage each other with ethical advice.[40]

A rationale is provided for indulging in these ethical exercises (621A–B): The virtuous life is a struggle and it requires practice in order to overcome the skill of one's opponents and to avoid defeat. The entire battle is internal, in intellectual activity; there is death for those who choose to see only external things. In struggles of this kind, as in wrestling, those with experience must train those who are inexperienced. In this contest the beginner must take his stand with self-control against gluttony which contends with the soul and incites the mad frenzy of lust. The man who surrenders to the pleasure of food is easily conquered by the condition of his paunch. Those who are advanced in acquired skills of self-control teach beginners since they know how to break the holds of their opponents.

The old man now turns from gluttony to vanity and arrogance, and in the process changes his metaphor from wrestling to the sailor stormed at sea (621C–624B). Men of accomplishment persuade themselves and each other to renounce vanity and arrogance. Like storm-tossed sailors, they have been alert to all kinds of danger, avoiding shipwreck by "huge waves of emotion and the surge of impure thoughts." But if they relax or become lazy when they approach the harbor, they strike hidden shoals and lose their entire cargo in sight of their port. Vanity deprives deeds of their rewards and makes effort unprofitable for those who have worked hard. Arrogance is equally damaging for it rejects God as a help-mate in good things and ascribes to itself the power of right actions. The case against vanity and arrogance is brought to a close by citations from the Old Testament together with a bit of apposite explication added for each citation (624C). Haggai 1.6 is quoted against vanity; Proverbs 3.34 against arrogance. As a closing for his excursus on the life of the Sinaitic solitaries, the old man compares them to Moses and Elijah (625A–C). They practice their unassuming ways and imitate their virtue. The experiences of Moses (Exod. 3.1–2; 19ff.) and Elijah (1 Kings 19.7–13) in Sinai are summarized and introduce the statements mentioned above regarding the extension of Moses as a lawgiver to all nations when grace came to the entire race, and concerning Elijah who "saw God in a light breeze and heard the voice prophesying what He had decreed. The first and last convincing proof of men's fortitude and perseverance."[41] In contrast to the Israelites who merely passed through the desert, who grumbled at the food sent by heaven, who could not endure the absence of their leader for forty days, and who abused their freedom and deserted their faith, "these men, although lacking the necessities of life, spend all their time studying philosophy (*emphilosophousi*) in the desert and are the teachers to themselves of piety."

Narratio IV: Having concluded his description of two contrasting modes of life, Bedouin and eremitic, the old man turns once more to the events that have recently taken place. The Bedouins launched a sudden attack just as the worshipers were finishing their hymns. The old man and his son happened at that time to be coming down from the "sacred mountain" to make their customary visit to the holy men at the church at the site of the Burning Bush.[42] The raiders swooped down, plundered the food stores, and cruelly and sadistically slaughtered a number of the holy men, a slaughter which is described in fine detail (625D–632A). The old man and some others were allowed to escape. Those who ran up the mountain were not pursued by the Bedouins since "they believed that God stood there and had once revealed himself to the people" (632A). The old man remained transfixed since his son Theodoulus was being held captive by the Bedouins; only when his son gave him a sign with his eyes, did he take steps to save himself. The agonizing sight of Theodoulus being led away captive prompts the old man to comment on the nature of the pain of separation. For those who have not experienced this kind of pain, he says that they can learn from the example of dumb animals. He cites the close relationship between the cow and her calf; how, when her calf is taken from her, the cow expresses her grief by bellowing and by the expression in her eyes. The calf also demonstrates its pain on being separated by moaning and by frenetically running around its mother.

Following the analogy of the cow and her calf, the old man cries out his own pain as he watches his son disappearing from sight. Bewailing his son's captivity and the massacre of the holy men, he begins his lament, and complaint, to God with these words (633C–636A):

> Oh, you who are blessed and thrice blessed, what profit have you gained from self-control? What point to your patience and endurance? Is this the crown you have received for your continuing struggle? Are these the prizes reserved for you on behalf of your long contest? Is not the course of Justice useless? Is not the toil and trouble of virtue pointless since divine Providence had abandoned you when you were helpless and about to be murdered, and Justice did not stand up against the murderers, but the lawless hand prevailed against hallowed bodies, and by the defeat of truth, insolent impiety boasts of its victory?

The old man continues his series of rhetorical questions by asking why the Burning Bush did not take fire once more and burn the attackers; why the earth did not swallow them up as it one time did with Korah and his tribe (Num. 16.30); why Mount Sinai did not strike terror into the hearts of the outlaws with its flashes of lightning and the sound of its thunder. The avenging power did nothing, "nor with its strong hand did it shield those who were wronged so that they could experience its wonder and learn the incredible might of its invincible power" (636B). The holy men received no help, and they fell near the Burning Bush and the Mountain of the Giving of the Law. Where, the old man asks, was the power that drowned the Egyptians (Exod. 14.28); where was the power that struck down the enemy of the Israelites with hailstones (Josh. 10.11), and at another time blinded the enemy (2 Kings 6.18) and had them attacking one another? It curbed ferocious lions (Dan. 3.20–27) and it quenched the fire that faced the young men (Dan. 6.16–22). "Why did this power cause the virtue of these men to be attacked on all sides? Why did it abandon them, leaving them helpless, and cause them to be considered unworthly of its care?" (636C–637A.)

As if to answer his own *cri de coeur*, the old man provides a kind of *consolatio* on the subject of suffering (637A–B). Sorrow and depression on the part of those who struggle to learn self-control lead to blasphemy; many utterances by those who suffer are made against their better judgment. Divine assistance often abandons the righteous and gives them over to torture and slaughter "so that the genuine manliness of those who make the fight might be brought to light, and so that the luminous power of faith might shine forth." Suffering, even if it leads to death, overcomes the madness of the tormentors. Hence, those who have survived the Bedouin attacks do not wish to withdraw from the desert and prefer death to the indifferent way of life in the cities. Those who were killed preferred to die rather than to endure a life of evil in the inhabited world. They knew that the death of the soul was harder to bear than that of the body, and that death in sin was more perilous than death by the sword: the one holds little and transitory pain; the other holds long-lasting punishment.

The narrative turns back once more to the subject of the Bedouin attack (637C–640B). With the coming of night, those who had sought safety on the mountain came down to bury the dead. Among the victims they found one old man who was still alive and able to speak. They sat down beside him to lament his misfortune and spend the night with him. The holy man begs them not to be disturbed by his suffering, which he said was not to be compared with that of Job. Speaking metaphorically, he says: "For the Judge of the Games, as he places athletes before the Antagonist, knows the nature of his decision, and he offers prizes and glorious awards to those who accept blows with equanimity." Then, adapting the words of the apostle Paul (1 Cor. 2.9) to suit his own beliefs, and to continue his metaphor, the dying man says: "For the eye has not seen and ear not heard, and it has not entered into the heart of man what things God has prepared for those who contend on his behalf, things which surpass the contests of piety and perception and intellect."[43] God rewards the contestants with crowns and prizes exceeding all expectation, and makes his favor the reward for outstanding honor. Shortly after having made his final statement, the old eremite died and was buried along with the others.

Theodoulus' father brings the account of these events to a close with the words "and because the darkness was still hiding our departure, we were able to come to you." This is followed by a statement (640C) that two of those who were killed were called Paul and John, and there was also the elder (presbyteros) Theodoulus.[44] "They died on the seventh day after the Epiphany, which is the 14th of January. Pious men are very interested in learning the time and the names, since they want to check this information with the memories of holy men. Others were killed some years before, whose memory they celebrate on the same day because of the length of the journey and the size of the assemblage."[45]

Narratio V: At this point in the narrative, word is heard, dramatically, that someone has escaped from the hands of the Bedouin and will soon be present. A panting and panic-stricken young man arrives. He is the slave of a military official (stratêgos) who had finished his service with the government and, with his son and some others, was on his way to Pharan by way of the desert (641A–644A). Asked how he escaped, the slave tells the old man that he and Theodoulus were to be sacrificed at dawn to the Morning Star—he had learned this through a fellow-captive who understood the language of the Bedouins—and he therefore made up his mind to escape. Theodoulus, on the other hand, was afraid of being caught and, willing to abide by God's decision, decided not to make the attempt. That night, when the Bedouins were in a deep drunken sleep, he slipped passed their guards and made good his escape.

The young slave then tells a tale of horror, of slaughter, deception and sadism, that took place immediately following his capture (644B–648B). One captive was torn limb from limb. The slave's master and his son were deceived into believing they could be ransomed. A short distance from camp, the son was tortured and killed before his father's eyes. The slave says that his master should have been prepared for death, since the night before the Bedouins had cruelly put to death another of his slaves. The assignment was given to a young Bedouin in order to accustom the youth to cruelty. After being struck several times with the Bedouin's sword, the slave, in pain and anguish, fell back into the burning coals of the camp fire and finally died from both sword and fire.

On the following day, the slave goes on to report, as the Bedouins wandered through the desert, they came upon a patch of grass and a spring. While they let their animals graze and they refreshed themselves, they noticed a cave fashioned into a small house. They dragged out a man who was "venerable both in bearing and appearance." They killed him by throwing him off a rocky precipice. Nearby, the Bedouins came upon a young man "pale, wasted, but still showing the traces of a civilized background." They killed him as he gave thanks for having had his life taken from him while he still possessed his virtue; nothing had turned him away from his chosen occupation "contrary to his agreement with God" (649B).

At a small oasis a short distance away, the Bedouins found another small building which housed a young solitary of such nobility of spirit (megalopsychon) that even the Bedouins were forced to admire him. Even though he was promised that no harm would come to him if he would tell the whereabouts of the eremitic dwellings (monastêria) of his fellow solitaries, he refused not only to give them the information they desired, but he also refused to come out of his cell or to remove his clothing. To give that information, he said, would be a betrayal, and to yield to those who would use violence would be cowardice. He went on to say (652A–C):

For those who practice nobility of spirit, it is not right to give way to fear, even if the threat seems to hold no small amount of danger. For this practice is the path to greater things. And once cowardice has learned to rule us, it bids us to despise great and good things, and it teaches us to abandon piety itself whenever the fear of danger discovers one's judgment prostrating itself before cowardice. For if I now surrender the complete and absolute control of my capability to reason, and if I fear imminent death, how, in the face of outrages lying in store for me, and under the threat of torture, shall I not desert to impiety, accustomed as I am to value freedom from pain to what is expedient? Wherefore, since you have not achieved the things you hoped for, do not hesitate to do what you wish; for I shall not reveal to you the places in which the lovers of God (*theophileis*) live, although I do indeed know them. And even though you command it, I shall not come outdoors, nor shall I take off my clothes lest, while I am still in possession of my faculties and I am still master of my own resolve, someone might see me naked and look upon my body which until now not even my own eyes have seen. After I am dead, each one of you may do whatever he wishes with regard to looking upon my remains; for my judgment is no longer subject to reproach, but involuntary suffering of what is not sensate does not bring into question the strength and propriety of one's reasoning power when it has long since departed. For that which is lifeless is completely without feeling and is devoid of the capability of suffering; and what is devoid of the capability of suffering, it is agreed, is free from the complaints in those things which have caused suffering and which, at one and the same time, are deprived of suffering and not suffering. Now then I shall die within my house, fully clothed, as I have decided, and shall do nothing against my better judgment, though I have been tyrannized as if I were a slave. In the furrow in which I made my fight, I shall die; and my tomb shall be this humble dwelling which has long received the sweat of my struggle for virtue and now receives the blood of my bravery.

The determination of the young solitary so angered the Bedouins that they struck him again and again, and they went away writhing in anger that they could not inflict more punishment upon his dead body. Frustrated in their desire, the Bedouins fell upon and slaughtered three people who were making their way through the desert. The savage manner in which they attacked these travelers is likened to wild beasts or hunting dogs which, when they lose the scent of their prey, and are provoked to an even greater fury when they pick up the scent once more. While the Bedouins stood holding their swords dripping with warm and steaming blood, they spotted two eremitic dwellings separated from one another by some distance. Splitting their forces into two, they brought down one of the solitaries with arrows. (The young slave had no knowledge of what happened to the other one.) Though their prey was mortally wounded, the Bedouins cut him open from his genitals to his chest, and when he was dead they disemboweled him. With this the young slave concludes his tale of the savage cruelty which the Bedouins wreaked upon desert solitaries and travelers while he was their captive. He ends by reporting to the old man that he did not know what happened to Theodoulus, but that his son had no practical hope of remaining alive "because of the whisperings about his death."

Narratio VI: The old man, hearing these final words of the slave, was heartbroken and limp. He still had in mind a dream of his in which he had received a letter from Theodoulus which, by its salutation, indicated that his son was no longer among the living. This dream, together with the report he had just received, removed any doubt in his mind that Theodoulus was dead. Petrified with grief and transfixed by his loss, he could neither wail nor shed tears. A certain woman of Pharan, whose son happened to have been killed in the raid, brought back the old man to his senses. She had put on bright clothing and changed her whole appearance to one of joy. She stretched out her hands to heaven and "spoke words of this kind (phônas toiasde)[46] to God the Savior" 657B–661B):

> I committed my son to your care, Lord,[47] and he has been saved for me both now and forevermore. I entrusted my boy to you, and he has been truly protected, safe and unharmed. For I do not believe that he has died and in any way whatever ended his life, but that he has escaped experiencing sin of every kind. I notice not that his body was covered with wounds and that he submitted to a bitter end, but that he brought his pure and spotless soul thither [to you] and placed in your hands his unblemished spirit. I reckon his wounds as prizes. I count the blows as crowns. If only your body had room for more blows, my son, so that your rewards might have been greater! Wherefore, render me the rewards of my pregnancy. Wherefore, compensate me for the pains of childbirth. Wherefore, grant me the honors for nursing. Share with me the prizes of my labors, for the pain was common to both of us. You strove, and I loved the wounds of your struggle. You contended, and I rejoiced in your contest. You withstood the savages' fury, and I battled against the tyranny of my natural feelings. You scorned death; I disdained my deepest feelings. You bore the pain of your fatal wounds with patience; I endured the torment of my heart being torn to pieces. My suffering is equal and not inferior to yours. By the bitterness of your pain you prevail, but I have more than my share of it due to the length of time involved. For though you suffered much, death was but for an hour, but my pain is long and drawn out. And while I philosophize (philosophousa) and bear it pretty well, I am not insensible to suffering, but perforce exercise control over my pain. I feel the pain of the bonds of my bowels as they are being broken, and I tear at the recesses of my womb. Yet with sober and sensible reasoning I prevail over the calamities which rise up against me. For what is the good of frenzied grief that, in the process of being dissipated, is resolved unnaturally? On that account I did not imitate those mothers of mortal flesh who ignobly make an emotional display of such misfortunes. I did not emulate those breeders of mortal bodies who think only of this life, who know nothing of the life to be, and find it terrible and difficult to be separated from their dearest ones in the here and now. I did not tear my clothing and beat my bared breasts. I did not tear out my hair, nor did I disfigure my face with my fingernails, since I believe that you live a pure life with God, and that I will join you there after a brief old age, whenever and in whatever way my earthly vessel is broken. Blessed am I among mothers, having set such an adversary by the side of God! Blessed and thrice blessed! For I truly dare to boast further, you have gone to....[48] fear that envy would cause me harm for having planned something dangerous with regard to your soul. But go on, my son, go on that beautiful journey, go on! For I shall not concede first place to the patriarch Abraham, if I were competing against him. Nor shall I be content with receiving second place after him, since, when he was ordered, he readily and dispassionately offered up his son as a sacrificial victim to God. It is uncertain whether after making such an offering he remained free of emotion, since there were also many others who kept firm their resolve in these assignments, and after the act were inclined to grief, and by this change of heart proved the weakness of their nature. But now I am acting courageously and I change my expression of distress and sorrow to one of good cheer. When time subdues all those others and proves them less brave because of the length of time of their suffering, it consumes the force of their perserverance little by little. When memory has brought back the pain anew, it gives to one's reasoning capability the leisure to consider the distress of suffering free from fear. For it is hard and quite difficult to maintain a correct decision for a long time and preserve it completely

unchanged, since the power of reasoning is easily impelled to the opposite of what has been held. I once lamented my widowhood, and, as if helpless, I bewailed the absence of your father's protective care. But now what need to weep, what need to wail when I have such a champion at the side of God who can from that place defend me amid misfortunes, who can provide for me quite bounteously when I am old and gray, who can with authority draw from everflowing kindnesses (*charitôn*) and bring me more honor than if he were still alive and in command of kingly treasuries? Once that is spent from the latter, they run dry since their capacity is limited; but from the former there is an abundance which gushes forth and rains down, and shall never be exhausted.

The words and the courage of the Pharanite woman put the old man to shame. He considers her wise and himself mad, and he confesses (661D): "I thought it was right to blame God for the things I suffered, but then I realized I had sinned when I learned by the example of this woman that assaults of every dire kind can be borne." He makes the further observation that the sobriety of one who has overcome suffering often helps another sufferer, who is depressed at what he considers unsupportable, to recover his good spirits, and it teaches him not to give in readily to his suffering.

With this statement, the old man returns to narrating succeeding events (661D ff.).[49] The council (*boulê*) of Pharan decides to take action against those who perpetrated the attack by making representations to Ammanes, the Bedouin chief with whom the Pharanites had a treaty. Two young men are equipped as couriers and are sent off to Ammanes. While they are on their way, the old man and others go out to collect the bodies of the solitaries who had been killed in the raid. They discover that although they have been dead for five days, the bodies of the holy men have neither decayed nor have been mutilated by wild animals. The old man gives the names of seven of the dead solitaries and the names of five places in the wilderness in which their bodies were found.

On the way back to Pharan, the burial party met the two couriers who were returning with written word from Ammanes, the Bedouin chief. They brought news that he wished to reconfirm the peace treaty and that he extended an invitation to the relatives of the prisoners who were still alive to come to him. In addition, he promised retribution for those who had been murdered and the return of the property to those from whom it had been taken. The Bedouin chief was anxious not to break the treaty, since he derived many material advantages by keeping on good terms with the people of Pharan. Envoys were dispatched to seek out Ammanes for the purpose of revalidating the treaty. The old man, clinging to the hope that his son was among the prisoners, joined the envoy and others who were making the long trek through the wilderness to the camp of the Bedouin chief.

The journey through the desert took twelve days. On the eighth day, the band of travelers were out of water and suffering from thirst. Those who claimed to have some knowledge of the region said there was a spring nearby. Upon hearing this all members of the party scattered in a frantic search for water. The old man, slowed down by age and wishing to maintain a shred of his dignity, was left behind by the eagerness of the others. By chance, however, he took a direct route to the spring and stumbled upon it only to find it surrounded by a band of hostile Bedouins. In the vain hope that he might find his son among them, and willing either to be enslaved along with his son or to end his life and grief, he allowed himself to be seized and to be dragged about in a most violent manner. The others of his party, seeing what was happening to the old man, beat a hasty retreat. It was only when the armed guard that accompanied the group came upon the scene that the Bedouins released the old man and ran for their lives. Four days later, and without further incident, the envoys and others in the party reached the encampment of the Bedouin chief. Ammanes received them with friendship and hospitality. Matters relating to the attack were taken care of in short order. The old man, with beating heart, fearfully awaited news of his son. His ears and eyes take in every sound and facial expression, so intent is he on hearing news of whether his son is dead or alive. When he thought he could read nothing in the expression of their faces but gloom, he was sure that those around him were trying to conceal some unpleasant news. In strong language he asks the Bedouins for the truth; he will not be put off, nor will he be deceived by lies or by statements designed to hide the pain of truth. In philosophic fashion he states his conviction that facial expression reveals the hidden state of the soul. Grief cannot be hidden by a forced smile; appearance is not strong enough to hide the sufferings of the soul. "Now then," the old man says (673B), "I entreat you, either tell me the clear and straightfoward truth, or acknowledge that it has already been spoken, as I have already said, by your faces. For what advantage can there be in deluding a person in distress for a short time with false consolation, when later he will be distressed even more when the painful truth is detected?"

The old man is assured with many oaths that his son was alive, and that he had been sold to someone in the city of Elusa. Although his grief was lessened by this news, it was not healed completely, for he was now troubled by the idea that if his son was a slave, he would have limited access to him. Sometime later, on his way to Elusa with two guides generously provided by Ammanes, the old man meets a young trader who had been at the Bedouin encampment and knew of the old man's predicament. At Elusa, he had gotten in touch with Theodoulus and was now bearing a letter from him to his father. In addition to delivering the letter—the contents of which are not made known—he brought news that Theodoulus was well and that (676A) he had been bought by "a priest of the holy Christian mysteries" and that he was now performing the duties of a sexton (neôkoros), of the lowest grade in the hierarchy of the church. The old man thanked the trader profusely and then says (676B): "I attributed everything to the God of Providence. I cried and gave Him thanks for my unexpected joy, since He had freed me from my misfortune, which seemed without remedy, and was returning me to my former good fortune."

When the old man arrived at Elusa, he went directly to the holy temple (hagion neôn) where he wept and filled the sanctuary (temenos)[50] of God with loud laments. From there he went to the house where his son was living. The inhabitants of Elusa, knowing in advance his reasons for being there, followed the old man with smiling faces and joyfully called out to Theodoulus that his father had arrived. Father and son greeted one another tearfully. Overcome by the emotions of the moment, the old man falls into a dead faint. When he is revived, he begins to blame himself for having taken his son from a peaceful environment and transporting him to a land which caused him so much misery, a land which had no fear whatsoever of treachery. The old man bursts out (678C): "For the telling of a past experience is no longer painful, for just as health after sickness, and healing after wounds cheers one up and causes no distress, so the narration of sad events after their passing gives much pleasure, perhaps as much as the experiences give pain."[51]

Narratio VII: Theodoulus picks up his father's figure of speech and replies with sighs and tears (680B):

> Father, what profit is there in recalling those experiences since the recollection of suffering usually scratches a festering wound? For if the telling charms the ears of a listener who is fond of stories, and if it especially gives pleasure to hear another's suffering, it does not, nevertheless, free from pain the one who experienced it. Similarly, it does not take much to stir up a sympathetic reaction to a past suffering, in the same way as one causes pain by touching a scar that has not completely healed.

In spite of these remarks, Theodoulus gives in to his father's wishes, but he first admonishes him not to cry out or to weep (680C) "so that my voice is hidden by the sounds of your wailing." He also states his unwillingness to repeat the details reported by the slave who escaped from the Bedouins and made his way back to Pharan. To do so would be a digression and mere idle talk. He then relates his experiences by telling what happened on the evening before he was to be sacrificed. Everything was in readiness: the altar, the knife, the drink-offering, the bowl, the frankincense. Death awaited him at dawn "unless God intended to prevent it, which he did." He lay on the ground and prayed in secret to God. He prefaces his prayer with the observation that when a person is secure, he thinks of secular pursuits—and names some twenty such, as business, voyaging, planting, begetting children, lawsuits, office-seeking, etc.—but when his security is threatened, he becomes obsessed with his troubles and he entreats God as the only one who can help free him from his difficulties. Theodoulus then recalls the words of his prayer (681C–684B):

> Lord, creator of every sentient and intelligent creature, you who hold in your hand the hearts of your creations, and turn provocation and senseless rage into compassion, whenever in your good judgment you wish to save those given up to death by the decree of authoritiy; you who tame the fierceness of wild beasts thrashing about for the flesh of human bodies; you who cast back the streaming rush of fire, and by your very command make the high flickering flame die down; you who protect unharmed those who have been condemned to die, and demonstrate by your mysterious and marvelous power that their hair and skin are stronger than fire; save him who has no hope of help from any other quarter; save him who has not as yet been deprived of life by the enemy's decision, who in all likelihood is already a corpse. Do not give them my blood as a drink-offering for their deities (*daimosi*), nor let their evil spirits (*pneumata ponêra*) take pleasure at the smell of my flesh. They have prepared to sacrifice me to the star that takes its name from sexual lust. Do not let my body, which has remained chaste to this very day, become an offering and a victim of their deity (*daimonos*) named for licentiousness, but make the bestial heart of the savages kind and gentle, you who softened the seething rage of Ahasuerus, king of Media, against Esther, and turned his cruel heart to compassionate pity. Save the soul that is dedicated to serving you, and restore to my elderly father, who is also your servant, his son who knows not [of evil] and who is intent on serving God according to his purpose. Not out of fear of danger do I offer this pledge, so that the promise of my safe return may be considered a recompense for it, for by my power to reason I have anticipated the necessity of suffering. Show that faith is a swifter means to safety than feet, and that hope is more trustworthy than flight.

Theodoulus continues his prayer by further contrasting that he has placed his trust in God's power whereas his fellow captive placed his in swiftness of foot and in the darkness of night that covered his escape. After passing a sleepless night in prayer and tears, he raised his head to find that dawn had come, and with the appearance of the Morning Star, the time for the ritual sacrifice had passed. Theodoulus reports that he offered a jubilant but silent prayer to God (685A):

> Lord, in dealing with me, make your mercy a thing of wonder, you who have the power over life and death, just as you made it a thing of wonder with the holy men when they were in distress and were saved from every affliction, in order that we may have the confidence to call upon you and to have no fear, since we shall be saved from misfortunes which befall us, and so have an example of your help.

Theodoulus goes on to cite instances in which God rescued holy men from their misfortunes: Isaac as he was about to be sacrificed by his father (Gen. 22.9–12); Joseph plotted against by his brothers (Gen. 37.18) and ultimately reunited with his father (Gen. 46.29); Jacob fleeing from the rage of Esau (Gen. 27.41–43); Moses when he was fleeing from the Egyptians (Exod. 2.15);

the two boys restored to life and their bereft mothers (1 Kings 17.22; 2 Kings 4.34). Theodoulus concludes his prayer with these words (685B):

> Lord, you alone are unchangeable and work miracles, now as well as then, with that same power. Give me back then to my father who has hope in your mercy, Sovereign Lord,[52] and with your help free him from his inconsolable grief, and let those who know not your name wonder at your might and your strength, O much praised King of all power!

Having concluded a verbatim report of his prayer, Theodoulus continues the story of his adventures following his capture (688A–C). The Bedouins were disturbed by the fact that the proper time for the sacrifice had passed. They also discovered that their other young captive had escaped during the night. When they did not threaten him further, Theodoulus acted more boldly. He refused, though ordered, to eat forbidden food (*miarophagein*), and he refused to sport (*prospaizein*) with their women.[53] So it was until they came to settled areas where he as taken to a village and offered up for sale. When no one bid more than two pieces of gold, the Bedouins took him outside the village, and placing a sword at his neck, threatened to behead him if no one purchased him. He pleaded most abjectly to passers-by until someone took pity on him and paid the Bedouins their price. Knowing that his father's tears and moans would spoil the joy of their reunion, Theodoulus brings his abbreviated report to a close and asks his father to glorify God for his unexpected and wondrous salvation.

The old man replies (688C–689B) that he, Theodoulus, had been saved by the grace of God, and though danger and death had awaited him, he had escaped unharmed. Yet, he goes on to say philosophically, experience and anticipation are the same; however, the anticipation of death is far more painful than the experience of a quick death-blow. Returning to his own situation, the old man tells his son that at the time of his affliction, he vowed to God that if Theodoulus were brought back alive, he would impose upon himself "the harsh servitude of self-control and other suffering." Since his prayer has had a happy end, he asks Theodoulus not to violate his agreement, nor deceive the One who fulfilled his vow.

Theodoulus readily agrees, saying that since he has escaped the experience of death while his father only that of grieving for him, he has all the more reason to accede to his father's wishes. He would render his thanks to God on behalf of his father even if he had to suffer something terrible for the favor He granted. In support of this, he cites the instance of Jephtha's daughter (Judges 11.37). If she willingly became a sacrificial victim for her father, why should he not rush to be a payer of his father's debt? This talk of favors, gifts, and payment of debts leads Theodoulus into a long and intricate metaphor on how God receives the payment of debts (689B–C):[54]

> I am going to repay this debt to God who knows how to reciprocate the payment of debts with a second favor (*chariti*). For He receives the debt that is paid back, not as a debt, but as a loan. And agreeing to be in debt for its repayment, He moreover makes an additional payment for the kind consideration of the debtor as a gift for the loan. He always pays out favors (*charitas*) in advance, and He always guarantees (*cheirographounti*) to be in debt to those who borrow his good services. Further, He considers full repayment of these debts a matter of honor so that He may have authority over favors forever, and as a debtor He may repay favors by virtue of the generous and honorable character of his nature. Wherefore, father, since you have [in me] an eager co-payer, begin your repayment.

Theodoulus assures his father that God will demand payment of their debts only in proportion to their ability to pay. The old man prayerfully hopes that his vow will have a happy end and that their efforts will be rewarded. For, he says, this is the end of every task done for God, that deeds are confirmed with rewards and crowns attest to the struggle. "Prizes are undisputed testimony of the contest" (692A).

With the conclusion of this dialogue, the old man rapidly brings the narrative to a close (692A–693B). The bishop of Elusa took care of him and his son for an extended period of time. He asked them to stay on, but so as not to appear to be forcing them to that decision by virtue of the price he paid for Theodoulus, he indicated that he would not insist upon the terms of the obligatory service contract (*paramonê*) which he held on the young man. He did insist, however, that they, father and son, assume "the yoke of priesthood." Theodoulus and his father protested that they were unworthy of such a burden which, they said, was hardly appropriate for holy men insofar as it accorded with their way of life. Even when these holy men were called, priesthood seemed to them to be a burden. They pleaded weakness and said that the honor was more than right for them. Although by their training, they were more capable than others in giving service to the Lord, they declined election to the office for a long time.

The bishop, acceding to the wishes of Theodoulus and his father to return to Sinai, provided them with provisions for their long journey and graciously sent them off with his prayers. With this, the events of the narrative are concluded. The writer then makes a simple final statement:

> Let my story (*logos*) thus come to an end, since my suffering has ended, and the experience, with God's grace, has provided the beginning of a more joyful life after much affliction.

New York University

---

[1] W. F. Albright, *Yahweh and the Gods of Canaan* (New York, 1968), 239–40.

[2] J. P. Migne, *Patrologia series graeca*, 79, cols. 589–693. Peter Possines, the seventeenth–century editor, arranged the text into seven episodes for the convenience of the reader (col. 584, n.2). This arrangement has no basis in the text tradition. As for the text itself, it has not, of course, been edited according to modern standards. Imperfect as it may be in some details, it is, however, remarkably consistent in terms of its content. But whoever was responsible for giving the title of *diêgêmata* to this work (cols. 583–584) had something in mind which I am not sure is conveyed by the Latin translation of *Narrationes*. *Narratio* is a common translation for *diêgêsis* (the statement of the facts in a case, narration, narrative). The word *diêgêma*, though translated as "tale" or as Latin *fabula*, has more the connotation of an elaboration, a setting out in detail, a description. Interestingly enough, the text itself uses the words *historia* (612A), *diêgêsis* (600A, 677C) and *logos* (693B) to convey such meanings as "description," "narration," "story." I would, therefore, translate the full title as: "Nilus, the desert solitary: His detailed account of the massacre of the monks on Mount Sinai and of the captivity of his son Theodoulus." However, since the word *Narrationes* has become attached to the text, I have used it consistently throughout this paper. I have avoided its singular form, *narratio*, except in dealing with individual episodes designated as such within the text.

[3] P. Mayerson, "The Desert of Southern Palestine according to Byzantine Sources," *Proceedings of the American Philosophical Society* 107.2, 160–72.

[4] E.g., R. Devréesse, "Le Christianisme dans la péninsula sinaïtique des origines à l'arrivée des Musulmans," *Revue Biblique*, 49 (1940), 222; B. Altaner, *Patrology*, trans. H. C. Graef (New York, 1961), 390; J. Quasten, *Patrology*, vol. 3 (Utrecht, 1966), 496–97.

[5] "Nilus der Asket und der Überfall der Mönche am Sinai," *Neue Jahrbücher für das klassische Altertum*, 37 (1916), 107–21. "Untersuchungen zu Nilus dem Asketen," *Texte und Untersuchungen zur Geschichte der altchristlichen Literatur*, 42.2 (1917), 123–59. For a summary of Heussi's position, see his *Das Nilusproblem* (Leipzig, 1921), 6–10, and his article "Neilus" in *Pauly's Real-Encyclopädie d. klass. Altertumswissenschaft*, 16.2, col. 2186.

[6] "Ist der sogenannte Nilus-Bericht eine brauchbare religionsgeschichtliche Quelle?" *Anthropos*, 50 (1955), 81–148. The article of V. Christides, "Once again the 'Narrations' of Nilus Sinaiticus," *Byzantion*, 43 (1973), 39–50, has just recently come to my attention. Christides opposes the extreme position take by Henninger and attempts to take a more balanced view of the *Narrationes*, particularly with respect to the ethnographical data dealing with human and animal sacrifice.

[7] *Op. cit.* (above, n. 3), 161. See also Albright, *op. cit.* (note 1), 239–40: "True adventures in the Arabian desert have often sounded quite incredible, as I know from my own earlier life."

[8] *Op. cit.* (above, n. 1), 239. In Albright's view, the writer of the narrative was no one other than the well-known Nilus of Ancyra.

[9] One need only read von Grunebaum's treatment of love and separation motifs in Greek romances to see how far removed this narrative is from the genre of romantic literature. G.E. von Grunebaum, "Greek Form Elements in the Arabian Nights," *Journal of the American Oriental Society*, 62 (1942), 277–92.

[10] I have carefully avoided translating *hagios* as "saint" in the belief that it would mislead some readers as to the character of the solitaries mentioned in the *Narrationes*. Hence, I have consistently used "holy man" as a more neutral and more accurate translation of the word.

[11] Col. 612. The context would seem to support the translation of "the superior life." Of course, the meaning could be "former life" and would be applicable if the writer were talking about the life of the holy men who had just been massacred.

[12] *Op. cit.*, (above, n. 4), 497.

[13] Quasten, *op. cit.* (above, n. 4), 175, 497.

[14] F. Degenhart, *Der heilige Nilus Sinaita* (Munster, 1915), 25–26.

[15] *Texte u. Untersuch.*, (above, n. 5), 151–52.

[16] For a detailed discussion of the synaxarion for 12 November and its relationship to the narrative, see Heussi, *Texte u. Untersuch.* (above, n. 5), 16–22. For various other synaxaria and menologies relating to Nilus and Theodoulus, see *PG 79*, cols. 26–34; 663–66; 692–93.

[17] *Propylaeum ad Acta Sanctorum Novembris. Synaxarium ecclesiae Constantinopolitanae*, ed. H. Delehaye (Brussels, 1902), col. 217. See also, Heussi, *Texte u. Untersuch.* (above, n. 5), 17–18.

[18] *Historia ecclesiae*, 14.54.

[19] Since we are in the dark as to the true identity of the writer, I designate him simply as "the old man" (col. 592B: *presbyta*, see also 668A and 684A), "the writer of the narrative," or "the father of Theodoulus." I have resisted calling him "the pseudo-Nilus." In my earlier article (above, n. 3) I sidestepped the issue and referred to the writer as Nilus.

[20] In *Horae Semiticae*, vol. 9. Agnes Smith Lewis, trans. (Cambridge, 1912), 1–14. The document is obviously a late fabrication (sixth century?). For a critique of the account, see Devréesse, *op. cit.* (above, n. 4), 216–19.

[21] It should be noted that our text is not so much a descriptive narrative as it is a series of speeches—"orations" might perhaps be a better word—linked together by brief descriptions of events. Approximately two-thirds of the *Narrationes* is made up of these speeches.

[22] Scriptural citations or allusions will be noted in the epitome that follows the conclusion of these observations. In terms of the books and numbers of times cited, they may be summarized as follows: Genesis, 8 times; Exodus, 2; Numbers, 1; Joshua, 1; Judges, 1; 1 Samuel, 1; 1 Kings, 4; 2 Kings, 4; Job, 1; Psalms, 1; Proverbs, 1; Daniel, 2; Haggai, 1; Matthew, 1; Corinthians, 1; Epistle to Hebrews, 1.

[23] 1 Corinthians 2.9 (col. 640A-B) and Hebrews 11.37 (col. 609A); for Herod, Matthew 2.16 (col 609B).

[24] Psalms 79.3 (col. 609A); Haggai 1.6 and Proverbs 3.34 (col. 624B-C).

[25] See *e.g.*, below, pp. 63, 67.

[26] See below, pp. 65, 66–7, 69.

[27] See below, pp. 60–62.

[28] Degenhart, *op. cit.* (above, n. 14), 86. See also Quasten, *op. cit.* (above, n. 4), 498. Quasten also calls attention to the fact that Nilus of Ancyra made ample use of allegorical interpretation of Scriptural passages. Our text has no suggestion of the use of allegory.

[29] A tantalizing bit of information. The writer does not give us a clue as to the nature of these divine mysteries. One can speculate, in view of the interest of the writer in the books of the Old Testament, that there may have been readings from the Scriptures, and possibly, as part of the "mystery" some allegorical exegesis. In the absence of Christological material, it is difficult to believe that the divine mystery represented any of the rituals, such as the taking of the Eucharist, associated with Christian practices. To take this one step further, if these solitaries had not congregated on a regular basis and shared a common ritual however slight, one might be inclined not to consider them as members of a sect but rather as individuals responding to an impulse of ethical and theosophical asceticism. In the latter respect, they are almost indistinguishable from Porphyry's perception of a philosopher (*de abst.* 2.49): "... the philosopher, as a priest of God who is over all things, abstains from all flesh of living creatures, earnestly striving to approach God through himself and without being disturbed by others around him—alone to the Alone—and he is circumspect, having inquired into the necessities of nature. For one who is really a philosopher is skilled in and observant of many things; he comprehends the works of nature, he is intelligent, decent, temperate, and in every respect the savior of himself."

[30] There is an inconsistency here which I believe can be explained. The writer of the narrative describes a lay community and a way of life for his desert solitaries that make no mention of churches, priests, and the singing of hymns (col. 613C–625C; below 60–62). However, it appears that he and his son were accustomed to visit the

holy men and their church at the site of the Burning Bush, this being a more conventional and organized group of Christians that ultimately developed into the celebrated Monastery of St. Catherine on Mount Sinai.

[31] Most scholars take it for granted that Theodoulus and his father were ordained as priests. The text, however, says much about the Bishop's pressing them and about their protests that they were unworthy of such a burden, but it says nothing explicitly to the effect that they accepted the Bishop's bid and were ordained.

[32] *Cf.* Eusebius, *Demonst. Evang.* 1.3.43: "Moses himself declares with reason that on account of these things another prophet will be raised like himself. He proclaims that this man will be a lawgiver for all nations. He speaks enigmatically of Christ...." Eusebius also makes the point (*ibid.*, 1.3.42; 1.4.1) that the Mosaic law could not be used by all as a model for their lives. Jesus, he says, bid his apostle not to teach the Mosaic law to all nations, but rather to teach all that is contained in the Gospels. Eusebius accepted the books of the Old Testament as "our own for they contain prophecies concerning us, the Gentiles."

[33] I have given a full translation of the lament of the Pharanite woman on the death of her son (657B–661B). I have done so in the belief that her speech is the narrative's best in terms of emotional appeal and in demonstrating the rhetorical skill of the writer. I also believe that the lament can rank among the finest in post-Classical Greek literature.

[34] It is obvious, for whatever purpose the writer had in mind, that the people being addressed here (*tines*) are not the inhabitants of Pharan. (See above, p. 54). They appear to be newcomers who knew very little about the region, Bedouin customs, or about the recent events which the writer is going to relate. The conversations between the writer and these people take place from the very beginning of the narrative to the time that an escapee from the Bedouin camp appears on the scene, that is, for the first four episodes (cols. 589–640).

[35] Reading *hagiôn* for *hagôn* or *agôn*, neither of which seems to make sense here. If *agôn* were in a different position within the sentence, one might translate: "through it (i.e., observation) it (a life of tranquillity) leads it (the soul) as it progresses systematically near the knowledge of God."

[36] This is the writer's justification for leaving his wife and pursuing the life of a solitary in the desert, It can hardly be described as a religious motive (see above, p. 56).

[37] See above, p. 55.

[38] I am particularly struck by the authenticity of this statement which is in keeping with the environment of the Sinai desert. These solitaries, unlike their opposite numbers in Egypt, cultivated patches of arable soil in the wadis close to their dwellings. We hear nothing of the reeds and marshes, of the weaving of baskets and palm leaf mats that one comes across in reading accounts of eremites in the deserts of Egypt. For a description of wadi-cultivation, see P. Mayerson, "The Ancient Agricultural Regime of Nessana and the Central Negeb," *Excavations at Nessana*, H. D. Colt, ed., vol. 1 (London, 1962), 233–41.

[39] I have translated *ekklêsian mian* as "one congregation." Possines (col. 620, note 53) indicates that *mian* in the manuscript is marked with an obelus. Apparently, there was some difficulty in thinking that the words meant "one church," which would not be meaningful in this context.

[40] See above, p. 56.

[41] *Ibid.*

[42] *Ibid.*

[43] The quotation, "the eye has not seen .... into the heart of man ...," which St. Paul quotes and apparently adapted for his own purposes, is also quoted and similarly adapted by Clement of Alexandria in *Protrep.* 10 and 12, and in *Div. Salv.* 23. It is difficult to know whether this old man or the writer of the *Narrationes* had 1 Cor. 2.9. in mind or whether the words came to him from another source, the likelihood being that they were widely circulated and lent themselves to a variety of occasions.

[44] Heussi, *Texte u. Untersuch.* (above, n. 5), 133, takes it for granted that the "elder Theodoulus" is a presbyter of the church. I believe that the writer merely wishes to make it clear that this Theodoulus should not be confused with his son who bore the same name. If he did not make some distinction, his audience would have been bewildered.

[45] If this statement is not an interpolation, it must be taken as an aside and for the information of his readers. However, it seems to be completely out of place, coming as it does after the writer finishes his description of past events and just before the dramatic opening words of the following episode: "While we were still speaking about this, we were told that someone had escaped..."

[46] The writer here gives us a clue to his rhetorical technique of making his speakers say what he believes is called for by each situation.

[47] The writer consistently uses the word *despotês* for "Lord" except when citing from the Scriptures where, naturally, *kyrios* is used. No such consistency is shown in the letters of Nilus of Ancyra, his major work, where the words *kyrios* and *despotês* are used without any apparent distinction.

[48] There is some textual difficulty at this point (660B) which is also reflected in the variant readings provided in the critical apparatus.

[49] For a rationalization of these and succeeding events, and how these events accord with local conditions of the period, see P. Mayerson, *op. cit.* (above, n. 3), 162–69.

[50] Did the writer observe something at Elusa that would cause him to use these word to designate a church in place of the more conventional word *ekklêsia,* or were they used for rhetorical effect? I raise the question since I maintain that the narrative reliably describes the early state of Christianity at Elusa (see above, n. 3, 167–68). Do we have evidence here of some pagan structure (temple?) being used as a church, or of a church in the process of being built?

[51] An unusual and striking outburst for a philosopher, but in keeping with the emotional temperament of the old man.

[52] *dynasta* (Sovereign Lord), an uncommon substitute for *despota* or *kyrie.*

[53] The Bedouins probably knew that solitaries like Theodoulus were pledged to vegetarianism and celibacy. They seem to be having a bit of fun at the young man's expense.

[54] There is something in this extraordinary metaphor which suggests that the writer had been a business man at one point in his life. The text, of course, gives us no indication of what his vocation was prior to his pursuing the life of a philosopher and a solitary.

AN INSCRIPTION IN THE MONASTERY OF ST. CATHERINE AND THE MARTYR TRADITION IN SINAI

Philip Mayerson

AN attempt to clarify an abbreviated numeral in an inscription in the Monastery of St. Catherine on Mount Sinai has raised several questions concerning the resolution of the abbreviation, the meaning of the inscription, and the character of the martyr tradition in Sinai. The text of the inscription has, of course, been known for many years, but only lately has it been reedited by Professor I. Ševčenko, the epigrapher of the Alexandria–Michigan–Princeton Archaeological Expedition to the Monastery of Saint Catherine at Mount Sinai.[1] The text is inscribed on a marble plaque located in the South Chapel of the monastery where, according to Professor Ševčenko, the slab protects "the relics of Sinai's Holy Fathers..., who rest in the basilica's South Chapel, a place often reserved for relics in the early churches of Syria."[2] The portion of the inscription relevant to this discussion reads:

† Τῆς δ̄ δεκάδος τὴν διὰ τοῦ αἵματος κο-
λυμβήθραν ζηλώσαντες οἱ ἰσάριθμοι ὅσιοι
π(ατέ)ρ(ε)ς | ἐνθάδε κατάκεινται κτλ.

According to Ševčenko, the text, "hitherto misunderstood, commemorates the 'four times ten' fathers (of Sinai) who had 'imitated the baptism by blood of an equal number of Martyrs.'"[3] Ševčenko derives the number "four times ten" or "forty" from δ̄ dekados; and although, as he reported to me in a telephone conversation, he has no epigraphic analogue or parallel for "four times ten," he was led to the number by a historical—rather, a questionable historical—account, namely Ammonius' *Forty Martyrs of the Sinai Desert*.[4] Professor Ševčenko dates the inscription to the late sixth century and cites it as "an epigraphic *pendant* to literary fabrications" of that time.[5] He is led to this conclusion by the absence of a clear historical reference to forty martyrs who could have provided the model for the Sinaitic monks. He rules out the martyrdom of the forty at Sebaste on the grounds that they met their end by freezing to death on a lake and not by a baptism of blood.[6] The one reference to forty martyrs with a Sinaitic provenance is found in Ammonius' account, a description of two almost simultaneous attacks on the monks at Raithou and Mount Sinai, which resulted in the violent deaths of forty solitaries at each site.[7] Although the narrative claims to be an eyewitness account of attacks by Saracens and Blemmyes late in the fourth century, it is, according to R. Devreesse,[8] of a late date and unreliable for the early history of Sinai. Professor Ševčenko, relying on the conclusions of Devreesse, cites the Ammonius narrative as having been "composed—perhaps by some learned Sinaitic monk—toward the end of the sixth century"; hence his view of the inscription as "an epigraphic *pendant* to literary fabrications undertaken roughly at the same time

---

[1] I. Ševčenko, "The Early Period of the Sinai Monastery in the Light of its Inscriptions," *DOP*, 20 (1966), 258, 263. See also summary in G. H. Forsyth and K. Weitzmann, *The Monastery of Saint Catherine at Mount Sinai. The Church and Fortress of Justinian* (Ann Arbor [1973], 20, pl. CII,d.

[2] Ševčenko, *op. cit.*, 258.

[3] *Ibid.*

[4] Forsyth and Weitzmann, *op. cit.*, 20; Ševčenko, *op. cit.*, 258.

[5] Forsyth and Weitzmann, *loc. cit.*; Ševčenko, *loc. cit.*

[6] Ševčenko, *loc. cit.*

[7] The Greek text, *Ammoniou monachou logos*, in *Illustrium Christi martyrum lecti triumphi*, ed. F. Combefis (Paris, 1660), 88–132; a Syriac text, dated to the seventh century, and English translation in *The Forty Martyrs of the Sinai Desert*, trans. A. S. Lewis, Horae Semiticae, IX (Cambridge, 1912), 1–14 (English), 2–53 (Syriac).

[8] "Le christianisme dans la péninsule sinaïtique, des origines à l'arrivée des musulmans," *RBibl*, 49 (1940), 219.

in order to provide the newly founded monastery—or at least its site—with martyrs of its own."[9]

Leaving aside for the moment the resolution of the abbreviated numeral in the inscription, Professor Ševčenko's conclusions could lead us to believe (a) that there were no martyrs in Sinai—that is, martyrdom achieved by falling victim to violence at the hands of non-Christians, in this case Bedouins, whether called Agareni, Saracens, or Blemmyes; and (b) that the Ammonius narrative was composed prior to the time that the inscription was put in place in the South Chapel. For the latter, there is simply no evidence whatsoever, other than Ševčenko's assumption that the inscription bears a number taken from the Ammonius narrative or from other fictional narratives, to prove that the narrative preceded the inscription. As for the matter of martyrdom, there is reasonably sound evidence of Bedouin attacks on the eremitic communities on and around Mount Sinai from the fourth century on.[10] Even Devreesse, upon whom Ševčenko relies for an appreciation of the Ammonius narrative, states that many of the details in the account were "fabricated toward the end of the sixth century by learned monks of Sinai to give a sensational context to a bloody incursion or to a massacre of peninsular monks unexpectedly occuring on a certain January 14th; the number of forty martyrs—eighty on an exact count—could even have been borrowed from another literary source."[11] To this we can add the "Nilus" *Narrationes*, which were most likely composed at an earlier date (late fourth or early fifth century) than the Ammonius narrative, and which, although treated as a piece of pious fiction with regard to the abduction and recovery of a certain Theodoulus, preserve the historical reminiscence of the massacre of a number of Sinaitic monks and solitaries at the hands of Bedouins.[12]

If the inscription in the South Chapel refers to those who imitated forty martyrs, who could the original forty have been? There are two possibilities. One, of course, is the forty of Sebaste; the other is the forty martyrs of Palestine, the most distinguished of whom was Silvanus, the bishop of the churches around Gaza, who at an earlier stage in his career had spent some time as a solitary on Mount Sinai.[13] It would seem plausible, therefore, that the forty martyrs from Palestine, who had indeed suffered martyrdom by a baptism of blood—they were beheaded—would, by their proximity to Sinai and by Silvanus' association with the region, have provided the model for the martyrs mentioned in the inscription. But, however plausible these forty might be, their martyrdom does not seem to have created a lasting tradition. If it had not been for Eusebius' mention of them, they might have been lost to history.

We are on far surer ground with the forty from Sebaste. We need not be deterred, as was Ševčenko, by the fact that these martyrs died by freezing to death and not by some form of violence; death by any means in the unrelenting pursuit of the Christian faith merits the accolade of "baptized by blood," a glory greater than that of "baptism by water."[14] Basil of Caesarea, who delivered a homily in a church erected in honor of these victims of Licinian repression, adds several other interesting details, including a "baptism by blood." He tells the story of one of the guards who, when one of the forty weakened in his faith, cried out that he was a Christian, and rushed out on the ice to take the place of the apostate, and thus

[9] Ševčenko, *op. cit.*, 258.

[10] P. Mayerson, "The Desert of Southern Palestine according to Byzantine Sources," *PAPS*, 107 (April, 1963), 161–62.

[11] Devreesse, *op. cit.*, 219–20.

[12] Mayerson, *op. cit.*, 160–72. See also *idem*, "Observations on the 'Nilus' *Narrationes*," *JARCE*, 12 (1975), 51–74.

[13] Sozomenus, *Ecclesiastical History*, VI, 32.8; Eusebius, *Ecclesiastical History*, VIII,13.5. Although Eusebius speaks here of "forty save one," the number becomes simply "forty" in his *History of the Martyrs of Palestine*, XIII,11. See Eusebius, *The Ecclesiastical History and the Martyrs of Palestine*, ed. H. J. Lawlor and J. E. L. Oulton, I (London, 1927), 399 (long recension), and Eusebius, *History of the Martyrs in Palestine*, ed. and trans. from the Syriac by W. Cureton (London, 1861), 48.

[14] See, e.g., "Baptism by Blood," in *Encyclopaedia of Religion and Ethics*, ed. J. Hastings, II (New York, 1955), 411–12.

"filled out the number [of forty]."[15] Of this martyr, Basil goes on to say: "He was baptized into Him, not by another, but by his own faith, not in water but in his own blood."[16] He adds further that the forty were burned while their stiffened bodies still showed signs of life. Within a fairly short period of time, relics and legends of the Forty of Sebaste increased in number, and churches in their name proliferated in both the East and the West.[17]

In Sinai itself, the evidence for the tradition of the Forty Martyrs of Sebaste is quite secure. The library of the Monastery of St. Catherine contains at least four accounts of their martyrdom. Although all of these are in the Arabic collection and date between the twelfth and fourteenth centuries, they are undoubtedly translations from Greek accounts of an earlier date.[18] Further, we have some more tangible evidence from a location near the monastery itself. In the Wadi Leja, at the foot of Mount Sinai, is a structure called Deir el Arbain, "The Monastery of the Forty." According to E. H. Palmer, it was used in his time as a resting place for the night by pilgrims who had ascended Mount Sinai and were preparing for the ascent of Mount St. Katherina on the following day.[19] S. C. Bartlett describes the spring and the rather extensive gardens surrounding the old monastery, but states that the building itself was small, its interior measuring only about twenty-two

by sixteen feet in front of the chancel.[20] Unfortunately, we have no information on the date of the construction of the monastery or on the date it was given the name of Deir el Arbain.

Having confirmed the existence of the tradition of the Forty Martyrs of Sebaste in Sinai, and, further, taking into account the biblical associations with the number forty and its significance for the residents of a monastery in Sinai, we can easily appreciate the influences which led Ammonius to fix upon the number forty for the martyrs at Raithou and Mount Sinai. The influence of the number forty in this narrative, however, does not prove that the inscription in the South Chapel is "an epigraphic *pendant*" to a literary fabrication.

Let us now return to this inscription. As stated above, Ševčenko would translate *d dekados* as "four times ten" and would relate the number to the forty martyrs cited in the Ammonius narrative or in some other unknown literary fabrication. I take a contrary view. I do not believe that the number can be supported either by other citations or by the normal expectation of anyone reading it as an equivalent of the number forty. In my view, one should read *d̄ dekados* simply as "fourteen" in the genitive case (*tessares kai dekados* or *tessareskaidekados*), *d̄* being the common abbreviation for the number four. The task before us is to find some explanation for the use of the number fourteen in the inscription even though it may present some difficulty in interpretation.

If we examine the martyr tradition of Sinai, one incident of violence and suffering— and only one—etched itself deeply into the memory of the early Christian inhabitants of that remote region: a Bedouin raid on January 14 which took the lives of a number of monks and solitaries on and around the Holy Mountain. The year cannot be pinpointed—it seems to have been sometime between 373 and 410[21]—but the date of

[15] *Homilia in Quadraginta Martyres*, PG, 31, cols. 520–21. (Gregory of Nyssa also delivered three orations on the Forty of Sebaste, in PG, 46, cols. 749–88.)

[16] *Loc. cit.*

[17] See, e.g., "Forty Martyrs," in *The Catholic Encyclopedia*, VI, ed. C. G. Herbermann et al. (New York, 1909), 153. For a legendary account of the discovery of the relics of the Forty in Constantinople, see Sozomenus, *Ecclesiastical History*, IX,2.

[18] M. Kamil, *Catalogue of All Manuscripts in the Monastery of St. Catherine on Mount Sinai* (Wiesbaden, 1970), 44–50, nos. 527, 537, 569, 574. Other references to this famous martyrdom are possibly to be found in the historical accounts, homilies, and martyrdoms in the Greek and Arabic collections which are not specifically catalogued as "The Forty Martyrs of Sebaste."

[19] *The Desert of the Exodus*, I (London, 1871), 119.

[20] S. C. Bartlett, *From Egypt to Palestine* (New York, 1879), 276–77. The frontispiece in Lewis, *op. cit.* (*supra*, note 7), is an illustration of the ruined Monastery of the Forty.

[21] Mayerson, "The Desert of Southern Palestine," 161–62 and note 11.

January 14 became firmly fixed in tradition. The exact number of martyrs, on the other hand, apparently did not become part of that tradition.

At this point we must return to the two narratives which, however much deprecated as historical sources, have a Sinaitic provenance and concern that one Bedouin *razzia*. That of "Nilus," in all probability the earlier of the two, recounts with considerable verbal flourishes and breast-beating the sudden attack by barbarous Bedouins, the abduction of Theodoulus, and the bloody slaughter of several monks and solitaries.[22] After mentioning the names of three who were killed in that attack, the writer of the narrative then states: "They died on the seventh day after the Epiphany, which is the 14th of January. Pious men are very interested in learning the time and the names, since they want to check this information with the memories of holy men. Others were killed some years before, the memory of whom they celebrate on the same day because of the length of the journey and the size of the assemblage."[23] The Ammonius narrative places the date of the celebrated raid and double massacre on the second of Tybi, according to the Egyptian calendar, which would convert to the 28th of December. The Greek text, however, reveals how firmly set was the date of January 14, since the writer makes the following statement: "These Holy Fathers and victorious men of Christ died on the 2nd of the month of Tybi at about the ninth hour; according to the Romans, their memory is celebrated on the 14th of the month of January."[24] The "Nilus"

and Ammonius accounts were the two prime and perhaps the only sources from which the compilers of Greek menologies and synaxaria excerpted both the dramatic details and the date of January 14 to commemorate, possibly with a Eucharist and a sermon, the Holy Fathers who were killed at Sinai and Raithou.[25] Admittedly, there are differences in dating the massacre which I believe may be attributable either to dating by the Egyptian calendar (i.e., Tybi 2) or to miscalculating the number of days after the Epiphany, the formula that seems to have been used. As to the latter, the date is cited either as the seventh (as in the "Nilus" narrative) or the eighth day after the Epiphany, which would place the date at January 13 or 14.[26] In the course of time, however, January 14 became the fixed date for the anniversary of the Sinaitic martyrs, so much so that a current calendar of the Greek Orthodox Church carries this notation under the date of January 14: "Fathers Killed in Sinai and Raitho."[27]

It is my opinion, then, that January 14 was a red-letter day in Sinai, and that the inscription in the South Chapel of the Monastery of St. Catherine had only to use the number 14 to communicate to the monks of the monastery a well-known event in the ecclesiastical history of Sinai. Citing it as such is a form of synecdoche which is commonly employed when a numeral has a clear and unambiguous association, such as the Pentecost, the Lenten Quadragesima, Shabuoth, or the Fourth (of July). To the inhabitants of the Monastery of St. Catherine, the *d dekados* of the inscription marked that tragic day of January 14 which saw the death of an unknown number of monks and solitaries at the hands of Bedouin

---

[22] The full account of the "Nilus" *Narrationes*, in PG, 79, cols. 589–693. It is generally agreed that the writer of the *Narrationes* is not Nilus of Ancyra, although the narrative appears under his name; hence the quotation marks.

[23] *Ibid.*, col. 640C. In "Observations" (*supra*, note 12), 73, note 45, I have raised the question of the place of this quotation in the narrative.

[24] Ed. Combefis, *op. cit.* (*supra*, note 7), 129. The Syriac version apparently dates the martyrdom according to the Egyptian calendar. It should be noted that the following statement is placed, unlike that of the Greek text, as a kind of coda to the narrative (Lewis, *op. cit.* [*supra*, note 7], 14): "The life of the Holy Fathers who were slain at Mount Sinai and

Raïtho, is finished, in the days of Pope Peter of Alexandria. But the memory of these holy ones is made in December in the months of the Romans, the 28th."

[25] PG, 79, cols. 25–26, 31, 663–65, 692–93; *Synaxarium CP*, cols. 389–91.

[26] See especially *Le calendrier Palestino-Géorgien du Sinaiticus 34 (Xᵉ siècle)*, ed. and trans. G. Garitte (Brussels, 1958), 129–30, 420.

[27] The 1975 calendar from SS. Constantine and Helen Greek Orthodox Church of West Nyack, New York.

raiders. The South Chapel itself was apparently dedicated to, or contains the relics of, those who at a later date (sixth century?) achieved martyrdom by falling victims to periodic Bedouin violence. I would, therefore, translate the full inscription as follows:

† Τῆς δ̄ δεκάδος τὴν διὰ τοῦ αἵματος κολυμβήθραν ζηλώσαντες οἱ ἰσάριθμοι ὅσιοι π(ατέ)ρ(ε)ς | ἐνθάδε κατάκεινται, ὧν ἡ εὐφροσύνη ἡ βάτος ἡ ἀληθινὴ ὑπάρχει· δι᾽ ὧν ὁ 9(εὸ)ς σῶσον ἡμᾶς †

"The Holy Fathers lie here, equal in number[28] to those who were killed on the 14th [of January], and imitating them through a baptism of blood. Theirs is the joyous and true Burning Bush;[29] through them, O God, save us."

[28] "Equal in number" (*isarithmoi*) perhaps expresses the uncertainty—it is a vague enough expression—over the exact number of martyrs who fell on January 14.

[29] "Burning Bush" (*batos*) has a wide range of symbolic meanings; see entry in *A Patristic Greek Lexikon*, ed. G. W. E. Lampe (Oxford, 1961), 294.

Pl. 9. The fortified monastery built by Justinian in Sinai, now known as the Monastery of St. Catherine.

Procopius or Eutychius on the Construction of the Monastery at Mount Sinai: Which Is the More Reliable Source?

PHILIP MAYERSON
New York University, New York, NY 10003

When it comes to describing the events which led Justinian to order the construction of a fortified structure and a church at Mount Sinai, it is Procopius' account (*de Aed.* 5.8) that is generally cited as *the* historical source for those events. It is considered to be more dependable than the one other existing account of Justinian's actions, that of the 10th-century historian Eutychius (Saʿīd ibn Batrīq) in his *Annales* (*PG* 1863: cols. 1071–72; see Forsyth and Weitzman [1973: 6] who refer to Eutychius only as "a later account" and in an earlier article make no mention of him whatsoever [1968: 1–19]), and quite understandably so, since Procopius was not only a contemporary of the emperor, but he was also the recorder of the accomplishments and character of Justinian. As for Eutychius, whose testimony comes about 400 years after the event, he appears to lack the reliability of the man who virtually stood at Justinian's elbow when he gave the order for the construction at Sinai, the mountain which late tradition said was the place where Moses received the Law.

In an earlier paper on the defensive installations of *Palaestina Tertia* prior to the first Muslim attacks in 633/34, I noted that Procopius' account of the construction of a military installation deep in Sinai did not jibe well with the general conditions or needs of the region at that time (1964: 182, n. 83). Upon looking into the account more closely, I now believe it is possible to demonstrate that Procopius' description is entirely misleading. From a historical point of view, the only fact that one may accept as reliable is that the monastery, now known as the Monastery of St. Catherine, was built on orders from Justinian. Where, or from whom, Procopius received his information is not known, but it is obvious that he had no intimate knowledge of the Sinai peninsula, either in terms of its geography or its inhabitants. Ironically enough, the 10th-century version of Eutychius accords far better with the circumstances surrounding the need for a protected monastic settlement.

Procopius' statement relevant to this discussion follows:

> In what was formerly called Arabia and is now known as "Third Palestine," a barren land extends a great distance, unwatered and producing neither crops nor any useful thing. A precipitous and terribly wild mountain, Sina [Sinai] by name, rears its height close to the Red Sea, as it is called. . . . On this Mount Sina live monks whose life is a kind of careful rehearsal of death and they enjoy without fear the solitude which is very precious to them. Since these monks had nothing to crave—for they are superior to all human desires and have no interest in possessing anything or in caring for their bodies, nor do they seek pleasure in any other thing whatever—the Emperor Justinian built them a church which he dedicated to the Mother of God, so that they might be enabled to pass their lives there in praying and holding services. He built this church, not on the mountain's summit, but much lower down, since constant crashes of thunder and other terrifying manifestations of divine power are heard at night, striking terror into man's body and soul. It was in that place, they say, that Moses received the laws from God and published them. At the base of the mountain this Emperor built a very strong fortress and established there a considerable garrison of troops, in order that the barbarian Saracens might not be able from that region, which, as I have said, is uninhabited, to make inroads with complete secrecy into the lands of Palestine proper. (English translation from Dewey and Downey 1954: 355, 357)

The main point of contention is the purpose for which Justinian constructed a "strong fortress." According to Procopius, it would appear as if the emperor ordered its construction as an extension of the *limes* of *Palaestina Tertia* which originally was designed to protect Palestine proper and its trade routes from Bedouin attacks. On the contrary, the geographical position of Mount Sinai (28:32 N; 33:59 E)—deep within Central Sinai and nowhere near the Red Sea or its two arms, and far removed from any significant trade route and from civilization in general—could hardly ever have supported, then or now, any large number of Bedouins who could have threatened Palestine proper. The most graphic—and convincing—evidence for how remote Mount Sinai is from Palestine is to be seen on the popular photograph taken by the Apollo spacecraft of the Sinai peninsula and neighboring regions. Mount Sinai is situated almost at the very apex of triangular Sinai and within a much smaller triangle of dense, deep brown granitic structures. More to the point is the fact that by the late 6th century the forts of the *limes* far to the north, in the settled and populated areas of *Palaestina Tertia* and on established trade routes (Nessana and Eboda, for example), no longer functioned as military installations but had been turned into hospices or monastic buildings (Mayerson 1964: 178–90). The *limitanei* themselves had been assimilated into the general population and had cast off any semblance of being an effective military force. And what is more, we possess an eyewitness account of the character of the Bedouins in the region north of the granitic mountain ranges of which Mount Sinai is a part. The *Itinerarium*, attributed to a certain Antoninus of Piacenza, describes the Bedouins that he and his companions encountered en route to Mount Sinai just five years or so (ca. 570) after the death of Justinian (Geyer 1898: 182–83). As they entered the "inner desert" from Nessana at the edge of the Tih desert, these western travelers came into contact with their first "Saracens": a bedraggled lot of beggars, hardly a band of hostiles. Their guide then volunteered a demographic statistic—to be given little credence—that the Bedouin of Sinai numbered 12,600 (Geyer 1898: 183; see Mayerson 1963: 171–72; 1964: 186–87). Although it is true that the route taken by Antoninus and his companions was not the common one for approaching Mount Sinai—there being a moratorium on raiding at the time—the threat of attacks on small parties traveling through the wilderness was always present. Still, Bedouin raids of this sort cannot be taken as a serious threat by organized bands of hostiles. Be that as it may, a military post at Mount Sinai by its very geographical position could not have prevented hostile Bedouins from infiltrating lands to the north if they had an inclination to do so. The conclusion of

Forsyth (1968: 18) that "as a fortress, the monastery had its assigned part to play in a vast theater of military operations along the eastern borders of Justinian's empire" cannot be sustained in light of the evidence at hand.

The *Itinerarium* of Antoninus does record the existence of a defensive installation in Sinai, an installation which best can be described as a police post. After Antoninus left the monastery at Mount Sinai, which he describes simply as a *monasterium circumdatum muris munitis,* he set out for Pharan where he found the town, the only organized community in Sinai worthy of the name, surrounded by a [mud-]brick wall. The town had a police unit of 80 mounted men, provisioned and housed at public expense, to patrol the desert and protect the monasteries and hermits against Bedouin attacks (Geyer 1898: 184 for Mount Sinai, 186 for Pharan; see Mayerson 1964: 182–83).

As for the considerable garrison of troops which Procopius claims Justinian stationed in the fort at Mount Sinai, the very architecture of the structure lacks the essential elements generally associated with a military installation. G. H. Forsyth (1968: 6; see Forsyth and Weitzman 1973: 6), the architect of the Alexandria-Michigan-Princeton Expedition to the Monastery at Mount Sinai, cites no archeological or architectural evidence to suggest that the structure housed "a considerable garrison of troops." He (1968: 6) further observes something missing in the structure and comments: ". . . the puzzling fact remains that Byzantine military engineers, famous for their skill in fortification and siegecraft, should have been content to encircle the fortress by a wall unprovided with effective flanking towers. Those on the lower side, facing northeast, are relatively modern; the original ones on the upper, southwest side, are mock towers, projecting too little to provide enfilading fire along the curtain wall." Forsyth also comments on the position of the structure as a military installation made vulnerable by its situation at the base of a slope and capable of being dominated by archers from the above heights. In every respect—in design, in strategic position, in geographical location—the structure called by Procopius a "very strong fortress" is at variance with what we know of military installations on the *limes* of *Palaestina Tertia* or on any other *limes.* Nor is it likely that the structure we now see at the foot of Mount Sinai ever housed "a considerable garrison of troops."

There are yet other inaccuracies or ambiguities that crop up in Procopius' account. Apart from the

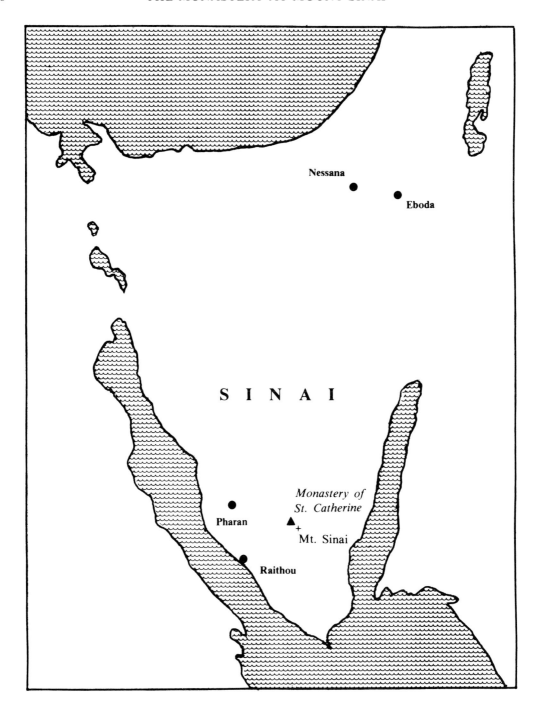

fact that Mount Sinai does not "rear its height close to the Red Sea," or that Third Palestine is not a barren place which produces no crops,[1] he describes its inhabitants as monks "whose life is a kind of careful rehearsal of death and they enjoy without fear the solitude which is very precious to them." All these statements are inaccurate. We possess two narratives which describe the lives of

the eremites at Mount Sinai and its environs, narratives attributed to a certain Nilus (*PG* 1865: cols. 589–694; see Mayerson 1975: 51–74 for a defense of the historicity of the *Narrationes*) and Ammonius (Combefis 1660: 88–132 for Greek text; Lewis 1912: 1–14 for Syriac text and English translation). Although both accounts have been challenged as being fictionalized versions of monastic life—a view

I do not entirely share—they were unquestionably written by two men who had spent time at Mount Sinai and who had the opportunity to observe the way of life of both Bedouins and eremites (see my forthcoming paper where I hope to demonstrate that the Ammonius narrative reflects a late 4th-century environment for monastic life in Sinai). Regarding the latter, theirs was not a preparation for death, no more so than that of any monk or hermit inhabiting the Egyptian deserts or of any Christian whose way of life is a preparation for entering the Kingdom of Heaven. The Sinaitic eremites, who dubbed themselves "Servants of God" and "Athletes of Christ," sought a life of tranquility through solitude and practiced a rigorous form of asceticism (*PG* 1865: cols. 589A–92A, 613C, 616A–C, 620C–621C; Combefis 1660: 89–91; Lewis 1912: 1–2). Although these eremites sought solitude, they did not as Procopius would have us believe "enjoy without fear the solitude which is very precious to them." Unless we interpret Procopius' words to mean that the monks did not fear solitude itself— which I do not believe Procopius had in mind—the isolated and defense-less monks did have something to fear, namely, harassment by Bedouins. We need only mention the Nilus (*PG* 1865: cols. 625–632A) and Ammonius (Combefis 1660: 91–95; Lewis 1912: 2–3) narratives which give vivid descriptions of how Bedouins periodically attacked the eremitic communities in Sinai.[2] Those monks who earned their martyrdom at the hands of the attacking Bedouins are commemmorated in synaxaries and menologies, in an inscription in the South Chapel of the Monastery of St. Catherine, and in the current calendar of the Greek Orthodox Church (Mayerson 1976: 375–79).

One additional and perhaps minor point, but one which again tells us something about the unre-liability of Procopius' account, is that Justinian built a church dedicated to the Mother of God not on the summit of Mount Sinai, but much "lower down," and that at the base of the mountain he built "a very strong fortress and established there a very strong garrison." We are led to believe by these two statements that the church was *not* within the fortress which housed the troops but was like a number of churches—really chapels but often referred to as churches—which can be found below the summit of the mountain. Forsyth (1968: 5) also comments on this inconsistency in Procopius' account.

If Procopius' information is unreliable, what of Eutychius' (*PG* 1863: cols. 1071–72)? Certainly the

reported conversations between the Emperor Justinian and his emissary are factitious but the rest of the account has a considerable measure of plausibility, if not certainty; and, as stated above, the account accords well with what we know of the conditions at the time the Sinaitic monks peti-tioned Justinian. Most important of all, Eutychius' description of the structure which Justinian ordered to be built has nothing to do with a military installation or with military strategy. What he describes for us is simply a monastic establishment surrounded by a protective wall. In other words, it is a fortified monastery, just as Antoninus described it: *monasterium circumdatum muris munitis* (Geyer 1898: 184). It is of a type similar to the kind which Antoninus came upon as he made his way from Mount Sinai to Palestine. At Surandela, he tells us:

> There is a small fort *(castellum modicum)* . . . having nothing within it except a church and its priest and two hospices for travelers . . . and at a place where the children of Israel crossed the Red Sea and pitched their camp, there too is a small fort within which is a hospice. (Geyer 1898: 187; Mayerson 1964: 183)

With this in mind, and with evidence in hand that there was no need to bolster security with imperial forces, Eutychius' account gives us a reasonable picture of the events which induced Justinian to order the construction of a fortified structure at Mount Sinai and the purpose which the structure was to serve. That part of Eutychius' account relevant to the above discussion follows:

> When the monks of Mount Sinai heard of the receptive disposition of Emperor Justinian and that he delighted in building churches and monasteries, they came to him and complained that the Ishmaelite Arabs injured them by devouring their provisions, and destroying their places (of habitation). Entering their cells they would pillage them of whatever was there, and breaking into churches they would gulp down the Eucharist. When the emperor asked them what they wanted, they said: "Oh king, that you build us a monastery in which we may be protected." (Before that time there was no monastery in which the monks could congregate, but they were scattered in the mountains and wadis around the Bush from which God spoke to Moses. Above the Bush they only had a large tower, which is still standing to this day, and within it is a church dedicated to St. Mary, and the monks would flee to this tower to protect themselves whenever anyone whom they feared approached.) The Emperor conse-quently sent a legate with full authority and with written instructions to the prefect of Egypt that he supply him (the legate) with as much money as needed, and that he pro-vide men and provisions from Egypt. The legate was also ordered to build a church at Clysma, and a monastery at Raya; and to build a monastery on Mount Sinai and to fortify it so that no better could be found in the entire

world, and to make it so strong that the monks or the monastery would not fear or suffer from any quarter.

The legate built the church of St. Athanasius at Clysma and the monastery at Raya; and then going to Mount Sinai he found the Bush located in a narrow place between two mountains, and in the same spot he found a tower built near the Bush and some running springs of water near it, and monks scattered about the wadis. It was his intention to build the monastery high up on the mountain and to leave the Bush and the tower (where they were). However, he rejected the plan because of the water since there was no adequate supply of water on the mountain. He therefore built the monastery close to the Bush and enclosed the tower within the monastery. The monastery was situated between two mountains and in a narrow spot, so much so that if anyone climbed the northern slope of the mountain and threw a stone, it would land in the middle of the monastery and injure the monks. Hence he built the monastery in this narrow spot, close by the Bush and the famous (biblical) monuments and a supply of water. On the mountain top, above the spot where Moses received the law, he built a chapel. The name of the abbot of the monastery was Doulas. The legate returned to Emperor Justinian and informed him of the churches and monasteries that he had built. He also described how he built the monastery of Mount Sinai. The emperor answered and said: "You made a mistake and you have harmed the monks and placed them in the hands of the enemy. Why did you not build the monastery on top of the mountain?" The legate answered: "I placed it near the Bush and close to the water supply; but if it had been built on the mountain top, the monks would lack water so much so that if they were at any time besieged, their water supply would be shut off and they would die of thirst. Moreover the Bush would be too far away from them."

Eutychius, whatever the source of his information, evidently had a clear sense of the topographical and political conditions of the time when the monks petitioned the emperor. Justinian, as we learn from Procopius himself, did take pleasure in building churches and monasteries, and the plea of the Sinaitic monks was one which spelled out their true concerns. From about the beginning of the 5th century to the time of the Muslim attacks on Palestine, we have no reports of difficulties with the "barbarian Saracens"; also the archeological evidence from the border region to the north, as indicated above, gives further assurance that that quarter of the world must have enjoyed a substantial degree of security (Mayerson 1964: 178–90). The attacks of the Ishmaelite Arabs (i.e., Bedouins) about which the monks complained at that time were more in the way of misdemeanors rather than felonies. If the monks petitioned for a monastery, the only two acceptable sites were the peak of Mount Sinai where Moses was said to have received the Law, or the Burning Bush close to the northern

escarpment of the Wadi ed Deir. As for the peak of Mount Sinai, it was completely unsuitable as a gathering place for the eremites who were scattered about the holy mountain. The site of the Burning Bush, on the other hand, had from early times been established as a place venerable in its own right, was easy of access, and had a good supply of water at hand. The Nilus account, a narrative of the late 4th or early 5th century, tells of a Bedouin attack at the time when the writer and his son "had come down from the sacred mountain to visit the holy men in the place of the [Burning] Bush" (*PG* 1865: col. 628A). The Ammonius narrative affirms the existence of a tower which was used as a refuge against attacking Bedouins: "Those (monks) who were found staying near the tower *(pyrgos)*, hearing the uproar and the tumult, ran into the stronghold together with the superior of the place, Doulas by name. He was truly a servant of Christ, for he had more patience and gentleness than anyone else; from this he was popularly called Moses"(Combefis 1660: 91). Both narratives also speak of the eremites gathering together once a week, presumably at the site of the Burning Bush.

There can be no doubt that the decision to build the monastery close to the northern escarpment of the Wadi ed Deir was determined by two factors: the site of the Burning Bush itself and the availability of a water supply. It would have been impossible to have satisfied these two conditions and at the same time to have built a military installation that would have been invulnerable from attacks from above. Hence the axis of the church in relationship to the surrounding walls could not have been as much a concern to the architect of the monastery as it is to modern architects. Eutychius is quite correct in stating that anyone climbing the northern slope of the Wadi ed Deir could throw a stone into the middle of the monastery, but in the light of the venerability of the site and the fact that the monks would be secure either from serious harassment or attacks by Bedouins, they were undoubtedly pleased to accept the design as it presently stands.

Finally, the monastery itself, in an opinion I base on several surveys of the region, is an anomaly in Sinai. No other settlement or monastery in the region—not at Pharan or at Raithou (Bir Abu Suweira-Tor of modern times), the two major settled monastic sites of Sinai—has a fortified structure or the remains of one like it. It is a tribute to Justinian's munificence and to its isolated position that the monastery has survived to this day.

NOTES

[1] As barren as Sinai may appear, one sees orchards *(bustānim)* at Mount Sinai and its environs and substantial palm groves at Pharan and Tor (see Mayerson 1962: 233–41 for the agricultural capability of a large area of *Palaestina Tertia*).

[2] It is also interesting to note that the peaceful scene in Egeria's account of a trip to Mount Sinai in which she describes having an evening meal with the monks in their garden is out of harmony with the two accounts attributed to Nilus and Ammonius (Prinz 1960: 6).

BIBLIOGRAPHY

Combefis, F., ed.
  1660   *Narrationes* of Ammonius. Pp. 88–132 in *Illustrium Christi martyrum lecti triumphi.* Paris.

Dewey, H. B., and Downey, Glanville
  1954   *Procopius VIII, Buildings* in *Loeb Classical Library,* ed. T. E. Page et al. Cambridge: William Heinemann.

Forsyth, George H.
  1968   The Monastery of St. Catherine at Mount Sinai: The Church and the Fortress of Justinian. *Dumbarton Oaks Papers* 22: 1–19.

Forsyth, George H., and Weitzman, Kurt
  1973   *The Monastery of St. Catherine at Mount Sinai: The Church and Fortress of Justinian.* Ann Arbor: University of Michigan Press.

Geyer, Paulus, ed.
  1898   *Itinera Hierosolymitana saeculi IIII—VIII.* Vol. 39 in *Corpus Scriptorum Ecclesiasticorum Latinorum.* Vienna: F. Tempsky.

Lewis, Agnes Smith, trans.
  1912   *The Forty Martyrs of the Sinai Desert and the Story of Eulogios.* Vol. 9 in *Horae Semiticae.* Cambridge: The University Press.

Mayerson, Phillip
  1962   The Agricultural Regime of Nessana and the Central Negeb. Pp. 233–41 in *Excavations at Nessana,* Vol. I, ed. H. D. Colt. London: British School of Archaeology in Jerusalem.
  1963   The Desert of Southern Palestine according to Byzantine Sources. *Proceedings of the American Philosophical Society* 107: 160–72.
  1964   The First Muslim Attacks on Southern Palestine (A.D. 633–634). *Transactions and Proceedings of the American Philological Association* 95: 155–99.
  1975   Observations on the "Nilus" *Narrationes:* Evidence for an Unknown Christian Sect? *Journal of the American Research Center in Egypt* 12: 51–74.
  1976   An Inscription in the Monastery of St. Catherine and the Martyr Tradition in Sinai. *Dumbarton Oaks Papers* 30: 375–79.

PG
  1863   *Annales* of Eutychius. Cols. 907–1156 in Vol. 111 of *Patrologiae Graecae,* ed. J.-P. Migne.

PG
  1865   *Narrationes* of Nilus. Cols. 589–694 in Vol. 79 of *Patrologiae Graecae,* ed. J.-P. Migne.

Prinz, Otto, ed.
  1960   *Itinerarium Egeriae.* Heidelberg: Carl Winter.

ANTI-BLACK SENTIMENT IN THE *VITAE PATRUM*

As more than occasionally happens in research, one comes upon material and ideas that are not related to the immediate field of interest but are so striking in their implications that they have to be pursued. Upon looking into the various editions of the *Vitae Patrum*,[1] this writer has come upon expressions of anti-black (i.e., Ethiopian or "Indian") sentiment in the early monastic communities of Egypt (third to fifth centuries). The evidence is not one of highly articulated prejudice; on the other hand, it is neither overly subtle nor subliminal. Further, the evidence, as I see it, runs contrary to the conclusions put forward by Professor Frank M. Snowden, Jr., who maintains that the early Christians continued the Greco-Roman tradition of considering no race superior or inferior to the other; that "color was inconsequential"; that "they regarded as black all men who had not been illumined by God's light and considered all men, regardless of color of skin, as potentially Christians."[2] These are legitimate conclusions derived from the exegetical speculations of theologians—such as Origen, Jerome, and Augustine—on passages from the Scriptures having to do with Ethiopia and Ethiopians, and of course, with the passage "I am black and beautiful . . ." from the Song of Solomon (1:15).

In further support of his thesis that black was viewed as beautiful, Snowden cites from the *Vitae Patrum* events in the life of Moses the Ethiopian, a brigand turned monk, who acquired the reputation of being a model of Christian virtue.[3] A closer reading of some of the episodes in the life of this Desert Father will show, I believe, that he was abused and subjected to discriminatory treatment because of the color of his skin. On one occasion Moses openly declares himself to be inferior

---

[1] For the purpose of this article I use *Vitae Patrum* as a generic title that covers the following works:

1. Athanasius, *Vita S. Antonii*, *PG* 26
2. *Apophthegmata Patrum* (Alphabetical Collection), *PG* 65
3. *Verba Seniorum* (Systematic Collection), *PL* 73
4. Palladius, *Historia Lausiaca*, *PG* 34
5. Palladius, *Historia Lausiaca*, *PL* 73
6. Rufinus, *Historia Monachorum*, *PL* 21
7. E. A. Wallis Budge, trans., *The Paradise or Garden of the Holy Fathers* [The Syriac version of ꜣAnān Īshōꜣ] (2 vols.; London: Chatto & Windus, 1907). Cited hereafter as "Budge" (contains the Syriac versions of the *Life of St. Antony* of Athanasius, the *Historia Lausiaca* of Palladius, the *Historia Monachorum* attributed here to St. Jerome, the *Verba Seniorum*, and the *Questions and Answers of the Holy Men*).

[2] *Blacks in Antiquity: Ethiopians in the Greco-Roman Experience* (Cambridge, MA: Harvard University, 1970) 196–217; 330–39.

[3] Ibid., 201, 209–11.

to his white brothers because he is black. In the *Vitae Patrum* these episodes are cited as examples of the black monk's humility and fortitude, qualities which earned for him a distinguished place in the annals of the Desert Fathers. But these incidents, regardless of how they were interpreted by the compilers of the *Vitae Patrum*, are clear evidence of anti-black sentiment.[4]

Abba Moses is the sole black among the Desert Fathers about whom we have any biographical information. The other blacks that are cited in the *Vitae Patrum* are demons or devils. These, as far as I know, have not entered into any discussion regarding the attitude of early Christians towards Ethiopians or blacks. It is true that in imagery "blackness" was associated with the darker side of human nature. But as far as demons go, the Desert Fathers, who encountered multitudes of them, never characterize them by color or race with the exception of those comparatively few that are cited as Ethiopian or black. Specifically citing a demon as black or as an Ethiopian must surely indicate a sentiment among some unlettered and theologically uninformed monks that black was not always beautiful.

With regard to Abba Moses, the evidence for the prejudicial treatment he received at the hands of his fellow monks or clerics is contained in four incidents. Moses is either insulted, treated with contempt, "tested," or reviled; he was subjected to treatment of a kind that was not inflicted upon other monks, even those of a lesser reputation for ascetical good works.

The clearest instance of color prejudice occurs on an occasion when the Fathers were gathered together, and because certain people wished to see Abba Moses, they treated him with contempt, saying, "Why does this Ethiopian come and go among us?" When Moses heard this he held his peace. And when the congregation was dismissed, they (the certain people?) said to him, "Abba Moses, were you not afraid?" And he said to them, "Although I was afraid, I did not say a word."[5]

The above is adapted with very little change from the Syriac version. The Greek text of the same incident makes no mention of "certain people wishing to see Abba Moses," but that "the Fathers, wishing to test him, treated him as an object of contempt, saying, 'Why does this Ethiopian come into our midst?' Later when the congregation was dismissed, they (the Fathers?) asked him, 'Abba, were you not in any way upset?' He replied, 'I was upset, but I did not speak.'"[6]

[4]See below (p. 128). Cf. Helen Waddell, *The Desert Fathers* (Ann Arbor, MI: University of Michigan, 1957) 59: Moses, "the long black man . . . liable to gibes about his colour."

[5]Budge, 2. 14.

[6]*PG* 65, col. 284; *PL* 73, cols. 970–71.

A similar, if not the same, incident is reported in the Syriac *Vitae Patrum* under the rubric of "Questions and Answers on the Ascetic Rule." In this instance it is "certain men" who revile Abba Moses. The purpose in recalling the incident is to interpret the words of the monk's reply: "Although I was troubled, yet I said nothing." The conclusion that is reached is that although Moses had demonstrated spiritual excellence in maintaining silence and in not showing his inner anger, he had not attained the perfect state of impassibility (*apatheia*?) by being angry neither inwardly nor outwardly.[7]

Abba Moses is subjected to two more "tests" at a time when he was an old man and had become a member of the clergy. The two incidents are combined in the Syriac and Latin systematic collections to illustrate the virtue of humility. The translation of the Syriac text is as follows:

> They used to say that when Abba Moses was one of the clergy he wore a long outer garment, and that the Bishop said unto him, "Behold, thou art wholly white, O Abba Moses." The old man said unto him, "Is the Pappa within or without?" And again wishing to try him, the Bishop said unto the clergy, "When Abba Moses goeth into the sacrarium drive him out, and go after him and hear what he saith." Now when he went into the sacrarium they rebuked him and drove him out, saying, "Get outside, O Ethiopian"; and having gone forth he began to say to himself, "They have treated thee rightly, O thou whose skin is dark and black; thou shalt not go back as if thou wert a [white] man."[8]

The Greek text of the alphabetical collection does not differ substantially from the Syriac or Latin versions, but the impact of the treatment that Moses receives at the hands of the Bishop (or Archbishop) and his fellow clerics can be felt more strongly.

> It is said of Abba Moses that when he became a member of the clergy and had been invested with the ephod, the Archbishop said to him, "See, Abba Moses, you have become entirely white." The old man said to him, "Outwardly, Lord and Father; am I also so inwardly?" Wishing to test him, the Archbishop said to the clergy, "Whenever Abba Moses comes into the sanctuary, drive him out and follow him so that you may hear what he says. The old man came in and they abused him and drove him out saying, "Get out, Ethiopian!" He went out and said to himself, "They have treated you properly, you soot-skinned black! Since you're not a man, why should you come into the company of men."[9]

Howevermuch these episodes were viewed in the past as demonstrations of Abba Moses's humility, they were also deliberate acts of humiliation directed against the man because of the color of his skin.

---

[7]Budge, 2. 325–26.

[8]Ibid., 2. 112. For the Latin version see *PL* 73, cols. 959–60.

[9]*PG* 65, col. 284; *PL* 73, col. 959. The Syriac version and some readings in the Greek MSS have "Bishop" instead of "Archbishop." Snowden (p. 210) cites him incorrectly as the "archbishop of Alexandria."

There can be no question but that the use of the word "Ethiopian" in these contexts is strongly deprecatory and is the equivalent of the most offensive word used against blacks in American society. The demoralizing effect that this treatment had upon Abba Moses understandably results in his denigrating appraisal of himself: ". . . you soot-skinned black! Since you're not a man, why should you come into the company of men." He of course means "in the company of white men." Further, the remark made by the Bishop, gratuitous at best, that Moses had become completely white because of his ephod stirs a hostile reaction within the black monk. His rejoinder—if it is accurately reported—is oblique yet pointed; he says in effect: "It seems that I am completely white outside because of my ephod, but do you think that I am completely white inside as well, and hence in every respect like you?"[10]

Whereas Abba Moses is attacked because of the color of his skin, black demons—or even the devil himself in the form of a black—attack the monks as they strive to attain spiritual and moral perfection. These black demons appear in the form of a woman, a man, or as young boys. Four of the seven instances cited in the *Vitae Patrum* represent demons of fornication or lust; the others represent arrogance or pride, disobedience, and distracting thoughts. The brief narratives that follow are so explicit in characterizing black or Ethiopian spirits as evil that they hardly require further commentary.

The biography of the earliest of the Desert Fathers, St. Antony the Great, provides us with the example of the devil assuming the appearance of a black boy. It is the saint's first encounter with a demon of any kind. The devil, seeing that he was unsuccessful in getting the youthful Antony to surrender to temptation, troubles him with maddening thoughts of lust. Through prayer and divine help, Antony maintains his equilibrium and his chastity. The devil then appears to him as a black boy and speaks to him in a human voice. Antony asks him who he is, and the black boy replies, "I am the friend of fornication; I trap and seduce the young, and I am called the spirit of fornication."

---

[10]There appears to be some confusion in the translation of Abba Moses's oblique retort (Ἄρα τὰ ἔξω, κύρι ὁ Πάπας, ἤ καὶ τὰ ἔσω). The Greek text, *PG* 65, col. 284, makes the remark exclamatory when it is clearly interrogatory. Cotelier's translation of the Greek is also misleading (*Utique exterius, domne papa, utinam et interius*). Snowden (p. 201) in his translation apparently follows the Latin of Cotelier: "Outwardly, holy Father, would that I were inwardly too." The Latin version of Pelagius in the *Verba Seniorum* (*PL* 73, col. 959) is closer to the Greek: "*Putas a foris, domne papa, aut deintus?*" A recent translation of the Greek text by Benedicta Ward (*The Sayings of the Desert Fathers* [London: Mowbrays, 1975] 117) gives a completely different meaning to the remark: "It is true of the outside, lord and father, but what about Him who sees the inside?" I find nothing in the Greek or Latin text to support this translation.

After giving an account of his powers, he is assailed by Antony: "You are utterly contemptible, for you are black-hearted and weak as a child." The black being, hearing this, fled and was henceforth afraid of coming near Antony.[11]

Under the rubric of fornication in the Latin systematic collection of the *Verba Seniorum*, the story is told of a man who went into the desert of Scete to become a monk and took with him his infant son. When the boy became a young man and the demons began to wage their war against him, he told his father that he had to go into the world because he could not bear the desire of lust that had overwhelmed him. To prevent his leaving, the young man's father urged him to spend forty days in the inner desert, taking with him forty days' worth of bread and work. The young man obeyed his father and lived a life of seclusion and hard work in the remote desert. Twenty days passed when, suddenly, he saw the work of the devil appear before him, "and it stood before him in the form of an Ethiopian woman, smelly and disgusting in appearance, so much so that he could not bear her smell. She then said to him, 'In the hearts of men I smell sweet, but because of your obedience and your labor, God does not permit me to lead you astray, but I have let you know my smell.'" When the young man returned to his father he said that he no longer wished to go into the world for he had seen the work of the devil and had smelled his foul odor. The young man's father replied that if he had stayed another twenty days deep in the desert, he would have seen a greater vision.[12]

Under the same rubric, but apparently given only in the Syriac version, is the story of a man who went into the desert to become a monk. The man was a virgin and did not even know that there was such a thing as whores in the world. "And when he was dwelling in his cell, the devils began to stir up in him the passion of fornication; and lifting up his eyes he saw the devils going round about him in the form of Ethiopians and they incited him to yield to the passion." After a brief prayer, a stone fell from the room and the monk heard, as it were, a sweet voice, and he enjoyed a short respite from his lustful thoughts. When seeking an explanation for these events, the monk was told by Abba Poemen that the stone that he had seen fall was the Calumniator, and that the voice which he heard was Lust. Supplication to God, he was

[11]*PG* 26, cols. 849–52; Budge, 1. 10–11. The Syriac version has the devil assuming the appearance of an "Indian boy" but is later described as a "black being." I have translated καὶ γὰρ μέλας εἶ τὸν νοῦν "for you are black-hearted." A more colloquial translation might be "for you have a dirty mind." Budge's translation of the Syriac has "for thou art black in thy nature."

[12]*PL* 73, col. 879; Budge, 2. 131.

told, was the way in which to contend with the devils and to free himself from the war of fornication.[13]

The story is also told of a certain young monk who was sorely disturbed by the demon of lust. He related his thoughts to an old man who himself was free of those thoughts. The old man, upon hearing the young monk's confession, was very angry and said that, since he had such thoughts, the brother was a wretch and unworthy of wearing the habit of a monk. The young man, taking this scolding very much to heart, left his cell and was on his way back to the world. Abba Apollo met the troubled brother and queried him about his sadness. After being told of what had happened, Apollo consoled him and advised him to return to his cell. Apollo then went to the cell of the old man who had caused his fellow monk to despair, and he prayed that the old man might learn in his old age what time had never taught him: to have compassion on those who are disturbed by temptations of this sort. "When his prayer was finished, he saw an Ethiopian standing close to the cell and shooting arrows at the old man; and as if pierced by them, the old man weaved to and fro like a man drunk with wine. And when he could bear it no longer, he left his cell and took the same road to the world that the young man had taken." Abba Apollo met him and lectured him on the need to comfort those who wage war with their passions. Apollo then made his prayer and immediately the old man was freed from the lustful desires that the Ethiopian had brought upon him.[14]

As an object lesson in obedience, Abba Herakles tells the story of a certain old man who had a disciple who for many years was exceedingly obedient. When the disciple was attacked by sinful desires, he begged the old man to make him a monk. He agreed and the disciple built a cell for himself a short distance away from his abba. The old man then gave him specific instructions on how to live, and told him not to come out of his cell until the Sabbath. For two days the disciple did as he was told, but on the third day he became depressed and decided against instructions to sing a great number of psalms. When he went to lie down on his mat in the evening, "he saw an Ethiopian lying there and gnashing his teeth at him." Terrified, he ran back to the cell of the old man and begged to be let in. Knowing that his disciple had not followed instructions, the old man would not admit him until the following morning, and then only out of compassion. The disciple burst in and said, "Father, I need you! I saw a black Ethiopian on my mat when I was about to go to bed." The old man told him that he had had this experience because he had not been obedient.[15]

---

[13]Budge, 2. 130.
[14]*PL* 73, cols. 874–75.
[15]*PG* 65, col. 185; Budge, 2. 54–55.

The black character of the demon of arrogance (or pride) is revealed in the story of a certain Abba Apollo who was in charge of a large monastery in the Thebaid and who was renowned for his ascetical labors and spirituality. At one point in his long life he heard the voice of God say to him that he, Apollo, would help destroy pagan knowledge and the worship of devils and that he would establish a race of holy people who would be exalted for good works. For fear that he would be punished for becoming excessively zealous in the performance of his task, he asked that his false pretensions be taken away. "And again he heard the divine voice and it said, 'Place your hand on your neck and whatever you grasp, bury it in the sand.' And when Apollo placed his hand on his neck, he grabbed a small Ethiopian [boy] and he buried him in the sand as the creature cried out and said, 'I am the demon of arrogance!' And again the voice came to Apollo saying, 'Go, and whatever you shall seek from God, you will receive.'"[16]

A long story is told of how Abba Macarius the Alexandrian came upon black demons that were responsible for the thoughts that distract monks when they are at prayer. It appears that Macarius was awakened one night by a demon knocking on the door of his cell. The demon urged him to go to the meeting of the monks who had come together for the nightly vigils. The demon insisted that Macarius was not aware that without demons there would be no such meeting, and he pressed Macarius to let him prove it to him. Prayerfully Macarius agreed and went to the assembly where the vigils were being held. "And, lo, he saw certain tiny, loathsome Ethiopian boys running about hither and thither as if they were borne about by wings. . . . Now these little Ethiopians hovered above (the monks) who were seated and if anyone pressed his eyes with his two little fingers, he immediately fell asleep; and if anyone touched his mouth with his finger, they made him yawn." And when the monks were kneeling in prayer, the little black demons caused some of them to see the image of a woman; and to others they appeared as if they were engaged in building or carrying something. And whatever the demons fashioned by their tricks, the monks busied themselves with these things in their thoughts as they prayed. Some monks, however, forcibly drove the demons away (from their thoughts), but the demons played over the backs and necks of those monks who were not intent on their prayers. When Macarius saw this, he wept. He brought the monks to him and they confessed that they had these thoughts when they were

---

[16]*PG* 34, col. 1137; *PL* 73, col. 1155. Budge (1. 340–41) has the monk pray to have his "pride" taken away, and has the demon cry out that he is the "spirit of pride." The Greek text has ἀλαζονία which I have translated as "false pretensions"; and I have also translated ὑπερηφανία as "arrogance."

at prayer. Macarius then perceived that the black demons cause all vain and needless thoughts, but that they are repelled by those who guard themselves against having these thoughts. Macarius also observed that when some of the brothers stretched out their hands to receive the sacraments from the priest, the Ethiopian demons put charcoal in their hands, but that the demons fled in fear when deserving monks held out their hands.[17]

As a postscript to the above notices of the third to the fifth centuries, we see that the black demon continued to disturb the psyches of men in a later period. It is reported that Petronas, the conqueror of the Arabs in 863, fell seriously ill after having an affair with a slave girl. After other means to cure him failed, he came to St. Antony the Young for help. He confessed that he had not behaved like a Christian and that, "an angry Ethiopian with a very eager look on his face came up to me at night [in a dream] and said, 'You are mine!'" Antony reassured him that he would sleep well that night. After certain rituals prescribed by Antony were performed, the black man no longer appeared to Petronas and he regained his health.[18]

PHILIP MAYERSON

New York University
New York, NY

---

[17]*PL* 21, cols. 453–55; a short redaction of this account is found in *PL* 73, cols. 765–66. In the latter, *nigros* is found instead of *tetros* ("loathsome"). This narrative is lacking in both the Greek and Syriac redactions.

[18]F. Halkin, ed., "Saint Antoine le Jeune et Pétronas le vainquer des Arabes en 863," AnBoll 62 (1944) 215–17.

THE AMMONIUS NARRATIVE: BEDOUIN AND BLEMMYE ATTACKS IN SINAI

PHILIP MAYERSON

NEW YORK UNIVERSITY

In late antiquity, during the several centuries in which the southern portion of the Sinai Peninsula flourished — if "flourished" is the correct word for life in that desolate part of the world — two events made a mark in the recorded history of the region: the construction of the celebrated fortified monastery at the site of the Burning Bush, and an attack, or a series of attacks, by Bedouins and Blemmyes on eremitic communities on Mount Sinai and at Raithou. Of the former, we have the evidence of two historians, Procopius and Eutychius,[1] and more importantly, we have the structure itself: the Monastery of Saint Catherine, as it is known today, with its inscriptions and mosaics, and its wooden doors and beams whose age can be determined by laboratory analysis. No one can doubt the words of Procopius and Eutychius that this was the structure that Justinian ordered to be built and that was completed in the middle of the sixth century. Of the latter, the raid on the two communities, we have an ironical situation. Scholars do not question that there was such a raid, or raids, sometime during the late fourth or early fifth century, but they hold that the two narratives describing them are wholly fictitious and of no historical value. One narrative, the *Narrationes* (διηγήματα) attributed to a certain Nilus,[2] has been treated fairly extensively by this writer.[3] I have attempted to give the narrative a more balanced reading and to

I wish to acknowledge the assistance of Irene Zajac, a graduate student, who skillfully performed the onerous task of preparatory work on the Greek text which has made my own task far less so.

[1] Cf. P. Mayerson, "Procopius or Eutychius on the Construction of the Monastery at Mount Sinai: Which is the More Reliable Source?" *BASOR* 230 (1978), 33–38.

[2] J. P. Migne, *Patrologia series graeca* 79 (Paris 1857–1866), cols. 589–693.

[3] P. Mayerson, "Observations on the 'Nilus' *Narrationes*," *Journal of the American Research Center in Egypt* 12 (1975), 51–74.

133

point out the limits that one must consider when faced with a document written by an apparently well-educated man but one who was neither historian nor anthropologist. Limiting factors aside, I remain convinced that the Nilus narrative was written by an unknown Sinaitic eremite who was a witness to a Bedouin attack on the community at Mount Sinai. I have gone so far as to suggest that the narrative contains evidence of an unrecorded Christian sect, short-lived most likely, that embraced a kind of philosophic asceticism and looked exclusively to the Old Testament for guidance and instruction.

The other narrative, a companion piece so to speak, the Ammonius λόγος (or διήγημα) "concerning the holy fathers killed by the barbarians on the mountain of Sinai and in Raithou," has suffered the same fate as the 'Nilus' *Narrationes*. It has been rejected by modern scholars, in particular by R. Devreesse,[4] and consequently it is virtually ignored when questions arise concerning the history of pre-Islamic Sinai. One reason why this narrative is rarely looked into is that text is nor readily available. In 1660, Combefis edited and published a Greek text of the narrative from codices that he obtained from Cardinal Mazarin and Pierre Séguier.[5] Unfortunately, the Combefis text is generally unavailable in major libraries outside of the Bibliothèque Nationale in Paris. Most scholars have relied on the Syriac version of the Greek text and its English translation by A. S. Lewis.[6] I have been fortunate to obtain photocopies of the Combefis text and of another Greek text of the narrative, *Sinaiticus Graecus* 267 (14th century?).[7] The latter has not been published nor is it available in the Library of Congress microfilms of the library of the Monastery of Saint Catherine. A comparison of the two Greek texts shows that the two are very similar, with only minor differences between them, and must have been derived from a common manuscript. The Syriac version, dated palaeographically to the seventh century, differs from the Greek in some important aspects that may bear on whatever historicity may be attributed to the narrative.

Availability of texts aside, we must return to Devreesse's appraisal of the value of the Ammonius λόγος as a historical document. He sums it up bluntly in these words: "Ammonius, if the expression be permitted me that best

---

[4] R. Devreesse, "Le christianisme dans la peninsule sinäitique des origines à l'arrivée des Musulmans," *RB* 49 (1940), 216–220. See also entries in recent encyclopedias and manuals of patrology.

[5] F. Combefis, *Illustrium Christi martyrum lecti triumphi* (Paris 1660), 88–132.

[6] Agnes Smith Lewis, *The Forty Martyrs of the Sinai Desert = Horae Semiticae* 9 (Cambridge 1912); translation on pages 1–14.

[7] The text, fols. 351r–358v, was graciously sent to me by Professor Ihor Ševčenko. I wish to express my thanks to Professor Ševčenko for putting it at my disposal.

expresses my feelings, Ammonius smells of falsehood *à plein nez*."[8] Devreesse pictures the writer of the narrative as having before him the Eusebius' *Ecclesiastical History* from which he has borrowed the names of Ammonius and Peter of Alexandria, two confessors of the faith during the persecution of Diocletian. From Sozomenus, according to Devreesse, the writer has taken the accounts of the conversion of Mauvia and the phylarch Zocom, and of a saintly man by the name of Moses who refused to be ordained by the Arian bishop of Alexandria, and from these he has fashioned elements of his narrative that speak of the death of a phylarch (which leads to the Bedouin raid on Mount Sinai) and of an eremite by the name of Moses who converted Obedianos, the chief of the Pharanites.[9] On the raid by the Blemmyes on Raithou, Devreesse makes no specific comment. He is however, willing to accept as authentic "that which relates to the life of the Sinaites, the fortified monastery, the hermitages, the name of Doulas. "Likewise," he continues, "let us retain the fact that Raithou was in the immediate vicinity of Elim and the palm trees, that there were hermitages at Raithou, a small fort and a church; that Pharan was guarded by Christian Arabs. All this was known previously. The rest was fabricated toward the end of the sixth century by the learned monks of Sinai to give a vivid account of a bloody incursion or a massacre of monks of the peninsula, occurring unexpectedly on a certain January 14; the number of 40 martyrs — 80, to count exactly — would even have been able to be borrowed from another literary source."[10]

My objection to this kind of historical analysis is that it is highly imaginative and based upon pure speculation, hardly upon the text. Are we to believe that some learned monks sat in the library of the Monastery of Saint Catherine shortly after it was completed and, having before them copies of the histories of Eusebius and Sozomenus, cribbed motifs for a semi-fictional narrative? And why is Devreesse so certain that a massacre occurred on January 14 when the text mentions both Tybi 2 (December 28) and January 14? Why not, rather, take Ammonius at his word that sometime during the bishopric of Peter of Alexandria (373–381) he made a pilgrimage to Mount Sinai, was caught in a Bedouin raid on the eremitic community there, and then returned to Egypt where he wrote of his experiences in his native language? This hypothesis is far less speculative than Devreesse's, although it should not be taken to mean that all details contained in the narrative are historical fact.

A prior question must, however, be raised that may bear upon the

[8] R. Devreesse, *op. cit.*, 218.
[9] *Ibid.*, 218–219.
[10] *Ibid.*, 219–220.

character not only of the Ammonius narrative but of the 'Nilus' *Narrationes* as well. The question is, simply, why were these narratives put into writing. The answer cannot be that Sinaitic ascetics, isolated and halfstarved in their devout austerity, were whiling away their time writing historical fiction, as has been claimed for the 'Nilus' *Narrationes,* or that they were engaged in dramatizing one particular raid out of the many that were part and parcel of life in that region. The answer must lie in the statements made by the writers themselves: namely, that they were strangers or recent comers to Sinai, that they witnessed a raid, and that they heard of others from information brought by other eye-witnesses. Apart from the desire to inform and edify the faithful, there were, I believe, yet other inspirational forces that led to these written accounts: that is, the topographical character of Sinai and the mores of the Bedouins and ascetics who inhabited the region. As seen through the eyes of strangers to the region, the extraordinary and dramatic setting of the land, as well as the contrasting lifestyles of the Christian eremites and the pagan Bedouins, must have stirred an interest in reporting those fascinating and marvelous sights to their communities back home. One need only review the *itineraria* of Egeria and Antoninus of Piacenza, of Felix Fabri and his companions, and of many others through the centuries to see how outsiders were inspired to put their experiences in Sinai into writing. The same may be said for Egypt, for what would we know of monastic life in the eastern and western deserts of Egypt if we had to rely on written accounts of the monks themselves, if we did not have reports on them from visitors to or temporary residents of those remote and inaccessible regions?

The point to be stressed here is that the Ammonius narrative and the *Narrationes* should, like so many others, be taken as reports coming from travelers who were strangers to Sinai. Unlike others, however, they tell of raids that had tragic consequences for eremitic communities: the *Narrationes* tell of a single Bedouin raid on Mount Sinai and its environs; the Ammonius narrative speaks of a similar raid and of one by Blemmyes on the community at Raithou. Whether the Ammonius narrative conflates two accounts of raids, one at Sinai and one at Raithou, at widely separated times, we have no sure way of knowing. If we were to take Ammonius at his word, he appears to have been an eyewitness to the raid at Mount Sinai and immediately thereafter to have received reports of the raid on Raithou. It is obvious from the amount of detail on the raid on Raithou that Ammonius — or whoever was responsible for conflating the two accounts — was far more taken by that event than the one at Mount Sinai. If a raid by some 300 Blemmyes from overseas did actually take place, we can well understand why he devoted so much of his narrative to its description. We should also anticipate a considerable amount of overdramatization of the events in a conflict between pagans and Christians as well as a eulogizing of the way of life of the ascetics and their bravery in the face of sure death. Although these eremites lived in a period free from religious persecution by imperial decree, their death at the hands of pagan marauders was considered martyrdom by a baptism by blood. And the coincidence of forty dead at each site should not be accepted as an actual body count but as a number that had emotional associations with the biblical number forty.

If the Devreesse thesis lacks cogency, as I believe it does, what is there in the account as we have it that would confidently place it in a fourth-century context and give some assurance that it is not a fabrication of late date? The text, like many others of its genre, provides no sure answer, especially since it is said to be a translation from the Coptic by a certain John the Presbyter who found it in the home of a hermit.[11] It is possible, however, to make some reasonable assessment of the narrative in terms of its plausibility and to judge whether or not it jibes with what we know of life on and around Mount Sinai during the early period of monastic development.

The narrative is written in the first person singular. It opens with Ammonius relating that he was a monk living in a cell at Canopus near Alexandria. Unhappy over the persecution of Bishop Peter and his followers, he resolved to travel to the Holy Land. After visiting and worshiping at all the holy places, he set out for Mount Sinai in company with other devout Christians. They reached their destination in eighteen days. There Ammonius spent his time in prayer and consultation with the eremites, who, through solitude and severe abstention, had achieved outstanding piety. A short time thereafter, the death of a Saracen sheikh precipitated a sudden attach by Saracens, who killed all those they could find in Gethrabbi, Chobar, Kodar, and other areas around the Holy Mountain. But those near a tower, together with Doulas, the "superior," ran inside for shelter. As the Saracens approached them, a great flame accompanied by much smoke appeared on the top of the mountain. The monks begged God to save them, and the terrified Saracens fled, leaving behind their shields and camels. The survivors then came out of the tower and took account of the slaughter of their companions. They found 38 dead: 12 in Gethrabbi and the rest in various other places. The bodies were quickly buried, and attention was given to two eremites, Isaiah and Sabas, who were wounded but still alive. Isaiah died that same evening, but Sabas, not having serious injuries, lingered on. This frustrated and upset him because he considered it a sign of his unworthiness to join the other martyrs. After having begged God to let him die, he finally had his wish fulfilled on the

---

[11] F. Combefis, *op. cit.,* 131–132.

third day following the massacre, which had taken place on the second of Tybi.[12]

This is a summary of the story that Ammonius tells of the Bedouin attack on Mount Sinai and its environs. In the Greek text of Combefis, the account occupies only eight pages out of a total of 45. It should be noted that the episode is recounted without excessive embellishment and without specific exempla of piety and fortitude such as are often found in the lives or the sayings of the fathers. Where one would expect an extended treatment concerning the ascetic way of life, it is summed up in these few sentences:

> Remaining in solitude for the entire week, they all gathered together in the Lord's house (τὸ κυριακόν) when the evening of the Lord's Day dawned (sic) for the sabbath; and when they had said their evening prayers together, and in the morning had taken part in the immaculate and life-giving mysteries of Christ, each one returned again to his own place. Their bodily form and way of life were angelic, for they were exceedingly pale in aspect and wasted away in body through excessive abstinences, being almost incorporeal. They possessed nothing of those things that bring pleasure and luxuriousness, neither wine nor olive oil nor bread at all, just a few date palms or some fruit trees with which they made do for their bodily needs. In consideration of strangers who were present for prayers, a few loaves of bread were stored away in the house of the "superior" (παρὰ τῷ προεστῶτι) of the place.[13]

Following this statement, Ammonius tells of the Bedouin attack. The cause was the death of the sheikh of the local tribe or confederation of tribes (φυλαρχία) with whom the ascetic community must have had some form of agreement guaranteeing its safety. With the death of their leader, the Bedouins apparently felt under no obligation to honor the agreement and fell upon the solitaries scattered about Mount Sinai. The result was that many were killed, except those who, finding themselves near a tower (πύργος), fled there together with the προεστώς Doulas whom Ammonius describes as "truly the servant of Christ for he had more patience and gentleness than anyone else, and from this people called him Moses."[14]

---

[12] *Ibid.*, 88–95.

[13] *Ibid.*, 90. The phrase παρὰ τῷ προεστῶτι, "in the house of the superior" must surely indicate that no organized monastic establishment existed at Mount Sinai at the time this document was written. I have placed the word superior in inverted commas to avoid it being confused with the formal head of a monastic establishment. As I indicate below (page 140), the προεστώς is merely the "leading man" or "chief." Later on in the account (*Ibid.*, 96), he is called the πρῶτος, the same word that is used to describe Obedianus and other Saracen sheikhs (*Ibid.*, 101, 128).

[14] *Ibid.*, 91. R. Devreesse, *op. cit.*, 219, sees in the name Doulas and the tower — which is also referred to as a "stronghold" (ὀχύρωμα), and not as a "fortress" as Devreesse would have it — as

The attack took place in a limited area around Mount Sinai. Three sites are named: Gethrabbi, Chobar, and Kodar. Gethrabbi is Beth Rabbeh, Rabbeh being the name of a peak located a very short distance from Mount Sinai at the mouth of Wadi Ledga.[15] Twelve bodies were recovered from a monastic dwelling ($\mu o\nu\acute{\eta}$) at this site. At present there is a garden and a chapel of the Twelve Apostles at the foot of this peak, possibly commemorating the twelve who were martyred there. Chobar is Choreb or Horeb, part of the Mount Sinai range, cited in the *itinerarium* of Antoninus of Piacenza as being separated from Mount Sinai by a valley.[16] Where Kodar was located is not known. The tower mentioned by Ammonius is also unknown. It could have been the tower cited by Eutychius as being near the Burning Bush,[17] or it could have been one of several others built by the monks for their safety. Surprisingly enough, no mention is made of deaths occurring at the holiest place on Mount Sinai, that of the Burning Bush; hence the likelihood is that the tower is not the one mentioned by Eutychius.

Ammonius then goes on to recount how the Bedouins were about to attack him and his companions when miraculously lightning flashed on the peaks — a not altogether uncommon occurrence at Mount Sinai during the winter months — frightening off the attackers. There follows a description of the atrocities committed by the Bedouins on the defenseless eremites, the burial of the dead, and the death of two wounded monks, Isaiah and Sabas. The latter, not seriously wounded according to Ammonius, prayed that he not be separated from "the holy fathers who died earlier, but in me let the fortieth number of your servants be filled." He died, says Ammonius, on "the third day after the death of the holy men, which was the second in the month of Tybi."[18]

An examination of this part of the narrative suggests nothing, in terms of

---

evidence of the writer's having derived from historical sources, Procopius and Eutychius, the information on the foundation of the Justinian monastery at Mount Sinai. The name Doulas should come as no surprise since the solitaries at Mount Sinai are often called servants ($\delta o\tilde{\upsilon}\lambda o\iota$) of God or of Christ. Theodoulus, for example, is a central figure in the 'Nilus' *Narrationes* (cf. above, note 2). And the name of the Saracen sheikh, Obedianus, is a Hellenized form of the Semitic Obadiah and Abdullah, the Servant of God.

[15] Cf. E. H. Palmer, *The Desert of the Exodus* (London 1871), 120–121. In the 'Nilus' *Narrationes* (cf. above, note 2), col. 664B, the site is called $\beta\epsilon\sigma\vartheta\rho\alpha\mu\beta\eta$, where one of the eremites died as a result of the Bedouin raid described in that narrative.

[16] P. Geyer, ed., *Itinera Hierosolymitana Saeculi IIII-VIII (Corpus Scriptorum Ecclesiasticorum Latinorum)* 39 (Prague 1898), 183–184.

[17] J. P. Migne, *Patrologia series graeca* 3 (Paris 1857–1866), col. 1071.

[18] F. Combefis, *op. cit.,* 95.

anachronism or terminology, of a date as late as the sixth century. The conventional hierarchy associated with organized monastic communities of that date is completely lacking. Normally, we would expect to find the names of the monks prefixed with the reverential title of "abba" and the superior of the monastic community called ἡγούμενος.[19] In place of these common elements the reverential title is completely absent, and Doulas is merely the προεστώς, "the leading man" or "chief".[20] The use of the substantive τὸ κυριακόν, "the Lord's house" is essentially a fourth-century usage for ἐκκλησία.[21] And most compelling, if this were a fictional account of martyrdom at Mount Sinai, we would expect to hear of a bloody massacre at the holiest of sites, that of the Burning Bush. No mention of it occurs whatsoever.

In sum, the evidence is admittedly *prima facie* for the most part, but strong enough, I believe, to overthrow the contention of a sixth-century date and to support the plausibility of the attack on Tybi 2 (December 28) sometime during the bishopric of Peter of Alexandria (373–381). If a case has been made, it would also support the conclusion that the translator of the narrative — if this portion of the account had originally been written in Coptic — was also a near contemporary of Ammonius.

In turning from the rather simple and straightforward account of the Bedouin raid on Mount Sinai to that of the Blemmye attack on Raithou, there are significant differences to be noted in narrative technique and terminology. First of all, the writer of the narrative was not an eyewitness to the Blemmye raid. The news of the raid is first brought to Mount Sinai by an "Ishmaelite" and then a full account is given by an eremite of Raithou who fled and sought safety at Mount Sinai.[22] The second narrator gives a dramatic turn to the events that he is called upon to describe. He embellishes his account with a vivid description of his fellow anchorites — for so he calls them — facing their martyrdom through a baptism by blood and of the atrocities perpetrated by the Blemmyes on the bodies of the fallen eremites.[23]

---

[19] Consistently so in the extant documents of the sixth and seventh centuries in the Negeb and Sinai. Cf. C. J. Kraemer, *Excavations at Nessana: non-literary papyri* 3 (Princeton 1958); F. L. Nau, "Le texte grec des récits du moine Anastase sur les saints pères du Sinaï," *Oriens Christianus*, 2 (1902), 60–89.

[20] See above, note 13.

[21] See citations in E. A. Sophocles, *Greek Lexicon of the Roman and Byzantine Periods* (New York 1900), and in other Greek dictionaries. Note that the *Concilium Laodicenum* (A.D. 343/381), Can. 28, makes a distinction between the two: "It is not necesary to prepare the so-called common meal either in Lord's houses (κυριακοῖς) or in churches (ἐκκλησίαις) . . ."

[22] F. Combefis, *op. cit.*, 95–130.

[23] The use of a second narrator to report on events that take place at a distance is also found in the *Narrationes* (cf. above, note 2). In that account (cols. 641–655; 680–688) the narrator receives

The use of the word "Ishmaelite" catches one's eye. Throughout this part of the narration, the common word for Bedouins or Arabs — that is, Saracens — is conspicuously absent although Arabs ultimately repel the attack of the Blemmyes and bury the bodies of the fallen eremites with great solemnity. They are referred to as "the people (λαϊκός) in the territory of the Pharanites," "the local residents" (οἱ ἐντόπιοι), and "the Ishmaelites of Pharan."[24]

By way of further contrast with the earlier account, the story of the attack by the Blemmyes is interrupted by a long digression describing the geographical location of the eremitic community at Raithou and depicting the extraordinary piety and asceticism of some of the resident hermits. Although there is a Herodotean quality to this kind of narrative, it must be kept in mind that these details are being related to strangers to the region, Ammonius and his companions, who had called upon the man to tell "precisely what happened to the holy fathers and how he himself escaped in safety from the barbarians, and with what virtues and deeds these holy men conducted themselves."[25]

The consistency of terminology that was noticed in the earlier part of the narrative dealing with Mount Sinai is lacking in the part dealing with Raithou. As the narrative progresses, the use of the reverential title "abba" begins to appear;[26] and although the word κυριακόν is most often used, the word ἐκκλησία makes its appearance four times in place of it.[27] It is possible that these inconsistencies — minor perhaps — crept into the later part of the text during the period of transmission; yet it is worth noting how free the earlier part of the text is of them.

Finally, prior to the epilog we are given the date of the martyrdom of the forty at Raithou. In the Combefis text it reads: "These holy, victorious (martyrs) of Christ died in the month of Tybi on the second, around the ninth hour; according to the Romans their memory is celebrated in the month of January on the fourteenth."[28] The text of *Sinaiticus* 267 reads: "These holy, victorious (martyrs) of Christ died in the month of January on the fourteenth

---

additional information of other Bedouin attacks from a young man who had escaped from the hands of the Bedouins, and from Theodoulus, the son of the narrator, when father and son were reunited.

[24] F. Combefis, *op. cit.*, 109, 110, 124. Does writer of the narrative wish to distinguish between the two: the Saracens, pagan Arabs, desert raiders and the enemy; the Ishmaelites, Christian Arabs (see below, note 47) and friendly to the small eremitic community at Raithou? Or is there another hand at work in this portion of the account? Note that the Syriac text (cf. above, note 6) uses the word "Saracen" throughout.

[25] *Ibid.*, 96–97.

[26] *Ibid.*, 104, 105, 129, 130.

[27] *Ibid.*, 99, 111, 118, 121.

[28] *Ibid.*, 129.

around the ninth hour."[29] Unlike the simple statement dating the Bedouin raid at Mount Sinai — that Sabas died "on the third day after the death of the holy men, which was the second day in the month of Tybi" — this elaborate dating formula strongly suggests an interpolation at a much later date to fit in with the day observed in the church calendar for the martyrdom of the monks at Mount Sinai and Raithou.[30]

Despite the fact that there are aspects in this part of the text that do not neatly fall into place, there is nothing within it by way of anachronism or ambiguity that would betray a late fourth-century date. The eremitic community at Raithou is described as being minuscule: only 43 souls who live in caves or in holes in the ground (i.e., burrows), "practising asceticism in solitude with God and known by him alone who knows the things that are hidden (τὰ κρυπτά)."[31] The text provides a fairly accurate description of its site: a two-day journey from Mount Sinai, close to the Red Sea (i.e., the Gulf of Suez), mountain ranges to the east, a stony plain between the mountains and the community, springs and palm trees linking Raithou with biblical Elim.[32] Recent archaeological surveys have identified Raithou with monastic remains at Bir Abu Suweira,[33] a short distance north of Tor, some 50 km. or so southwest of Pharan, and roughly 80 km. southwest of Mount Sinai.

There is no evidence of monastic organization within this tiny community,

---

[29] *Sinaiticus Graecus* 358[r].

[30] I have also suggested the possibility of an interpolation for a more elaborate statement in the *Narrationes* (P. Mayerson, *op. cit.*, [note 3], 64 note 44). The statement (col. 640 C) reads: "They died on the seventh day after the Epiphany, which is the 14th of January. Pious men are very interested in learning the time and the names, since they want to check this information with the memories of holy men. Others were killed some years before, whose memory they celebrate on the same day because of the length of the journey and the size of the assemblage."

In the Syriac version (see above, note 6), the date of the massacre is not mentioned — not even that at Mount Sinai — until the very end of the document. It was unquestionably appended by the translator, giving further support to our view that this date at least is an interpolation in the Greek text. The translation of the Syriac text (page 14) reads: "The life of the Holy Fathers who were slain at Mount Sinai and Raîtho, is finished, in the days of Pope Peter of Alexandria. But the memory of these holy ones is made in December in the months of the Romans, the 28th."

On the matter of the date and its relationship to the church calendar, cf. P. Mayerson, "An Inscription in the Monastery of St. Catherine and the Martyr Tradition in Sinai," *Dumbarton Oaks Papers* 30 (1976), 375–379.

[31] F. Combefis, *op. cit.*, 107.

[32] *Ibid.*, 96–98.

[33] Personal communications from Dr. Yoram Tsafrir, Department of Archaeology, The Hebrew University, Jerusalem. I have also visited the site of Abu Suweira, where I have seen remains of monastic dwellings and chapels. Raithou shares with at least one other site, Wadi Gharandel (Surandela or Arandara in ancient itineraries), springs and palm trees, and hence the identification of both sites with biblical Elim.

not even a προεστώς. Paul, a native of Petra, is apparently the most revered member of the group, and is simply described as "our most holy father."[34] Other members that are mentioned in the narrative come from Pharan (Moses),[35] the Thebaid in Egypt (Psoes),[36] Aila (Joseph)[37] and Rome (Domnos).[38] The eremites have a church (κυριακόν, ἐκκλησία) and a "meeting place" (συνακτήριον),[39] if the two are not one and the same. The church is walled around with "bricks" — in this region, most likely blocks of stone —up to twice the height of a man, and hence was considered a "so-called fort" (τὸ λεγόμενον κάστρον).[40]

This is the setting of the story prior to the attack of the Blemmyes, who are also called Moors (Μαῦροι).[41] We then hear that two men, apparently Christian seamen, arrive at Raithou and report that their ship, which had sailed from Aila, lay at anchor in a port in the territory of Ethiopia when it was seized by a band of about 300 Blemmyes. They demanded to be taken to Clysma. With the threat of death hanging over the crew, "we promised them to do this, and we waited for a day on which the south wind would arise, so that we might sail."[42] The two men escaped and made their way across the gulf to warn the community at Raithou. Spotters were stationed near the sea. A day later they saw a ship headed in their direction. The local residents, "as many as were found in the territory of the Pharanites," prepared to fight "for the sake of their women, children, and herds of camels." The monks fled into their fortified church.[43]

The Blemmyes entered the harbor and spent the night near the mountain.

---

[34] F. Combefis, *op. cit.*, 111.

[35] *Ibid.*, 99.

[36] *Ibid.*, 102.

[37] *Ibid.*, 102.

[38] *Ibid.*, 128. Omitted in Sinaiticus Graecus 358ʳ but retained in the Syriac version.

[39] *Ibid.*, 98–99.

[40] *Ibid.*, 110.

[41] *Ibid.*, 95, 109, 110, 123. The association of Μαῦροι (i.e., Blacks or Nubians?) with Blemmyes is to my knowledge unrecorded.

[42] *Ibid.*, 107–108. While we cannot identify the Ethiopian port, Epiphanius (*Haereses* 2.46 = J. P. Migne, *Patrologia series graeca* 42 [Paris 1857–1866] col. 29) mentions three ports on the Red Sea (Aila, the fort of Clysma, and Berenice) where ships unloaded their cargoes from India for transshipment within the Roman empire. Note the confusion in the Syriac text (see above, note 6, page 7): ". . . the Blemmyes . . . seized a boat which was beyond Elath . . ."
The Syriac version also has the two men crossing the sea "on boats of palm-wood." The Greek text has them crossing "on foreign timber" (ἐπάνω ξενικῶν ξύλων), "timber (ξύλα) belonging to Ethiopian territory." I believe what is meant here is a craft of some sort, a raft or dugout canoe; or, less likely, by metonymy, "on a foreign ship."

[43] *Ibid.*, 109.

In the morning they put all their hostages ashore except one whom they left behind on the ship with a Moor to guard him. In the initial battle that followed, the Moors killed 147 men, captured the women and children, and held them prisoners near the springs. They then turned their attention to the church, thinking to find money and other valuable possessions stored there. Terrified by the sound of the howling barbarians as they circled the walls, the monks lost heart until Paul of Petra strengthened their resolve to die as martyrs. The Blemmyes brought long poles, scaled the protecting wall, and burst into the church. Angered both by the attitude of the eremites as they prayerfully awaited their martydom and by the absence of anything of value, they cruelly slaughtered everyone in sight and filled the whole church with blood. The narrator took advantage of the Blemmyes' occupation with Paul to hide under a pile of palm branches in a corner.[44]

Since their raid had proven completely useless, the Blemmyes returned to the springs, intending to continue on to Clysma. An unexpected complication awaited them. The Christian hostage who had been left behind had killed his Moor guard, sank the ship by running it aground, and then escaped to the mountain. Insane with frustration and rage, the barbarians killed all the women and children prisoners and burned down the palm trees.[45]

Meanwhile, since word of the raid had gotten about, a force of 600 select archers from Pharan gathered and marched on the Blemmyes. Seeing the superior force of Pharanites and their own impossibility of retreat, the Blemmyes stood their ground bravely and fought till they were all killed. The Pharanites lost 84 of their men.[46]

The narrator continues his story with the aftermath of the massacre. He came out of his hiding place and took stock of the disaster. All the holy men were dead except three, and of the three only one was seriously wounded. The Pharanites, led by Obedianus — a sheikh ($\pi\rho\tilde{\omega}\tau\sigma$, $\dot{\alpha}\rho\chi\dot{\eta}$) converted to Christianity after having been miraculously cured by the hermit Moses of Pharan[47] — buried their dead in caves on the mountain and then helped the survivors to bury the martyred eremites. Adorned with costly garments brought by the

---

[44] *Ibid.*, 109–123.

[45] *Ibid.*, 123–124.

[46] *Ibid.*, 124–125.

[47] *Ibid.*, 99–101. Moses of Pharan, as related by the refugee from Raithou, was an aged solitary to whom "God. . .had given. . .power over unclean spirits so that he cured many and converted to Christianity nearly all the people living on the borders of the Ishmaelites who inhabit the region of Pharan." Obedianus was similarly cured of an evil spirit — one that attempted to deter Moses from isolating himself completely during Lent — as he approached the cell of the holy man.

Pharanites and accompanied by psalm singing and palm branches, the 39 martyrs were carried to their final rest. The mortally wounded eremite, who died that same evening, was buried with the others. The date of the martydom of the 40 is then given: January 14, or Tybi 2. Two of the survivors were unable to decide whether to remain at Raithou; but the narrator, because of the desolation of the place and traumatized by memories of the massacre, decided to leave and seek sanctuary with the monks at Mount Sinai.[48]

This is a summary of the Blemmye attack on Raithou and its consequences. Once again, it is difficult to sort out what is fictional, exaggerated or historically accurate. That there was a community of eremites at Raithou is beyond dispute. That the Blemmyes continually harried the Roman frontiers of Egypt during the fourth century and extended their raids into the eastern desert along the coast of the Red Sea is also beyond dispute.[49] That they attempted a piratical raid on Clysma at the head of the Gulf of Suez is certainly not beyond belief. The story told by the men who escaped and made their way to Raithou has the ring of verisimilitude. The strategy of the Blemmyes was to capture a ship and to force the crew to sail them to their destination. However, as the men reported "we waited for a day on which the south wind would arise so that we might set sail." Keeping in mind that the date of the massacre at Raithou was late December (Tybi 2 = December 28) or mid-January and the fact that the south wind in the Red Sea blows mainly during the winter months,[50] if then at all, the least that can be said is that the narrative contains some accurate information concerning sailing conditions in the Red Sea and the Gulf of Suez. If the south wind is so unreliable — near Tor the northwest wind predominates throughout the year — the ship carrying the Blemmyes could easily have been blown toward Raithou where it would await a favoring breeze rather than attempt to beat against stiff northwest winds. It is also possible that Tor — a very short distance south of Raithou and the first good harbor en route north — may have been the Blemmyes' intended port of call before proceeding on to Clysma.

The strategy used by the Blemmyes in attacking the monks is equally striking in its plausibility. The church — which was surrounded by a wall twice the

[48] *Ibid.,* 125–130.

[49] See the article "Blemyes" in G. Wissowa, ed., *Pauly's Real-Encyclopädie der classischen Altertumswissenschaft* 3:1 (Stuttgart 1897), cols. 565–568. Cf. also W. B. Emery and L. Kirwan, *The Royal Tombs of Ballana and Qustul* 1 (Mission archéologique de Nubie 1929–1934; Cairo 1938), 10–11.

[50] Cf. "Physical Geography of the Red Sea with Sailing Directions by Captain W. Kropp," *United States Hydrographic Office — Bureau of Navigation Publication* 39 (Washington 1872), 9–10; 19. Cf. also *British Admiralty: Red Sea and Gulf of Aden Pilot* (London 1944), 48–49.

height of a man, say about three meters — was hardly a serious obstacle to the attackers. Using long poles of palm logs (ξύλα μακρά) they scaled the wall and overpowered the 43 inhabitants with ease.[51] The Blemmyes, long known as a fighting force capable of overrunning settlements as large as cities — they were prepared in this instance to attack Clysma — could hardly have been fazed by the "so-called fort" (τὸ λεγόμενον κάστρον) designed to protect the handful of eremites against Bedouin attacks. It is the kind of installation that is reported in the sixth-century itinerary of Antoninus of Piacenza. At Sur-andela (Arandara), present day Wadi Gharandel to the north of Raithou, Antoninus and his companions came upon a fortified monastery (castellum) containing a church, its priest, and two hospices; and farther along the route towards Egypt, they came upon another castellum and a hospice.[52] At Mount Sinai, by way of contrast, a simple tower was all that was used by the eremites to protect them from Bedouin attacks. And it is well documented that Bedouins found it difficult to surmount an obstacle of any size.[53] Further, at Bir Abu Suweira, the site of Raithou, there can still be seen — as I myself have observed — a stone wall about three meters high protecting the entrance to a small chapel of unknown date.

On a far lesser scale of credibility is the matter of numbers and coinci-dence. The coincidence of 40 eremites being martyred at each site may, as stated above, be written off as a number that had emotional associations with the biblical number forty. And whether the two events occurred on the same day is also highly questionable, although there is no way of proving it one way or the other. As to the number of Ishmaelite casualties involved in the incident at Raithou, it is quite possible that the Blemmyes did kill 147 men in the first of the two battles and 84 in the second. These are precise numbers and may represent an actual body count although a better estimate of their reliabi-lity could be made if we knew more about the size of the lay communities either at Pharan or at Raithou. However, the number 600 representing the select archers from the territory of Pharan can mean nothing more than "a large number"; the number 600 is the proverbial figure often given for an indeterminately large group. Whereas there is no qualification given to the number 600, the "about 300" Blemmyes reported as seizing a ship is a num-ber that at least could be transported by a merchant vessel without difficulty.

With the report from the refugee from Raithou concluded, the narrative is

---

[51] F. Combefis, op. cit., 115.

[52] P. Geyer, ed., op. cit., 187.

[53] Cf. P. Mayerson, "The First Muslim Attacks on Southern Palestine (A.D. 633-634)," Trans-actions and Proceedings of the American Philological Association, 95 (1964), 180-184.

quickly brought to an end. The eremites at Sinai then recounted their own experience and they wondered at the coincidence of both disasters happening on the same day and at the same time, with an equal number of dead in both cases. The προεστώς Doulas arose, praised the martyrs, and called his fellow monks to prayer. Ammonius then reports that he himself returned to Egypt, not to his old location at Canopus, but to a tiny house near Memphis, where he wrote of his experiences. He concludes with these words: "Here I live and continually read the accounts of the noble martyrs of Christ, rejoicing in their struggles and sufferings for the glory of the Father and Son and Holy Ghost." As a postscript there is a statement by John the Presbyter (or Elder), who "found this with God's help at the home of an anchorite, an old man, near Naucratis, written in Egyptian, which I translated into Greek since I am very familiar with the language of the Egyptians."[54]

It is this final statement that leads Devreessee to an exclamation of disbelief: "La déclaration finale devait déjà mettre en éveil: un récit composé par un lecteur d'Actes des martyrs et traduit du copte de grec!"[55] I, on the other hand, find the statement convincing, convincing in that the detail concerning Ammonius' new location near Memphis serves no literary artifice, and that Ammonius' dedication to reading the accounts of martyrs is not at all extraordinary. After having barely escaped being a martyr himself, why should he not have been interested in reading about coreligionists who suffered martyrdom? As to the statement of the translator, John the Presbyter, I do not find it beyond belief that Ammonius, an Egyptian, should write in Coptic and that his work should be put into the lingua franca of the Near East. Compared to the writer of the *Narrationes*, Ammonius obviously has none of the literary pretensions or formal training of a well educated man.[56] Or, to put it simply, even though he may have known Greek, he may have felt more comfortable writing in Coptic. Of course, if one considers the entire account to be a work of fiction, then every statement becomes suspect.

In conclusion, the Ammonius narrative in my view is not a work of fiction or semi-fiction of the sixth century. The account, all of it, appears certainly to have been written at about the time that the events described in it occurred —

[54] F. Combefis, *op. cit.*, 130–132.

[55] R. Devreesse, *op. cit.*, 218.

[56] I am also struck by the complete absence of any quotation from the Scriptures in that part of the narrative concerned with the attack on Mount Sinai. For Raithou there is only one quotation, Math. 11.28, (F. Combefis, *op. cit.*, 114) when, miraculously, a voice came from the altar in reply to the prayer of Paul of Petra saying, "Come unto me, all ye that labor and are heavy laden, and I will give you rest." One might suspect that Ammonius was truly a humble monk who was acquainted more with asceticism than with the Scriptures.

that is, the late fourth century. The description of the eremitic form of life is consistent with what we know of the development of early monasticism. I have also observed nothing in terms of language or terminology that would arouse any suspicion that the narrative was composed in the sixth century or later. I remain convinced that the story of the Bedouin attack at Mount Sinai is highly plausible, if not certain. The account of the Blemmye attack at Raithou is another matter. There are elements within the report that are equally as plausible as that of the attack on Mount Sinai. There are other elements, such as the coincidence of the time and number slain at both sites, that are not reasonable to accept as historical fact. It may very well be that the writer of the narrative took the story of this raid from another source, if in fact another hand may not have appended it to the account of the raid on Mount Sinai. Since, however, we possess so little information about the Blemmyes, whatever we do come across should not be casually set aside but rather analyzed with care. And finally, it must be recognized — as I have stated once before[57] — that experiences in the desert *are* dramatic, and very often read like fiction. These adventures are sometimes difficult for scholarly critics to appreciate or evaluate.

[57] P. Mayerson, "The Desert of Southern Palestine according to Byzantine Sources," *Proceedings of the American Philosophical Society* 107:2 (1963), 161 note 8. Cf. also W. F. Albright, *Yahweh and the Gods of Canaan* (New York 1968), 240.

Mauia, Queen of the Saracens
A Cautionary Note

PHILIP MAYERSON

New York University

THE story of Mauia (or Mavia),[1] queen of the Saracens during the reign of Valens (364–378 C.E.), fascinated church historians from the time it was set down by Rufinus of Aquileia early in the fifth century. Modern historians have likewise been attracted to Mauia — largely, I suspect, in their desire to fill in lacunae in the events of the late fourth century or to flesh out a skimpy statement appearing in an inscription or in some ancient writer. The result has not always been a happy one for historiography, especially when assumptions tend to be taken as historical fact. So it is that on the one hand we find Mauia described as the wife of the chief of a very powerful tribe of Saracens (i.e. Bedouin) at Pharan, deep in Sinai,[2] while on the other hand she is said to be an Arian convert carrying out military operations in the region of Umm el-Jemal and Deir el-Kahf in Syria.[3] We hear of her as having been 'une belle fille chrétienne, que les Sarassins avaient enlevée'; and that it was she who had provided the troop of Saracens for the defence of Constantinople mentioned by Ammianus Marcellinus.[4]

A brief sentence concerning Saracens in the *Expositio Totius Mundi et Gentium* — 'And they say that women rule over them' — leads the editor of the text to assume that the writer was alluding to the reign of Mauia.[5] It also occasions an imaginative reconstruction of her life: she was a Christian slave, married to a Saracen sheikh; after her husband's death (*c.* 355–358) she gradually gained control over a large number of tribes and became powerful enough to wage a war in Roman territory; she attacked Syria in *c.* 370, at which time she had a nubile daughter about fifteen years of age who, according to the terms of the agreement to conclude the hostilities against Valens, was married off to Victor, the *magister militum*; she was a believer in the Nicene Creed.[6] A

---

[1]   Mauia or Mavia does not appear to be a common Arabic name. F. Altheim and R. Stiehl: *Die Araber in der Alten Welt*, V. 2, Berlin, 1969, p. 328, give as its meaning, 'die (brünstige) Hündin, die Hunde anheulen'. See also E. Littman: *Thamūd und Ṣafā*, Leipzig, 1940, p. 74.

[2]   A. Couret: *La Palestine sous les Empereurs grecs, 326–636*, Grenoble, 1869, p. 73. As a point of reference I have used, for the most part, the secondary material cited by A.A. Vasiliev: Notes on Some Episodes Concerning the Relations between the Arabs and the Byzantine Empire from the Fourth to the Sixth Century, *Dumbarton Oaks Papers* 9–10 (1956), p. 307, n. 3.

[3]   G.W. Bowersock: Limes Arabicus, *Harvard Studies in Classical Philology* 80 (1976), pp. 223, 226. Professor Bowersock has informed me that he was mistaken about Mauia's conversion to Arianism.

[4]   A. Piganiol: *L'Empire chrétien, 325–395*, Paris, 1947, p. 169, n. 2.

[5]   J. Rougé (ed.) in *Sources chrétiennes*, CXXIV, Paris, 1966, pp. 154, 234.

[6]   *Ibid.*, p. 25.

similar attempt to place Mauia in a fuller historical context included her in an unin-
terrupted succession of phylarchs in Rome's service from the time of Imrū al-Qays (d.
328) to Jafna, the reputed founder of the Ghassanid dynasty under Emperor Anastasius
(491–518).[7] And when the name of a certain Mauia appeared in a dedicatory inscription, dated to 425, in a church in Syria, it was attributed to 'Maouia II... née du mariage
politique conclu en 373'.[8] Finally, since her husband's name is not known, Mauia is
linked in marriage to Obedianus, a desert chief of Pharan in Sinai, or to the little-known
Ghassanid emir, Harith II (360–373).[9]

The question raised by this confusion of interpretations is whether we have evidence in
hand strong enough to sustain any of them. My answer is in the negative, and I wish to
put forward the proposition that the story of Mauia as it appears in the church
historians — our only source — is of limited historical value and should be used with
considerable caution. I would further maintain that the interest of the church historians
lay less in Mauia than in a certain hermit by the name of Moses, who fearlessly attacked
the heresy known as Arianism and its chief advocate and enforcer in Alexandria. And
since it is Rufinus' narrative that was taken up by succeeding church historians —
Socrates, Sozomenus and Theodoretus in the main — who adapted and enlarged upon
the story, it is his account, and the context in which it is placed, that should for the most
part determine how much credence ought to be given to Mauia and her activities.

Sometime late in 401, Rufinus undertook to translate the *Ecclesiastical History of
Eusebius*, to which he added two books (X and XI) to bring the history down to the
death of Emperor Theodosius.[10] In the preface to these two books, he says that he composed them 'partly from the traditions of former generations and partly from the facts
within my own memory'.[11] The story of Mauia is found in Book XI, and the events that
lead up to it deal exclusively with the persecution of the orthodox and the atrocities
committed against them by the Arian Emperor Valens and by the Arian Bishop of
Alexandria, Lucius.[12] Lucius, who succeeded Athanasius in 373 after driving the latter's
successor, Peter, and other orthodox bishops into exile, is described by Rufinus, playing
on his name, as a 'wolf' who 'swept down on the sheep'.[13] He then describes how the
Arian supporters of Lucius pillaged and burned the orthodox communities and how the

---

[7]   Altheim and Stiehl (above, n. 1), p. 332: 'Die Reihe der arabischen Phylarchen in römischen Diensten
reicht lückenlos von Imru'ulkais über Mavia's Gatten und diese selbst zu Zokomos, und von diesem im
Haus der Daǧā'ima bis zur Einsetzung Ǧafna's durch Anastasios.'

[8]   R. Mouterde and A. Poidebard: *Le Limes de Chalcis*, I, Paris, 1945, pp. 194–195.

[9]   *Ibid.*, pp. 194, n. 3; 195, n. 1, cited as rejected views of Le Beau and Caussin de Perceval.

[10]   Text in T. Mommsen (ed.): *Die Griechischen christlichen Schriftsteller der ersten drei Jahrhunderte*,
IX.2, Leipzig, 1908 (hereafter *GCS*); the text can also be found in Migne, *Patrologia Latina* (hereafter *PL*),
XXI, cols. 465–540.

[11]   *GCS*, p. 952: *...partim ex maiorum traditionibus, partim ex his, quae nostra iam memoria comprehen-
derat.*

[12]   *GCS*, pp. 1002–1010.

[13]   *GCS*, p. 1003.

army was used to invade the hermitages of the monks.[14] The mention of the persecution of the Egyptian solitaries leads Rufinus, who spent some time among them shortly after the death of Athanasius, to describe their virtues and their miracles.[15] The account of the persecution of the monks is then followed by the story of the Arian 'pogrom' at Edessa in Mesopotamia, where Valens had ordered the slaughter of all those who opposed his Arian beliefs. The willingness of a woman to suffer martyrdom along with her child led the prefect, who was ordered to carry out the slaughter, to persuade the emperor to control his madness.[16]

These are the events recorded by Rufinus that lead up to the story of Mauia. It must be kept in mind that Rufinus, a believer in the Nicene Creed, was in Alexandria at the time and was a witness to the persecution of the monastic communities. 'I was there,' he says, 'and I speak of the things I have seen; and I report the deeds of those whose sufferings I have been privileged to be associated with.'[17] After describing the incident that took place at Edessa, Rufinus goes on to say:

> At this time, the church, as if by the fanning of the fires of persecution, gleamed brighter than gold. Its beliefs were not tested by anyone's words but by exiles and jails, because it was not by honour that it was Catholic, but by pain. This was especially so at Alexandria, where the faithful had not even the unhindered opportunity of burying the corpses of their dead. While Lucius acted with every kind of arrogance and savagery, Mauia, the queen of the Saracen nations, began to harass the border cities of Palestine and Arabia, and at the same time to lay waste the neighbouring provinces. And when she had weakened the Roman army with constant wars, caused large losses of men, driven those remaining into flight, she promised, when urged to do so, to make peace on condition that a certain Moses, a monk of her nation, be ordained bishop. [This Moses] passed his life as a solitary in a neighbouring desert, and he was widely known for his virtue and kindness, and for the miraculous works which God effected through him.[18]

The remaining portion of Rufinus' account of this episode describes the dramatic confrontation of Moses, an adherent of the orthodox creed, with Lucius, the Arian heretic, a confrontation that is made vivid by *oratio recta* and one that culminates in a happy ending for the vigorous supporter of the orthodox faith.

---

[14] *GCS*, p. 1004.
[15] *GCS*, pp. 1004–1008.
[16] *GCS*, pp. 1008–1010.
[17] *GCS*, p. 1005: *quae praesens vidi, loquor et eorum gesta refero, quorum in passionibus socius esse promerui*. See also, F.X. Murphy: *Rufinus of Aquileia, 345–411 (The Catholic University of America, Studies in Medieval History*, N.S., V), Washington, D.C., 1945, pp. 40–44.
[18] *GCS*, pp. 1010–1011.

[Mauia's] request was made known to the Roman emperor, who ordered it to be carried out without delay by our commanders who had fought there with such an unhappy turn of events. As was the custom, Moses was brought to Alexandria to assume the priestly office. Lucius, to whom had been assigned the task of ordination, was present. When Moses saw him, he said to the commanders who were present and urging him [to be ordained] and to the people, 'I do not believe that I am worthy of such a priestly office, but, notwithstanding my unworthiness, if any holy dispensation is thought to be fulfilled in me, I call upon our Lord, the God of heaven and earth, that Lucius not touch me with his hands that are polluted and stained with the blood of the saints.' When Lucius saw that he was branded with so grave a charge in the eyes of many, he said, 'Moses, why do you so readily condemn one about whose creed you know nothing? Or if anyone has declared to you otherwise concerning me, listen to my beliefs and place your trust in yourself rather than in others.' Then he [Moses] replied, 'Don't assault me with those fraudulent thoughts of yours. Your creed is known to me: the servants of God condemned to the mines testify [to them]; bishops driven into exile; presbyters and deacons banished to habitations unknown to Christians; some given over to wild beasts, yet others to flames. Can your creed be held truer to ears than to those things which are seen by the eyes? I am sure that those who believe Christ rightly do not do these things.' And so dishonoured by a greater shame, since consideration for the needs of the State demanded it, [Lucius] was forced to give in so that [Moses] was inducted into the priestly office by the bishops who had been driven into exile. When he had assumed the office, he kept the peace of a most fierce nation and preserved inviolate the community of Catholic faith.[19]

These are the 'facts' that Rufinus recalled from memory almost three decades after the events he described. What his source was for the story of Mauia is, of course, not known, but his intent patently was to condemn the Arian atrocities committed by Valens and Lucius, not necessarily to make an accurate historical statement. Rufinus' own traumatic experience in Egypt at the time of the persecutions and his own commitment to the Nicene Creed, must surely have coloured his perception of the events that he recalled from memory. It is also evident that he knew far more about Moses than about Mauia, and we can only surmise that his information came from friends in the monastic community or from other orthodox believers in Alexandria.

This is not to say that there is no truth whatsoever in the reporting of a Bedouin raid, or a series of raids, against Roman territory. Bedouin raids were a fact of life on the borders of the empire, and there is evidence that such raids did take place in the late fourth and early fifth centuries. What must be called into question, however, is whether we have in Rufinus an account of sporadic raids or full-scale wars, and whether Mauia — if she is a historical figure — was able to organize and unify Bedouin tribes for a ma-

---

[19] *GCS*, pp. 1011–1012.

jor assault on the Roman empire.[20] Rufinus' description of the attack is so generalized and wide-ranging — 'border cities and towns of Palestine and Arabia, and... neighbouring provinces' — that it must be taken as hyperbole. Jerome indulges in a similar kind of overstatement. In a letter dated to 411, he says: 'In this year... a sudden attack by barbarians... ran through the borders of Egypt, Palestine, Phoenicia and Syria like a torrent carrying everything along with it....'[21] Surely all statements of this kind must be taken with a grain of salt. For who would expect a victorious Bedouin chieftain to make terms with the defeated enemy on the sole condition — we know of no other — that a hermit be made bishop? And is it not extraordinary that Moses, a Bedouin who lived his life as a hermit in 'a neighbouring desert',[22] should be aware of the fine theological distinctions between the Arians and the orthodox, and of the goings on in Alexandria? In short, the historicity of Mauia and her activities, as we have it from Rufinus' memory, does not appear to rest on very substantial evidence.[23] If the reliability of Rufinus is called into question, is not that of Socrates, Sozomenus and Theodoretus also suspect?

Rufinus' story of Mauia is reported in varying detail by the above-mentioned church historians, who were contemporaries or near contemporaries of Rufinus. Their setting for the narrative is more or less the same as that of Rufinus: the accession of Valens and his persecution of the orthodox; the installation of Lucius as Bishop of Alexandria; the attack upon the monastic communities; an account of the monks, their piety and their miracles; and then the story of Mauia and the confrontation between Moses and

---

[20]   More typical of Bedouin tactics are raids on isolated and vulnerable communities. Cassian reported such a raid (*Collationes*, VI. 1, in *PL*, XLIX, cols. 643–645), in which monks in the neighbourhood of Thecue, modern Tekoa, were suddenly attacked and murdered by thieving Bedouin (*... repente discurrentibus Saracenorum latrunculis interempti*). A building inscription found in the Syrian desert and dated to 334 records a similar attack and that 'many of the men manning the outposts had been ambushed and killed by Saracens while fetching water for themselves...' (J.H. Iliffe: A Building Inscription from the Syrian Limes A.D. 334, *QDAP* 10 [1944] pp. 62–64). For raids in Palaestina Salutaris (Tertia) and Sinai, see P. Mayerson: The Desert of Southern Palestine according to Byzantine Sources, *Proceedings of the American Philosophical Society* 107 (April, 1963), pp. 161–162. Ammianus Marcellinus, a most reliable source for the character of the Saracens during the late fourth century, describes them as 'more adapted to stealthy raiding expeditions than to pitched battles...' (31.6.5); or 'adapted for guerilla warfare (*ad furta bellorum appositi*)...' (23.3.8). Nothing that Ammianus has to say about Saracens — and it is all uncomplimentary — agrees with Rufinus' description of Mauia as a kind of Christian 'noble savage' (see 14.4.1–7; 24.2.4; 25.6.10). Further, in all the source material cited by Vasiliev (above, n. 2), there is only one mention of a city, Arbela in Persian territory, that was taken and looted by Bedouin.
[21]   *PL*, XXII, col. 1086.
[22]   The clear implication here is that Moses did not live in one of the Egyptian deserts. A desert neighbouring those in Egypt would appear to be one in the Sinai Peninsula. It is possible that Rufinus had in mind that Moses was a hermit at Pharan or Mount Sinai. Theodoretus (Migne, *Patrologia Graeca* [hereafter PG], LXXXII, col. 1181) states specifically that Moses lived on the borders between Egypt and Palestine. Be that as it may, it is difficult to see how Moses was able to keep in touch with the day-to-day events in Alexandria.
[23]   On the disputed reputation of Rufinus as an historian, see Murphy (above, n. 17), pp. 163–175.

Lucius. These three historians had Rufinus' narrative before them — if not the Latin, then a Greek version.[24]

Socrates, closest in time to Rufinus, calls attention to the fact that Rufinus was among the monks at the time they were being persecuted by the Arians at Alexandria and that 'he was not only a witness to the cruelties, but also one of the sufferers.'[25] He amplifies the account of Rufinus by relating that 'the Saracens, who had·been in alliance with the Romans, revolted and were led by Mauia, whose husband was then dead. All the regions of the East were at that time laid waste by the Saracens.' The remainder of the narrative follows Rufinus, including the dispute between Moses and Lucius in *oratio recta*. The confrontation ends with the friends of Moses taking him 'to the mountain so that he might be ordained by those [bishops] who were in exile there'. Mauia kept the peace and 'gave her daughter in marriage to Victor, the *stratēlatēs*'. After the death of Valens, Socrates reports that when the Goths attacked Constantinople (378), 'a few Saracens that had been sent by Mauia under the terms of a treaty, helped the inhabitants in the defence of the city.'[26]

This is the first we hear of a daughter of Mauia, which is not as surprising as Socrates' reporting that she was married off to Victor, a very high officer in the Roman army. We do not know how Socrates came by this bit of information, but why Victor, undoubtedly a sophisticated Roman officer, should want to take a Bedouin woman in marriage — even the daughter of a Saracen queen — is difficult to understand. It is all the more difficult to accept in light of the contemporary view, as expressed by Ammianus Marcellinus, that the Saracens were treacherous, uncivilized vandals, 'desirable neither as friends nor as enemies'.[27]

Seeck takes Socrates at his word and identifies this Victor with the Sarmatian who was an orthodox Christian and who held high office under five Roman emperors. After the death of Valens, according to Seeck, Victor spent some time at Antioch where he married Mauia's daughter.[28] J. Rougé, on the other hand, believes that the marriage was arranged by Valens as one of the terms of the accord between Mauia and himself. Rougé agrees with Seeck that Mauia's daughter was married to Victor, the *magister militum*. He also adds, citing a general statement of Ammianus Marcellinus, that it was a body of Mauia's Saracens that distinguished itself in the defence of Constantinople when the city was threatened by the Goths.[29] A hard look at the evidence once again

---

[24]   The question of whether Rufinus' history was a translation from the Greek of Gelasius or whether it was an original work has been treated by Murphy (above, n. 17), pp. 160–164. Regardless of the outcome of this debate, Greek versions of the history were available soon after it was written (*ibid.*, p. 175).

[25]   *Historia Ecclesiastica* (hereafter *HE*), 4.24; in Migne, *PG*, LXVII, col. 524. For the account of Mauia and Moses, see *HE*, 4.36 (*PG*, LXVII, cols. 556–557).

[26]   *HE*, 5.1 (*PG*, LXVII, cols. 565–567).

[27]   14.4.1 (see above, n. 20).

[28]   O. Seeck: *Die Briefe des Libanius zeitlich geordnet (Texte und Untersuchungen zur Geschichte der altchristlichen Literatur, neue Folge XV)*, Leipzig, 1906, pp. 312–313.

[29]   Rougé (above, n. 5), p. 24. Ammianus (31.16.5–7) does not specify that these were Mauia's troops;

raises the question of whether these unqualified conclusions, based upon reportage of doubtful quality, can reasonably be taken as historical fact.

The story takes a new turn with Sozomenus.[30] Although he has borrowed much from Rufinus and Socrates (his account of the confrontation between Lucius and Moses has been borrowed almost entirely from Rufinus), he details the military campaign against Mauia, adds an anthropological excursus on the origins of the Saracens and their way of life, and appends the story of Zokomos, a childless Bedouin sheikh who converted to Christianity when a monk convinced him that through prayer and a belief in Christ he would have a son. Mauia, whom Sozomenus calls 'Mania', is described as the widow of a Saracen king. After the death of her husband and the abrogation of the treaty with the Romans, Mauia gained control of her people and 'laid waste the cities of Phoenicia, Palestine, even as far as those of Egypt... in the region called Arabia'. She became so powerful and difficult to subdue that the commander (hēgemon) of the troops in Phoenicia called upon the general (stratēgos) of the entire cavalry and infantry of the East for assistance. The latter, laughing at the call, ordered his subordinate to take no part in the battle. Mauia, acting as her own general, met him in battle. The general was routed and was barely rescued by the commander of the Palestinian and Phoenician troops who, acting against orders, rushed upon 'the barbarians' and gave the general time to escape by keeping the Saracens at bay while he slowly retreated. 'These [events],' reports Sozomenus, 'are still now remembered by people living here and by the Saracens in their songs.'

Then follow the episode of Lucius and the proposed ordination of Moses 'who at this time was practising philosophy [i.e. Christian asceticism] in a nearby desert'. Moses, however, refused to be ordained by the Arian Lucius. 'The Roman commanders interceded and took him to the bishops in exile who ordained him. Moses went to the Saracens and reconciled them to the Romans. He passed his life there among them, acting as their priest. He prepared many to live a Christian life, but found few of them who shared his beliefs.' After describing the origins and mores of the Saracens and the conversion of Zokomos and his tribe, Sozomenus concludes with the statement that the Saracens became formidable opponents to the Persians and to other Saracens.

It is the story of Zokomos that is particularly attractive to Musil, who sees a direct historical connection between Zokomos and Mauia.[31] He identifies Zokomos with a family, Ḍoj'om or Ḍajā'ima, mentioned by Arab historians. According to Musil, after Zokomos' death, all his tribes were at war with the Romans. Then Mauia, 'who was

---

they could just as well have been Saracens under the control of some other phylarch. The actions of the Saracens described by Ammianus were particularly bloodthirsty, and it is doubtful that he had Christian Arabs in mind.

[30] Sozomenus, HE, 6.38; in Migne, PG, LXVII, cols. 1408–1413. Because of the fullness of detail in his account, Sozomenus is most often cited by historians; e.g. Vasiliev (above, n. 2), p. 307, cites only Sozomenus in the body of his article and relegates Rufinus to the footnotes under the rubric of 'Brief account'.

[31] A. Musil: Ḳuṣejr 'Amra, I, Vienna, 1907, p. 130.

perhaps descended from this same family of Ḍoj'om, placed herself at its head and laid waste the provinces of Phoenicia, Palaestina Secunda and Tertia, and overran the entire Sinai Peninsula up to the Nile.' After Rome sued for peace, Mauia organized the Christian hierarchy under her tribes. She had the hermit Moses ordained by the orthodox bishops who were languishing in the copper mines of Phenom; then Moses travelled with Mauia as a bishop of the camp *(episcopos parembolēs)* and his priests went along with the other Bedouin tribes.

If we follow Musil's reconstruction of the events recorded by Sozomenus, Zokomos and Mauia were in some way related and Mauia was responsible for the conversion and ecclesiastical organization of all the Bedouin tribes of the Near East. Such a synthesis, as I see it, has no historical validity. This is not to say that Mauia's desert hermit or that a phylarch by the name of Zokomos may not have existed, but that the interest of church historians in citing stories of conversion of pagans lay primarily in demonstrating the powerful influence that monks and other committed Christians had on non-Christians.[32] The *gesta* of holy men are a *topos* in patristic literature. The influence of other holy men on Bedouin in Palestina Salutaris (Tertia) can be seen in Hilarion's missionary work at Elusa[33] and in the conversion of Obedianus, the Bedouin chief at Pharan.[34]

For Theodoretus, the narrative of Mauia and Moses closes his chapter on the crimes perpetrated by Lucius upon the orthodox in Alexandria.[35] It is preceded by a long and highly tendentious report cited from a letter of Peter, the exiled bishop of Alexandria. After vivid horror stories of mob rule, rape, pagan orgies defiling the church altar and atrocities committed against the orthodox by Lucius and other Arian zealots,[36] Theodoretus gives a summary account of Mauia's activities, and, once again in direct discourse, the dispute between Lucius and Moses. It was at this time, states Theodoretus, that 'the tribes of the Ishmaelites [i.e. Saracens or Bedouin] approached [the territories under] Roman rule and laid waste the countryside. They were led by Mabia [*sic*], a woman who did not regard [the sex] that nature had given her and conducted herself like a man. After many struggles she made peace; and then having received the light of the knowledge of God, she asked that a certain Moses, who was encamped on the borders between Egypt and Palestine, be appointed high priest for her nation.' Valens agreed and had Moses taken to Alexandria to be ordained, since Alexandria was closest to where he lived. There follows the dispute between Moses and Lucius, ending with Lucius 'the murderer', afraid to be the cause of the renewal of war, having Moses ordained by the exiled orthodox bishops. 'After receiving the high-priestly

---

[32]   Murphy (above, n. 17), p. 169. See also P. Brown: The Rise and Function of the Holy Man in Late Antiquity, *Journal of Roman Studies* 61 (1971), pp. 80–101.

[33]   Jerome, *Vita Hilarionis*, in *PL*, XXXIII, col. 41. See also Mayerson (above, n. 20), p. 167.

[34]   See the Ammonius narrative in F. Combefis (ed.): *Illustrium Christi martyrum lecti triumphi*, Paris, 1660, pp. 99–101.

[35]   *HE*, 4.20; in *PG*, LXXXII, col. 1181.

[36]   *HE*, 4.19, cols. 1168–1180.

grace of our most worthy faith, Moses returned to the people who asked for him, and by his apostolic teaching and miracles led them in the way that leads to truth. In Alexan dria, then, these were the things that were perpetrated by Lucius and that were dis pensed by divine foresight.'

In sum, the four church historians provide the only evidence of any substance that can be brought to bear on the activities of Mauia. Later accounts, such as those of the ninth-century historians Georgius Monachus[37] and Theophanes,[38] contribute little and distort the picture further by adding a romantic touch — that Mauia, the Christian queen of the Saracens, was a Roman by birth who was taken prisoner, and because of her beauty was considered a suitable match for the king of the Saracens. Nicephorus Callistus, a fourteenth-century historian, takes his version part and parcel from Sozomenus.[39] We are left, then, with a rather vague description of the area in which Mauia conducted her military operations. Was it the border cities and towns of Palestine and Arabia as well as the neighbouring provinces, as Rufinus reports? Was it all the regions of the East, as Socrates would have us believe? Or was it the cities of Phoenicia, of Palestine, and of Egypt east of the Nile, as Sozomenus would have it? As vague as these reports are concerning the range of Mauia's activities against the Romans, they are remarkably consistent on these points: that a confrontation took place in Alexandria between an orthodox monk and an Arian bishop; that the Arians committed heinous crimes and atrocities against the believers of the Nicene Creed; that Moses, a desert hermit, was willing to be martyred rather than be ordained bishop by Lucius the Arian; and that Lucius, by force of circumstances, had to knuckle under to the demands of Roman officials that Moses' orthodoxy be accommodated. Finally, the account of the two incidents — Mauia's raids and the ordination of Moses originates in Rufinus, and it was out of his personal experience in Alexandria and among the solitaries in the Egyptian deserts that he framed not so much a record of historical events as a powerful anti-Arian statement. In this respect, he is essentially followed by Socrates, Sozomenus and Theodoretus. For these four writers, Mauia's conversion and Moses' battle against heresy were exemplars of the strength of the Catholic church. Whether they were historical fact is another matter.

---

[37] De Boor (ed.): *Chronicon*, II, p. 555. In *PG*, CX, col. 682, Mauia is called 'Mauias, a Christian who was king of the Saracens'.

[38] De Boor (ed.): *Chronographia*, I, p. 64.

[39] *HE*, 40.46; in *PG*, CLXVI, cols. 732–736.

17
THE CLYSMA-PHARA-HAILA ROAD ON THE PEUTINGER TABLE

PHILIP MAYERSON

During the past twenty-five years there has been a revival of interest by historical geographers and archaeologists in tracing the ancient road systems leading from Aila to the north and northwest toward the Mediterranean.[1] Where literary and epigraphic sources provided the names of sites, investigations were centered on the identification of way stations which were not as securely known as such places as Oboda, Elusa, or Beersheba. One stretch that was intensively investigated and surveyed produced twelve milestones or markers and evidence of the road having been cleared of stones and bordered with curbstones;[2] another survey revealed the construction of steps where the gradient of the slope was over 20 percent and the erection of 3 m. high walls to protect the edges of the road against erosion.[3]

As in all surveys of this kind, the Peutinger Table—the map said to reflect the main lines of communication in the Roman road system of the fourth and first half of the fifth centuries A.D.—figured largely because it gives the names of sites and the distances between them in Roman miles, as, for example, between Aila and Lysa (fig. 1): *Haila xvi Ad Dianam xvi Rasa xvi Gypsaria xxviii Lysa*. Strangely enough, however, when one turns to a neighboring road system pictured on the Peutinger Table, that which leads from Aila (modern Aqaba) to Clysma (Suez), one finds virtually no discussion of it since the publication of Miller's study of the Table in 1916;[4] and even Miller has little to say about the road other than to identify the sites between Aila and Clysma, Phara and Medeia. The distances, recorded in Roman miles, are as follows: from Clysma to Medeia (*-deia* or *-ocia*) 40 *(xl)*, from Medeia to Phara 80 *(lxxx)*, from Phara to Haila 50 *(l)*. The site of Phara is located under a representation of Mount Sinai (*Mons Syna*), and above the symbol for the mountain are the words *Hic legem acceperunt i(n) monte syna*. Above this inscription, in bolder letters and covering a much larger space, are these words: *Desertum u(bi) quadraginta annis erraver(un)t filii isr(ae)l ducente Moyse.*

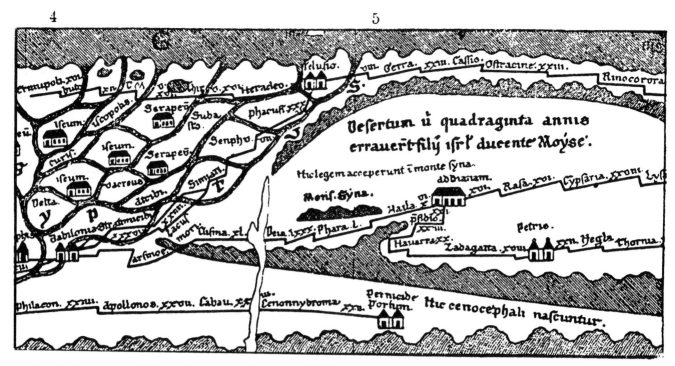

Fig. 1. The roads of Sinai, detail of the Peutinger Table.

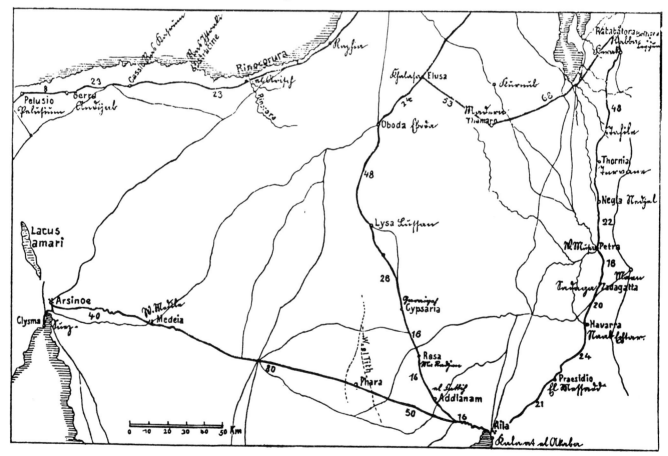

Fig. 2. Sketch map of the Clysma-Aila road. Reproduced from K. Miller,
Itineraria Romana (Stuttgart 1916) cols. 813-14.

174

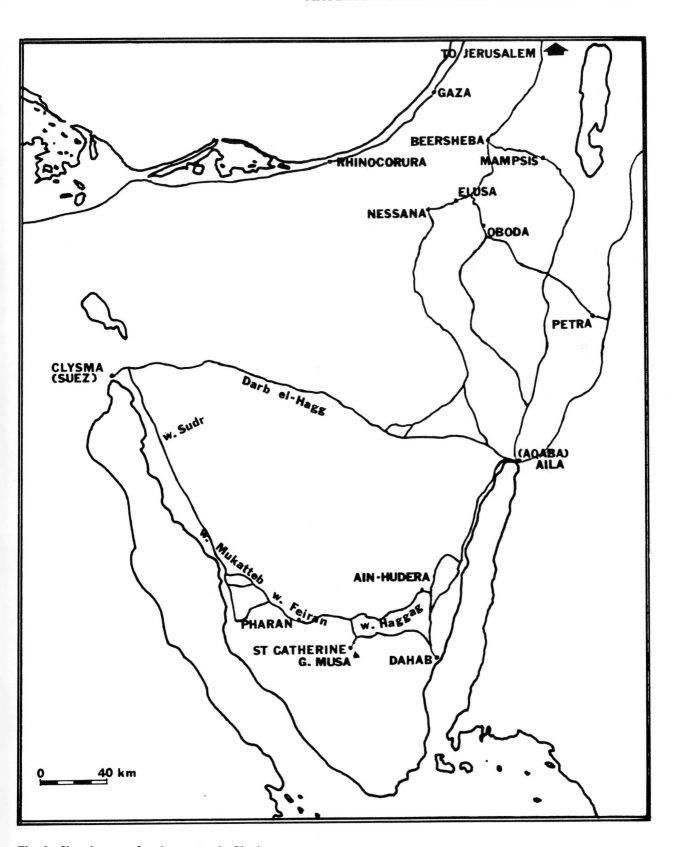

Fig. 3. Sketch map of major routes in Sinai.

According to Miller's sketch map (fig. 2)—apparently influenced by or adapted from J. L. Burckhardt's map in his *Travels in Syria and the Holy Land* (1822)—the road leads in almost a straight line from Clysma to Aila, as if it were identical with the Darb el-Hagg which Moslem pilgrims en route to Mecca once traveled from Suez to Aqaba. Miller identifies Medeia with remains in Wadi Medila and locates Phara just west of Wadi et-Tih.[5] No citation is given in support of these two identifications. Aharoni appears to agree with Miller's interpretation, placing Phara in northern Sinai at eth-Themed, a way station on the Darb el-Hagg, and states: "On the Roman *Tabula Peutingeriana* eth-Themed is called Phara (i.e., Paran). It is probable that this name is given here with the addition of the name of the desert in which it was located, like El(ath)-Paran and that on the Roman map only the second part of the name is preserved."[6]

The interpretations of Miller and Aharoni face a serious obstacle, and that is the identification of Phara, or Pharan, as it is more commonly known. Of all the sites in Sinai, one, and only one, has an enduring history. That is the Pharan cited by the second-century geographer Ptolemy as a *komê* situated deep in the Sinai peninsula (fig. 3),[7] and in the third century called by Eusebius a *polis* "situated to the south beyond (the boundaries of) Arabia."[8] Pharan is the site at which the peripatetic nun Egeria, in the late fourth or early fifth century, stopped on her way to and from Mount Sinai.[9] Pharan is also cited by other pilgrims or monks who traveled to or lived near the "Mountain of God."[10] It is now known by its Arabic name as Feiran, and the remains of a considerable community can still be seen on a high bank overlooking the Wadi Feiran. Ceramic remains from the site provide evidence that it was inhabited as early as the eighth or seventh century B.C.,[11] and probably earlier since the locale has the richest supply of perennial water in all of Sinai. Unquestionably, it was its water supply that made Pharan a center for human habitation over so many centuries.

Why, then, should Pharan be placed far to the northeast in one of the most barren places of the Sinai peninsula? The scholarly dilemma seems to have arisen from attempting to rationalize the figures given on the Peutinger Table for the distances cited for the two sites between Clysma and Aila. One thing is certain: the Pharan that is so well known is no fifty Roman miles from Aila. Medeia, whose identification could help in pointing out the general direction of the route from Clysma, is simply unknown from any source. Its identification by Miller with a wadi with a vaguely similar name is hardly secure evidence for locating the site.[12] One must come to the conclusion that there is something wrong with the figures given on the Peutinger Table.

If the Clysma-Aila road on the Table is examined closely and compared with those leading north of Aila, it will be noted for the latter that the distances between sites are given in very precise numbers, whereas the distances for the Clysma-Aila road are given in round numbers. Take, for example, the road from Aila to Elusa (see fig. 1). There are six stations between the two points, with distances of 16, 16, 16, 28, 47, and 24 Roman miles (220 km.).[13] The Clysma-Aila road, on the other hand, covers 170 Roman miles (250 km.) with only two intervening stations between the termini.

It is clearly evident that the Clysma-Aila route was not a major line of communication during the fourth century, and it is most likely that the cartographer of the Table either had no detailed information regarding this route, or that he only wished to give a schematic notion of it in terms of distances and intervening stations. He did, however, know what he was about in drawing the line of the road as he did. At the very least, his intention is quite clear.

The most prominent feature on the Table for the area under discussion—its only vignette, so to speak—is Mount Sinai, together with the inscriptions bearing on the biblical associations with the mountain and with the Exodus. It would be asking too much of the cartographer to expect, as does Aharoni,[14] that he was locating a general biblical expanse known as the desert of Paran. The map itself is quite explicit in designating Phara (or Pharan) as a geographical place no different from Clysma or Aila. And placing Pharan just under the representation of Mount Sinai must surely indicate that the cartographer associated one with the other. In short, we must accept Phara of the Peutinger Table to be Pharan, an established community in southern Sinai and in close proximity to the mountain which, at the time the map was drawn, was believed to have been the place where Moses received the Law. As to the distance between Clysma and Pharan, 120 Roman miles, I believe it is possible to show that it is reasonably accurate. The 50 Roman miles between Pharan and Aila is another matter and cannot be rationalized.

If, then, Phara of the Peutinger Table is to be identified with Pharan deep in the Sinai peninsula and some thirty-five Roman miles from Mount Sinai, the route from Clysma must head south-southeast (see fig. 3) and not east-southeast, as shown by Burckhardt and Miller. This southern route was the one generally taken by pilgrims on their way from Egypt to the "Mountain of God," and until the fortified monastery at Mount Sinai was constructed in the sixth century on orders from Emperor Justinian, Pharan was the point at which pilgrims could find shelter and refreshment on their way to and from the mountain, where facilities must surely have been limited.

The *itinerarium* of Egeria, dated to the late fourth or early fifth century, is instructive on this point. Although the text of the account is broken and opens with Egeria's approach to Mount Sinai, we hear that she had arrived there from Pharan;[15] after receiving a guided tour of the holy places at Mount Sinai, she returned to Pharan, "which is thirty-five miles from Sinai, and we had to stop there for two days in order to rest."[16] She then describes the return journey to Clysma without mentioning specific stages along the route. At one point she remarks that "there is no road there at all, only sands of the desert all around," and goes on to comment on the skills of the Pharanites in traveling through the roadless desert.[17] Finally, she states, "we arrived at Clysma by the same route and by the same stages by which we had come."[18]

Some twenty-five years after the construction of the fortified monastery at Mount Sinai, now known as the Monastery of Saint Catherine, an *itinerarium* (ca. 570) attributed to Antoninus of Piacenza records yet another route to the Holy Mountain.[19] Antoninus traveled from Gaza to Elusa and then to Nessana, whence he set out on a six-day trek through the waterless "inner desert" on a direct route to Mount Sinai, thereby bypassing Clysma, Aila, and Pharan.[20] At Mount Sinai he learned that the moratorium on raiding by Bedouins had come to an end and that no travelers should remain in the desert through which they had come. Hence, "some returned to the Holy City through Egypt and some through Arabia. From Mount Sinai to the city of Arabia, which is called A(b)ila, is eight stages."[21] Antoninus and his companions decided to return to Jerusalem via Egypt. They traveled to Pharan, which Antoninus describes as a city fortified with walls made of brick and having a police force which patrolled the desert in order to protect monasteries and hermits against Bedouin attacks.[22] En route to Clysma from Pharan, they stopped at Surandela (Arandara)—to Antoninus the site of biblical Elim—where they found a small fortified monastery *(castellum)* containing a church, its priest, and two hospices *(xenodochia)* for the use of travelers.[23] They rested there for two days to recover from the exhaustion of desert travel. Further along the way to Clysma, at a place "where the Children of Israel marked out their camp after passing the Red Sea," Antoninus and his companions came upon another *castellum* with a hospice.[24]

The Antoninus *itinerarium* outlines the two main, and relatively secure, routes from Mount Sinai as drawn on the Peutinger Table. In the fourth century there was no fortified monastery at the Holy Mountain, and Pharan—one day's distance from Mount Sinai and itself considered to be the biblical site where the Israelites battled with the Amalekites—was the center of activity for pilgrims and a "Saracen" community. As we learn from the Antoninus itinerary, travelers from Palestine could go directly either to Mount Sinai and Pharan without making their way to Clysma or Aila; but although the route was much shorter, the risk was greater. The Clysma-Pharan route, on the other hand, offered pilgrims the opportunity of touring Israelite sites both in Egypt and Sinai. Egeria's record of her journey shows that she wanted to be shown the physical sites of biblical events, especially those associated with the Exodus, and she wanted to do so in safety. She traveled the long route from Pharan to Clysma and Egypt; she was escorted by Roman troops ''as long as we were traveling through unsafe places''; and after touring Egypt, she returned to Pelusium and reached Palestine ''by the same stages of Egypt by which we had come.''[25]

If the evidence is secure that Phara of the Peutinger Table is Pharan in southern Sinai and a short distance from Mount Sinai, how accurate is the distance given on the Table (40 Roman miles to Medeia and another 80 to Phara, for a total of 120 Roman miles) between Clysma and Phara? As was stated above, the site of Medeia cannot be located with any certainty. If the conventional route is taken from Clysma to Pharan, Medeia should perhaps be located at a point near Wadi Sudr where there is water and evidence of habitation. We are on a surer footing with the 120 Roman miles between Clysma and Pharan. If we were to use the mileage provided by the *Guide Bleu* for the trip from Suez to the oasis of Feiran via Wadi Maghara (i.e., Wadi Sidri)—there being no one road, since a number of tracks may be taken after leaving the proximity of the coast of the Gulf of Suez—the distance is given as 196 km.[26] At a conversion rate of 1.482 km. to a Roman mile, the distance between Suez and Feiran—or Clysma and Pharan—is 132 Roman miles. This figure, I believe, is close enough to the round number 120 provided by the Peutinger Table. Further, not only is the accuracy of the Table confirmed for this leg of the route, but the correlation of the two mileages also confirms the direction of the route from Clysma: south-southeast.

There remains the final leg of the route as given on the Peutinger Table: Phara to Haila, 50 Roman miles. As was stated above, 50 Roman miles for this stretch of the road cannot be rationalized if the initial section went south-southeast from Clysma to Pharan. If we were to assume that the cartographer omitted a roman numeral, say a *c* before the *l*, it could be possible to rationalize a distance of 150 Roman miles or 222 km. between Pharan and Aila. However plausible it may be to assume this or some other error in text tradition, an emendation would neither prove anything nor be anything other than a hypothetical correction. What can be stated with assurance is that a well-traveled route (hardly a road) did exist between Aila and Pharan-Mount Sinai. The Antoninus *itinerarium* has already been cited to indicate that Aila was an eight-day journey from Mount Sinai.[27] The itinerary of Theodosius (ca. 530), slightly earlier than that of Antoninus, also calls for eight stages betwen Aila and Mount Sinai, "if you are willing to travel through the desert, but if you go through Egypt, it is 25 stages."[28] No other ancient itinerary at hand records a trip along this route, although Eusebius says that "Aila is a three-day trip in an easterly direction" from Pharan.[29] This is an extraordinarily short amount of time to travel a distance of about 250 km. over very difficult terrain. It is interesting to note, however, that the 1895 edition of Baedeker's *Egypt* agrees more with the itineraries of Theodosius and Antoninus in estimating a journey of approximately nine days between Mount Sinai and Aqaba.[30]

In spite of the lack of extant itineraries on the route from Pharan, or Mount Sinai, to Aila, we possess a clear epigraphic record from pilgrims and other travelers en route either from Mount Sinai or Aila. The Wadi Haggag (The Wadi of the Pilgrims), situated a short distance from the spring of Ain Hudera and on the Aila-Mount Sinai route (see fig. 3), holds over 400 Nabataean, Greek, Latin, Coptic, Armenian, and Hebrew-Aramaic inscriptions, the greater number of them being Christian and in Greek. Some of the Christian inscriptions have been dated as early as the fourth century.[31]

It is clear, then, that the weight of the evidence favors identifying the Clysma-Phara-Haila road on the Peutinger Table with the route taken by pilgrims from either entrance, Clysma or Aila, to the "Desert where the Children of Israel wandered for forty years under the leadership of Moses." To identify the road as identical with, or paralleling, the Darb el-Hagg of Moslem pilgrims lacks any support in terms of purpose, of archaeological or epigraphical evidence, or of its representation on the Peutinger Table. Further, the Table gives only a schematic representation of the road, which in no way could serve as a useful guide for travelers to the Holy Mountain. In point of fact, there was no "road" between the points given on the Table; at best it should be called a route or track. The distances cited on the Table are similarly general and of no practical use.

But what is exceptionally graphic on the Peutinger Table is that the route from Pharan-Mount Sinai proceeds to Aila and then to Elusa, and from that point, without any further stages indicated, directly to Jerusalem. Undoubtedly it is one of the two routes which were recommended to Antoninus of Piacenza for his return to Jerusalem.[32] More than any other, it is the itinerary of Theodosius which provides us with a verbal description of the route pictured on the Table. "Near Mount Sinai is Pharan where holy Moses fought with Amalek. From Jerusalem to Elusa there are three stages; from Elusa to Aila, seven stages. . . . From Aila to Mount Sinai, eight stages."[33]

NOTES

1. Y. Aharoni, "The Roman Road to Aila (Elath)," *Israel Exploration Journal* 4.1 (1954) 9-16; M. Harel, "The Roman Road at Ma'aleh 'Aqrabbim ('Scorpions' Ascent')," ibid. 9.3 (1959) 175-79; A. Negev, "The Date of the Petra-Gaza Road," *Palestine Exploration Quarterly* 98 (1966) 89-98; Z. Meshel, "The Roads of the Negev According to the Geography of Ptolemy and the Tabula Peutingeriana," *Excavations and Studies in Honour of S. Yeivin*, ed. Y. Aharoni (Tel Aviv 1973) 205-9 (in Hebrew); Z. Meshel and Y. Tsafrir, "The Nabataean Road from 'Avdat to Sha'ar-Ramon," *Palestine Exploration Quarterly* 106 (1974) 103-18; ibid. 107 (1975) 3-21, with bibliography earlier than 1954.

2. Meshel and Tsafrir (n. 1 above) 106-18.

3. Harel (n. 1 above) 177.

4. K. Miller, *Itineraria Romana* (Stuttgart 1916).

5. Ibid. col. 820. For the confusion in determining the precise location of Medeia, see R. Weill, *La presqu'île du Sinai* (Bibliothèque de l'École des Hautes Études Sciences historique et philologique, fasc. 171 [Paris 1908]) 115, n. 2.

6. Y. Aharoni, *The Land of the Bible: A Historical Geography* (London 1968) 52, n. 30. For the same identification based on the similar distance between Aqaba and eth-Themed, see J. Ball, *Egypt in the Classical Geographers* (Cairo 1942), p. 157.

7. *Geograph.* 5.16.

8. *Onomasticon*, ed. Klosterman (Leipzig 1904) 166.

9. *Itinerarium Egeriae (Peregrinatio Aetheriae)*, ed. O. Prinz (Heidelberg 1960) 2.3, 5.11.

10. See P. Mayerson, "The Desert of Southern Palestine According to Byzantine Sources," *ProcPhilAs* 107.2 (1963) 160-72; "The First Muslim Attacks on Southern Palestine (A.D. 633-634)," *TAPA* 95 (1964) 155-99.

11. Aharoni (n. 6 above) 183: "remains from Iron Age (ca. seventh century B.C.) up to the Arab period without any noticeable gap." Cf. B. Rothenberg and Y. Aharoni, *God's Wilderness* (London 1961) 166: "at the very least, from the Iron Age, *c.* 9th-8th centuries B.C., through the Persian-Hellenistic and Roman-Byzantine periods up to the early Arab period."

12. Miller (n. 4 above) col. 820.

13. See Aharoni (n. 1 above) 15, without his emendations.

14. See n. 6 above.

15. *Itin. Eg.* (n. 9 above) 2.4: *venientes a Faran.*

16. Ibid. 6.1: *Ac sic ergo cum pervenissemus Faram, quod sunt a monte Dei milia triginta et quinque, necesse nos fuit ibi ad resumendum biduo immorari.*

17. Ibid.: *via enim illic penitus non est, sed totum heremi sunt arenosae.*

18. Ibid. 6.4: *nos autem eodem itinere et eisdem mansionibus quibus ieramus, reversi sumus in Clesma.*

19. *Itinera Hierosolymitana Saeculi IIII-VIII (Corpus Scriptorum Ecclesiasticorum Latinorum)*, ed. P. Geyer (Vienna 1898) 39. For the sake of simplicity we shall refer to the writer as Antoninus, although the account was written by some unknown person.

20. Ibid. c. 36 (p. 183). Note that Antoninus and his companions arrived at Mount Sinai on the eighth day. The six-day trip undoubtedly was through the waterless stretches of the desert during which water, carried by camels in leather skins, was carefully rationed. For an analysis of the itinerary and of conditions in the region, see Mayerson, "Byz. Sources" (n. 10 above) 169-72.

21. Ibid. c. 39-40 (p. 185): *alii per Aegyptum, alii per Arabiam reverterentur in sanc-*

tam civitatem. De monte Sina in Arabia in civitatem, quae vocatur Abila, sunt mansiones octo.

22. Ibid. c. 40 (p. 186).
23. Ibid. c. 41 (p. 187).
24. Ibid.
25. *Itin. Eg.* (n. 9 above) 9.3, 9.7.
26. M. Baud, *Les Guides bleus: Égypte* (Paris 1950) 694-96.
27. *Itin. Hier.* (n. 19 above) c. 39-40 (p. 185).
28. "De Situ Terrae Sanctae," *Itinera Hierosolymitana* (n. 19 above) c. 27 (p. 148): *De Aila usque in monte Syna mansiones VIII, si compendaria volueris ambulare per heremum, sin autem per Aegyptum, mansiones XXV.*
29. *Onomasticon* (n. 8 above) 166.
30. *Egypt* (Lower Egypt and the Peninsula of Sinai), ed. K. Baedeker (London 1895) 279-80.
31. A. Negev, "The Inscriptions of Wadi Haggag, Sinai," *Qedem* 6, (1977) 1-2, 76-77. For a mention of other inscriptions along the northern part of the route to Aila, see Rothenberg-Aharoni (n. 11 above) 83-86. See also B. Rothenberg, "An Archaeological Survey of South Sinai," *PEQ* 102 (1970) 14 (figs. 7-8), 18-19. He traces the route from Aila to Mount Sinai and Pharan, calling it a major Nabataean-Roman road, and, somewhat grandly, "the Aila-Feiran Highroad." In March of 1979, this writer visited the site of Wadi Haggag and, some distance away, Wadi Marrah, and observed the numerous inscriptions carved into brittle mesalike structures. Apart from the inscriptions, I was impressed with the fact that at these sites the terrain is flat enough so that caravans or travelers are not restricted to a "road." It was also apparent that travelers coming up the steep escarpment from Ein Hudera, or before descending to it, must have rested at Haggag, Marrah, or at other sites nearby where they took the opportunity to record their names, unwittingly doing so for posterity and epigraphers.
32. *Itin. Hier.* (n. 19 above) c. 39-40 (p. 185).
33. *Itin. Hier.* (n. 28 above) c. 27 (p. 148): *Iuxta montem Syna in Fara civitate ibi sanctus Moyses cum Amalech pugnavit. De Hierusalem in Elusath mansiones III, de Elusath in Aila mansiones VII. . . . De Aila usque in monte Syna mansiones VIII.*

The Pilgrim Routes to Mount Sinai and the Armenians

PHILIP MAYERSON

New York University

A RECENT survey along the conventional pilgrim routes to Mount Sinai and its renowned monastery, the Monastery of St. Catherine as it is now known, has yielded a bumper crop of Armenian inscriptions — 'an astonishing discovery' in the words of Michael Stone, the leader of the survey team.[1] Although several Armenian inscriptions were known before the survey was made, they were fortuitous discoveries by investigators who were more knowledgeable about — or more interested in — the Greek and Nabatean inscriptions that were scratched into the rocks along the routes to the Holy Mountain. These same rocks also bore notices in Thamudic, Latin, Syriac, Arabic and Georgian characters.

The survey conducted by Stone in 1979 took in Wadis Mukatteb and Maghara in the western portion of the Sinai peninsula as well as the route leading eastwards to Feiran, ancient Pharan. In addition, the main pass, Naqb Raqna, leading from the Tih plateau south to Mount Sinai from Gaza, was also screened for inscriptions. In the eastern portion of the peninsula, Wadi Haggag and the routes leading from that point of Mount Sinai were also surveyed, including Leja, a wadi in very close proximity to the Holy Mountain and intersecting it and Jebel Katerina. Although all sites contained numerous Greek and Nabatean inscriptions, the distribution of those in Armenian script was quite unexpected. The tally of the 64 Armenian inscriptions is as follows:

Wadi Mukatteb	4
Wadi Maghara	1
Maghara to Feiran	0
Naqb Raqna	0
Wadi Haggag	55
Wadi Leja	4

---

[1] M. Stone: *Armenian Inscriptions from Sinai: An Intermediate Report with Notes on Georgian and Nabataean Inscriptions*, Sydney, 1979, pp. 1–21. In a personal communication to this writer Professor Stone reports that on a later visit to Mount Sinai, on 23–25 February 1980, an additional 23 Armenian inscriptions were found near the chapel and mosque on the summit and four others carved in the sixth-century door of the church of St. Catherine.

Stone would date the main body of the inscriptions from Wadi Haggag between the seventh and tenth centuries; those in the Wadi Mukatteb are paleographically later than those in Haggag. One of the Haggag inscriptions is dated to 420 of the Armenian Era, which corresponds to 971–2 C.E.; another is interpreted to say 'I have gone around Moses' and is taken to mean Jebel Musa or Mount Sinai. Yet another may refer to St. Catherine. And one on the path up Mount Sinai reads: 'I saw Jerusalem'.[2]

Without underestimating the importance of these inscriptions for Armenian onomastics and paleography, their most striking feature — to this writer at least — is their distribution: 55 in Wadi Haggag (Wadi of the Pilgrims) on the eastern route to Mount Sinai and only five on the western. To Stone this is a 'mystery' since 'the accepted route' was 'to travel down from the land of Israel along the coast of the Mediterranean to Pelusium and then to bear roughly south through Clysma and east through the wadis to Firan and then on through Wadi Sulaf and the Naqb el-Hawa pass to Mount Sinai'.

The fact that there is no evidence of Armenians' having travelled from Gaza by way of the pass of Naqb Raqna is also 'by way of deepening the mystery'.[3] Apart from other considerations, the discovery of these 55 Armenian inscriptions at Wadi Haggag draws our attention emphatically to the eastern route from Palestine to Sinai and the Holy Mountain. Although the statistic of 55 *versus* five may not be conclusive in solving the 'mystery' of why there are so many Armenian inscriptions on the eastern route and so few on the western side of the peninsula, it must have a bearing on the preferred route for reaching Mount Sinai from the borders of Palestine. The statistic also raises the question of whether the western route was in reality the accepted and shortest route from Palestine to Mount Sinai.

These conclusions would seem to fly in the face of the two most often cited *itineraria* of pilgrims to the Holy Mountain and the reports of investigators of the past two centuries. As to the latter, we have an imbalance in the amount of data on routes in Sinai, since the interest of investigators focused so sharply on tracking the route of the Israelites from Egypt to the mountain where Moses was said to have received the Law. As a consequence, relatively little was explored in the region to the east of Mount Sinai. Whereas the inscriptions in Wadis Mukatteb and Maghara were well publicized for many years, virtually nothing was known of those on the eastern side of the peninsula

---

[2]   *Ibid.*, pp. 3–5, 12. The history of the Armenian Bishop Sebeos (661?) is very enlightening on the main points of interest for Armenian pilgrims. Following the capture of Jerusalem by the Persians in 614, Modestus, the leading priest of Jerusalem, writes to Kumitas, the archbishop and metropolitan of Armenia. He recalls the pilgrimages previously made by the Armenians to the holy places of Jerusalem and how their coming warmed his heart. He reassures Kumitas that the holy places have been rebuilt and that religious services are again being conducted in all the churches of Jerusalem. In his reply to Modestus, Kumitas acknowledges that these pilgrimages were salutary for his people, that pilgrims baptised their bodies in the holy waters of the Jordan, and that 'they shed the anguish of their hearts about Mount Sinai'; F. Macler (trans.): *Histoire d'Héraclius par l'évêque Sebéos*, Paris, 1904, pp. 70–74.

[3]   Stone (above, n. 1), pp. 10–11.

until twenty years ago.[4] Hence, one was easily led to believe that the western route was the *grande route ordinaire* to and from Mount Sinai.[5] As for the two *itineraria*, that of the nun Egeria (*c.* 400) and the one attributed to Antoninus of Piacenza (*c.* 570), they reflect primarily the interest of two pilgrims in touring holy places in Sinai and Egypt, and hence their routes were determined by what they wanted to see and not by what route was most convenient or even the safest. However, the incidental information contained in these travel memoirs provides useful data concerning conditions along the routes that these two pilgrims travelled.

The itinerary of Egeria is a record of a trip from Egypt to Mount Sinai and a return to Egypt to tour biblical sites associated with the Exodus.[6] Her text opens as she is on her way from Pharan to Mount Sinai. After her stay at the Holy Mountain, she was accompanied back to Pharan by monks who served as her guides. From Pharan, where she rested for two days, she made her way (via Wadis Mukatteb and Maghara?) with the help of Pharanite guides to the coast and Clysma. Her journey from Clysma to the city of Arabia (Thou or Phacusa?) required a four-day trip across the desert, going from fort to fort (*de castro ad castrum*) in the company of a military escort.[7] At the city of Arabia, Egeria dismissed the soldiers who had accompanied her through dangerous places (*per loca suspecta*) since there was a public highway nearby that went towards Pelusium. She reached the frontier of Palestine by the same stages (*mansiones*)[8] by which she had come. The remainder of her trip to Jerusalem was uneventful and is reported in a single sentence.

The journey that Antonius of Piacenza reports in his *itinerarium* is not a typical one, since he and his companions used neither the eastern nor the western route to Mount Sinai. Apparently hiring a dragoman or professional guide at Gaza, a city whose inhabi-

---

[4]   For a summary of the scholarly interest in the inscriptions along the routes to Mount Sinai, see A. Negev: *The Inscriptions of Wadi Haggag, Sinai* (*Qedem* 6), Jerusalem, 1977, pp. 1–3. Professor Negev observes (p. 79) that 'the western routes leading from Egypt to the same Holy Mountain, crossing the large wadies Mukatteb and Feiran, are almost void of Christian inscriptions, although Nabatean graffiti entirely cover the rocks there'. Interestingly enough, the Nabatean inscriptions have been published (*Corpus Inscriptionum Semiticarum*, II, 1–2) but to my knowledge there has been no publication of the Greek.

[5]   Stone (above, n. 1), p. 10, has also been led to this conclusion. Negev (above, n. 4), p. 77, also concludes that 'most pilgrims to the newly created holy places took the shorter and safer route from Egypt...' See also R. Weill: *La presqu'île du Sinai* (*Bibliothèque de L'École des Hautes Études Sciences historique et philologique*, Fasc. 171), pp. 119, 227. For the confusion in determining the precise location of Medeia, see *ibid.*, p. 115, n. 2.

[6]   *Corpus Christianorum, Series Latina* 175, pp. 37–50. For the same identification based on the similar distance between 'Aqaba and eth-Themed, see J. Ball: *Egypt in the Classical Geographers*, Cairo, 1942, p. 157.

[7]   *Ibid.*, pp. 45–46.

[8]   *Ibid.*, pp. 49–50. The word *mansiones* is usually translated as 'stages' or 'staging-posts'. In inhabited areas a *mansio* implies an overnight stop after a day's trip at a hospice or a lodging of some kind. In the Sinai and other uninhabited desert areas, the word should be taken to mean a 'camp-site'.

tants he cites as 'friendly in every way, lovers of travellers', he made his way to Elusa.[9] After a stop at a hospice 20 miles from Elusa, he entered the 'inner desert', making his way on foot over the waterless desert of the Tih plateau on a direct line to Mount Sinai. The journey along this route, which took eight days, was possible only because of a religious festival of the Saracens (*i.e.* Bedouin) that enjoined them from their traditional occupation of trading and raiding.[10] After having witnessed the character of monastic life on the Holy Mountain, and having been informed of the people, places and things associated with biblical events, Antoninus and his company were ready to leave. 'Because the Saracen holy days were coming to an end', however, 'an announcement was made that no one should remain in, or return through, the desert by which we had come. Some returned to the Holy City through Egypt, and some through Arabia. From Mount Sinai to the city of Arabia which is called A(b)ila is eight stages. ...We however decided to return through Egypt.'[11]

En route to Egypt, Antoninus' first stop was at Pharan where he was greeted by women and children singing a hymn in Egyptian (*i.e.* Coptic). He also observed a police unit of 80 publicly domiciled men (*condomae*) who along with their families received a food and clothing allowance from Egypt. (The unit patrolled the desert, protecting monasteries and hermits against lawless Saracens.) En route from Pharan to Clysma, Antoninus stopped at two fortified monasteries, each described as a *castellum* with a church and a hospice or two within its walls.[12] From Clysma, Antoninus and his companions made a most unusual trip down the eastern shore of Egypt to the desert retreat that once housed the celebrated Egyptian monk, St. Paul. He then made his way from one reputed biblical site to the next until he reached Alexandria. We next find Antoninus in Jerusalem without any indication of how he arrived there.[13]

The itineraries of Egeria and Antoninus point unmistakably to the fact that Pharan was oriented toward Egypt. The people spoke 'Egyptian', and the police unit received its

---

[9] P Geyer (ed.): *Corpus Scriptorum Ecclesiasticorum Latinorum: Itinera Hierosolymitana Saec. III–VIII* 38, pp. 180–181.

[10] *Ibid.*, p. 183. For an analysis of the itinerary and of conditions in the region, see P. Mayerson: The Desert of Southern Palestine according to Byzantine Sources, *Proceedings of the American Philosophical Society* 107 (1963), pp. 169–172. The Nessana papyri P. Colt 72 and 73, dated to the late seventh century, record two orders to the administrator of Nessana from the Muslim governor at Gaza to provide a guide to conduct two individuals — in one instance a man and in the other the governor's wife — to Mount Sinai; C. J. Kraemer (ed.): *Excavations at Nessana: Non-Literary Papyri*, III, Princeton, 1958, pp. 205–208. It is possible that the guide followed a route similar to that taken by Antoninus. It is equally possible that the guide proceeded to Mount Sinai via Aila since that route was easily accessible from Nessana. Be that as it may, what is more striking about these two documents is the fact that two people from Gaza, one of whom was the wife of the governor himself, were directed to travel to Mount Sinai not through Egypt but by one of the routes through the interior of Palestine.

[11] Geyer (above, n. 9), p. 185.

[12] *Ibid.*, pp. 185–187.

[13] *Ibid.*, pp. 188–190.

supplies from Egypt. For Egeria it was a halting place on her way to and from Mount Sinai, and it was at Pharan that she hired guides to take her back to Clysma and Egypt. Because of its rich supply of water, Pharan developed into the sole urban centre in Sinai during the heyday of pilgrimages to the Holy Mountain. Some time after 400, it became an episcopal seat as well as a centre for monks and hermits. Pilgrims stopping at Pharan believed they were at the site of biblical Raphidim where Moses and the Israelites fought against the Amalekites.

In determining the common or preferred route for pilgrims making their way to Mount Sinai from Palestine, one must consider the roads that led from Jerusalem — the *sine qua non* attraction for any pilgrim in Palestine — to the entrances to the Sinai peninsula: Aila on the east and Clysma on the west. Equally deserving of consideration are the travelling conditions (security, ground surfaces and water resources) in Palestine, Egypt and Sinai. Our evidence, of course, is generally concerned with major routes, and it is more than probable that there were a number of minor routes available to guides, who for any number of reasons may have preferred them to those that were well established. This is particularly true in Sinai where there were no roads in the accepted sense of the word but, rather, routes or tracks.

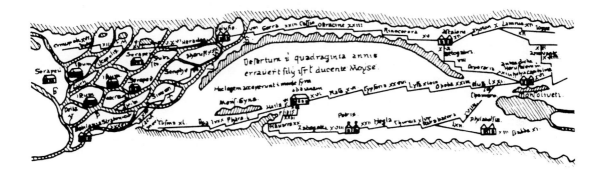

Fig. 1. Part of the Peutinger Table showing route from Jerusalem to Aila.

The Peutinger Table — the map said to reflect the main lines of communication in the Roman road system of the third or fourth century C.E. — illustrates in a most graphic fashion the preference for the Jerusalem-Aila route (Figs. 1, 2). There are in fact two such roads to Aila. One road leads south from Jerusalem to Elusa in the Negev, at which point it heads south-south-east to Aila by five stages (Oboda, Lysa, Gypsaria, Rasa, Ad Dianam).[14] Another road, branching off the Jerusalem-Elusa way, heads east to Jordan via Thamara and joins the Philadelphia-Aila road, where by seven stages (Rababatora, Thorma, Hegla, Petra, Zadagatta, Haurra, Praesidium) it leads to Ad

---

14 K. Miller: *Itineraria Romana*, Stuttgart, 1916, Cols. 833–834.

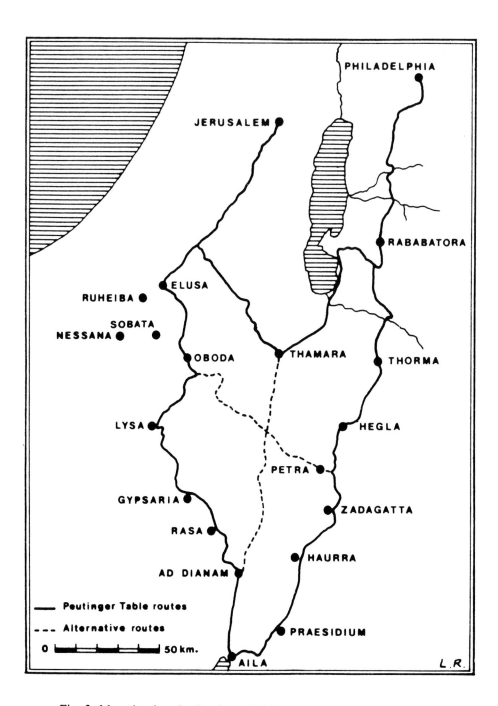

Fig. 2. Map showing the Peutinger Table route and alternative routes.

Dianam and thence to Aila.[15] According to the Table, the milage for the trip from Jerusalem to Aila via Elusa is 220 Roman miles (=mp); via Thamara, 288 mp. As for the route to Clysma, the Peutinger Table shows no direct approach to it. The road from

---

[15] *Ibid.*, Cols. 819–820, 836. The Table omits the distance between Thorma and Negla, and there is an apparent copyist's error in showing the road as leading from Praesidio to Ad Dianam instead of going

Jerusalem to Ascalon and the coast road are clearly marked by three stages. From Ascalon to Pelusium, the Table follows the coast road but omits the key city of Gaza and inaccurately records the distances between various stages. (It gives, for example, the milage between Ascalon and Rhinocorura as 15 mp!) From Pelusium the road heads to Egyptian Babylonia via Phacus, Senphu and Simiati. From Babylonia another road heads east to Arsinoë and, finally, to Clysma. The distances between Babylonia, Arsinoë and Clysma are not given.[16]

The corrective for the rather sketchy information shown on the Peutinger Table for the Jerusalem-Clysma route is provided by the *Itinerarium Provinciarum Antonini Augusti*, the Antonine itinerary of the late third century (Fig. 3). The distance between Jerusalem and Ascalon is covered in two stages of 44 mp. From Ascalon to Pelusium there are seven stages (Gaza, Rafia, Rhinocorura, Ostracena, Cassio, Pentascino) for a distance of 150 mp, or a total of 194 mp for the distance between Jerusalem and Pelusium.[17] The Antonine itinerary then marks out a route from Clysma due north to Pelusium (via Serapiu, Thaubasio, Sile, Magdolo) for a distance of 110 mp, making a total of 304 mp from Jerusalem to Clysma.[18] In terms of comparative distances, the Jerusalem-Clysma road is about 84 mp longer than the Jerusalem-Aila route via Elusa, or approximately the same length as the Jerusalem-Thamara-Aila route.

By the end of the fourth century, these two lines of communication had to do more with the needs of the military and the merchant than with the passage of pilgrims. Some time during the reign of Aurelian or Diocletian, the *Legio decima Fretensis* was posted to Aila, the border control point at the crossroads of key highways into Syria and Palestine. At the beginning of the fifth century, as we learn from the *Notitia dignitatum*, points along the roads leading to Clysma and Aila were manned by auxiliary military units (*limitanei*) to defend against desert marauders. Along the route to Clysma, there were units in place at Rhinocurura, Gerra, Pelusium, Sile and Thaubasio. The Jordan route to Aila had forces stationed at Thamara, Rababatora, Thorma, Zadagatta, Haurra, Praesidium — and the Tenth Legion at Aila, the only city in the three Palestines in which the Romans stationed a legion.[19]

Somewhat later, in the fifth and sixth centuries, the trans-Negev route to Aila was also reinforced with auxiliary units. About the mid-fifth century, a fort and a mobile border force, a camel corps, were put in place at Nessana, about 20 mp south of Elusa at the edge of the 'inner desert'. In the sixth century a fort was built at Oboda, which

---

directly to Aila. The total mileage, however, is reasonably accurate. See Y. Aharoni: Tamar and the Roads to Elath, *IEJ* 13 (1963), pp. 39–42.

[16]   Miller (above, n. 14), Cols. 812–814, 835–836, 858–859.

[17]   G. Parthey and M. Pinder (eds.): *Itinerarium Antonini Augusti*, Berlin, 1948, pp. 91, 96.

[18]   *Ibid.*, p. 76.

[19]   O. Seeck (ed.); *Notitia Dignitatum*, Berlin, 1976, pp. 59–60, 73–74. For the strategic importance of Aila, see P. Mayerson: The First Muslim Attacks on Southern Palestine (A.D. 633–634), *Transactions and Proceedings of the American Philological Association* 95 (1964). pp. 169–171.

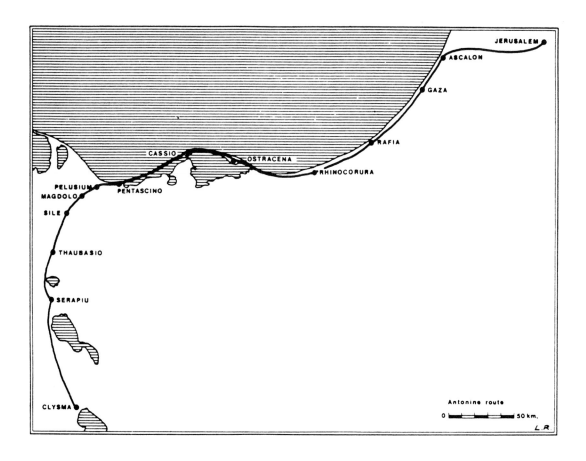

Fig. 3. Map showing the Antonine route.

presumably housed a unit similar to that stationed at Nessana, while at Elusa we hear of military personnel mentioned in an official edict.[20] Providing protection along these routes not only controlled desert raiding and secured safe passage for caravan traffic, but also encouraged a renewal of sedentary life in the Negev to a degree that had not been seen since the time of the Nabatean monarchy. Added to this was the spread of Christianity into the region. Monasteries and hermitages sprang up in increasing numbers, and building activity, particularly of ecclesiastical structures, during the sixth and seventh centuries turned such desert sites as Elusa, Ruheiba (ancient name not known), Sobata and Nessana into what might legitimately be called urban centres. Security and stability within the Negev were such that even after the border forces were withdrawn or disbanded some time late in the sixth century, the region continued to prosper and grow. The Church assumed, or was compelled to take on, the administrative affairs of these

---

[20] For Nessana and Oboda, see Mayerson (above n. 10), pp. 166–167; for Elusa, see A. Alt: *Die griechischen Inschriften der Palaestina Tertia westlich der Araba*, Berlin and Leipzig, 1921, p. 5.

communities; and it is then — if we can take Nessana as a paradigm — that the local ecclesiastical authorities turned military fortifications into monastic dwellings or hostels for pilgrims.[21]

If this is a reasonable vignette of the developments along the routes to Aila and Clysma, a century or so of imperial concern for their security made it possible for pilgrims and their guides to travel them without fear of harassment by marauding Saracens. The pilgrims were not only anxious to visit the Holy Mountain where Moses received the Law and where Elijah went into retreat; they were also interested in observing at first hand eremitic and monastic life in the deserts of the Negev and Jordan. Antoninus of Piacenza, for example, was told, on reaching Elusa, of a remarkable pious woman who lived in the region of Segor (Zoar) near the Dead Sea. He and his companions took time out from their trip to Mount Sinai to visit the site where they found a convent of some sixteen or seventeen impoverished young women. It was here that one of the pilgrims offered to buy, for the not insubstantial sum of 100 *solidi*, an extraordinary tame lion that was said to lead a little donkey to pasture. The offer was rejected. Determined to be of help, the pilgrim sent to Jerusalem and provided the women with food and clothing. Upon returning to Elusa, Antoninus and his company resumed their journey to Mount Sinai.[22]

If the experience of Antoninus is a typical one, other pilgrims *en route* to Sinai must have come well provided with money and were solicited for donations to churches and monastic orders at places where they stopped or visited. This would in part explain the reason for the large number of ecclesiastical structures that one finds among the remains of relatively small communities. As for the Sinai peninsula south of Aila and Clysma, there were no military installations along the routes to Mount Sinai, and, with the exception of Pharan, there were no settlements that could be considered even organized villages. The statement of Procopius that the Emperor Justinian had a fort constructed at the foot of Mount Sinai and stationed a considerable garrison of troops there to prevent Saracen incursions into Palestine proper cannot be supported either by archaeological evidence or, more to the point, in terms of military strategy. What Justinian had built was not a fort to house military personnel, but, on the petition of the monks of the Holy Mountain, a fortified monastery on a grand scale.[23]

It is evident then that Sinai proper at this time was not a major thoroughfare for the soldier or the trader and that the Saracen population, either because of its numbers or because of pacification through imperial payments, did not offer a serious threat to

---

[21]   Mayerson (above, n. 10), pp. 169–171; idem (above, n. 19), pp. 174–176. For churches in the Negev, see C.L. Woolley and T.E. Lawrence: *The Wilderness of Zin*, London, 1936, pp. 92, 97, 108, 116, 122, 129, 130, 133, 141.

[22]   Geyer (above, n. 9), pp. 181–182.

[23]   P. Mayerson: Procopius or Eutychius on the Construction of the Monastery at Mount Sinai: Which is the More Reliable Source? *BASOR* 230 (1978), pp. 33–38.

travellers or to the lands that bordered the peninsula.[24] Egeria, for example, was escorted from Mount Sinai to Pharan by monks of the Holy Mountain, and it was only when she reached Clysma that she spoke of soldiers and forts. Hence, travellers making their way to Mount Sinai or Pharan must have been led by guides who not only knew the tracks through the wilderness but also could deal with the Saracen tribes encountered along the way. It is possible too that armed guards, or even military personnel, may have accompanied groups of pilgrims in the uninhabited areas beyond the *oecumene*.[25]

If these were the conditions as we described them, then the matter of distance, surface conditions, and the availability of potable water had to be considerations in determining whether to go to Mount Sinai via Egypt (*i.e.* Clysma) or through Palestine (*i.e.* Aila). The itinerary of Theodosius (*c.* 530) is informative. It outlines a route from Jerusalem by means of the trans-Negev road to Aila that harmonizes with the Peutinger Table. The 71 mp that is given on the Table as the milage between Jerusalem and Elusa is covered in 3 stages; the remaining 149 mp to Aila is covered in 7 stages, or a realistic average of 20 mp per day for the journey from Jerusalem to Aila. From Aila to Mount Sinai, a distance of some 150 miles, the Theodosian itinerary goes on to state that '...there are 8 stages if you wish to take the short route through the desert.' The itinerary then adds this unelaborated and simple statement 'but if you wish to go through Egypt, there are 25 stages'.[26]

In short, there are 18 stages between Jerusalem and Mount Sinai via Aila, and 25 stages for the route through Egypt. The 18 stages coincide precisely with the number of days that it took the Egyptian monk Ammonius late in the fourth century to travel from Jerusalem 'through the desert' to Mount Sinai in a caravan of 'devout Christians'.[27]

The Theodosian itinerary calling for 25 stages for the journey between Jerusalem and Mount Sinai gives us no indication of the route that a traveller would take once he reached the borders of Egypt. Peter the Deacon's *de locis sanctis* (1137 C.E.) provides more detailed information. Deriving his account in part from Bede's compilation and, as is generally believed, from the lost portion of Egeria's itinerary, the monk of Monte Cassino reports that the journey from Jerusalem to Mount Sinai can be covered in 22 stages, and that 'from Pelusium to Mount Sinai, it is 12 stages'.[28] These are reasonable figures, for if we take the milage from Pelusium to Clysma (110 mp) and from Clysma

---

[24] This is not to say that the roads were always free of marauders. Two incidents are recorded for the seventh century when the route from Palestine to Mount Sinai was blocked by hostile Bedouin; see Mayerson (above, n. 19), p. 191.

[25] For one such instance, see P. Mayerson: Observations on the 'Nilus' *Narrationes, Journal of the American Research Center in Egypt* 12 (1975), p. 67.

[26] P. Geyer (ed.): *De Situ Terrae Sanctae* in *Corpus Scriptorum Ecclesiasticorum* 39, p. 148: 'De Hierusalem in Elusath mansiones III, de Elusath in Aila mansiones VII... De Aila usque monte Syna mansiones VIII, si compendiaria volueris ambulare per heremum, sin autem per Aegyptum, mansiones XXV.'

[27] F. Combefis: *Illustrium Christi martyrum lecti triumphi*, Paris, 1660, p. 88.

[28] *Corpus Christianorum, Series Latina*, 175, p. 100: 'Ab Ierusalem autem usque ad montem sanctum Syna sunt mansiones viginti duo... A Pelusio autem usque ad montem Syna sunt mansiones duodecim.'

to Mount Sinai via Pharan (165 mp), the average number of miles covered in one day
would be about 23 mp. The 194 mp from Jerusalem to Pelusium would be covered in 10
stages and would average about 20 mp per day.

Peter the Deacon also provides us with some general information concerning travelling conditions between Arabia (*i.e.* Arabia Petraea) and Palestine. After stating that
Egypt is very fertile, even more so where the children of Israel lived, he goes on to say:
'The part of Arabia which joins Palestine has an impassable road; for although there
are 15 stages along this road, yet these places are without water'.[29] While this statement
is not as precise as we would like it to be, it does point to the difficulties in travelling
from Palestine to Sinai via Egypt: shifting sands that make roads impassable and the
lack of sources for water. The coastal road west of Rhinocorura (modern el-Arish) cuts
through a region of sandy wastes;[30] and the road from Pelusium south to Clysma runs
through dune belts and salt marshes. Although this route may not be considered impassable, it does offer difficulties, perhaps not so much for the camel as it does for the
donkey and the man on foot. Pliny the Elder characterizes the desert road between
Pelusium and the Red Sea as being 'across sands, a road that, unless reeds are fixed (in
the sands) to show the way, is lost from sight due to winds that immediately cover the
track'.[31]

South of Clysma, on the western side of Sinai, the scarcity of potable water is also a
problem. For the 63 miles between Clysma and Wadi Gharandel, the site of ancient
Surandela, the terrain is parched and dry: '...a barren wilderness... with water supply
which, except at two favoured sites (Ayun Musa and Wadi Gharandel) consists of no
more than a few brackish pools'.[32] And a guidebook of the turn of the century speaks of
the coastal route between Ayun Musa and Wadi Gharandel as 'le désert de trois jours
sans eau'.[33]

The traveller from Egypt had of necessity to bear these hardships before heading into
the sandstone interior (most likely from Abu Zuneima on the coast to Naqb Budra,
Maghara, Mukatteb and Feiran), where reasonably good supplies of water were
available. The traveller from Palestine, on the other hand, had the advantage of making
his way to Aila through the stony desert of the Negev, which provided sure footing for
man and beast, as well as water from wells, cisterns and reservoirs. At Aila, where

---

[29] *Ibid*: 'Egyptus autem cum sit ubertissima, loca tamen, que tenuerunt filii Israhel sunt meliora. Pars
Arabiae que iungitur Palestine, inaccessibile iter habet; nam licet mansionibus quindecim iter habeat, loca
tamen ipsa sine aqua sunt.'

[30] For an appreciation of the quality of this road for caravans, see W.F. Albright: Abram the Caravaneer:
A New Interpretation, *BASOR* 63 (1961), pp. 37–38.

[31] *Nat. Hist.*, 6. 29. 166–167.

[32] C.W. Wilson and H.S. Palmer: *Ordinance Survey of the Peninsula of Sinai*, I, Southampton, 1869, p.
80. Egeria, apparently speaking of this stretch of the road (above, n. 6, p. 46) describes it as '... no road
whatsoever, but only the sands of the desert' (via enim illic penitus non est, sed totum heremi sunt
arenosae.)

[33] B. Meisterman: *Guide du Nil*, Paris, 1902, p. 53.

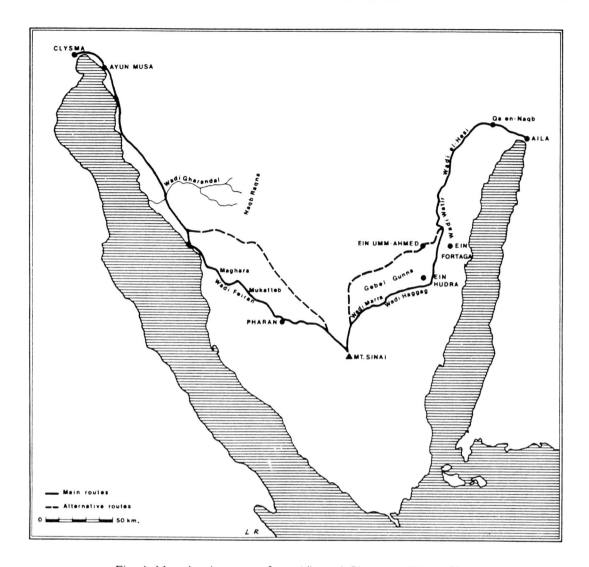

Fig. 4. Map showing routes from Aila and Clysma to Mount Sinai.

there is an excellent supply of water, the traveller could refresh himself before undertaking the final leg of his journey to Mount Sinai (Fig. 4). Undoubtedly there were arrangements also to be made at Aila for new guides and a change of transport animals. If conditions warranted, it was possible to make a direct connection with the Sinai route at Qa en-Naqb in north-eastern Sinai and thus to avoid backtracking to that point from Aila. Whatever course was selected, the traveller found not only good supplies of water *en route* to the Holy Mountain but also sure footing on the sandstone and granitic formations of eastern Sinai.

At this point, it may be best to cite the experience of Avner Goren, the Archaeological Staff Officer for Sinai, who trekked back and forth over the routes from modern Elat to Mount Sinai, where he lived, as well as those routes from Mount Sinai to the Gulf of Suez. These are his observations:

The conventional route went through the large wadis parallel to the Gulf of Elat (Aqaba), and afterwards turned toward the interior of the country. A coastal route never developed because mountains reach the sea at several places, and because of poor supplies of water and difficult terrain. The route began at Qa en-Naqb, the plain overlooking Elat from the west (800 m. above sea-level), and required a climb from Elat (Naqb Aqaba), but those coming from the trans-Negev route came directly to the Qa. The Qa contains wells, and in the ravine of Wadi Umm-Sidra at the edge of the Qa, there are hollows that fill with water most of the year. The ravine offers shelter from the sun and wind. It contains many rock inscriptions, including some in Greek.

From the western end of the Qa, the route descends southward to Wadi el-Hesi, which later becomes Wadi Watir. There are sources of water along the way (*e.g.* Bir Hesi and Bir Swere), and the wadis are wide, straight, and make for easy passage. The route then crosses from the Watir into Wadi Lat'hi to the middle of Wadi Ghazala, but it is possible to continue for several kilometers in the Watir to the border of the large oasis, Ein Fortaga, where there is a small rivulet that flows all year round. Wadi Ghazala flows into this oasis, and the route rises to the very top of the Ghazala. From there the way crosses west to the Haggag 'valley' among the sandstone hills that are covered with inscriptions. There is no doubt that Haggag was a wayside stop on track to Mount Sinai. Ein Hudra provided the water for this encampment, but it was necessary to send camels to transport the water. Although Wadi Hudra flows into Ghazala, and it would appear to be a shortcut to Haggag, it is in fact impossible for a caravan to pass that way because the Naqb which goes up to Haggag (Naqb Shie) is steep and sandy, and can be traversed only by camels carrying half-loads.

From Haggag, the route continues to the base of Gebel Gunna and parallel to it by way of Wadi Marra where there is a rock with Greek and other inscriptions. Thence to the Ilu el-Agramia plains. The passage consists of three easy climbs, and there are several water sources that make possible a number of parallel passages. (In this area, the new motor road to the Monastery of St. Catherine is almost entirely in line with the ancient route.) From Ilu el-Agramia, the route descends to Wadi es-Sheikh, the major feeder of Wadi Feiran, and conveniently enters the foothills of Mount Sinai to the valleys and monastic establishments there. This region is rich in supplies of water.

There are alternate ways in several places. A secondary route crosses Wadi Watir by way of Ras el-Qalb to Ein Umm-Ahmed in Wadi Zalacka. It continues up through the entire length of the wadi to the top where it leads to the plains of Ilu el-Agramia and connects with the main route.[34]

---

[34] Personal communication. Investigators of the Sinai owe Mr. Goren, archaeologist, guide and conservationist, a deep debt of gratitude. He has selflessly and unstintingly shared his considerable knowledge of the terrain and archaeology of the region — as he has with this writer on many an occasion — with all those who have sought it.

In sum, then, all the evidence — inscriptions, security, travelling conditions, relevant itineraries — provides us with a convincing *prima facie* case that the shortest and preferred route from points in Palestine to Mount Sinai led toward Aila and the eastern side of the Sinai peninsula. To this should be added the evidence of the relationship of the monastic community at the Holy Mountain with Aila. An inscription on one of the beams of the basilica roof identifies a certain Stephanus, an architect or builder (τέκτων) who hailed from Aila.[35] The inscription is dated to the years between 548 and 565. And Anastasius, a monk who lived at Mount Sinai and its environs about the mid-seventh century, reports that Sergius, the bishop of Aila, sat by the side of Abba Orentios and heard his last words before he died.[36] Anastasius also tells the story of a renowned monk who, when he lay ill in his cell and knew that his end was near, sent a Saracen to Aila to summon one of his spiritual brothers. The distance, according to Anastasius, was 200 miles, and the Saracen returned with the friend of the old man in 12 days.[37]

Finally, returning to the Armenian pilgrims, it is this same Anastasius who reports that it was their custom to come often to Mount Sinai. He goes on to say: 'Twenty years ago, they came in a great crowd of almost 800 souls, and while they were on the holy summit in order to see from a distance the holy stone where Moses received the Law... the holy summit and all of them were enveloped in flame'.[38] To what extent Anastasius is given to hyperbole in terms of numbers and miracles we cannot say, but it is certain that these Armenians travelled along the route outlined above and even may have paused at Wadi Haggag to rest and to inscribe a name or two on the sandstone rock, like so many others who had preceded them from Palestine.

---

[35] I. Ševčenko: The Early Period of the Sinai Monastery in the Light of its Inscriptions, *Dumbarton Oaks Papers* 20 (1966), pp. 257, 262.

[36] F. Nau (ed.): Le texte grec des récits du moine Anastase sur les saints pères du Sinai, *Oriens Christianus* 2 (1902), p. 71.

[37] *Ibid.*, p. 67.

[38] *Ibid.*, pp. 81–82.

The City of Elusa in the Literary Sources
of the Fourth–Sixth Centuries

PHILIP MAYERSON

New York University

SOME 50 km. south-south-west of Gaza and 20 km. south-west of Beer-sheba lies the ancient city of Elusa. In the available works of reference either this city's existence passes completely unnoticed, or, as in the case of Pauly-Wissowa's *Realencyclopädie*, it is given a note so brief that the city would seem to merit no distinction whatsoever. In this standard work of reference, we are given the following information: according to the Peutinger Table, Elusa is 71 Roman miles from Jerusalem on the road to Aila; the Piacenza pilgrim cites it as being at the head of the wilderness extending to Sinai; Ptolemy mentions it as one of the cities of Idumea west of the Jordan. To this are added two citations from St. Jerome, with virtually no comment, that its bishops took part in the Councils of Ephesus and that 'Der eigentümlich heidnische Kult des Ortes ist von mehreren Kirchenvätern beschrieben'.[1] This and very little more.

It is Jerome who informs us of Elusa's 'eigentümlich' pagan cult. In his biography of Hilarion, Palestine's proto-monk (*c*. 300–371) — Hilarion is thought to have visited Elusa in 350 or thereabouts — we read as follows:

> The extent of Hilarion's zeal in not slighting a single brother, no matter how humble or poor he might be, is shown in his going to the desert of Cades to visit one of his disciples. On that occasion, accompanied by a great procession of monks, he arrived in Elusa by chance on the day that a solemn festival had brought all the people of the town to the temple of Venus. Now the Saracens worship the goddess because of the Morning Star, and their race is dedicated to her cult. But also the town itself is semi-barbarian for the most part because of its location.[2]

The key word in Jerome's description of Elusa is *semi-barbarus*. To him the town is for the most part 'semi-barbarian' or 'half-civilized' because of its location. Its people are 'Saracens' — a word most often used pejoratively to mean pagan Arabs, settled or

---

[1] *S.v.* Elusa, 5.2, col. 2457. As for other works of reference on Elusa, only one other dealing with the literary sources has come to my attention: *Dictionnaire d'histoire et de géographie ecclésiastiques*, col. 265, where Elusa is cited as a city of no importance. On the other hand, *EAEHL* II, pp. 359–360, contains an article summarizing the exploration, history and archaeology of the site.

[2] J.-C. Migne (ed.): *Patrologia Latina* 23, col. 41. The association of the goddess Venus with the Morning Star is certainly not strange or peculiar; see e.g. J. Hastings (ed.): *Encyclopedia of Religion and Ethics* 9, pp. 593–594.

197

unsettled (i.e. Bedouin), who inhabit desert regions. The picture drawn for us by Jerome was patently designed to exalt the missionary work of Hilarion, whose miraculous cures helped convert many pagans to Christianity. It is possible, of course, that Hilarion had no contact with people other than Bedouin or that Bedouin came to Elusa to worship the goddess along with other members of the community. Be that as it may, Jerome left the impression that Elusa was a half-civilized pagan town in the desert.

But was Elusa a half-civilized town in the middle of the fourth century? To Libanius (314–c. 393), the most celebrated man of letters of late antiquity, the city of Elusa must have appeared quite civilized. From his letters and orations we learn that it was the desert town of Elusa that produced Zenobius, a professor of rhetoric in Antioch and Libanius' own teacher. A great rhetorician in his own right, Zenobius rose to become the sophist of the city of Antioch, a position to which Libanius succeeded when Zenobius died in 345.[3] A cousin of Zenobius, Argyrius, who must also have had his origins in Elusa, equally made a name for himself in Antioch as a well-known rhetor of curial rank.[4] Where Zenobius and Argyrius learned their skills is not known, although it is possible that they left their birthplace at an early age to study in another city. We do know, however, that rhetoric was taught in Elusa at about the same time that Hilarion visited the city.

In a letter dated to 359, Libanius wrote to Eutocius, a leading councillor of Elusa, asking that the imperial stipend in kind (βασιλικὴ τροφή) granted to Eudaemon, the local sophist, be converted into money.[5] This Eudaemon was an Egyptian of wide reputation who together with his cousin practised law in Elusa in 357. He received his instruction in rhetoric at Elusa, and at the time of Libanius' letter, he was established there as a sophist (i.e. as a public teacher).[6] In Libanius' view, the fact that Eudaemon was a recipient of an imperial grant redounded to the reknown of the city of Elusa.

Elusa was also civilized enough to have a Guardian of the Peace, an Irenarch (εἰρήνης φύλαξ), a police officer of curial rank who was appointed by the governor of the province. On two occasions Libanius, presumably responding to pleas from appointees to the office in Elusa, attempted to use his influence with high-ranking imperial officials to rectify injustices, as he understood them, to two relatives of the aforementioned Zenobius. In 356, Libanius wrote to Firminus, the provincial governor, asking him to restore Boethus, a cousin of Zenobius, to the office of Irenarch from

---

[3]   R. Foerster (ed.): *Libanii Opera*, X, *Epistolae*, Leipzig, 1921 (hereafter *Ep.*), 101 (p. 102); see also O. Seeck: *Die Briefe des Libanius zeitlich geordnet* in Gebhart-Harnack: *Texte und Untersuchungen*, Neue Folge 15 (1917), pp. 315–316; A.F. Norman (ed. and trans.): *Libanius' Autobiography, Oration I*, Oxford, 1965, p. 60.

[4]   Seeck (above, n. 3), pp. 222, 315, 458. See also P. Petit: *Libanius et la vie municipale à Antioche au IVᵉ siècle après J.-C.*, Paris, 1955, p. 326; A.F. Norman: The Family of Argyrius, *Journal of Hellenic Studies* 74 (1954), p. 45, n. 2.b.ii.

[5]   *Ep.* 132 (p. 132); Seeck (above, n. 3), p. 151. See also H.W.G. Liebeschuetz: *Antioch: City and Imperial Administration in the Later Roman Empire*, Oxford, 1972, pp. 88–89.

[6]   Seeck (above, n. 3), p. 131.

which he had been removed.[7] Three years later, in 359/60, he wrote to Modestus, the Comes Orientis, and to his Assessor, Urbanus, to use the weight of their offices to put right an unstated injustice to a certain Zenobius, a relative of the famous rhetor of the same name.[8] In this particular case, we learn that Modestus was due to arrive in Elusa and that he would see for himself the nature of the difficulty. And the fact that the Comes Orientis was to make an official visit to Elusa — as did other high-ranking imperial officials — would indicate that the city was in the mainstream of imperial life.[9]

The intimate relationship that Libanius of Antioch had with the inhabitants of the desert town of Elusa is all the more surprising in view of the distance between the two cities and the fact that his correspondence and orations rarely cite other major cities of Palestine or Arabia. Elusa is cited by name six times; Gaza twice; Ascalon once; Caesarea twice; Petra once; Bostra twice.[10] While not in themselves conclusive, these bare statistics at least show not only that Elusa was more than a half-civilized desert outpost of the Roman empire during the fourth century, but also that the recipients of Libanius' letters were fully aware of the city and of its cultural and political setting.

For the hundred years following the death of Libanius we hear very little of Elusa. Toward the end of the fourth century, or somewhat earlier, the name of Elusa appears in a narrative attributed to a certain Nilus who lived as an eremite at Mount Sinai. The narrative tells of a Saracen raid that resulted in the death of a number of Sinaitic monks and the abduction of Nilus' son Theodoulus. Theodoulus, after several hair-raising adventures, was ransomed by the bishop of Elusa who bound him to an obligatory service contract, a παραμονή, and set him to work as a νεωκόρος to perform menial chores for his church.[11] Elusa at this point in time was turning from paganism to Christianity, and by 431 one of its bishops — oddly enough, Theodoulus by name — attended the Council of Ephesus.[12]

Recent archaeological work at Ḥaluṣa, the site of ancient Elusa, has uncovered a probable link with the city's school of rhetoric that is alluded to by Libanius. Excavations at the site have uncovered a theatre dating from the period of the Nabatean kingdom.[13] In itself the discovery of a theatre indicates a cultured population at Elusa during the early years of the Christian era. On the basis of finds associated with it,

[7]   *Ep.* 532 (p. 501).

[8]   *Ep.* 101–102 (pp. 101–103).

[9]   Seeck (above, n. 3), p. 214. Elusa was an administrative centre of the province, if not its capital; Y. Dan: Palaestina Salutaris (Tertia) and its Capital, *IEJ* 32 (1982), pp. 134–137, and as such it was undoubtedly visited by members of the civil and military hierarchy; L. Casson: The Administration of Byzantine and Early Arab Palestine, *Aegyptus* 33 (1952), pp. 54–60.

[10]   Foerster (above, n. 3), XII, *Index*, Leipzig, 1923.

[11]   P. Mayerson: Observations on the 'Nilus' *Narrationes, Journal of the American Research Center in Egypt* 12 (1975), pp. 68–71.

[12]   Idem, The Desert of Southern Palestine according to Byzantine Sources, *Proceedings of the American Philosophical Society* 107 (1963), pp. 167–169.

[13]   A. Negev: Survey and Trial Excavations at Ḥaluza (Elusa), 1973, *IEJ* 26 (1976), pp. 92–93, Pl. 20:B C; idem, Les Nabatéens au Négev, *Le Monde de la Bible* 19 (1981), pp. 17–19.

Negev states that the theatre was also in use during the Late Roman and Byzantine periods. An important find was a Greek inscription that commemorated the repaving of the floor of the theatre and stated that it was undertaken by Abramius the son of Zenobius. The date given on the inscription is equated to 454/5.[14]

The reappearance of the name Zenobius in the mid-fifth century is enough to raise an eyebrow, for it would be possible to see the family of the Zenobii as continuing the tradition of rhetorical training at Elusa. (We know of another Zenobius from Elusa, probably the son of Zenobius the Irenarch, who in 360 studied rhetoric with Libanius.[15]) By 454 the descendants of the renowned rhetor of Antioch had undoubtedly converted to the new faith; hence the appearance of the biblical name of Abramius. However, putting aside this supposition as speculative, we can safely assume that the theatre in the mid-fifth century and earlier served, as it did in other communities, as an outdoor 'lecture hall' for occasional public recitations and sophistical displays.[16]

At about the time that the floor of the theatre at Elusa was being repaved, another distinguished sophist, Procopius of Gaza (c. 450–526) was born. The correspondence of this Christian man of letters tells us little of the practice of rhetoric or politics at Elusa, but his proximity to the city made him especially knowledgeable about its physical environment. Procopius had a close relationship with an inhabitant of Elusa, a certain Jerome, who like Procopius was a sophist and teacher, and who at one time may have been one of his pupils. Jerome had gone to Egypt to practise his profession but travelled back and forth to Elusa where his wife and child were living.[17] It is from the correspondence between these two friends that we can extract some observations concerning contemporary conditions at Elusa at the beginning of the sixth century.

In several letters Procopius chides Jerome in a paternal way for his fascination with Egypt. In one, in which he writes to Jerome in Elusa expressing his surprise at finding him there, he repeats his friend's complaints about living conditions in his native town.

> I had high hopes of seeing you again, and naturally I was happy that you appeared in your blessed native town for at least a short time. You seem to me to be jesting when you complain about your native town. I would not deny that the air overhead is just as you say it happens to be, and that those who drink of its water are reminded of the sea, and that our (wheaten) bread is indiscriminately mixed with barley (flour). But out of consideration for your native town you have understated your complaints. Nevertheless, my very good friend, you should be grateful that you have trained your mind in philosophy so that some day you may learn to disdain the luxuries of Egypt.[18]

---

[14] *Ibid.*, p. 18, Fig. 23.

[15] Seeck (above, n. 3), p. 318.

[16] J.W.H. Walden: *The Universities of Greece*, New York, 1909, pp. 266–269.

[17] A. Garzya and R.-J. Loenertz (eds.): *Procopii Gazae Epistolae et Declamationes* in *Studia Patristica et Byzantina* 9 (1963), pp. xxxi–xxxii. A letter (*Ep.* 87, p. 41) to a certain Agapeto, a rhetor and resident of Elusa, informs us at least that the profession was actively practised in the city.

[18] *Ep.* 2 (p. 4, lines 12–20).

Two of Jerome's complaints, virtually given verbatim by Procopius, provide a sure indication, if not proof positive, that conditions at Elusa have not changed since the sixth century. That the well-water at the site is brackish and barely palatable can be testified to by this writer. Bedouin pasturing their flocks near Ḥaluṣa use its well only for their animals; they themselves seek their drinking water from pipelines serving Israeli settlements in the vicinity. Elusa, like neighbouring ancient communities, depended largely for its drinking water on rainwater gathered in cisterns and reservoirs.[19] However, there must have been times of the year, or periods of drought, when the inhabitants had to rely for their drinking water solely on available wells. As for the air — perhaps better yet, the haze — hanging overhead, this too is a common occurrence during a large part of the year, due either to the intense heat of the *hamsin* or to winds that cloud the air with minute particles of sand that tend to obscure the sun.

Jerome's complaint that his bread was laced with barley flour — apparently as was Procopius' at Gaza — is an expression of his unhappiness with the standard of living at Elusa, or even at Gaza. However, the fact that flour milled from wheat was the essential ingredient of bread baked at Elusa is in itself an indication of a high standard of living for a desert town. Barley bread, as we learn from Libanius, was fare for the poor or was eaten when nothing better was available.[20] Libanius, of course, was referring to Antioch in the Fertile Crescent, where one could take for granted the availability of fine bread. But at Elusa, where conditions for the cultivation of cereals favoured barley over wheat, inhabitants like Jerome expected their bread to be made exclusively from flour milled from wheat. As surprising as this may sound, there is support for Jerome's expectations, at least in terms of the availability of the preferred cereal. The evidence comes from the site of Nessana, some twenty miles south of Elusa and deeper in the desert. The sixth–seventh-century papyri discovered there, of which a good number are concerned with cereals, confirm the preference of wheat over barley: only two documents mention barley, while all the others deal with wheat.[21] And one unusual document, an account of wheat and barley sown and reaped at various places near Nessana, records that five times more wheat than barley was sown.[22]

In yet another letter to Jerome, who at this time was in Egypt, Procopius takes him to task for living in the lap of luxury and for putting on airs. But he, Procopius, will have the last laugh, for when Jerome returns to his home town he will be shocked at what he will find. This letter is particularly informative, even more so than the one written to Jerome at Elusa, for Procopius provides us with a contemporary view of conditions, both physical and climatic, experienced by Elusa at the time he wrote the letter, presumably at the turn of the century.

---

[19] See e.g. C.L. Woolley and T.E. Lawrence: *The Wilderness of Zin*, London, 1936, pp. 52, 78, 91.
[20] Norman (above, n. 3), I. 8 (p. 6); T. Frank (ed.): *An Economic Survey of Ancient Rome*, IV, Baltimore, 1938, p. 129.
[21] P. Mayerson: The Ancient Agricultural Regime at Nessana and the Central Negeb, in H.D. Colt (ed.): *Excavations at Nessana*, I, London, 1962, pp. 227, 259–262.
[22] *Ibid.*, pp. 221, 261.

Once more Egypt, luxury, and in comparison with you we are poor, and there is no reason for your absence. It's of no consequence. Only smile when you see the Nile flowing with gold. And even if you continue to put on airs, we shall tolerate and overlook it completely. For there will be a day when you will see Elusa again and you will weep at the sand being shifted by the wind and stripping the vines naked to their roots. The nymphs of the dry land and of the sea, and Zeus the Bringer of Rain, are nowhere there at all. Then I shall laugh and mock your fate. However, putting aside the fact that the Nile provides you with luxury, do write and call us an insignificant and a low-down creature. For even when you write in this manner, we shall enjoy it, and we shall excuse your pretentiousness with the hope of a better outlook (for you).[23]

It is quite obvious from this letter that Jerome has been away from Elusa for some time and has neglected corresponding with Procopius. Leaving aside whatever rhetorical devices Procopius has employed to cover his pique at having been neglected, he informs Jerome that since he left his native town of Elusa there have been drastic changes.

Simply put, Procopius tells Jerome that Elusa is in the grip of a severe drought and that winds and sands have damaged, if not destroyed, its vineyards. By 'the nymphs of the dry land and of the sea' (νύμφαι ξηραί τινες καὶ θαλάττιαι), Procopius certainly refers to water resources, but not to springs since there are no springs in the vicinity of Elusa. By 'nymphs of the dry land' I believe that Procopius was referring to the flood waters that periodically flow in dry streambeds (wadis) or in runoff areas as a result of winter rains. These are the waters that the ancient inhabitants of this arid region directed onto the fields to grow their crops and diverted into reservoirs to provide themselves with a supply of potable water.[24] As for 'the nymphs of the sea', if Procopius attached any specific meaning to the phrase, he may have been referring to brackish well-water; as he remarked in the previously mentioned letter to Jerome, 'those who drink of it are reminded of the sea'. Severe droughts deplete subterranean water-levels which in turn affect water-levels in wells. If, then, the nymphs of the sea and Zeus the Bringer of Rain did not come to Elusa — as Procopius puts it — its wells, which used to hold water saline to the taste, could have run dry.

The combination of drought and wind has highly erosive effects on soil, particularly on the light aeolian soils that surround Elusa; hence, 'the sand being shifted by the wind and stripping the vines naked to their roots'. There is yet one other consideration that must be taken into account; namely, that Procopius' letter may provide us with a *terminus a quo* for a radical change in the physical environment in the region around Elusa: the encroachment of sand dunes on its cultivable lands. Current maps of Israel (e.g. 1:250,000 South) show the ancient site of Elusa surrounded by deep sandy areas. One such area to the west of the town is even called *Ḥolot Ḥaluṣa*, 'the Sand Dunes of Ḥaluṣa'.

---

[23] *Ep.* 81 (p. 43).

[24] Mayerson (above, n. 21), pp. 233–249.

Further, with Procopius' statement in hand, one made by the Piacenza pilgrim some fifty years later can be interpreted as supporting the view that shifting sands had indeed invaded the region around Elusa. In his itinerary (*c. 570*) the Piacenza pilgrim writes that he set out from Gaza *en route* to Mount Sinai, and arrived at Elusa 'at the head of the desert that extends to Sinai' (*in caput heremi qui vadit ad Sina*).[25] To a European, as the writer unquestionably was, who may never have had the experience of seeing a true desert of sand or stone, the sight of sandy wastes as he approached Elusa would naturally indicate to him that he had entered one.

Additional support for the possibility that Procopius may have unwittingly given us evidence for this change at Elusa and its environs comes from recent excavations at the coastal site of Deir el-Balah, just west of Gaza, where large deposits of Byzantine pottery were uncovered under sand dunes 13 m. high. Nothing of a period later than Byzantine was found.[26] The relationship of these dunes to others in the region is a subject of investigation by geologists associated with the Deir el-Balah expedition.

At the moment, the question of whether Procopius' enticing statement may be regarded as hard evidence for establishing the time when sands began to move into Elusa must be held in suspense pending further investigation by the archaeologist and geologist. However, the sophist of Gaza, in his two letters to Jerome, provides more certain evidence that climatic conditions at Elusa were no different at the turn of the sixth century than they are today. And further, since a climate both harsh and variable made civilized life difficult, it is understandable that those of the city's inhabitants who were able to do so — Zenobius, Argyrius, Jerome and others — sought to improve their lot by moving to more favourable locations.

[25]   P. Geyer (ed.): *Corpus Scriptorum Ecclesiasticorum: Itinera Hierosolymitana Saec. III–VIII* 38, p. 181.

[26]   Trude Dothan: Deir el-Balah, 1977–1978 (Notes and News), *IEJ* 28 (1978), p. 267; idem, Deir el-Balah, 1979, 1980, *ibid*. 31 (1981), pp. 127–129; personal communications with Prof. Dothan. Of interest in this connection are the observations made by Woolley and Lawrence (above, n. 19), pp. 24, 126, 127, as they investigated the region around the site of Elusa just before the First World War. They commented that as one approaches the site 'the stony hills are exchanged for wide sand-dunes...' and that 'the roads to Saadi and Raheiba were clearly defined by their overgrown hedges and piled sand-drifts'. It is also of interest to note that the modern road runs quite a distance to the west of the ancient track that at one time connected Elusa with towns to the north and the south. Undoubtedly, the intention of the modern road-builder was to avoid the drifting sands and dunes that cover the old road.

P.OXY.3574: "ELEUTHEROPOLIS OF THE NEW ARABIA"

A petition, dated securely to *ca.* 314-318, P.Oxy.3574,[1] fortuitously informs us of the existence of a certain "Eleutheropolis of the new Arabia." The details of the document concern, briefly, a request by a petitioner, Aurelian Malchus son of Ionathes, "from the confines of Eleutheropolis of the new Arabia," (ἀπὸ ὁρίων Ἐλευθεροπόλεως τῆς νέας Αραβείας), to the *praeses* of Aegyptus Herculia regarding a claim against a man from Bubastos who held in distraint a quantity of wine on behalf of a sum of money that the petitioner had guaranteed for a man from Scenae extra Gerus. The money was not repaid and the wine went bad, even though the petitioner was willing to pay. Hence, the *praeses* was asked to provide a judge against the man from Bubastos.

On the basis of this document, T.D. Barnes has attempted to resolve the tantalizing crux of the Verona List — *arabia item arabia* — by taking the *nea Arabia* of P.Oxy.3574 as one of the two Arabias of the List and by stating that the words *arabia item arabia* show that "when the province of Egypt was divided in 314/5, it was not divided into two provinces but into three provinces of Aegyptus Iovia, Aegyptus Herculia and Arabia Nova." P.Oxy.3574, he further states, "attests the existence of a province named Arabia Nova between 314/5 and 318 and implies that a town called Eleutheropolis in Arabia Nova is close to Aegyptus Herculia." Barnes acknowledges that his interpretation of the papyrus relies entirely upon that of G.W. Bowersock and, without any indication of uncertainty, he places "Arabia Nova (created 314/5)," after Aegyptus Herculia, in the list of provinces cited by the Verona List for the diocese *Oriens.*[2] J.R. Rea, the editor of P.Oxy.3574, has adopted a more cautious position in interpreting the document. After reviewing the position of Barnes and Bowersock, i.e., that *nea Arabia* was the name of an Egyptian province and that Eleutheropolis was an unknown Egyptian place, he still favors his original view that

> Eleutheropolis here is the only known place of that name and that it fell at this period in a province called New Arabia which is to be identified with one of the two Arabias of the Verona List. The Semitic name of the petitioner [Aurelian Malchus son of Ionathes] agrees well with an origin from the only known Eleutheropolis . . . Contact between Eleutheropolis in Palestine and Oxyrhynchus is already attested. The doubts arising from the geographical names used by Eusebius, from the differences in spelling and wording between 1722 and 3574, and the existence of a nome called Arabia, seem less weighty.[3]

---

1) Dr. J.R. Rea, responding generously to my request, provided me with a copy of the text and commentary of P.Oxy. 3574 that he sent to the printer for the forthcoming Volume L of *The Oxyrhynchus Papyri*.

2) T.D. Barnes, *The New Empire of Diocletian and Constantine* (Cambridge, Mass., 1982) 205-206, 211, 213-215. P.Oxy. 29 4B.48/G(6-7), cited by Barnes on p. 205 (n.13), is an earlier inventory number for P.Oxy. 3574.

3) Above, note 1. For P.Oxy. 1722, see nn. 5 and 11 below.

In attempting to sort out the pros and cons of these two positions, we are
caught on the horns of a dilemma. On the one hand, the abundant papyrological
evidence attests to changes in the administrative structure of Egypt practi-
cally from one year to the next. Between 295 and 338, we know the names of 37
provincial governors for the several provinces into which Egypt had been
carved (Barnes, loc. cit. [above, n.2] 147-152). We also know, for example,
that the province of Aegyptus Herculia lasted but a decade, from 314 to 324,
and that other changes were afoot by 341, when the province of Augustamnica
apparently absorbed Aegyptus Herculia.[4] For Palestine, on the other hand, we
are in less fortunate position. For the regnal years of Diocletian and Constantine, we know the names of only four governors, three of them provided by
Eusebius and the other found in an inscription from Scythopolis (Barnes, 152).
Nor have we any information concerning administrative changes that might have
taken place in Palestine during the volatile years of the late 3rd and early
4th centuries, and we would truly be in the dark without P.Oxy.1722[5] and,
possibly, 3574.

As for Eleutheropolis itself, the situation is quite different. The city
of Eleutheropolis in Palestine is well documented. It is cited in the literature; it minted its own coins; and its physical remains can be seen at the
site of Beit Jibrin.[6] Eleutheropolis was so well known that Eusebius cited
it some 40 times in his Onomasticon in order to provide orientation for the
identification of biblical sites. And, most important, it was a city with a
large associated territory. In Egypt, however, despite the many place names
that have cropped up in papyri, there is no evidence of a city or a district
named Eleutheropolis. Hence, Barnes would maintain that P.Oxy.3574 "implies
that a town called Eleutheropolis is close to Aegyptus Herculia" (Barnes, loc.
cit. [above, n.2] 213-214). Why Eleutheropolis should be close to Aegyptus
Herculia is not stated. I see no reason why a man called Aurelian Malchus
could not have been a wine merchant or money lender from the well-known city
of Eleutheropolis, who conducted business with individuals in Egypt and who
perhaps even had the petition drawn up while he was traveling in Egypt. Be
that as it may, we have no knowledge of a city by that name in Egypt, or even
of its possible whereabouts with respect to Aegyptus Herculia.

The association of nea Arabia with the former nome of Arabia in northeastern
Egypt is undoubtedly the source of one of the arguments that led Barnes and

----

4) A.H.M. Jones, The Cities of the Eastern Provinces (Oxford 1971) 336 and 489 (n.50).

5) P.Oxy. 1722, a fragment of an agreement dated to the 3rd or 4th century, mentions one
of the parties as having come ἀπὸ Συρίας 'Ελευθεραπόλεως. Rea suggests that the phrase might
be translated as "from Syria (more precisely) Eleutheropolis," and he cites 1722 as evidence
for the contact between Eleutheropolis of Palestine and Oxyrhynchus.

6) Jones, loc. cit. (above, n. 4), 279 and 463 (n. 71). A. Calderini-S. Daris, Diz. dei
nomi geogr. e topogr. dell' Eg. Gr.-Rom., s.v.

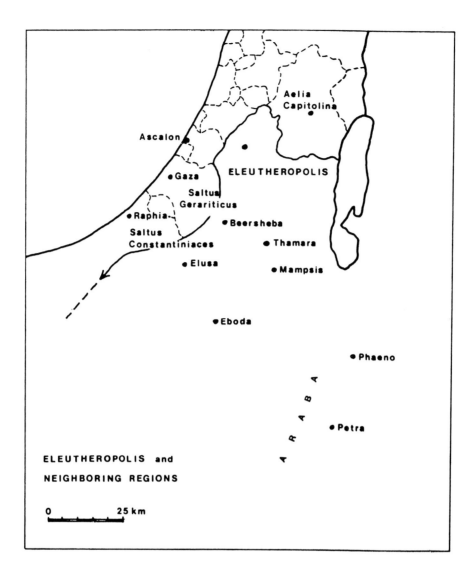

Bowersock to conclude that *nea Arabia* was the third Egyptian province. That
there was a nome by the name of Arabia and that its metropolis was Phacusa
are fully attested. A.H.M. Jones, discussing the conversion of nomes into
cities during the early years of the 4th century, comments that although usage
varied from place to place, in a number of instances the name of the metropolis superseded the name of the nome as the name of the city. On the other
hand, he states that Arabia (the nome) was preferred as a city name over Phacusa (its former metropolis).[7]

   Perhaps more germane than the Byzantine city lists cited by Jones for Arabia is the account of an eyewitness, the peripatetic nun Egeria, who visited

───────────
   7) Jones (above, n. 4), 299-300, 336-337, 479 (n. 21), and 489-490 (n. 51).

Egyptian Arabia during her tour of biblical sites sometime late in the 4th century. After visiting Mount Sinai and Pharan in Sinai, she made her way to Clysma, at which point she believed that she was entering the biblical land of Goshen. *Desiderii ergo fuit*, she writes, *ut de Clesma ad terram Gesse exiremus, id est ad civitatem quae appellatur Arabia, quae civitas in terra Gesse est; nam inde ipsum territorium sic appellatur, id est terra Arabiae, terra Iesse, quae tamen terra Egypti pars est, sed melior satis quam omnis Egyptus est.* [8]

It is conceivable that the information provided to Egeria by an attending monk or guide — "the city of Arabia is in the land of Goshen, and the region takes its name from it; that is, the land of Arabia" — is a recollection or a reminiscence of Arabia either as a nome or as a province of Egypt. However, the phrase "the land of Arabia is the land of Goshen" and others associating the land of Goshen with the land of Egypt are taken by annotators of the text to be paraphrases of various passages in Genesis (45.10, 46.34, 47.6, 47.11) of the Septuagint. [9] The experience of Egeria with Egyptian Arabia involved only the city itself or its bishop.

The itinerary of Egeria is instructive on another score, namely, the confusion attending the use of the name "Arabia." No sooner had Egeria finished touring biblical sites in Egypt, than she made her way to Palestine and Jerusalem via the public road "from the Thebaid to Pelusium, which passed through the city of Arabia." After some time, she was "taken once more with the desire to go to Arabia, to Mount Nebo": *fuit denuo voluntas accedendi usque ad Arabiam, id est ad montem Nabau* (10,1 p. 50). The Arabia of Mount Nebo is, of course, the Roman province of Arabia east of Palestine, but Egeria seems to have been unaware of the distinction between the two Arabias.

A confusion of a different kind occurred at a later date, when the southern portion of the province of Arabia had been organized as part of Palaestina Tertia. The itinerary of the Piacenza pilgrim (*ca.* 570), like that of Egeria, describes a pilgrimage to Mount Sinai. After completing his stay at the Holy Mountain, the Piacenza pilgrim and his companions were informed that they could not return to Jerusalem by the same route they had come. "Some," he reports, "returned to the Holy City through Egypt and some through Arabia. From Mount Sinai in Arabia (*in Arabia*) to the city which is called A(b)ila is 8

---

8) *Itinerarium Egeriae* 7.1 (*CCSL* 175, 46-47). For *omnis = refera omnis*, see E. Löfstedt, *Philol. Kommentar zur Per. Aeth.*, Uppsala 1911, 174.

9) See, e.g., *Egeria: Diary of a Pilgrimage*, G.E. Gringras (trans. and annot.) in *Ancient Christian Writers*, XXXVIII, 180-181. Egeria's itinerary is cited here as the nun's observation of the former nome of Arabia at firsthand. That the region was known as Arabia by some writers — as a region but not necessarily as the name of a province — is attested to by Sozomenus (ob. post 450) in his account of Mauvia, the Saracen queen (*Hist. Ecc.* 6.38.1-2). During the reign of Valens (364-378), she was said "to have laid waste the cities of Palestine and Phoenicia, even as far as (the region) of Egypt that is on the lefthand side as one sails up the Nile (i.e., the eastern Delta). The inhabitants call the region "The Arabian (τὸ Ἀρά-βιον).

stages" (*Antonii Placentini Itin*. 40,*CCSL* 175, 149). Another recension reads:
"From Mount Sinai to the city of Arabia (*in Arabiam civitatem*) which is called
A(b)ela is 7 stages" (*ibid*. 40, pp.171-172). To the Piacenza pilgrim or his
informants, either Aila or Mount Sinai was in Arabia, and even though both
sites had been part of the province of Palaestina Tertia for some 200 years,
the tradition of their earlier situation prevailed.

It is with the confusion of provincial names — Palaestina vs. Arabia —
in mind that the evidence, such as it is, for locating Eleutheropolis and *nea
Arabia* in Palestine merits further investigation. Barnes, relying primarily
on the work of Brünnow and Damaszewski, states that the southern part of the
Trajanic province of Arabia had been incorporated into Palestine before 314,
and that both recensions of Eusebius' *Martyrs of Palestine* (composed in 311 and
313) state that the area around Petra — specifically Phaeno — belonged to
Palestine in 307.[10] Therefore, if Phaeno was located in the province of Palestine, *nea Arabia* could not have been within the borders of that province.
It may very well be that Phaeno and the southern half of the Trajanic province
had been incorporated into Palestine some time early in the 4th century. However, that fact does not preclude the possibility of the creation of a province out of part of Palestine, a province that had no relationship with the
"Palestine" of Petra and Phaeno. The evidence for such an event may be only
circumstantial, yet it is more substantial and bears more strongly on the
problem than an unknown Eleutheropolis and a *nea Arabia* in Egypt.

The region that bears consideration as the *nea Arabia* of P.Oxy.3574 is that
portion of Edom in Palestine known as Idumea. In early times it was inhabited
by Edomite Arabs, and it continued to be inhabited by people of Arab stock,
many of whom were converted to Judaism during the reign of Hyrcanus, including
the ancestors of Herod the Great. Aurelian Malchus the son of Ionathes of P.
Oxy.3574, whose name is not only Semitic but almost beyond question Jewish,
could have been a descendant of a converted Edomite Arab.[11] The Idumean en-

---

10) Barnes, *loc. cit.* (above, n. 2), 214. R.E. Brünnow and A. v.Domaszewski (*Die Provincia
Arabia* III, Strasbourg 1909, 273-274), summarizing the views of several scholars on the question of the date for these events, are not as specific as Barnes. The situation is confused
by the sources — some of which are quite late and none of which are local in origin — that
speak of a Petra in Arabia or a Petra in Palestine. One is unavoidably put in the position of
having to assume that the writers of the 4th and 5th centuries were acutely aware of administrative changes taking place at a distance in space and time from the point at which they were
writing. T. Nöldeke, cited by Brünnow and Domaszewski, perhaps puts it best: "Nun ist aber
auch in Wirklichkeit der offizielle Name der südlichen Provinz im vierten Jahrhundert gar
nicht mehr "Arabien", sondern "Palaestina". Denn da an sich ersterer Name für dies Land nach
Geschichte und Beschaffenheit durchaus passend ist, so begreift es sich sehr wohl, daß der-
selbe auch nach einer offiziellen Umtaufung noch zuweilen vorkommt; dagegen wäre die Anwen-
dung des Namens "Palaestina" auf die Gegend bis ans rothe Meer unerklärlich, bevor dieselbe
durch einen Act der Gesetzgebung festgestellt war."

11) The name Malchus was also adopted by Jews, and its association with Ionathes (Jonathan)
makes it virtually certain that "Aurelius Malchus the son of Jonathan" was a Jew from the
region of Eleutheropolis. Rea has suggested that there might be a connection between P.Oxy.

clave covered a major portion of Palestine south of Jerusalem and Judea. Just
how extensive these lands were prior to the transformation of Bethogabris
(Beit Jibrin) into Eleutheropolis by Septimus Severus in A.D. 200 can be ap-
preciated from Ptolemy's *Geography*. To Ptolemy, all of Idumea was west of the
Jordan River (i.e., west of the Dead Sea and the Araba). He lists five sites for
Idumea, two of which have not been located; the other three are Birsama, Elusa,
and Mampsis (cap.15.6). All three sites are in the Negev south of Beersheba.
Curiously enough, Ptolemy places in Arabia Petraea several other towns in the
Negev that were close to Elusa and Mampsis, viz. Eboda, Maliatha, Lysa, Gubba,
Gypsaria, and Gerasa (cap.16). Whether Ptolemy's information is accurate, we
have no way of knowing, but his arrangement of sites in Idumea and Arabia
Petraea offers the possibility — or even probability — that the lines defining the borders of Arabia and Palestine were drawn in such a manner that
neighboring sites were located side by side in different provinces. Be that
as it may, the region dominated by Eleutheropolis in the 4th century was extensive, the largest in Palestine and large enough to have been considered a
province. It encompassed what had been Idumea as well as two former Judean
toparchies. It extended into the Negev, but just how far south is not known.
On the west, it ran along the borders of Gaza southward into the lands that
later became the imperial estate of Gerara and the Constantinian estate.[12]
That the town of Beersheba and others in its environs may have fallen under
the administrative jurisdiction of Eleutheropolis is strongly suggested by
the appearance, as late as the 6th and 7th centuries, of a substantial number
of inscriptions dated by the era of Eleutheropolis (A.D. 200) and the menology
of Arabia.[13]

What is being suggested here is the likelihood that sometime during the
reign of Diocletian a province similar to that of Idumea was carved out of
Palestine and out of part of Palestinian Arabia Petraea (i.e., the Negev).
Eleutheropolis was designated its administrative center, just as Marissa, a
short distance away, had been the capital of Idumea prior to its destruction
in 40 B.C. I would also suggest that the Edomite tradition was strong enough
in the region for the name *nea Arabia* to be given to the newly created province
or else that the name was used to distinguish a Palestinian Arabia from the

1722 (above, n. 5) and 3574. In attempting to emend the very fragmentary text of 1722, he
sees the possibility of restoring the name to read "Aurelius Malchus the son of Jonathan and
the grandson of Ananias" (the papponymic is meant e.g. [Rea's letter of March 30th, 1983]).
If this reading should be essentially correct, it would make it even more certain that the
petitioner of P.Oxy. 3574 was a Jew. On the name Jonathan, see *Beth She'arim: The Greek Inscriptions* II, M. Schwabe and B. Lifschitz, eds. (Jerusalem 1974), 119 and 120 (n. 6).

   12) M. Avi-Yonah, *The Holy Land: A Historical Geograpgy* (Grand Rapids 1966) 123 and 159-
162; see also *idem, Map of Roman Palestine* (Jerusalem 1940) 20; Jones, *loc. cit.* (above, n.
4), 279; G. Beyer, *Zeitschrift des Deutschen Palästina-Vereins* 54 (1931) 210-271; M. Burrows,
Journal of the Palestine Oriental Society 12 (1932) 142-148.

   13) E. Schwartz, *NGWG* (phil.-hist.Kl. 1906) 349 and 377-383. See also, A. Alt, *Die Griechischen Inschriften der Palaestina Tertia westlich der Araba* (Berlin-Leipzig 1921) 18-21.

former Petraean Arabia (cf. Avi-Yonah, *loc. cit.* [above, n.12] 96).

What is also being suggested here is that there was a need for the creation
of such a province during the late 3rd or early 4th century. We know little
of the development of Idumea during this period, but if we are to judge by
the emphasis placed upon Eleutheropolis by Eusebius, it is likely that the
city grew in importance from the time it was founded by Septimius Severus and
that it became the administrative center of the towns of the former territory
of Idumea. Further, if *nea Arabia* extended into the Negev, it is no coincidence
that the organization of that province corresponds with the revival of former
Nabataean communities within the region. At Eboda (Oboda), farthest removed
from Eleutheropolis, inscriptions record a surge of building activity starting
in the mid-3rd century. One inscription dated to 293/4, reports the building
of a tower that the excavator of the site believes to have been part of the
administrative complex of the late Roman town.[14] A hoard of coins discovered
at Mampsis attests to considerable activity at the site at the beginning of
the 3rd century, which probably continued on into the 6th century.[15] Elusa,
ultimately to become an administrative center for Palaestina Salutaris (Tertia), tells another story. Its surface barely scratched by archaeologists,
Elusa stands as the most promising site in the entire region. That it was no
backwater in the 3rd century is apparent from the correspondence of Libanius
(314-*ca*.393), the most celebrated man of letters of late antiquity. From his
letters and orations, we learn that the desert town of Elusa produced Zenobius,
a professor of rhetoric and Libanius' own teacher. Zenobius died in 354. A
cousin of Zenobius, Argyrius, who must have had his origins in Elusa as well,
also made a name for himself in Antioch as an orator of curial rank. Elusa
still flourished as a center for rhetoric into the 6th century. Despite
Jerome's claim that when Hilarion, Palestine's proto-monk, visited Elusa (*ca.*
350) the town was "*semi-barbarus* for the most part because of its location," it
must have been quite civilized at the time *nea Arabia* was organized and it no
doubt shared in the growth of the region along with its sister towns.[16]

Finally, we may only speculate on the possibility that the military garrisons at Beersheba and Thamara cited by Eusebius had some bearing on an imperial motive for organizing a new Arabia.[17] The province must have existed
for only a relatively short time, however, for by *ca.* 358, Palaestina Salutaris
(Tertia) encompassed all of what had been the southern half of the Trajanic

---

14) A. Negev, "Eboda," in *Encyclopedia of Archaeological Excavations in the Holy Land* II,
M. Avi-Yonah, ed. (Jerusalem 1976) 345 and 350; *idem, The Inscriptions from the Negev in
Studium Biblical Franciscanum (Collectio Minor* 25; Jerusalem 1981) 11-27.

15) A. Negev, "Kurnub", in *Encyclopedia of Archaeological Excavations* III, M. Avi-Yonah
and E. Stern, eds. (Jerusalem 1977) 726-728.

16) See my forthcoming article, "The City of Elusa in the Literary Sources of the IV-VI
Centuries," *Israel Exploration Journal*.

17) *Onomastikon der Biblischen Ortsnamen*, E. Klosterman, ed. (Leipzig 1904) 8 and 50.

province of Arabia. Eleutheropolis and its surrounding region, on the other
hand, became part of Palaestina Prima at this time or earlier.

In sum, the evidence at present does not favor the position taken by Barnes
and Bowersock that Eleutheropolis of *nea Arabia* is to be located in Egypt close
to Aegyptus Herculia, a position at best controversial and which should be
cited as uncertain. The evidence does favor the view of J.R. Rea, the editor
of P.Oxy.3574, even though he thinks it "too patchy for a firm conclusion";
I hope that the material presented above has made it less so.

Postscript

I may add a postscript on the question of whether P.Oxy.3574 has a direct
relationship with the problematic *arabia item arabia* of the Verona List now that
augusta libanensis has been removed from any association with the latter of the
two Arabias. Barnes, changing his previous position on the question of the
unity of the List, takes the *nea Arabia* of P.Oxy.3574 as the former of the two
Arabias of the List and cites it as evidence of the List's homogeneity (*loc.
cit.* [above, n.2] 205). I would submit, however, that the three words *arabia
item arabia* are as yet unexplained and remain a conundrum. The Verona List is
very explicit in naming the imperial provinces. Provinces having the same name
are distinguished from one another with such characterizing or qualifying
words as *superior, inferior, augusta, prima, secunda, nova,* or *vetus*. It is only *arabia
item arabia* that lacks a similar modifier. If *nea Arabia* were known to the compiler of the List, it would be a reasonable expectation to find it designated
as *arabia nova* or *augusta arabia*. It is apparent that the compiler of the List
did not know the official name of the two Arabias, or that whatever official
document that he had in hand did not provide him with the correct information.
Hence, I believe that P.Oxy.3574 has not given us the answer to *arabia item
arabia*.

New York University   Philip Mayerson

*The monastery of Saint Catherine in the mid-19th century. Lithograph by the great Holy Land artist, David Roberts. From George Croly, **The Holy Land, Syria, Idumea, Arabia, Egypt and Nubia** (1855–56). Courtesy of the Rare Books Collection, Perkins Library, Duke University.*

Codex Sinaiticus: An Historical Observation

by Philip Mayerson

After a number of years of news reports of a newly discovered hoard of ancient manuscripts in the Monastery of St. Catherine at the foot of Mount Sinai, we now possess a preliminary report from the hands of a reliable scholar, Professor J. H. Charlesworth (1981). There can be no doubt that the discovery of several thousand fragments, including at least 8 of the Codex Sinaiticus, is a spectacular one, not only for paleographers and theologians, but for historians as well.

It is as an historian that I would like to raise a question or two with regard to statements in the preliminary report regarding the Codex Sinaiticus and a fragment of the "Ladder of Paradise" of St. John Climacus. It is true that we are dealing with a preliminary report and can anticipate further refinements of the views put forward by Professor Charlesworth and, as reported by Charlesworth, those of Professor L. Politis. However, unless exceptions are taken to some of these views at the outset, we run the risk of having them accepted prematurely as hard fact. I also recognize that the report is almost exclusively paleographical, but paleographical conclusions must fit comfortably into a reasonable historical context. I find that some do not.

With regard to the Codex Sinaiticus, Professor Charlesworth provides us with a translation of a news release prepared by Professor Politis, a well-known paleographer. Professor Politis, in describing manuscripts of the uncial style, makes this statement (Charlesworth 1981: 36):

> The uncial script was used, as we said, for books (codices) chiefly from the 4th century and later. An exceptional example of a codex of the uncial script (more specifically of the style which we call "biblical uncial"), which itself also originates from Sinai, is the Sinaiticus Codex of the Bible (Old and New Testament), which specialists date to the third quarter of the 4th century.

Unless Professor Politis' statement has been garbled in the translation, we are given to believe that a form of uncial script, and the Codex Sinaiticus itself, originated in Sinai in the 4th century. Professor Charlesworth appears to agree with this statement in his appreciation of a fragment of Genesis from the new finds, which he says is "in a very early uncial script, which probably dates from the late 4th century." He goes on to say: "The script is, therefore, almost as old as the Codex Sinaiticus. Both date from approximately the same time and possibly were produced in the same monastery" (Charlesworth 1981: 11).

The bones of contention, as I see them, are the attribution of the Codex Sinaiticus and the style in which it is written to the late 4th century, and the claim that these originated in Sinai, presumably at the present site of the Monastery of St. Catherine. I raise no objection to the date of the manuscript, but I do to the place, namely Mount Sinai, that is claimed to be its *fons et origo*.

The major question to be asked is whether conditions at Mount Sinai in the late 4th century were such that would stimulate the creation of a style of script and that would facilitate the production of codices on vellum of the size and quality of Sinaiticus. The answer must be strongly in the negative. If our sources give us a reasonably accurate picture of life at Mount Sinai late in the 4th century, the monastic community—that is, the organized monastic community, such as it was—was small and scattered. Life itself for the Sinai solitaries was a struggle to provide the means for keeping body and soul together and to survive the periodic attacks of marauding bedouins, whom they referred to as Saracens.

In the late 4th or early 5th century, there was, as we learn from the report of the traveler Egeria, a small community of monks scattered about the environs of Mount Sinai. When the peripatetic nun Egeria made her celebrated visit to the Holy Mountain, she found no monastery but a community of solitaries living in cells (*monasteria*, i.e., hermits' quarters of a kind in which solitaries lived). After spending a night in a church (most likely in Wadi el-Leja and very much like the one that at present can be seen at the foot of the mountain), Egeria was escorted to the top of Mount Sinai, as she says, "by the presbyter (or priest) of the church and the monks who lived there" (*Corpus Christianorum* 175: 39). Upon descending from the Mountain of God, she came to the church at the site of the Burning Bush, the site of the present Monastery of St. Catherine. Some time later, after being given a tour of the biblical places associated with the Exodus, Egeria set off for Egypt by way of Pharan, some 35 miles from Mount Sinai. "Most of the holy men," she says, "who live at the Mountain of God or in its environs were good enough to escort us all the way to Pharan—at least those who were strong enough" (*Corpus Christianorum* 175: 45).

Egeria has told us something about the size of the monastic community about Mount Sinai. We have an indication of the character of the church and the community at the site of the Burning Bush from Eutychius, patriarch of Alexandria. In his *Annales* he informs us that prior to the construction of the Justinian monastery in the 6th century, the church at the site of the Burning Bush, dedicated to St. Mary, was situated in a tower, and that "there was no monastery in which monks could congregate, but they were scattered in the mountain and the wadis around the Bush..." (Migne 1863: 1071; Mayerson 1978: 33–38). Hence, not only was the community a small and scattered one in the 4th century, but it held no monastic structure or church of a size that would be suitable for the production of biblical manuscripts or codices.

Egeria's brief stay at Mount Sinai was a peaceful one. But all was not peaceful at the Holy Mountain. We possess two other accounts of the late fourth or early fifth century that not only describe the harsh ascetic life pursued by the Sinai solitaries, but also document in vivid detail the dangers resulting from periodic raids by the local Saracens. One account, attributed to a certain Nilus, an inhabitant of the eremitic community, tells of a raid during which a number of solitaries at Mount Sinai and its environs were killed (Migne 1865: 589–693; Mayerson 1975: 51–74). The other account, reported by an Egyptian monk, Ammonius, who like Egeria was on a tour of holy places and happened to be at Mount Sinai when the Saracens attacked, tells of yet another slaughter of monks (Combefis 1666: 88–95). Leaving aside the question of the accuracy of the description of the atrocities committed by the bedouins, both accounts leave no doubt that life at Mount Sinai during the early years of the monastic community was, at best, precarious. It was so even into the 6th century when the monks, as we learn from Eutychius, petitioned Emperor Justinian for protection against the ever-present misdemeanors and felonies of the Saracens (Migne 1863: 1071). The deaths of monks in this region have been commemorated as a holy day in the Greek Orthodox Church, and its current calendar carries the notation for January 14th, "Fathers killed in Sinai and Raithou" (Mayerson 1976: 375–79). The Nilus narrative is more informative. It contains the following statement, an interpolation of a somewhat later date: "They (the holy fathers) died on the 7th day after the Epiphany, which is the 14th of January. Pious men are very interested in learning the time and the names, since they want to check this information with the memories of holy men. Others were killed some years before, the memory of whom they celebrate on the same day because of the length of the journey and the size of the assemblage" (Migne 1865: 640c; Mayerson 1975: 64).

Under these conditions it is difficult to imagine Mount Sinai, or any other site in the Sinai Peninsula, as a center for the production of manuscripts of the kind represented by the Codex Sinaiticus.

Unless Professor Politis' statement has been garbled in the translation, we are given to believe that a form of uncial script, and the Codex Sinaiticus itself, originated in Sinai in the 4th century. Professor Charlesworth appears to agree with this statement in his appreciation of a fragment of Genesis from the new finds, which he says is "in a very early uncial script, which probably dates from the late 4th century." He goes on to say: "The script is, therefore, almost as old as the Codex Sinaiticus. Both date from approximately the same time and possibly were produced in the same monastery" (Charlesworth 1981: 11).

The bones of contention, as I see them, are the attribution of the Codex Sinaiticus and the style in which it is written to the late 4th century, and the claim that these originated in Sinai, presumably at the present site of the Monastery of St. Catherine. I raise no objection to the date of the manuscript, but I do to the place, namely Mount Sinai, that is claimed to be its *fons et origo*.

The major question to be asked is whether conditions at Mount Sinai in the late 4th century were such that would stimulate the creation of a style of script and that would facilitate the production of codices on vellum of the size and quality of Sinaiticus. The answer must be strongly in the negative. If our sources give us a reasonably accurate picture of life at Mount Sinai late in the 4th century, the monastic community—that is, the organized monastic community, such as it was—was small and scattered. Life itself for the Sinai solitaries was a struggle to provide the means for keeping body and soul together and to survive the periodic attacks of marauding bedouins, whom they referred to as Saracens.

In the late 4th or early 5th century, there was, as we learn from the report of the traveler Egeria, a small community of monks scattered about the environs of Mount Sinai. When the peripatetic nun Egeria made her celebrated visit to the Holy Mountain, she found no monastery but a community of solitaries living in cells (*monasteria*, i.e., hermits' quarters of a kind in which solitaries lived). After spending a night in a church (most likely in Wadi el-Leja and very much like the one that at present can be seen at the foot of the mountain), Egeria was escorted to the top of Mount Sinai, as she says, "by the presbyter (or priest) of the church and the monks who lived there" (*Corpus Christianorum* 175: 39). Upon descending from the Mountain of God, she came to the church at the site of the Burning Bush, the site of the present Monastery of St. Catherine. Some time later, after being given a tour of the biblical places associated with the Exodus, Egeria set off for Egypt by way of Pharan, some 35 miles from Mount Sinai. "Most of the holy men," she says, "who live at the Mountain of God or in its environs were good enough to escort us all the way to Pharan—at least those who were strong enough" (*Corpus Christianorum* 175: 45).

Egeria has told us something about the size of the monastic community about Mount Sinai. We have an indication of the character of the church and the community at the site of the Burning Bush from Eutychius, patriarch of Alexandria. In his *Annales* he informs us that prior to the construction of the Justinian monastery in the 6th century, the church at the site of the Burning Bush, dedicated to St. Mary, was situated in a tower, and that "there was no monastery in which monks could congregate, but they were scattered in the mountain and the wadis around the Bush..." (Migne 1863: 1071; Mayerson 1978: 33–38). Hence, not only was the community a small and scattered one in the 4th century, but it held no monastic structure or church of a size that would be suitable for the production of biblical manuscripts or codices.

Egeria's brief stay at Mount Sinai was a peaceful one. But all was not peaceful at the Holy Mountain. We possess two other accounts of the late fourth or early fifth century that not only describe the harsh ascetic life pursued by the Sinai solitaries, but also document in vivid detail the dangers resulting from periodic raids by the local Saracens. One account, attributed to a certain Nilus, an inhabitant of the eremitic community, tells of a raid during which a number of solitaries at Mount Sinai and its environs were killed (Migne 1865: 589–693; Mayerson 1975: 51–74). The other account, reported by an Egyptian monk, Ammonius, who like Egeria was on a tour of holy places and happened to be at Mount Sinai when the Saracens attacked, tells of yet another slaughter of monks (Combefis 1666: 88–95). Leaving aside the question of the accuracy of the description of the atrocities committed by the bedouins, both accounts leave no doubt that life at Mount Sinai during the early years of the monastic community was, at best, precarious. It was so even into the 6th century when the monks, as we learn from Eutychius, petitioned Emperor Justinian for protection against the ever-present misdemeanors and felonies of the Saracens (Migne 1863: 1071). The deaths of monks in this region have been commemorated as a holy day in the Greek Orthodox Church, and its current calendar carries the notation for January 14th, "Fathers killed in Sinai and Raithou" (Mayerson 1976: 375–79). The Nilus narrative is more informative. It contains the following statement, an interpolation of a somewhat later date: "They (the holy fathers) died on the 7th day after the Epiphany, which is the 14th of January. Pious men are very interested in learning the time and the names, since they want to check this information with the memories of holy men. Others were killed some years before, the memory of whom they celebrate on the same day because of the length of the journey and the size of the assemblage" (Migne 1865: 640c; Mayerson 1975: 64).

Under these conditions it is difficult to imagine Mount Sinai, or any other site in the Sinai Peninsula, as a center for the production of manuscripts of the kind represented by the Codex Sinaiticus.

The historical considerations cited above should be taken together with the paleographical observations made by H.J.M. Milne and T.C. Skeat: that "copies of literary works were multiplied commercially by groups of scribes working simultaneously from dictation"; that the Codex Sinaiticus was produced by the same method; that it was the product of at least 3 hands; and that from internal evidence Caesarea in Palestine was most likely its provenance (1979: 29, 55–59, 66–69).

It would, therefore, be more reasonable to account for the presence of this renowned codex of over 700 pages of vellum in the Monastery of St. Catherine as having arrived there at some unknown date, either as a gift or accompanying a new member of the monastic order. This would apply not only to the Codex Sinaiticus but also to other prime codices. In effect, we should think of these codices as being no different from the celebrated icons of the Monastery of St. Catherine in the sense that they were produced in other parts of the Byzantine empire and then were brought to Sinai, where, fortunately, they have been preserved to this very day.

With respect to a fragment in uncial script of St. John Climacus' "Ladder of Paradise," Professor Charlesworth—relying on Professor Politis, who dates the piece paleographically to the 7th century—considers the text to be contemporaneous with the author himself. "It could have been written," he states, "by St. John Climacus himself or perhaps even be the autograph of the *klimax tou paradeisou*" (1981: 11, Pl. II).

It is hardly conceivable, in my view, that John Climacus, whether composing the "Ladder of Paradise" in a cell near Mount Sinai (where he spent a part of his life), or whether doing so in the newly-constructed Justinian monastery, would write a major work of this kind on vellum and in uncial script. Further, since the fragment is dated paleographically—it could easily be off by a century more or less—we have no assurance that the text is contemporaneous with the author himself. Above and beyond these considerations, the fragment appears clearly to be the work of a skilled scribe.

A brief word concerning the "period of great silence," the period from the mid-7th to the 9th centuries, from which so few Greek manuscripts have been preserved (Charlesworth 1981: 10, 37). That period of silence has been broken somewhat by the discovery at the site of Nessana, 150 miles or so north of Mount Sinai, of remains of literary, biblical (New Testament), theological, and legal manuscripts (Casson and Hettich 1950). These manuscripts written on papyri date to between the 5th and 8th centuries—8 of the 13 pieces can be placed between the 7th and 8th centuries—and are probably representative of the kind of manuscripts that were on hand in the Monastery of St. Catherine during its early years.

Bibliography

Casson, L. and Hettich, E. L.
  1980   *Excavations at Nessana.* vol. 2. *Literary Papyri.* Princeton: Princeton University Press.
Charlesworth, J. H.
  1981   *The New Discoveries in St. Catherine's Monastery: A Preliminary Report on the Manuscripts.* ASOR Monograph Series 3. Cambridge, MA: American Schools of Oriental Research/Winona Lake, IN: Distributed by Eisenbrauns.
Combefis, F., ed.
  1666   *Christi martyrum lecta trias.* Paris: Fredericum Leonard.
Corpus Christianorum.
  1965   *Series Latina.* vol. 175. Turnholti: Typographi Brepols.
Mayerson, P.
  1975   Observations on the 'Nilus' Narrationes. *Journal of the American Research Center of Egypt* 12: 51–74.
  1976   An Inscription in the Monastery of St. Catherine and the Martyr Tradition in Sinai. *Dumbarton Oaks Papers* 30: 375–79.
  1978   Procopius or Eutychius on the Construction of the Monastery at Mount Sinai: Which is the More Reliable Source? *Bulletin of the American Schools of Oriental Research* 230: 33–38.
Migne, J.-P., ed.
  1863   *Patrologia Graeca.* vol. 111. Paris: J.-P. Migne.
  1865   *Patrologia Graeca.* vol. 79. Paris: J.-P. Migne.
Milne, H. J. M. and Skeat, T. C.
  1979   *Scribes and Correctors of the Codex Sinaiticus.* London: The British Museum.

Antiochus Monachus' Homily on Dreams:
An Historical Note

NEW YORK UNIVERSITY

> ". . . the lamentations of the monk Antiochus whose one
> hundred and twenty-nine homilies are still extant, if what no
> one reads may be said to be extant." (Edward Gibbon, *The
> Decline and Fall of the Roman Empire*)

Despite Gibbon's characteristically arch *obiter dictum,* at least one of
the homilies of Antiochus Monachus, his homily on dreams (περὶ
ἐναπνίων)[1] deserves to be revived, read, and reviewed. Not that what
Antiochus has to say about dreams will add anything to the annals of
Freudian psychology, nor is his one and only story to illustrate the danger
of dreams particularly worthy of incorporation into a corpus of anti-
Semitica. What deserves raised eyebrows is the citation of two towns or
cities, Noara and Libyas, as the "headquarters of the Jews".[2] This
statement is, I believe, of some significance both historically and
topographically. Antiochus, a monk of the monastery of Mar Saba and a
witness to the fall of Jerusalem to the Persians in A.D. 614, can be
considered a reliable source for this incidental and fortuitous piece of
information, for whatever prejudice he had with regard to dreams and
Jews, it is not likely that he had any ulterior motive in citing Noara and
Libyas as the Jewish headquarters.

As for the homily itself, since Antiochus was undoubtedly aware that
there was biblical support on both sides of the question of whether dreams
are a boon or a bane to man, his sermon is strongly admonitory rather than
an outright condemnation of all dreams as the work of evil demons. He
advises those who give credence to dreams that they "are nothing other than
things of the imagination and hallucinations of a mind led astray. They are
the illusions of evil demons to deceive us and result from their enticements
with the attendant purpose of carrying off a man to (sinful) pleasure." In
support of this view, Antiochus cites Jude 3, Ecclesiastes 5.3 and 5.6-7, and
Ecclesiasticus 34.1 and 34.7.[3] "Now then", he goes on to say, "if a light or

---

[1]   J. B. Migne, *Patrologia graeca,* 89, cols. 1688-1692.

[2]   *Ibid.,* col. 1692A " τῶν Ἰουδαίων" The accompanying Latin translation has *asyla
Judaeorum,* "the sanctuaries of the Jews." *Asyla* cannot be supported by any citations for the
Greek τὰ ὁρμητήρια

[3]   *Ibid.,* col. 1688C-D.

216

some shape in the form of fire appears to one of those who strive (for a spiritual life), let him in no way whatsoever admit this vision. It is a patent delusion of an inimical and wicked scheme. It is this that the apostle teaches us, saying that he (Satan) is transformed 'into an angel of light'." Antiochus then recommends a bedtime prayer, which he has composed, that would save one's soul and rid one of the deceit of the evil demon.[4]

Following the prayer, Antiochus takes another tack and acknowledges, citing Job 33.14-15, that dreams may result from divine revelation. However that may be, his advice is not to trust or give assent to them. "Even though, as is likely, a vision may have been sent down to us by divine revelation, let us not pay attention to it lest we accept smoke in lieu of light. In this way we do not stir up the Lord's anger, but rather (by not accepting the vision) He may also approve our guarding, with the help of fear, the treasure (i.e., the divine revelation) entrusted by Him to us."[5]

At this juncture Antiochus feels obliged to illustrate his thesis. He has he says, "many stories, old and new, concerning the illusions arising from dreams and of (people) suffering pitiably from them.[6] He decides, however, to tell only one, a tale that will sum up the point he has been trying to make. This is it.[7]

> There was a certain monk, a model solitary, on Mount Sinai who exhibited extraordinary ascetic discipline and for many years remained shut up in his cell, Later he was deceived by diabolical visions and dreams, and he succumbed to Judaism and the circumcision of the flesh. Moreover, the Devil showed him truthful dreams many times, and through them he (the Devil) won over his confused state of mind. Later he showed him the host of martyrs, and the apostles, and all the Christians in the dark and filled completely with shame. As against this, he illuminated with a bright light Moses, the prophets, and the hateful-to-God Jewish people, and (showed them) living joyously and full of cheer. Perceiving these things, the wretched man straightaway rose up and left the Holy Mountain. He went to Palestine, to Noara and Libyas, the headquarters of the Jews, and told them that he had been greatly honoured by the appearance of diabolical illusions. He embraced Judaism, took a wife, and in the sight of all, taught anti-Christian doctrine on behalf of the Jews.

Antiochus then relates that he and many other monks had observed the event. The apostate monk, however, did not live long after his conversion but died a painful death. "It was indeed a pitiful sight," says Antiochus, "a man who has completely grown grey and old in monastic life and its hardships, sporting with women, tasting the vile flesh of the Jews, speaking unseemly words, blaspheming Christ, and mocking the sanctity of baptism. From such things the impious Jews called him a second Abraham".[8]

---

[4]   *Ibid.,* col. 1689A-C.
[5]   *Ibid.,* col. 1689C-D.
[6]   *Ibid.,* col. 1689D.
[7]   *Ibid.,* cols. 1689D-1692D.
[8]   *Ibid.,* col. 1692D.

Why Antiochus chose this particular story from his well-stocked repertoire, we cannot say, unless he was concerned about a trend toward conversion to Judaism, or was expressing common patristic hostility against Jews. It is possible, however, to rationalize the likelihood of such dreams and visions occurring to an impressionable monk living at the site where it was believed that God revealed himself to Moses and the Israelites, and where Elijah heard "a still small voice". Putting aside all these speculations, we are left with the compelling statement that the monk left Mount Sinai and "went to Palestine, to Noara and Libyas, the headquarters of the Jews".

What Antiochus has quite innocently told us is that Noara and Libyas were centres of Jewish life in the seventh century. Both sites are known to us – one more so than the other – but that they were regarded as "the headquarters of the Jews" is not. To be sure, the *Onomasticon* of Eusebius cites the Naarath of Joshua 16.7 as " now Norath, a town ($\kappa\dot\omega\mu\eta$) of the Jews 5 miles from Jericho".[9] Jerome translates the citation as "Naorath, a *villula* of the Jews . . . ."[10] But between Eusebius in the fourth century and Antiochus in the seventh, we hear nothing about Noara save a mention in Talmudic midrashim on Lamentations 1.17, and in the anonymous life of Chariton, the proto-monk of Judaea. In the latter, we read of a certain Elpidius who enlarged the hermitage founded by Chariton near Jericho, and that "he put an end to the insults against it which the Hebrews, who at that time inhabited Noeron – as the place was called – let loose in their distress and hostility".[11] The Talmudic midrashim of Lamentations 1.17 cite five pairs of towns that were enemies of one another, including Jericho and "Naaran".[12] The cause of the enmity is not stated, but the midrashim most likely reflect religious differences between the Jewish and non-Jewish populations.

In support of these limited citations may be added an equally limited archaeological observation. At 'Ain Dûk, the site identified with ancient Noara, there are the remains of an impressive mosaic of a synagogue that has been dated to the sixth century.[13] Although the synagogue, as well as the town itself, is covered over and obliterated by cultivation, the mosaic at least attests to a Jewish presence at the site and bears upon Antiochus' statement that Noara was an important centre of the Jews.

As for the Libyas of Antiochus, it was a well-known city ($\pi\dot o\lambda\iota s$) on the

[9] E. Klostermann (ed.), 136.24.
[10] *Ibid.,* 137.27.
[11] *Acta Sanctorum,* Tome 7 (September 28), 618.
[12] Mid. Rabbah on Lamentations 1.17 (no. 52); Mid. Rab. on Leviticus 23.5; Mid. Rab. on Song of Songs 2.2 (no. 5).
[13] See art. "Na'aran" and accompanying bibliography in M. Avi-Yonah and E. Stern, *Encyclopaedia of Archaeological Excavations in the Holy Land,* 3, 891-892. For Elpidius and his connection with 'Ain Dûk, see Dom C. Butler, *The Lausiac History of Palladius* (Cambridge, 1904) 2, 142; 225. See also C. Clermont-Ganneau, *Archaeological Researches in Palestine* (London, 1896), 2, 21-22.

east side of the Jordan, and a relatively short distance from Jericho and Noara.[14] But well known as it was, our sources reveal no connection whatsoever with a Jewish community of any size or importance, until we read of it in Antiochus' homily. The city was identified with Beth-haran of Numbers 32.36 and Joshua 13.27, and the site was important enough in the first century to be honoured with the name of Augustus' wife Livia, later Julia after her adoption into the Julian family. Josephus informs us that Herod "threw a wall . . . about Betharamphtha which he called Julias after the name of the emperor's wife", and that "Nero bestowed on Agrippa Julias, a city in Peraea and fourteen villages that go with it."[15] Subsequent writers called the city Livias, Levias, Libias or Libyas – as did Ptolemy[16] and Antiochus. At present, the site is identified with modern Tell er-Rameh. Eusebius, interpreting Numbers 32.36, cites Beth-haran as "a city of the tribe of Gad, near Jordan, Bethramphtha of the Syrians but now called Libias."[17] To Eusebius the city was well known enough to be cited six times as a means of locating other nearby places.[18]

A local tradition, apparently not recorded earlier than the late fourth century, links Livias with Moses and the Israelites of the Exodus. Egeria travelled to "Libias" where she was shown "the foundations of the camp of the children of Israel and of their dwellings . . . ."[19] A local priest conducted the peripatetic nun to a spring some six miles from Livias where the monks of the neighbouring monastery informed her that it was "the water which holy Moses gave to the children of Israel in the desert".[20] Late in the fifth century, Peter the Iberian, weakened by his austerities, visited Livias to bathe in "the hot springs of holy Moses". He did not, however, find the baths hot enough to give him any relief.[21]

In the sixth century, Livias was visited by two notable pilgrims, Theodosius and Antoninus of Piacenza. Theodosius (c. 530) reports that "the city of Levias is beyond the Jordan, twelve miles from Jericho. In this Levias Moses struck the rock with his staff, and waters flowed out, and from that place flows a large stream which irrigates all Levias. There they grow the large Nicholas date. There too Moses departed from his life, and there are also the warm waters in which Moses bathed, and in the warm waters lepers are cleansed".[22] Antoninus of Piacenza (c. 570) also speaks of

---

[14] See art. "Libias" in *Pauly's Real-Encyclopädie d. class. Altertumswissenschaft,* 3, cols. 111-112.

[15] *Ant.* 18.27; 20.159 (Loeb ed. 25; 475). See also *Bell. Jud.* 2.59; 2.252 (Loeb ed. 345-6; 423).

[16] *Geogr.* 5.16.9 Libyas and Livias will be used here interchangeably; the former when referring to Antiochus' statement, the latter as a common referent for other sources.

[17] E. Klostermann (ed.), *Onomasticon,* 48.14-15.

[18] *Ibid.,* 12.23; 16.26; 44.17-18; 48.4; 48.17; 168.26.

[19] *Corpus Christianorum, series Latina,* 175, cap. 10.4 (p. 50).

[20] *Ibid.,* cap. 10.8 (p. 51); cap. 11.2 (p. 52).

[21] R. Raabe (ed.), *Petrus der Iberer* (Leipzig, 1895), 81-82.

[22] *Corpus Christianorum, series Latina,* 175, cap. 19 (p. 121).

the hot baths of Livias "which are called the baths of Moses where also lepers are cleansed". He adds: "And not far from the Salt Sea into which the Jordan flows . . . there is a spring of very sweet water which is drunk as a cathartic and heals many sicknesses. In this (Salt) Sea lepers lie all day throughout the months of July and August and up to mid September; but in the evening they wash in the very baths of Moses."[23]

Gregory of Tours (c. 585) also comments on the claim that lepers were cured in the baths of Moses and adds the statement that Joshua was accustomed to bathe in them.[24] Nothing more is heard of Livias until Antiochus wrote his homily in the early decades of the seventh century and informed us that the city was the headquarters of the Jews.

Brief though these citations are, and almost completely dependent on Christian sources, we may be reasonably certain that Noara and Libyas were, as Antiochus informs us, important centres of Jewish life in the seventh century. Jewish tradition, which may have been faulty,[25] held that both sites rested on the inheritance granted by Moses and the Torah. As for Noara, it was long known as a Jewish town, as Eusebius' citation and the Talmudic midrashim emphasize, and the hostility recorded by the biographer of Chariton most likely had something to do with the encroachment of Christian ascetics on nearby land. The town itself was also richly supplied with the water of a spring, now called 'Ain Dûk,[26] capable of irrigating plantations of date palms and of supporting a substantial population. The story of Livias is quite different. None of the sources, save that of Antiochus, reports anything specifically Jewish about the inhabitants of the city. Its association with biblical Beth-haran and its position on the Plains of Moab gave rise to a number of tangled local traditions concerning Moses and Joshua.[27] We can only speculate that the city's most

[23]   *Ibid.,* 10 (p. 134). Through convention the name of Antoninus has been attached to the itinerary although it has been attributed to an anonymous writer.

[24]   J. P. Migne, *Patrologia latina,* 71, col. 721.

[25]   An archaeological survey of both sites has revealed no evidence of Iron Age occupation from the time of Joshua. At Tell er-Rameh, identified with ancient Livias-Bethramphtha, no evidence earlier than the Roman period could be found. See N. Glueck, *Explorations in Eastern Palestine, IV* (The Annual of the American Schools of Oriental Research, Vols. XXV-XXVIII for 1945-1949) 108; 391.

[26]   *Cf.* Josephus. *Ant.* 17.34 (Loeb ed. 529): "(Archelaus) also rebuilt the royal palace in Jericho . . . and diverted half the water that served to irrigate the village of Neara, leading it into a plain that had been planted by him with palm-trees."

[27]   *Cf.* M. Avi-Yonah, *The Madeba Mosaic Map* (Jerusalem, 1954) 32-33: "The adoption by Christianity of the Old Testament as a part of its Bible in addition to the Gospels made inevitable the use of Jewish traditions for the identification of most of the Biblical sites, for there were no others. These Jewish traditions were in themselves the product of the two centuries following the destruction of the Second Temple, the Fall of Beth-Ther and the Hadrianic persecution. The leaders of Palestinian Jewry at that time were most anxious to keep alive the veneration of the Holy Land in the hearts of those Jews who still clung to their ancestral soil. They also tried to revive the stream of Jewish pilgrims from the Diaspora, which had been much reduced with the destruction of the Temple and subsequent political troubles."

celebrated attraction, the baths of Moses, originated among the Jews of
Livias, and that the healing qualities of the spa was spread abroad by
Christian pilgrims. Be that as it may, there can be no doubt that Jews as well
as Christians sought out the spa, and that members of the Jewish
community of Livias had entrepenuerial interests in the baths or in
providing accommodations and services of various kinds, if not for the
Christians, then for the Jews who came for the cure. Other members of the
community must also have had interests in the plantations that grew the
reputed food staple, the large Nicholas date as well as the caryota date.[28]

In sum, Antiochus' statement that Noara and Libyas were centres of
Jewish activity during the seventh century has the ring of more than mere
verisimilitude and, *pace* Gibbon, it deserves recognition as a legitimate piece
of evidence for the history of the period.[29]

[28]   On the fine quality of these dates, see Pliny, *N.H.* 13.9.44-45.
[29]   A postscript comment must be made with regard to the statement of Antiochus that
"the impious Jews called (the apostate monk) a second Abraham." The monk evidently
merited the epithet since both he and Abraham had worshipped "false gods" before coming to
terms with the God of Israel. There is another interpretation which must be approached with
due caution. In the Jewish apocryphal writings (*e.g.,* 4 Esdr. 3.14; Apoch. Baruch 4; Jubilees
15.17) Messianic glories were revealed to Abraham during his life on earth. With the revival of
Messianic hopes in Palestine before the fall of Jerusalem to the Persians, it is possible that the
Jews of Noara and Libyas looked upon the apostate monk as one who, like Abraham, had
conversed with God – his visions on Mount Sinai could easily have been taken as his having
heard the voice of God – and that he had been sent to restore the glory of Israel.

WHEAT IN THE ROMAN WORLD: AN ADDENDUM

J. K. Evans' well-documented article, 'Wheat production and its social consequences in the Roman world', correctly makes the point that 'the evidence with regard to wheat yields is at once meagre and plainly contradictory'.[1] The difficulty in assessing yields arises, of course, from the character of the available source material; namely, literary sources. The information comes from the hands of men such as Cicero and Varro who were concerned with matters other than specific data on the cultivation and production of grains, and who probably never sowed or reaped a *modius* of wheat. What was lacking until recently was a bona-fide document from the hands of a farmer or a community intimately concerned with the growing of wheat. We now have one such document, P. Colt 82 of the seventh century A.D., that fills a gap in the evidence for yields for both wheat and barley.

Ironically enough, P. Colt 82 comes from an arid region of the Roman empire, from a town in *Palaestina Tertia*, in a region known today as the Negev of Israel, where the average annual rainfall is 100 mm and less. The document, written on papyrus, records the exact amounts of wheat, barley, and *aracus* sown and reaped at six sites in and around a place that is still called Birein. Along with other documents relating to agriculture, it was uncovered at the site of Auja Hafir in Southern Palestine by archaeologist H. D. Colt. Written during the sixth and seventh centuries, the documents revealed that the name of the ancient Byzantine town was Nessana. The site is now called Nitsana, and the Birein referred to in P. Colt 82 is but a short distance to the south of Nitsana. An analysis of the agricultural evidence contained in these documents has been published by this writer in the archaeological report, *Excavations at Nessana*, and in a separate monograph.[2]

Place	Modii sown	Modii reaped	(Yield – fold)
Ragorion to Kat	40 wheat	270	6·7
Malalkani	40 wheat	288	7·2
Alphag	180 wheat	1225	6·8
Alphag	50 barley	402	8·0
Birein	40 barley	350	8·7
Birein	30 *aracus*	97	3·2
Seram	100 wheat	Unrecorded	
Malzemarche	90 wheat	Unrecorded	

[1] *CQ* n.s. 31 (1981), 429. See also K. D. White, 'Wheat farming in Roman times', *Antiquity* 37 (1963), 207.

[2] P. Mayerson, 'The ancient agricultural regime of Nessana and the central Negeb', in H. D. Colt (ed.), *Excavations at Nessana* 1 (London, 1962), pp. 211–69 (*The Ancient Agricultural Regime of Nessana and the Central Negeb*, British School of Archaeology and the Colt Archaeological Institute [London, 1961], pp. 1–57). For the documents themselves see C. J. Kraemer, Jr. (ed.), *Excavations at Nessana: The Non-Literary Papyri*, III (Princeton, 1958).

It will be sufficient for the purpose of this note to provide a translation of P. Colt 82 in the form of a summary.[3]

An analysis of the agricultural regime of Nessana and its environs (i.e. topography, soils, rainfall, water resources, land organizations, floodwater installations, crops) can readily be found in the publications cited above. I would like, however, to caution against making sweeping generalizations based on the evidence from Nessana. The yields, for example, have no relevance to areas some 30 or 40 miles away to the north or west where, although rainfall may be greater, topographical conditions do not permit the accumulation of winter floods, and the fertilizing silt carried by their waters, to ensure or produce similar yields. At Nessana and its environs we are essentially dealing with patch-cultivation – the only arable soil lay in wadi-bottoms – and to think of these patches as fields of wheat stretching to the horizon would be misleading.

The evidence provided by the Nessana papyri also shows that the inhabitants of this Byzantine town in the desert had decided preference for wheat over barley – only two documents of the entire collection mention barley – and contradicts the point of view of such scholars as Jasny and Jardé that barley was the major grain crop in classical antiquity.[4]

In sum, P. Colt 82 and other Nessana papyri provide us with precise evidence for grain yields and for the preference for the cultivation of wheat over barley. Taken together with archaeological sightings, the documents also reveal how the ancient inhabitants integrated the local peculiarities of land and water into a productive agricultural system. It must be borne in mind, however, that the evidence applies to one corner of the empire, to Nessana and its environs, or to other marginal regions of the empire possessing similar characteristics of topography and climate.

New York University   PHILIP MAYERSON

---

[3] ibid. pp. 227–8, 261 (pp. 17–18, 51).
[4] ibid. p. 227 (p. 17).

ZEITSCHRIFT FÜR PAPYROLOGIE UND EPIGRAPHIK

"PALAESTINA" VS. "ARABIA" IN THE BYZANTINE SOURCES

The appearance of the words "Eleutheropolis of Nea Arabia" in an Oxyrhynchus document (P.Oxy. 3574), dated securely to A.D. 314-318,[1] has opened a Pandora's box with regard to several assumptions that have been made concerning the provincial organization of what had formerly been a part of Provincia Arabia. The central issue raised by the surfacing of Nea Arabia in P.Oxy.3574 is whether we know anything certain regarding the reorganization of the province of Palestine during the first eight or nine decades of the 4th century. Not only is there a question of precisely when and what part of the southern portion of the province of Arabia was incorporated into Palestine, but also whether Palaestina Salutaris (later, Tertia), was organized c.358, a date that is consistently cited as a given for that event.[2]

The problem set forth in P.Oxy.3574 is that if we are to accept Eleutheropolis as the well-known city of Palestine, and Nea Arabia as the territory of which it was a part, it would seriously upset inferences derived from statements made by Eusebius as to the time the southern portion of the province of Arabia was severed and incorporated into Palestine. Hence, the view of Professors Barnes and Bowersock that Eleutheropolis of Nea Arabia was an unknown site and that Nea Arabia was to be located somewhere in Egypt encompassing the former nome of Arabia.[3]

The view taken by the editor of P.Oxy.3574, J.R. Rea, is quite different. He holds that Eleutheropolis is the well-known site in Palestine and that a province called Nea Arabia was created early in the 4th century with Eleutheropolis as its administrative center. This writer also supports the view of the editor and has offered evidence to support the suggestion that the area covered by the province of Nea Arabia was similar to that described by Ptolemy as Idumea (ZPE 53, 1983, 251-258).

The bone of contention between these two points of view has to do with the reliability of the information provided by Eusebius and later writers as to whether two cities, Petra and Phaeno, were in Palestine or in Arabia. If in

---

1) To be published in the forthcoming volume 50 of The Oxyrhynchus Papyri. J.R. Rea, the editor of 3574, generously provided me with a copy of the text and his commentary.

2) To my knowledge the date has not been challenged since the publication of R.E. Brünnow and A. v.Domaszewski, Die Provincia Arabia III (Strassburg 1909). In this monumental work, hereafter cited as PA, Brünnow and Domaszewski have assembled most of the available evidence, making it necessary only to cite fuller contexts or material that has more recently come to light.

3) T.D. Barnes, The New Empire of Diocletian and Constantine (Cambridge, Mass., 1983), 205 and 211. G.W. Bowersock, Roman Arabia (Cambridge, Mass., 1983), 145-146. P.Oxy. 29 4B. 48/G (6-7) cited by Barnes and Bowersock is an earlier inventory number of P.Oxy. 3574.

Palestine, then Eleutheropolis of Nea Arabia would of necessity be elsewhere
other than in Palestine, unless of course Nea Arabia was carved out of a portion of Palestine.

Barnes has laid great weight on Eusebius' knowledge of changes in provincial organization that were taking place during his lifetime. A statement made
by Eusebius in the *Martyrs of Palestine* for the year 307, to the effect that
Phaeno and its coppermines lay in Palestine, is to Barnes evidence that the
Diocletianic province of Arabia Petraea was incorporated into Palestine, "not
only before 314, but also, unless Eusebius is guilty of an anachronism, in or
before 307."[4]

As for Petra, the problem is somewhat more complex. In his *Onomasticon* Eusebius cites Petra four times with provincial designations. Three of the citations place Petra in Arabia, while one describes the city as being part of
Palestine. Barnes finds that "both descriptions were accurate at the time of
writing — that is Arabia Petraea was incorporated in Palestine while Eusebius
was engaged on compiling the gazetteer in the 290s."[5]

The evidence for these conclusions is derived almost exclusively on inferences derived from statements made by Eusebius on matters other than political
organization. The assumption that is made by Barnes and others is that since
Eusebius was a contemporary of Diocletian and his successors, his information
on what was happening at the time is more accurate than that provided by later
writers. This may be true, but not necessarily so in every instance. There is
also the assumption based on inference that Eusebius was aware of what was

---

4) T.D. Barnes, *ZPE* 16 (1975) 277. Bowersock adds (above, n. 3, p. 146) that the well-known
Eleutheropolis near Jerusalem "lay far outside the confines of Old Arabia and its successor
province. It belonged to Palaestina Prima." There is, so far as I know, no evidence that
Palaestina Prima existed as a province as early as 313-318. Palestine underwent a number of
territorial and administrative changes in the years between P.Oxy. 3574 and the *Notitia Dignitatum* (c. 395-413) in which we first learn of a tripartite division of Palestine. See also
a similar dubious statement (p. 143): "The whole southern part of Arabia, on both sides of
the 'Araba, became known as Palaestina Tertia by the mid-fourth century."

5) Above, note 3, p. 214, Eusebius, *Das Onomastikon der biblischen Ortsnamen*, ed. E. Klostermann (Leipzig 1904), pp. 36,13; 112,8f.; 142,7; 144,7. The entry (36,13), in which Eusebius appears to cite *Ant.* IV 82 (= 4.7 [I p. 240, ed. B. Niese, Berlin 1887]) of Josephus,
equates biblical Arcem with Petra. Josephus mentions the site as χώριον ὃ μητρόπολιν αὐτῶν
Ἄραβες νενομίκασι, πρότερον μὲν Ἄρκην λεγομένην, Πέτραν δὲ νῦν ὀνομαζομένην. Eusebius does
not quote Josephus verbatim but says that κατὰ Ἰώσιππον αὕτη ἐστὶν Πέτρα πόλις ἐπίσημος τῆς
Παλαιστίνης. If Eusebius had used the actual words of Josephus, except for those terms which
had become historically obsolete, a better case could have been made for his knowing that
Petra was no longer a part of the province of Arabia. F.-M. Abel (*Géographie de la Palestine*
II [Paris 1938], 169-170) was also impressed by this entry and states that when Eusebius
"fait de Pêtra une ville illustre, il use du langage administratif et cela balance tous les
passages ou suivant l'usage traditionnel il met cette ville en Arabie." Accordingly, Abel
places the date at which the southern portion of Trajanic Arabia was made part of Palestine
at *c.* 295. There is yet the possibility that Eusebius simply nodded or was mistaken, or that
some early copiest emended the entry. In connection with the latter, note that in another
entry dealing with *Kadês Barnê* (p. 112,8), Petra is called "a city of Palestine" in the Codex
Vaticanus, but the correct reading of "a city of Arabia" was provided by Jerome and Procopius
of Gaza. See also *PA*, p. 273.

happening, almost on a year to year basis, as boundary lines were being shifted this way and that during one of the most volatile periods of Roman imperial
administration. There is further assumption that Eusebius' knowledge of the
geography of a region far removed from his desk in Caesaria was more accurate
than other writers who had the experience of living in the southern region of
Palestine.

Let us take Phaeno and Aila as an illustration of how problematic it may
be to accept unconfirmed contemporary citations as hard fact. For Phaeno's
location in Palestine, we have to rely exclusively on Eusebius' statement in
the *Martyrs of Palestine*.[6] No other writer names the province in which it is
located. In the *Onomasticon* (p.168,7-10; see n.5), Eusebius correctly states
that Phaeno is situated between the city of Petra and Zoara. As for Aila, a
city far to the south on the shore of the eastern arm of the Red Sea, its
bishop attended the Council of Nicea (325) and his name is listed under the
province of Palestine.[7] However, the bishop of Sodoma also attended the Council of Nicea, but he is listed under the province of Arabia (*PA*, p.334). Sodoma is identified by Eusebius as a city near Zoara, and like Zoara situated at
the southern end of the Dead Sea.[8] Accepting all these citations as fact would
mean that Sodoma, a city of Arabia, would lie northwest of the "Palestinian"
cities of Phaeno and Aila, as well as Petra. If that were so, the boundary
line between the two provinces would be incomprehensible and a question would
have to be raised regarding the accuracy of listing the city of Aila under
the province of Palestine. Errors have been made in the conciliar lists and
one could easily have been made either by some secretary in Nicea in dealing
with a little-known bishop from the remote city of Aila, or by a later tran-
scriber of the original roster of bishops.[9]

Despite the confidence placed in the authority of Eusebius and the Nicean
roster of cities and provinces, equal trust is not given to other conciliar
lists and ecclesiastical writers who, on the key question of Petra's political
position, place the city in the province of Arabia rather than in Palestine.
While it is true that Petra and Arabia are almost synonymous, and that critics
have minimized the ecclesiastical sources that cite Petra as part of the province of Arabia,[10] it does not necessarily follow that every citation should

6) 7.2 in short and long recensions. See also Barnes (above, n. 4), p. 277 and (above, n. 3), p. 214.

7) *PA*, pp. 262, 273. It should be noted that Eusebius (above, n.5, p. 6,17f.) confuses the kingdom of Elam with the city of Ailath/Ailan. (cf. Jerome's translation, p. 7,25f.).

8) *Onom.* (above, n. 5), pp. 94,2; 150,10. *PA*, pp. 253, 263, 280.

9) See *e.g.*, Barnes (above, n. 3), pp. 210-211. Note the confusion in some of the Latin mss. concerning the city in which Petrus, the supposed bishop of Aila, was said to have re-presented (*Patrum Nicaenorum nomina*, ed. M. Gelzer, Leipzig 1898, 12-13).

10) *PA*, p. 276. Abel (above, n. 5), p. 169 concludes that "Arabia et Pétra etaient telle-ment liés qu'il fallait certainement faire un effort pour admettre la fantaisie du prince qui situait cette ville en Palestine."

be cast out as being irrelevant. The conciliar list for the Council of Serdica
(343-4) is a case in point. The roster of bishops under the rubric of Arabia
carries the name of Asterius of Petra (cols. 652f.; 656).[11] And as late as
362, at the time of the Council of Alexandria, the name of Asterius is still
associated with "Petra of Arabia" (cols. 729f.; 737). That Asterius came from
the city of Petra and that Petra was located in Arabia is also supported by a
contemporary, Athanasius (c.293-373), and the church historian Theodoretus.[12]

Epiphanius (c.315-403), I also believe, deserves a better hearing than he
has had in the past. Born and reared near Eleutheropolis in the heart of
Palestine — most likely the Eleutheropolis of Nea Arabia of P.Oxy.3574 —
Epiphanius may be presumed to have had a general knowledge of conditions in
the region sometime during the second half of the 4th century. In his *Panarion*,
written during the years 374-377, he describes the pagan festival and rituals
associated with Kore and the birth of Aion from the virgin goddess. He goes
on to say that "this also takes place in the city of Petra — the metropolis
of Arabia, which is Edom in the Scriptures — and that from her Dousara was
born, that is, the only begotten of the Lord. This also takes place in the
city of Elusa on the same night that it does in Petra and Alexandria."[13] The
phrase "the metropolis of Arabia" is virtually official language for Petra as
the capital of Arabia or the administrative center, if not for the entire
province, at least for a segmented portion of it.

In a later work, dated to 392, *de mensuris et ponderibus*, a kind of dictionary
of the Bible, Epiphanius unambiguously locates Petra in Palestine. In his
entry on Reqem (that is, Petra), he makes the following comment: "It is among
the Kingdoms. In Isaiah, then, it is called Reqem. It exists, then, as a city,
large and famous, which is in Arabia. It is considered part of Palestine. It
is, moreover, named Edom in Scripture."[14]

---

11) *Acta Conciliorum et Epistolae Decretales ac Constitutiones Summorum Pontificum*, ed. J.
Hardouin, I (Paris 1715). *PA*, p. 273.

12) Athanasius, *Apol. c. Arianos* (PG XXV, col. 333); *Tomos ad Antioch.* (PG XXVI, col. 807).
The confusion of names and provinces in the *Hist. Arianorum ad monachos* (PG XXV, col. 715),
is clearly a textual error. Theodoretus, *Hist. Eccles.* 2.8.30. See also *PA*, p. 273.

13) *Panarion* 51, 22, 10-11 (II pp. 286f., ed. K. Holl in GCS XXXI, Leipzig 1922). There
is yet another reference in the *Panarion* (66.1,1-7 [III pp. 13-14, GCS XXXVII, Leipzig 1931])
that relates ambiguously to the Palaestina-vs.-Arabia question. In his introduction to the
heresy of Manicheanism, Epiphanius describes the early years of Manes who was born at Eleutheropolis with the name of Cubricus. He was the slave of a man by the name of Scythianus,
who, Epiphanius says, "was of Saracen origin, and who was brought up on the borders of
Palestine, that is, Arabia." We cannot be sure whether Epiphanius is referring to his own
time or to that of Scythianus, or that he is merely indicating the region or province that
bordered Palestine (i.e., Arabia and not Syria). I am inclined to believe that he meant the
latter (cf. L. Koenen in *Das röm.-byz. Ägypten* [Aeg. Treverensia, Mainz 1983], 96).

14) *Epiphanius' Treatise on Weights and Measures: The Syriac Version*, ed. J.E. Dean
(Chicago 1935) p. 74. Dean's translation of the Syriac appeared to me to be quite ambiguous
("Concerning Rekem. Rekem, which is in Kingdoms, but called Rekem in Isaiah. It was, however,
a great and famous city that was reckoned to be in Arabia-Palestine, which is also called

We now go back to the years 357/358, so often cited as indicating a new development in the provincial organization of Palestine, and, specifically, the creation of Palaestina Salutaris out of the southern portion of the former province. The evidence for this change is derived essentially from several letters of Libanius (c. 316-395) to Clematius, governor of the province of Palestine. These letters are for the most part personal in nature and are subtly expressed requests to Clematius for the use of his influence on behalf of friends and fellow rhetoricians. As important as these letters are, the historical resonance emanating from them is rather weak and consequently they have been submitted to considerable interpretation.

In two letters, *Epp.* 315 and 321 (X pp. 293 and 301 [ed. R. Förster, Leipzig 1921]), dated to 357, Libanius writes to Clematius in the interests of Dynamius from the city of Petra, and of Eunomus and Eudaimon from the city of Elusa. The assumption is made that both these cities fell within the jurisdiction of Clematius, governor of the province of Palestine at that time, although there is no indication of what Clematius was asked to do or where he was expected to use his influence. In *Ep.* 334, dated to 358, Libanius writes again to Clematius, a flattering letter, commending his friend Hieronymus to him even though he and Hieronymus are aware that the city of Elusa is no longer governed by Clematius "due to a division of jurisdictional authority" (κατὰ τὴν τομὴν ἀρχῆς; X pp. 314f.). Since Petra and Elusa are located in the southern portion of Palestine and Arabia, these three letters are often cited as evidence that in 358 the region encompassing these two cities was organized as a separate province known as Palaestina Salutaris, later to be designated as Palaestina Tertia.[15]

There is no doubt that a split or a division of some kind took place in the year 358 during the reign of Constantius II that placed Elusa beyond Clematius' political influence, but the precise nature of it is not known. We also have no explicit evidence that the split or division (τομή) created a Palaestina Prima, or a Secunda, or a Salutaris. There seems to have been another division or administrative shift in the year 361/2 of which we have no details other than what we learn from Libanius. In a letter addressed to Cyrillus, (*Ep.* 686), Libanius speaks elliptically of his having been transferred (?) εἰς ἀρχὴν ἐξ

Edom in the Scripture"). Professor Baruch Levine was kind enough to translate and transliterate the Syriac text, and to answer my question as to whether the quotation was in the present or past tense. He replied in part: "There are no verbs in the past tense. All are either present participles, or we find elliptical constructions in nominal clauses....My translation is purposely stilted for precision." The transliterated Syriac text provided by Professor Levine is as follows: *Reqem: hiy da- b^emalk^ewoto'. be-'eša'yo' deyn Reqem metqaryo'. 'iytiyho deyn m^ediynto' (read: m^ediytto') rabto wa- y^ediy'ato' da-b^e'arabiyo'. hiy l^ewot Palastiyno' methasbo'. hiy d'op 'edum ba-k^etobo' meštamho'.*

15) *PA*, pp. 277-278. See also Barnes (above, n. 3), p. 214; *The Breviarum of Festus*, ed. J.W. Eadie (London 1967), p. 159.

ἀρχῆς, εἰς Παλαιστίνην ἐκ Παλαιστίνης (p.622).[16] However, from Epiphanius'
point of view some years later, c.374, Petra was "the metropolis of Arabia"
(above p.226). And to the pagan historian Zosimus (Hist. nova 4.41 [II p.309
ed. F. Paschoud, Paris 1979]), the orator Hilarius was given rule over "all
Palestine" in the year 379 because the emperor Theodosius had been so impressed with his eloquence. Some years later again, in 392, Epiphanius informs us
that Reqem (Petra) "is considered part of Palestine" (above, p.226). To complicate matters further, the conciliar lists for the years between 358 and
381 — Seleucia (359), Alexandria (362) and Constantinople (381) — give no
hint of a change in the nomenclature for the province of Palestine (cols.725f.;
737f.; and 814 Hardouin [above, n.11]). In short, we have no evidence of substance for the volatile eight or nine decades of the 4th century that can give
us a reasonably accurate picture of what administrative or territorial changes
were being affected in the provinces of Palestine and Arabia. The picture for
Palestine is particularly unclear. Apart from P.Oxy.3574 we do not have a document or an inscription to help us out of this quandry.

It is Jerome (c.347 - c.420) who provides us with the first bit of hard
evidence in connection with Palaestina Salutaris. He is in fact the first
writer to use the words "Palaestina Salutaris." In his Commentary on Genesis, composed sometime between the years 389 and 392, Jerome comments on the birth of
Isaac in the region of Gerar, and amplifies the description of the region by
saying: "ubi et Bersabee usque hodie oppidum est. quae provincia ante non grande tempus ex
divisione praesidum Palaestina salutaris est dicta. huiusrei scriptura testis, quae ait 'et
habitavit Abraham in terra Philistinorum!" (Hebr. quaest. in Gen. 21,30f. [CCSL LXXII
p.26]).

The key words here are ante non grande tempus: "not long ago" or "a short time
ago". It is an expression that usually has the connotation of time anywhere
between several months and a year or two, certainly not as long as thirty
years. Nöldeke's interpretation of the context of ante non grande tempus that it
"kann an einer Stelle, wo er von den uralten Zeiten Abrahams spricht, wohl ein
Jahrhundert umfassen" (Hermes 10, 1876, 168) is simply not supportable. The
words huiusrei have no connection with ante non grande tempus but relates to Jerome's
proof that Isaac was born in Gerar and not in Mamre. And the sentence " quae
provincia... Palaestina salutaris est dicta" informs the readers of the Commentary,
presumably Jerome's contemporaries, that the province in which Gerar and Bersabee were located was recently organized under the name of Palaestina Salutaris.

The date, therefore, for the organization of the province of Palaestina

---

16) It is interesting to note that although Libanius mentions the province of Palestine
some 40 times, he does so without any modifying term that would indicate his awareness of
changes in the official terminology for the province. PA, 278f. places Cyrillus as governor
of Palaestina Salutaris in 360 and of Palaestina in 361/2.

Salutaris should be *c.*390: that is, it took place during the reign of Theodosius I (379-394) rather than that of Constantinus II (337-361). It should be noted once again that Epiphanius considered Reqem (Petra) as part of Palestine in 392, whereas earlier, *c.*374, he cites Petra as being the metropolis of Arabia. That it was Theodosius' act that was responsible for creating this new province is also enhanced by the appearance in the Nessana papyri of a military unit bearing the emperor's name and, undoubtly one that was activated by the emperor. The unit, a *numerus*, based at Nessana, the southernmost fortified community west of the Arabah, bore the name "the Very Loyal Theodosians".[17]

Following Jerome's comment on the organization of Palaestina Salutaris, all the ambivalence that is found in the sources prior to the year *c.*390 vanishes. The citations from the last decade of the 4th century to the 6th consistently cite the province that embraces the southern portions of Palestine and Arabia by its new name or Palaestina Salutaris, later Palaestina Tertia. The tripartite division of Palestine is recorded in the *Notitia dignitatum* (*c.*395-413) as Palaestina, Palaestina Secunda, and Palaestina Salutaris.[18] The list of bishops who attended the Council of Ephesus (431) cites the bishop of Phaino as "Saidas of Palaestina Salutaris" (col. 1380 Hardouin; above, n.11). Finally, *Codex Theodosianus* VII 4.30 for the year 409, the *Synecdemus* of Hierocles, and the *Descriptio orbis Romani* of Georgius Cyprius give numerical modifiers to the province undicating a Prima, Secunda and a Tertia.[19]

In sum, the province of Palaestina experienced a number of territorial and administrative changes during the first eight or nine decades of the 4th century. If our analysis of P.Oxy.3574 is correct, the document is evidence for only the earliest of these changes. As for the letters of Libanius, they provide us with evidence of changes within the province, but they do not charac-

17) *P.Ness.* III (ed. C.J. Kraemer, Jr. [Princeton 1958]) pp. 41-42. The editor attributes the founding of the military unit to Theodosius II "some years before 450 at a time when the archaeological evidence suggests that considerable new activity was taking place..." The excavation of the site dealt mainly with the structures on the hilltop of Nessana. It is far more likely that the *numerus* was stationed at Nessana some years before the building activity took place. A date in the time of Theodosius I would be more appropriate.

18) *Notitia Dignitatum Orientis*, ed. O. Seeck (Berlin 1876), pp. 48-49. On the date of the document, see A.H.M. Jones, *The Later Roman Empire*, (Oxford 1964), III 351 and 381.

19) *PA*, pp. 255-256; 277. By the time of the church historian Evagrius Scholasticus (*c.* 563 - *c.* 600), the several Palestines are cited in a number of contexts as "the region of the Palestines"; "the three Palestines"; "Petra on the outer limits of the Palestines"; "the Palestines"; "one of the Palestines" (*Hist. Eccl.* 2,6; 2,18; 3,32; 3,36; 4,7). Malalas, *Chronographia* XIII (p. 219) claims without further elaboration that Constantine (307-338) "made a third province of Palestine" (τρίτην Παλαιστίνης ἐποίησεν ἐπαρχίαν). Does Malalas, refer to Palaestina Tertia? Or does he mean that there had been a division and that Constantine made yet another, a third? We can only speculate — no more than that — that the third province may have been the Nea Arabia cf. P.Oxy. 3574 whose dates fall within the reign of Constantine.

terize the changes, nor can they be used to specify the date for the organization of Palaestina Salutaris or for the designations Prima and Secunda. It is
the compelling remark of Jerome and the appearance in the Nessana papyri of a
military unit bearing the emperor's name that leads to the conclusion that
the province of Palaestina Salutaris was organized *c*.390 during the reign of
Theodosius I.

New York University   Philip Mayerson

Urbanization in Palaestina Tertia: Pilgrims and Paradoxes

PHILIP MAYERSON
New York University

When, in A.D. 106, L. Cornelius Palma, acting on orders from Trajan, "acquired Arabia" and "made it into a province", he took possession of a vast piece of territory that Nabataean kings had controlled for almost four centuries. The development of the province under Roman auspices in the succeeding centuries was, of course, determined by political and economic considerations operative within and without the empire. In spite of these common considerations, urbanization took place apparently under exceptional circumstances in one part of the new province, *Palaestina Tertia*, organized in the mid-fourth century. Although it is commonplace to attribute urban growth to sites positioned along secure and prosperous commercial routes, in *Palaestina Tertia* this growth is not at all evident along its most renowned road system, the *Via Nova Traiana*, which possessed more than adequate supplies of water. This situation would not be so remarkable if we did not observe substantial sites along lesser known routes that lacked perennial water and that were not in any respect trading marts or transshipment centers.

This is the essential paradox in the urbanization of *Palaestina Tertia* as can be observed in the arid areas south of the Dead Sea. While trade and security may be in part responsible for the growth of some communities, the unusual growth of communities in unfavorable locations is rooted, we believe, in special circumstances that arose during the fifth and sixth centuries: monasticism and pilgrimages associated with the veneration of saints and martyrs. Monks and pilgrims - and their guides - used roads, and the roads they chose to use had to do not only with security, but also with the physical character of the land through which the roads ran. These factors do not loom large in regions blessed with favorable living and trading conditions, but in the marginal and semi-arid areas that comprised *Palaestina Tertia*, topography is a vital consideration. As for the paradox of finding an exceptionally favorable location - specifically, Ain Qudeirat, biblical Kadesh Barnea - completely lacking in the development that characterizes nearby sites, there simply may be no answer beyond mere speculation.

When Trajan annexed the territory of his former clients, the Nabataeans, it had a certain homogeneity: it virtually had no clear borders. From its principal city, Petra, it extended on all cardinal points of the compass to the termini of trade routes. In the north, the realm that originally encompassed ancient Edom extended far beyond Wadi Mujib; in the east, to the desert and the wadis (Sirhan and Ramm) that run down to Saudi Arabia; in the south, to the Hejaz and Red Sea ports; and in the west, to the Negev and the *entrepôts* on the Mediterranean. The Nabataeans blanketed their territory with forts, watchtowers and cisterns, ostensibly to protect the trade routes and the caravans that plied them. In their numerous settlements, sedentary Nabataeans traded, cultivated the soil, mined copper, or practised the ordinary pursuits of townsfolk. Other Nabataeans pastured their flocks on the hills and mountain ranges, and undoubtedly served as guides for travelers through the uncharted wilderness.

It was this extraordinary piece of territory that Trajan ordered to be annexed as a province of Rome. Bostra became the administrative and legionary headquarters of the new province, and under its governor, C. Claudius Severus, a north-south arterial road was built *a finibus Syriae usque ad mare rubrum*: a refurbishing, so to speak, of the biblical Kings' Highway. From Aila at the Gulf of Aqabah (Eilat), the *Via Nova Traiana* ran north to Petra, Philadelphia, Bostra, and to the network of roads radiating from Damascus. Nabataean defensive installations along this main highway and its branches were taken over and manned by Roman units. As far as Petra and its satellite settlements were concerned, however, their development was stunted, not only because Bostra became the political and commercial center of the annexed province, but also because of the competition of Palmyra when it opened up more convenient routes to the Persian Gulf, thus depriving Petra of its Indian trade.

The above is a brief summary of the well-known events, hardly requiring documentation, that led to the establishment of the new province and the subsequent decline of Petra and the Nabataeans as a vital force in the region that once had been under their control.[1] This is not to say that trade petered out completely, or that military units posted along the *Via Nova* and its branches did not continue to protect the province and trading caravans from marauding Bedouin. According to an archaeological survey along the so-called *Limes Arabicus* in modern Jordan, between the years A.D. 135 and 284 the number of fort sites increased from 9 to 14, and from A.D. 284 to 324, from 14 to 30.[2] The latter increase is meaningful, for with the defeat of Zenobia and the reduction of Palmyra in 273, and with the consequent disruption of the Tigris-Euphrates routes by the constant hostilities between Roman and the Sassanids, old trade routes were revived and protected as they had been under the Nabataeans. It is of interest to note that the survey cites the years 284 to 392 as "the time of the greatest strength and complexity of the *Limes Arabicus*".[3] It was some time between these years that two legionary camps were set up at Lejjun and Odruh, and that the *Legio decima Fretensis* was posted to Aila at the head of the Gulf of Aqabah. All these factors taken into account, settlements along the *Via Nova* and its branches remained small. With the possible exception of Aila, the legionary settlements did not seem to have attracted substantial populations.

In the middle of the fourth century, *ca.* 358, a reorganization of the province of Arabia took place. The sector south of the Wadi Mujib in the Trans-Jordan, together with the Negev and the Sinai in the west, was severed from Arabia and became a new province, *Palaestina Tertia* (or *Palaestina Salutaris*, as it was earlier called). The exact reason for and the precise date of its creation are not known, but it is generally attributed to the military and civil reforms initiated by Diocletian and completed by his successors.

However much administrative sense it made to divide the province Arabia this way, from a topographical point of view it was a most curious division, for it pieced together two quite dissimilar land masses with dissimilar resources. The dividing line between them is the Wadi Arabah, the great rift valley that runs from the southern end of the Dead Sea to the Gulf of Aqabah. To the east, towering 5,000 feet (1,500 m.) and more above the floor of the valley, are Nubian sandstone and granitic cliffs, in which winter storms have eroded deep and well-nigh impassible gorges that offer few possibilities of a route from the Arabah onto the high tablelands above. In contrast to the dramatic precipices and gorges facing the Arabah, the tableland falls away gently to the barren lands of the eastern desert. Its surface is cut by two deep river canyons, the Wadi Mujib (biblical Arnon) and el Hasa (biblical Zered), neither of which is easy to ford from the *Via Nova*, the highland road that ran along the western edge of the plateau.[4]

On the other side of the Arabah, facing the Mediterranean, lay the Negev and its extension into Sinai - the western part of *Palaestina Tertia*. Unlike the region to the east, the Negev is topographically more varied and less dramatic in its geological development. Bounded on the north by a line running from the southern end of the Dead Sea through Beersheba toward Rhinocorura (modern el-Arish), the region shares certain characteristics of the country to the north. From the coastal plain of sand and loessial deposits, the land rises in troughs and ridges to the Negev highlands, a series of mountain ranges, 1,000-2,000 feet (300-600 m.) in height running from the north-east to the south-west. These highlands, with their intervening plains and valleys, are generally made up of calcareous formations (limestone, dolomite, chalk and marl). The region is drained by broad, negotiable wadis, most of which ultimately reach the Mediterranean.

To the east of the Negev mountains, following once more their north-east to south-west axis, the land falls sharply and precipitously into the Wadi Arabah. These are the "badlands" of the Negev, and the steep gradients associated with them offer some difficulties in passage to and from the western watershed. Further south, a short distance from modern Eilat, the region, including its extension into eastern Sinai, assumes the features of the Trans-Jordan sector: sandstone and granitic structures.

A network of roads ran through this western sector of *Palaestina Tertia*, as it did for centuries prior to Roman occupation of the region. Without the historical fanfare of the *Via Nova*, these roads may have borne more traffic than the "grand" highway to the east.[5] Linking up with the Jerusalem-Hebron road, the main arterial system continued south along the uplands of the Central Negev to Elusa. Here, one branch continued further south to Nessana, where it connected with northern Sinai routes that linked Aila with Mediterranean and Egyptian ports. Another road branched off from Elusa and headed in a south-easterly direction to Eboda. Perched near the point where the tortuous track up the western scarp of the Arabah led to the highland plateau, Eboda at one time had served Nabataean traders coming from Petra en route to the Mediterranean ports of Gaza and Rhinococura. Another road from Eboda bypassed the difficult descent to the Wadi Arabah and proceeded in a south-south-easterly direction onto the Sinai plateau and then made its way to Aila. In addition to the Eboda-Petra route, another road connected the eastern and western sections of the province. Branching off the Jerusalem-Elusa road, it crossed the northern end of the Wadi Arabah and joined the *Via Nova* at or near Charachmoba (modern Kerak). Yet another branch led to Mampsis (modern Kurnub) - perched like Eboda on a height - where the road came up from the Arabah via the Scorpion Ascent. This was one of the subordinate routes that ran the length of the Wadi Arabah to Aila. All roads, it should be noted, led to Aila, not only a port and a legionary station, but also a staging area for travelers to Sinai.

Related to the nature of the landscape and the road systems associated with it is the issue of water resources. As land masses on either side of the rift valley are different from one another, so is the availability of water. By virtue of their height, the Trans-Jordan plateau and steppelands receive a mean annual rainfall of 8 to 16 inches (200-400 mm.). The deep layers of impervious Nubian sandstone hold subterranean water reservoirs that produce a fair line of springs along the western ridge of the highlands.

On the other side of the Arabah, in the Negev and its extension into Sinai, seasonal rainfall decreases both southward and eastward from the Mediterranean coast: from 8 inches (200 mm.) at Beersheba to 4 inches (100 mm.) or less at Nessana. As for springs, there is scarcely one in the entire Central Negev worthy of the name. The best perennial water source in the entire region is to be found at Ain Qudeirat in northern Sinai, and to a lesser degree at Ain Qadeis, a short distance away. However, the Wadi Arabah itself possesses some of the strongest springs in the region, since it stores most of the water that cascades down the scarps flanking both sides of the rift valley. The better known ones are at the sites of Ghor es-Safi (ancient Zoara), Feife (ancient Praesidium), Tlah (ancient Toloha), Feinon (ancient Phainon), Gharandel (ancient Arindela), Yotvata (Ghadyan, ancient Ad Dianam) and Aila.[6]

Given this topographical and historical setting for *Palaestina Tertia*, the normal expectation for any kind of urban growth - if predicated on the increase of trade along established commercial routes - would be on both sides of the Wadi Arabah. The Trans-Jordan sector, in fact, should be given the edge in this expectation since the *Via Nova* provided a secure and direct route from the port of Aila, or for caravans from the Hejaz, to transshipment centers in the north. Further, with the availability of ample supplies of perennial water, the means to sustain good size communities were present. The fact is that urban development is virtually lacking south of Kerak and the Wadi el Hasa in the period under discussion, and little more can be said for the region south of the Wadi Mujib to el Hasa. Archaeological surveys have brought to light numerous sites and associated defensive installations of the Byzantine period, but none, with the possible exception of Aila and Petra, can be called a city or substantial townsite. Even Petra itself does not show much evidence of having had a vigorous life during the Byzantine period. It is even more remarkable that there is not a structure in Petra that can be called a church or a monastery. If the bishops of Petra had not ascribed their names to the lists of those who attended various synods of the church - and if an inscription on one of the Nabataean tombs concerning a bishop by the name of Iason had not come to light - we might have had some doubts whether Petra had been a Christian community.[7] To pursue this point one step further, it is equally remarkable that in the region of the Trans-Jordan highlands south of the Wadis Mujib and el Hasa, the remains of churches and monasteries have virtually gone unreported, while a short distance north of the Mujib, at Madaba, there are remains of at least fifteen churches and monasteries - not to mention those in the cities further to the north.

In the Wadi Arabah, the story is much the same: despite good water supplies along commercial tracks, there are only small installations. Two exceptions should be noted. Ghor es-Safi, the probable site of Byzantine Zoara, situated at the outlet of the Wadi el Hasa just south of the Dead Sea, may well have been a large site, but its physical remains have been completely obliterated by later Arab and medieval occupations. Hardly a structure survives that would attest to the fact that, as Jerome informs us, Zoara was heavily populated, had a garrison of Roman soldiers, and was known for its cultivation of the date palm and balsam.[8] Zoara, reputed to have been the place where Lot fled from burning Sodom, was an important point on the road linking the eastern and western parts of the province. It was an episcopal see, and several of its bishops were present at various synods of the Church.[9] The other exception is Phainon. Situated in the Wadi Feinan near a fine fresh-water spring, Phainon is now a mass of ruined buildings, among which the remains of a monastery and three churches can be observed.[10] As an episcopal see, its bishops, like those of Zoara and Petra, attended several prominent synods of the Church.[11] The site itself was not only important as a copper mining or refining center, but also served as a penal settlement.

At the time of the Arian persecutions, Orthodox opponents were sent to work the mines of Phainon.[12] The martyrdom of the Orthodox and the association of the site with Punon of the Old Testament could easily have made Phainon an attraction for pilgrims.

In contrast to the eastern portion of *Palaestina Tertia*, the urban picture regarding the western section is quite different. Clustered within the foothills and highlands of the Central Negev the remains of six conspicuous urban sites are to be found, as well as numerous hamlets and agricultural installations associated with them. The word "clustered" is appropriate, for over the vast stretch of territory encompassed by the western portion of the province, these six sites are located a day's journey, more or less, from one another. They are situated along roads leading south and east in the general direction of Aila, or north and west from Aila to Jerusalem and the Mediterranean. All are south of the line of manned garrisons reported in the *Notitia dignitatum* (*ca.* 400), and all have been built in part on Nabataean foundations.

The area is easily outlined: on the north, a line extending from Halutsa (Khalasa, ancient Elusa) to Kurnub (ancient Mampsis); on the east, Kurnub to Avdat (Abda, ancient Eboda or Oboda); on the south, Avdat to Nitsana (Auja Hafir, ancient Nessana); and on the west, Nitsana to Rehovot (Ruheiba, ancient name unknown) and to Halutsa. Included in this irregular rectangle of some 2,000 km.² is the site of Shivta (Isbeita, Soubeita, ancient Sobata). The clustering of these six sites is best illustrated by the following mileage table expressed in Roman miles (1 Roman mile = 1.482 km. or 0.921 English statute mile).[13]

	Elusa	Ruheiba	Sobata	Eboda	Nessana	Mampsis
Elusa	--	7	20	29	23	33
Ruheiba	7	--	15	37	15	40
Sobata	20	15	--	17	15	37
Eboda	29	37	17	--	29	34
Nessana	23	15	15	29	--	51
Mampsis	33	40	37	34	51	--

A study of the population of Western Palestine has provided estimates on the size and population of these six sites.[14] The following figures are very rough estimates and cannot be taken as a constant for any period other than "Early Byzantine". However, it can safely be assumed from the archaeological evidence that the floruits of these sites range from the sixth to the seventh centuries.

Site	Size (hectares/acres)	Population
Elusa	35/86	10,000
Nessana	15-18/37-44	4,000
(Ruheiba)	12/30	4,000
Eboda	(300-400 caves)	3,000
Sobata	11.5/28.5	2,000
Mampsis	4/10	1,500

All six sites are located in an area of extremely limited water resources. Rainfall is scanty and irregular, springs are non-existent, and whatever wells there are have a high chloride content. Eboda and Ruheiba each had a well that was dug to extraordinary depths; Ruheiba's, the deepest in the Negev, was 100 m. in depth; Eboda's was 60 m. deep. These apparently provided water for the nearby baths. Nessana had a number of shallower wells, as did Elusa, but since their water is brackish, it is likely that the water was used for animals (as is common today). It is also possible that they furnished water for baths, the remains of which have not yet been uncovered. Sobata, without a well or a spring, had to conserve water from its only source: a meager and unreliable rainfall that could vary sharply year by year from its average annual precipitation of less than 100 mm. To provide water for domestic purposes, the inhabitants utilized the runoff areas of roofs and streets to fill household cisterns and two large open-air reservoirs in the town center. At Mampsis, on the other hand, retaining dams (Byzantine?) were built in a deep wadi adjacent to the town to catch and store floodwater, but these had the disadvantage of silting up and rapidly losing their storage capacity. For all six towns, natural sources of water were so scarce that the inhabitants had to rely almost exclusively on collecting rainwater in household cisterns and reservoirs.[15]

However great the effort spent by the inhabitants of these six towns to guarantee a supply of water for domestic purposes, it cannot be compared with the extraordinary energy expended in making it possible to cultivate patches of soil that lay in wadi beds or on the flood plains of large wadi systems. Literally thousands of kilometres of dry-stone walls were painstakingly erected to gather, check, spread, or to divert water accruing solely from winter rains onto these patches of soil, thus making it possible to grow a variety of crops. It is estimated that each unit of arable land required a runoff area of some 20 times its size. And still visible are the remains of farmsteads, towers, wine-presses and covered reservoirs (*harabas*) that were carved into the limestone hills.

The phenomenon of an agricultural regime under arid conditions in the Central Negev has been extensively investigated and need not be amplified here.[16] The papyrological documents from Nessana mention crops of wheat, barley and *arakos*, of vineyards and of orchards of olives, figs, dates, and presumably of pomegranates and almonds. A unique document, reporting the amounts of wheat and barley sown and reaped, reveals yields that compare favorably with regions with a far greater rainfall than that of the Negev. The same document informs us that the inhabitants of Nessana cultivated a crop of barley as far away as Birein, 11 km. from the town.[17] Each town appears to have been the nucleus of a large agricultural area to assure its inhabitants of an adequate supply of food to carry them through the year and even through periods of drought.

The inventory of the unusual features of these six communities has one more item that has attracted the eye of the traveler and the spade of the archaeologist: the prominent remains of numerous churches. Within the 2,000 km.² of the Central Negev there are at present 20 known churches and related structures (attached monastic buildings, martyria). Of those listed below, 11 have been excavated or are in the process of being cleared; the remains of nine others have been sighted.[18]

Elusa:	(3)	One very large on the outskirts of the city; possibly as many as six.
Ruheiba:	(4)	One large, north-east of the town.
Nessana:	(5)	Two on the acropolis, one below; two others claimed to have been sighted in the town.
Sobata:	(4)	Two within the town, one on the outskirts; one situated a short distance away at Mishrefa.
Eboda:	(2)	On the acropolis of the town.
Mampsis:	(2)	Within the town.

It is these churches, I believe, that are the key to understanding the unparalleled urban development within this limited area of western *Palaestina Tertia*. Although trade from the port city of Aila may account for part of the growth, we have no way of knowing whether the bulk of that trade went through the roads of the Negev by way of the *Via Nova Traiana* or by the eastern desert route north to Bostra and Damascus. However, since these towns of the Negev were neither trading marts nor transshipment centers, no great economic advantage could have been gained by servicing caravans en route to such centers. Further, with limited water supplies available - especially true of Sobata - it is doubtful that large numbers of sizeable caravans could be handled at these sites.[19] It is also possible that the inhabitants profited from the sale of their agricultural surplus - if they had any for sale - or from the cultivation of the grape that helped make Gaza famous for its wine. That, too, could hardly account for the growth of these towns. The answer must rest in the advent of Christianity and in the spread of monasticism to the reputed desert of "Cades". Consequently, the region attracted pilgrims who wished to visit biblical sites, to observe the saintly life of monks and to worship at the shrines of those who became martyrs in the pursuit of that life. In time, the monastic center at Mount Sinai, deep in the Sinai Peninsula, at the site where Moses was thought to have received the Law and that was later to become the refuge of Elijah, became, after Jerusalem, the prime objective of great numbers of pilgrims. To reach the "Holy Mountain" from Palestine, most pilgrims made their way through the Central Negev.

Christianity came to the region in the middle of the fourth century, at about the time the province of *Palaestina Tertia* was organized. Our knowledge of its beginnings we owe to Jerome's biography of Palestine's protomonk and great exorciser of demons, Hilarion (*ca.* 300-371). Jerome informs us that Hilarion was responsible for the spread of monasteries throughout Palestine and that his reputation for piety and asceticism attracted a great number of monks to follow a way of life he had learned in Egypt. As many as two thousand monks followed him in his travels from one monastery to another "on the appointed days before the vintage" to give them his blessing. Jerome then reports:

> The extent of Hilarion's zeal in not slighting a single brother, no matter how humble or poor he might be, is shown in his going to the desert of Cades to visit one of his disciples. On this occasion, accompanied by a great procession of monks, he arrived at Elusa on the very day that a solemn festival had brought all the people of the town to the temple of Venus. The Saracens, moreover, worship this goddess as the Morning Star and their race is dedicated to her cult. The town itself is, for the most part, semi-barbarian because of its location.[20]

Since Hilarion had healed many Saracens before this time, he was met by swarms of men, women and children who cried out for his blessing. Having given it and having urged them to give up the worship of idols

> ... he promised them that if they believed in Christ, he would come to them often .... They did not allow him to leave until he planned a church for them.[21]

From the next hundred years we possess little in the way of specific testimony for the development of the towns of the Central Negev. Toward the end of the fourth century, or the very beginning of the fifth, we hear of Sobata and Elusa as still being half-civilized and of the newly-established church in Elusa as having difficulty in gathering a congregation for itself.[22] Mount Sinai, on the other hand, appears to have had an active monastic community and to have been an attraction for pilgrims. The peripatetic nun Egeria, who made her way to Sinai from Egypt toward the close of the fourth century, gives us one of the most detailed accounts of her reception at the hands of the monks. She climbs the "Mountain of God", attends Mass and is given a guided tour of the region around the mountain and its association with the events and personalities described in *Exodus*, *Numbers* and *Kings*. As she dines with the monks in the garden near the church of the Burning Bush, the scene is one of serenity. The monastic community is very small. Egeria visits all the holy men who live there, and when she leaves for the town of Pharan 35 miles away, she is accompanied the entire distance by "most of the holy men who lived at the Mountain of God or near it - at least the ones who were strong enough."[23]

All, however, was not peaceful at Mount Sinai or in other parts of *Palaestina Tertia*. The isolation sought by eremites in the desert made them vulnerable to Saracen (i.e. Bedouin) harassment of all kinds, from mischievous misdemeanors to bloody massacres. The monks who lost their lives during Bedouin incursions were viewed no less as martyrs through a "baptism by blood" than those who suffered martyrdom under the decrees of Roman emperors. These were "the saints"; their relics became the object of veneration, and the places where they met their deaths were sought out by pilgrims.

A record of the martyrdom of "the holy fathers" at Mount Sinai is preserved in two narratives - the pseudo-Nilus and the Ammonius - in an inscription in the South Chapel of the basilica in the Monastery of St. Catherine, and in the current calendar of the Greek Orthodox Church. While the two narratives have been impugned by some scholars as fictional biography, the historicity of Bedouin attacks mentioned in these narratives has not been challenged. Fiction or not, both narratives were written by people well acquainted with the region of Mount Sinai and with the dangers involved in living in unprotected isolation.

The writer of the Nilus narrative describes himself as one who voluntarily chose a life of self-denial and solitude in the Sinai wilderness.[24] He witnesses a sudden and brutal Bedouin attack that resulted in the deaths of 12 monks at Mount Sinai and its immediate environs. He also hears of an attack on a party of travelers (pilgrims?) making their way to Pharan. Following a description of the savage attack of the Bedouin, the narrative makes this statement - a later interpolation, in my belief.

> They died on the seventh day after the Ephiphany which is the 14th of January. Pious men are very interested in learning the time and the names, since they want to check this information with the memories of holy men. Others were killed some years before, the memory of whom they celebrate on the same day because of the length of the journey and the size of the assemblage.[25]

The writer of the Ammonius narrative claims to be an Egyptian monk.[26] After having completed a pilgrimage to the Holy Land, he made his way to Mount Sinai, in company with a number of other devout Christians. While he was visiting the monastic community there, Bedouin attacked and massacred 40 of the eremites. Ammonius barely escaped with his own life. He then heard of a Blemmye attack on the monastic settlement at Rhaithou, where a similar number of monks were slain. Appended to the text of the narrative is the statement:

> These holy fathers and victorious men of Christ died on the 2nd of the month of Tybi (i.e. December 28th) at about the ninth hour; according to the Romans, their memory is celebrated on the 14th of the month of January.[27]

The Nilus and Ammonius accounts were the two prime and perhaps only sources from which the compilers of Greek menologies and synaxaria excerpted both the dramatic details and the date of January 14th to commemorate the eremites killed at Mount Sinai. The words in the Nilus narrative - "Others were killed some years before, the memory of whom they celebrate on the same day because of the length of the journey and the size of the assemblage" - are compelling evidence of the large number of pilgrims who travelled to the renowned mountain to pray at the sanctuaries of the saints and to venerate their relics. January 14th, in fact, became a red-letter day in Sinai, and still remains one in the Greek Orthodox Church, for its calendar for this date carries the notation: "Fathers killed in Sinai and Raitho".

Security for the monks at Mount Sinai came about when Emperor Justinian ordered the construction of the fortified monastery, now known as the Monastery of St. Catherine. The South Chapel of the basilica church contains the remains of other Sinaitic eremites who had achieved martyrdom by falling victim to periodic Bedouin violence. A marble plaque in the chapel bears a commemorating inscription (late sixth century?) that reads:

> The holy Fathers lie here, equal in number to those who were killed on the 14th (of January), and imitating them through a baptism by blood. Theirs is the joyous and true Burning Bush; through them, O God, save us.[28]

Relatively few years after the construction of the fortified monastery, there was a flourishing eremitic community at Mount Sinai and its environs, well organized to accommodate pilgrims from virtually every corner of the known world. An *itinerarium* (*ca.* 570), attributed to Antoninus of Piacenza, graphically describes the moving reception given to a group of Italian pilgrims as they approached the Holy Mountain. "Suddenly", the account reports, "a multitude of monks and a horde of hermits, carrying a cross and singing hymns, blocked our way. Throwing themselves on the ground, they greeted us with great respect. We did the same and we wept."[29]

Within the monastery, the pilgrim from Piacenza noted that there were "three Fathers who were learned in Latin and Greek, in Syriac and Egyptian, and in Bessan (Persian? perhaps Armenian?), and there are many there who can translate uncommon languages."[30]

On their way to Egypt and the monastery of St. Paul, the Italian pilgrims stopped at Pharan, where they were greeted by, as the Piacenza pilgrim informs us, "women with their children, carrying in their hands palms and flasks of radish oil. Throwing themselves at our feet, they annointed our soles and heads, and in the Egyptian language they sang the hymn, 'Blessed be you by the Lord, and blessed is your coming: Hosanna in the highest.'" At the same time, the pilgrim noted that Pharan had a mounted police force of 80 men who had been posted to guard the monasteries and hermits against Saracen attacks.[31]

These emotional greetings after days of traveling through a desert, as dramatic as the setting of the monastery itself, could not but touch the deepest emotions of the pilgrims. Unquestionably stirred by the display of pious asceticism, visitors must have made donations for the support of the monks and hermits, as well as offerings on their own behalf. Many of the pilgrims came well provided with money, as we learn from the pilgrim of Piacenza. His account tells of a side trip to a convent near Segor (i.e., Zoara) and of the offer by one of the pilgrims of the very large sum of 100 *solidi* for the purchase of two unusual animals. When the offer was not accepted, the pilgrim sent to Jerusalem and provided the convent with food and clothing.[32] There can be little doubt that this pilgrim and others in his company were most generous in their donations to the monastic establishments at Mount Sinai and Pharan.

A more specific reference to financial transactions at Mount Sinai is found in one of the documents from the Nessana archive, from about the same time or somewhat later than the journey of the Piacenza pilgrim. P. Colt 89, an account of a small trading company of Christian (monks?) that made its way to the Holy Mountain, records a donation of 17 *solidi* on behalf of two communities and of a small offering on its own behalf. The trading company also received from a certain abba Martyrius the very large sum of 270.5 *solidi*, most likely amassed from donations and offerings and given to the traders for deposit elsewhere.[33]

Mount Sinai continued to attract large numbers of pilgrims even after the Muslim conquest of Palestine. The *apophthegmata* attributed to the monk Anastasius (post-650) describes a miraculous event experienced by a group of Armenians on a peak of the Holy Mountain. The description is prefaced with the statement: "It was the custom of the Armenians, as everyone knows, to come often to the Holy Mountain. At all events, twenty years ago a great caravan of them came, about 800 souls."[34]

Armenian pilgrims, like those mentioned by Anastasius, paused en route to Mount Sinai at a wadi above the spring of Ain Hudra and inscribed their names on the sandstone rocks. The Armenian inscriptions are dated palaeographically to between the seventh and tenth centuries. One is dated to 420 of the Armenian era, which would correspond to 971-972. These same rocks bore other notices in Greek, Latin, Syriac, Arabic and Georgian characters, mute testimony to the many pilgrims who journeyed through the western portion of the peninsula to the Holy Mountain. The wadi of the inscriptions was appropriately named by the Bedouin, "Wadi Haggag" (Wadi of the Pilgrims).[35]

Mount Sinai and its monastic community has to be considered the key to understanding the development of urban sites in *Palaestina Tertia*. For very many pilgrims the *via sacra* began at the river Jordan and Jerusalem and ended at the mountain of Moses the Law Giver and the dwelling places of the "athletes of Christ" and their martyrs. It was certainly so for Armenian pilgrims. Kumitas, archbishop and metropolitan of Armenia, replying to a letter (*ca.* 614) from the vicar of Jerusalem, acknowledges that pilgrimages to the holy places of Jerusalem were salutary for his people, that they baptized themselves in the river Jordan, and that they "shed the anguish of their hearts about Mount Sinai".[36]

It is true that towns in the "desert of Cades" (i.e., the Central Negev) attracted monastic communities, but their growth into substantial settlements must be due mostly, as stated above, to pilgrim traffic along the route from Jerusalem to the Holy Mountain, rather than to trading caravans coming up from the port of Aila or from the Arabian peninsula. Not only did these communities have to house, feed and provide other services for travelers, but they also had their own saints, martyrs and holy places to attract the devotional interests of pilgrims.

Following - or perhaps even preceding - Hilarion's missionary work, monasticism took hold in the wilderness of Cades. At the time of the protomonk's visit to "half-civilized" Elusa, Palestine proper was protected against Bedouin incursions, as the *Notitia dignitatum* indicates, by a line of manned garrisons that encompassed the Central Negev on the north, east and west.[37] For anyone attempting to follow the precepts of the "new" religion, marauding Bedouin must have made this biblical desert a danger to life and limb. How many monks and hermits earned the name of saint and martyr through a "baptism by blood" is not known; their martyrdom apparently did not create a lasting tradition as it had for others at Mount Sinai. Our knowledge of these saints and martyrs comes from the work of archaeologists over the past half century.

Excavations at five of the six towns in the Central Negev have uncovered at each site inscriptions mentioning martyria or reliquaries that at one time held the relics of local saints. At the sixth site, Elusa, work has not progressed enough to indicate whether it too celebrated its own saints and martyrs, but as an episcopal see, Elusa must surely have had the remains of the earliest and most prominent martyrs of the region.

At Mampsis, the East Church, dated to the late fourth or early fifth century and called by the excavator the Church of Saints and Martyrs, held two reliquaries and a small altar associated with one of them.[38] On the acropolis at Eboda, two churches of the late fifth or early sixth centuries contained reliquaries. An epitaph in the South Church of a certain Zacharias son of John notes that he was buried "in the martyrium of St. Theodore". The same saint is mentioned in other inscriptions found by the excavator in various places on the site.[39] At Ruheiba, where archaeological work has virtually been limited to a large church (dated to the last quarter of the fifth century), the major discovery was a large crypt containing a reliquary.[40] At Sobata, the South Church had niche-like apses and the church "was dedicated to the cult of the martyrs".[41]

The evidence from Nessana is far greater than that from any of the other sites. In the North Church, dedicated to the soldier saints, Sergius and Bacchus, a white marble reliquary cover was discovered. The excavator describes it as follows: "The presence of oil stains on the square raised area of the underside, and on the edges and sides of the hole passing through it, suggests that the square compartment of the box contained the bones of some holy person. It was the practice for oil to be poured through the hole, to pass over the bones, and then to be distributed to the faithful in small vials or flasks."[42]

Room 16 of the North Church complex contained a burial inscription (dated to 464) of a priest who "was laid to rest in this holy Martyrium"; another inscription in the room (dated to 475) was of a deacon, whose burial is noted as being "in this holy place". In other rooms and courts of this church complex, prayers (of pilgrims?) to saints and and martyrs were cut, scratched, or painted on various architectural members, as, for example: "St. Stephen, help us..."; "Holy martyrs, help..."; "Lord and St. Sergius and Stephen, help..." Scribbled on the voussoir of the Martyrium (i.e., Room 16) was a list of seven saints, eight Fathers (*abbas*) and three Our Mothers (*ommana*).[43]

The early martyrs of the Central Negev, whose relics were reverently preserved and venerated by the local population and the pilgrims, undoubtedly fell, like those in Sinai, to raiding Bedouin during unsettled times in this unpoliced area of Palestine. It was sometime during the late fourth or early fifty century that the central government felt it necessary to provide greater security for the region. Whether it planned added protection to the trans-Negev route to Aila for military or commercial purposes, or whether it was responding to pleas from the monastic communities for protection against Bedouin attacks is simply not known. However, during the reign of Theodosius II (408-452), or possibly even as early as Theodosius I (379-395), a fort and a mobile border force - a camel corps with the name of the Very Loyal Theodosians - were put in place at Nessana, at the junction of roads that led to Sinai and Egypt.[44] Somewhat later, around A.D. 500, a fort of substantial size was built at Eboda, possibly connected with an auxiliary unit similar to that stationed at Nessana.[45] In addition, at Elusa and Mampsis, an official edict mentions military personnel.[46]

Providing protection along the routes on which these towns were situated not only controlled desert raiding and secured safe passage for caravans, whether of merchandise or of pilgrims, but it also encouraged the sedentarization of the local population and an influx of people from other regions. An onomasticon composed from inscriptions and papyri would show a mixed population: although most of the names are Semitic, biblical, or martyrological, others are typically Egyptian, Greek, or Roman. A dedicatory inscription from the East Church at Nessana (dated to 601) illustrates the interest taken by a distant and prominent family from Emesa-Homs in Coele Syria (and new residents?) in this remote desert town. The inscription reads in part: "For the salvation of the benefactors Segius, ex-assessor and monk, and Pallus his sister, and John the deacon, her son curialis of the metropolitan city of Emesa..."[47]

The process of pacification that began in the fifth century became felt in the sixth and seventh centuries. To judge from the evidence of dated inscriptions and papyri, these two centuries represent the period during which the towns of the Negev were at the peak of their development. At Nessana, dated inscriptions (i.e., epitaphs) range from 464 to 630; at Ruheiba, from 485 to 555; at Sobata, from 506 to 679; at Eboda, from 541 to 617; and at Elusa, from 426 to 603.[48] We have no dated inscriptions from Mampsis, but in the excavators' opinion, the period of the sixth and seventh centuries was one of intensive building activity.[49] As for the Nessana papyri, the earliest document is dated 505 and the latest 689. Approximately half the dated documents come from the sixth century; the other half from the seventh.[50]

To this should be added the mute evidence of the agricultural installations. The extension of the cultivated area far beyond the immediate vicinity of the towns could only have been a gradual development as the population grew and traffic increased. The building of kilometer upon kilometer of stone walls required to conserve soil and water in the wadi beds and flood plains required many hands, considerable time and well-organized communities. Numerous farmsteads were found in remote and isolated wadis, with no indication that they were fortified to fend off attackers.

By the time the pilgrim from Piacenza and his fellow pilgrims made their way through the Negev on their way to Mount Sinai (ca. 570), the desert of Cades had become open country, free from the danger of mass attack. Border forces had been withdrawn, and the fort at Nessana - and presumably the one at Eboda - had been converted to other uses.[51] The Piacenza itinerary is informative on this score and on the kind of monuments that were pointed out by guides to touring pilgrims. They were not only shown places associated with biblical events, but also monasteries and the tombs of celebrated monks and martyrs.

Upon leaving Jerusalem, the pilgrims struck out for the coastal road via Eleutheropolis. Along the way their guide pointed out sites mainly connected with Old Testament personalities: David and Goliath, Samson, Zachariah, Abraham and Jacob. At Ascalon, they were shown the tomb of the three martyred brothers called "The Egyptians"; at Maiuma, the tomb of the martyr Victor; and a short distance from Gaza, the tomb of Hilarion. Gaza itself is eulogized in the itinerary as being "magnificent, delightful; its inhabitants most respectful, friendly in every way, lovers of travelers".[52] There is no doubt that Gaza was one of the staging areas for pilgrims traveling to Mount Sinai via the Negev, and that the city profited handsomely from housing them and providing them with guides and transport.

Arriving at Elusa, cited by the itinerary as being "as the head of the desert extending to Sinai", the pilgrims met the bishop of the city, who told them of a remarkable woman who lived as a hermit in the desert near Zoara.[53] As related above, the pilgrims made a side trip to the region near the Dead Sea, where they observed a convent, and where one of the wealthy pilgrims provided the women with food and clothing. They then returned to Elusa to continue their journey. (It is of interest to note that the pilgrims' guide decided, for any number of reasons, to backtrack to Elusa, rather than to make for the *Via Nova*, a short distance away, which could have taken him and his charges to Aila and then to Mount Sinai.)

The itinerary goes on to state that "twenty miles from Elusa there is a fort in which there is a hospice (*xenodochium*) of St. George in which travelers have something of a shelter and hermits their keep."[54] The pilgrims at this point have arrived at Nessana, where the fort that once served the border force of the Very Loyal Theodosians was now put to use as a shelter for pilgrims. The limited number of rooms that abutted the walls of the fort were probably occupied by monks or hermits; the pilgrims must have had to make do with the open area of the fort. It is also probable that a similar situation existed at Eboda, where there were no rooms in the fort except a chapel which could have been used by the pilgrims for their devotions.)[55]

From Nessana, the Piacenza pilgrims travelled through the arid desert of the al-Tih plateau on a direct route to Mount Sinai, possible only because of a Saracen festival that enjoined them from raiding. However, when the pilgrims were ready to depart from Mount Sinai, they were informed that the Saracen festival had reached its end and that they could not return to Jerusalem by the same route. "Some", the itinerary reports, "returned to the Holy City through Egypt, and others by way of Arabia. From Mount Sinai to the city of Arabia that is called Aila is eight stages."[56]

By the sixth century, of the two routes to Mount Sinai from Jerusalem and other points in Palestine, the preferred route ran through the Central Negev.[57] The itinerary of Theodosius (*ca.* 530), with hardly a word about the route through Egypt, makes this point very clear. "From Jerusalem to Elusa", the account states tersely, "there are three stages, and seven from Elusa to Aila... From Aila to Mount Sinai there are eight stages if you wish to take the short route through the desert; but if you wish to go through Egypt, then there are twenty-five stages."[58] The eighteen stages coincide precisely with the number of days it took the Egyptian monk Ammonius at an earlier time to travel from Jerusalem "through the desert" to Mount Sinai in a caravan of "devout Christians".[59]

Apart from security considerations, the stone desert of the Negev and Sinai had the advantage of providing sure footing for man and beast, as well as reasonably good supplies of water from wells, cisterns, and reservoirs. At Aila, where there is an excellent supply of water, the traveler could refresh himself before undertaking the final leg of his journey to Mount Sinai. The route to Sinai through Egypt, on the other hand, was a difficult one. The coastal road west of Rhinocorura (modern el-Arish) to Pelusium cuts through a region of sandy wastes; and from Pelusium to Clysma (modern Suez), the route runs through dune belts and salt marshes. From Clysma to Mount Sinai water is scarce until the traveler reaches the sandstone region in the interior.

Travel through the Central Negev to Mount Sinai continued even after the Muslim conquest of Palestine. Two documents from Nessana, dated to the late seventh century, record orders to the administrator of the town from the Muslim governor at Gaza to provide a guide to conduct two individuals to Mount Sinai.[60] What is striking about these two documents is the fact that two people from Gaza, one of whom was the wife of the governor himself, were directed to travel to Mount Sinai not through Egypt, but through one of the routes through the interior of Palestine.

From the meager evidence for the period following the Muslim conquest of Palestine in 640, it is known that at least two of the towns continued to flourish well into the seventh century. At Nessana, as its documents show, organized economic activity continued as late as 690.[61] From sherds of Arab pottery and from coins of the Ummayad period (661-750), it can be reasonably assumed that the town maintained itself into the eighth or ninth century.[62] At Sobata, a new floor in the South Church, bearing a dedicatory inscription dated to 640, showed signs of considerable use. The clergy continued to be buried in a chapel of the North Church between 646 and 679. A mosque was built near the South Church with care taken not to damage the adjoining church structure. Sherds of Arab pottery similar to those at Nessana also indicate that the town continued to function in the eighth or ninth century.[63] The fate of the other towns in the Central Negev is unknown.

The tolerance of the new Arab rulers toward Christians changed under later Khalifs. As stricter sanctions were imposed, there were conversions to the new religion or an exodus of non-Muslims from the region. Pilgrims, however, continued to pass through the Negev on their way to Mount Sinai, as is witnessed by late Armenian, Georgian and Arabic inscriptions in Wadi Haggag, but the region gradually lost its settled population. Churches were abandoned, local saints and martyrs were forgotten, and the desert nomad reclaimed the land that had been taken from him some five hundred years earlier.

As an epilogue, so to speak, to the vagaries of urbanization in *Palaestine Tertia*, there remains the paradox of Ain Qudeirat, at present identified with biblical Kadesh Barnea. Situated one day's travel (about 40 km. or 27 Roman miles) south-east of Nessana, on or close to the road leading to Aila, Ain Qudeirat contains the best perennial supply of water in the western sector of the province. The site holds an impressive fort of the Israelite period and the poor remains of a small town with evidence of Nabataean-Roman occupation. The location would be ideal either for a monastic community or a military outpost, yet there is not a sign of a later - i.e., Byzantine - community of any size in its vicinity. Why urbanization ceased to the south of a line extending from Clysma to Aila is not known. There were no military installations along the routes to Mount Sinai, and, with the exception of Pharan, no settlements that could even be considered organized villages. We can only speculate that Ain Qudeirat was in the hands of a formidable Saracen tribe that resisted intrusion by church or state. The tantalizing reference to a "newly appointed phylarch" in a fragmented Nessana document[64] may indicate that the Saracens of Ain Qudeirat and other parts of Sinai were pacified through imperial payments or other arrangements.

Notes

1   The standard work for the Roman province is that of R. Brünnow and A. von Domaszewski, *Die Provincia Arabiae*, Vols. I-III (Strassburg: Trübner, 1901-1904). For Nabataean and earlier periods, see N. Glueck, "Explorations in Eastern Palestine", *AASOR* (1934-1951). See also G.W. Bowersock, "A Report on Provincia Arabia", *Journal of Roman Studies* 61 (1971), pp. 219-242.

2   S.T. Parker, "Archaeological Survey of the *Limes Arabicus*: A Preliminary Report", *Annual of the Department of Antiquities of Jordan* 21 (1976), pp. 26-27.

3   *Ibid.*, pp. 27-28. Cf. D.F. Graf, "The Saracens and the Defense of the Arabian Frontier", *BASOR* 229 (1978), p. 13.

4   For the relief features of the region, see D. Baly, *The Geography of the Bible*, New York, 1974, pp. 32-34, 206-208, 233-236, 241-251.

5   On the roads and highways that ran through the province, see Y. Aharoni, *The Land of the Bible: A Historical Geography*, London, 1966, pp. 39-53; Baly (above, n. 4), pp. 97-99, 251. See also Z. Meshel and Y. Tsafrir, "The Nabataean Road from 'Avdat to Sha'ar-Ramon", *PEQ* 105-106 (1974-1975), pp. 103-118, 3-21; B. Rothenberg, "An Archaeological Survey of South Sinai: First Season 1967/1968, Preliminary Report", *PEQ* 102 (1970), pp. 4-22; Y. Aharoni, "The Roman Road to Aila (Elath)", *IEJ* 4 (1954), pp. 9-16; M. Harel, "The Roman Road to Ma'aleh 'Aqrabbim (Scorpions' Ascent), *Israel Exploration Journal* 9 (1959), pp. 175-179; P. Mayerson, "The Clysma-Phara-Haila Road on the Peutinger Table", *Coins, Culture, and History in the Ancient World: Numismatic and Other Studies in Honor of Bluma Trell*, Detroit, 1981, pp. 167-176.

6   Baly (above, n. 4), pp. 206-209, 247-249. M. Evenari *et al.*, *The Negev: The Challenge of the Desert*, Cambridge, MA, 1971, pp. 31-35. Mean average rainfall figures are often misleading since they do not take into account the extreme variability of precipitation in an arid region, where there may be extreme drought one year and heavy rainfall the next.

7   *Oriens Christianus*, Paris, 1740, III, Cols. 724-726. Brünnow and Domazewski (above, n. 1), p. 345. P.C. Hammond, *The Nabataeans - Their History, Culture and Archaeology in Studies in Mediterranean Archaeology* (Gottenburg) 37 (1973), p. 56: "...the inscription of one Jason 'the pious' in A.D. 447 mentions a *numerus* stationed at Petra... Much has been made of reference to Petra as a Christian center in this later era, citing the attendance lists of Church councils and other contemporary sources. However, it should be noted that the 'See of Petra' in these sources refer to Kerak and not to Nabataean Petra, and the latter's role is thus not as significant as it appears in the sources commonly cited. Some Byzantine materials are to be found at Petra, to be sure, including the Ed-Deir inscription, pottery and some sculptural fragments, but the Byzantine occupation must have been relatively light. After the inscription of 447, no other dated history of Petra is extant, until the Crusader period." P.C. Hammond, "New Light on the Nabataeans", *Biblical Archaeological Review* 7/2 (1981), p. 32: "(At Petra) we found no objects marked with crosses or Christian symbols... The Christian influence so long assumed to exist at Petra because of the two tombs' reuse as churches, must now be rethought."

    While surveys in southern Trans-Jordan have focused upon Nabataean and earlier periods, none, to my knowledge, has detailed post fourth-century habitation in the region. Unlike the Negev to the west, where even before excavations were undertaken, one could clearly observe a heavy Byzantine overlay of earlier sites. Nothing comparable in magnitude has been reported along the *Via Nova*. The survey of A. Musil graphically illustrates the contrast between the two sectors of the province. To the east of the Wadi Arabah, Musil draws plans of only two sites: Petra and Feinan (ancient Phainon); to the west of the Rift Valley, he draws plans of five of the six urban sites described below (*Arabia Petraea* II.1-2, Vienna, 1907-1908). Lately come to my attention is the report of B. MacDonald, "The Wadi el Hasa Survey, 1981", *American Schools of Oriental Research Newsletter* 3 (November 1981), p. 14: "The number of Byzantine (A.D. 324-640) sites in the area was surprisingly low. They are generally small and are mostly located in the western portion of the survey area."

8   *Eusebius, Das Onomastikon der biblischen Ortsnamen* (ed. E. Klostermann), Hildesheim, 1966, p. 43.

9   *Oriens Christianus* (above, n. 7), Cols. 744-746.

10   Personal observation. For a description and a sketch plan of the site, see F. Frank, "Aus der 'Arabah", *Zeitschrift des Deutschen Palästina-Vereins* 57 (1934), pp. 221-224, Pls. 19, 21; A. Musil (above, n. 7), II.1, pp. 278-287, Fig. 150. To Jerome, the biblical city "is now a small town (*viculus*) in the desert where copper is mined as a punishment for the condemned". (*Onomastikon*, [above, n. 8], p. 169.)

11   *Oriens Christianus* (above, n. 7), Cols. 745-748.

12   *Ibid.*; Musil (above, n. 7), p. 310.

13   The distances between these sites can vary since there are several routes, or tracks, that one can take between them. The distances were provided by two knowledgeable Israelis: one an archaeologist; the other a geographer.

14   M. Broshi, "The Population of Western Palestine in the Roman-Byzantine Period", *BASOR* 236 (1979), pp. 1-3. My own estimates are far more conservative. See P. Mayerson, "A Note on Demography and Land Use in the Ancient Negeb", *BASOR* 185 (1967), pp. 39-43.

15   Summarized in P. Mayerson, "The Ancient Agricultural Regime of Nessana and the Central Negeb", *Excavations at Nessana* (ed. H.D. Colt), London, 1962, I, pp. 221-222.

16   *Ibid.*, pp. 231-249; Evenari *et al.* (above, n. 6), pp. 95-119.

17   Texts and analysis in Mayerson (above, n. 15), pp. 227-231, 259-262.

18   Personal conversations with Prof. A. Negev, who is currently conducting excavations at Elusa. The evidence for churches at Eboda, Mampsis, Nessana, Ruheiba, and Sobata-Mishrefa is summarized in A. Ovadiah, *Corpus of Byzantine Churches in the Holy Land*, Bonn, 1970, pp. 23-26, 134-136, 145-151, 154-155, 166-173, 188-189. See also Y. Tsafrir, "Rehovot (Kh. Ruheibeh)", *Revue biblique* 84 (1977), pp. 422-426.

19   Certainly the huge caravans from Mecca, with as many as 2,500 camels and 100-300 men, could not have used the trans-Negev route. See art. "Mecca" in *Encyclopaedia of Islam* (ed. M. Th. Houtsma *et al.*), London, 1936, III, p. 440. Surveys and excavations in the Negev have not brought to light any evidence of caravan traffic for the period under discussion.

20   "Vita S. Hilarionis" in Migne, *Patrologia Latina* XXII, Cols. 42-43. To Eusebius and Jerome, the biblical desert of Cades extended into the Negev as far north as Arad and Thamara. See *Onomastikon* (above, n. 8), pp. 8-9, 14-15.

21   *Ibid.*

22   See P. Mayerson, "The Desert of Southern Palestine according to Byzantine Sources", *Proceedings of the American Philosophical Society* 107 (1963), pp. 167-168.

23   "Itinerarium Egeria" in *Corpus Christianorum, Series Latina* CLXXV, pp. 38-45.

24   "Nili Monachi Eremitae Narrationes", in Migne, *Patrologia Graeca* LXXIX, Cols. 589-694. For an analysis of the narrative, see P. Mayerson, "Observations of the 'Nilus' Narrationes", *Journal of the American Research Center in Egypt* 12 (1975), pp. 51-74.

25   *Ibid.*, Col. 640C; Mayerson, p. 64.

26   The Greek text, "Ammoniou monachou logos", in *Illustrium Christi martyrum lecti* (ed. F. Combefis), Paris, 1660, pp. 88-132. For an analysis of the account, see P. Mayerson, "The Ammonius Narrative: Bedouin and Blemmye Attacks in Sinai", *The Bible World: Essays in Honor of Cyrus H. Gordon*, New York, 1980, pp. 133-148.

27   *Ibid.*, p. 129.

28   P. Mayerson, "An Inscription in the Monastery of St. Catherine and the Martyr Tradition in Sinai", *Dumbarton Oaks Papers* 30 (1976), pp. 375-379.

29   "Antonini Placentini Itinerarium", in *Corpus Christianorum, Series Latina* CLXXV, par. 37, pp. 147-148.

30   *Ibid.*, p. 148.

31   *Ibid.*, par. 40, pp. 149-150.

32   *Ibid.*, par. 34, pp. 145-146: "Quibus per me centum solidos offerebat ille christianissimus, cum quo fui,

sed noluerunt accipere." For a more believable version, in which the offer was made to one of the pilgrims and was refused, see the alternate recension (*Ibid.*, par. 34, p. 169): "Quem et offerebant nobis pro centum solidis. Sed pater Antoninus suscipere noluit."

33   *Excavations at Nessana: non-literary papyri* (ed. C.J. Kraemer, Jr.) III, Princeton, 1958, pp. 251-260.

34   "Le texte grec des recits du moine Anastase sur les saints pères du Sinai" (ed. F. Nau), *Oriens Christianus* 2 (1902), pp. 81-82.

35   M. Stone, *Armenian Inscripitons from Sinai: An Intermediate Report with Notes on Georgian and Nabataean Inscriptions*, Sidney, 1979, pp. 3-5, 12. See also P. Mayerson, "The Pilgrim Routes to Mount Sinai and the Armenians", *IEJ* 32 (1982), pp. 44-57.

36   *Histoire d'Héraclius par l'évèque Sebeos* (trans. F. Macler), Paris, 1904, p. 74.

37   *Notitia dignitatum ... in partibus Orientis et Occidentis* (ed. E. Bocking).

38   A. Negev, "The Churches of the Central Negev: An Archaeological Survey", *RB* 81 (1974), p. 404, Pl. 21; *idem*, "Kurnub" in *Encyclopedia of Archaeological Excavation in the Holy Land* (eds. M. Avi-Yonah and E. Stern), Jerusalem, 1975-1978, pp. 729-730.

39   Negev (above, n. 38, "Churches"), pp. 406-407, Pl. 20; *EAEHL* (above, n. 38), art. "Eboda", pp. 351-352.

40   Tsafrir (above, n. 18), p. 425.

41   Negev, "Subeita", *EAEHL* (above, n. 38), pp. 1121-1122.

42   *Nessana* I (above, n. 15), p. 60, Pl. XXVI.12-13.

43   *Ibid.*, pp. 137-163.

44   *Nessana* III (above, n. 33), pp. 5-6, 40-41. Cf. Negev (above, n. 38, "Churches"), p. 409.

45   Negev (above, n. 38, in *EAEHL*), p. 351; Mayerson (above, n. 22), p. 166.

46   A. Alt, *Die griechischen Inschriften der Palaestina Tertia westlich der Araba*, Berlin and Leipzig, 1921, p. 5. Cf. P. Colt 39 in *Nessana* III (above, n. 33), pp. 119-125.

47   *Nessana* I (above, n. 15), pp. 173-174.

48   Negev (above, n. 38, "Churches"), pp. 405-407; (above, n. 38, *EAEHL*), p. 360.

49   Negev (above, n. 38, *EAEHL*, p. 724.

50   *Nessana* III (above, n. 33), pp. 1-9.

51   P. Mayerson, "The First Muslim Attacks on Southern Palestine", *Transactions and Proceedings of the American Philological Association* 95 (1964), pp. 184-185.

52   *Corp. Christ. Lat.* (above, n. 29), par. 31-34, pp. 144-146. Later, at Alexandria in Egypt (par. 45, p. 152) they were shown tombs of Sts. Athanasius, Faustus, Epimachius, Antony, Mark ... "and many other bodies of holy men".

53   *Ibid.*, par. 34, p. 145.

54   *Ibid.*, par. 35, pp. 146-147.

55   Mayerson (above, n. 22), pp. 170-171.

56   *Corp. Christ. Lat.* (above, n. 29), par. 39, p. 149. See also Mayerson (above, n. 50), pp. 186-187.

57   See Mayerson (above, n. 35).

58   "De Situ Terrae Sanctae", in *Corp. Christ. Lat.* (above, n. 29), par. 27, p. 123. See also Mayerson (above, n. 5), pp. 173-174.

59   Combefis (above, n. 26), p. 88.

60   P. Colt 72 and 73 in *Nessana* III (above, n. 33), pp. 205-208.

61   *Ibid.*, pp. 30-35.

62   *Nessana* I (above, n. 15), p. 23.

63   Negev (above, n. 38, *EAEHL*, pp. 1116, 1118. Baly, "S'baita", *PEQ* (1935), p. 173.

64   P. Colt 160 in *Nessana* III (above, n. 33), p. 330.

Pl. 10. Shifta (ancient Sobata): Aerial view of the excavated town. Note reservoir and church near the center of the town.

Pl. 11. The South Church of Shifta.

Pl. 12. The Central Church of Shifta.

Pl. 13. The North Church of Shifta.

Pl. 14. Ruheiba/Raheiba (ancient name unknown): Aerial view of the town. Note the excavated church in the upper left of photograph.

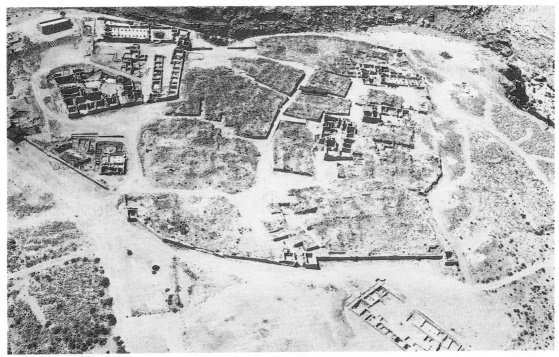

Pl. 15. Kurnub (ancient Mampsis): Aerial view of the excavated town with its two churches. Note the building outside its walls (caravanserai?).

Pl. 16. Khalasa (ancient Elousa): Aerial view of the town, former administrative center of *Palaestina Tertia*, now robbed of most of its stone and covered with sand.

The Wine and Vineyards of Gaza in the Byzantine Period

PHILIP MAYERSON
Department of Classics
New York University
New York, NY 10003

The reputation of the city of Gaza as producer of a vintage of export quality to the west has long been known. However, the factors that made the name of Gaza synonymous with its wine in the 5th and 6th centuries are not so well known. Recent archaeological work, in conjunction with citations from literary sources, bear on the social and economic causes for the increased production and popularity of Gazan wine. With the advent of Palestinian monasticism, Gaza and its far-reaching environs experienced a fast-growing population of consumers and producers of wine. The appearance of extraordinarily large wine presses in the hinterland (the Negev) is evidence that the region was a major producer. Gaza, port of call for merchants and pilgrims to the Holy Land from the western provinces, was also the port for shipment of products to the west. Undoubtedly the ships that carried pilgrims to their home ports also carried cargoes of the same Gaza wine that pilgrims savored during their stay in Palestine and Sinai.

It is well known that during the 5th and 6th centuries, the city of Gaza gained a reputation as a producer of a vintage of export quality. Equally well known are the supporting literary sources that are so often cited by economic historians—Sidonius Apollonaris, *Carmina*, 17.5; Corippus, *In Laudem Justini*, 3.88; Ven. Fortunatus, *Vita S. Martini*, 2.81–82; Gregory of Tours, *Hist. Franc.*, 7.29; *In Gloriam Confess.* c. 64; Cassiodorus, *Variae*, 12.12 (Heichelheim 1938: 139, 204; Sperber 1975: 439–41). Not so well defined, however, are the factors that went into making the name of Gaza synonymous with its wine (*vinum Gazetum, Gazetina, Gazeticum*): the sources of the commodity, the reasons for its appearance on the export market, and the range of its distribution. The writers cited mention only the vintage bearing the city's name; they do not state or even hint at the cause of its popularity. Nor is it enough to postulate that after an earlier decline, viticulture, along with Palestinian agriculture in general, experienced "some kind of improvement" during the course of the 4th century (Sperber 1975: 439).

Both literary and archaeological evidence bears directly on the social and economic causes for the increased production and popularity of Gazan wine. Simply put, the rise in production of Gazan wine must have had something to do with demand for the product, and the strong demand in the 5th century and later must be related to events both in and around Gaza. The evidence points to a burgeoning population and to the appearance of a number of large wine presses in the hinterland. To this must be added the fact that Gaza, the southernmost city of Palestine, became a port of call for travelers—and not only merchants—from the western provinces of the empire.

It is no coincidence that the popularity of Gazan wine rose almost simultaneously with population increases in both the environs of the city and in the western portion of Palestine (i.e., the Negev), which became known in the late 4th century as Palaestina Salutaris. The initial impetus for this growth was the rise of monasticism during that century. One man stands out in that movement, Palestine's proto-monk Hilarion (ca. 300–371), an exorciser of demons and a worker of miracles. He was born at Tabatha, some five miles south of Gaza. After his initiation into eremitic life under Anthony of Egypt, Hilarion returned to the vicinity of Gaza, where he established a monastery and attracted a large number of followers. His reputation spread through the cities of Palestine, Egypt and Syria, and beyond to distant provinces. All this we learn from Jerome's biography of the holy man, the *Vita Hilarionis* (*PL* 23: 29,42). Of all the agricultural activities recorded in the *Vita*, it is vintage (*vindemia*) and vineyards (*vineae*) to which most references are made. Hilarion made a point of visiting his fellow monastics on "fixed days before the vintage" (*statibus diebus ante vindemian*), presumably to bless the new crops of grapes before they were sent to the wine presses. He was escorted, so Jerome reports, from monastery to monastery by as many as 2000 monks (*PL* 23: 42).

On one occasion, Hilarion was invited into the vineyard of a monk named Sabas. When the holy man blessed the vineyard, it produced 300 jars (*lagenae*) of wine; originally the yield had been estimated at only 100 jars (*PL* 23: 43).

We are further told that Hilarion also visited Elusa, an important city in the Negev some 50 miles southeast of Gaza, possibly to bless the vintage of some monastic outpost (*PL* 23: 42). The populace of the city was pagan at the time of his visit; but, undoubtedly influenced by the miraculous cures he effected, it soon after converted to Christianity. Late in life, when Hilarion reviewed his great monastery, the multitude of brothers dwelling with him, and the crowds of those who sought to benefit from his curative powers, he saw the desert for miles around filled with all kinds of men (*PL* 23: 44).

This is the story of Hilarion's activities in and around Gaza during the mid- and late 4th century. Making full allowance for Jerome's exuberance and hyperbole, his *Vita Hilarionis* provides evidence to confirm the increasing population in the region and viticulture as a principle occupation of that population.

Toward the end of the 5th century, another monk, Peter the Iberian, spent some time in the neighborhood of Hilarion's monastery. Peter's biographer, with customary hyperbole, relates a tale of the miraculous effectiveness of the holy man's blessing, and in the process shows that the inhabitants of the region were engaged in the production of wine (Raage 1895: 95–96). A certain Christian inhabitant of Gaza reported that the vineyards around each village produced only a little wine— and that of poor quality—because the soil was sandy and thin. The monk Peter was taken to the vineyards and asked to pray over and bless each of them; afterwards, no one who worked that soil could remember the vineyards ever producing such an abundance of grapes or a wine so strong.

Material remains of the ancient wine industry near Gaza have not surfaced. However, several miles to the west, at Deir al-Balah, archaeologists excavating a Late Bronze site unexpectedly came upon a large deposit of Byzantine sherds. A wadi, long since covered over by sand, had apparently carried the sherds from an unknown locus and deposited them on the surface of the Late Bronze site. All the sherds turned out to be fragments of wine jars (Dothan 1978: 267; 1981: 127–29).

We also hear of viticulture at Elusa in the Negev. The information comes from the sophist Procopius of Gaza (ca. 450–526) in a letter to a certain Jerome, a sophist and teacher like himself, who was a native of Elusa but who had gone to Egypt to practice his profession. In this letter, Procopius takes Jerome to task for living in the lap of luxury and for putting on airs. But he, Procopius, will have the last laugh, for when Jerome returns to his hometown he will be shocked at what he will find. Procopius writes: "There will be a day when you will see Elusa again and you will weep at the sand being shifted by the wind stripping the vines naked to their roots" (ἔσσεται γὰρ ἦμαρ, ὅτε πάλιν ὄψει τὴν Ἐλοῦσαν, καὶ δακρύσεις ψάμμον μεθισταμένην τοῖς πνεύμασι καὶ γυμνοῦσαν εἰς ῥίζας τὴν ἄμπελον.. Garzya and Loenertz 1963: 43; see also Mayerson 1983: 251–52). Apart from the fact that Procopius may have been recording both physical and climatic conditions at the turn of the 6th century, the mention of vines indicates that the inhabitants of Elusa were engaged in viticulture.

On the basis of this bit of literary evidence alone, we might not be justified in concluding that Elusa was a wine-producing center. However, a short distance from the site of the city, a wine press of substantial proportions and extraordinarily fine workmanship was uncovered (figs. 1–2). The structure was built of extremely well-cut and precisely-fitted ashlar stones. The treading floor measured 28.50 m^2. Its paving slabs were well matched, creating "a completely waterproof surface." A drainpipe led to two receiving vats, each of which measured 2 m in diameter (Mazor 1981: 54).

At other sites in the Negev to the south and east of Gaza and Elusa, in and around the ancient towns of Sobata and Eboda, similar large-scale presses were uncovered: three at Sobata and five at Eboda (figs. 3–4). Two of the presses, one from each site, were enlarged by the addition of more space for treading and collecting (fig. 3). The

Fig. 1. Wine press near Elusa. (Photograph: P. Mayerson).

average measure of these treading floors, including the one at Elusa, was 33 m². Each press contained one or two receiving vats that were fed by a sophisticated drainage system. The volume of these vats ranged from 2.60 m³ to 8.80 m³. (In terms of U.S. gallons, this would mean between 590 and 2000 gallons.) Provision was also made for the storage of grape baskets and some structures had room for storing wine jars near the treading floor. The maximum capacity of the floors is estimated at 20 m³ of grapes; for efficient pressing, it is likely that only about half that amount was used at a time. The capacity of the receiving vats provides a dependable standard for the optimal amount of grapes that could be trodden in one pressing, 8–13 m³ on the average (Mazor 1981: 51–52, 55, 59).

These nine wine presses are the only ones that have been uncovered by archaeological investigations. Many others of similar dimensions undoubtedly lie undiscovered at sites that have not been as fully explored as ancient Sobata and Eboda. Towns and villages such as Ruheiba, Saadi and Nessana, all situated in a region that abounds in evidence of agricultural exploitation, have yet to be surveyed for installations of this kind. However,

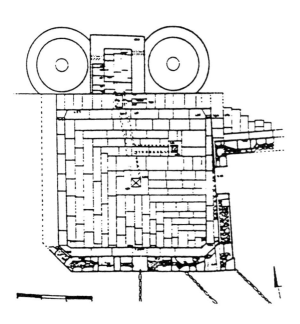

Fig. 2. Wine press near Elusa (after Mazor 1981: 51).

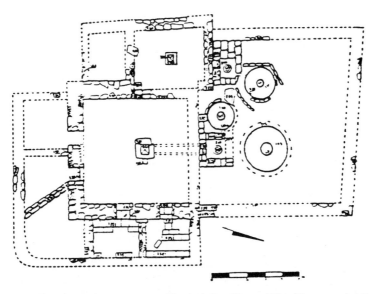

Fig. 3. Enlarged wine press near Eboda (after Mazor 1981: 53, upper right).

Fig. 4. Wine press at Sobata (after Mazor 1981: 54, lower right).

the size of the wine presses currently known leaves no doubt that the farmers of the Negev were engaged in the large-scale production of wine.[1] It is certainly possible to speak of these presses, if not as industrial operations, then as corporate or cooperative ventures, most likely undertaken by monastic communities distributed throughout the central Negev. It is equally reasonable to assume that part of their output satisfied the needs of local inhabitants, and that part—especially in years with harvests of high yields—was sold to wine merchants in Gaza.[2]

That there were wine merchants in Gaza in the 4th century we learn from the *Expositio Totius Mundi et Gentium* (Rougé 1966: 162) and from Marcus Diaconus' *Vita Porphyrii* (Soc. Phil. Bonn. Sod. 1895: 49), but their business was apparently conducted with Egypt and Syria. The question that these sources do not answer is how the popularity of Gazan wine spread to the western provinces. Although explicit evidence is still lacking, the answer must involve a major consequence of the rise of monasticism—pilgrimage. Beginning in the 4th century and continuing into the 6th, pilgrims came to the Holy Land in ever increasing numbers from the Latin west: from Spain, France, and Italy. They came to visit biblical sites, to see and touch holy things, to witness the extraordinary devotion of monks living lives of piety and self-denial, and to worship at the shrines of those who became martyrs in the pursuit of that life.

Egeria came from Spain, Cassian from France, and "Antoninus" from Piacenza in Italy. These three pilgrims from the Latin west left memoirs of their experiences in the Holy Land; most did not. There can be no doubt that for multitudes of the pilgrims, the city of Gaza was a staging center where arrangements were made for guides to the biblical sites of Egypt and Sinai. It must have been at Gaza that these western pilgrims tasted the *vinum optimum* mentioned in the *Expositio* and a demand for it was created when they returned home to the west.

The journey of "Antoninus" and the Piacenza pilgrims (ca. 570) can be taken as a paradigm of the route and the points of interest for many travelers from the western provinces. After a tour of the Holy Land proper, they set out for the celebrated monastery at the foot of Mount Sinai and for sites in Egypt. En route from Jerusalem,

they stopped at Gaza and were so taken with the city that the writer of the account eulogized it in these words: "Gaza is a magnificent city, delightful; its inhabitants are most respectful, distinguished in every way by their friendliness, and love for people from foreign parts" (*Gaza autem civitas splendida, homines honestissimi omni liberalitate decori, amatores perigrinorum. CCSL* 175: 145).[3]

Without the experiences of pilgrims like these, it is doubtful that the name of Gaza would have been ranked with the highly touted vintages of Falernum in Italy and Chios in the Aegean. And it is not far-fetched to suggest that the same ships that carried pilgrims to their home ports also carried cargoes of Gaza wine. Be that as it may, *vinum Gazetum* became during the 5th and 6th centuries—and not earlier—a *topos* for poets such as Sidonius Apollonaris, Corippus and Venantius Fortunatus, as well as a symbol of quality for such influential writers as Gregory of Tours and Cassiodorus. With the Muslim occupation of Palestine in the 7th century and the consequent Islamic prohibition against the drinking of wine, we hear no more about the once-renowned vintage of Gaza; nor is anything further known about viticulture of Elusa and the other towns of the Negev.

NOTES

[1]To the evidence must be added the kilometer upon kilometer of stone heaps found on the slopes in the agricultural belt of the Negev. The Bedouin call them *tuleilāt el-ᶜanab* or *rujūm el-kurūm* (vine heaps). The function of these heaps has been the subject of much debate. This writer has maintained that they are properly named: the heaps of stone, found singly or in long rows, are the remains of up-castings, i.e., the remains of holes or furrows dug into the slopes in which vines were planted and which provided small catchment basins for runoff and other operations associated with viticulture. With the abandonment of the region, the holes and furrows filled up, leaving only the heaps in patterns which, when viewed on aerial photographs, are identical with those of active vineyards in other areas.

An opposing view suggests an unparalleled agricultural practice. It maintains that the stone heaps resulted from stripping the slopes to expose the soil to the crusting effects of rain to make more effective the flow of runoff into the terraced wadi beds below. If the Bedouin tradition is correct, here is the material evidence for the vast fields of vines that were cultivated in the Negev during the Byzantine period. (See P. Mayerson, [1962:

249–57], and M. Evanari *et al.* [1982: 127–47]).

Mention must also be made of the papyrological documents of the 6th and 7th centuries that were discovered in the process of excavating two churches on a high hill overlooking the ancient town of Nessana. Many deal with properties given over to agriculture, with vineyards prominent among them. One document, P. Colt 34, mentions a vineyard furnished with stakes or props and newly set out. For a summary of the documents relating to agriculture, see Mayerson (1962: 259–62).

[2]In fairly recent times, interestingly enough, "Gaza barley," famous as a malting barley, came to Gaza from the Bedouin farmers of the Negev (Lowe, 1944: 32).

[3]The sites shown the pilgrims on their way from Jerusalem to Gaza via Eleutheropolis were mainly those connected with Old Testament personalities: David and Goliath, Samson, Zechariah, Abraham, and Jacob. At Ascalon they were shown the tomb of the three martyred brothers who were called "The Egyptians"; at Maioumas, the tomb of the martyr Victor; and a short distance from Gaza, the tomb of Hilarion. (See also Mayerson 1982: 44–57.)

BIBLIOGRAPHY

CCSL
175   *Antonini Placentini Itinerarium* in *Corpus Christianorum, Series Latina,* Vol. 175.

Dothan, T.
1978   Deir el Balah 1977–1978. *Israel Exploration Journal* 28: 266–67.
1981   Deir el Balah 1979, 1980. *Israel Exploration Journal* 31: 126–31.

Evanari, E. *et al.*
1982   *The Negev: The Challenge of the Desert.* Cambridge, MA: Harvard.

Garzya, A. and Loenertz, R-J., eds.
1963   *Procopii Gazae Epistolae et Declamationes* in *Studia Patristica et Byzantina,* Vol. 9.

Heichelheim, F. M., ed.
1938   *An Economic Survey of the Ancient World.* Vol. 4. Baltimore: Johns Hopkins.

Lowe, B. A.
1944   "Dry Farming in the Beersheba District of Palestine." P. 32 in *Middle East Supply Centre Agricultural Report No. 6.* Cairo.

Mayerson, P.
1962   "The Ancient Agricultural Regime at Nessana and the Central Negeb." Pp. 249–57 in *Excavations at Nessana,* Vol. 1, ed. H. D. Colt. London: British School of Archaeology in Jerusalem.
1982   The Pilgrim Routes to Mount Sinai and the Armenians. *Israel Exploration Journal* 32: 44–57.
1983   The City of Elusa in the Literary Sources of the Fourth–Sixth Centuries. *Israel Exploration Journal* 33: 247–53.

Mazor, G.
1981   Wine Presses in the Negev. *Qadmoniot* 14: 51–60 (Hebrew).

PL$_{23}$ *Vita S. Hilarionis,* in *Patrologia Latina,* J-P Migne, ed. Vol. 23.

Raage, R., ed.
1895   *Petrus der Iberer.* Leipzig: J. C. Hinrichs'sche Buchhandlung.

Rougé, J., ed.
1966   *Expositio Totius Mundi et Gentium* in *Sources Chrétiennes,* Vol. 124. Paris.

Soc. Phil. Bonn. Sod.
1895   Societatis Philologae Bonnensis Sodales, eds., *Marci Diaconi Vita Porphyrii Episcopi Gazensis.* Leipzig: Teubner.

Sperber, D.
1975   *Agrarian Life in Roman Palestine I,* in *Aufstieg und Niedergang der Römischen Welt.* Vol. 2.8. Berlin: Walther de Gruyter.

NEA ARABIA (P.OXY. 3574): AN ADDENDUM TO ZPE 53

In my article in *ZPE* 53 (1983), pp.251-258 "P.Oxy.3574: Eleutheropolis of the New Arabia," I took exception to the position held by T. Barnes and G.W. Bowersock that Nea Arabia of P.Oxy.3574 occupied the space of the Egyptian nome Arabia and that Eleutheropolis is an unknown city there. I sought to establish — on the principle of the *lectio difficilior* — that Eleutheropolis was the well known city in Palestine and that Nea Arabia corresponded to the region previously known as Idumea and the Palestinian portion of Arabia Petraea.

In *ZPE* 56 (1984), pp.221-222, G.W. Bowersock took issue with my statement (p.255) that "in early times (Idumea) was inhabited by Edomite Arabs, and it continued to be occupied by people of Arab stock." Edomites, he states, were not Arabs, and that I was the first serious scholar to call them Arabs. Secondly, that the region extending into the Negev could not have been called New Arabia since "no province of the Roman or Byzantine Empire received its name without reference to local traditions of the nomenclature of people or places." These two statements I believe represent the essence of Bowersock's objections to the evidence I had cited in favor of considering Eleutheropolis as the well known city in Palestine, and Nea Arabia as having been carved out of the region formerly known as Idumea and its extension southwards into Palestinian Arabia.[1]

As to the first objection, I wish to respond only by saying that scholars more serious than myself — *e.g.*, M. Avi-Yonah and I. Shahid[2] — have considered Idumaeans as Arabs. In fact, G.W. Bowersock, in a private communication, now refers me to Uranius, the geographical author of the third or fourth centuries A.D. (J.M.I. West, *HSCP* 78 [1974] 282-284) who, according to Stephanus of Byzantium, is said to have written that the Idumeans (Ἐδουμαῖοι) were an ἔθνος Ἀράβιον (FGH IV 525, fr.22). This confirms my conclusion from the second-century geographer Ptolemy who in his description of the extent of Idumea includes three sites in Palestinian Arabia Petraea (*i.e.*, the Negev); and in his description of Arabia Petraea, he names six other sites in Palestinian Arabia Petraea. I believe it would be reasonable to call the inhabitants of these

1) In *ZPE* 56 (1984) p. 224, n. 4, I have also taken issue with Bowersock's statement in his *Roman Arabia* (p. 146) that Eleutheropolis "lay far outside the confines of Old Arabia and its successor province. It belonged to Palaestina Prima." I replied, among other things, that so far as I knew there was no evidence that Palaestina Prima existed as a province as early as 313-318.

2) M. Avi-Yonah, *The Holy Land; A Historical Geography* (Grand Rapids, Mich., 1966), 25-26, 61-62, 65; I. Shahid, *Rome and the Arabs. Prolegomena to the Study of Byzantium and the Arabs* (Dumbarton Oaks 1984), pp. xxi 13, 61 n., 96 n., 153.

towns Arabs.[3)]

I may add an additional note on the physical description of Idumea of a date somewhat later than P.Oxy.3574. Jerome (*c.* 347 - *c.* 420), in his commentary on *Obadiah* 5.6 and Jeremiah 49.9-10 (*CCL* 76, pp.359/60), has this to say concerning the Idumea of Esau: *omnis australis regio Idumaeorum de Eleutheropoli usque Petram et Ailam, haec est enim possessio Esau.* Jerome's statement, taken together with Ptolemy's, proves, conclusively I believe, that what had been known of Idumea in the first century B.C. as a region bordering on Beersheba to the south, was viewed in the second and fourth centuries A.D. as extending deep into the region known as Arabia — "from Eleutheropolis all way to Petra and Aila" — the Arabia that embraced both Palestine and Transjordan.

The preceding discussion answers, implicitly, the objections concerning the nomenclature of both people (or at least, part of the people [cf. n.3]) and the tradition that justified naming the new province Nea Arabia.[4)] That portion of Nea Arabia that encompassed first-century B.C. Idumea lay cheek by jowl to "Old" Arabia; the remaining portion had already been part and parcel of the province of Arabia. Its people in the second and fourth centuries A.D. — at least those in places cited by Ptolemy (Birsama, Elusa, and Mampsis) and by Jerome (Petra and Aila) were certainly Arabs. I therefore believe that the weight of evidence makes southern Palestine the more reasonable choice for "Eleutheropolis of Nea Arabia" than the former Egyptian nome of Arabia.

New York University   Philip Mayerson

---

3) The present argument concerns the question of how the region of Idumea, and the people who inhabited it, were seen at a later date. Their ethnic origin as close kin to the Hebrews (*Genesis'* Esau/Edom; cf. Strabo 16, 2, 34: Idumaeans as Nabataeans who, after an unsuccessful sedition, joined the Judaeans and shared their customs) and the mixed stocks of people in the area (Egyptian, Arabian, and Phoenician tribes according to Strabo) need no discussion in the present context. Admittedly, my reference to "early times" (p. 255) was misleading.

4) G.W. Bowersock, *ZPE* 56 (1984) 221 concedes that the new province could have been named "Νέα 'Αραβεία" if it had been inhabited by Edomite Arabs.

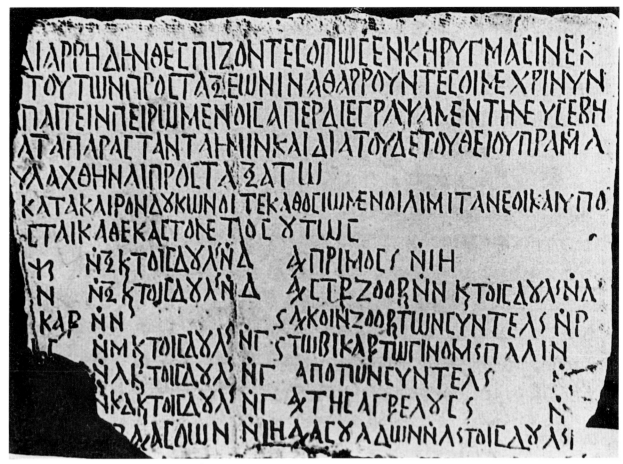

Pl. 17. The "Beersheba" inscription.

THE BEERSHEBA EDICT

During the opening decade of the twentieth century, four fragmentary inscriptions of the Byzantine period were purchased or otherwise fell into the
hands of members of the Palestine Exploration Fund and the École biblique.
One was acquired from an old Arab known for his clandestine excavations;[1]
one from an undeclared source;[2] another from the ruins of a town (Byzantine
Beersheba?) east-north-east of the new town of Beersheba;[3] and yet another
presumbly from the same site.[4] These four inscriptions have been given their
most definitive editing to date by A. Alt.[5] Since they appear to be fragments of one or more imperial rescripts, Alt placed them under the rubric of
"Amtliche Publicationen" and numbered them one to four. He also observed,
from place names that have been preserved or reasonably restored, that Inscr.
1 and 2 have to do exclusively with Palaestina Tertia (pp.7,9-10). Inscr. 3,
an additional fragment of which turned up at a later date,[6] mentions sites
in Palaestina Prima, Secunda and Tertia, as does Inscr. 4.

Inscr. 1 contains a portion of an imperial edict and a schedule of annual
payments in terms of solidi (νομίϲματα). Lacking as it does the name of the
emperor issuing the edict and the official to whom it was addressed, the inscription deprives us not only of the date of the rescript, but also of a
clear understanding of the purpose for the schedule of payments. The payments
are listed by towns in a formula of X number of solidi "from" (ἀπό) town Y
and X number of solidi "for" (ὑπέρ) certain personnel called δοῦλοι. After a
group of towns, a sum of solidi was designated for a Vicarius. Apart from
these amounts we do not know the recipient of the sums allocated to each town.
Inscr. 2, unlike 1, lacks any portion of an edict. It is a list of 18 towns
in trans-Jordanian Palaestina Tertia that follows the above formula with the
exception that no sum is indicated for a Vicarius. Inscr. 3, together with
the added fragment, lists sums allocated to towns and sums for δοῦλοι and a
Vicarius. Inscr. 4 contains no sums of solidi; it records a Vicarius of Palaestina Secunda, a κοινὸν ἀρχιφύλων, ϲυντελεϲταί, and place names in the three

---

1) F.-M. Abel, *Revue biblique*, 1909, 89; cf. B.W. Robinson, *AJA* 12 (1908) 343.

2) M.I. Clermont-Ganneau, *Revue biblique*, 1906, 412.

3) R.A. Stewart Macalister, *Palestine Exploration Fund Quarterly Statement*, 1902, 236.

4) M.I. Clermont-Ganneau, *Revue biblique*, 1906, 86-90.

5) "Die griechischen Inschriften der Palaestina Tertia westlich der Araba" in *Wissenschaftliche Veröffentlichungen des Deutsch-Türkischen Denkmalschutz-Kommandos* II (Berlin and Leipzig), 4-13.

6) F.C. Burkitt, *Palestine Exploration Fund Quarterly Statement*, 1920, 19-20. F.-M. Abel,
Revue biblique, 1920, 260-265; A. Alt, *Zeitschrift des Deutschen Palästina-Vereins* 46 (1923)
52-55; *SEG* VIII 282.

Palestines.

Setting aside for the moment any speculation regarding the purpose of the schedule of payments, we are on surer ground in examining the amounts in Inscr. 1 and 2 to see what they mean in real terms — in terms of the purchasing power of the solidus — and thereby gain a more meaningful understanding of the magnitude of the obligation imposed on the communities of Palaestina Tertia. For this purpose we turn to the Nessana papyri which are nearest in time and place to the above two inscriptions. Nessana, a town of Palaestina Tertia, 32 miles southwest of Beersheba, on the route to Aila and Mount Sinai, was active — a better word for this desert town than flourished — in sixth and seventh centuries. The documents discovered during the course of excavation of the site provide us with the prices of such commodities as wheat and oil, camels, donkeys, and slaves.

> 1 solidus was the *adaeratio* rate for 15 modii of wheat and 15 sextarii of oil = 4 US bushels of wheat and 4 gallons of oil (*P.Ness*.III 64, 65, 69);
>
> 3 solidi purchased a slave girl (*P.Ness*. III 89);
>
> 6 solidi purchased a slave boy (*P.Ness*. III 89);
>
> 5 solidi was the average price of a camel (*P.Ness*. III 89);
>
> 2 1/3 - 5 1/3 solidi for a she-donkey (*P.Ness*. III 89);
>
> 3 1/2 solidi for a Saracen guide to the Holy Mountain (*P.Ness*.III 89).

Other amounts given in the Nessana documents provide some additional perspective on the magnitude of the taxes cited in the two schedules: *P.Ness*. 33 - the return of betrothal gifts of 15 gold solidi and women's jewelry valued at 15 gold solidi; *P.Ness*. 36 - amounts ranging from 91 to 3 solidi in a military account; *P.Ness*. 56 - 30 solidi to secure the release from an indenture of general services; *P.Ness*. 58 - 37 1/2 solidi for a land survey.

To return to Inscr. 1, the annual assessments in column II, omitting the 50 solidi for the Vicarius and the small sums for the δοῦλοι, are 60, 40, 30, 20, and 100; in column III 18, and then 50 from the soldiers (cτρατιωτῶν) of Zoara and 100 from the association of tax collectors of Zoara (κοιν[οῦ] --- τῶν cυντελ[εcτῶν]). In Inscr. 2, the amounts associated with the names of 16 of the 18 communities are 65, 43, 32, 24, 15, 42, 30, 24, 15, 15, 15, 15, 15, 12, 5, and 20 solidi. The sums allocated for the δοῦλοι have not survived.

For the purposes of comparison with the Nessana papyri, the largest figure of 100 solidi which is assessed to Zoara would be sufficient to purchase 1500 modii of wheat and 1500 sextarii of oil. Zoara, however, is amply supplied with perennial water and probably was the most fertile and productive site in Palaestina Tertia (Abel, *loc. cit.* [n.1], 100-101). Nessana, situated in a region less fertile than Zoara by far, produced in one area alone (Birein) 1780 modii of wheat (*P.Ness*. III 84).[7] The remaining amounts, excluding the two

---

7) Since it is likely that Nessana's name occupied one of the lacunae in Inscr. 1, it would have had a considerably smaller assessment than that of Zoara.

connected with Zoara, are considerably smaller, and in terms of purchasing power could buy anywhere from 3 to 8 camels, and from 270 to 600 modii and sextarii of wheat and oil. The same observation would apply to Inscr. 2. The two largest sums, 65 and 43 solidi, are connected with Adrou and Auara (modern Humayma) respectively, both of which have good supplies of water and give evidence of having supported substantial populations.[8] Robatha, with an assessment of 42 solidi, has not been securely identified. The remaining sums, 30 to 5, fall short of these three communities. We would have to conclude, judging alone from the value of the solidus in the Nessana papyri, that the annual assessments indicated in these two inscriptions are modest and certainly not excessive.

Returning to the more difficult question of the specific purpose of the tax, and for whom it was designated, we note that the preserved portion of the *forma* preceding the *notitia* reads] κατὰ καιρὸν δουκῶν οἵ τε καθοσιωμένοι λιμιτάνεοι καὶ ἀπο[τεταγμένοι --- συντελε]σταί, presumably indicating those who are to pay the amounts listed in the *notitia* "year by year as follows:" Abel has restored οἱ δοῦλοι to precede δουκῶν in the lacuna;[9] Alt, on the other hand, has not attempted to fill it. I would suggest [οἱ στρατιῶται τῶν] --- δουκῶν; that is, the field troops (*comitatenses* or *pseudocomitatenses*) under the command of the *dux* as distinguished from the frontier troops (*limitanei*).[10] It is clear from the citation for Zoara that the στρατιῶται and the συντελεσταί are two distinct tax-paying classes. Zoara, as we learn from Eusebius, had a garrison of soldiers (Φρούριον στρατιωτῶν)[11] and the *Notitia dignatatum* records that a cavalry unit (*Equites sagittarii indigenae*) was stationed at the site at the opening of the fifth century.[12] The inscription also mentions an "outpost" (ἀγράρεα) of Elusa, most likely a unit of στρατιῶται, stationed outside the town.[13] The sum for Elusa itself is undoubtedly in the missing portion of the inscription. We can only assume that these two towns, both of which were on important road systems of Palaestina Tertia, had military units posted in installations *extra muros*, and, like the inhabitants of Zoara and

---

8) R.E. Brünnow and A. von Domaszewski, *Die Provincia Arabia* I (Straßburg 1904) 462; J.W. Eadie and J.P. Oleson, "The Watersupply Systems of Nabataean and Roman Humayma," *BASOR* (forthcoming).

9) Abel, (*loc. cit.* n.1), 91; he held (p. 95) that the *dux*, his *officium* and the *limitanei* "reçoivent l'annone et que les provinciaux la paient chaque année suivant le tariff annexé au présent décret."

10) A.H.M. Jones, *The Later Roman Empire* II (Oxford 1964) 665. In the Nessana papyri, the *numerus* of the Very Loyal (καθωσιωμένων) Theodosians are cited as στρατιῶται. According to C.J. Kraemer (*P.Ness.* III p. 22), they are both *limitanei* and "regulars" as well as tax payers. Jones (III, p. 202, fn. 111) considers the unit to be *pseudocomitatenses* "no doubt the Balistarii Theodosiaci of the Eastern field army (*Not. Dig. Or.* VII 57)."

11) *Das Onomastikon der biblischen Ortsnamen*, E. Klostermann, ed. (Leipzig 1904), p. 42.

12) *Notitia Dignitatum Orientis*, O. Seeck, ed. (Berlin 1876), p. 73.

13) Cf. Ammianus 14.3.2: *Mesopotamiae tractus praetenturis et stationibus servantur agrariis...*

Elusa, were subject to the tax. If these assumptions are reasonable, Inscr. 1
cites three taxable classes: the military regulars, the settled frontier militia, and the general population. And where a community did not have a unit
of the first two classes, or that for tax purposes the *limitanei* were considered part of the general population, the schedule cited one amount, as in the
case of Mampsis, Asoa, and Asouada,[14] there being no need to distinguish between one class and another.

Inscr. 2, when compared to 1, is less complex. No part of its *forma* has survived, but its original edge is preserved on the left, and on the top and
bottom. The right portion is lost, as are the amounts assessed for the δοῦλοι.
Whether the columns of the lost portion contained assessments to be paid by
the ϲτρατιῶται and ϲυντελεϲταί, as in 1, is of course not known. Inscr. 2, unlike 1, 3 and 4, also does not preserve an assessment for a Vicarius. It
should be noted, however, that of the 18 place names in Inscr. 2, ten are
known from the *Notitia Dignitatum* (Auara, Zadakatha, Ammatha, Ariddela, Sobeia,
Robatha, Aphro, Sirtha=Cartha? Toloana, Praesidio [pp.73-74]); one (Adrou) was
the site of a legionary camp of the time of Trajan or Diocletian;[15] two according to Eusebius, had a φρούριον (Karkaria, Thomara=Thamara [*Onom. bibl.*
Ortsn. (n.11) pp.116 and 8]); and five are not known to have had any military
installation (Ellebena, Phaino, Eiseiba, Moa, and Ainautha). Although a century or more may separate the *Notitia* and Eusebius from the time of Inscr. 2,
there can be little doubt that the greater majority of these sites represented
the eastern frontier of Palaestina Tertia and were manned by *limitanei* who were
taxable subjects along the non-military population.

The issue at hand, once more, is the purpose of the tax and the recipient
of the assessments. The epigraphical material and imperial legistation cited
by Abel and Alt (e.g., Waddington 1906a = *SEG* IX 356; *PAES* IIIA, no.20; *C.J.*
1.27) as bearing on the missing portions of the *forma* of Inscr. 1 have lead
them to view the assessments as subsistence requisitions for the army (*annona*
militaris) converted into money. Alt, taking his lead from Abel (*loc. cit.* [n.1],
pp.92 and 96), interprets Inscr. 1 — his interpretation also applies to the
other three inscriptions — as being concerned with three taxes (*loc. cit.* [n.
5], p.7): "first, the main tax, not otherwise identified, which is collected
everywhere, the old *annona militaris* for the imperial army and the civil service,
now converted into money. Then a surtax for the δοῦλοι, which probably
means the civil service of the provincial authorities, collected only where
the main tax reaches a certain level and increasing proportionally with it;
and finally, a special tax for the Vicarius, perhaps the governor of Palaesti-

---

14) The *Notitia Dignitatum* (n. 12), p. 73 lists a frontier unit at this site, the *ala*
prima miliaria Sebastena.

15) A. Killick, *Levant* 15 (1983) 125. S. Thomas Parker, in a forthcoming publication,
holds that the camp should be dated to the time of Diocletian.

na Tertia, limited to groups of taxable subjects particularly able to pay. The various items are presumably combined into appropriate groups relative to the administrative system, the level of the tax amounts determining the order."

We are here at the heart of the issue. Does the edict, as Abel and Alt believe, represent assessments on behalf of the *annona militaris*? And are the inscriptions and imperial legislation that they cite as parallels relevant for an understanding of the assessments contained in the several *notitiae* of the Beersheba inscriptions? With respect to the latter question, Waddington 1906a, *PAES* IIIA. 20, and *C.J.*1.27 have no relevance for the Beersheba *notitiae*; they are concerned with the rights and duties of provincial officials and with the regulation of payments, in terms of *annona* and *capitum* (fodder ration), for the military and civil service. The Beersheba inscriptions, unlike any of the above, simply list assessments community by community;[16] there is no indication of *annona* or *caput* nor of the regulation of officials. In this respect they are quite different from all other epigraphical material or imperial ordinances that have come to hand. And since it appears that the στρατιῶται and *limitanei* were taxable, it would be strange indeed to find them taxed for their own rations. As to the annual assessments themselves, apart from their limited purchasing power mentioned above, they could not support a *cohors* or *ala* of frontier troops. In Egypt, the value of the *annona* is estimated at 12 solidi;[17] in North Africa, Justinian established the *adaeratio* value of the *annona* at 5 solidi and 4 solidi per unit of capitum.[18] At this latter rate, a military unit of 500 men would require 500 *annonae* and 500 *capita* converted into 4500 solidi. If we were to take all the assessments preserved in Inscr. 1, 2, and 3 — excluding the sums for the Vicarii and the δοῦλοι — and double, treble or quadruple them, they would only amount to some 2500, 3800, or 5100 solidi. If we are to examine some of the smaller sums in Inscr. 2, they are, in terms of *annona* and *caput*, not very compelling: an assessment of 5 solidi for Thomara (Thamara), 12 solidi for Praesidio, 15 solidi for Karkaria, Phaeno, Moa, Tolana and Eiseiba, and 24 solidi for Ammatha, Aphro and Sirtha. As mentioned above, Thamara was the site of a military installation, and Praesidio, Toloana, Ammatha and Sirtha are cited in the *Notitia dignitatum* as having either an *ala* or a *cohors*. Phaeno, a center for the mining of copper, was a town of some size with several churches or monasteries.

It is a specific action taken by Justinian in A.D. 536 that I believe relates more directly to all aspects of the Beersheba inscription, including

16) C.J. Kraemer views *P.Ness.*III 39 (pp. 122-124), an account of allotments by Villages of Palaestina Prima and Tertia, as having some relationship with the Beersheba Edict and the *annona militaris* suggested by Alt. However, major differences between the two documents compelled the editor of the papyrus to leave the question of the relationship unanswered.

17) A.C. Johnson and L.C. West, *Byzantine Egypt: Economic Studies* (Princeton 1949) 226-227.

18) *Ibid.*, 227. *C.J.* 1.27.1, par. 22ff.

the Vicarii and the δοῦλοι. In Novel 103, Justinian ordered a sweeping change in the power structure of Palestine. He decreed that the governor of Palaestina Prima be given the title of Proconsul with the rank of spectabile (περί-βλεπτος). He was to hear appeals in cases not exceeding 10 lbs. of gold (720 solidi) in value "from each of the Palestines" (ἐξ ἑκατέρας Παλαιστίνης). He was to have a large number of soldiers at his disposal. His salary or subsistence allowance (κατὰ δὲ σιτήσεων πρόφασιν) was to be 22 lbs. of gold (1584 solidi) which he was to divide between himself, his assessor, and the loyal members of his staff (τὴν πειθομένην αὐτῷ τάξιν). The Proconsul was to notify the emperor of how the sum of 22 lbs. of gold was to be distributed so that he could confirm the arrangement with an imperial mandate.[19]

The Novel goes on to state (*caput II*) that the *dux* of Palestine (ὁ κατὰ καιρὸν περίβλεπτος τῶν τόπων δούξ) was not to have anything to do with civil cases or with the collection of taxes. The Proconsul was to maintain order in the cities and see that no violent disturbances took place there because of differences in religious worship. "And if it becomes necessary for him to visit Palaestina Secunda for the purpose of suppressing disorder, he is not to yield nor do anything untoward there, especially in that province since we know that widespread disturbances exist there, the results of which are no small matter."

In the event of need (*caput III*), the Proconsul could coopt soldiers stationed in the province, and the *dux* was prohibited from depriving the Proconsul of the military authority conferred upon him. The *dux* was to be in command of the *limitanei*, the *foederati*, and the entire body of soldiery in the province with the exception of those allotted to the service of the Proconsul. In matters relating to public taxes and incitment against legal authority, the Proconsul was to have undisputed authority.

A companion piece to Novel 103, and of the same date, is Novel 102. In language expressing concern over the internal stability of the province of Arabia — oddly enough consistently called "the land of the Arabs" (ἡ Ἀράβων χώρα) in the text — Justinian ordered a reorganization of authority within the province. His mandate traces the causes of the difficulties to the weakness of civil authority and to the fact that for a long period of time there was no civil authority. It was the military (ἡ στρατιωτική) that performed civil functions as well as its own, but it did so inefficiently and for its own profit. As a consequence the emperor mandated the installation of a governor with the title of Moderator and with the rank of *spectabile* so that he would in no way be inferior to the office of the *dux* (ἡ δουκική). The governor

---

19) It should be noted that two years after *C.J.* 1.27.1 no mention is made in this Novel of units of *annona* and *capitum* converted into solidi. Jones (op. cit. [n. 10]), p. 461 comments appropriately that Justinian "assigned salaries in solidi or pounds of gold to the new posts he created, but other salaries were still in his reign calculated according to the old rules."

was not to allow the *dux*, nor the phylarch (φύλαρχος), nor any other person of power and influence to inflict losses upon the taxpayers of the province. The Novel goes on to state that the governor was to see to it that taxes were duly collected and that the population of Bostra and other people did not take part in public uproars or incitements against legal authority. The governor was also to have soldiers under his command. He was granted an allowance (cίτηcιc) of 14 lbs. of gold (1008 solidi) and 2 lbs. of gold (144 solidi) for his assessor, and the same amount for his staff (τάξιc). The imperial mandate also called for soldiers to be stationed in the province subject to the command of the governor; the *dux* would have no control over them nor over any civilian. The governor and the *dux* were to keep themselves strictly within the limits of their authority.

The radical changes ordered by Justinian in the administration of the three Palestines also required financial adjustments to support the newly created office of Proconsul of Palestine. Novel 103 called upon the Proconsul to inform the emperor how the 22 lbs. of gold for cίτηcιc was to be distributed between himself, his assessor, and his staff so that payment could be authorized by imperial decree. There was yet another step to be taken over and above the allocation of the 22 lbs. of gold. Since the Proconsul was newly vested with certain judicial powers and with the command over a number of troops for purpose of maintaining peace and order within the three provinces that constituted Palestine, a request for additional funds was undoubtedly sent to the emperor accompanied by a *notitia* of assessments upon the communities of the three Palestines. In my view, the Beersheba Edict is the imperial decree of Justinian approving the assessments and commiting the communities throughout the Palestines to make annual payments in support of the office of the Proconsul. It was in effect an extraordinary tax. The publication of the decree, a copy of which reached Beersheba — or Elusa, an administrative center of Palestina Tertia[20] — was carved in stone and displayed in a public place. The fragments that were found in or near Beersheba need not be, as Alt maintained, pieces of different edicts;[21] they may be part of one decree that gave imperial approval of assessments throughout the several Palestines

---

20) Alt (*loc. cit.* [n. 7], p. 51, fn. 1) citing *Nea Sion* 12 (1920) 127, notes that a certain Greek physician had copied numerous inscriptions at the ancient site of Elusa but that they had never been published. It is quite possible that the inscriptions had made their way to Beersheba where they were ultimately discovered or sold.

21) Alt (*loc. cit.* [n. 5], p. 9) comes to this conclusion on the basis of various differences, palaeographic and stylistic, between Inscr. 1 and 2, although he admits that different sections of the inscription could have been assigned to different stonemasons. He concludes: "Once a beginning had been made in Bir es-Seba' to publish imperial edicts in stone, new inscriptions would have had to replace old ones as soon as they were invalidated by new edicts." It is difficult for me to see assessments community by community to be carved into stone on the occasion of every new imperial edict. It is far more likely such assessments were communicated on papyrus, an example of which we find in *P.Ness.* 39. The fragments that comprise the Beersheba Edict represent, in my view, a consequence of Justinian's Novel 103.

to provide for the newly appointed office of Proconsul.

With Novel 103 in mind, the sums designated for the Vicarii and their role in the provincial organization become more understandable. Contrary to the view suggested by Alt in connection with Inscr. 1, the Vicarius was not the governor of Palaestina Tertia. The new powers granted the Proconsul required representatives to exercise his authority and to carry out his orders in the several provinces of Palestine. These would be the Vicarii. It is of no small significance that Inscr. 4 specifically mentions a Vicarius of Palaestina Secunda, the very province that Justinian cited as being exceptionally disorderly. The Vicarii, in addition to performing other duties in the name of the Proconsul, undoubtedly commanded the troops that were under the control of the Proconsul. Hence, the money designated for the several Vicarii was needed to support them and their offices as vicars of the Proconsul of Palestine.

As to the small assessments allocated for δοῦλοι, these must be taken as providing support for certain personnel of the Proconsul who did not fall into the officially designated titles for provincial staff positions. A year prior to Novel 103, in A.D. 535, Justinian issued Novel 8 which prescribed salaries or perquisites (cυνήθειαι) for various officials who served bureaucratic functions under provincial governors. In the three Palestines, each governor (ἄρχων) was to pay a total of 63 solidi for 3 chartularii, a Primicerius of the tribuni notarii and his adjutant, and for the bureau of prefects. The δοῦλοι of the Beersheba Edict, on the other hand, should be considered part of the enlarged *officium* of the newly appointed Proconsul as "aides" or even more literally as "servants."[22]

In essence, the Beersheba Edict, as I see it, is an extraordinary tax placed upon the communities of the three provinces comprising Palestine following Justinian's reorganization of the power structure within the region as detailed by Novel 103. The creation of a Proconsul of Palestine with civil and military responsibilities within the three provinces, required the additional personnel — Vicarii and δοῦλοι — indicated in the inscription. I believe the edict was issued to provide the support for the enlarged *officium* of the Proconsul. Accordingly I would date the Beersheba Edict to A.D. 536 or very shortly thereafter.

New York University   Philip Mayerson

---

22) The precise function of the δοῦλοι is unclear. I have found no citation for them as members of the civil service. Various dictionaries have not been helpful; only Lampe's *Patristic Lex*. has an entry that would bear upon the meaning in the context of the inscription (*s. v.* δοῦλος, A 2): "of imperial officials as δ. of emperor *CG-Cl* 1.1 (Corinth 527–565)." However, *CG-Cl* 1.1 is a lauditory inscription, presumably by an official of Justinian, and the words πιcτὸν αὐτοῦ δοῦλον mean little more than "his (Justinian's) faithful servant" (cf. Preisigke, *Wörterb*. I and IV *s.v.*). Cf. the archaic "Yours faithfully" or "Your faithful and obedient servant."

Choricius of Gaza on the Watersupply System of Caesarea

THE major watersupply system of Caesarea Maritima consisted of two aqueducts — dubbed the high-level and low-level aqueducts by Conder and Kitchener[1] — and has been the subject of considerable archaeological investigation. The field reports have focussed on the sources of supply, methods of construction and repair, and on several inscriptions.[2] The high-level aqueduct is composed of two channels, which are fed by the Shumi springs some 8 km. from Caesarea and by the springs in the 'Ammiqam-Avi'el area, about 7.5 km. to the north-east of those at Shumi. By tunnel and channel, water flowed south to the city over a distance of 12 km. The low-level aqueduct took its waters from the Zerqa River (Naḥal Tanninim) and its sources, and ran some 5 km. to Caesarea. In the absence of literary sources — Josephus (*Ant.* xv.331) describes the city's sewer system but makes no mention of the aqueducts — the dating of the initial construction of the watersupply rests on the assumption that it was constructed at the time that Herod undertook to build a new town on the site of Strato's Tower. Hence, the eastern channel of the high-level aqueduct is thought to have been built at the end of the first century B.C.E. or the beginning of the first century C.E.; the western channel a short time later,[3] or according to another view, during the reign of Hadrian.[4] The date of the construction of the low-level aqueduct is not known. From epigraphic evidence, it appears that the western channel was repaired in the second century by units of the Legio II Traiana Fortis and by the Legio X Fretensis,[5] and the 'double aqueduct' (τὰ δύο ὑδραγώγια) by the end of the

---

[1]   C.R. Conder and H.M. Kitchener: *The Survey of Western Palestine*, II, London, 1882, pp. 18–23.

[2]   A. Reifenberg: Caesarea — A Study in the Decline of a Town, *IEJ* 1 (1950–51), pp. 26–29; H. Hamburger: A New Inscription from the Caesarea Aqueduct, *IEJ* 9 (1959), pp. 188–190; A. Negev: The High Level Aqueduct at Caesarea, *IEJ* 14 (1964), pp. 237–249; D. Barag: An Inscription from the High Level Aqueduct of Caesarea — Reconsidered, *IEJ* 14 (1964), pp. 250–252; A. Frova *et al.*: *Scavi di Caesarea Maritima*, Rome, 1966, pp. 274–275; A. Negev: A New Inscription from the High Level Aqueduct at Caesarea, *IEJ* 22 (1972), pp. 52–53; Y. Olami and J. Ringel: New Inscriptions of the Tenth Legion Fretensis from the High Level Aqueduct at Caesarea, *IEJ* 25 (1975), pp. 148–150; L.I. Levine: Roman Caesarea: An Archaeological-Topographical Study, *Qedem* 2 (1975), pp. 30–36; Y. Olami and Y. Peleg: The Water Supply System of Caesarea Maritima, *IEJ* 27 (1977), pp. 126–137.

[3]   Negev (above, n. 2, 1964), p. 249.

[4]   Olami and Peleg (above, n. 2), p. 136; see also Levine (above, n. 2), pp. 31–36.

[5]   Negev (above, n. 2, 1964), p. 249; Negev (above, n. 2, 1972), pp. 52–53.

fourth century.[6] Finally, citing Choricius of Gaza, it is believed that the aqueduct was repaired once more in the reign of the Emperor Justinian.[7] We shall consider this latter assumption here.

Choricius of Gaza (*fl.* 530), orator and teacher of rhetoric, provides us with the sole literary statement concerning the watersupply system of Caesarea. In his encomium to Stephanus, the governor of *Palaestina Prima*, dated to 534/6, he praises the steps taken by Stephanus to improve the supply of water to the city.[8] Abel cites several lines from Choricius in his brief report on Caesarea and his statement is repeated by Reifenberg;[9] Levine provides the passage in Greek and a translation of this text.[10]

A full account of Choricius' statement and its interpretation has, to my knowledge, never been published.[11] First a few facts about Stephanus' achievements should be given. In a highly rhetorical style characteristic of the period, Choricius informs us of the outstanding accomplishments of the governor of *Palaestina Prima*: he had a hand in suppressing the revolt of the Samaritans in 529; he checked a raid of Saracens entering his province from Egypt; he helped clear the roads of his province from brigands; he quelled rumours of famine in Caesarea; he suppressed political unrest arising out of factional disputes in the city; and he was generous in assisting Gaza in its extensive building programme.[12] Stephanus' reputation as an able administrator also came to the attention of the Emperor Justinian who, in his reorganization of Palestine in 536, raised him to the rank of proconsul, with an increase in stipend and staff and the added authority for the entire province of Palestine in the collection of taxes and in controlling civil disorder.[13] The work carried out by Stephanus on the watersupply system may not rank as his greatest achievement, but to Choricius it was one of a list of activities of an able administrator, and yet another opportunity for him to display his oratorical talent. After mentioning Stephanus' handling of the threat of famine in Caesarea, Choricius proceeds to the problem of the failing watersupply of the city.

44. As a counterbalance to what has been mentioned, I now come bringing forward another good deed of yours from the same city. Springs of clear and salubrious water — fifty *stadia* to the east, so I believe — meet one on his leaving the city. From that point a way (ὁδός) has been constructed

---

[6]   Hamburger (above, n. 2), pp. 189–190.

[7]   Reifenberg (above, n. 2), p. 27; Negev (above, n. 2, 1964), p. 249, n. 34.

[8]   R. Foerster and E. Richtsteig (eds.): *Choricii Gazaei Opera*, Leipzig, 1929, pp. 60–62, par. 44–49.

[9]   F.M Abel: *Géographie de la Palestine*, I, Paris, 1933, p. 449; Reifenberg (above, n. 2), p. 27.

[10]   Levine (above, n. 2), p. 31, n. 223.

[11]   Mention should be made of the unpublished dissertation of F.K. Litsas: *Choricius of Gaza: An Approach to his Work*, University of Chicago, Chicago, Illinois, 1980. For his treatment of the aqueducts of Caesarea, see pp. 166–167, 263–265.

[12]   *Choricii Gazae Opera* (above, n. 8), pp. 51–52, par. 10–13; pp. 57–60, par. 33–43; p. 64, par. 60–62.

[13]   *Ibid.*, pp. 63–64, par. 57–59; R. Schoell and G. Kroll (eds.): *Corpus Juris Civilis (Novellae)*, III, Berlin, 1895, pp. 496–499. See also P. Mayerson: Justinian's Novel 103 and the Reorganizations of Palestine, *BASOR* (forthcoming).

conducting the gift of the springs to the city by means of public fountains that have been built to receive the water. 45. Such things need to have very frequent care; consequently, since there was neglect, there was no longer as unhindered (ἀκώλυτος) a passage (πόρος) for the flowing water as before, but the movement of the water (ὑδάτων φορά) was checked (προσέπταιεν) in many places and the water flowed slower than usual. As a result, it came about that it passed by some fountains made idle by the lack of water, and the drawing of water from others yielded less than was needed. And what is more, men in the prime of life were in fierce competition with those who were pushing one another in their wish to draw water. 46. At any rate, women, old men, and children came back, some with empty vessels; for some a great struggle produced half-filled ones to carry away, while many children went off crying because their vessels had broken. 47. As a consequence, with the lack of water increasing the desire for it, and with the desire making the scarcity of it even greater, and with both elements helping to increase each other, the evil was unbearable on all sides. 48. And at that time, someone given to poetry would have said that Caesarea was 'a much thirsting city', although Argos — for the poets call it so — made its inhabitants blameless since it had a natural lack of water; but for the people of Caesarea, the springs kept flowing as a reproach to their neglect, and consequently it induced a despair more galling. For pleasant things are not as distressful when they are out of sight, as they are when seen and people are not able to enjoy them. 49. Who then is the one who delivered us from this misfortune? Who is the one who opened and freed the way (ὁδός) for the flowing water and eliminated those old hindrances (κωλύματα) with workers skilled in such matters? Who is the one who added still more fountains, since the rush of flowing water is superior to the former amount? They know who have the experience of it![14]

From Choricius' description, the springs he refers to as being about 50 *stadia* (9 km.) east of Caesarea are the Shumi springs, and the aqueduct must therefore be the high-level aqueduct. Choricius praises Stephanus for removing obstacles that prevented the free flow of water from the springs to the public fountains in Caesarea. No doubt these obstacles were caused by the accumulation of debris — sediments of various kinds, living and decaying vegetation, garbage — which, if not cleared periodically, would reduce the flow of water in the tunnels and channels leading from the springs to the public fountains. One other impediment to the free flow of water may have been illegal and surreptitious tapping of water for irrigation or private use.[15] The action of the governor was purely one of maintenance.

It is surprising that Stephanus employed skilled workers to clear away obstructions in the aqueduct that had accumulated over a period of time. Apparently this critical work had been neglected by previous governors — a neglect that Stephanus undertook to remedy. But what of the legal obligations imposed on certain inhabitants to perform such public services? An edict in the Theodosian Code (15.2.1), retained in the Justinian Code (11.23.1), imposes such service upon 'landholders over whose lands aqueducts pass'. They were to be exempt from other liturgies 'so that by their work they may cleanse the aqueducts when they are choked

---

[14]   Above, n. 8. Translated by the present writer.

[15]   Cf. the several citations in the Theodosian Code (15.2.2–6 = Justinian Code 11.23.2–3) warning against this practice, which must have been widespread.

with dirt (*sodes* = dirt, trash, filth). The landholders... shall not be subject to other burdens of any superindiction lest they be occupied in other matters and should not be present to clean the aqueducts'.[16]

The obligation to perform such public service in Palestine during the sixth century is attested in a town in *Palaestina Tertia*, some 100 miles to the south-south-east of Caesarea. A number of ostraca, uncovered at the ancient town of Sobata (Shivta, Subeita), proved to be receipts certifying labour in a 'cistern' (κιστέρνα).[17] Sobata had two open-air reservoirs of considerable size that were undoubtedly for public use, and the obvious connection of the receipts is with the cleaning (i.e. periodically removing the accumulated sediment) or the repair of the reservoirs.

It should be noted that Choricius, probably for stylistic reasons, does not employ a single technical word commonly used to designate a device for the conveyance of water. Where one would expect to read ὑδραγώγιον for aqueduct or waterchannel — a word that appears in the fourth century inscription mentioned above, or in the Nessana papyri that are close in time to Choricius[18] — he uses such non-specific words as ὁδός and πόρος. In general, Choricius provides us with an impressionistic view of Stephanus' achievements in connection with his work on the watersupply system. As with other actions and events in his political career, details as specific as historians would like are not provided. Stephanus, according to Choricius' encomium, improved the watersupply system of Caesarea by maintenance work, clearing the high-level aqueduct's channels of obstructions. However, Choricius' statement does not support the attribution to Stephanus of the repairs and reconstructions observable in the field.

---

[16]   *The Theodosian Code*, trsl. by C. Pharr, Princeton, 1952, p. 430.
[17]   H.C. Youtie: Ostraca from Sbeitah, *AJA* 40 (1936), pp. 452–459.
[18]   C.J. Kraemer (ed.): *Excavations at Nessana: Non-Literary Papyri*, Princeton, 1958, pp. 98, 102.

The Saracens and the *Limes*

PHILIP MAYERSON
Department of Classics
New York University
New York, NY 10003

*Roman fortified positions (*limes*) on the eastern frontier and Saracen phylarchs serving as Roman allies have been under recent investigation. The question of whether the* limes *comprised a coordinated system of border garrisons is reviewed in terms of evidence from the western sector of Palaestina Tertia; the conclusions are applied to the eastern sector. Saracens both within and beyond the line of fortified positions, were a constant threat, and Roman strategy was designed to protect not borders, but the thinly settled populations and their lines of communication.*

The word "frontier" is a more meaningful term than "border" for defining the function of the limes *and* limitanei *in the provinces of Palestine, Arabia, and possibly Syria. "A sufficient force" would be gathered from one or more garrisons to defend against large numbers of attacking Saracens, and the* castra *and* castella *on the frontier also served as a refuge for the settled population in the event of attack. Saracen phylarchs, on the other hand, when not allied with the Romans against their enemies, were employed, or bought off, to keep the peace in the uninhabited fringe regions. Understanding the* limes *as "frontier" and recognizing the meaning of the "inner desert" clarifies the meaning of "inner* limes,*" uninhabited desert reaches controlled by Saracen phylarchs, and, in times of difficulty, their traditional haven of safety.*

During the past decade or two, the eastern frontier of imperial Rome, particularly that portion between the Dead Sea and the Red Sea, has been the subject of renewed investigation by archaeologists and historians. Sherds have been collected and inscriptions recorded; literary sources have been reviewed and reinterpreted. The remains of forts, fortlets, watchtowers, and roads have been surveyed, and selected sites have been excavated. These investigations have cleared the air somewhat, but as is often the case, differences of interpretation have cast a long shadow of historical uncertainty as to the meaning of the evidence. Regarding this southern sector, we have no precise knowledge of where the actual border was, or if there ever was one. Further north, in the region where Rome and Persia persistently opposed one another, the situation is quite different. The written works of Ammianus Marcellinus, Zosimus, Procopius, and Agathias provide a fair idea of where the boundary—at least the military boundary—was between these two opposing states as they fought one another

over some 300 years. We possess no such reportage for the southern sector of the eastern frontier. Hence, Bowersock (1976: 222) has rightly questioned whether the military installations along the *Via Nova Traiana* during the Late Roman and Early Byzantine periods were part of the *limes* in the sense of a coordinated system of frontier defenses. The *Via* was simply too far west to be a border between the province of Arabia and the desert lands to the east. Bowersock concludes that the system in this region was one of defense in depth rather than of a defensive line. However, the absence of a fortified line raises the question of how incursions from the eastern and southern deserts of Arabia were prevented. Graf (1978: 20), on the basis of the Rawwafa inscriptions, dated to A.D. 166–69, which report friendly relations between Rome and the Thamudic confederation in the Hejaz, believes that the enigmatic gap in the militarized zone along the southeastern Arabian frontier was closed by formal arrangements between Rome and tribal federations. As *foederati*, Arab tribesmen took over the task of patrolling the borders and "as a result, they absolved Rome from the heavy demands and fiscal responsibility of an intensive fortified zone between Aqaba and Jebel al-Shera" (cf. Sartre 1982: 28–29).

However, the policy indicated in an inscription does not necessarily obtain for other regions or for later centuries. It should be noted that in 473 under Emperor Leo I, Amorcesus, a Saracen from Persia, operating against other Saracens (*foederati*?) was able to penetrate the southern portion of Palaestina Tertia and take over the Roman custom-house on the island of Iotabe as well as other islands controlled by nearby towns. He wanted, as Malchus of Philadelphia informs us (FHG: 4, 113), to conclude a treaty with the Romans, "and become a phylarch of the Saracens in Petraea [i.e., the eastern portion of Palaestina Tertia] who were subject to the Romans." He was the guest of the emperor to Constantinople, where he shared the imperial table and was honored with many distinctions and gifts, including the right to possess Iotabe and many other towns. The island was not recovered by Rome until 498 (Theophanes; de Boor 1883: 141).

While the information provided by Malchus would indicate the absence of opposition by Roman regulars or *limitanei*, there is the question of whether there was any opposition at all by Arab *foederati*. It does not appear that there was, not even by the *Legio X Fretensis* based at Aila at the time. The manner in which Leo knuckled under to the demands of Amorcesus and ceded to him control of strategic trade routes both on land and sea—Amorcesus controlled them for 25 years—would also indicate that the so-called *foederati* either were not an effective deterrent to an adventurer like Amorcesus or that they did not exist at all. Add to this the fact that Amorcesus, by exacting custom duties, made himself wealthy at the expense of the imperial fisc.

I believe that the story of Amorcesus invites us to act cautiously in attempting to justify, on the basis of limited evidence, a broad conclusion, or a conclusion as to the purpose of the central authority in Constantinople. In the absence of more cogent evidence, conditions on the eastern frontiers of Palaestina Tertia remain enigmatic. However, if there is some relationship or connection in the strategy employed in the western portion of the province, where literary and epigraphic evidence gives us a fairly clear picture of defensive arrangements, we may be able to arrive at a better

understanding of those employed on the province's eastern "border."

There remains another cautionary note before proceeding, and that has to do with the word Saracen. It can be best expressed by slightly altering a response to a question posed by Huck Finn in Mark Twain's *Tom Sawyer Abroad* (chapter 13):[1] "They was all Saracens, Tom said, and when I asked him what a Saracen was, he said it was a person that wasn't a Presbyterian." This statement is not far off the mark as it applies to what we know about the so-called Saracens. Latin and Greek sources, on which we are so dependent, hardly ever designate a nomadic or seminomadic Arab by any term other than Saracen; only on very rare occasions do we hear of the tribe to which they belonged. (Other equally nonethnic designations are Nomads, Tent-Dwellers, Agareni, and Ishmaelites: i.e., descendants of Hagar and Ishmael.) Those who converted to Christianity still bore the name Saracen; others who were pagan were sometimes referred to as *barbaroi*. In the view of the settled Christian community, the transition of Saracens from paganism to the new faith is best summed up in the statement from Cyrillus' *Vita Euthymii* (Schwartz: 24): "Those who were formerly called the wolves of Arabia . . . became members of the spiritual flock of Christ."

It must be remembered that the habitat of the Saracens was not exclusively beyond the pale. In the eastern provinces, including Egypt, Saracens were found everywhere; they were an integral part of the population that dwelt on the fringes of the *oikoumenē*. In fact, for many, their homeland was the very region occupied by Rome. They undoubtedly could also be found, as Bedouin are today, in the major centers of the population. Hence in the province under consideration, we cannot think of the *limes* as a border in the modern sense of the term—as a line between "us" and "them"—nor as a line of fortifications designed to keep out the enemy known as the Saracens. The Romans, to be sure, were concerned with the movements of large Arab tribes, but they could not prevent small groups or individual Saracens from infiltrating or moving about the provinces. These Saracens included not only the traditional raiders— "the wolves of Arabia"—but also traders, guides, messengers, members of the Roman armed forces, and mercenaries within the Roman military establishment. And at one time or another, a Saracen could have served in all these capacities.

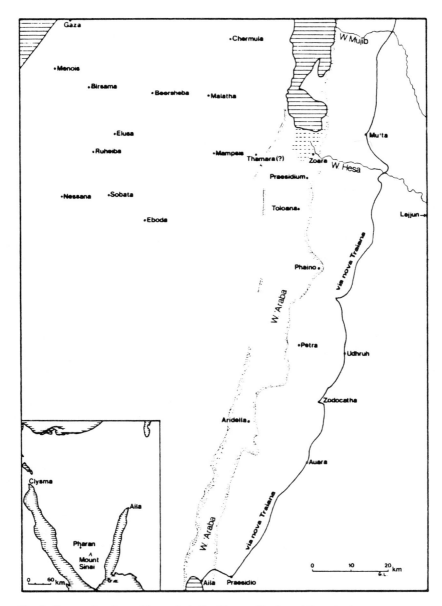

Fig. 1. Roman frontier settlements in the Negev, Sinai, and Transjordan.

In examining conditions in the western portion of Palaestina Tertia, the region now generally known as the Negev and its extension into Sinai, our best evidence derives from the fourth and fifth centuries (for locations of the sites under discussion throughout, see fig. 1). The northern portion of the province, stretching from the Dead Sea to a point where it abuts the Saltus Geraticus and Palaestina Prima, was a fortified area and has been called by some the *Limes Palaestinae* (*inter al.*, Gichon 1980: 843–64). Although the date of establishment for this *limes* is still under debate—and there is even some discussion as to whether the name should

apply to the western portion of the province (Bowersock 1976: 229)—we do possess firm evidence for the existence of a line of military positions, not necessarily fortifications, by the end of the fourth century. The *Notitia Dignitatum* (ca. 393–405) cites military detachments at Menois, Birsama, Beersheba, Malatha, and Thamara(?) (Seeck 1876: 73–74). Earlier in the same century, Eusebius (ca. 330) mentions, in connection with biblical Beersheba, that a military installation (φρούριον στρατιωτῶν) was located in the town (Klostermann 1966: 50). He also cites a similar installation at Thamara, one day's distance from

Mampsis and on the road from Hebron to Aila (Klostermann 1966: 8). That at least two of these garrisons (Menois and Birsama) were manned by *limitanei* is supported by a decree of Theodosius II (7.24.30) for the year 409.

The normal expectation would be to consider this line of military detachments as a means of protecting Palestinian communities north of the line from Saracen inroads from the south. This was the perception of Procopius of Caesarea (*Aed.* 5.8.5) when he commented that the Emperor Justinian constructed at Mount Sinai "a very strong fortress . . . in order that the barbarian Saracens might not be able . . . to make inroads with complete secrecy into the lands of Palestine proper (ἐς τὰ ἐπὶ Παλαιστίνης χωρία)." Procopius was in error in his perception, since a fort deep in the Sinai peninsula, and removed from Palestine proper, could not have prevented Saracen raids to the north (Mayerson 1978: 33–36). "Palestine proper" in the late fourth century—let alone in the sixth—did not begin north of the "*Limes Palaestinae*" since substantial communities existed south of the garrisoned line: Elusa, Mampsis, Eboda, Sobata, Ruheiba, and Nessana. The most important of these was Elusa.

Elusa, some 20 km southwest of Beersheba, was a thriving city (*polis*) early in the fourth century. Formerly a Nabataean town, as were all the others, Elusa was not the half-civilized town described by Jerome when Palestine's protomonk and missionary Hilarion visited the site ca. 350 (Mayerson 1983: 247–53). It was quite civilized, as we learn from the letters of Libanius (314–ca. 393). Antioch's celebrated professor of rhetoric and Libanius' own teacher, Zenobius (ca. 345), was from Elusa, as most likely was his cousin Argyrius, a well-known rhetor of curial rank at Antioch. The city housed a school of rhetoric and had an Irenarch, a police officer of curial rank, who was appointed by the governor of the province. Elusa was important enough to be visited by Modestus, the Comes Orientis (ca. 360) and other high ranking officials. And of no small significance is the city's prominent position on the *Peutinger Table* (ca. fourth century). It is cited without intervening stations as being 71 Roman miles from Jerusalem.

A relatively short distance south and southeast of Elusa (10 km and 30 km) lay two imposing sites, Ruheiba (ancient name unknown) and Sobata (modern Shivta, Soubaita), each of which covers ca. 30 acres. With Elusa they share a common

characteristic: they show no evidence of having a military installation, a φρούριον στρατιωτῶν, or any structure that could serve to defend against attack. Early investigators, Woolley and Lawrence (1936: 91, 125, 129), noted that the towns of Elusa, Sobata, and Ruheiba had nothing that resembled a city wall; their protection, such as it was, appears to have been continuous lines of houses and garden walls.[2]

Three sites south of the so-called *Limes Palaestinae* are known to have had military installations (i.e., forts). These are Nessana (modern Nitsana, Auja Hafir) and Eboda (Oboda, modern ꜥAvdat, ꜥAbde), but both are late. Nessana, 52 km southwest of Beersheba, had a fort of substantial size and a Camel Corps (a *numerus* of the Very Loyal Theodosians). On evidence contained in papyrological finds, the military establishment is dated to the time either of Theodosius I or of Theodosius II (Kraemer 1958: 22; Mayerson 1983: 229). The fort at Eboda, 63 km south-southeast of Beersheba and Elusa, has been dated as late as the sixth century (Negev 1976: 351; cf. Negev 1983: 162–63), but it may be somewhat earlier. The situation at Mampsis (modern Kurnub) was different from its sister towns of the Negev. Situated 40 km northeast of Beersheba and one day's distance from the garrison at Thamara, the town was positioned at the strategic point where the road emerged from the Dead Sea–Wadi ꜥAraba region. Early in the third century a detachment of the Third Cyrenaica legion was based at the site. There is no further evidence that the town housed a military unit during the fourth to sixth centuries, although a protective wall surrounded its perimeter during the Late Roman and Byzantine periods (Negev 1977: 728–29, 734; cf. Negev 1983: 165).

These urban sites, except for Mampsis, were the nuclei of extensive agricultural lands. But like the towns themselves, there is no evidence that the numerous farmsteads of the region were fortified in any way to fend off raiders and attackers; and many of these farmsteads were situated quite far from the populated centers. In short, the western portion of Palaestina Tertia to the south of the "*Limes Palaestinae*" was open country (Mayerson 1964: 184).

If this evaluation is correct, what was the function of the military units based to the north of the communities? How, for example, was Elusa able to flourish, as it did in the mid-fourth century, some 20 km south of the nearest military post at Beersheba? How did it cope with Saracen raids, which certainly must have occurred from time to time, raids of the kind reported by Rufinus (*HE* 2.6) for ca. 374 ("cities and towns of the Palestinian and Arabian *limes*"), and by Jerome (*PL* 22: col. 1086) for 411 ("a sudden attack by barbarians . . . ran through the *limes* of Egypt, Palestine, Phoenicia and Syria")? What is certain is that a military border, a *limes*, did not and could not contain these raiders. Nor, in my view, was it meant to do so.

When we recognize that many of these raids originated *within* a military or a political border, it becomes apparent that the military strategy in the region was not so much to defend "borders" as to defend communities against Bedouin attacks. Borders, whether political or military, were meaningless when the "enemy" lived and moved freely within them. Even in Palaestina Prima, a province that possessed clear political borders, monastic communities in the Judaean desert just a few miles south of the Jerusalem–Jericho road were periodically subjected to Saracen raids. During the reign of Emperor Anastasius (491–518), the celebrated camp (*Parembolē*) of converted Saracens (established by Euthymius ca. 420) was attacked by *barbaroi* and had to be abandoned. The raiders then attacked their new encampment near the monastery of Abba Martyrius, killing and taking prisoners, leaving the survivors to find refuge in various towns (Schwartz 1939: 67–68). Again in ca. 503, when Mundhir, the Saracen client of the Persians, invaded the provinces of Arabia and Palestine, "a great number of barbarians who were scattered through that (Palestinian) desert" threatened the retreat of John the Hesychiast in the remote part of the Judaean desert called Rouba (Schwartz 1939: 211). Perhaps raids of this kind caused Sabas, the founder of the Great Lavra, to urge Justinian to build a fort (*Kastron*) in the desert near his monasteries to protect them against Saracen incursions (Schwartz 1939: 175). Somewhat further south, close to the main road between Bethlehem and Hebron, John Cassian records (*PL* 49: cols. 643–45) that the Saracens made an incursion into Palestine (ca. 429) and massacred great numbers of eremites at Thecue (modern Tekoa). The Judaean desert of Palaestina Prima, from the eastern watershed to the Dead Sea, was, like much of Palaestina Tertia, open country, thinly populated, and subject to sporadic Saracen attacks. In connection with this Palestinian province, a recent survey of the Judaean desert re-

vealed a line of fortifications— two forts, seven fortlets, and four watchtowers— dated by ceramic finds to the fifth century. They extended from modern Tekoa to the vicinity of Chermula (Hirschfeld 1979: 78–84). These installations may have been manned by detachments from the garrison at Chermula.

It is necessary, I believe, to discard the association of the term *limes* with the words "border" or "boundary" or "fortified line" in its application to both sectors of Palaestina Tertia, to Palaestina Prima, and to the province of Arabia as well. For many, these words are so closely associated with a line of separation, whether it be of states, provinces, armies, ethnic groups, etc., that they do not serve to describe the military or political situation in this part of the Roman empire. Certainly the *limitanei* of Menois and Birsama cited in the Theodosian Code, positioned as they were in the westernmost part of Palestine, can hardly be thought of as "border" militia. It seems best, rather, to translate the term *limes* as "frontier" in the sense that it is used in the United States: i.e., as the land that forms the furthest extent of a country's settled or inhabited region. The analogy with the "American frontier" is appropriate since the problems were similar to those that existed in Palaestina Tertia and its neighboring provinces: thinly settled populations subject to raids, and threatened lines of communication. To meet these problems, a series of forts was gradually extended into the territory as settlement developed. The forts were manned with garrisons of mounted troops that protected lines of communication and operated against raiders the forts themselves served as sanctuaries for the settled population when raiders came in large numbers. The much-quoted statement of Malalas on Diocletian's strategy in the east (Bonn: 308) is best interpreted in light of this definition: namely, that he "also built forts (κάστρα) for the frontiers (εἰς τὰ λίμιτα) from Egypt as far as the borders (ὅρων) of Persia and stationed frontier troops (στρατιώτας λιμιτανέους) in them."

What the imperial government found necessary for the Roman east was the defense of the *oikoumenē*, the inhabited world, and in the fifth century, the *oikoumenē* for western Palaestina Tertia began not north of the "*Limes Palaestinae*" but to its south, at the cluster of settled communities. The cavalry units cited in the *Notitia Dignitatum* helped protect not only the towns to the south, but also communities to the north, which could also be subject to Saracen raids.

Organized communities could also be widely separated. Pharan, for example, deep within the Sinai peninsula, was at least an eight-day trek through a wilderness inhabited only by Saracens and occasional eremites. It was defended, as we learn from the sixth-century itinerary of the Piacenza pilgrim (*CCSL* 175: 149), by a mounted unit of 80 *condomae* who "patrolled the desert protecting monasteries and hermits against Saracen attacks." These *condomae* were in effect a mounted police unit. The cavalry units of the "*Limes Palaestinae*" to the north served the same function as these *condomae*, but on a larger scale.

When communities were widely separated from one another, either the imperial government or the communities themselves provided armed escorts for travelers through lands infested with hostile Saracens. In the late fourth century, the peripatetic nun Egeria traveled from Clysma, at the head of the Gulf of Suez, to the city of Arabia in Egypt, a four-day trip through the desert. In the company of a military escort, she went from fort to fort (*de castro ad castrum*); and when she reached the city of Arabia, she dismissed the soldiers who had accompanied her *per loca suspecta*, "through dangerous places" (*CCSL* 175: 49).

A more dramatic account of the hazards of traveling through Saracen badlands is provided by the narrative of a resident of the Sinaitic desert, a certain Nilus. A sudden Saracen attack on the monastic community at Mount Sinai resulted in the death of a number of the eremites and the abduction of Nilus' son Theodoulus. With a number of others Nilus set out from Pharan to find his son (Mayerson 1975: 67; Conca 1983: 38–40). After an exhausting journey of eight days, he became separated from his group and was captured by a band of marauding Saracens, only to be saved in the nick of time by an armed troop (οἱ τῆς ὑμετέρας δυνάμενως μάχιμοι).[3] "They [the armed troop] appeared," Nilus wrote, "high on a hill and caused much confusion among the savages. As they made their presence known by shouting, none [of the Saracens] remained there; the whole area, which a short time ago had been full of people, became bare." Nilus ultimately found his son at the city of Elusa. Theodoulus recounted the hardships and indignities that he suffered at the hands of the Saracens (Mayerson 1963: 166; Conka 1983: 49) until "we came near the rest of the inhabited world

(*oikoumenē*) . . . and they [the Saracens] entered a town called Soubaita (i.e., Sobata) and announced to the inhabitants that I was up for sale."

The itinerary of Egeria and the Nilus narrative record the experiences of two individuals as they made their way to the *oikoumenē* through regions populated with marauding Saracens. The reaction of the imperial government to Saracen raids is reported by Choricius of Gaza (*Laud. Steph.*: 57–58; Mayerson 1964: 181). In his eulogy (ca. 535–40) to Stephen, the governor of Palestine, Choricius praises him for his forthright action in checking the incursions from Egypt of Saracens who disturbed the peace and committed injustices against the border cities: "For gathering a sufficient force, you chastized the evil of these people who were deprived in every way of your forgiveness."

The phrase "gathering a sufficient force" is the key to understanding the military strategy employed to meet the threat of large numbers of attacking Saracens. An armed escort would be sufficient to scare off a band of raiders, as we learn from the Nilus narrative; but a military force of some size would be necessary to counter the menace of a large body of attackers. This would mean sending messengers or messages by a system of signals to nearby garrisons, which would provide the needed men and materiel. The strategy of "gathering a sufficient force" is confirmed by a later incident in the eastern sector of Palaestina Tertia. As reported by Theophanes for the year 629 (de Boor: 335), Muhammad had appointed four emirs to wage war against the Christian Arab tribes. They marched against a town called Moucheon, in which Theodorus the Vicarius was stationed. Learning of this from a member of the Quraish tribe, Theodorus "gathered all the soldiers from the desert garrisons" (συνάγει πάντας τοὺς στρατιώτας τῶν παραφυλάκων τῆς ἐρήμου), and met the enemy in a region called Mothous (Muᶜta), where his forces killed three of the emirs and most of the enemy.

It is now appropriate to discuss the situation further east, to the great Rift Valley known as the Wadi ᶜAraba and to the eastern sector of Palaestina Tertia. But unlike the evidence available for the western sector, we have to rely more on surface surveys and on the very limited excavations in this region. The *Notitia Dignitatum*, to be sure, lists a number of military detachments and the sites at which they were posted, but not all can be located with reasonable certainty. However, the placement of those that can be located indicates communication with the communities along the *Via Nova Traiana*, and with the ᶜAraba as well (Abel 1938: 181–82). A mounted troop was stationed at the well-known site of Zoara, at the southern end of the Dead Sea. Then along the eastern bank of the ᶜAraba detachments were posted at Praesidium (el-Feife), Toloana (et-Tlah), and Aridella (Gharandel). The locations of these four are fairly certain; the others—Calamona, Iehibo, Hasta, Asuada, Moahile—are less sure, but on the basis of toponomical similarities are considered to be in the ᶜAraba. Because these units are west of the *Via Nova*, they represent a series of posts to protect individual communities served by the springs of the Rift Valley, or those like the town of Phaino, that mined and smelted copper ore. They also protected lines of communication, not so much those along a north–south route through the ᶜAraba—a subject of much debate (Rothenberg 1971: 211–23)—but those that crossed the region in a general east–west direction.

Atop the escarpment east of the Wadi ᶜAraba and the Dead Sea lay the *Via Nova Traiana*, the main north–south line of communication of the eastern frontier. The *Notitia* cites ten or more units believed to have been posted along this road. Of these, only three can be placed with reasonable certainty: Hauana (Hauarra or Auara of the *Peutinger Table*, modern Ḥumayma), Zodocatha (Zadagatta of the *Table*, modern Sadaqa) and Praesidio (modern Kirbet el-Khalde) (Abel 1938: 182–84). Tarba may be Gerba, a short distance north of Udhrûh, and Sabure or Veterocaria may be the Carcaria that is cited by Eusebius as being a day's journey from Petra. It has generally been assumed that those units that could not be located with some precision, were nevertheless posted on the *Via Nova*. It is possible, however, that one or more of these were sited at or near communities to the east, or even to the west, of the road.

Recent surveys and excavation by S. T. Parker (1976: 26–28; 1980: 865–74; 1981: 171–78; 1982: 19–22; 1985: 19–22) along the *Via Nova* have uncovered a considerable number of military installations, which he has dated by ceramic finds (surface sherding) to the Antonine, Severan, Diocletian, and Justinian periods. It is Parker's view that these installations represent the Palestinian portion of a coordinated line of defensive fortifications that he calls the *Limes Arabicus*. For the period contemporary with the *Notitia*, he has mapped ten auxiliary forts (*castella*) and a legionary camp (Udhrûh) between the Wadi Ḥesa and Aila; and north of the Ḥesa to the Wadi Mujib, four *castella* and a legionary camp (Lejjûn). Parker dates these installations to the years 284–450 and considers them part of the "*Limes* of Diocletian."

Apart from the *Notitia Dignitatum*, we have no literary evidence for the region, nothing to indicate unsettled conditions or pressure by external forces on the *Via Nova Traiana*, or on the regions to its east or to its west. To the north of the Ḥesa, along the Arnon (modern Wadi Mujib), Eusebius reports (Klostermann 1966: 10) that in that extremely rugged ravine—as it was in his day and still is today—"there are garrisons of soldiers to keep guard from all sides because of the fearful nature of the area" (φρούρια πανταχόθεν φυλάττει στρατιωκὰ διὰ τὸ φοβερὸν τοῦ τόπου) As for the Ḥesa (ancient Zered), Eusebius says only that it is a ravine (i.e., a wadi) in the region of the desert (Klostermann 1966: 92). Eusebius and other writers have nothing to say regarding the security of the region south of the Ḥesa. Epigraphic evidence of any consequence is also lacking. From the time of the *Notitia* and for about a century later, the eastern sector of Palaestina Tertia is truly *terra obscura*; we are left only with the remains of military installations.

It is therefore fortunate to have the preliminary results of a survey that is being carried out at the site of Ḥumayma (Humeima) to shed some light on conditions in the southern portion of the province. Ḥumayma has been reliably identified with Auara of the *Notitia* and the *Peutinger Table*. According to the report of Eadie (Eadie and Oleson, this issue), the director of the survey, the distances provided by the *Table* between Zadagatta (Sadaqa) and Praesidio (Khirbet el-Khalde), 20 and 23 Roman miles (30 km and 36 km) respectively, are the exact distances between Sadaqa-Ḥumayma and Ḥumayma-Khirbet el-Khalde. The name of Auara also crops up in the Beersheba Edict, which records assessments on towns and villages of the three provinces that comprised Palestine. The Edict, about a century later than the *Notitia*, shows that Auara was assessed the second highest sum of any of the towns in the eastern sector: 43 *nomismata*, exceeded only by the 65 for the settlement at Adrou-Udhrûh near Petra. Situated on the *Via Nova*, Auara is the largest site between Petra and Aila; and like towns in the Negev, Roman–Byzantine Auara lies over an earlier

Nabataean town.

The most significant point for this discussion is that Ḥumayma is similar in a number of other ways to the towns in the western sector of the province. From the abundance of characteristic later pottery on the surface of the site, Eadie considers the landscape of Ḥumayma Byzantine. The town was unwalled, but a *castellum*, a "fort," and a watchtower were located nearby. From the bare outline of the *castellum*, a *tetrapyrgos*, it would appear that it should be dated to the time of Diocletian or somewhat later. The "fort," an enclosure of imposing dimensions (204 m × 147 m), and as yet unexcavated, is, in the opinion of Eadie, a bona fide military installation and not a caravanserai. The area also held two churches. To the east and west of the site, wadis were terraced with check-dams to allow winter floodwater to percolate into the soil. The town even shared a similar isohyet with towns in the Negev, 90 mm. But what Ḥumayma did not share with them was a number of springs, the water of one of which was conducted by an aqueduct of some 15 km. We do not know if this aqueduct, which shows evidence of Nabataean construction, was in use during the Byzantine period; but the strong likelihood is that an excellent source of perennial water would not have been permitted to go to waste. All in all, Ḥumayma, like its sister towns to the west, appears to have been a vigorous Byzantine community. Positioned in open country, it possessed the means to protect itself and its lines of communication from attacks by raiding bands of Saracens. In the event of a major attack by marauders from the eastern desert, the fort would also have served as a refuge for the town's population.

Two other sites remain to be considered: Adrou-Udhrûh and Aila. The former, some 10 km east of Petra, is not listed in the *Notitia*, but the site contains the impressive remains of a legionary camp that is currently under excavation. The director of the excavation, A. Killick (1983: 125), dates the fort on stratigraphic grounds to the time of Trajan. Parker (1985: 21) suggests a date in the late third or early fourth century. Within the fort itself, there is a small church or chapel built at a later time in what had been the *principium*; another church has been found outside the southeast tower of the fort. Although Stephen of Byzantium cites *Adrara* as a large *komē* of Palaestina Tertia, and Islamic sources give prominent mention to the town (Killick 1983: 110–11), we possess little mean-

ingful information on the physical character of the ancient site, except that there were the remains of houses and that the land was cultivable (Brünnow and Domaszewski 1904: 462). The existence of a strong spring and a pool would indicate that the site could support a substantial population.

Aila presents a problem of a different kind. Eusebius and the *Notitia* both record the presence of the *Legio X Fretensis* at Aila, but no material evidence of the legion has been uncovered. The likelihood is that the late town of Aqaba has obliterated the remains of the legion's camp. Who was responsible for transferring the legion from Jerusalem to Aila, and why, are not known. Some attribute the action to Diocletian, others to Aurelian. However, the fact that the only legion assigned to the three Palestinian provinces was based at Aila is significant. Aila, a port on the Gulf of Aqaba (Eilat) and the anchor town of the *Via Nova*, was important strategically, both in military and commercial terms. The port, as we learn from Epiphanius (*PG* 42: col. 29) and the Piacenza pilgrim (*CCSL* 175: 149), received merchandise from the east. Situated at the outlet of the Wadi Yutm, a passageway from the highlands to the sea, Aila was a *stomion* into Palestine proper (Mayerson 1964: 169–71). In addition, good supplies of potable water were available at the site.

As for the legion's responsibilities, we can only speculate that it supported the units posted along the *Via Nova* and its vicinity, and that in the event of a serious threat to the communities on the edge of the *oikoumenē*, the prefect of the legion would, as Theodorus the Vicarius did in 629, "gather all the soldiers from the desert garrisons" to meet and repel the enemy. Detachments of the legion must also have provided escorts for caravans of merchants traveling north along the *Via Nova*, or north-west along the route indicated on the *Peutinger Table* that led to Elusa and Jerusalem. Aila was also a station on the route from Jerusalem to Mount Sinai, and if escort was needed by travelers heading in either direction, elements of the legion could have provided it. Despite these speculations, however, we remain in the dark as to the actual activites of the *Legio X Frentensis* at Aila.

In sum, there are serious reservations in considering the military installations of Palaestina Tertia as a "line" of defensive fortifications designed to preempt the enemy (in this case Saracens) from making inroads into Palestine proper. Equally misleading is the consideration of *limitanei* of this province as "border" troops, since it leads to a view of men positioned along a line of demarcation separating them from the enemy. The entire province, thinly settled, submarginal in terms of rainfall and cultivable land, and lacking a fixed eastern boundary, should be considered a frontier province in the sense defined above. As such, scattered communities required protection from raiding Saracens who lived within and outside the province. The military units provided the customary functions necessary for policing a frontier territory: patrolling, scouting, escorting, and pursuing. Because these communities existed in open country, *castra* and *castella* could also have served as places of refuge for local populations and for travelers.[4]

The use of the military and its installations was one means of meeting the Saracen threat; another was negotiating with the leader of an Arab tribe, or group of tribes, either to serve as an ally (*foederatus*), or to protect a community against attacks by members of the tribe under his control. In regions of the eastern provinces that were the scene of major military actions between Rome and Persia, Arab tribes were employed by both sides as auxiliaries for their regular armed forces. The historical sources, particularly for the sixth century, are fairly replete with the names and titles of Saracen chiefs (*phylarchoi*) with whom the governments of Rome and Persia negotiated to assist them in their wars against one another. Shahîd (1984: 393) calls these federated tribes Rome's "Arab shield" and says that they "performed an important function, sometimes a threefold one: participation in the Persian Wars, the maintenance of law and order in certain zones within the *limes*, and the protection of the *limes* against inroads from the Arabian peninsula."

As far as Palestine is concerned, we know of the appointment of phylarchs for the province—such as Harith b. ᶜAmr, Abukarib, Imrulqays—and we know that the Romans called on the phylarch of Palestine to help quell the Samaritan revolt of 529 (Sartre 1982: 169). In Palaestina Tertia, however, we know little or nothing of the movements or activities of such well-known federated tribal groups as the Salihids, Tanukhids, Kindas, Lakhmids and Ghassanids. The general assumption, extrapolated from the actions of these tribal federations in the northeastern provinces, has been that one of these tribal groups was responsible for patrolling the frontiers of Palaestina Tertia beyond its fixed military positions. In these areas of the frontier,

the imperial government or individual communities either did not wish to expend the effort, or could not effectively control the movement of desert tribes. Hence, the central government or local governments entered into a formal treaty or an arrangement with a tribal authority—a phylarch—that explicitly defined him and members of his tribe as friends rather than enemies. This arrangement guaranteed the tribe certain advantages, usually an allowance in money or in kind. The initiative to conclude these arrangements did not always lie in the hands of the Romans, for a powerful tribal leader could impose his demands on the imperial government or on individual communities, as witnessed by the actions of Amorcesus in 473 and by Muhammad in his negotiations with Aila and Udhrûh in 630 (Mayerson 1964: 171–73). However, despite formal treaties, there were sporadic hostilities by members of a tribe acting without the sanction of the tribal authority, though sometimes with the tacit approval of that authority.

Of the imperial government's treaty with a tribal leader, literary and epigraphic material have nothing to say regarding its specific terms; mention is made of the tribal leader's appointment as a phylarch and the province or region in which he was to serve as phylarch, presumably as a *foederatus*. There is more detailed evidence in dealings between communities and individual tribal leaders. The arrangement between Muhammad and the cities of Aila and Udhrûh has been treated fully. A fragment from the Nessana papyri (Kraemer 1958: 323) has a tantalizing reference to a "new phylarch" or a "newly appointed phylarch" and to supplies of various commodities. The Nilus narrative, on the other hand, has left us a unique account of a raid by an "outlaw" band of Bedouin and the actions taken by the community of Pharan and the tribal leader Am(m)anes to heal the breach in the treaty between the two. The account also reveals the extent of the area controlled by the tribal leader: it took 12 days for the envoys to travel from Pharan in Sinai to the Bedouin encampment somewhere in the Negev near the town of Elusa, a distance of approximately 250 to 300 miles. The narrative picks up the story after the attack and murder of a number of solitaries in the environs of Mount Sinai (Mayerson 1975: 67; Conca 1983: 37): "After they heard the news, the council [*boulē*] of the inhabitants of Pharan decided not to remain silent about the outrage, but to inform the king [*basileus*] about it. They sent two of those who are called couriers to complain about the violation of the established treaty." While the couriers were on their way, the narrator and others went out to collect and bury the bodies of the solitaries who had been killed. On the way back to Pharan, the burial party met the couriers who were returning with written word from the Bedouin leader (*hēgoumenos*) (Conca 1983: 38).

> As we were on our way to Pharan, we met the men who had been sent ahead, and they were bringing a letter from him (the *hēgoumenos*), which confirmed the peace [treaty] and asked those who had been wronged to come to him, especially the kinsmen of the prisoners who were still alive. Further, if anyone wanted vengeance for those who had been murdered, he said he was ready to punish the guilty. He also agreed to return the spoils to those people from whom it had been stolen. He was unwilling to violate the terms of the peace treaty, so he indicated, being satisfied with the agreement that he had reached with them [the people of Pharan], because of the (material) encouragement that he received from them. For their dealings with each other brought no small gain to those [the barbarians] who were helped by the resources of the other party [the Pharanites] in the necessities which they lacked. They [the Pharanites] then prepared gifts and appointed envoys for the renewal of the broken peace treaty.

The narrator, Nilus, whose son had been abducted by the raiding Bedouin, was a member of the party that sought redress from the Bedouin chief. Eight days away from Pharan, Nilus had, as mentioned above, a narrow escape from a band of hostile Bedouin. He then went on to say (Conca 1983: 41):

> After we had traveled four more days, we reached the camp. When the envoys had been announced, they were called to meet with Am(m)anes, for this was the name of the barbarian king. When they brought gifts, they received a favorable response, and took the tent next to his and enjoyed much hospitality, until a direct question brought the matter clearly to the reason for the brutal attack.

What the local community or the central government gained—purchased might be a better word—through the payment of money, or its equivalent in kind, was the phylarch's guarantee that his tribe would not engage in hostile actions against the community or the state. And a military unit stationed near a town or on a vital road was helpful in checking any impulse on the part of the phylarch to authorize a raid in violation of the treaty. To the phylarch, payment was a form of tribute and the recognition of his status as a power—or a power broker—in the region under his control. Whether a treaty stipulated that the phylarch was to be responsible for patrolling the frontier, is not known; it is unlikely to have been the case. There was, to be sure, the matter of "territorial imperative." A phylarch who was the overlord of a region would certainly take quick action against any intruding tribe that would imperil the largess he was receiving from local or central governments. If payments were not forthcoming, however, the phylarch did not feel bound to honor his contractual obligations; all the more so if there were no armed forces in the vicinity. It was the cessation of payments and the absence of the military in 633/634 that encouraged the first attacks of Muslim forces in Southern Palestine (Mayerson: 1964), and ultimately led to a new definition of what previously had been known as the *limes*.

As an addendum to the above, I would like to lend a measure of support for Bowersock's (1976: 220–27) rejection of the contention of Brünnow and Domaszewski and others that there was a double line of defensive installations in the eastern provinces, i.e., an "inner" and an "outer" *limes*. If the definition of *limes* as "frontier" presented here is a valid one, then an "inner *limes*" refers to that part of the frontier that is more distant or further removed from settled habitation. It is, so to speak, the deeper part of the frontier. In the statements of Ammianus, Malalas or Theophanes, "inner" as a modifier of *limes* cannot be taken to mean "closer" or "nearer," or as the opposite of "outer." That this is so is made clear in those citations having to do with the "inner desert," for in the eastern provinces, the frontier (*limes*) was the desert (*eremus*)! An "inner desert" was conceived as one that was at a considerable distance from the *oikoumenē*. The itinerary of the Piacenza pilgrim provides an unambiguous example of the meaning of "inner" in the context of a desert (*CCSL* 175: 145–47; Mayerson 1963: 171–72). En route from Gaza to Mount Sinai, he made his way to Elusa in the Negev, which he says is "at the head of the desert (*in capite heremi*) that stretches to Sinai." Leaving Elusa, he and his companions went into the desert (*ingressi heremum*), and 20 miles further they stopped at a fort (Nessana) in which there was a hospice for travelers. From that point, the last organized community on the way to Mount Sinai, they "entered the inner desert (*interiorum heremum*)"; that is, the Tih desert which was inhabited only by Bedouin.

As for Ammianus 23.5.1, in which he reports that Diocletian encircled Cercusium with walls and high towers, the rest of his statement might read, "at the time when he was putting in order (militarizing?) the more remote frontiers (*interiores limites*) in the very vicinity of the barbarians (*barbarorum confiniis*) so as to prevent the Persians from overrunning Syria." Finally, the two citations of Malalas that are so often quoted, when examined in terms of their physical setting and the character of the personalities involved, leave no doubt that the "inner *limes*" to which he refers can only mean the uninhabited desert reaches. On one occasion, when the Saracen phylarch Arethas feared the hostility of the *dux* of Palestine, he fled to the inner *limes* (Bonn: 434); on another, when Mundhir the phylarch raided Syria to the very borders (ὅρων) of Antioch, he quickly withdrew to the inner *limes* before he could be overtaken by a superior force of Byzantines (Bonn: 445; de Boor: 178). There can be no question that these two Arab chiefs sought their traditional haven of safety—the open desert, far removed from forts and urban populations.

NOTES

[1]The scene takes place in Cairo. I have substituted the word Saracen for Moslem.

[2]According to the Beersheba Edict (Alt 1921: 5), Elusa appears to have had a (military) outpost (*agrarea*). Its location is unknown.

[3]ὑμετέρας in Conca's edition does not make sense in this context. ἡμετέρας of *PG* 79: col. 669, line 6) is preferable, since it would suggest that the mission from Pharan to the Bedouin camp—of which the old man was a part—was accompanied by an armed guard; in the words of the old man, "our armed guard."

[4]The interpretation of the words *castrum* and *castellum* as it applies to this part of the world requires some reconsideration. Although the two words bring to mind military installations, some actually had no connection with the military. When the monastic community at Mount Sinai and Sabas of the Great Lavra petitioned the emperor for a "fort," they had in mind a wall to protect their monasteries from Saracen attack, a "fortified" monastery of the kind observed by the Piacenza pilgrim at Mount Sinai (*CCSL* 175: 148): *monasterium circumdatum muris munitis.* This same traveler, en route from Mount Sinai to Clysma at the head of the Gulf of Suez, also described two *castella* that were little more than waystations (*CCSL* 175: 150; Mayerson 1978: 36): at Surandala, a "*castellum modicum* . . . having nothing within it except a church and its priest, and two hospices for travelers . . . and at a place where the children of Israel crossed the Red Sea and pitched their camp, there too is a *castellum modicum* within which is a hospice." Although a Camel Corps was stationed at Nessana, excavation of the fort revealed no evidence that it ever served to house men of the unit or its officers. The Piacenza pilgrim describes it (*CCSL* 175: 146–47) as a *castrum* "in which there is a hospice . . . in which travelers have a sort of shelter or hermits their keep." That, in addition to providing a shelter for the town's population against attack, may have been the original function of the fort. Similarly at Eboda, excavation of the fort uncovered no architectural detail or artifact that might associate the structure with the military (Mayerson 1964: 185).

BIBLIOGRAPHY

Abel, F.-M.
   1938   *Géographie de la Palestine*, II. Paris: J. Gabalda.

Alt, A.
   1921   *Die griechischen Inscriften der Palaestina Tertia westlich der ʿAraba.* Wissenschaftliche

Veröffentlichungen des deutsch-türkischen Denkmalschutz Kommandos 2. Berlin and Leipzig: Vereinigung wissenschaftlicher verleger.

de Boor, C., ed.
1883   *Theophanes: Chronographia.* Leipzig: Teubner.

Bowersock, G. W.
1971   A Report on Arabia Provincia. *Journal of Roman Studies* 61: 219–42.
1976   Limes Arabicus. *Harvard Studies in Classical Philology* 80: 219–29.

Brünnow, R. E., and A. von Domaszewski
1904   *Die Provincia Arabia* I. Strassburg: Trübner.

CCSL
175   *Corpus Christianorum, Series Latina.* (Itinerarium Egeriae, eds. A. Franceschini and R. Weber; Antonini Placentini Itinerarium, ed. P. Geyer), 175. Turnhout, 1953.

Conca, F., ed.
1983   *Nilus Ancyranus Narratio.* Leipzig: Teubner.

Eadie, J.
In press Humayma 1983: The Regional Survey. *Annual of the Department of Antiquities of Jordan.*

FHG
4   *Fragmenta Historicorum Graecorum,* IV. Ed. C. Muller. Paris, 1885.

Gichon, M.
1980   Research on the *Limes Palestinae:* A Stocktaking. *Roman Frontier Studies 1979* in *BAR International Series* 71: 843–64.

Graf, D. F.
1978   The Saracens and the Defense of the Arabian Frontier. *Bulletin of the American Schools of Oriental Research* 229: 1–26.

Hirschfeld, Y.
1979   A Line of Byzantine Forts along the Eastern Highway of the Hebron Hills. *Qadmoniot* 12: 78–84 (Hebrew).

Killick, A.
1983   Udrûh—The Frontier of an Empire: 1980 and 1981 Seasons, A Preliminary Report. *Levant* 15: 110–31.

Klostermann, E., ed.
1966   *Eusebius: Das Onomastikon der biblischen Ortsnamen.* Hildesheim: Georg Olms Verlagsbuchhandlung.

Kraemer, C. J., Jr., ed.
1958   *Excavations at Nessana: Non-Literary Papyri,* III. Princeton: Princeton University.

Laud. Steph.
1975   *Choricius Gazeus: Opera.* Eds. R. Foerster and R. Richsteig. Leipzig 1975.

Mayerson, P.
1963   The Desert of Southern Palestine According to Byzantine Sources. *Proceedings of the American Philosophical Society* 107:.2: 160–72.

1964   The First Muslim Attacks on Southern Palestine (A.D. 633/634). *Transactions and Proceedings of the American Philological Association* 95: 155–99.

1975   Observations on the 'Nilus' *Narrationes:* Evidence for an Unknown Christian Sect? *Journal of the American Research Center in Egypt* 12: 51–74.

1978   Procopius or Eutychius on the Construction of the Monastery at Mount Sinai: Which is the More Reliable Source? *Bulletin of the American Schools of Oriental Research* 230: 33–38.

1983   The City of Elusa in the Literary Sources of the Fourth–Sixth Centuries. *Israel Exploration Journal* 33: 247–53.

Negev, A.
1976   Eboda. *Encyclopedia of Archaeological Excavations in the Holy Land,* eds. M. Avi-Yonah and E. Stern, 2: 343–55. Jerusalem: Massada.

1977   Kurnub. *Encyclopedia of Archaeological Excavations in the Holy Land,* eds. M. Avi-Yonah and E. Stern, 3: 732–35.

1983   *Tempel, Kirchen und Zisternen.* Stuttgart: Calwer Verlag.

Parker, S. T.
1976   Archaeological Survey of the *Limes Arabicus:* A Preliminary Report. *Annual of the Department of Antiquities of Jordan* 21: 19–31.

1980   Towards a History of the *Limes Arabicus.* Pp. 865–78 in *Roman Frontier Studies 1979,* eds. W. S. Hansens and L. J. F. Keppie. Oxford: British Archaeological Reports.

1981   The Central *Limes Arabicus* Project: The 1980 Campaign. *Annual of the Department of Antiquities of Jordan* 25: 171–77.

1982   Preliminary Report on the 1980 Season of the Central *Limes Arabicus* Project. *Bulletin of the American Schools of Oriental Research* 247: 1–26.

1985   Preliminary Report on the 1982 Season of the *Central Limes* Project. Pp. 1–34 in Preliminary Reports of ASOR-Sponsored Excavations 1981–83, Walter E. Rast, ed. *BASOR* Supplement No. 23. American Schools of Oriental Research. Winona Lake, IN: Eisenbrauns.

PG
42   *S. Epiphanii Adversus Haereses* in *Patrologiae cursus completus, Series graeca* 42. Ed. J.-P. Migne.

79   *Nili Monachi Eremitae Narrationes* in *Patrologiae cursus completus, Series graeca* 79. Ed. J.-P. Migne.

PL
22   *S. Eusebii Hieronymi Epistulae* in *Patrologiae*

cursus completus, Series latina, 22. Ed. J.-P. Migne. Paris: L. Migne.

49   *Joannis Cassiani Collationes* in *Patrologiae cursus completus, Series latina* 49. Ed. J.-P. Migne. Paris: L. Migne.

Rothenberg, B.
1971   The ꜥArabah in Roman and Byzantine Times in the Light of New Research. Pp. 211–23 in *Roman Frontier Studies 1967*. The Proceedings of the 7th International Congress. Tel Aviv University.

Sartre, M.
1982   *Trois études sur l'Arabie romaine et byzantine*. Collection Latomus 178. Brussels: Revue d'etudes latines.

Schwartz, E., ed.
1939   *Kyrillos von Skythopolis*. Leipzig: J. C. Hinrichs.

Seeck, O., ed.
1876   *Notitia Dignitatum*. Berlin: G. Lange.

Shahîd, I.
1984   *Byzantium and the Arabs in the Fourth Century*. Dumbarton Oaks Research Collection and Library. Washington, D.C.: Dumbarton Oaks.

Woolley, C. L., and Lawrence, T. E.
1936   *The Wilderness of Zin*. London: J. Cape.

ZEITSCHRIFT FÜR PAPYROLOGIE UND EPIGRAPHIK

LIBANIUS AND THE ADMINISTRATION OF PALESTINE

The appearance of the words "Eleutheropolis of Nea Arabia" in *P.Oxy.* 3574, dated firmly to 314-318, has, at least for this writer, resulted in a reexamination of the administrative arrangements in Palestine during the fourth century. In *ZPE* 53 (1983) 251-258 and in *ZPE* 64 (1986) 139-140, I have maintained that Eleutheropolis was the well known city of Palestine, that the province of Nea Arabia was carved out of southern Palestine, and that it covered an area similar to that described by Ptolemy as Idumea. In *ZPE* 56 (1984) 223-230, I attempted to sort out the shifting boundaries of Palestine and Arabia with particular emphasis on the location of Petra in one or the other province. This led me to Libanius and to Jerome, and to the conclusion that Palaestina Salutaris (later Tertia) came into being, not in the commonly accepted date of 358, but in c. 390. There is one more step to be taken: a review of earlier studies of Libanius' letters to the administrative officials of Palestine. What follows challenges a number of assumptions contained in these early studies that many scholars, myself included, have accepted uncritically.

Palestine in the fourth century was far removed from the scene of the major political events taking place in the Near East. Ammianus Marcellinus, our best source for the period 353-378, barely mentions the name Palestine — certainly not in any significant historical context — and does not name a single governor of the province. If it were not for the correspondence of Libanius (314-c.393) we would have no knowledge whatsoever of who governed Palestine between the years 353 and 382, the year 363 being an exception. Libanius, celebrated orator, teacher, and *éminence grise* of later antiquity, maintained an extraordinary correspondence with prominent citizens and imperial officials, as well as friends, kinsmen, former students, and professional colleagues. He was literally a man of letters — over 1500 of them have survived to this day, all, unfortunately, undated. It is largely from this correspondence and other works of his that scholars such as Sievers and Seeck, and doctoral candidates (v. Rohden and Silomen)[1] have sought to fill in the lacuna not only of the administrative officials of Palestine but also of those in other provinces to which Libanius' network of personal relationships extended.

---

[1] G.R. Sievers, *Das Leben des Libanius* (Berlin 1868); hereafter, Sievers. O. Seeck, *Die Briefe des Libanius zeitlich geordnet* (Leipzig 1906), T.U. 30; hereafter, Seeck. P. von Rohden, *De Palaestina et Arabia Provinciis Romanis Quaestiones Selectae* (Berlin 1885). H. Silomon, *De Libanii Epistularum Libris I-VI* (Göttingen 1905).

Howevermuch Libanius' publications are vital for the reconstruction of the ambience and the history of the period in which he flourished, the bulk of his personal correspondence does not provide the kind of firm evidence that historians have an affection for: not only do the letters lack any kind of dating formula, many are vague, particularly letters of recommendation, official titles are absent as are patronymics of the addressees and comments about events of the time or public affairs.[2] Despite these handicaps, Sievers has written a history of the life and times of the famed Antiochene personality that is based in large part on connecting the addressees of his letters with known historical figures. Included in this seminal work is an appendix, "Clematius und die Provinz Palestina", which bears on the administration of Palestine. There he proposes the year 358 as the year in which Palestine was divided into two provinces.[3]

Siever's work on the correspondence of Libanius was followed by Seeck's study (see n.1), a scholarly tour de force. Seeck, like Sievers, working primarily through internal evidence and inference, organized the correspondence of Libanius into a framework that is regarded at present as fundamental for the chronology and prosopography of Libanius. Silomen (see n.1) has raised a number of questions in his dissertation regarding the dates assigned by Seeck to certain letters. For example, Seeck's letter 258, dated by him to 360/1, is dated by Silomon to 357/8 and accepted by Foerster in his edition that is now standard for the works of Libanius.[4] This example is offered to illustrate the point, often overlooked, that the

---

[2] On this point, see J.H.W.G. Liebeschuetz, *Antioch, City and Imperial Legislation in the Later Roman Empire* (Oxford 1972), 17-23.

[3] Sievers, 241-242: "Clematius, a friend of Libanius, became governor of Palestine through the influence of Anatolius, Ep. 478, perhaps shortly before the time that Aristaenetus and Modestus received their high rank. Nothing is said that Strategius, whose friend he was, Ep. 1185, had a hand in it. He was governor at the time that Sebastianus was commander in Egypt, which was the case in the years 357 to 359 (cf. introd. par. 17 to the Hist. ac. Athan.). We come to this conclusion by comparing Ep. 510 with 511, Ep. 320 with 321, and Ep. 352 with 353 (the letters of Rhetorius himself seem to belong to the period of Julian). So we may assume that Clematius was governor of Palaestina in the years 357 or 358, and that Ep. 320 was addressed to him during this time....The most important one is Ep. 337 in which we can see that during his time as governor a division of the province Palaestina took place and in such a way that Elusa, which in Ep. 325 still belonged to it, was torn away from the province which he kept. That is, he remained governor (later called consularis) of Palaestina I whereas another (perhaps Eupaterius, Ep. 338) received the governorship of Palaestina II to which was allocated Elusa as well as Petra which in Ep. 324 still stood under Clematius...."

[4] Seeck, 131, 175; Silomen, 44; *ep.* 255 in *Libanii Opera (Epistolae)*, X, R. Foerster, ed. (Leipzig 1921). Sievers' and Seeck's system of numbering the letters is derived from the edition edited by J.C. Wolfe, *Libanii Sophistae Epistulae* (Amsterdam 1738). We shall follow the numbering system adopted by Foerster and in brackets cite the letters as they appear in Sievers and Seeck. It should also be noted that Rohden (above, n.1), 41-48, uses approximate dates in his list of governors where additional support is not found in other sources, such as the Theodosian Code. In general where Sievers and Seeck use such cautionary modifiers as "vielleicht" and "wahrscheinlich", they are often passed over, tending to turn their assumptions into facts.

chronology of Libanius' correspondence, having been arrived at mostly through inference and assumption, cannot be taken as definitive. The same caveat applies to other historical aspects that have been siphoned from the correspondence. However, in the absence of firmer evidence, the chronology provided by both Sievers and Seeck has to be taken as a basis — a working basis — in utilizing Libanius' work as historical evidence.

Along with the difficulty of establishing a fixed chronology is the attribution by Sievers and Seeck of official titles to certain administrators known solely through Libanius, titles which are not cited by Libanius or in other source material. Seeck's assignment of such titles as *praeses* and *consularis* for eleven governors of Palestine have no authority attached to them since Libanius uses the rather vague and generic word ἄρχων,[5] if he uses it at all.

Having posed these general reservation to some of the earlier Libanian scholarship, I turn to a consideration of the governors of Palestine that are known solely through Libanius' correspondence, and more narrowly to an interpretation of the letters that have been taken as evidence for the division of the province in 358. Prior to this date, Seeck lists four governors *consulares*: Araxius, c. 350; Clematius I, 353/4; Syncletius, 355; and Firminus I, 356 (summarized on p. 487). A few questions have arisen concerning these four. *The Prosopography of the Later Roman Empire* (=*PLRE*) questions whether Syncletius held the title of *consularis*, and considers that Firminus was "probably" governor (*consularis*). As for Clematius I, since Ammianus Marcellinus (14.1.3) describes the death of a certain Clematius of Alexandria in 353/4, *PLRE* appropriately questions the date of his governorship in Palestine (I [Cambridge 1971] 871, 339, 213).

Beginning with the year 357/8, a considerable amount of confusion sets in, essentially because of three letters addressed to Clematius II. Clematius II is said to have been the governor of all Palestine in 357 and to have had administrative control of two cities in the southern part of the province, Elusa and Petra. In *Epp.* 315 and 321 (318 and 324), Libanius writes to Clematius on behalf of Dynamius from the city of Petra and of Eunomus and Eudaemon from the city of Elusa. The assumption is made by Sievers (p. 241) and Seeck (pp. 111, 342) that both these cities fell under the jurisdiction of Clematius. In *Ep.* 334 (337), dated to 358, Libanius writes again to Clematius, commending his friend Hieronymus of Elusa to him even though he and Hieronymus are aware that the city is no longer under his jurisdiction. Since Elusa and Petra were assumed to be under Clematius' control in 357 and that later in the year Elusa was not, these three letters are cited as evidence that the province of Palestine was split into two in 358 (or late 357), into a Palaestina Prima and a Palaestina Secunda (or a Palaestina Salutaris according to Nöldeke (*Hermes* 10 [1876] 168). The situation is made more confusing by attributing official titles of *consularis* and *praeses* without

---

[5] On Libanius' use of this word and ἀρχή, see P. Petit, *Libanius et la vie municipale à Antioche au IV° Siècle apres J.-C.* (Paris 1955), 47, 72-74, 254-255.

supporting evidence to the governors of Prima and Secunda (Salutaris). The following outline illustrates the assumption made primarily by Seeck (p. 487) and then interpreted by the *PLRE* (I. 1108).

	Seeck:	*PLRE* :
357/8 Clematius	Consularis Primae	Prima
357/8 Eupaterius	Praeses Secundae	Praeses Salutaris
360/1 Hypatius	Consularis Primae	Consularis Primae
360/1 Cyrillus	Praeses Secundae	Salutaris
361/2 Cyrillus	Consularis Primae	Consularis (?) Primae
361/2 Entrechius	Praeses Secundae	Salutaris (?)
362/3 Leontius	Praeses Secundae	Salutaris (?)
	Consularis Primae	Consularis Palaestinae
364 Priscianus	Consularis Primae	Consularis (?) Primae
365 Apophobius	Consularis Primae	(?) Primae or Salutaris
ante 382 Proculus	Consularis Primae	Palestine

The basis for this administrative structure derives essentially from the three letters mentioned above. A closer examination of these letters, however, warrants interpretations substantially at variance with those Seeck and Sievers. The first issue concerns the early part of the year 357/8, during which time the governor Clematius is said to have the cities of Elusa and Petra under his jurisdiction. *Ep.* 315 (318) is a petulant letter to Clematius concerning two friends and fellow rhetors, Eunomus and Eudaemon, "from Elusa", reminding him that he had previously written and had asked him to place them in a position to plead cases (cυναγορεῖν). The phrase "from Elusa" (ἐξ 'Ελούcηc) need not mean, as Seeck indicates, that they were residents of Elusa at the time, but simply that Elusa was their home town. They may have been living in Caesarea, the capital of the province and the center of political and economic activity, and were now seeking a position in the provincial administration through the governor's, and Libanius', influence.[6] There are examples of other rhetoricians

---

[6] *Cf. Ep.* 533. Libanius, when referring to Boethus, a resident of Elusa, writes βοηθὸc πόλεωc 'Ελούcηc, but when he refers to his teacher Zenobius in Antioch, he says that he comes ἐξ 'Ελούcηc. A tangled situation arises out of the reference to Eudaemon and Elusa in *Ep.* 315 (318). Eudaemon, and presumably his cousin Eunomus, came from Pelusium in Egypt — he is several times called "the Egyptian" — and were schooled rhetors. For the critical years 357/60, Seeck assumes (p. 131) that Eudaemon and his cousin practised their profession solely in Elusa, and that the letters sent to Clematius and Cyrillus, governors of Palestine, related to their position at Elusa. Even a certain Eutocius, to whom Libanius addresses *Ep.* 132 (132), requesting a letter of recommendation from his as a distinguished "professor" of rhetoric so that Eudaemon might secure an imperial grant (βαcιλικὴ τροφή), is viewed by Seeck (pp. 151, 195) as a resident of Elusa. What is certain is that Libanius had an extremely high regard for Eudaemon as a rhetor, a stylist, and a man of letters, as is reflected in *Epp.* 255 and 132, and he used his influence with governors and other imperial officials to see that both Eudaemon and his cousin received the best possible positions in provincial centers. But to think that Libanius would have

who left their home city of Elusa to improve their lot. Zenobius, Libanius' teacher, is one of those whose native city was Elusa and rose to become a famous rhetor in Antioch (παρ' ἡμῖν μὲν οἰκῶν, ὢν δὲ ἐξ Ἐλούσης).[7] In short, Ep. 315 may date not early in Clematius' administration, but later, say in the year 358.

The situation regarding Petra is clearer. Ep. 321 (324) to Clematius, dated to 357, concerns a certain Dynamius with whom Libanius developed a friendship at Athens. "Since coming here (ἥκων)," writes Libanius, "he has sung your praises and asks me to write you a letter. I would have done so even if he hadn't asked for it so that I would please you and that you would take pleasure in seeing him." A certain Eusebius joins with Libanius in wishing that Dynamius obtain the "goodwill" (εὔνοια) of Clematius. The letter concludes with the statement: "then do both of us a favor and repay the praises of Dynamius and show yourself to be a cultivated person to the one who adorns (τῷ κοcμοῦντι) Petra."

It is apparent that Dynamius was in Antioch at the time Libanius wrote his letter, and was either on his way to Petra and wished to enjoy the hospitality of the governor of Palestine before proceeding to Petra, or, less likely, was seeking a position in Palestine. The phrase "to the one who adorns (or honors) Petra" merely indicates that Dynamius was an outstanding rhetor, a star in the firmament of rhetoricians of Petra; not that Petra was part of the province of Palestine and under the jurisdiction of Clematius.

In ZPE 56 (1984) 224-226, I have taken issue with the conclusion that Arabia Petraea was incorporated into Palestine early in the fourth century. Despite earlier statements on both sides of the issue by Eusebius of Caesarea, and the signature of the bishop of Aila at

---

Eudaemon spending much of his life at Elusa, an isolated city in the semi-arid wastes of southern Palestine, is difficult to maintain. Elusa may not have been the half-civilized (semibarbarus) town described by Jerome in his life of Hilarion (PL 23, col. 41), but it certainly was not on the leading edge of activity for a rhetor with the reputation and ability that Libanius ascribes to Eudaemon. See my article, "The City of Elusa in the Literary Sources of the Fourth-Sixth Century," Israel Exploration Journal 33 (1983), pp. 248-249, in which I, unfortunately, relied too heavily on Seeck's interpretation.

The letters addressed to Clematius (Ep. 315) in 357, and to Cyrillus (Ep. 164) in 359/60 should be viewed as letters of introduction to newly appointed governors of Palestine. In Ep. 164, Libanius states pointedly that he introduced Eunomus to Modestus, comes Orientis, and that "many governors are their supporters (of Eunomus and Eudaemon) nor do they have any regrets." As for Eutocius, who taught Eudaemon the art of rhetoric, he undoubtedly practiced his profession in the well-known rhetorical schools that were located in Gaza or in Caesarea. Seeck arguing for Elusa as the residence of Eutocius states (p. 151, on the basis of Ep. 1279 [1363]): "Dazu paßt es, daß Leute, die aus Antiochia nach Aegypten reisen, unterwegs seine Gastfreundschaft in Anspruch nehmen." It is far more likely that Eutocius lived in Gaza, a city on the coast road to Egypt, rather than in Elusa which is inland—it is some 50 km. south-south-west of Gaza—and certainly not an avenue to Egypt.

[7] Ep. 101 (100). See also Libanius' Autobiography, Oration 1, A.F. Norman, ed. & trans. (Oxford 1965), p. 60.

the Council of Nicaea in 325, Petra, at least between the years 343 and 374, was within the bounds of the province of Arabia. This is not to say that Palestine did not undergo a territorial change earlier in the fourth century, but that does not mean that other changes did not take place later in that century. Barnes maintains that the Diocletianic province of Arabia Petraea was incorporated into Palestine "not only before 314, but also, unless Eusebius is guilty of an anachronism, in or before 307" (*ZPE* 16 [1975] 277). This may very well be, but by 314/18, as we learn from *P.Oxy.* 3574, we have evidence of another change, the creation of Nea Arabia in southern Palestine.

One must reasonably conclude that in the fourth century both Palestine and Arabia underwent a number of territorial changes in which cities of their southern regions were shifted back and forth. As for *Ep.* 321, since Petra was part of Arabia between the years 343 and 374, the letter cannot be taken as evidence that the city was under the jurisdiction of Clematius, the governor of Palestine for the year 357/8.

There remains *Ep.* 334 (337), dated once more to 357/8. Libanius writes again to Clematius concerning a schoolmate of his, Hieronymus, who resided in the city of Elusa. Hieronymus had complained that Libanius had neglected to write Clematius on his behalf and had insisted that he do so. Libanius goes on to say that a letter is useless since "he (Hieronymus) is under another's jurisdiction (ὑπ' ἄλλῳ) due to the division of the administrative office (κατὰ τὴν τομὴν ἀρχῆc). And yet he named you his governor even if someone should divide Palestine further..." There is no ambiguity here. Elusa, situated in southern Palestine (the Negev), is clearly stated to be under the jurisdiction of someone other than Clematius of Palestine. It is on the basis of this letter, and the two mentioned above, that Sievers and Seeck argue that Petra and Elusa were under Clematius early in 357/8, and that later, when Elusa was no longer administered by him, a division of two provinces took place: the southern part was called Palaestina Secunda, while the rest of Palestine was designated Palaestina Prima.

Sievers and Seeck took their assumptions one step further. Since Libanius in *Ep.* 335 (338) addressed a letter to a certain Eupaterius in which he recommended the rhetor Hieronymus in the highest possible terms and asked Eupaterius to take an interest in him, they came to the conclusion that he had been designated as governor of the newly created province of Palaestina Secunda, although the letter mentions neither an administrative title nor the name of the province.[8]

As for the substitution of the name Salutaris for Secunda, it was perceived by citations in later sources that the southern region of Palestine carried the name of Salutaris rather than

---

[8] It should be noted that Sievers (p. 241) adopts a word of caution when he says "vielleicht Eupaterius." Seeck (pp. 135, 347), on the other hand, has no doubts in citing him as "praeses Palaestinae Secundae."

Secunda. Of special significance was the statement of Jerome, written c. 389/92, that Palaestina Salutaris was created *ante non grande tempus*, a statement that Nöldeke interpreted as being able to comprise "wohl ein Jahrhundert."[9] In any event, the year 358 became crystallized as the date for the division of Palestine into two provinces and resulted in the complex administrative organization outlined above.

The major difficulty in accepting the administrative arrangements posed by Sievers and Seeck is, simply, that there is no supporting citation in any historical or literary source other than Libanius' *Ep.* 334 (337). Even Libanius himself, who cites the name of the province of Palestine some forty times in his letters and orations, never uses a modifying term that would indicate his awareness of a change in the official terminology for the province. For these reasons, and for the evidence cited below, it is the writer's conclusion that the province of Palestine was not split into a Prima and a Secunda (or a Salutaris) at the time Clematius' governship in 357/8, and that it remained a single province until c. 390 when it was divided into three provinces: Prima, Secunda, Salutaris (later Tertia).

There yet remains the stark statement contained in *Ep.* 334 (337) that Elusa "is under another's jurisdiction (ὑπ' ἄλλῳ) due to a split (or a separation) of the administrative office." Some split or division or separation did take place during Clematius' term as governor, but it does not necessarily mean that there was a division of the province into two distinct Palestines. There is another option which was not considered by Sievers and Seeck; namely, that the southern region, which included the city of Elusa, was separated from Palestine and was incorporated, for some unknown administrative reason, into the province of Arabia. The rationale for suggesting this option centers on the fact that Petra was part of Arabia, not of Palestine, during the years 343/77 and later, and that southern Palestine was traditionally "Arab," as Ptolemy, *P.Oxy.* 3574, and Jerome give us to believe.[10] There is a strong suggestion that Elusa was incorporated into the province of Arabia in another statement, late though it may be. Stephanus of Byzantium says that "Elusa, formerly of Arabia, is now a city of Palaestina Tertia" (*Ethnica,* A. Meineke, ed. [Graz 1958] 269). Of course, we have no idea of Stephanus' source for this statement, but it is of interest to note that when he cites trans-Jordanian cities of Adara, Arindela, Charachmoba, and Rabathmoba, he does not say that they were formerly in the province of Arabia, but merely that they are in Palaestina Tertia (*ibid.* 26, 118, 541, 687). Similarly, Procopius of Caesarea, in describing the cis-Jordanian region says that it "was formerly called Arabia and is now known as Palaestina Tertia."[11]

---

[9] I have treated this issue in *ZPE* 56 (1984) 228, but without suggesting how the province was organized. See also below, p. 259.

[10] *ZPE* 53 (1983) 255-257; 56 (1984) 225-228; 64 (1986) 139-140.

[11] *Buildings* 5.8.1. The editor of the Loeb edition has a footnote (p. 355) attributing the division of Palestine into three provinces to Constantine. It is apparent that the editor relied on a

These are tantalizing hints, but there is a letter of Libanius to Urbanus, *Ep.* 102 (101), dated to 359/60, that offers stronger evidence. The letter concerns a certain Zenobius, a relative of Libanius' teacher. Libanius calls upon Urbanus, the assessor (?) of the *comesOrientis*, to rectify an injustice committed against Zenobius who had been deprived of his position as chief of police in Elusa by a man who is known to have purchased it. He asks Urbanus to see to it that Zenobius' position is restored to him and that he mollify the governor (ἡγεμών = *praeses*) either by speaking to him or by writing him. It should be noted that Libanius does not mention the name of the governor, the likelihood being that he did not know the name of the governor of Arabia for the year 359/60, but he certainly knew the governor of Palestine for that particular year. A similar situation had taken place three years earlier. Boethus, a cousin of the famous Zenobius, had been removed from his position as chief of police (Irenarch) of Elusa. Libanius wrote directly to Firminus (*Ep.* 132) the probable governor of Palestine, asking him to restore Boethus to his previous position. Had he known the governor of Arabia it follows that he would have addressed a letter to him to demand that Zenobius be given back his position.[12]

A short time later, in the year 363, an edict of Theodosius (12.1.55) was addressed to Leontius, *consular(is) Palaestinae*. There is no modifying term to indicate that Leontius governed one of the two Palestines, which the edict would surely have indicated if that had been the case. And shortly before the date of the edict, we have another letter of Libanius, *Ep.* 686 (599), dated to 361, in which he congratulates Cyrillus with this clever and cryptic remark: χαίρω ὅτι εἰς ἀρχὴν ἐξ ἀρχῆς, εἰς Παλαιστίνην ἐκ Παλαιστίνης. Seeck and others have interpreted these words to mean that Cyrillus had been advanced from *praeses* of Palaestina Secunda (or Salutaris) to *consularis* of Palaestina Prima.[13] But if in 363 Leontius

---

statement made by Malalas (Bonn, p. 319) to the effect that the emperor created the province Palaestina Tertia. Malalas (p. 347) makes another curious statement that Theodosius "separated Palaestina Secunda from Prima and made it a province."

[12] Libanius had also written to Modestus (Ep. 101), *comes Orientis*, regarding the same case and asked him to look into it, presumably when he arrived at Elusa. Apparently, Libanius expected Urbanus to attend to the details of restoring Zenobius to his office as peace officer. See also Liebeschuetz (above, n. 2), 122-123.

[13] Seeck, 112, 388; *PLRE*, 238-239. The fact that two letters, both quite vague, were written concerning people living in Elusa, does not necessarily mean that they were beyond the range of Cyrillus' influence, especially if Libanius did not have an acquaintanceship with the governor of Arabia. *Ep.* 166 (166), dated to 358/61, is addressed to the governor of Phoenicia, asking to send, by the messenger who brought this particular letter, a note to Cyrillus to help a relative of Libanius' administrator who lived in Elusa. In *Ep.*170 (170), dated to 359/60, Libanius writes to Cyrillus, alerting him that a certain Zenobius, a student of his in Antioch, may come to him asking help for his father, a resident of Elusa. There are a number of ways in which Cyrillus might have been of help to the young man, if the matter did not involve stepping on another governor's political toes. It must be kept in mind that Elusa was far more accessible from Caesarea or another city in Palestine than from Petra in Arabia.

was governor of all Palestine, it is not likely that there were two Palestines in 361. The simple solution to the elliptic statement of Libanius is that Cyrillus was governor of Palestine with the title of *praeses*, and that he was advanced in title to *consularis*, the same title that Leontius held two years later.

To add a further point, I return to Jerome's citation of Palaestina Salutaris (above, p. 257) as it suits best a division of Palestine late in the fourth century. In his *Commentary on Genesis*, composed c. 389/92, Jerome comments on the birth of Isaac in the region of Gerar, and amplifies the description by saying, "*ubi et Bersabee usque hodie oppidum est. Quae provincia ante non grande tempus ex divisione praesidum Palaestinae salutaris est dicta.*" The division that Jerome speaks of need not mean that Salutaris was carved solely out of Palestine; it could very well have included the southern portion of the province of Arabia on both sides of the Jordan Rift which contained the cities of Elusa and Petra.[14] As to the words *ante non grande tempus*, "not long ago", they have the connotation of a relatively short time, hardly as long as thirty years or the century proposed by Nöldeke. Jerome is informing the readers of his *Commentary*, presumably his contemporaries, that the province in which Gerar and Bersabee were located was recently organized under the name of Palaestina Salutaris (above, n. 9).

The most convincing evidence of all—the key to the problem, so to speak—appears in an edict of Justinian dated to 536. His Novel 103, decreeing a change in the title and authority of the governor of Palaestina Prima from *ordinarius* to Proconsul *spectabilis*, contains a brief statement regarding the prior organization of Palestine into three provinces. In the preface of the edict, Justinian calls attention to his practice of upgrading the authority of provincial governors by increasing their stipends and staffs, and by advancing them in official titles. He then singles out for special attention Palaestina Prima and its capital Caesarea, and states that the province

> should also enjoy greater distinction above others for the reason that the province was previously governed by a Proconsul. It was an official of this rank that administered the province. The proconsulship changed from a very prominent one to a lesser one when the whole of Palestine, formerly one province, (μίας μὲν ἔμπροσθεν τῆς ὅλης οὔσης Παλαιστίνης) was divided into three. The proconsulship did not survive, but the office has been reduced at the present time to one that is called *ordinarius* (*Novellae* in Corpus Iuris civilis III, R. Schoell and G. Kroll, etc.).

---

[14] Note that Sievers (p. 228) says that Elusa was situated in the province of Arabia ("Arabiens wo Elusa lag"). Although he provides no support for the citation, he was undoubtedly influenced by Wolfe (above, n. 4) who cites (p. 53, n. 6) Stephanus of Byzantium. Equally interesting is Foerster's citation in his index (vol. XII, p. 30): Ἔλουσα Ἀραβίας.

If there is substance in the historical précis contained in Novel 103, then Palestine was one province when its governor held the title of Proconsul; and that when it was divided into three provinces, the governors of Prima, Secunda and Salutaris (Tertia) were reduced in rank to *ordinarii*. The Theodosian Code confirms the fact that a Proconsul governed a unified Palestine late in the fourth century: for the years 383, 384, and 385 imperial decrees (11.36.28; 11.30.42; 10.16.4) were directed to the "Proconsul of Palestine." And when Paula the Elder arrived in Palestine in 385/6, Jerome writes (*Ep.* 108 in *Pl.*22, col. 884) that the *proconsul Palaestinae* knew her family very well. Presumably some time after 363, when Leontius held the rank of *consularis*, the governor of Palestine was given the rank of Proconsul. By 390/2 Palestine — probably including a portion of Arabia — was divided into three. From that date on, but not before, our sources (e.g., *Notitia dignitatum* of 395-413, *Codex Theodosianus* 7.4.30 for the year 409) provide numerical modifiers for Palaestina, indicating a Prima, Secunda, and a Salutaris (or Tertia).

New York University   Philip   Mayerson

Justinian's Novel 103 and the Reorganization of Palestine

PHILIP MAYERSON
Department of Classics
New York University
New York, NY 10003

Justinian's edict of ca. 536 (Novel 103) merits close attention since it bears directly on events within Palestine that are separated by almost two centuries. The Novel contains an historical précis relating to the division of the province into three provinces, and provides additional support for a date of 390/392. The body of the edict deals with the reorganization of the province to repair the consequences of civil disorder and economic upheaval caused by religious dissension. To that end Justinian upgraded the rank and staff of the governor of Palaestina Prima and gave him the responsibility for the maintenance of public order and the collection of taxes within all three Palestinian provinces. In addition to providing the governor with an armed force, the edict clarified the responsibilities of both the governor and the dux *with respect to internal affairs within the province.*

In ca. 536, Justinian issued an edict (Novel 103) decreeing a change in the title and the authority of the governor of Palaestina Prima from *ordinarius* to Proconsul *spectabilis* (ἀνθύπατος περίβλεπτος). This decree is noteworthy in that it contains a brief statement regarding the prior organization of Palestine into three provinces, the naming of the administrative officer who would assume the proconsulship, and an indication of unrest within the borders of Palestine. In addition, the edict offers some insight into Justinian's attempt to clarify the responsibilities of both the governor and the *dux* with respect to internal affairs. Although Novel 103 has by no means gone unnoticed, its bearing on the date of the tripartite division of Palestine in the fourth century has been passed over, as have the specific causes for the unrest to which Justinian alludes in the text of the edict. When Novel 103 is correlated with the evidence from the Theodosian Code, Cyril of Scythopolis, Zosimus, Malalas, Procopius, and Choricius of Gaza, it provides a clearer picture of events within Palestine that are separated by almost two centuries.

THE TRIPARTITE DIVISION OF PALESTINE

As for the edict itself, Justinian calls attention in the preface to his practice of upgrading the authority of provincial governors by increasing their stipends and staffs and by advancing them in official titles. He then singles out for special attention Palaestina Prima and its capital Caesarea, and states (Schoell and Kroll 1895: 496) that the province

should also enjoy greater distinction above others for the reason that the province was previously governed by a Proconsul. It was an official of this rank that administered the province. The proconsulship changed from a very prominent to a lesser one when the whole of Palestine, formerly one province, was divided into three parts. The proconsulship did not survive, but the office has been reduced at the present time to one that is called *ordinarius*.

If the edict is accurate in stating that when Palestine was governed by a Proconsul it had not

294

yet been divided into three provinces and that when it was, the office of proconsul was eliminated, this datum should have some bearing on the date when the province was so divided. In an earlier paper, I have taken issue with the oft-quoted date for the division of ca. 358, which has been accepted as a given for that event (Mayerson 1984: 222–30). The evidence for ca. 358 was essentially based on a letter of Libanius (ca. 316–395) to Clematius, governor of Palestine, requesting that he use his influence on behalf of a friend and fellow rhetorician. In *Ep.* 334, (Foerster 1921: 315) dated 358, we read that the city of Elusa in southern Palestine was no longer administered by Clematius due to a split or a division of his office (κατὰ τὴν τομὴν ἀρχῆς). In another letter, *Ep.* 686, (Foerster 1921: 622) dated to 361/2, Libanius writes to a certain Cyrillus and alludes to his having been transferred or advanced (?) "from office to office, from Palestine to Palestine" (χαιρὼ δὲ ὅτι εἰς ἀρχὴν ἐκ ἀρχῆς εἰς Παλαιστίνην ἐκ Παλαιστίνης). Libanius gives us evidence of some changes in Palestine during the years 358 and 361/2, but he does not necessarily prove that it was divided into three or even two provinces. It is possible, for example, that in 358 Elusa and the southern portion of Palestine, now known as the Negev, were severed and joined for a period of time to Arabia. And as to the elliptically clever remark to Cyrillus, we cannot be sure of what Libanius meant, other than that some administrative change took place. To complicate matters further, Zosimus (Mendelsohn 1887: 284) informs us that Hilarius was given rule over "all Palestine" in the year 387.[1]

It is certain, amid all the conflicting evidence, that the boundaries of Palestine were in considerable flux during the fourth century. As early as 318, a papyrus document, P.Oxy. 3574, mentions Eleutheropolis "of New Arabia" (τῆς νεᾶς Ἀραβείας). This "New Arabia" was most likely carved out of Palestine and consisted of a good portion of what had formerly been Idumea (Mayerson 1983: 251–58; 1986b: 139–40). In all likelihood, the lifespan of "New Arabia" as a province was a short one, and it must have fallen to the many changes in Palestine during that volatile century.

The first specific evidence of a change appears in Jerome's *Commentary on Genesis*, dated 389/392, in which he informs his readers that biblical Gerar is to be located in the province that was recently (*ante non grande tempus*) organized under the name of Palaestina Salutaris. By about the same time, or a bit later, the *Notitia Dignitatum* cites the division of Palestine into a Prima, a Secunda, and a Salutaris (see fig. 1). Hence, the tripartite division of Palestine can be dated to ca. 390 (Mayerson 1984: 228–30).

To this evidence must now be added the historical précis contained in Novel 103. If there is substance in Justinian's statement, Palestine was one province when its governor held the title of Proconsul; when it was divided into three provinces, the governor of Prima was reduced in rank to that of *ordinarius*. The Theodosian Code confirms the fact that a Proconsul governed a unified Palestine late in the fourth century: for the years 383, 384, and 385, imperial decrees (11.36.28; 11.30.42; 10.16.4) were directed to the "Proconsul of Palestine" (Pharr 1952: 282, 328, 338). Accordingly, the sum total of evidence for dating the division of Palestine into three provinces at ca. 390 (or 393) far outweighs the date of ca. 358, which consists primarily of the oblique information provided by Libanius.

THE JUSTINIAN REORGANIZATION OF 536

Following the preface, the edict in chapter 1 (Schoell and Kroll 1895: 497–98) spells out the organization and the perquisites of the newly mandated office of the Proconsul of Palaestina Prima. The Proconsul was to hear appeals in cases not exceeding ten pounds of gold in value "from each of the Palestines." His allowance was to be 22 pounds of gold, which he was to divide among himself, his assessor, and members of his staff. The Proconsul was to notify the emperor of how the gold was to be distributed so that he could confirm the arrangement with an imperial mandate.

In chapter 2 (Schoell and Kroll 1895: 498) the edict ordered the *dux* of Palestine not to have anything to do with civil cases or with tax collection. The Proconsul was to decide all public and private litigation and to see that public revenues were paid in full. "And the fact that Stephanus *spectabilis* has become the first Proconsul of the province, and has already distinguished himself as its guardian, we are persuaded that he will again discharge his duties as he has previously."

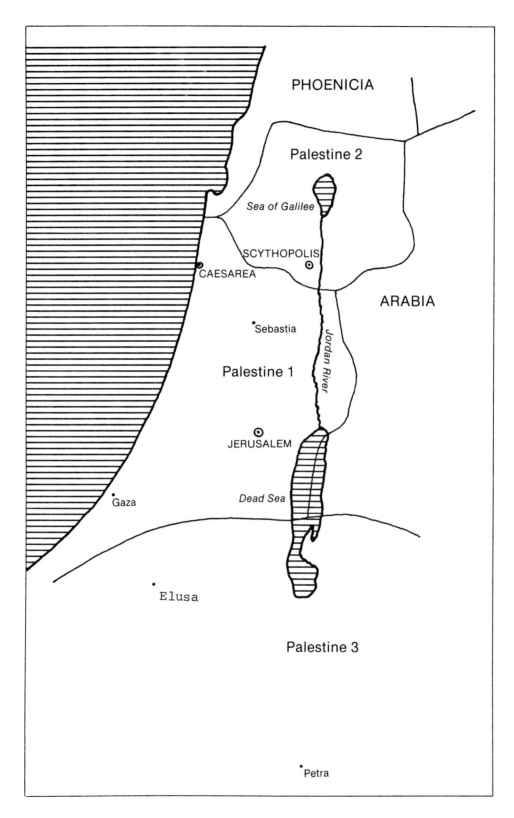

Fig. 1. The divisions of Palestine into three segments can be dated to ca. 390.

The Proconsul, the edict goes on to state, was to maintain order in the cities so that no violent disturbances took place there because of differences in religious worship. "And if it becomes necessary to visit Palaestina Secunda for the purpose of suppressing disorder, he is to be firm and not do anything untoward, especially in that province since we know that there are widespread disturbances there, the results of which are not insignificant." If necessary (Schoell and Kroll 1895: 495–99), the Proconsul could coopt soldiers stationed in the province to preserve peace and order in the cities and in the countryside and for the collection of taxes. The *dux* and the commanding general (στρατηγός) were prohibited from depriving him of the soldiers assigned to him "lest henceforth any disorder may arise in the cities." The *dux* was to be in command of *limitanei*, the *foederati*, and the entire body of soldiery in the province with the exception of those soldiers in the service of the Proconsul. In matters relating to public taxes and civil disorder, the Proconsul was to have undisputed authority.

As can be seen from this summary, Novel 103 is concerned with civil disorder in the several provinces of Palestine—Palaestina Secunda is especially noted—and with increasing the authority of the Proconsul with respect to the collection of taxes and the maintenance of law and order. As for the *dux* and all those subordinated to him, he was ordered not to abridge the newly authorized powers of the Proconsul.

The edict specifically cites differences in religious worship as being one of the causes of civil disorder. Those differences can only refer to the upheavals caused by the Samaritan revolt of 529. The uprising extended over the whole of Samaria from Scythopolis in Palaestina Secunda to Caesarea in Palaestina Prima. Impelled by repressive imperial legislation and conflicts with local Christians, the Samaritans, according to Cyril of Scythopolis, sacked and burned churches, murdered the Bishop of Neapolis and many priests and others, and proclaimed an emperor of their own sect (Schwartz 1939: 172–73). Malalas adds that the governors of Palestine (ἄρχοντες Παλαιστίνης) and the *dux* Theodorus informed the emperor of the insurrection, and that Theodorus, together with a Saracen phylarch, suppressed the revolt, killing as many as 20,000 Samaritans.[2] For his part in the operation, the Saracen phylarch took 20,000 captives who were sold as slaves in Persia and India (Dorpfeld 1831: 446). Those were the events following 529. However, the Samaritans, despite their reverses, continued their opposition, for in 555/556 they arose in yet another rebellion.

There can be no doubt that Novel 103 reflects Justinian's concern over the continuing conflict with the Samaritans and the resulting political and economic upheavals. As related by Cyril of Scythopolis, the situation had been dramatically brought to the emperor's attention in 531 by the mission of the monk Sabas, who, along with several ecclesiastical dignitaries, petitioned the emperor at Constantinople to remit the taxes of Palaestina Prima and Secunda due to the devastation caused by the Samaritans (Schwartz 1939: 175). Justinian ordered a commission comprised of bishops of Palestine to make an inspection of the buildings destroyed by the Samaritans in the two Palestines. He likewise ordered the governors of Palestine to "forgive the taxes for the ninth and tenth indictions [530/1–531/2] in proportion to the damage done in each place [Palaestina Prima and Secunda] equivalent to 13 *centenaria* of gold." The emperor further ordered the commission to inspect the churches that had been burned and to decide the sums to be given for reconstructing each of them; the money would be taken either from the public treasury or from the assets of the Samaritans. Stephanus, *comes clarissimus*, was charged with providing the money and with giving the bishops as much help as they needed.[3] The commission came back with the recommendation that there be a remission of taxes for Palaestina Prima, which comprised all Samaria, in the amount of 12 ·*centenaria*; they recommended only one *centenarium* for the region around Scythopolis in Palaestina Secunda since the destruction of property there had not been heavy. The bishops then took a large sum (from the public treasury?) to rebuild and appropriately decorate the churches that had been burned (Schwartz 1939: 181–82).

The sum of 13 *centenaria* of gold, if Cyril's information is accurate, represents 1300 pounds of gold, or the equivalent of 93,600 *solidi*, over a two year period. The 13 *centenaria* set aside to repair the damage caused by the Samaritan revolt, plus other charges against the public treasury for the reconstruction of churches, represent more than 1.6 percent of the global revenues of the

Eastern empire, estimated at 400 *centenaria* per year (Jones 1964: 463). As another measure of its magnitude, 1300 pounds of gold represent more than 1 percent of the 11,000 pounds that Justinian paid Chosroes upon signing a treaty of eternal peace in 532 (Jones 1964: 272–73). The 13 *centenaria*, hence, represented a substantial loss of income to the province and to the imperial government. In light of those circumstances, Justinian had good cause to place a high priority on maintaining order in the province and on efficiently collecting taxes.

With the name of Stephanus we come back to Novel 103. Although the name is common, this Stephanus is surely the same governor whom Justinian, in recognition of his distinguished service, rewarded with new powers, an increased stipend, and the rank of Proconsul *spectabilis*. The character of Stephanus' service, however, is set out in more detail by Choricius of Gaza (fl. 530) in an encomium to him and the *dux* Aratius. With all the elegance and ornamentation of a rhetor and sophist, Choricius praises the governor of Palaestina Prima for his diplomacy, tact, and forthrightness in handling difficult situations. In an obvious reference to the Samaritan unrest and Justinian's repressive legislation against "heretics," Choricius describes the manner in which Stephanus averted an open revolt: "There was recently a (hostile) act of impious people who plundered the region of Caesarea . . . It was necessary for the emperor to prescribe by law the cure for the impiety and for you (Stephanus) "to sprinkle soothing medications" (Homer, *Il.* 11.830). . . . Nevertheless, you did not exact justice by force, but you eased their anger by the nobility of your character" (Foerster and Richtsteig 1929: 51–52).

Stephanus was equally formidable in handling two chronic problems: an occasional raid by Saracens (i.e., Bedouin) and the blockage of roads by brigands (Foerster and Richtsteig 1929: 57–58). The mention of an action taken by Aratius against some Saracens calls to Choricius' mind that when Stephanus was governor, a band of Saracens from Egypt "ran aground of imperial decrees and committed offenses against nearby cities . . . and collecting a sufficient force you (Stephanus) chastened their intemperate actions." When brigands were active, "the roads between cities were unsafe because of the ambushes of criminals, and which even an armed man did not

have the courage to use, [but] now even a child travels without danger."

It was in Caesarea that Stephanus also distinguished himself in quelling disorder and riots that were produced by rumors and factionalism (Foerster and Richtsteig 1929: 59–60). A fire broke out—possibly an act of arson due to political or religious unrest—that resulted in mass confusion. Stephanus calmed the anxieties of the populace by "inspecting everything and attending to everyone lest any hidden spark somehow escape." Choricius goes on to speculate on the nature of riots brought about by factions (δῆμοι), "for factions quarreling with one another are more contentious than enemies, especially when they take to bearing arms, their brutishness leading them into continuous conflict. And besides, a quarrel of members of the same family against one another is terrible and difficult to heal."

After recording several other benefactions performed for Caesarea, Choricius, with a rhetorical flurry, tells how Justinian was informed of Stephanus' achievements (Foerster and Richtsteig 1929: 63–64):

> The emperor has heard from every side, from men who never lie, the results of your efforts. For a delegation was dispatched [to the emperor] consisting of three priests, the most powerful of the priesthood [i.e., bishops]. How then was the emperor disposed toward the delegation? Was it evident that he was overjoyed and not at all amazed that your achievements should testify on your behalf? Did he know of your greater exploits? What particular ones did he not know? Have you not performed the greatest commissions for him? Did you not bring to these assignments the keenest acumen?

The appointment of Stephanus as Proconsul of Palaestina Prima with added powers and responsibilities for all Palestine was clearly Justinian's response to the administrative weakness created by the tripartite division of the province toward the end of the fourth century. Part of that response may also be seen in the Beersheba Edict, which has been attributed to follow-up legislation detailing the structure and the means of financing the new arrangements (Mayerson 1986a: 141–48).

There remains Justinian's apparent dissatisfaction with the earlier relationship between the *dux* and the governor of Palaestina Prima, as expressed in chapters 2 and 3 of the edict. It is not enough to say (Jones 1964: 282), that "Justinian upheld the principle of the division of civil and military power in the frontier areas where the *duces* had a real strategic task; in Armenia I and IV, and in Phoenice Libanensis, Arabia and Palestine the *duces* and the civil governors remained separate and coordinate, and in the last three provinces the status of the latter was enhanced expressly in order to prevent their falling under the power of the *duces* as hitherto had been the case."

The events in Palestine do not conform with this model. Choricius, for one, gives no hint that Stephanus the governor had in any way fallen under the influence of the *dux* Aratius. Each of the two had his own spheres of responsibility, Stephanus mainly with the body politic within the province, Aratius with actions against external forces (raiding Saracens and the occupation of the island of Iotabe by the enemy). The situation in Palestine was unlike that in Arabia, where Justinian ordered a reorganization (Novel 102) because of the weakness of civil authority. In Arabia the military performed civil functions as well as its own, but did so inefficiently and for its own profit.

Palestine's special problem is clearly reflected in Novel 103: internal dissension caused by religious revolutionaries. Justinian was attempting to rectify the disastrous consequences of the Samaritan revolt of 529 and the unrest that continued unabated. When the Samaritans arose in Scythopolis of Palaestina Secunda in 529, the governor Bassus, having no armed force under his command, failed, much to his misfortune, to quell the insurrection (Malalas = Dorpfeld 1831: 445). It was necessary for the combined forces of the *dux* Theodorus and the Saracen phylarch, presumably based on the eastern frontier, to enter the heart of the province and put down the revolt. They did so with a heavy hand, killing 20,000 Samaritans and giving 20,000 young people of both sexes to be sold in the slave markets of Persia and India. To Justinian and the province, this action meant the loss of a large number of tax-paying inhabitants and another large number of future tax-paying inhabitants. Procopius (*S.H.* 11.29–30), after citing the killing of 100,000 Samaritans, states that " . . . the land, which is the finest in the world, became as a consequence destitute of farmers." There was, in addition, the cost of repairing the damage to buildings and churches.

The loss of public revenues and public confidence must have been enormous. Justinian recognized that Palestine, with three civil governors, low in rank (*ordinarii*) and weak in authority, could not cope with insurrections that spread beyond the borders of their individual provinces. The emperor's strategy was to strengthen the authority of the governor of the most vital of the three provinces, Palaestina Prima, and to concentrate in his hands not only the collection of public taxes for all Palestine, but also command of an armed force, drawn from the regular army, to deal with unrest within the several provinces. In effect, Justinian was authorizing the creation of a special service unit to control riots and other forms of public disorder. Novel 103 is explicit on this point. It prohibits the *dux* and the *strategos* from depriving the Proconsul of the soldiers assigned to him "lest henceforth any disorder may arise in the cities." Following those words Justinian sums up his political philosophy in this statement: "This very thing [public disorder] will never take place if the Proconsul controls the office of civil affairs, if the collection of taxes is efficient, if he has an auxiliary force of soldiers, and if he punishes the disorderly conduct of these soldiers and others." Hence, in matters relating to public taxes and civil disorder, Justinian decreed that the Proconsul was to have undisputed authority. As for the *dux*, as was proper for a military commander, his authority was to command the *limitanei*, the *foederati*, and those soldiers not assigned to the Proconsul.

Exactly how successful was Justinian's reorganization of 536, our sources do not say. Samaritan unrest continued, ultimately breaking out in 555/556. According to the account of Malalas (Dorpfeld 1931: 487), the Samaritans, joined by the Jews of Caesarea, rose in revolt, killing many Christians and destroying their churches. Stephanus, "the governor of the city," (the same Stephanus?) attempted to stem the insurrection but was killed in his praetorium. Upon the appeal of Stephanus' wife, Justinian dispatched Amantius, the "governor" of the East (*magister militum*?) to Caesarea, and he suppressed the uprising ruthlessly. The best that one can say for Justinian's reorganization is that, with the appointment of Stephanus, an able and experienced administrator, it apparently functioned well for two decades in maintaining public order within the several provinces of Palestine.

NOTES

[1] G. W. Bowersock has called to my attention that Jones *et al.* 1971: 435 and Paschoud 1971: 433 place the date of Hilarius' tenure as governor at 392/3. This may very well be and would not conflict with the date of Jerome's composition of his *Commentary on Genesis.* However, the date of 392/3 rests on several assumptions made by Seeck (1906: 178–79) about several letters of Libanius, particularly *Ep.* 1053 and *Ep.* 1105. Since Libanus' letters are notoriously vague—i.e., they were not written for the benefit of historians of later antiquity—they must be approached with caution. The list of governors (Jones *et al.* 1971: 1108) has no name attached to the year 387/8. In an earlier paper (Mayerson 1984: 228), I cited the date as 379, a typographical error, which should have read 387.

[2] For a summary of the events of 529, see Montgomery, 1907: 114–17. Of all the sources that bear on the revolt, those of Cyril of Scythopolis and Malalas are the most coherent. The *Chronicon Paschale* (Dindorf 1832: 619) places the uprising at 530 and states that Iranaeus the *stratēlatēs* was called in to restore order. According to Procopius, *S.H.* 11.29, most likely with considerable exaggeration, the number killed was 100,000.

[3] The title of *comes clarissimus* cited by Cyril (Schwartz 1939: 177) provides no definite indication of the administrative post held by Stephanus since such titles were loosely employed. (See Festugière 1962: 106, n. 240.)

BIBLIOGRAPHY

Dindorf, L., ed.
   1832   *Chronicon Paschale* in *Corpus Scriptorum Historiae Byzantinae.* Bonn: Weber.

Dorpfeld, L., ed.
   1831   *Ioannes Malalas: Chronographia* in *Corpus Scriptorum Historiae Byzantinae.* Bonn: Weber.

Festugière, A.-J.
   1962   *Les Moines d'Orient,* III.1, Paris: du Cerf.

Foerster, R., ed.
   192   *Libanii Opera,* vol. 10. Leipzig: Teubner.

Foerster, R. and Richtsteig, E., eds.
   1929   *Choricii Gazei Opera.* Leipzig: Teubner.

Jones, A. H. M.
   1964   *The Later Roman Empire 284–602.* 2 vols. Norman, OK: University of Oklahoma.

Jones, A. H. M. *et al.,* eds.
   1971   *The Prosopography of the Later Roman Empire.* Cambridge, Eng.: Cambridge University.

Mayerson, P.
   1983   P.Oxy. 3574: "Eleutheropolis of the New Arabia." *Zeitschrift für Papyrologie und Epigraphik* 53: 251–58.
   1984   "Palaestina" vs. "Arabia" in the Byzantine Sources. *Zeitschrift für Papyrologie und Epigraphik* 56: 223–30.
   1986a   The Beersheba Edict. *Zeitschrift für Papyrologie und Epigraphik* 64: 141–48.
   1986b   Nea Arabia (P.Oxy. 5374): An Addendum to *ZPE* 53. *Zeitschrift für Papyrologie und Epigraphik* 64: 139–40.

Mendelsohn, L., ed.
   1887   *Historia Nova.* Leipzig: Teubner.

Montgomery, J. A.
   1907   *The Samaritans.* Philadelphia, PA: Ktav.

Paschoud, F., ed.
   1979   *Zosime: Histoire Nouvelle,* vol. 2. Paris: Budé.

Pharr, C., trans.
   1952   *The Theodosian Code.* Princeton, NJ: Princeton University.

Schoell, R. and Kroll, G., eds.
   1895   *Novellae,* in *Corpus Juris Civilis,* vol. 3. Berlin: Weidmann.

Schwartz, E.
   1939   *Kyrillos von Skythopolis.* Leipzig: Hinrichs.

Seeck, O.
   1906   *Die Briefe des Libanius Zeitlich Geordnet.* Leipzig: Hinrichs.

A Note on the Roman *Limes*:
'Inner' versus 'Outer'

PHILIP MAYERSON

New York University

FOR decades it has been taken for granted by many historians and archaeologists that the Romans organized a double line of defensive installations along the eastern provinces of their empire — an 'inner' and an 'outer' *limes*. Bowersock, on the basis of his readings of 'inner' and 'outer' *limes* in Ammianus Marcellinus, Malalas, and Theophanes, rejected the double-line concept put forward by Brünnow and Domaszewski and others, stating that 'no writer of antiquity can be shown to refer to an outer *limes*'.[1] In coming to this conclusion Bowersock believed that Theophanes[2] preserves a more accurate reading of Malalas,[3] using the word 'inner' (ἐσωτέρου) whereas Malalas has 'outer' (ἐζωτέρου).

I hold the contrary view — namely, that Malalas' statement is accurate as it stands, and that Theophanes misunderstood Malalas and changed 'outer' to 'inner' or, less likely, that he had something else in mind. Part of the problem in Bowersock's interpretation of the word *limes* and the two modifying words is that he viewed the *limes* as a fortified zone or territory rather than a non-specific frontier without any associations with military installations.[4] To Malalas the word meant simply 'frontier', and he had in mind two geographical aspects of an ill-defined region: an inner frontier that was the furthest removed from settled habitations, and an outer frontier that was closer to the *oikoumenē*, the settled or developed territory.

Although this interpretation seems to run contrary to the usual meaning of the words 'inner' and 'outer', it can stand the test of usage in late antiquity. Since there is a clear understanding of the word 'inner', whether applied to the frontier

---

[1] G.W. Bowersock: Limes Arabicus, *Harvard Studies in Classical Philology* 80 (1976), p. 228. Although Bowersock rightly challenged the concept, he mistakenly reasoned that 'the sense of "inner" is revealed to be simply "inside" the frontier'. Since it has been shown that the word 'inner' in the cited texts does not mean 'closer' or 'inside' but rather 'more remote' or 'further removed' Bowersock has corrected his interpretation in his *Roman Arabia*, Cambridge, Mass., 1983, p. 104, n. 41. On this point, see P. Mayerson: The Saracens and the *Limes*, *BASOR* 262 (1986), pp. 44-45.

[2] *Chronographia* (ed. C. de Boor), Leipzig, 1883, p. 178, line 15.

[3] *Chronicon* (ed. L. Dindorf), Bonn, 1832, pp. 448, line 6.

[4] Bowersock (above, n. 1, *HSCP*), p. 228; *Roman Arabia*, p. 104. On the meaning of the word *limes* as 'frontier' in its broadest sense without any connection with a line, system or zone of fortifications, see Mayerson (above, n. 1), p. 39. B. Isaac, in a wide-ranging article on the use and misuse of the word, comes to a similar conclusion in: The Terms 'Limes' and 'Limitanei', *Journal of Roman Studies* 78 (1988), forthcoming.

or to the desert, as meaning 'further out', 'deeper', or 'more remote', it is logical to assume that there would be a need for a word to describe a region or a place that is nearer or closer. That this is the case is unambiguously stated by Athanasius (*c.* 296-373) in his life of the Egyptian proto-monk Antony, in the Latin translation by Evagrius, a friend of Jerome, and in the *Apophthegmata Patrum* (late fifth century) concerning events in the life of the monk Sisoes.

In Athanasius' *Vita S. Antonii*, Antony sought an isolated retreat and found a deserted *parembolē* on a mountain 'across the [Nile] river'.[5] However, he soon found his solitude disturbed by crowds of admirers, and after he had considered going to the Upper Thebaid, a voice told him to go 'to the inner desert' (εἰς την ἐνδοτέραν ἔρημον).[6] Joining a Saracen caravan, Antony was brought to his famous retreat (now known as the Monastery of St. Antony) in Egypt's eastern desert near the Gulf of Suez. It was there, Athanasius states, that he remained alone on the 'inner mountain' (εἰς τὸ ἔσω ὄρος).[7] Occasionally he returned to his former dwelling place 'on the outer mountain' (ἐν τῷ ὄρει τῷ ἔξω) where he was visited by various people and where he customarily visited monks living there.[8] After responding to people who asked his views on Christian doctrine, he returned 'to the inner mountains' (εἰς τὸ ἔνδον ὄρος).[9]

Antony's influence spread to Sisoes, a monk from Scetis who settled on the inner mountain late in the fourth century. The *Apophthegmata Patrum* records a number of his experiences on the inner mountain, which is cited simply as 'Abba Antony's mountain' (τὸ ὄρος τοῦ ἀββᾶ 'Αντωνίου).[10] On one occasion, Sisoes went from Antony's mountain 'to the outer mountain of the Thebaid' (εἰς τὸ ἐξώτερον ὄρος τῆς Θηβαῖδος), and when some people heard that he had come 'to the outer mountain' (εἰς τὸ ἐξώτερον ὄρος), they asked to see him.[11]

With this evidence in hand, attesting to the use of 'inner' and 'outer' as geographical terms meaning 'further away' or 'far removed' (from civilization) and 'closer' or 'nearer' (to civilization), I now turn to Malalas and Theophanes. In Malalas we read that when the Saracen phylarch Arethas feared the Roman *dux*, he fled 'to the inner *limes* toward the Indies' (εἰς τὸ ἐνδότερον λίμιτον ἐπὶ τὰ 'Ινδικά).[12] Arethas sought, as I have pointed out, the traditional haven of safety, the open desert, far removed from forts and urban populations.[13] The words ἐπὶ

---

[5] *Patrologia Graeca* 26, col. 861.

[6] *Ibid.*, cols. 913-915. Evagrius' translation: *ad interius desertum*. The editor notes (col. 914, n. 83) that almost all manuscripts have ἐσωτέραν, which he changes to ἐνδοτέραν. Cf. n. 17, below.

[7] *Ibid.*, col. 918. Evagrius: *deserti interiora*.

[8] *Ibid.*, cols. 944-945. Evagrius: *in exteriori monte*.

[9] *Ibid.*, col. 969.

[10] *Patrologia Graeca* 65, cols. 393, 396, 398, 400.

[11] *Ibid.*, col. 405.

[12] Above, n. 3, p. 434.

[13] Mayerson (above, n. 1), p. 45.

τὰ Ἰνδικά leave no doubt that Arethas fled far to the east (into or near Persian territory?) where he fell into the hands of the Persian phylarch, who killed him. Theophanes reproduces Malalas' statement virtually verbatim.[14] However, when Mundhir raided Syria as far as the suburbs of Antioch, Malalas states that after he knew that the Roman army was proceeding against him, he gathered all his booty and fled 'through the outer *limes*' (διὰ τοῦ ἐξωτέρου λιμίτου).[15] Theophanes adds a number of details concerning the damage inflicted in the regions surrounding Antioch, and then says that he fled with his booty and prisoners 'through the inner *limes*' (διὰ τοῦ ἐσωτέρου λιμίτου).[16]

The point to be considered here is the fact that the raid by Mundhir took place deep within the Syrian *oikoumenē*, up to the outskirts of Antioch. In geographical terms, his actions were within the 'outer frontier' — that is, in the western portion of the frontier close to the city of Antioch and civilization. When Mundhir withdrew, Malalas states he went *through* (διὰ), not *to* (εἰς), the outer frontier in order to reach safety in the eastern desert. Theophanes, on the other hand, has Mundhir fleeing, not *to*, but *through* the inner frontier after retreating from his raid on the territory of Antioch and other sites in Syria. Apparently either Theophanes, or a copyist, did not recognize the geographical distinction that Malalas clearly made in his description of Mundhir's withdrawal. It is also possible that Theophanes had in mind that Mundhir fled 'through the inner *limes*' in order to reach a secure haven deep in Persian territory. However, he cites Malalas so literally (lines 5-7) that he appears to be uncertain as to his use of 'outer'. In any event, it is possible to make a case for both readings as they stand without emending either text, although I consider that Theophanes' text has the far weaker of the two readings.[17]

A final point: it is not a matter of coincidence that Ammianus, Evagrius, and Malalas use the words 'inner' and 'outer' in the same geographical sense. All three were natives of Antioch and Malalas himself was living in Antioch at the time of Mundhir's raid.

---

14 Above, n. 2, p. 179.
15 Above, n. 3, p. 445.
16 Above, n. 2, p. 178.
17 See also R. Devreesse: *Le Patriarcat d'Antioche*, Paris, 1945, p. 271, who makes this critical assessment of Theophanes' handling of readings in Malalas: '...ces deux textes [of Malalas] ont eu la malchance de tomber sous le main de Théophane, qui a changé ἐνδότερον en ἐσώτερον (De Boor, p. 179, 17) et ἐξωτέρου en ἐσώτερου (p. 178, 15), ce qui est plus grave, de même qu'il a ajouté (p. 174, 14) un ἐσώτερον au texte relatif à Palmyre (Malalas, 426). Laissons Théophane de côté, qu'il soit responsable de l'addition ou qu'elle retombe sur un copiste, pour nous arrêter à Malalas, seul digne d'être ici pris en considération'. Devreesse then attempts to rationalize — unsuccessfully, in my opinion — the meaning of 'inner' and 'outer' in accordance with the accepted meaning of the two words.

ZEITSCHRIFT FÜR PAPYROLOGIE UND EPIGRAPHIK

P. Ness. 58 and Two *Vaticinia ex Eventu* in Hebrew

A recent article on the impact of the Arab conquest on agriculture has brought to the attention of this writer–quite by chance–two *vaticinia ex eventu*, written in Hebrew, on the coming of the Arabs to Palestine.[1] The two texts brought to mind *P. Ness.* 58, a post-Conquest document having to do with a sum of money for "γεωμετρία of the Saracens" and γεωμορία of an Arab tribe called the bani Ouar. The editor of the papyrus, C.J. Kraemer, Jr., dated the piece to the late seventh century and believed that it represented a receipt for tax on assigned land. To give an understanding of the document as a whole, he paraphrased it as follows: "You, Sergius, have given us, the collectors 37½ solidi which you owe following the Arab survey. The money is due on lands formerly listed as belonging to the Beni War but transferred to you by order of the Governor" (*P. Ness.* III [Princeton 1958] p.169).

P. Ness. 58, along with some 40 other documents–about half of all the Nessana papyri–and archaeological data fall within the Umayyad period (660-750), a period during which the new ruling dynasty adopted not only the political but also the economic infrastructure of the pre-Islamic world. Agriculture was one aspect of that economic organization which the Umayyads actively fostered and encouraged.[2] Although the inhabitants of the conquered lands continued to call the invaders "Saracens" and "Ishmaelites" they were not the nomadic raiders often cited under those names in the Roman-Byzantine sources. As F.M. Donner has pointed out, Muhammad and his successors had rigorously subordinated the nomadic tribes to the sedentary ruling elite of the Hijaz, and that to become a Muslim, one had to lead a settled life (*The Early Islamic Conquests* [Princeton 1981] 79-80).

It is against this background, which has been generalized mostly from source material concerning Syria and Iraq, that *P. Ness.* 58 provides the evidence, in its particularity, for an action taken by the Muslims to settle on land in a rural community in the semi-arid Negev of Southern Palestine. As for the Hebrew *vaticinia*, they provide parallels for the two technical

---

[1] B.Z. Kedar, "The Arab Conquests and Agriculture: A Seventh-Century Apocalypse, Satellite Imagery, and Palynology," *Asian and African Studies* 9 (1985) 3-4.

[2] O. Grabar, summarizing the work of J. Sauvaget on the *Châteaux Ommeyades de Syrie*, states that the so-called "palaces" were centers for agricultural exploitation and that these centers "literally cover the whole area between the desert and sown extending northwest or west of a line drawn from the Euphrates around Raqqah to Damascus through Palmyra and through the mountains of Hawran down to the Gulf of 'Aqabah in an ill-defined fashion approximated by a straight line from the present oasis of Azraq to the modern town of 'Aqabah" (*Studia Islamica* 18 [1963] 8). On the western bank of the Wadi 'Arabah, I have been shown an Umayyad qanat system, which has been published (Y. Porath, *Qadmoniot* 20 [1987] 106-115 [Hebrew]), and other work in progress on Umayyad agricultural settlements. Y.D. Nevo has collected and published a large number of Umayyad inscriptions in Arabic in the settled region of the Negev (*Papers presented to the 3rd International Colloquium: From Jahiliyya to Islam* [1985]).

terms γεωμετρία and γεωμορία that are central to a new understanding of the Nessana document.

The unknown writers of these two prophecies, have cloaked themselves with the authority of renowned and legendary rabbis of the 1st and 2nd centuries A.D. (Eliezer the Great, Ishmael ben Elisha, and Simon ben Yokhay) and present an apocalyptic vision of the coming of a messiah, a deliverer who will establish an eternal kingdom. The historical context, however, is the 8th century, the post-Conquest period of the Umayyads, during which time the new rulers settled Muslims on Jewish lands. The deliverer that was sought by the Jews was one who would free them from the Umayyad caliphs.

In the relevant portion from *Pirqe de Rabbi Eliezer* (The Chapters of R. Eliezer), dated variously from the eighth to the early ninth century, there is this "prophetic" vision:

> Rabbi Ishmael says, Fifteen things are the Children of Ishmael going to do in the Land (of Israel) in the latter days, and they are as follows: They will measure the land with ropes, and make the cemetery into a dunghill where the flock rests, and they will measure them upon the tops of the mountains, and falsehood will multiply...

The historian H. Graetz claimed that the above passage was derived from an earlier Hebrew "prophesy," *Nisterot Rabbi Shim'on ben Yokhay* (The Secrets of R. Simon b. Yokhay), which he dates between August and October 750.[3]

> Also, Rabbi Simon used to say that he heard Rabbi Ishmael (say), when he heard that the Kingdom of Ishmael was approaching. "They are going to measure the land with ropes, as it is said, 'and he shall divide the land for a price' (Dan. 11:39). And they make cemeteries into pasture for flocks. And when one of them dies, they bury him wherever they find a place, and later they plough the grave and sow over it."

Both statements attributed to Rabbi Ishmael mention that the invaders will "measure the land with ropes" and in the *Nisterot* there is added the biblical citations from the Book of Daniel "and he shall divide the land for a price."[4] There can be little doubt that measuring the land with ropes by the Ishmaelites is the equivalent of γεωμετρία τῶν Σαρακηνῶν in *P. Ness.* 58 and that dividing the land is the same as γεωμορία.

Kraemer, relying mostly on early parallels from Egypt, viewed the money given for γεωμετρία of the Saracens as a tax on land rather than a fee for the survey of property. He was also led by the difficulties in interpreting lines 9-11 to take γεωμορία as "land-holding" and to suggest further that the land owned by the bani Ouar had been presented or assigned to Sergius by the order of the governor and that Sergius was paying the tax on the property.

---

[3] The date has not gone unchallenged. See Kedar (above, n. 1) p. 4, fn. 10.

[4] What R. Ishmael had in mind by the biblical phrase "for a price" is not clear, although from his apocalyptic utterance it would appear that he meant that Jews would have to pay the cost for dividing the land. Since the phrase is not used with measuring the land with ropes, it is possible that the land was taken away by "eminent domain" for less than its real value.

The two *vaticinia*, taken together with the policy of the Umayyads in encouraging settlement on the newly conquered lands, give us a new insight into developments that were taking place in Nessana in the late seventh century. The two activities of survey and division are interrelated. The document records a sum of money for a survey, and, in a modern real estate term, for a sub-division of the property that had been surveyed. The text of the receipt can hardly be said to be good Byzantine Greek; nevertheless the writer considered that he was composing a legal document and he indulged in a bit of legal redundancy in lines 8-10.

The core of *P. Ness.* 58, lines 6-11, is as follows: --- ἔςχομεν ---

6 παρὰ coῦ κύρω Σεργίου Γεωργίου τὰ δοθέν-
τα ὑμῖν χριcοῦ νομίcματα ν[ο(μ).] λζ Ϛ ἀρ(ί)θ(μια)

8 ἐκ τῆc γηωμετρίαc τὸν Σαρακινὸν+
ἐκ τὸν δοθέντο cυ ἐκ τοῦ δεcπότου ὑμὸν
Μεcλεμ cυμβούλου, ἐκ τῆc γεομορίαc τ[ὸν]
β(αν)υ Ουαρ +

---

6 κυρίου   7 ἡμῖν(?), χρυcοῦ   8 γεωμετρίαc τῶν Σαρακηνῶν   9 τῶν δοθέντων coι, ἡμῶν(?)   10 γεωμορίαc τ[ῶν]

The commission, representing the community (of landholders and taxpayers?) of Nessana affirms that it has received "from you, Sergius son of George Esq., the 37$\frac{1}{2}$ gold nomismata that were given to us in consequence of the land survey of the Saracens; (and) in consequence of the moneys given you by our lord Meslem the governor in consequence of the sub-division of the property of the bani Ouar."

Lines 7-8 attest only that the commission has received the 37$\frac{1}{2}$ solidi from Sergius for the survey; lines 9-11 attest that the money was given to Sergius by the governor and that it covered the sub-division of property connected with the bani Ouar. The writer of the receipt unfortunately did not make crystal clear that the sum of money given to the commission by Sergius covered both the survey and the sub-division of the property. However, there seems to be no question that the receipt contained all aspects for which the money was given, and that the money was given to Sergius by the governor. Hence, *P. Ness.* 58 cannot be viewed as a receipt for tax on assigned land.

If the above presentation is on the right track, it may be possible to reassemble some of the elements that led to the move of the Umayyad governor to survey and sub-divide property at Nessana. The town of Nessana was an economically viable community in semi-arid Southern Palestine. Despite limited amounts of rainfall and no perennial springs, the town sustained itself agriculturally by diverting run-off to plots of land in the numerous wadis surrounding the town.[5] Cereals and olives were grown in sufficient quantity not only to feed the inhabitants but also to furnish, as the Nessana *entagia* (*P. Ness.* 60-63; 65-67) show, supplies of wheat and olive oil that were requisitioned by the Umayyad administration. It is

---

[5] For a description of the hydrological system and the Nessana papyri relating to agriculture, see P. Mayerson in *Excavations at Nessana* I, H.D. Colt, ed. (London 1962) 231-246; 227-231; 259-263).

also more than probable that the vineyards of the town supplied the grapes that help make the name of Gaza famous for its wine (P. Mayerson, *BASOR* 257 [1985] 75-80). Yet another source of income was derived from pilgrim traffic to Mount Sinai which continued unabated under the Umayyads (*idem, Israel Expl. Journal* 32 [1982] 44-57). *P. Ness.* 72-73, dated to 684? and 683?, represent orders from the Arab governor to provide the services of a guide to escort two individuals to the Holy Mountain. Additional revenues were also possible, if, as *P. Ness.* 92 and 93 suggest, an Arab garrison or military command had been posted to Nessana–the town had a Roman fort and a *numerus* had been stationed there during the fifth and sixth centuries.

The Sergius of *P. Ness.* 58 had risen from presbyter to father-superior of the monastic community, and as such was one of the town's leading men, if not the leading man as is indicated by the honorific title of κύριος in line 6.[6] It was he to whom the governor Meslem, presumably of Gaza, gave the sum of money with instructions for the town to conduct a survey and a sub-division. Whose money was involved is of course not known: it may have been provided by the governor to purchase land for the bani Ouar, or it may have been payed to the governor by the tribe. It is also quite possible that the "survey of the Saracens" was on a large scale and not intended solely for the bani Ouar but for settling other tribes as well on the surveyed land. Equally unknown is the kind of land that was surveyed: abandoned land? land taken by force? by treaty with the town? purchased for Muslim settlement?[7] We cannot say other than to point out that productive tillable land in this region required long lines of stone walls, somewhat similar to terrace walls, to secure sufficient moisture for growing crops. Land previously cultivated would have been the most desireable. All that can be assumed is that the survey was conducted by the town and the Sergius was turning over the money to the commission to dispense it as had been agreed upon. As for the sub-division, whether for part or all the land surveyed, it surely concerned the tribe, since for tax purposes the land given to or purchased by the bani Ouar had to be sub-divided in order to determine which individual was to be responsible for the tax on the land assigned to him.

It appears evident that *P. Ness.* 58 fits neatly into the picture of Umayyad settlement in Palestine. Apart from the two *vaticinia*, the scores of Umayyad inscriptions that are found throughout the Negev, and the archaeological material that is being brought to light–all of which attest to the Umayyad policy of settlement on newly conquered lands–the Nessana document is unique in that it provides direct evidence of a transaction that put that policy into effect.

New York University   Philip Mayerson

---

[6] Sergius is a presbyter in *P. Ness.* 57, dated to 689; in *P. Ness.* 77, dated to c. 685-690, he is ἡγούμενος. See also *P. Ness.* III pp. 6-7. In *P. Ness.* 68,70,74, all dated prior to 686, the same honorific title is given to George, the *dioecetes* of Nessana. It appears that Sergius took over this administrative post having to do with finances, and as *dioecetes* he would be in communication with the governor.

[7] See F.M. Donner, *The Early Islamic Conquest* (Princeton 1981) 240.

ZEITSCHRIFT FÜR PAPYROLOGIE UND EPIGRAPHIK

The Meaning of the Word *Limes* (λίμιτον) in the Papyri

In the past several decades there has been such a spate of interest in the *limes* that a colleague of mine has called it "the *limes* industry." This interest has been occasioned largely by surveys and excavations of military installations in the Roman provinces of Palestine and Arabia. From the time of Mommsen, Brünnow and Domaszewski to the present, the preoccupation with military installations and military organization has led investigators to interpret the word *limes* as meaning a fortified line of defense, and to formalize their conclusions by coining or using such terms as *Limes Arabicus*, *Limes Palaestinae*, Antonine, Severan, Diocletian, Justinian *Limes*.[1]

In an article on the Saracens and the *limes*, this writer has taken the position that, in its application to Palestine and Arabia, it is necessary to discard the association of the term *limes* with the words "border" or "boundary" or "fortified line"; that it is best to take the word as a broad geographical term meaning "frontier" (*BASOR* 262 [1986] 39). Among other citations in support of my view I pointed out that Malalas makes clear this meaning of the word when he relates (Dindorf, 434) an incident concerning the Saracen phylarch Arethas who, fearing the hostility of the *dux* of Palestine, fled "to the inner *limes* toward the Indies"; that is, he fled to the interior frontier region, the traditional haven of safety for raiding Arabs, far removed from forts, urban populations and civilization.[2]

B. Isaac, in a wide-reaching article on the meaning of the words *limes* and *limitanei*, has argued persuasively that for every period, from the first century to the sixth, the word *limes* had no specific connection with a fortified line of defense, whether linear or in-depth, and that from the fourth century the term became an "administrative concept denoting a frontier district administered by a military commander (*dux*) ... In time this formal term came to be used in an informal manner, to indicate the 'frontier district' (*JRS* 78 [1988] forthcoming)." In arriving at his conclusions, Isaac investigated the use of the word in literary and epigraphic sources. He did not, however, examine the use of the word in the papyri; hence, this opportunity to test both our positions on this very sensitive issue in which there is a heavy investment in scholarly publications.

---

[1] See *e.g.*, S.T. Parker, "Toward a History of the Limes Arabicus," *BAR International Series* 71 (1980) 865-877; *idem*, *BASOR Supplement* No. 23 (1985) 1-24; I. Shahîd, *Byzantium and the Arabs in the Fourth Century* (Dumbarton Oaks 1984) 476-483 *et passim*; M. Avi-Yonah, *RE* suppl. 13 (1973) s.v. Palaestina, cols. 417-418; 448.

[2] *loc. cit.* 45. See also P. Mayerson, "A Note on the Roman *Limes*: 'Inner' versus 'Outer'," *Israel Exploration Journal* (forthcoming). From a Roman point of view, the inner part of the frontier district was more remote than the outer parts, at least one of which bordered upon the Roman oikoumenē.

It is natural to turn first to Maspero's seminal work on the military organization of Byzantine Egypt. Maspero accepts the traditional meaning of the word *limes* as a system of defense, but he is confronted by a dilemma when comparing the defense-in-depth system described by Diehl for Africa and its absence in Egypt. It leads him to raise this question:

"Existe-t-il un *limes* semblable en Egypt au vi⁰ siecle? Il nous en reste très peu de té-moignages écrits; encore sont-ils des plus succincts. En général, l'expression de λίμιτον a ce sens très large de 'province frontière' .... Parfois pourtant elle se restreint, et, en Thébaïde au moins, désigne cette sorte de *marche* des confins qui est à cette époque le véritable limes."[3]

Maspero, in spite of being influenced by the traditional meaning of *limes*, has, in the face of the evidence, touched upon this writer's conclusion for the eastern provinces and Isaac's general statement for the late empire. Maspero's term "*marche* des confins" is the equivalent of "borderlands" or "border region" and is quite close in meaning to "frontier" or "frontier district." The fact that he reserved the word "frontière" to qualify "province" apparently did not provide the meaning he sought in connection with the Thebaid. As for defining *limes* as "frontière province," the phrase cannot serve as a general term to describe such provinces as Palestine, Phoenicia, and Syria. Maspero's *marche*, however, appears to have influenced the editors of *P. Abinn.* 1.5-6, who translate *comes limitis* as "count of the Mark." E. Bernard uses "marche" in *J. Philae* 194 but "province-frontière" in *J. Philae* 220-222 although all three refer to the Thebaid.[4] G. Zefereli translates *limes* as "Mark" and as "Grenzgebiet" (*Aegyptus* 9 [1928] 115 and 117). In *P. Mert.* I 43.17, however, where mention is made of a στρατοπεδάρχης τοῦ Αἰγυπτιακοῦ λιμίτου, the editor, relying on Maspero, notes (p. 143): "For λίμιτον, used either of a frontier province, or as probably here, of an area marked by a line of fortified posts."

P. Abinn. 1.5-6 (340/1), *P. Mert.* I 43.17 (V?) and nine others represent all the citations of the word *limes* in Egyptian documents prior to the Islamic era: *Stud. Pal.* XX 143.2 (435); *W.Chr.* I 6.15 (425/450); SB IV 7433.1.20 (468); *BGU* XII 2162.3; *P. Ryl.* IV 609.1 (505); *SB* VI 9598.3 (V); *P. Monac.* I 6. 11 and 28f. (VI); *BGU* II 670.4 (byz); *P. Cair. Masp.* I 67076.13 (byz). For the Islamic period, there are two, dated to 708: *P. Lond.* IV 1332.23 and 1333.25. In addition to the above, there are four inscriptions from Philae (194 and 220-222) that are often cited in discussions of the word *limes* in Egyptian documents (see n. 4).

In all instances, with the exception of *P. Cairo Masp.* I 67076, *P. Monac.* I 6, and *P. Lond.* IV 1332 and 1333, the word *limes* appears as part of the title of the *comes* together with the name of the province: τοῦ Θηβαϊακοῦ λιμίτου or τοῦ Αἰγυπτιακοῦ λιμίτου or its Latin equivalent. In *P. Monac.* 6, a certain tribune (?) Menas is cited as τοποτηρητὴς τοῦ λιμίτου, and *BGU* XII 2162, 2f. is directed to a certain *commentariensis*, ἀπὸ κομ[μ]εντα-ρησίων [---]ης στρ[α]τιωτικῆς τάξεως τοῦ θηβαϊκ[οῦ λι]μίτου.

---

[3] *Organization militaire de l'Égypte byzantine* (Paris 1942) 19.

[4] *Les Inscriptions grècques et latines de Philae II* (Paris 1967). His numbers 194, 220, 221, and 222 refer to *Rec.* 592, 598, 599, and 600 respectively in G. Lefèbvre, Recueil des inscrip-tions grecques-chrétiennes d'Egypte, Cairo 1907.

There is no question that in the several provinces of Egypt the *comes* --- occasionally called *comes et dux, comes rei militaris*, or *dux* --- was the imperial officer in command of the armed forces and military installations. However, the fact that the word *limes* was attached to his title cannot be taken as a formal imperial designation. The eleven citations that have come to light represent a statistically low number of occurences. A sampling from Preisigke's "Besondere Wörterliste" (pp. 126-7; 206) shows that out of some 80 citations for *comes*, only 4 are followed by *limes*; out of 45 citations for *dux*, only one, and that is also cited under *comes*. Interestingly enough, however, the words τῆc Θηβαίων χώρας appear 4 times under the listing of titles for *dux*. I see here a close association in meaning between *limes* as "frontier" and χώρα in a more general sense as "region."

In *P. Lond.* IV 1332 and 1333, dated to the early Islamic period, an Arab official is charged with the duty of searching for fugitives and is ordered to go εἰ(c) λίμιτ(ον). The use of the word without a qualifying place name has created somewhat of a dilemma as to its location. The editor of the papyrus believes that it probably represented one of the two Thebaids which appears in Justinian's Edict XIII 22.1; or that it is the border district between Arcadia and the Thebaid.[5] Maspero, on the other hand, believes that it can only be the fortified zone facing the Nubian frontier (*op. cit.* [n. 3], p. 19). I would like to suggest another alternative. The two documents cite three distinct regions for which Arab officials were ordered to search for fugitives: the Thebaid, Arcadia, and λίμιτον. Wherever λίμιτον was, the Arab official knew where it was. If it was one of the two Thebaids, it would have been so stated. It is possible, I believe, that over time, a region that was loosely called "the frontier" became formally known as a distinct region called The Frontier. (cf. the degeneralization of castrum becoming Chester.)

P. Cair. Masp. I 67076, a letter, is a compelling one since the critical word is not part of the title of a military commander, but deals with quantities of wheat, a money allowance, and the phrase "to send wheat from the *limes*" i.e., from the frontier. Maspero considers that the Thebaid is to be understood with the phrase (*ibidem* p. 19, n. 1). It is possible, however, that, as in *P. Lond.* IV 1332 and 1333, the writer was referring to a region known as The Frontier.

It should also be noted that no citation for the word *limes* appears in any of the Egyptian documents earlier than the fourth century. Isaac has observed that the term became extremely common after the army reorganization of Diocletian and Constantine, and that from the fourth century and later it was used in the sense of a frontier district and that it was used frequently (*JRS* 78 [1988], forthcoming). The word soon entered the vocabulary of Rufinus (*HE* 2.6) when he reported Saracen raids (ca. 374) on "cities and towns of the Palestinian and Arabian *limes* ... and neighboring provinces." Jerome (PL 22.1086), in a letter dated 411, writes: "a sudden attack by barbarians ... ran through the *limes* of Egypt, Palestine, Phoennicia and Syria." To this may be added the much-quoted statement of Malalas (Dindorf 308)

---

[5] p. xx; *JHS* (1901) 120, n. 42.

regarding Diocletian's reorganization of the eastern provinces, that he "built εἰς τὰ λίμιτα κάϲτρα from Egypt to the borders of Persia (ἕωϲ τῶν Περϲικῶν ὅρων).

It would appear that, from the fourth century or somewhat earlier, the imperial chancellory required a word that would more closely define the relationship between lands that were controlled by Rome and those that were not. In regions where there was a fixed, or perceived, line between the two, the word *fines* (boundary) was appropriate. By the fourth century, apparently, boundaries were difficult to define, and hence the world *limes* (frontier) more accurately described the situation in such provinces as Egypt, Africa, Arabia, and Syria. It is significant to note that in Justinian's edict 1.27, dated to 534, directed to the praetorian prefect of Africa and Belisarius as *magister militum Orientis*, the word *fines* is used 6 times in 27.4 in urging the army to recover lands "to that point where the Roman state had its boundaries (*fines*) before the invasion of the Vandals and the Moors." In the paragraphs which follow, (27.5-17), which specify the actions required by the prefect and Belisarius to maintain the frontier, the words *limes* and *limitaneus* are used exclusively, some 13 times.

To elaborate further on my opening statement to this paper, I have taken the position that, with respect to the eastern provinces, it is best to translate the word *limes* as "frontier" in the sense that it is used in the United States: i.e., as the land that forms the furthest extent of a country's settled or inhabited region (*BASOR* 262 [1986] 39). The word "frontier" is an elastic one and does not require sharp definition in terms of boundaries or lines of separation between states, provinces, ethnic groups, etc. A frontier lies at the hither edge of a desert, or of a region incapable of habitation or penetration; it is a region that is thinly settled, if at all. Because of the hostile nature of the environment, a frontier usually requires a system of defense to protect its inhabitants, to provide sanctuary in forts, fortlets, or towers in the event of attacks in force, and to keep open lines of communication between settlements and commercial entrepôts. Hence, we can speak of a frontier of settlement and a frontier of military defense. When Rufinus and Jerome speak of raids and use the word *limes* they are unquestionably referring to frontiers of settlement; Malalas' statement, on the other hand, refers to the action taken by Diocletian to organize the military defenses on the frontiers facing Persia and the east.

As for Egypt, the armed forces listed in the *Notitia Dignitatum* for the diocese, the military titles that crop up in the documents, and the physical evidence of forts and towers direct our attention forcibly to the military frontier, while little is known of the scattered settlement, monasteries, and habitations of ascetics that lay beyond the pale of the organized system of defense. Such was the case of the monastic settlements at Scetis and Nitria in the western desert, and the monasteries of St. Anthony and Paul in the eastern desert. In other words, the two frontiers do not necessarily coincide. This is perhaps truer for Egypt than for most other provinces since one does not have to go far to find the Egyptian frontier. All the lands to the east and west of the narrow belt of cultivation along both banks of the Nile, and several oases, represent the Egyptian frontier. Maspero has put it succinctly when he states: "Chaque ville, en un certain sens, est ville frontière puisqu' à travers les solitudes de sable ou de montagnes qui longent de si près chaque rive du Nil, les bandes pillages de nomades peuvent toujours circuler inaperçues et opérer une razzia dans les nomes les plus inattendus et en apparence les mieux protégés" (above, n. 3, p. 10).

To sum up,it is evident that there is ambiguity and confusion in giving meaning to the term *limes* as it appears in the Egyptian documents and other sources. One cannot use words meaning "border" where there are no borders in the conventional sense of the term, but only outlying districts of civilization or undefined tracts of land. Confusion is added when *limes* is taken without qualification as a line of military installations. To clarify what has become a muddied situation, it would be helpful to translate *limes* as "frontier," or "frontier-district" and their equivalent in other languages. It would help even more if it were possible to be more specific by distinguishing between the two different kinds of frontiers: frontiers of settlement and military frontiers. There may also be occasions where it would be useful to use the term "political frontier" when, for example, describing an uninhabited and unfortified region (*limes interior*?) that is under the apparent control of a governing power.

One additional item. If the view put forward by Isaac and myself has merit, it would be unfortunate should the word *limes* continue to be listed in further supplements of Preisigke's *Besondere Wörterliste* under Abschnitt 10: "Militär" without some cautionary note. The same would apply to the multi-fascicled entry "Limes" in the *Dizionario Epigraphico de Antichità Romane*.

New York University   Philip Mayerson

Saracens and Romans: Micro–Macro Relationships

Department of Classics
New York University
New York, NY 10013

Banning (1986) and Parker (1987) have put forward contrasting viewpoints on the relationship of the nomadic population (Saracens) to the settled inhabitants (Romans) in the late Roman-Byzantine era, based essentially on their interpretations of different kinds of archaeological evidence. This paper takes the position that the true temper of the relationship can only be assessed by an analysis of the literary sources, which are particularly rich for that period. The complexities of that relationship are demonstrated in detail: there was both conflict and symbiosis between Roman and Saracen and a Pax Romana *never existed between the two. As to the position that Roman military strategy was to monitor and control the movement of Arab tribes, there is no evidence that it ever did or indeed that it was designed for that purpose.*

Anthropologist E. B. Banning has presented a theoretical and methodological model based on the data of the 1979 season of the Wadi el Hasa survey (Banning 1986: 25–50). As an alternative model to the traditional view of a Roman-nomad conflict, the conflict between the agriculturist and the nomad raider, Banning suggested (1986: 44) that "there was no ethnic conflict at all, implying that all the Roman-Byzantine sites within the study area belong to a fairly homogeneous society with an agricultural base." Hence, the use of such words as *Pax Romana* and "mutualism" in the title of his paper. Similarly, on the basis of his finds, S. Rosen (1987) suggested that "a pastoral society functioned in complement to a settled urban/agricultural society of the Byzantine period in the Negev."

S. T. Parker, an historian, rebutted most of Banning's assumptions, citing literary and epigraphic evidence detailing conflict between the sedentary populace and Arab nomads along the entire eastern frontier (Parker 1987: 35–51). To this he added his own archaeological survey of military installations of what he has dubbed the *Limes Arabicus* and came to these conclusions (1987: 48): "The Roman objective was to monitor and control any raiding by tribes along the frontier.... The control of Arab movement was one means of maintaining regional security. A second means was diplomacy. Diplomatic methods of control included treaties and payment of subsidies to nomads."

It is clear that Banning has presented us with a micro view of the possible relationship between the nomad and the settled population that is based on a survey of 100 km². Similarly, Rosen, in the Ramon Crater of the Negev, has surveyed some 200 km² and has suggested a peaceful relationship between the pastoralist and the agriculturalist. Parker, although he acknowledges that such relationships did exist, states that they did so because the Roman government pursued an aggressive policy in "monitoring and controlling the movement of Arab tribes" (Parker 1984: 48). In essence, he has given a macro view of the relationship between the Saracen[1] (i.e., the nomad or the bedouin) and the Roman (i.e., the settled inhabitant) based on literary sources that refer to events that took place within the several Roman provinces on the eastern frontier.

The question arises whether or not the two views are compatible, or whether the conclusions of both Parker and Banning are flawed in some respect. The "micro" views Banning and Rosen

313

presented are limited by the nature of the surveys on which they are based and can be accepted only as they apply to those areas. Their application to other areas of the frontier can be taken only as hypothetical models—and have been presented as such—and must await further testing in the field. The two surveys, however, have directed our attention to the more humble archaeological remains (small ceramic scatters, pens, campsites, nonagricultural installations) that have been passed over but which nonetheless are part of the historical mosaic.

Banning's and Rosen's limited surveys aside, the true temper of the relationship between the Romans and the Saracens can be assessed only by an analysis of the literary sources. Archaeological finds (ceramic collections, details of military installations), while valuable in providing support for the literary evidence, are, naturally, silent on the question of how the two sides related to each other. The literary sources, on the other hand, are contemporary or near contemporary accounts of actions and counteractions between the two societal (if not ethnic) groups. It must be remembered, though, that the sources present only the Roman side of the picture, which is often unfavorably disposed toward the Saracen. Those accounts, however, are quite varied in character and scale. Historians, such as Ammianus Marcellinus, Procopius, Evagrius and Malalas, give us a view of events taking place on a large scale—battles between Rome and Persia and their respective Saracen allies, actions taken by generals, emperors and kings—and focus on regions where major actions were taking place, generally north of the 34th parallel. Then there are the reports or memoirs with a more limited view, the micro view: the accounts of travelers, monks, and ascetics who relate their personal experiences as they came into contact with Saracens or who communicate the account of another's experience. Although the scale of reportage is narrower, such reports reveal a more intimate relationship between the Roman and the Saracen. That is particularly true of the European pilgrim or traveler for whom the Saracen was an exotic figure and an item of great interest for his community.

THE FRONTIER (*LIMES*)

We should discard the conventional view that the eastern frontier where Romans and Saracens

came into contact was a line or a border or a zone separating Romans and Saracens. The eastern frontier encompassed more than those regions east of the *via nova Traiana* and the military installations extending to the Euphrates; the frontier (*limes*) also included the regions—usually marginal or semimarginal in terms of habitable capability—that were thinly settled and had extended lines of communication between settled populations. (On the meaning of the word *limes*, see Isaac 1988; Mayerson 1986: 39; Mayerson in press.) It was within the interstices of those settled areas that the Saracen was found. He lived and roamed both within and beyond whatever fortified zone the Romans had developed. The frontier in this sense applies to areas deep within the Roman provinces of Egypt, Palestine, Arabia, Syria, and Mesopotamia. That this is so is clearly reflected in the memoir of the peripatetic nun Egeria. En route from Clysma in Sinai to Egypt (ca. 385), she was escorted from one fort to another; and after visiting "biblical" Pithom, which was also a fort, she states (*CCSL* 175.48) that she then "entered the borders of Egypt and left behind the lands of the Saracens (*fines Egypti intravimus, relinquentes iam terras Saracenorum*)." And the writer of the Nilus narrative, a Sinaitic eremite (ca. 400), declares that the Saracen "nation inhabits the desert from Arabia as far as Egypt's Red Sea and the River Jordan" (Conca 1983: 12). We even possess a statistic on the number of Saracens who wandered through the "inner desert" of Sinai. As the Piacenza pilgrim and his companions were making their way through the desert to Mount Sinai (ca. 578), they were told, presumably by their guide, that the Saracens numbered 12,600 (*CCSL* 175.147). All Palaestina Tertia, of which Sinai was a part, can be said to have been a *limes*, a frontier zone. According to a Theodosian edict (7.4.30) dated to 409, there were also frontier troops (*limitanei milites*) in the other two provinces of Palestine.

Saracen Raiding and Trading

Prior to the Muslim invasions of the seventh century, Arab tribes that were given to raiding did so in pursuit of plunder and prisoners; they had no interest in taking possession of territory, cities, or provinces.[2] Nor was there any need to, since they were reasonably free to pursue their traditional occupation of raiding communities deep

within the imperial lands of the east. From the
fourth to the seventh century there are reports,
expressed in broad terms, of raids on the provinces of Egypt, Palestine, Arabia, Phoenicia, and
Syria. Rufinus, in his account of the Saracen
queen Mauia, tells of her "harassing the frontier
(*limes*) cities of Palestine and Arabia and at the
same time laying waste the neighboring provinces"
(*PL* 21: col. 515). Jerome, in a letter dated ca.
411 (*PL* 22: col. 1086) reports that "a sudden
attack by barbarians ran through the frontiers
(*limites*) of Egypt, Palestine, Phoenicia, and Syria
like a torrent carrying everything before it." And
in his life of the monk Malchus, Jerome vividly
describes (*PL* 23: cols. 55–56) the capture of
Malchus, who was traveling in a convoy close by
a public road that led from Beroea (Aleppo) to
Edessa. He was seized by marauding Saracens
and enslaved. Other raids that clearly originated
within the Roman provinces of Palestine and
Egypt have been recorded by Cyril of Scythopolis,
John Cassian, Evagrius, Choricius of Gaza, and
Theophanes (Mayerson 1986: 39; 1964: 181; Isaac
1984: 193, n. 108). In 619, following the Persian
occupation of Palestine, Sophronius brought the
body of John Moschus from Rome for burial at
Mount Sinai; but when he reached Ascalon he
found the road to the Holy Mountain blocked
"because of the tyrannical incursions of those who
are called Agareni" (*PL* 74: col. 121). One source
even informs us that a region within Palaestina
Tertia was off limits to travelers because it must
have been, as Egeria put it, *terrae Saracenorum*.
When the Piacenza pilgrim made his way to
Mount Sinai, he took a direct route from the
town of Nessana through central Sinai to the
Holy Mountain. At Mount Sinai he learned that
it was not safe to return by the same route since
the Saracen festival, during which there was a
moratorium on raiding, was over and pilgrims
were advised to take the safer routes to Jerusalem
by way of Egypt or Arabia (*CCSL* 175: 149;
Mayerson 1982: 46–47). To the monks of the
Judaean desert, the raiding Saracens were "the
wolves of Arabia". . . ."uncivilized (*barbaroi*) in
conduct; intent on doing evil." (Schwartz 1939:
24, 97).

Raiding was one aspect of the relationship
between Roman and Saracen; trading was another. Trading, like raiding, was a means of
acquiring resources and income; and as settled
communities and travelers grew in number, op-

portunities arose for local Saracens to profit by
providing a variety of services. In fact, as populations swelled, there was a concomitant increase in
the migration of tribes to the frontiers of the
eastern provinces, where there were opportunities
for brigandage or peaceful coexistence.

Accounts of major profitable arrangements between tribal leaders and Roman emperors are well
documented; those on a smaller scale, and rather
mundane, are rarely recorded. Historians are quiet
on such micro matters; but travelers, eremites,
and papyrological documents record a number of
transactions in which Saracens provide transport
or serve as messengers, guides, and sellers of
animals. Anastasius, a monk who lived at Mount
Sinai, tells of a renowned eremite who, when he
lay ill in his cell and knew that his end was near,
sent a Saracen to Aila to summon one of his
spiritual brothers. The distance, according to
Anastasius, was 200 miles, which the Saracen
covered in 12 days (Nau 1902: 67). The Nessana
papyri mention a Saracen who delivered a letter
to Nessana from the bishop of Aila (Kraemer
1958: 146). Another document, a fragmentary
statement of transactions of a group of merchants
or pilgrims, records an exorbitant payment of 3½
solidi "to the Saracen who took us to the Holy
Mountain," and another 1½ *solidi* "to the Saracen
ᶜAdi, the money we borrowed for the wool." The
same document also records purchases of camels,
horses, and a donkey, presumably from the Saracens (Kraemer 1958: 256). In the Judaean desert,
the *oikonomos* of Sabas' Great Laura hired Saracen camels and a Saracen camel-driver to transport wheat from Machaerus on the Dead Sea
(Schwartz 1939: 186).

To those commonplace transactions we may
add elements in the Nilus narrative that combine
raiding and trading. The community of Pharan in
Sinai had a treaty with a tribal leader named
Am(m)anes. It was broken by an outlaw band of
his tribesmen who killed a number of solitaries in
the environs of Mount Sinai and took some
prisoners, among them Theodoulus, son of Nilus.
The council of Pharan sent couriers to Am(m)anes
to complain that the treaty had been breached.
Am(m)anes reassured them that the treaty was
still in force, that he would punish the guilty and
return the prisoners who were still alive as well as
the booty that had been taken. He did so because
the arrangement with the community of Pharan
was profitable. "For their dealing with each other

brought no small gain to those (members of his tribe) who were helped by the resources of the other party (the Pharanites) in providing the necessities which they lacked (Mayerson 1986: 261–62). As for Theodoulus, he was taken to the Negev, to the town of Soubaita (Sobata), where he was put up for sale, and "when no one offered more than two pieces of gold (2 *solidi*), the barbarians threatened to kill him until someone paid their price" (Conca 1983: 49–50; Mayerson 1975: 70).

Somewhat earlier in Egypt, the famed monk Antony, seeking an isolated retreat in which to practice his asceticism, was directed to a group of Saracens heading toward the eastern desert. They provided transport to his new retreat, and for a time supplied him with bread (*PG* 26: cols. 913; 916). In 357, however, Jerome records (*PL* 27: cols. 689–90) that (other?) Saracens raided his monastery and killed one of his disciples.

The proximity of monks and Saracens in the remote regions of the frontier brought them together in a relationship that had little to do with trading or raiding. It is not likely that the nomads were impressed with the monks' austere and solitary life or by their religious doctrines; it was their miracle-working cures, their ability to exorcise demons that convinced the nomads to turn from paganism to Christianity. Tribes often converted en masse, following the example of their chiefs. When Hilarion, the protomonk of Palestine, traveled to the isolated communities of the Negev (ca. 350), he came into contact with Saracens in or near the city of Elusa. It was there, as Jerome relates (*PL* 23: col. 42), that "he had often cured many Saracens who were possessed by an evil spirit . . . and they would not let him depart until he had planned a church for them." At about the same time, a Sinaitic eremite named Moses cured the tribal leader Obedianus and "converted to Christianity all the people living on the frontiers of the Ishmaelites who inhabit the region of Pharan" (Combefis 1660: 99–101). Another sheikh, Zokomos, unable to beget a son, was told that if he believed in Christ he would have one. Upon the birth of a son, Zokomos and his tribe converted to Christianity and he "was regarded with fear by the Persians and other Saracens" (Sozomenus *H.E.* 6.38). Cyril of Scythopolis tells of how Euthymius (d. 473) healed Terebon, the ailing son of the phylarch Aspestos, by marking him with the sign of the cross. Aspestos and his tribe were so struck by the miracle that they begged Euthymius to convert them to Christianity (Schwartz 1939: 20).

In addition to those friendly contacts between eremites and Saracens, there were the occasional happy experiences of travelers as they came upon nomads. The Piacenza pilgrim records one such experience as he traveled through the deep desert to Mount Sinai. He gives an age-old picture of bedouin poverty and hospitality (*CCSL* 175: 147): "The children and wives of the Saracens came from the desert and sat weeping by the road. They spread out their bundles in front of them and asked the passers-by for bread. Their husbands also came and brought skins of cool water from the remoter parts of the desert and gave us some. They accepted bread and offered us stems and roots (i.e., dried herbs) whose sweet smell was superior to any fragrance. They asked nothing for them since they considered them a gift and were celebrating a religious festival."

The intimate contacts between Romans and Saracens prove that there were both conflict and symbiosis between them. But Banning's statement that "there was no ethnic conflict at all"—even though the statement is applied only to his study area—is flawed in terms of its use as a model for other areas. Equally difficult to sustain in light of the evidence are the unmodified words *Pax Romana* and "mutualism" in the title of his article.

We return to Parker's broad view of Rome's military strategy, namely, that the Roman objective along the eastern frontier was "to monitor and control" raiding by nomadic tribes. He states his conclusion as follows:

> It is evident that the Roman frontier was not designed as a military barrier against nomadic tribes. The tribes were expected to pass through the frontier on their semiannual migrations along natural routes of communication. Therefore, nomads could be found along both sides of the military zone and even in the zone itself. The Roman objective was to monitor their movements and control any raiding by tribes along the frontier. A reconnaissance system of watchtowers and patrols would alert the larger garrisons in the towns and forts of the region of any nomadic raid. Some Roman units would continue to garrison strategic points, denying the invaders food, water, and fresh mounts. A mobile strike force

would meanwhile attempt to intercept and destroy the raiders (Parker 1987: 48).[3]

The major objection to that point of view is that we do not possess a recorded instance of a military unit "controlling" a nomadic raid; nor do we have a citation of Romans denying invaders food, water, and fresh mounts, nor of a mobile strike force taking preemptive action to intercept and destroy raiders. On the other hand, there are more than ample citations, (above) to demonstrate the inability of the Romans to control raids by Arab tribes. It is apparent that the Romans were aware that they could not do so, for the military strategy that Diocletian initiated was designed not to control the movement of tribes, but to react defensively to attacking forces. As Malalas informs us (Dorpfeld 1831: 308), Diocletian "built forts for the frontiers (*limita*) from Egypt as far as the borders of Persia and posted frontier troops in them, and he appointed *duces* for each province to be stationed within the forts with considerable forces for their safety." Parker cites an inscription that records the construction of a reservoir by the protector Vincentius because so many outlying pickets had been killed by Saracens while procuring water (Parker 1987: 45; 1986: 144). But it is clear that the Saracens, not the Romans, were in a position to deny the Romans access to water.

Let us take this issue of control a step further. Parker (1986: 45) cites Procopius (*B.P.* 1.17.41–42; 45–47) to explain Justinian's strategy in entering an alliance with the Ghassanid Arethas (Ḥarith) to serve as a counterpoise to the Lakhmid Alamoundaras (al-Mundhir), the Persians' Saracen ally. A closer reading of Procopius, even if one were to discount much of what he says as overstatement, makes clear that the army of Roman regulars, let alone the *limitanei milites*, could not prevent hostile Saracens from penetrating the frontier of the eastern provinces. This is how Procopius tells it.

> . . . beginning with the boundaries of Egypt and as far as Mesopotamia, he (al-Mundhir) plundered the whole country, pillaging one place after another, burning buildings in his track and making captives of the population by the tens of thousands on each raid, most of whom he killed without consideration, while he gave up the others

for great sums of money . . . so suddenly did he move . . . he was already off with his plunder when the generals and soldiers were beginning to learn what had happened and to gather themselves against him . . . he was always able to make his inroad with the whole army wherever he wished in the Roman domain; and neither any of the commanders of the Roman troops, whom they call *duces*, nor any leader of the Saracens allied with the Romans, who are called "phylarchs," was strong enough with his men to array himself against Alamoundaras; for the troops stationed in different districts were not a match in battle for the enemy. (Loeb translation)

I emphasize the word "controlling" and the inability of the Romans to control the movement of Arab tribes. Monitoring is another matter, if it means observing the movement of tribes so as to be on the alert against attacks. Towers, of course, would be used for that purpose. Monitoring in that sense would be a defensive action; it would give the local inhabitants time to seek safety in a tower or a fortified place. One such example of the use of a tower is found in the Ammonius narrative dated to the fourth or fifth century (Combefis 1660: 91; Mayerson 1980: 138). A horde of Saracens, their leader having recently died, swooped down on the monastic community at Mount Sinai and slaughtered a number of monks; "but those who were found near the tower (πύργος) hearing the uproar and the tumult, fled into the secure place (ὀχυρώμα)" and survived the attack.[4]

The southern sector of the eastern frontier was open country; the scattered towns were by-and-large unwalled, and the *castra* and *castella* served a double function of housing the military—if a unit was assigned to the area—and as places of refuge for local populations and travelers in the event of an attack. (Mayerson 1986: 40–41, n. 4) The military provided armed escorts for travelers making their way through regions infested with hostile Saracens; and when faced with raiders in large numbers, they countered the menace by assembling "a sufficient force" from various garrisons. Even Gaza, the largest and richest city in the region, had allowed its city wall to deteriorate to such an extent that, according to Choricius (Foerster and Richtsteig 1929: 32), it was a wall in name only. Under the leadership of Bishop Marcian (fl. 510), the wall was rebuilt and provided with a defensive trench "even though the enemy was at peace."

The northern sector presents a different picture. Large urban sites such as Bostra, Gerasa, Philadelphia, and Circusium were walled (Ammianus Marcellinus 14.8.13; 23.5.2). However, those conventional defenses were not raised against Saracen attacks, for as Procopius (*B.P.* 2.19.12; *Bldgs.* 4.9.4) and Ammianus Marcellinus (25.6.8) tell us, Saracens were incapable of storming a wall or even a barricade made of mud. Walled cities of that kind sought protection against well-organized foes, such as the Persians, armed with siege machinery. And it was the Persians, not the Saracens, who overran them in 611–14.

The hostile relationship between Romans and Saracens was offset by a somewhat more amicable and mutually beneficial arrangement between them. Saracens were taken into the military establishment as soldiers serving under Roman officers, or as *foederati*, contingents serving under tribal leaders known as phylarchs. With respect to the former, three cavalry units bearing the name of Saracens are listed in the *Notitia Dignitatum* (ca. 400): one in the province of Egypt and two in the province of Phoenicia (Seeck 1876: 59, 68). None was posted in Arabia nor in any province on the eastern fringes of the frontier; all three were stationed in the western sector, removed, it appears, from proximity with their fellow tribesmen. Apart from their mention in the *Notitia*, we know nothing more about them. Many units bearing the designation *indigenae* in the *Notitia* were stationed on the eastern limits of the frontier and most likely were drawn from the locally settled population of Arab stock (cf. Shahīd 1984: 56–63). The exception is *Equites Saraceni indigenae*, posted at Betproclis in Phoenicia, which—if it is not a case of dittography in the manuscript tradition—may have been drawn from the local nomad population. In any event, the fact that only three Saracen contingents served under Roman officers—we know of no others—may indicate either that the Romans placed little trust in them or that the Saracens were unwilling to submit to Roman discipline.

Alliances between Roman emperors and tribal leaders, *foederati*, enabled the Romans to neutralize the aggressive actions of the Saracens and to employ them as auxiliaries (i.e., mercenaries) in the armed forces.[5] The "marriage" between the two sides, however, had its pitfalls, as it had with individual communities. Benefits did accrue to each, but the Saracens profited more from the relationship. The cost to the empire for acquiring a federated alliance was money or commodities in kind (*annonae foederaticae*) and titles and dignities (e.g., King, Patricius, *clarissimus, spectabilis*) conferred upon tribal leaders. In return, the Romans gained a force to counter the Saracen allies of the Persians and ostensibly to prevent renegade elements from attacking settled areas within the provinces. The Romans recognized the skill of the Arab tribes in desert warfare: Ammianus (23.3.8), despite his aversion toward the Saracens, remarks that they were suitable for the stealthy stratagems of war (*ad furta bellorum appositi*); and Evagrius (*H.E.* 5.20), with some admiration, says that they "are invincible by any other than themselves, on account of the fleetness of their horses; when hemmed in they cannot be captured and they outstrip their enemies in retreat."

Loyalty and military discipline were another matter. In those things tribal mores and not western standards guided the Saracens. In 364, the emperor Julian, who had granted the Saracens an alliance, found them attacking his men (and siding with the Persians?) because he had denied them the pay and numerous gifts (*salaria muneraque plurima*) that they had received in the past (Ammianus 25.6.9–10). A similar situation in the third decade of the seventh century led to the first attacks by Muslim forces in southern Palestine. When the emperor Heraclius refused to pay the Arabs (in Palaestina Tertia?) their customary money allowances, they guided the Muslim commanders to the district of Gaza where they defeated the Roman troops sent to interdict them (Theophanes in Mayerson 1964: 157–58). For the year 635, Nicephorus reports that Heraclius refused to pay 30 pounds of gold in the form of commodities to the Saracens. As a consequence, the Saracens "began to inflict outrages on Roman territory" (Mayerson 1964: 158). Somewhat earlier, in 528, an apparently serious dispute, of unknown nature, arose between the *dux* of Palestine and the phylarch Arethas. The phylarch fled to the "inner *limes* in the direction of India (i.e., to the east)" where he was killed by Mundhir, the Saracen allied to the Persians. Justinian organized a large force to pursue Mundhir. Failing to find him in the distant eastern frontier, the Romans went into Persian territory where they overran Munhir's camp; took numerous men, women, and children as prisoners; and carried off whatever dromedaries they found, along with other kinds of chattel (Malalas in Dorpfeld 1831: 434–35).[6]

Another instance of difficulty for the Romans in dealing with their *foederati* occurred during the reign of the emperor Tiberius. The phylarch Mundhir—not to be confused with the Persian ally—refused to cross the Euphrates and support the *comes* Mauricius against "Scenites" subject to the Persians. As a consequence, the emperor banished him, his wife, and some of his children to the island of Sicily. His son Naaman when Mundhir was captured, "filled the empire with countless evil deeds, and by the hands of his followers plundered the provinces of Phoenicia and Palestine, and sold the inhabitants into slavery" (Evagrius *H.E.* 5.20; 6.2); for a more vivid account see John of Ephesus *H.E.* 3.40–43).

On the other side of the ledger, the Saracens profited materially from the money and food the Romans provided; and by the assumption of royal titles and dignities, they enhanced their position within the bureaucracy and among their fellow tribesmen. They also had the opportunity to legitimize their predilection for plunder as they operated in association with Roman officers. During the Samaritan revolt of 529, the *dux* Theodorus, accompanied by the forces of the phylarch of Palestine, put down the rebellion. According to Malalas (Dorpfeld 1831: 427) the Saracen phylarch took 20,000 young Samaritan men and women as booty and sold them in Persia and India. John of Ephesus provides a broader view of the kind of booty the Saracens carried off. In addition to men and women, Naaman son of Mundhir carried off "gold and silver, and brass and iron, dresses of wool and cotton; wheat, wine, and oil; troops of baggage animals of all kinds,

whatever fell into their hands, and herds of oxen, and all their flocks of sheep and goats" (*H.E.* 3.42). Much of that booty, John goes on to say, was stored in the city of Bostra. Joshua the Stylite, speaking of the siege of Amida in 505, comments that "to the Arabs on both sides (Roman and Persian), this war was a source of much profit and they worked their will on both kingdoms" (Wright 1882: 64). To sum up, the day-to-day contact of individuals and small communities with the Saracen population produced no symbiotic relationship that can be described as lasting or as leading to a *pax Romana*. Communities and individuals employed Saracens in a variety of tasks; but when threatened by tribal hostility, they defended themselves with whatever armed forces were at hand (Mayerson 1986: 40) or came to terms with the tribal leader by paying tribute in the form of money or food supplies. Perhaps the best-known agreement of that kind is the one exacted by Muhammad from the community of Aila. For an annual contribution of one *solidus* per resident adult, the agreement gave the people of Aila, among other considerations, the right of protection (against raids) by Muhammad and the tribes under his control (Mayerson 1964: 172–73).

In connection with the difficulties Rome faced in dealing with the Persians and their Saracen allies, it was a case of fighting fire with fire. The Roman armies simply were no match for the combined forces of Persia and their desert warriors. Circumstances compelled the Romans to use other Saracens to counter those whom the Persians employed. It is doubtful that they would have entered into an alliance with a coalition of Arab tribes if they had had another option. But it is quite clear that the Romans never were able, or committed, to control the movement of Arab tribes. At best, they could only react to situations, both small and large, as they arose.

NOTES

[1]In Latin and Greek sources, the Saracens are known also by such names as Scenites, Agareni, Ishmaelites, and barbarians.

[2]The exception is Amorcesus, the Saracen from Persia, who held the island of Iotabe and several neighboring islands from 473 to 498 (Mayerson 1986: 36).

[3]The statement has an inconsistency. If there were no kind of military barrier, how could the Romans "control any raiding by tribes . . . denying them food, water, and fresh mounts . . . intercept and destroy the raiders"?

[4]Vööbus (1960: 164–65, n. 21) cites a number of towers that monks used. Although he believes that they

were used to watch the activities of the bedouin, they undoubtedly also served as dwellings and as a means by which the monks protected themselves against raiding bedouin.

[5]The political relationships between the federated Saracens and the Romans, as well as the ethnic relationships among the Saracens, has been treated in depth by Shahīd (1984: 585–86 for bibliographical references) and by Sartre (1982: 121–203).

[6]This is one of the rare citations in the sources that speak of Saracen women and children, a subject about which virtually nothing is known for the period under discussion.

BIBLIOGRAPHY

Banning, E. B.
    1986   Peasants, Pastoralists and *Pax Romana*: Mutualism in the Southern Highlands of Jordan. *Bulletin of the American Schools of Oriental Research* 261: 25–50.

Combefis, F., ed.
    1660   *Illustrium Christi lecti triumphi.* Paris.

Conca, F., ed.
    1983   *Nilus Ancyranus Narratio.* Leipzig: Teubner.

CCSL
    175   *Corpus Christianorum, Series Latina.* (Itinerarium Egeriae, eds. A. Franceschini and R. Weber; Antonini Placentini Itinerarium, ed. P. Geyer), 175. Turnhout, 1953.

Dorpfeld, L., ed.
    1831   *Ioannes Malalas: Chronographia* in *Corpus Scriptorum Historiae Byzantinae.* Bonn: Weber.

Foerster, R., and Richsteig, E., eds.
    1929   *Choricii Gazei Opera.* Leipzig: Teubner.

Isaac, B.
    1984   Bandits in Judaea and Arabia. *Harvard Studies in Classical Philology* 88: 171–203.
    1988   The Meaning of the Terms *Limes* and *Limitanei. Journal of Roman Studies* 88: 125–47.

Kraemer, C. J., Jr., ed.
    1958   *Excavations at Nessana: Non-Literary Papyri*, III, Princeton: Princeton University.

Mayerson, P.
    1964   The First Muslim Attacks on Southern Palestine (A.D. 633/634). *Transactions and Proceedings of the American Philological Association* 95: 155–99.
    1975   Observations on the "Nilus" *Narrationes*: Evidence for an Unknown Christian Sect? *Journal of the American Research Center in Egypt* 12: 51–74.
    1980   The Ammonius Narrative: Bedouin and Blemmye Attacks in Sinai. Pp. 133–48 in *The Bible World. Essays in Honor of Cyrus H. Gordon.* New York: Ktav.
    1982   The Pilgrim Routes to Mount Sinai and the Armenians. *Israel Exploration Journal* 32: 44–57.

    1986   The Saracens and the *Limes. Bulletin of the American Schools of Oriental Research* 262: 35–47.
In Press   The Meaning of the Word *Limes* (λίμιτον) in the Papyri. *Zeitschrift für Papyrologie und Epigraphik.*

Nau, F., ed.
    1902   Le texte grèc des récits du moine Anastase sur les saints pères du Sinai. *Oriens Christianus* 2: 58–89.

Parker, S. T.
    1986   *Romans and Saracens: A History of the Arabian Frontier* (American Schools of Oriental Research Dissertation Series, No. 6). Winona Lake, IN: Eisenbrauns.
    1987   Peasants, Pastoralists, and *Pax Romana*: A Different View. *Bulletin of the American Schools of Oriental Research* 265: 35–51.

PG
    26   *S. Athanasii Alexandrini Archiepiscopi Vita S. Antonii* in *Patrologiae cursus completus, Series graeca* 26. Ed. J.-P. Migne. Paris: Migne.

PL
    21   *Rufini Aquileiensis Presbyteri, Historiae Ecclesiasticae Libri duo* in *Patrologiae cursus completus, Series latina*, 21. Ed. J.-P. Migne. Paris: Migne.
    22   *S. Eusebii Hieronymi Epistulae* in *Patrologiae cursus completus, Series latina*, 22. Ed. J.-P. Migne. Paris: Migne.

PL
    23   *S. Eusebii Hieronymi de Viris Illustribus* in *Patrologiae cursus completus, Series latina*, 23. Ed. J.-P. Migne. Paris: Migne.

PL
    27   *S. Eusebii Hieronymi Chronicon* in *Patrologiae cursus completus, Series latina*, 27. Ed. J.-P. Migne. Paris: Migne.

PL
    74   *Vitae Patrum sive Historiae Eremiticae* in *Patrologiae cursus completus, Series latina.* 74. Ed. J.-P. Migne. Paris: Migne.

Rosen, S. A.
    1987   Byzantine Nomadism in the Negev: Results
            from the Emergency Survey. *Journal of Field
            Archaeology*: 28–41.

Sartre, M.
    1982   *Trois études sur l'Arabie romaine et byzan-
            tine*. Collection Latomus 178. Brussels: Re-
            vue d'études latine.

Schwartz, E., ed.
    1939   *Kyrillos von Skythopolis*. Leipzig: Hinrichs.

Seeck, O., ed.
    1876   *Notitia Dignitatum*. Berlin: Lange.

Shahīd, I.
    1984   *Byzantium and the Arabs in the Fourth
            Century*. Dumbarton Oaks Research Collec-
            tion and Library. Washington: Dumbarton
            Oaks.

Vööbus, A.
    1960   *History of Asceticism in the Syrian Orient*,
            II = *Corpus Scriptorum Christianorum Ori-
            entalium*, XVII.

Wright, W., ed.
    1882   *The Chronicle of Joshua the Stylite*. Re-
            printed 1968. Amsterdam: Philo.

ZEITSCHRIFT FÜR PAPYROLOGIE UND EPIGRAPHIK

The Word Saracen (Σαρακηνός) in the Papyri

Prior to the Islamic conquest, the word "Saracen", so prominent from the fourth century on in western literary sources, was a catchall to designate an Arab nomad (i.e., a bedouin) who could be found ranging at large within and beyond the eastern frontiers of the empire. To the settled populations that came into contact with Saracens, they were a bane and a boon, but mostly a bane. In general, Saracens were either raiders or traders: they raided settlements for prisoners and plunder; they fought against Roman and Persian forces, and at other times they served as mercenaries in units of both camps. On the other side of the ledger, Saracens served as messengers, as guides, as sellers of animals, as suppliers of provisions for travelers and remote settlements, and as providers of transportation for people and commodities.[1] As a paradigm for this uncommon polarity, there are two events in connection with the monastery of St. Antony in Egypt's eastern desert that illustrate the contrasting lifestyles of the Saracens. In Athanasius' biography of the proto-monk of Egypt, we learn (PG 26.913; 916) that when a voice told Antony to go to the inner desert, he joined a Saracen caravan that brought him to his famous retreat, where, for a period of time, Saracens provided him with a supply of bread. Some years later, Jerome records (PL 27.689-690) that in 357, Saracen marauders raided Antony's monastery and killed one of his disciples. However, despite some of the more socially acceptable pursuits of the Saracens, rarely did anyone have a good word to say for them. Cyril of Scythopolis (24, 97 ed. Schwartz) called these pagan nomads "the wolves of Arabia … barbaric in conduct; intent on doing evil."

Both aspects of the Saracen character are reflected in the papyri, although references to them are hardly plentiful. The lack of citations is understandable since most documents deal with the legal and commercial concerns of settled individuals and communities, and with their relationship with officials representing the imperial government.

Of a total of some 15 Greek documents that cite the Saracens, 9 or 10 are pre-Islamic.[2] Of these, *SB* I 4769.3 (byz), is a fragment without a meaningful context. Similarly, *P. Fuad I Univ.* 29.17-18 (IV?) refers without a context to the "cloaks of the Saracens" (παλλίων Cαρακηνῶν). The remaining documents reflect the Janus-like aspect of the Saracens' service and disservice to settled populations. *SB* XVI 1.12284.4-5 (VI/VII) is an order to a *notarius* to see to it that a herd of goats, the property of the *dux*, was to be taken from a Saracen (goatherd?) who was in Singkerē (ἀποcπάcῃ τὰ αἰγίδια … ἐκ τοῦ Cαρακηνοῦ τοῦ ὄντος εἰς Cιγκερή).

---

[1] See P. Mayerson, "Romans and Saracens: Micro-Macro Relationships," *Bulletin of the American Schools of Oriental Research* (1989) [forthcoming].

[2] In addition, *Stud. Pal.* VIII 703.3 (V) has been suspected of hiding Σαρακηνῶν behind the spelling Σαλαγηνϛ. This is very unlikely. T. Gagos was kind enough to send me two additional citations for the word Saracen from *O. Douch* 85.7 and 86.3 (IV), both in uncertain contexts and with variant spellings of Cαραγη[óc and Cαραχηνóc.

Stud. Pal. VIII 780 and 945 (VII), apparently connected with monastic establishments, are orders in which Saracens are used to pick up money and quantities of wheat and oil. *P. Ness.* 51, dated by the editor to the early VII, is a letter from the bishop of Aila to a resident of Nessana and refers (line 2) to something that the resident "received from the Saracen" to give to a church in Nessana and Elusa. It is clear that the Saracen was the messenger who brought the letter and its attachment from Aila to Nessana.

Another document from the same archive, *P. Ness.* 89, is an unusual one for it takes us directly into the milieu of the desert and the Saracen nomad. Dated to the late VI or early VII, the document, barely literate, is an account of a caravan of traders — or quite possibly of pilgrims — making its way to and from the Holy Mountain (Mount Sinai) during which time a number of transactions were conducted with nomads. In addition to the purchase of a slave boy and a slave girl, and of camels and donkeys, presumably from desert nomads, the account mentions a substantial sum of money, $3^1/_2$ *solidi*, paid to a Saracen. The transaction is stated in these words (lines 22-23): δοθ(έντα) τῷ Caρακαινῷ cικοφαντέcαντι ἐμᾶc ic τὸ ἅγιον ὄροc (νομ.) γ. To give full force to the meaning of the participle cυκοφαντήcαντι, I translate the sentence as follows: "Paid to the Saracen who extorted $3^1/_2$ *solidi* from us (en route) to the Holy Mountain." The likelihood is that the Saracen was not a passing nomad but the sheikh of a tribe who demanded the money so that the caravan would travel under his protection and be free from harassment, or worse, by his tribesmen. It is unlikely that the money was given for the services of a guide since *P. Ness.* 72 and 73 show that the town of Nessana provided guide service to the Holy Mountain. At a later time, following the visit to the monastery at Mount Sinai, it appears that the caravan recovered the sum of 4 *solidi* (line 35) in lieu of a camel that was stolen by the Saracens of the bani al-Udayyid. On the credit side, however, the account records (line 40) that $1^1/_6$ solidi was paid to the Saracen 'Adī for "the money we borrowed for the price of wool."

The two remaining pre-Conquest documents are more in accord with the popular view of the Saracen's character as often expressed in literary sources. *P Cairo Masp.* I 67009 (VI) is a complaint of the residents of Antaeopolis directed to the *dux* of the Thebaid concerning an officer who had not responded to their grievances, one of which had to do with the "nefarious Saracens" (line 23) [ἀλιτηρί[ω]ν Caρ[α]κηνῶν]. The pejorative ἀλιτήριοc is applied to other offending raiders such as the Blemyes, Nobades, and *barbaroi*. On the verso of the same document (lines 18-19) is the complaint made against the "nefarious barbaric Blemyes," ἀλιτη[ρί-ων] Βλέμυων βαρβάρων (see also *W. Chr.* I 6,5 [V]). The antagonism of the settled population against Saracens, as well as the Blemyes, was put into verse by the poet Dorotheus of Aphrodito (fl. 560) in his eulogy of the *dux* Athanasius, praising the result of his campaigns against them (*P. Cairo Masp.* I 67097 C, 1-2): "You will no longer see the race of the Blemyes nor that of the Saracens. You will not gaze with fear upon the murdering thieves."

The Islamic conquest in the decades following the 630's produced another kind of Saracen, a Muslim who was dedicated to the principles of Islam which held that nomadic life was incompatible with Islam, and that to be a Muslim one had to live a settled life.[3] Unlike the Saracen

---

[3] F.M. Donner, *The Early Islamic Conquests* (Princeton 1981) 79-82.

nomad who attacked settlements but never occupied them, the Muslim Saracen overran the Roman provinces and settled on the land. To the conquered population, however, there was no distinction between the two; the Arab, whether a nomad or a settled Muslim, was called a Saracen. In the post-Conquest documents none has surfaced with the telltale words ἀλιτήριοc Cαρακηνόc although the free-ranging nomad — pagan or Muslim — must have continued his nefarious practices.[4]

In general, the Greek papyri employ the word Saracen when the Arab name was not known, or when the writer had no need or inclination to provide it. This can best be seen in an early bilingual document dated 22 A.H. (643 A.D.).[5] The Greek portion states, "I have taken over from you the maintenance of the Saracens being with me in Herakleopolis, 65 sheep ..."; the Arabic on the other hand is considerably expanded: "This is that what has taken 'Abdallah ibn Gabîr and his mates of the sheep of Ehnâs: we have taken from the representative of Teodhoraq, the younger son of Abû Qîr, and from the representative of Iṣṭafan, the elder son of Abû Qîr, 50 of the sheep for slaughter and 15 other sheep."

Similarly, *P. Lond.* IV 1433, an extensive account dated to 706-707, records requisitions of various kinds from a number of χωρία, and lists some 17 unnamed Saracens who were to be provided with wages in connection with travel by ship (lines 56, 83, 172, 190, 220, 239, 259, 273, 335, 394, 408, 414, 429, 442, 514, 525 [545]. Two entries (lines 360 and 433) concern the δαπάνη of a certain Arab official, Szourae son of Al-Ouasel "through the Saracen of Szourae" (his courier?) or "through (his) Saracen." Szourae son of Al-Ouasel surfaces once more in *P. Lond.* IV 1521.10, a Coptic[6] guarantee-declaration dated to 709 where he is cited as "Szourae son of Al-Ouasel, the Saracen set over the Thebaid" (i.e., the Muslim administrator of the Thebaid). Since the writer of the guarantee-declaration records that certain families had been sent home on the authority of an official, it was necessary for him to provide his name.

P. Lond. IV 1518, 7-8 (708/9), a Coptic guarantee-declaration refering to fugitives, names another Arab administrator, "Abdella son of Shourae the Saracen" who was "set over" the nome of Ptolemais. Two other Coptic documents *P. Lond.* IV 1508.15 and 1509.2,5, cite a certain "Garah the Saracen" who apparently was an official concerned with payments for workmen. Somewhat like the above, 1510.3, a fragment of a Coptic declaration, mentions a Saracen.

The remaining citations from *P. Lond.* IV, all in Greek, are isolated words or names. In 1441.53, the name Cελημ‾ Cαρακιν′ appears, unlike others in the same document, without a patronymic. In 1464, the word "Saracen" has no context; and in 1457.24 there is a questionable restoration.

---

[4] See e.g., "Le text grec des récits du moine Anastase sur les saints pères du Sinaï," F. Nau, ed., *Oriens Christianus* II (1902). Written after 650, the monk records (p. 65) that "barbarians" controlled the road to Mount Sinai and caused a scarcity of oil on the Holy Mountain. He also tells (pp. 75-76) of a Christian who was enslaved by a Saracen. (Cf. Jerome, PL 73.55-56.)

[5] A. Grohmann, *From the World of Arabic Papyri* (Cairo 1952), 113-114 = *SB* VI 9576.

[6] Cited here are only those Coptic documents in *P. Lond.* IV that offer sufficient context.

P. Apoll. 33 (c. 713?) contains a tantalizing reference (1. 16) to someone who is annoyed by Saracens (ὁ δεcπότηc ἡμῶν ὁ Πανεύφημοc ᾿Αμιρᾶc χάριν τῶν ναυτ[ῶν (x letters)] αὐτὸc παρενοχλεῖται ἐκ τῶν Cαρακηνῶν). The editor notes (p. 84) that "la remarque serait intéressant si nous savions qui est représenté par αὐτόc."[7] In the same collection, *P. Apoll.* 37.10, reference is made to messages carried for the Emir "by four Saracens of the Emir of the Believers" regarding the purchase of several articles.

SB I 5609, a conveyance of a house, is dated (line 8) by this unusual formula: "in the year of the Emperor Diocletian 451 and in the year of the Saracens 114," ἔτουc Διοκλη[τιανοῦ] βαcιλεὺc $\overline{υνα}$ καὶ ἔτουc Cαρακηνῶν $\overline{ριδ}$, i.e. 734.[8]

There remains among the Egyptian documents *BGU* II 366 (arab), a guarantee regarding the delivery (lines 12-14) "... for the account of the Saracens, one τονάχιον and three cτρώματα according to Saracen specifications," ... εἰc λόγον τῶν Cαρακηνῶν τονάχιν ἕν καὶ cτρώματ[α] τρ[ί]α τῷ μέτρῳ τῶν Cαρακηνῶν. The three cτρώματα "according to Saracen specifications" seem to be something other than simple mattresses. Since failure to deliver on the due date would result in a heavy penalty — 3 *solidi* for each cτρῶμα— I suggest that the mattresses referred to are "saddle blankets" of the kind that are stuffed with straw and that are used on mules and camels.[9] The word τονάχιον, which in the form τοναχίου also appears in line 18 and *BGU* II 403.6, is unattested. In spite of the fact that it altogether occurs three times, it may well be a poor spelling for γονάχιον, the prayer-carpet that is found several times in papyri of the Arab period.[10] In any case, the object was of value. Failure to deliver it on the due date would incur a stiff penalty of 6 *solidi*.

The documents up to this point show the Umayyad calphs occupying Egypt, taking over the administrative machinery of the Byzantines, and exploiting, as had their predecessors, the resources of the country. To this extent the Arab conquerors settled on Egyptian land, but they did not work the land. The situation is different in Palestine where the Muslims not only settled but worked the land.[11] *P. Ness.* 58 (late VII), from the semi-arid Negev of Southern Palestine, when taken together with two false prophesies and recent archaeological work in the region, provides a specific instance — a very early one, if not the earliest — of Muslim Arabs

---

[7] In spite of the preceeding lacuna, it is tempting to see the Emir as the one being troubled by the Saracens, probably in matters concerning shipping.

[8] Cf. the 7 bilingual *entagia*, *P. Ness.* 60-66, where the dates are cited by indiction and by the "year according to the Arabs," κ[α]τ᾿ ῎Αραβ[αc] ἔτουc.

[9] See *'ukâf* "saddle" in E.W. Lane, *An Arabic-English Lexicon* (Beirut 1968) I 71. H. van Herwerden in *Lexicon Graecum suppletorium et dialecticum* (Leiden 1910) II 1461, offers "lectulus?" without any meaningful support other than its association with cτρῶμα.

[10] This is Preisigke's suggestion (Wörterbuch s.v. τονάχιον. To the examples he quotes for γονάχιου we may add *P. Apoll.* 49 r. 4 and 50 r. 1; cf. also Lampe, *Patr. Greek Lex.* who with reference to Leontius Neop., *vita Iannis Elem.* 21 (p. 38.9f. and 39.14) explains the word as "covering, prob. cloak." Otherwise, an Arabic word may be hidden here and the word refer to another article "according to Saracen specification" connected with a Saracen mount.

[11] Cf. the art. "Israel, Land of (History)" in *Encyclopedia Judaica* IX col. 261: "The conquest was followed by the migration of Arabs into the area... The number who became landlords and engaged in agriculture increased when Mu῾āyia became governor of Syria and Ereẓ Israel. Arabs bought estates, settled down and became peasants throughout the country."

settling into an agricultural community.[12] The document from Nessana records (lines 8, 10) a sum of money given by Meslem the governor[13] "in consequence of the land survey of the Saracens" (ἐκ τῆc γεωμετρίαc τῶν Cαρακηνῶν) and "in consequence of the sub-division of (the property of) the bani Ouar," ἐκ τῆc γεωμορίαc τ[ῶ]ν β(αν)υ Ουαρ.

In sum, although the documents cited above are limited in number, they illustrate all the characteristics attributed to Arabs prior to and following the Muslim Conquest. They also reveal the semantic transition of the word Saracen from a nomadic Arab to the occupying and settled Arab following the conquest.

New York University   Philip Mayerson

---

[12] See P. Mayerson, "*P. Ness.* 58 and Two Vaticinia ex Eventu in Hebrew," forthcoming in *ZPE* 77, 1989, 283-286. This writer has taken this position rather than viewing the document, as has the editor, as a receipt for tax on assigned land. The two Hebrew prophesies and the archaeological evidence are discussed in the same article.

[13] τοῦ δεcπότου ἱμῶν (read ἡμῶν) Μεcλεμ cυμβούλου. This may be better translated as "our Lord the Muslim governor." The scribe did obviously not know his real name.

Towards a Comparative Study of a Frontier

PHILIP MAYERSON

New York University

In the past decades there has been a spate of interest in the *limes*, occasioned largely by surveys and excavations of military installations in the Roman provinces of Palestine and Arabia. From the time of Mommsen and Brünnow and Domaszewski to the present, the preoccupation with military installations and organization has led investigators to interpret the word *limes* as if it were a formal term used in the Roman military establishment, and to use or coin such terms as *Limes Arabicus* and *Limes Palaestinae* as if they were part of a military vocabulary designating a fortified system of defence. In the last few years, however, a number of articles have appeared that have challenged this interpretation, maintaining that the word in Latin or Greek had no specific connection with a fortified line of defence, and that from the fourth century onwards it was used as a geographic term meaning 'frontier' or 'frontier district'.

In an article on the meaning of the words *limes* and *limitanei*, Isaac has argued that from the first to the sixth centuries, the word *limes* was never used to mean a fortified line of defence, and that by the fourth century, the term had become 'an administrative concept denoting a frontier district administered by a military commander (*dux*)... In time this formal term came to be used in an informal manner to indicate the "frontier district".'[1] Isaac did not, however, define the character of a *limes*. In an earlier article,[2] this writer reviewed the question of whether the *limes* comprised a coordinated system of border garrisons, taking as examples the western and eastern sectors of *Palaestina Tertia*. I came to the conclusion that it was necessary to discard the association of the term *limes* with 'border', 'boundary' or 'fortified line' in its application to *Palaestina Tertia* as well as *Palaestina Prima* and *Arabia*; and that it was best to translate the term as 'frontier' in a more generalized sense, i.e. the land that forms the farthest extent of a country's settled or inhabited region. An analogy with the American frontier seemed appropriate since its problems were similar to those in *Palaestina Tertia* and its neighbouring provinces: sparsely settled populations subject to raids and threatened lines of communication. To meet these problems, a series of forts was gradually extended into the territory as settlement developed. The forts were garrisoned with mounted troops, who protected lines of communication and operated against raiders. These installations also served as sanctuaries for the settled population against raiders who came in force.

---

[1] B. Isaac: The Meaning of the Terms *Limes* and *Limitanei, Journal of Roman Studies* 78 (1988), pp. 125–147.

[2] P. Mayerson: The Saracens and the *Limes, BASOR* 262 (1986), p. 39.

In two subsequent articles I supported my view of this meaning of the word *limes* as a broad geographical term meaning 'frontier' or 'frontier district'. Turning to the question of whether there were 'inner' and 'outer' parts of a frontier district, I argued with quotations from historical sources that the 'inner' part of a frontier district was a region more remote from the Roman *oikoumenē* than the 'outer' part.[3] Since Isaac had not investigated the meaning of *limes* in the Egyptian papyri, I undertook an examination of the documents, all of which dated from the fourth century and later, and found that the word was used to designate a frontier district without any specific connection with military installations. The editors of the documents gave a variety of interpretations or translations of *limes*, many of which touched upon its meaning as a frontier district: e.g. 'marche de confines', 'frontière province', 'march', 'Mark', 'Grenzegebiet'. I also took the opportunity to refine my definition of a frontier: 'The word "frontier" is an elastic one and does not require definition in terms of boundaries or lines of separation between states, provinces, ethnic groups, etc. A frontier lies at the hither edge of a desert or of a region incapable of habitation or penetration; it is a region that is thinly settled if at all. Because of the hostile nature of the environment, a frontier usually requires a system of defense to protect its inhabitants, to provide sanctuaries in forts, fortlets, or towers in the event of attack in force and to keep open lines of communication between settlements and commercial entrepôts. Hence, we can speak of a frontier of settlement and a frontier of military defense.'[4] The evidence from Egypt clearly shows that the two frontiers did not necessarily coincide.

The interpretation of the word *limes* as a frontier or frontier district leads to an investigation on a broader scale: a comparison of two or more frontiers of different historical periods in order to learn what they have in common, or what distinguishes them, and whether this can help to reveal a general historical process at work. In essence, we are speaking of comparative frontier history in its application to the ancient world. Two such studies have recently appeared.[5] However, these essays lack an organizing principle or common factor of analysis, since each author gave his own meaning of the term 'frontier'.[6] In their book on historical frontiers, Thompson and Lamar, after giving a summary of the progress of comparative historiography, attempt to define their concept of a frontier in universal terms and to explain its application at different levels of analysis.

---

[3]   P. Mayerson: A Note on the Roman *Limes*: 'Inner' versus 'Outer', *IEJ* 38 (1988), pp. 181–183.

[4]   P. Mayerson: The Meaning of the Word *Limes* in the Papyri, *Zeitschrift für Papyrologie und Epigraphik* 77 (1989), pp. 287–291.

[5]   J. Eadie: *Civitates* and Clients: Roman Frontier Policies in Pannonia and Tingitana, in D.H. Miller and S.O. Steffen (eds.): *The Frontier: Comparative Studies,* Norman, Oklahoma, 1977, pp. 57–80; D.H. Miller and W.W. Savage, Jr.: Ethnic Stereotypes and the Frontier: A Comparative Study of Roman and American Experience, in *ibid.,* pp. 109–137.

[6]   L. Thompson and H. Lamar (eds.): *The Frontier in History: North America and South Africa Compared,* New Haven, 1981, p. 6.

We regard a frontier not as a border or line, but as a territory or zone of interpenetration between two previously distinct societies. Usually one of the societies is indigenous to the region, or at least has occupied it for many generations; the other is intrusive. The frontier 'opens' in a given zone when the first representatives of the intrusive society arrive; it 'closes' when a single political authority has established hegemony over the zone.[7]

The essays in this book deal with frontiers which are well documented and date from the recent past. However, documentation is often lacking for ancient frontiers, since archaeologists have in the main excavated major urban sites, and regional surveys have only recently been undertaken. Further, most historians and archaeologists specialize in one period, if not in one region. It is necessary, therefore, to start with what is known best and to attempt to make a cogent comparison with another region or another historical period. It is likely, of course, that matching attributes will come to mind which should serve to illuminate a particularly apt comparison, but 'the high level of abstraction' recommended by Thompson and Lamar must await comparisons on a broader scale.

More than this must be said, however. An alien group intruding into a frontier zone may exert only a limited amount of control over a portion of that zone. This may be seen in the occupation of areas by nomadic or semi-nomadic tribes that lack the power, organization or desire to control or occupy an entire frontier zone effectively.[8] Tribal societies generally lack the well-developed political organization that would be needed for such control; they are often content with exploiting the resources of a region. A good example is provided by the nomads whom the Romans called Saracens. They inhabited wide regions of the Roman-Byzantine frontier, one of which was known as *terrae Saracenorum*, but raided and traded without a thought of occupying the territory controlled by the Roman state.[9] Even when organized groups of Saracens — the Lakhmids and Ghassanids, for example — allied themselves with the Romans or the Persians, they never attempted to take possession of cities or provinces. All this changed with the advent of Islam; tribalism gave way to pan-Arabism and the call to occupy the land of the enemy. An earlier version of this trend may be found in the leadership of Moses, on whom Muhammad modelled himself.[10] As biblical tradition has it, Moses unified the Israelite tribes for

---

[7] *Ibid.*, p. 7.

[8] See e.g. C. Bailey: The Negev in the Nineteenth Century: Reconstructing History from Bedouin Oral Tradition, *Asian and African Studies* 14 (1980), pp. 35–80; idem, Dating the Arrival of the Bedouin Tribes in Sinai and the Negev, *Journal of the Economic and Social History of the Orient* 38 (1985), pp. 20–49.

[9] P. Mayerson: Saracens and Romans: Micro-Macro Relationships, *BASOR* 274 (1989), pp. 72–74.

[10] P. Crone: *Meccan Trade and the Rise of Islam*, Princeton, 1987, p. 247. On pan-Arabism and the call to occupy land, see F.M. Donner: *The Early Islamic Conquests,* Princeton, 1981, pp. 79–80. See also P. Mayerson: *P. Ness.* 58 and Two *Vaticinia ex Eventu* in Hebrew, *Zeitschrift für Papyrologie und Epigraphik* 77 (1989), pp. 283–291.

the purpose of settling them in a divinely ordained land. This movement ultimately led to the creation of a state under Saul, David and Solomon with the political and military authority to impose its will on the inhabitants of the frontier.

I turn now to ancient Palestine and the southern sector of the region known as the Negev. Palestine is an appropriate area for comparative study, since it has been investigated more thoroughly than any other region in the ancient Near East. The Negev, identified in part with the biblical Negeb, the southland of Palestine, is part of the vast desert which extends to the south and east of the Fertile Crescent. Unlike the more favoured lands of Palestine, whose frontiers over time oscillated between expansion and contraction, the Negev remained a frontier area during all periods of recorded history, limited as it was in terms of water resources, productive land and numbers of inhabitants.

The indigenous population of the Negev, like that of neighbouring deserts, consisted of nomads whose movement within and beyond the region was conditioned by a number of factors: the availability of pasturage and water; the political environment; and the opportunity of obtaining resources by raiding other tribes or settlements, or by providing services for settled communities and governments.[11] During several periods, people settled in and cultivated certain marginal lands of the Negev. The location of their settlements was determined by the availability of arable land and by the means to augment meagre quantities of rainfall through the control of runoff water. These agricultural settlements appear to have been deliberately placed near larger communities and administrative centres, probably for economic, religious and defensive reasons.

Evidence on which to base a meaningful conclusion is to be found in the physical traces (houses, forts, terrace walls and pottery) which can be related to historical documents. There are to be sure remains which pre-date written sources, and about which no definitive statement can be made regarding their place within a larger socio-political framework.[12] Hence, I exclude from consideration those periods of history in which there are remains of habitation — possibly due to the process of sedentarization of nomads — but which for lack of recorded evidence cannot be placed in a particular historical context. I omit from consideration the evidence from the Early Bronze Age II (third millennium B.C.E.) in southern Sinai and the Negev, representing perhaps the indigenous population of the desert. I also omit from consideration the numerous small settlements in the Negev highlands, the el-Tih Plateau and northern Sinai, which have been dated to the Intermediate

---

[11] Mayerson (above, n. 9).

[12] The absence of both forms of evidence need not mean that a region capable of some form of habitation was devoid of population. It simply means that products of human activity that were subject to decay have disappeared from view. This would be especially true of transhumant groups, whose use of animal and vegetable materials would be difficult to identify archaeologically. See I. Finkelstein and A. Perevolotsky: Processes of Sedentarization and Nomadization in the History of Sinai and the Negev, *BASOR* 279 (1990), pp. 67–68.

Bronze Age (*c.* 2350/2300–2000 B.C.E.). There are no traces of habitation from the succeeding Late Bronze Age. This, however, was a well-documented period of transition and movement, with unsettled conditions in Egypt and Canaan that created an opportunity for movement by the Israelites and their kindred tribes into the 'open' frontiers of Canaan — i.e., the hill country of Palestine and the northern Negev. In explaining the success of the semi-nomadic Israelite tribes in penetrating Canaanite territory, Malamat sums it up as follows:

> The impoverishment of Canaan as a result of Egyptian exploitation, the unstable security situation (clearly reflected in the El-Amarna tablets and in Papyrus Anastasi) and above all, the incessant internal strife among Canaanite city-states — these bickerings had been intensified by Egyptian policies of 'divide and rule' which, prior to the advent of the Israelite, left the country fragmented with its towns divided.[13]

By the beginning of the Iron Age (*c.* 1200 B.C.E.), the clans kindred to Judah had made their way to the less marginal regions of the Negev and had taken up positions in various sections of the territory. The Negev, like other areas occupied by Israelite tribes, was not safe from raids by hostile tribes. The insecurity of the Israelites is best illustrated by the attack, described in Judges 5–7, of the camel-riding Beduin — the Midianites, Amalekites and 'Sons of the East' (*bene Qedem*). They ranged far and wide in Palestine, from the valley of Jezreel 'all the way to the neighbourhood of Gaza', plundering the land of crops and cattle until Gideon and a small force counter-attacked and pursued the raiders into the southern desert of Transjordan.[14]

After some 200 years of uncertain occupation of newly acquired territory, and in the face of old and new enemies pressing upon the Israelites from the east, west and south, the need arose to replace the loose tribal confederacy with a central and permanent authority under the leadership of a king. Saul was anointed ruler of Israel and spent his reign in wars defending tribal territory against encroachment from without. In the Negev to the south lay the traditional enemy of Israel, the Amalekites, whose continued incursions threatened the people of Judah and Simeon. Amassing a large army, together with a contingent of Judahites, Saul defeated the Amalekites in a series of wide-ranging actions and took possession of their flocks and cattle (I Sam. 15). Despite Saul's victory, attacks by Amalekites and other tribes of the southern desert continued. It was left to David to finish what Saul had attempted to do. Surrounding himself with a small force of roving

---

[13] A. Malamat: Canaan — Before and During the Israelite Conquest, in H.H. Ben-Sasson (ed.):*A History of the Jewish People,* Cambridge, Mass., 1976, p. 57.

[14] Although many scholars consider the early biblical narratives quasi-historical, legendary or factitious, they provide a fairly accurate tableau of ancient nomadic and semi-nomadic lifestyles and attitudes.

fighters,[15] and employing the hit-and-run tactics and the moral values of Beduin raiders, David struck a telling blow against the desert marauders.[16]

Biblical tradition concerning the Amalekites and other southern desert tribes as a serious threat to Israel ends with the action taken by David. In I Chron. 4:42–43, we read that five hundred Simeonites went to Mount Seir and destroyed the Amalekites that had escaped. By the time of the United Monarchy of David (1004–965 B.C.E.) and Solomon (968–928 B.C.E.), the neighbouring peoples of Moab, Edom, Ammon and Aram had been conquered or neutralized, so that tribal movement into the Negev from the south-eastern desert was limited. As for the Philistines on the west, the territory of Judah remained free from their attacks until after the death of Uzziah. The campaigns of David and Solomon had established political hegemony over the Negev, and in particular over the Negeb of Judah. Sealed off from free-moving hostile tribes, the territory became a 'closed' frontier.

The closing of the frontier, brought about by the military and political actions taken by the United Monarchy, stabilized the region and encouraged the growth of settlements in the highlands of the central Negev, the only sizeable area capable of sustaining some form of settled life. The growth of public security and economic opportunity attendant on an increasing population provided incentives for the sedentarization of nomadic and semi-nomadic groups, as well as for the migration of other people into the region. It is a process that has been repeated in Palestine during periods in which a central authority establishes firm control over a region formerly subject to raids by nomads and consequent insecurity.[17]

Archaeological survey and excavation, from Kadesh-Barnea and Makhtesh Ramon in the south to the Beer Sheva basin in the north, have revealed a concentration of settlements, dated by means of ceramic finds and archaeological features to the period of the United Monarchy (Iron Age II). The settlements,

---

[15] Biblical tradition has unquestionably compressed the events of this critical period. It is significant to note, however, that small mobile forces are more effective than armies in controlling Beduin raiding. The Romans, as is evident from the disposition of their forces as detailed in the *Notitia Dignitatum* (*c.* 395 C.E.), learned this lesson when they reorganized their imperial forces into mobile field units and frontier garrisons. The large legionary forts at Lejjun (Betthorus) and Udruḥ (Adrou) in Transjordan are an anachronism in the fourth century and later. As for the Tenth Legion posted at Aila, we know nothing of its installation or its activities on the frontier.

[16] For a composite picture of pre-monarchical David and his strategy against the southern nomads, see J. Bright: *A History of Israel* (2nd ed.), Philadelphia, 1972, pp. 172–173.

[17] D.H.K. Amiran: The Pattern of Settlement in Palestine, *IEJ* 3 (1953), pp. 65–78, 192–209, 250–260, has shown how the pattern of settlement has closely followed the up-and-down cycle of public security. The Beduin frontier, i.e. the region open to Beduin raids, extended as far north as Bethlehem; in 1480 Jerusalem was raided, its shops looted and its governor attacked, and Nablus was plundered by Beduin in 1280 (p. 70). One need not go beyond Palestine to find parallels for the correlation between public security and the rise of settlements. See also D.H.K. Amiran and Y. Ben-Arieh: Sedentarization of Beduin in Israel, *IEJ* 13 (1963), pp. 161–181.

primarily agricultural, are made up of enclosed areas, houses, threshing floors, silos, cisterns, animal pens and terraced wadis. There are over 40 of these enclosed areas, almost all of which have associated settlements and are concentrated in an area of approximately 50 × 40 km. in the central Negev (Fig. 1). South of Makhtesh Ramon there are no remains of similar communities with enclosed areas.[18]

Investigators have focused on the type of enclosed area located on a hilltop, or with the walls running around the circumference of a hill. These enclosures, ranging in size from 380 m.² to 3,100 m.², are surrounded by strong double-line (casemate) walls or single-line walls, and contained sizeable open spaces (courtyards) with a number of interior rooms abutting the walls (Fig. 2). Structures of this kind have been dubbed 'forts' and 'fortresses', with the inference that they served a military function. Aharoni, one of the earliest investigators of the region, cites them as 'forerunners of the *limes*' and views them as part of the building activity of Israelite kings (Solomon, Jehoshaphat and Uzziah) who were concerned with controlling the trade routes from the Red Sea along the 'highways' of the Negev.[19] Subsequent investigators, with the exception of Finkelstein, have continued to call these enclosed areas forts and fortresses, and describe them as built by 'royal initiative' or 'royal enterprise'. It is often asserted that 'the forts were intended to defend caravans plying the routes of the Way of Spies, the Way of the Hill Country and Amorites, and the Way of the Red Sea'.[20] Finkelstein, however, holds that these 'courtyard sites', which he dates to the Iron Age I or early Iron Age II, represent the work of sedentarized desert nomads, whose economy was based on pasturage.[21]

There are difficulties in accepting the interpretation of these enclosed areas as forts or fortresses, supposedly built by royal initiative to protect roads and caravan traffic. There are more than forty of these Iron Age installations within a limited area of the central Negev, most as close as three to five km. to one another, while two of them

---

[18]   R. Cohen: The Iron Age Fortresses in the Negev, *BASOR* 236 (1980), p. 78; idem, The Fortresses King Solomon Built to Protect his Southern Border, *Biblical Archaeology Review* (1985), pp. 56, 58, 61, 63.

[19]   Y. Aharoni: Forerunners of the *Limes*: Iron Age Fortresses in the Negev, *IEJ* 17 (1967), pp. 1, 11–13. The use of the word 'highways' implies main arteries for passage or transportation, whereas the central Negev can be traversed by a variety of routes or tracks. Even the word 'road' suggests a smooth or paved surface, of a sort which is not found in the Negev before the twentieth century. On the use of the word 'highways', see also Cohen (above, n. 18, *BASOR*), pp. 61–62.

[20]   Z. Herzog: Enclosed Settlements in the Negev and the Wilderness of Beer-Sheba, *BASOR* 250 (1983), p. 48; R. Cohen: Did I Excavate Kadesh-Barnea?, *Biblical Archaeology Review* (1981), p. 33. The phrases 'royal initiative' and 'royal enterprise' are frequently used. See Z. Meshel: Ḥorvat Ritma — An Iron Age Fortress in the Negev Highlands, *Tel Aviv* 4 (1977), p. 132; R. Cohen: Excavations at Ḥorvat Ḥaluqim, *ʿAtiqot* 11 (1976), p. 49; idem, *Archaeological Survey of Israel: Map of Sede-Boqer-West (167)*, Jerusalem, 1985, p. xii; M. Haiman: *Archaeological Survey of Israel: Map of Har Ḥamran — Southwest (198)*, Jerusalem, 1986, p. 19.

[21]   I. Finkelstein: *The Archaeology of the Israelite Settlement*, Jerusalem, 1988, p. 244.

Fig. 1. Map showing principal Iron Age I-II forts in the central Negev. From
R. Cohen (n. 17, *BASOR* 236), p. 62.

are only 1.5 km. apart.[22] None has been found south of Makhtesh Ramon on the
routes leading to ports on the Red Sea. If forts were needed to protect caravans,
why were others not built in the open areas of the Negev and Sinai, which were
highly susceptible to Beduin raiding? Further, caravans generally used armed guards

---

[22]   Z. Meshel and R. Cohen: Refed and Ḥatira: Two Iron Age Fortresses in the Northern
Negev, *Tel Aviv* 7 (1980), p. 70. It should be noted that the disposition of military garrisons cited
in the *Notitia Dignitatum* and the distances between stages given in the *Tabula Peutingeriana* are
at least some 16 Roman miles, or 24 km., apart. See Y. Aharoni: The Roman Road to Aila
(Elath), *IEJ* 4 (1954), pp. 9–16; idem, Tamar and the Roads to Elath, *IEJ* 13 (1963), pp.
31–42.

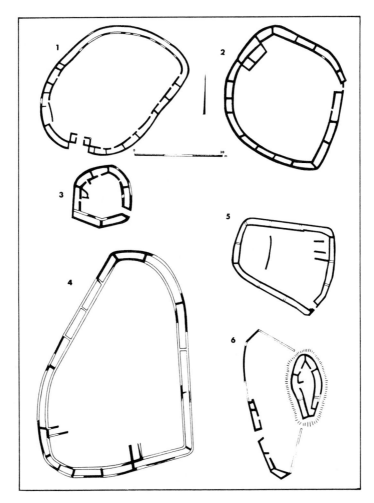

Fig. 2. Oval installations in the central Negev; 1) ʻEn Qudeis; 2) ʼAtar Haroʻa;
3) Ḥorvat Ḥaluqim; 4) Ḥorvat Raḥba; 5) Ḥorvat Ketef Shivta; 6) Ramat Maṭred Fort 146. From
R. Cohen (n. 17, *BASOR* 236), p. 65.

for their protection or paid some form of tribute or impost for safe passage through regions controlled by unfriendly people. Pliny is instructive on the nature of caravan traffic.[23] He reports that caravans of frankincense traversed 1487½ Roman miles from Timna (Thomna) to Gaza in 65 stages with stops for camels, presumably about 23 miles between daily stops; '... all along the route they keep on paying, at one place for water, at another for fodder, or charges for lodgings at halts, and for various imposts'. He mentions stops for camels (*mansiones camelorum*) and various imposts (*variis portoriis*), but nothing about the use or need for forts or protection. Later, in the Byzantine or early Umayyad period, a Nessana document, *P. Ness.* 89, an account of a caravan of traders making its way through

---

[23]   Pliny: *Natural History,* 12. 23, 64–65.

the Sinai frontier to Mount Sinai, has this entry: 'Paid to the Saracen who exorted 3½ *solidi* from us [en route] to the Holy Mountain.' The Saracen could not have been a passing nomad, but rather the sheikh of a tribe who demanded money so that the caravan could proceed under his protection and be free from harassment, or worse, by his tribesmen.[24] It is also significant to note that during the time that the Nabateans and Byzantines controlled the Negev frontier, there was no similar concentration of fortified structures to compare with those claimed for the Iron Age; in fact, there were very few such sites.

As for 'royal initiative' or 'royal enterprise' in constructing these enclosed areas, it is likely that initiative came from the settled population in need of protection from Beduin raids that certainly persisted, even after the Amalekite threat had been greatly reduced by the actions of Saul and David. If we turn to the Byzantine period, there are two instances that may serve as a paradigm for the way in which a central government may be pressured to construct a fortification of some sort. Cyril of Scythopolis tells of an appeal made by the celebrated monk Sabas to Justinian to build a fort (*castrum*) in the wilderness below his monasteries with a garrison of soldiers to protect them against Saracen raids.[25] The orders were given, but apparently the fort was never built. The same emperor was approached by the monastic community of Mount Sinai with a similar appeal. Justinian provided the means for the construction of the fortified monastery at the foot of Mount Sinai, which survives to this day.[26]

It is also instructive to cite another parallel regarding the strategy that brought about the positioning of outposts on the American frontier. Huntley holds '... that these forts represented less a deliberate plan than erratic responses to communities for security and local markets. The forts, incidentally, encouraged settlers to move beyond the range of military protection, stirred up the Indians, and led to still more forts — many beyond effective logistical support.'[27]

Turning back to the Iron Age, excavation within the enclosed areas and other installations has revealed a great variety of wheel-made pottery (bowls, cooking pots, storage jars, juglets, lamps, flasks, *pithoi*), but no military artifacts. On the other hand, the evidence of agricultural activity near the enclosed areas presents a convincing picture of settled agricultural communities for whom the enclosed areas could provide sanctuary and protection during periodic raids by marauding nomads. Similarly, the excavation of the Byzantine forts at Nessana and ᶜAvdat,

---

[24] P. Mayerson: The Word Saracen in the Papyri, *Zeitschrift für Papyrologie und Epigraphik* 79 (1989), p. 284.

[25] E. Schwartz (ed.): *Kyrillos von Skythopolis,* Leipzig, 1939, par. 73, p. 175.

[26] See P. Mayerson: Procopius or Eutychius on the Construction of the Monastery at Mount Sinai: Which is the More Reliable Source?, *BASOR* 230 (1978), pp. 33–38.

[27] R.M. Huntley: The Frontier and the American Military Tradition, in P.A. Hutton (ed.): *Soldiers West,* Lincoln, Neb., 1987, p. 4.

both of substantial size and with all the hallmarks of having been constructed by royal initiative, produced no evidence of occupation by the military. We learn from the Piacenza Pilgrim, who visited Nessana in about 570 C.E. on his way to Mount Sinai, that the fort (*castrum*) served as a hospice (*xenodochium*) for hermits and travellers.[28]

This is not to say that there was no royal initiative whatsoever in the area during The Iron Age. The towered fortresses at Kadesh Barnea in the south and Ḥurvat ʿUzzah (Khirbet Ghazza) in the northern Negev appear to have been constructed on the initiative of a central authority.[29] It must be mentioned, however, that the fort at Kadesh Barnea, although strategically positioned on the southern flank of the biblical Negeb, was located near the best supply of water in the entire Negev and Sinai. A perennial spring of water — the only one in the region worthy of the name — irrigated a large part of an area filled with Iron Age and Byzantine sites and remains of agricultural settlements. The number of sites far exceeds others to the north, showing that the region supported a substantial population.[30] Despite the absence of finds of a military character, the fort at Kadesh Barnea may have housed a garrison to protect the surrounding settlements; in times of crisis the fort undoubtedly provided refuge and protection for the local inhabitants. What is unusual and enigmatic at this particular site is the fact that the Byzantines felt no need to build an equivalent installation, whereas the Israelites rebuilt the fort twice after it had been destroyed. The explanation may lie in the development of corporate communities, such as those at Nessana, ʿAvdat, Shivta, Khalasa and Ruheiba during the Nabatean hold on the Negev. This trend was greatly enhanced during the Byzantine period. Secondly, the level of security during the latter period may have been such that the inhabitants were able to cultivate lands that were marginal from a security point of view and that were at a distance from their home settlements. The contrast in development between the two periods can be attributed to the fact that the Iron Age settlements had a short lifespan — brought to an end by Shishak's invasion (*c.* 920 B.C.E.) or another force[31] — while the Nabatean

[28] Mayerson (above, n. 2), p. 45, n. 4.
[29] Y. Aharoni: The Negeb of Judah, *IEJ* 8 (1958), pp. 33–35; R. Cohen (above, n. 20), pp. 20–33; idem, Excavations at Kadesh-Barnea, *BA* (1981), pp. 93–107.
[30] From the two archaeological survey reports in hand, it is interesting to note that the southwestern region (Har Ḥamran) lists 80 Iron Age II, 16 Nabatean-Roman, and 118 Byzantine-Early Arab sites (Haiman [above, n. 20], pp. 17–23, 34), whereas the survey of Sede-Boqer-West produced only 19 Iron Age, 18 Nabatean-Roman and 41 Byzantine sites (Cohen [above, n. 20], pp. xi-xiv, xx).
[31] Meshel (above, n. 20), p. 133, attributes the brief lifespan of the Negev strongholds to the fact that they represented 'the initial conquest of the desert and a "show of force" on the part of the central authority. When the local inhabitants recognized the existence and permanency of this authority, they accepted it and either integrated themselves into it or lived quietly on its borders. As the need for these Negev strongholds diminished, they were abandoned.'

and Byzantine occupation of the region provided the time and economic opportunity for the growth of towns and villages, and even a provincial administrative centre at Elusa.

There remains Finkelstein's view that the elliptical enclosed areas, which he calls 'courtyard sites', represent settlements of desert nomads whose primary economic activity was herding. While it may be true that these elliptical enclosed areas (the most common type of all) were modelled on Beduin encampments, there are a number of objections that stand in the way of accepting his interpretation of the function of these sites.[32] First and foremost, the construction of the enclosed areas far exceeds the needs, or the organizational capability, of a herding society. The height of the walls as they now stand reaches up to 1.7 m., and the size and weight of the stones are unusually large and heavy. A comparison of Nabatean and Byzantine stonework with that of the modern Beduin is revealing. During the two earlier periods, large and roughly shaped stones were used in the construction of houses and wadi terrace-walls, indicating the availability of a well-organized body of people to work and handle large, heavy pieces of stone. The modern Beduin rarely if ever use stone of any size and weight, and when they mend ancient terraces or construct them anew, they use small stones which can be handled by one person. The character of Beduin terrace walls is in sharp contrast to those of the Nabateans and Byzantines.

Further, there is abundant evidence of agricultural activity near the enclosed areas. It may be, since Finkelstein dates these sites to the Iron Age I and early Iron Age II, that the hill-top enclosures represent an early stage in the sedentarization of herding nomads, and that the agricultural activity represents a later stage. However, if there is any correlation between ancient and modern lifestyles, it is worth noting that modern Beduin avoid conspicuous hilltops for their encampments, preferring slopes where they are protected from the wind and unwelcome visitors.[33]

Finally, something must be said about the towers that yield ceramic material of the three major occupants of the region. There is no doubt that such installations could have served both military and civilian populations, to monitor the movement of hostile elements and to take appropriate action against them. For the local inhabitants it would give them time to seek safety in some secure place. It is not often recognized, however, that the towers themselves were used as places of refuge and safety in the event of attack by raiders. During the Byzantine period

---

[32]   Finkelstein (above, n. 21), pp. 242–244. The attribution by Finkelstein of these sites to the Iron Age I or early Iron Age II (eleventh-tenth centuries B.C.E.) rests on the date of the wheel-made pottery found in excavations and surveys. Since there is no consensus among archaeologists that would help refine the dating of the ceramic material, and in the absence of biblical or extra-biblical documentation, the enclosed areas are variously attributed to the Amalekites, the Edomites, Saul, Solomon, or as late as Uzziah. On this issue see Cohen (above, n. 18), p. 77.
[33]   See Amiran and Pen-Arieh (above, n. 17), p. 164.

there is evidence that towers were havens of safety, and that monks would flee to them when anyone whom they feared approached. The tower at Mount Sinai, prior to the erection of the fortified monastery, is also said to have housed a church dedicated to St. Mary.[34]

To sum up, this comparative study of the Negev frontier, focusing on the Iron Age and its relationship to elements of the Nabatean and Byzantine periods, has attempted to demonstrate that frontiers share certain characteristics that bear upon one another, and that to discuss one period in isolation from others, especially those that have ample documentary evidence, may lead to faulty conclusions. The use of comparative material provides a reasonable approach to the interpretation of archaeological and documentary evidence, and adds a significant dimension to the history of a region. To take this approach one step farther, a comparative study of the frontier in Transjordan east of Wadi ꜤArabah would yield striking similarities and contrasts to the Negev.

[34] See Mayerson (above, n. 9), pp. 75, 77–78, n. 4; idem (above, n. 26), p. 36.

The Words τονάχιον and γονάχιον in the Egyptian Papyri

In a forthcoming *ZPE* article on the Saracens in the papyri this writer stumbled across the word τονάχιον in two documents (*BGU* II 366. 14,18; 403.6). Preisigke's *Wörterbuch* gave no clue to its meaning, stating: "(Sinn unklar). Sollte... γονάχιον zu lesen sein?" Under γονάχιον Preisigke offers "Gebetsteppich der Muhammedaner" and four citations from the seventh and eighth centuries. This definition is clearly owed to the interpretation of the editor of *P. Lond.* 1414 whose note to line 12 reads: γον^{χ}ν^{χ}: γονάχια; '*Pulvinus qui genubus substernitur*,' Ducange. Perhaps a prayer-carpet such as is used in Mohammedan countries." What the editor of *P. Lond.* had expressed as a possibility or a conjecture was taken as a fact by Preisigke and by the editor of *P. Apoll.* 49 and 50, dated to 703-715, who viewed the two documents as a "Demande de tápis de prière."

Although it is tempting to see in these several documents the earliest mention of the use of prayer rugs among Muslims—and I pursued it as such—a closer investigation shows that γονάχιον cannot mean a prayer rug. There is no evidence that prayer rugs were in general use in the early years of Islam, not before the ninth century (see art. Sa*djdj*âda in *Enc. of Islam*). More compelling is the fact that the entry of γονάχιον in Du Cange's *Glossarium* is quite confused and gives no specific citation for a prayer rug. His definition (*Pulvinus qui genubus substernitur*) appears to have been influenced by the Greek word γόνυ. Apart from some completely unrelated meanings, Du Cange cites only τάπις and πάλιον.

Even more compelling is the citation of γονάχιον in Lampe, *Patr. Greek Lex.* in which reference is made to the *Vita Sancti Joannis Eleemosynarii* of Leontius Neapolitanus (d. 620/630, ed. H. Gelzer, *SAQ* 5 [1893]). In the ninth century, the life was translated into Latin by Athanasius. Leontius relates that when a certain wealthy man observed thāt John was covered with a torn and threadbare γονάχιον, he sent for a γονάχιον worth 36 *solidi* (p. 38.9-10). When John begins to consider this gift in terms of the poverty of his fellow monks, he refers to it with the word (p. 38.17) παλλίν (= παλλίον). The word γονάχιον is mentioned once again with its price (p. 39.14). Athanasius accordingly translates these words with Latin *opertorium, coopertorium, pallium*, and *coopertorium* (*PG* 93: col. 1631). It is obvious that in the above contexts, the word γονάχιον means a covering, a cloak, or a blanket-like wrap;[1] it may be a "rug" in the sense of a thick piece of cloth that is used as a wrap or a coverlet.[2]

---

[1] See also Ar. ḥayk in R. Dozy, ed., *Supplément aux dictionaire arabes* (Beirut 1968) I, 345: "Afrique, *grand manteau de laine* ordinairement blanc, qui sert de vêtement pendant la jour et de coverture pendant la nuit."

[2] Although Leontius uses the word παλλίον in place of γονάχιον without any change in meaning, the scribe of *P. Lond.* 1414 does make a distinction between the two words. In line 112, he cites the cash equivalent (ἀπαργυρισμός) of 4 γον(άχια) at 2 $^1/_3$ *solidi* each and one παλλί(ον) at 2 *solidi*. What the precise difference is between the two is unclear, unless the material of a

But if the word γονάχιον means a wrap or a cloak or a cover of some sort, how did it get its meaning? It is apparent that the word is not rooted in Greek. I inquired of specialists in Arabic, Persian and Coptic but they reported that the word had no connection with these languages. It was a Semitist, Professor J. Greenfield of Hebrew University, who provided the answer. In an informal note, which I have edited slightly, he states as follows:

More fitting (than another word) is a word that is recorded twice in the Targum (Aramaic translation to the Minor Prophets). For "and she covered him with a blanket" (Heb. śemīkā), the Targum has *gunkha*. In *2 Kings* 8, 15 "and he took a *makhber* and dipped it in water and spread it over his face and he died," the Targum has *gunkha*. The meaning of *makhber* is not known but it may be a net, a blanket, etc. Now J. Levy, *Chaldäisches Wörterbuch über die Targumim* (Leipzig 1867) 149 compared Latin *gaunaca, gaunaces*. The word appears in Syriac. C. Brockelmann, *Lexicon Syriacum* (Halle[2] 1928), 109 records two occurrences, but does not translate, but compares Greek *gaunakes*. There is a Late Babylonian word *gunaku*, a cloth or a garment, which is compared by the lexica with Greek *kaunakes* and Aramaic *gunkha* (which for all one knows should be vocalized *gunakka*). I should add that *gunkha* is taken by Rav Hai Gaon (939-1038) to be a robe or a blanket made of wool, with tufts and fringes and rather thick.

With this statement in hand, the resolution to the meaning and source of γονάχιον becomes crystal clear. Derived from the Semitic,[3] it is an orthographic variant of Greek γαυνάκη(c) or καυνάκηc. Citations and related compounds of these words are well supported in Preisigke and in Greek and Latin dictionaries as early as the third century B.C. The editor of *P. Cair. Masp.* 67288.5 adds that the word καυνάκηc is frequently found in the Coptic papyri (Crum, *Copt. Dict.* 824a *s.v. cωναc*).

There remains the question of a connection between γονάχιον and τονάχιον. For this we turn to *BGU* II 366 (arab), a guarantee regarding the delivery (lines 12-14) "... for the account of the Saracens one τονάχιον and three cτρώματα according to Saracen specifications." Because of the heavy penalty (3 *solidi* for each cτρωμα and 6 for the τονάχιον) in the event of failure to deliver on the due date, I originally believed (*ZPE* forthcoming) that the cτρώματα (mattresses or bed rolls) might have been something like "saddle blankets" and that τονάχιον had a connection with an Arab mount. However, in light of the clarification in the meaning of γανάχιον, and the close association of cτρώμα with τονάχιον, the word τονάχιον is clearly a misspelling (if not a misreading) of γονάχιον, and like the latter means a cloak or a wrap that can either serve as an article of clothing or as a blanket.

New York University   Philip Mayerson

γονάχιον is heavier and thicker (*v. infra*) than a παλλίον. As for their function, both items can serve as a garment, a blanket, or a cover.

[3] Since Aramaic was one of the two official languages of the Achaemenid empire, there is no need for the widely accepted derivation from Iranian **gauna-ka*; see B. Hemmerdinger, *Glotta* 48 (1970) 50f.

The Use of the Term *Phylarchos* in the Roman-Byzantine East

During the past several decades, interest has focused on the role of the Arab nomad, generally known as Saracens, within the political and military structure of the provinces of the Byzantine East. Roman authorities, as is well known, enrolled Arab tribes as *foederati* to keep peace along the broad frontiers of the eastern provinces and to serve as an auxiliary fighting force in Rome's wars against the Persians and Goths. Some scholars have perceived a change from the fourth century on in the way in which Rome organized these relationships by giving one tribal chief authority over other tribes; that is, giving him control over other tribal chiefs. For the designated chief Roman authorities used the term "phylarch" (φύλαρ-χος) as an official administrative title, a title derived from Greek historical antecedents.

M. Sartre found the first indication of this process in Cyril of Scythopolis' account of the Persian phylarch Aspebetos who, unhappy over the Persian treatment of Christians, defected with his tribe (c. 420) to the Romans. Anatolius, then *magister militum* of the East, received the tribe, enrolled its members as *foederati*, and conferred upon Aspebetos the position of phylarch (φυλαρχία) in Arabia. Sartre remarks that Aspebetos became "le chef de *tous* les Arab nomades" in the Roman province of Arabia, and "pour la première fois, un phylarque arab étend son authorité sur d'autres tribus que la sienne propre grâce à Rome; pour la première fois, la φυλαρχία est un titre administratif romain, répondant à une charge précise et confiée par Rome dans le cadre d'une province romaine. C'est une étape intéressant car elle marque un pas de plus vers l'integration des tribus nomades dans l'organization militaire et administrative de l'Empire. De simple alliés admis en territoire romain, les nomades devienne, au temps d'Aspébet, l'une des composantes de l'administration romaine en Arabie." Sartre was aware of the ambiguity in the term phylarch since it was used to denote a tribal chief not only of Saracens but of other tribal organizations; but, "il est des cas où ce titre, reconnu par Rome, acquiert un valeur officielle et le phylarchat devient un titre romain."[1]

I. Shahid pursued this same theme in several of his studies on the relationships of the Arabs to Byzantium. In his view, the word *phylarchos* became, towards the end of the fourth century, the standard term designating the Arab tribal chief allied to Rome.[2] The transliteration of the Greek word into Latin *phylarchus* "reserved the use of the term to the Arab chief and

---

[1] M. Sartre, *Trois études sur l'Arabie romaine et byzantine* (Brussels 1982), 150 and 152. See also Theodoretus of Cyprus, *H.R.* 26.15 edited by P. Canivet and A. Leroy-Molingen in *Sources Chrét.* CCLVII,II (1979), 193. With the appearance of the word phylarch, the editors note: "Titre donné aux chefs de tribus arabes fédèrées (Saracènes) avec mission d'assurer la garde du *limes* correspondant au titre de *dux*. In *R.E.* Suppl. XI (1968) F. Geschnitzer has presented an almost exhaustive survey of the appearance of the word *phylarchos* in a variety of historical sources. He does not, however, enter into a discussion of the term as an official administrative title.

[2] *Rome and the Arabs: A Prolegomenon to the Study of Byzantium and the Arabs* (Dumbarton Oaks 1984), 31.

this contributed to the emergence of the phylarchate as a distinctive military office."³ Shahid was aware, as was Sartre, that there was some ambiguity in the use of the word in Greek sources and cites Sozomenus *H.E.* 6.38.14-16 where the term is used in the literal sense of a tribal chief but with the suggestion that he was also a *foederatus* of Rome.⁴

In a work dealing with the fifth century, Shahid is more explicit in stating that the term phylarch emerges clearly "as a technical term that designated the Arab chief who was a federate of Byzantium." He goes on to say that in the sixth century, "the phylarchate became an office in the Byzantine administrative system in the Orient, and when the title phylarch is used in texts that document Arab-Byzantine relations, it almost certainly means an Arab official in the services of Byzantium, a *foederatus*, not a tribal chief, a *sayyid* or *shaykh*. This is seen in the use of the term νέος in one of the Nessana papyri."⁵ To Shahid, Zokomos, rather than Aspebetos, became "a phylarch in the new sense of the term as an administrative title" (*ibid.* 44, n. 99). The significance of the two words νέῳ φυλάρχῳ in the undated fragment, *P. Ness.* 160.6 is, in Shahid's view, a reference not to a tribal chief (*shaykh*), but to a "Byzantine phylarch in the technical sense" (*ibid.* 144-145), i.e. to an Arab newly appointed by the Romans as a *foederatus*.

A further development took place in 530/1. Justinian, in an attempt to counteract the military successes of Mundhir, the Saracen ally of the Persians, decided to, in Procopius words, "put in command as many tribes as possible, Arethas, the son of Gabalas, who ruled over the Saracens of Arabia, and bestowed upon him the dignity of king" (*Bell.* 1.17.47). Shahid viewed this decision of Justinian as creating a hierarchy among Saracen tribal chiefs: "a unified organization comprising all his Phylarchs under the leadership of one Phylarch, consequently around the year 530 A.D. he (Arethas) was made Supreme Phylarch."⁶ In using the term Supreme Phylarch, Shahid was adopting Nöldeke's description of Arethas' new status as "Ober-Phylarch."⁷

The above outlines the position of Sartre and Shahid with respect to the development of the word *phylarchos* as an official administrative title. This writer takes a contrary position, namely that the word was not part of the official terminology of the Roman government, and that the word means, in dealing with Saracens, a tribal chieftain, a *sayyid* or a *shaykh* or a *malik* (king). I take this position despite the two statements of Procopius on the issue. In speaking of the successes of Mundhir, he mentions the inability of the Roman *duces* and any leader (ἡγούμενος) of the Saracens allied (ἐνσπόνδων) with the Romans, who are called "phylarchs" (φύλαρχοι) to cope with the Persian Saracens.⁸ On another occasion, after re-

³ *Byzantium and the Arabs in the Fourth Century* (Dumbarton Oaks 1984), 516.

⁴ *Ibid.*, n. 211. *Cf.* p. 298 for an unsupported inference that the deceased head of a tribal organization (*phylarchia*) deep in Sinai had been a *foederatus* of Rome.

⁵ *Byzantium and the Arabs in the Fifth Century* (Dumbarton Oaks 1989), 500-501.

⁶ *B.Z.* 50 (1957), 46, 56, 61, 63. See also *op. cit.* (above, n. 3) 20, 46.

⁷ *Die Ghassânischen Fürsten aus dem Haus Gafna's* (Berlin 1887), 12.

⁸ *Bell.* 1.17.46: "...neither any commander of the Roman troops, whom they call 'duces' nor any leader of the Saracens allied with Romans who are called 'phylarchs'..." The *ut appelant(ur)* formulas in this citation of Procopius has led P.H. Lammens to believe that Justinian "créa pour eux (the Ghassanids) la dignité de *phylarque.*" (La Mecque à la veille de l'hégire, ix, fasc. 3 [1924], 244). As A. and A. Cameron have demonstrated,

ceiving the Palm Groves as a present from Abocharabus, the ruler (ἄρχων), Justinian appointed him phylarch (φύλαρχον) over the Saracens in Palestine (*idem*, 1.19.10). The third and last reference in Procopius to the term phylarch comes in connection with a pagan Saracen tribe known as the Maddeni who were subject to the Homeritae. Justinian sought the latter as an ally in his war against the Persians and suggested that the fugitive Caïsus be appointed phylarch over the Maddeni since he was by birth of "phylarchic rank" (ὁ δὲ Καΐσος οὗτος γένος μὲν ἦν τοῦ φυλαρχικοῦ).[9] It is clear from this reference that Caïsus was a descendant of men who held the rank of phylarch, not as *foederati* of the Romans, but as *shaykhs* or kings of the Maddeni. An even more compelling statement on the issue of appointment is provided by Theophanes, who reports for the year 563 that Arethas, patricius and phylarch of the Saracens, went to Byzantium to inform the emperor which of his sons should hold his position in the tribal organization as phylarch (φυλαρχία) (*Chronogr.* [de Boor], 240).

As for the words νέῳ φυλάρχῳ in *P. Ness.* 160.6, the fragmentary condition of the document does not lend itself to be taken as evidence of a newly-appointed federate of Rome. Secondly, the editor of the document, who used the word "newly-appointed," upon which Shahid based his interpretation, mistakenly considered that the fragment related in some way to a liturgical official with the title of phylarch, a title used in Egypt that did not survive the third century.[10] At best, the Nessana document appears to have been part of a letter requisiting certain foodstuffs to be given "to the new phylarch" for an unknown purpose.

Phylarchs, insofar as they were Arab tribal chieftains, were not appointed by government officials, but acquired the title by right of succession. This was the case, among others, of Mauia who succeeded her husband at his death, of Terebon, the son of Aspebetos, of Mundhir, the son of Arethas, of Naaman, the son of Mundhir. The position of a phylarch as a *foederatus* was determined by a treaty or contract (ὑπόσπονδος), written or oral, in which the amount and kind of *annona* —in money (ῥόγα) or in kind (ῥουζικόν)—that he would receive from the government for his services and that of the tribe (or tribes) under his control. The treaty might also have included the right to raid enemy territory and to keep the booty acquired during his service as a *foederatus*. It is in this connection that the political administration considered the chieftain the ἄρχων of his tribe(s) φύλη. He was answerable to the government in consideration of the *annona* that was granted him; and when that was not forthcoming, the phylarch considered that he was no longer bound by the treaty.[11]

---

historians of the late empire have employed these formulas as a display of erudition in imitation of earlier writers (*Class. Quart.*14 [1964], 324-327).

Procopius was certainly not unfamiliar with the term "duces" as military officers, and with "phylarchs" as tribal leaders. The context of 1.17.46 deals with Saracen phylarchs who were allied with the Romans and not with phylarchs in general.

[9] *Idem*, 1.20.10. See also E. Honigman, *CSCO* 146, Subsidia 7, 136.

[10] *Excavations at Nessana* III, C.J. Kraemer, ed. (Princeton 1958), 323. The document is dated paleographically to VI/VII.

[11] *E.g.*, Naaman, the son of the Ghassanid Mundhir, rose up against the Emperor Tiberius and plundered Roman territory, not only for imprisoning his father, but also because Tiberius "cut off our food supplies (*annona*) so that we have no means of living" (John of Ephesus, *H.E.* III 42, *CSCO* 106, *Scriptores Syri* 55,

It is also doubtful whether the Roman government, on its own authority, could place tribes under the leadership of one phylarch without the willingness of the tribal leaders themselves. The statement of Procopius that Arethas was placed in command of *as many tribes as possible*, is an indication that Arethas had to negotiate his position with other tribal leaders who, for a variety of reasons, especially the consideration of material benefits, may or may not have agreed to serve under him. The idea that Arethas could exercise effective control over *all* Saracen tribes federated with Rome, is difficult to accept if one considers the geographical distribution of Arab tribes over the vast eastern frontier. From Justinian's point of view, his primary objective was to amass an army of Saracens large enough to neutralize the activities of Mundhir in the area of the Persian conflict. Equally difficult to accept is the view of Sartre that Aspebetos, a recent Persian ally, could receive the obeisance of *all* the Arab nomads in the Roman province of Arabia.

In the matter of usage, the term phylarch has a long history, from the Classical period on, during which time its meaning changed in accordance with the character of the group of persons under the leadership of an individual. In a general sense, a phylarch was the head of a group of families, or of a body of people united by ties of descent from a common ancestor, or of an official in charge of a tribal unit of operation including a political division. During late antiquity, the term had no precise specific meaning that would limit its use to a particular organized group of people, a fact that militated against it becoming an official title in the Roman hierarchy. A prime example can be found in Sozomenus whom Shahid cites as providing the first suggestion of the use of the term phylarch as an official administrative title. In *H.E.* 6.38.14 Sozomenus refers to Zokomos, the Saracen converted to Christianity, as a phylarch; but at the outset of his history (1.1.3), Sozomenus cites Judah, the son of the biblical patriarch, as a phylarch. Similarly, John Chrysostom uses the word phylarch in connection with biblical tribal leaders, but he also employs the word, in the usage of the Classical period, as a military officer.[12] Libanius, demonstrating his knowledge of the historical past, also uses the word for an officer of a cavalry unit.[13] For Epiphanius, the term phylarch is applied solely to the tribal leaders of the Hebrew Bible,[14] while Dio Cassius cites Sporaces as the phylarch of the city of Anthemousia in Mesopotamia.[15] Five hundred years later, Nicephorus calls Omar, the Umayyad Caliph, "phylarch of the Saracens" (*op. cit.* [n. 11], 24 and 26).

As for restricting the meaning of phylarch to Roman federates, the word is found in association with a variety of other ethnic tribal groups, including Saracen allies of Persia. Comes Marcellinus reports for the year 536 that Chabos and Hesidos, phylarchs serving under the Persian Saracen Mundhir, attempted to move into Roman territory with their tribes.[16]

---

132). For other examples of Romans reneging on their agreement, see Theophanes, *Chronographia* (de Boor), 336; Nicephorus, *Opusc. hist.* (de Boor), 23.

[12] *P.G.* 48, col. 922; *P.G.* 57, cols. 74 and 179; *P.G.* 61, col. 582.

[13] *Or.* 25, 58.3 (R. Foerster); *Decl.* 26, 16.10.

[14] *Haer.* (K. Holl) 25, 187.21; 37, 127.8; 37, 464.18.

[15] *Hist.* 68.21. For the city of Edessa, see J.B. Segal, *Edessa* (Oxford 1970) 17.

[16] *P.L.* 51, col. 943. See also Theophanes *Chronographia* (de Boor), 141, who notes for the year 497/8 that the Saracen allies ((ὑπόσπονδοι) of the Persians "were of the tribe (φυλῆς) of the phylarch Naaman."

The *Bibliotheca* of Photius provides a wide range of phylarchs who cannot be considered Roman *foederati*. Mundhir, the Persian Saracen is cited as a phylarch, as well as a phylarch(s) of Goths, of Blemmyes, of Burgundians, and of Slavs.[17]

The documents from Roman Egypt add yet another wrinkle to the way in which between 245/8 and 285/7 the term phylarch was used for liturgical officers of the city of Oxyrhynchos which was divided into φυλαί. In the year in which a φυλή provided the liturgical services, its officer was called ὁ τῆς πόλεως φυλάρχος (sc. of the city of Oxyrhynchos; *P. Harr.* 64.4-11).[18]

Some years later (c. 500), several documents from Nubia dealing with Blemmyes and Noubades attach quite a different meaning to the term. According to T.C. Skeat, local tribal leaders appear to have been called "Kings" (*Basileis*), who owed allegiance nominally to the Chief King (*Basiliskos*). The sons of these tribal rulers were called phylarchs and *hypotyranni* (princes and princelings).[19] In sum, the use of the term phylarch in Greek historical literature shows considerable variation in meaning and in application which, if used as an official administrative title, could only lead to misinterpretation and confusion. Viewed in another way, the word φύλαρχος is no more a Roman-Byzantine administrative term than ἄρχων is or ἡγούμενος.

There is an even more compelling argument, an argument *ex siletio* to be sure. If, as Nöldeke and Shahid believe, Greek terms of such Roman ranks as *illustris, spectabilis, clarissimus,* and *gloriosissimus* were translated into Syriac,[20] there should be the reasonable expectation that the term *phylarchos* would also be translated if it were an official title. It is not found. Writers in Syriac—for example, Zacharias Rhetor, John of Ephesus, Joshua Stylites—who record the conflict between Rome and Persia and their Saracen allies in Mesopotamis, do not employ any term suggesting a translation of Greek *phylarchos*. Tribal leaders of the Tayyaye (Saracens) were generally called *riše* or *rišane*, simply meaning "head(s)," the Syriac equivalent of ἄρχων and ἡγούμενος. The other designation in Syriac for a tribal leader is *malkā'* "King." Perhaps the best example of the proper use of both "King" and "phylarch" is to be found in Ammianus Marcellinus (24.2.4) when he refers to the Saracen Podosarces as the "Malechus Podosarces tribal chieftain of the Assanitic Saracens" (... *malechus Podosarcis nomine*, phylarchus Saracenorum Assanitarum).[21]

New York University   Philip Mayerson

---

[17] R. Henry, ed. (Paris 1959), I, 4, 30; 167, 42; 179, 2; 181, 39; 182, 10-11; 172, 30; 9, 11-12.

[18] Before 245/8 the officer was called amphodogrammateus, after 285/7 systates. The phylarch was also involved in the administration of the dole. For this office see A. Moscadi in his introduction to *P. Oxy.* 3137; D. Hagedorn introd. to *P. Köln* II 87; J.R. Rea, introd. to *P. Oxy.* vol. 40, pp. 6-8; N. Lewis, *The Compulsary Public Services of Roman Egypt*, Pap. Flor. XI, Firenze 1982, 52 *s.v.* φυλάρχης; and P. Mertens, *Les services de l'état civil*, Acad. Royale de Belgique, Mem. 53.2, Bruxelles 1958, 16-30.

[19] *JEA* 63 (1977) 164. See also J. Rea, *ZPE* 34 (1979) 147-162.

[20] *Op. cit.* (n. 7) 13-16; *BZ* 52 (1959) 334-337.

[21] Lately R. Paret's note on a passage of Malalas concerning Arab phylarchs (*Islamica* 5 [1958] 251-262) which, among other issues, shares the main point of this paper has come to this writer's attention.

The Gaza 'Wine' Jar (*Gazition*)
and the 'Lost' Ashkelon Jar (*Askalônion*)

PHILIP MAYERSON

New York University

IT IS well known — perhaps too well known — that the wines of Gaza had earned an international reputation during the Byzantine period, particularly during the fifth and sixth centuries C.E. when pilgrimage to the Holy Land reached its peak. This writer undertook some years ago to provide the social, economic and archaeological evidence that went into making the name of Gaza synonymous with its wine.[1] A significant number of factors entered into the process that attached the name of Gaza to a vintage, the grapes of which were mostly grown far in the hinterland and crushed by large complex presses in proximity to the vineyards. That Gaza did not produce all the wine known as 'Gaza wine' is not unusual. A modern analogy might be appropriate: not all Jaffa oranges are grown in Jaffa — the oranges earned their reputation from the merchants, and, particularly, from the port from which they were shipped. The same process undoubtedly applies to the wine shipped from the port of Gaza (i.e. Maioumas) to western Europe, where Latin poets and writers gave it a good 'press'. The reputation of Gaza wine is also aided by economic historians and others, this writer included, who often cite these literary sources in support of related positions.[2] It is but a short step from the literary evidence to the archaeological, and there's the rub.

Archaeologists excavating Byzantine strata at sites such as Caesarea, Deir al-Balaḥ and Ashkelon on the Mediterranean coast have uncovered large numbers of storage-jar sherds, which they, or their ceramists, have dubbed 'Gaza wine jars' or 'Gaza storage-jars'. The association of the name 'Gaza' with the jar has largely been influenced by the accolades given 'Gaza wine' by European writers of the fifth and sixth centuries. Riley, examining storage-jars from Caesarea, states: 'There are strong grounds for a hypothesis that Caesarea's type 2 is from the Gaza region and is either the container or the forerunner of the container for Gaza wine. The arguments are as follows: First, the type is found throughout the Mediterranean and as far north as Britain in the fourth, fifth and possibly sixth centuries. Second, fifth and sixth century authors writing in the western Mediterranean praise the wine from Gaza. Third, the archaeological evidence points to the Gaza region as its area

1 P. Mayerson: The Wines and Vineyards of Gaza in the Byzantine Period, *BASOR* 257 (1986), pp. 75–80.
2 F.M. Heichelheim: Roman Syria, in *Economic Survey of Ancient Rome,* IV, Baltimore, 1938, p. 139, n. 124; J.A. Riley: The Pottery From the First Session of Excavation in the Caesarea Hippodrome, *BASOR* 218 (1975), p. 30, n. 20; Mayerson (above, n. 1).

of greatest concentration.'[3] Riley further notes that the pottery had their interiors smeared with pitch, suggesting that they were used for the storage and transportation of wine.

During the excavation of the Late Bronze Age settlement at Deir al-Balaḥ, a considerable amount of Byzantine sherds were discovered in the fill of the wadi which cut through the Late Bronze strata and in the topsoil loci. An analysis of the most numerous ceramic material was undertaken by Ann Killebrew, who concluded, citing Riley and the literary evidence, that the material was the so-called 'Gaza' amphora or storage-jar. More importantly, however, she states: 'Though only fragments of this storage-jar type were recovered, this group can be subdivided into two types based on the general shape of the vessel, rims, and bases' (Fig. 1).[4]

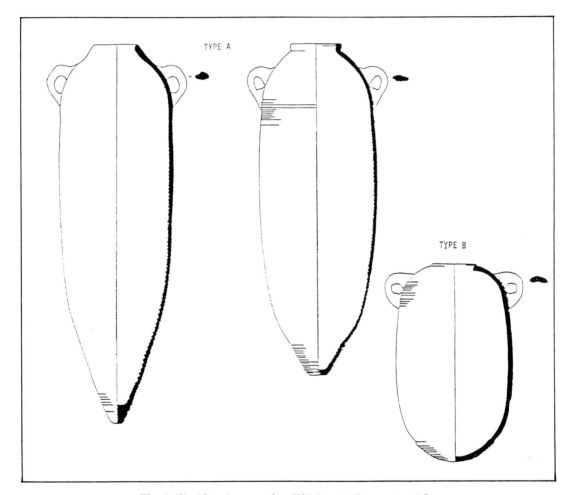

Fig. 1. The 'Gaza' storage-jar, Killebrew's Types A and B.

---

3 Riley (above, n. 2), p. 30.
4 Ann Killebrew's study will appear as part of the publication of the excavation report of Deir al-Balaḥ in *Qedem* (in preparation). I wish to thank Prof. Trude Dothan, the director of the Deir al-Balaḥ expedition, for permission to use material from the forthcoming publication.

Stager, the director of the major excavation underway at Ashkelon, provides us with some preliminary observations on the storage-jar under discussion. Citing Riley's exemplars from Caesarea (Type 2), he reports: 'Our excavations at Ashkelon have now confirmed that these storage jars were used as transport amphorae for exporting local wines. Dr. Barbara Johnson, our staff ceramist and director of the Ashkelon Laboratory in Jerusalem, has studied literally hundreds of thousands of potsherds from the fourth to sixth centuries C.E. recovered from our excavations. A very high percentage of these sherds comes from so-called Gaza-type — perhaps now, we should add Ashkelon-type — wine jars.'[5] An illustration in the text identifies the storage-jar as a Gaza wine jar of Killebrew's Type B.[6]

The one major cipher lacking in the investigation — one so often overlooked — is the evidence from the published papyri and ostraca. These humble documents introduce us with conspicuous prominence, although without the publicity which European writers gave to Gaza wine, to another jar, the *askalônion* (ἀσκαλώνιον). To be sure, the documents mention the Gaza jar (γαζίτιον), but, as readers will note in the inventory below, the *askalônion* does not take second place to the *gazition*.[7]

Before detailing the documents from the papyri and ostraca, several other items, which may have escaped the notice of archaeologists and ceramists, require mention. Stephanus of Byzantium in his *Ethnika* calls attention not only to the pottery of Gaza (οἱ κέραμοι λέγεγεται Γαζίται), but also to that of Ashkelon ('Ασκαλωναῖα κεράμια).[8] A choice reference to the *askalônion* jar is made in Leontius Neopolitanus' *vita Joannis Eleemosynarii*. This seventh-century Greek writer records that St. John sent Modestus, the patriarch of Jerusalem, a large sum of money, various supplies and a thousand *askalônia* of wine (χίλια ἀσκαλώνια οἴνου) for the purpose of restoring a church destroyed by the Persians.[9] One final observation: both the *askalônia* and the *gazitia* held not only wine, but a wide variety of other products.[10] While it is true that as early as Herodotus (3.5.6) all empty wine jars were put to other uses, it is likely that not all storage-jars were manufactured for first use as wine containers. Smearing the inside of the jar with resin or pitch would protect any liquid product other than wine.

---

5 L.E. Stager: *Ashkelon Discovered: From Canaanites and Philistines to Romans and Moslems,* Washington, 1991, p. 52.

6 *Ibid.,* p. 53.

7 There is not a hint of the existence of an amphora with this name in D.P.S. Peacock and D.F. Williams: *Amphorae and the Roman Economy, an introductory guide,* London — New York, 1986, or in A. Zemer: *Storage Jars in Ancient Sea Trade,* Haifa, 1978.

8 Stephan von Byzanz, *Ethnika,* A. Meineke (ed.), Graz, 1958 (Berlin, 1849), p. 132, 1. 10; p. 194, 1. 9.

9 H. Gelzer (ed.): *Leontios von Neapolis, Leben des heiligen Iohannes des barmherzigen Erzbischofs von Alexandrien,* in *Sammlung ausgewählter kirchen- und dogmengeschichtlicher Quellenschriften* 5, Freiburg i. B. — Leipzig, 1893, p. 37, 1. 19.

10 The citations for *gazition* in H.G. Liddell and R.S. Scott *et al.* (eds.): *Greek–English Lexicon,* Oxford, 1966, p. 257, as a measure, and for *askalônion* in G.W.H. Lampe (ed.): *A Patristic Greek Lexicon,* Oxford, 1962, p. 243, as a measure for wine are misleading. They should be taken as storage-jars, amphorae, or containers for a variety of products.

The following is an inventory of *askalônia* and *gazitia* and their contents, from published papyri and ostraca.

ASKALÔNIA

30 *askalônia*	*P. Got.* 17.r.4
— *ask(alônia)*	v.7
1 *askalônion* of mixed sweetmeats	r.18–19
5 *askalônia* of sweetmeats	v.18–19
4 *askalônia* of wine	*P. Herm.* 23.3
1 *askalônion* of sweetmeats	.4
20 *askalônia* of wine	*P. Laur.* 4.184.5
3 *askalônia* of wine	*P. Oxy.* 16.1924.3
1 *askalônion*, empty	.9
1 *askalônion* of beans	*P. Oxy.* 56.3862.25
2 *askalônia* of fish	*P. Prag.* 1.92.2
1 *askalônion* of fish sauce	90.8
6 *askalone* of cheese	*O. Sarga** 196.2
16 *askalone* of cheese	198.2–3
12 *askalone* of cheese	203.1–2
56 *askalone* (jars)	275.4

* Coptic ostraca

GAZITIA

39 *gazitia* of wine	*P. Got.* 17.4.14
1 *gazition* of groats of rice-wheat (*zeia*)	.20
1 *gazition* of choice bread	.21
— *gaz(itia)*	17.v.8
— *gaz(itia)*	.10
39 *gazitia* of wine	.17
15 *gazitia* of sweetmeats	.18
9 new *gazitia* of wool (?)	*P. Iand.* 6.103.r.8
1 *gazition*	*P. Ness.* 3.85.1
2 *gazitia* of salted fish	.3
2 *gazitia* of cakes	.4
1 *gazition* of wheat meal	.7
7 *gazitia* of pickled fish	*P. Oxy.* 16.1924.2
1 *gazition*, empty	.10
1 *gazition* of pickled food (?)	*P. Vind. Worp.* 11.10
1 *gazition* of black (?) pistachios	.14
1 *gazition* of white (?) pistachios	.15
— *gazition*	.16
— *gazitia*	.17

Although the identification of the *askalônian* should properly be left to the archaeologist and the ceramist, I venture to suggest that Killebrew's Type B (Figs. 1, 2) is the 'lost' *askalônion* storage-jar, which is so prominently mentioned in the papyri and ostraca. Another important datum for this identification is found in the ninth-century Latin translation of Athanasius of Leontius' *vita Joannis Eleemosynarii*. Athanasius translates the Greek χίλια ἀσκαλώνια οἴνου into the Latin *mille vascula vini* — 'a thousand small jars of wine'.[11] Killebrew, who has surveyed all

Fig. 2. One of the 'lost' Ashkelon
storage-jars, found at Be'er Manoaḥ.

the known examples of Types A and B, has found that Type A averages 70–85 cm. in height, whereas the shorter and broader Type B has an average height of 40–55 cm. Type B is, therefore, slightly over half the size of Type A, which has been securely identified as the Gaza storage-jar (Fig. 3), and, compared with the Gaza amphora, might well be called a *vasculum*. Without straining the evidence further, I would also suggest that the illustration provided by Stager is an example not of a Gaza wine jar, but of a local product of Ashkelon, one of the 'lost' *askalônia*.[12] There are other considerations to be taken into account in the comparison of the two types, which must be left to the archaeologists and ceramic specialists.

Fig. 3. A Gaza storage-jar (Killebrew's Type A), found
at Ramat ha-Nadiv. Courtesy of Y. Hirschfeld.

---

11 J.P. Migne (ed.): *Patrologia Graeca*, Paris, 1857–1866, Vol. 93, col. 1631.6. We cannot be certain that the word *vasculum* maintained its diminutive force in the ninth century. It surely did not among the native speakers of Latin in the West, where the word could not even be used to describe the features of an amphora. It must, however, be borne in mind that Athanasius, a Greek, was seeking some word to describe to Latin readers a virtually unknown term. Hence, I believe that he chose *vasculum* (plucked from some classical dictionary?) to convey the meaning of 'a small amphora'.

12 Stager (above, n. 5), illustration, p. 53.

The Island of Iotabê in the Byzantine Sources: A Reprise

PHILIP MAYERSON

Department of Classics
New York University
New York, NY 10003

The recorded history of the island of Iotabê in the Red Sea spans a brief 60 years, during which time it changed hands at least four times. The island served, not to control shipping, but to tax merchandise coming from the region(s) known at that time as India, and then to transship it to Roman ports. Iotabê has persistently been identified with the island of Tiran even though archaeological investigation has ruled out that possibility. Identification of Iotabê with any island, ancient or modern, remains in doubt.

The history of an island with the name of Iotabê begins with a fragment from the work of a sophist and critic of the Emperor Leo, and ends only a little more than a half-century later with a eulogy to a military commander by another sophist.[1] What the name of the island was before and after those two writers is unknown, and equally problematic is its identification; but it is fairly certain that during its short history Iotabê changed hands at least four times.

The story of Iotabê opens with the diatribe of Malchus of Philadelphia against Emperor Leo and his mishandling of the activities of a wily Persian Saracen named Amorkesos. In 473 C.E. Amorkesos set out for Roman Arabia, took possession of the island of Iotabê, evicted the Roman tax collectors (δεκατηλόγοι), and by collecting taxes (τέλη) became wealthy (Blockley 1983: 2.404–6). That is the first known citation for an island called Iotabê and it records the fact that at one time it had Roman customs officers whom Malchus calls by the rare term (δεκατηλόγοι).[2] In order for Amorkesos to take possession of the island, marine transport would have been necessary for an amphibious assault. Regrettably, Malchus is silent on how Amorkesos, a Saracen, managed that feat.

The island is brought to our attention again by Theophanes (de Boor 1883: 141) who reports on the activities of Romanus, commander of forces (*dux*) in Palestine. During the reign of Anastasius (ca. 498), Romanus undertook a punitive expedition against Scenite (i.e., Saracen) sheiks, whose raids were causing serious damage in the province. Theophanes comments that the island of Iotabê in the Red Sea had at one time produced considerable tax revenue for the Roman emperor before its occupation by Scenites. After some intense fighting, Romanus liberated the island and turned it over "to Roman traders (πραγματευταῖς) to live there as an autonomous community, to export (ἐκπορεύεσθαι) cargoes (of merchandise) from India, and to produce regular revenues for the emperor" (de Boor 1883: 141:15–18). Theophanes, like Malchus, does not tell how a naval assault was mounted against the island.

It is significant that in Theophanes' account Iotabê once more became a Roman trading colony that taxed cargoes coming from India and then transshipped the merchandise to other ports. The traders lived as an independent community under its own laws (αὐτονόμως), a clear indication that the island during the reigns of Leo and Anastasius was beyond the bounds of Palaestina Tertia. Procopius, in his description of the island before it fell under Roman control, uses the same term (αὐτονόμοι) for the Jews "who lived there from old" (B.P. I.19.4). It is apparent that between Romanus' conquest and Justinian's reign Iotabê was in the hands of Jews, presumably traders. That there was a Jewish population on the island is also attested by an Aramaic inscription written in Nabataean script. Found in northeastern Sinai in association with

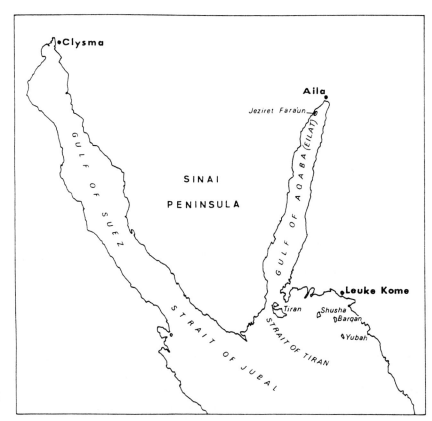

Fig. 1. North end of the Red Sea.

representations of Jewish ritual objects, the inscription reads, "Akrabos son of Samuel of Maqna, of son-of-Sadia of Iotabê" (Rothenberg and Aharoni 1961: 181; Vasiliev 1950: 371–72 presents the reason for the increased presence of Jews in the Hijaz and on Iotabê).

Procopius says nothing about Justinian's reason for taking the island, but it undoubtedly coincides with the action taken by Aratius, *dux* of Palestine (ca. 534), to recover Iotabê from "an unholy people." In his encomium to Aratius, Choricius (Foerster and Richtsteig 1929: 65–67) praises his deeds in punishing the "unholy ones" for setting fire to the church of the Mother of God, and for depriving the emperor of his income by appropriating the taxes on the merchandise brought to the island. After fierce fighting and victory, Aratius turned Iotabê over "to trusted men who were appointed to levy taxes for the emperor" (67:17–19). Of the island itself, Choricius says that "it served as a port for cargoes from India, the taxes on which were considerable" (65:22–23). Although Choricius has much to report on Aratius' strategy and success in laying siege to the formidable fortress that guarded the island from without, he, like Malchus and Theophanes, makes no mention of how

the *dux* mounted his amphibious assault and landed on the island. After the action taken by Aratius, we hear no more of Iotabê, except the name of its bishop, Anastasius.

In addition to traders, cargoes from India, customs officials, and taxes, Iotabê had a community of Christians even before Amorkesos arrived on the island in 473. The Council of Chalcedon in 451 cites "Marcianus, the most reverent bishop of Iotapê (= Iotabê)" along with three other bishops from Palaestina Tertia. In 536, shortly after Iotabê had been secured by Aratius, Anastasius, the bishop of Iotabê, attended the Synod of Jerusalem (Abel 1938: 533–34).

Taking all of the above into account, the question now arises as to the location of the island (fig. 1). Relying primarily on Procopius' description that the island lay not less than 1000 stadia (130 miles) from Aila (B.P. 1.19.3–4), most scholars, citing Abel's analysis of the question (1938: 510–38), designate Tiran as the site of ancient Iotabê. In 1956 and 1957, however, archaeologists landed on Tiran, and after having made a survey of the island, found no evidence of buildings, fort, harbor installations—nothing, not even of the most humble kind. Lacking a supply of water, Tiran also could not support a community of any size (Roth-enberg and Aharoni 1961: 162; see also Bourdon's communication in Abel 1938: 538). Tiran, lying at the entrance to the Gulf of Aqaba (Eilat) from the Red Sea, had other disadvantages. About 6–7 km from the Sinai peninsula and some 7 km from the Hijaz, the island is surrounded by reefs with only a narrow channel between them. In addition it is buffeted by persistent strong northerly winds blow-ing down the gulf, making navigation very difficult for sailing vessels,[3] not to speak of merchant ships or naval vessels attempting to make an amphibious landing. As for the details provided by Procopius, they are reasonably accurate for Tiran—and he may have had Tiran in mind—but that island does not suit the needs of a trading community that re-ceived and transshipped merchandise from the east.

There is yet another consideration. The point is often made that Iotabê controlled traffic into the Gulf of Aqaba or the Gulf of Suez. Sartre (1982: 116, nn. 4–5), for example, passes over the fact that Tiran contained no evidence of habitation, and relying on Procopius and Abel, states that the island "est le port d'attente avant de gagner Clysma (at the head of the Gulf of Suez) en même temps qu'elle permet de con-trôler tout le trafic à destination du fond golfe de ᶜAqaba." There is nothing in the sources, however, to suggest that Iotabê was a safe harbor for ships pro-ceeding to Clysma, or that it controlled traffic enter-ing the Gulf of Aqaba from the Red Sea.[4] Vasiliev (1950: 365, 367), also citing Abel, declares flatly that Iotabê "has been definitely identified with . . . Tiran," and that it controlled shipping to Clysma and Aila (at the head of the Gulf of Aqaba).

Aharoni, one of the archaeologists who investi-gated Tiran, seeing in the name Iotabê some remi-niscence of biblical Jotbathah and a wadi named Taba, suggested that the small island of Jazirat Faraᶜun, ten miles southwest of ancient Aila, was ancient Iotabê. However, the physical remains on that island are mostly Mamluk and Crusader; no clear case could be made for a Byzantine installa-tion that would correspond to Iotabê as described in the sources. In addition, the difficulties of sail-ing into the Gulf of Aqaba in the face of the strong northerly winds that predominate throughout the year make it unlikely that the small island, only about 190 m in length and half that in width, could have served as an autonomous trading community.

In the face of the evidence, Tiran must be ruled out as the site of ancient Iotabê, nor can any island in the Red Sea be confidently identified with the Roman trading colony without further archaeologi-cal investigation.[5] There remains the possibility that Iotabê is one of the islands formerly inhabited by Nabataeans who, according to Strabo (16.4.18) used small craft or rafts and "plundered vessels of people sailing from Egypt." The Aramaic inscrip-tion, indicating a Jewish presence on Iotabê and written in Nabataean script, appears to suggest that possibility. It can be said with more confidence that Iotabê was an entrepot that off-loaded cargoes coming from the east on large merchant vessels that could not, or did wish to, risk navigating the difficult waters of the two gulfs. Merchandise was then transshipped by means of smaller craft, such as coastal vessels and lighters, for transportation to ports in the Red Sea and the Gulfs of Aqaba and Suez. Those same vessels undoubtedly brought back merchandise to Iotabê to be loaded onto mer-chant ships returning to their home ports in the south and east. In the process of importing and ex-porting, customs duties were imposed by imperial officials, Saracens, or Jews.

It is further evidence that Rome used Iotabê to intercept the income that Ethiopian and other mid-dlemen derived from receiving, taxing, and trans-shipping foreign merchandise to Roman ports (see n. 4). Judging from the checkered political career of the island, it was not a very successful enter-prise. Since the island was "autonomous" and re-moved from imperial territory and influence, it lay exposed to alien forces eager to profit from the ac-tive trade entering the Red Sea.

NOTES

[1] If we take into account the names of two bishops "of Iotabê" who attended church councils in 451 and 536, the chronology of the island may be stretched to 85 years.

[2] The word that Malchus, a sophist, borrowed from Demosthenes (Or. 23.177) has no connection with the specific amount levied on cargoes coming into the port. The data bank of the Thesaurus Linguae Graecae cites only three writers who used the word: Demosthenes;

Harpocration, who provides a gloss on Demosthenes; and Basilius of Caesarea, a trained sophist like Malchus. During this period, customs duties on imports and ex-ports were charged at the rate of 12.5 percent—an eighth (octava) of the value of the merchandise received or shipped (see Jones 1986: 409, 1175).

[3] For the difficulty sailing vessels had navigating in the Gulf of Aqaba, see Wellstead 1832: II. chapters vii,

viii, ix. Besides the difficulty of the strong contrary winds, the gulf offers few good anchorages, and the exceptionally deep waters throughout its course, ranging from 250 to 750 fathoms, made it impossible for ancient vessels to drop anchor if caught offshore. The gulf is little more than a deep trough through which the predominating northerly winds are funnelled (See Schick 1958: 122–25).

[4]The assumption made by Sartre (1982: 117), based on inscription 9046 which mentions Clysma but not Iotabê, that " . . . le commercarius avait un droit de contrôle sur Iotabé" is not supported by any evidence. Equally so are similar assumptions made by Letsios (1989: 530). Although ancient writers from the fourth century on cite both Clysma and Aila as ports that receive ships and products from India, we do not know whether those writers are referring to cargo vessels that originated in the east or local craft transshipping merchandise off-loaded at other ports. The most detailed report of the harbor at Clysma is that of Peter the Deacon (ca. 1137), purportedly derived from the itinerary of Egeria (ca. 382) and generally accepted as such. Although it is atypical for Egeria to describe in detail a site having little to do with ecclesiastics, the church, and places mentioned in the Bible, the account, from whatever source, is informative on Clysma as a trading port. "It is a port for India, which is to say that it receives ships from India, for ships coming from India can come to no other port but this in Roman territory. And ships there are numerous and great, since the official (*agens in rebus*) known as the *logothete* has his residence there, the one who goes on an embassy each year to India by order of the Roman emperor, and his ships lie there" (Wilkinson 1971: 206; CSEL 39: 116). However, Bury (1923: 2.318) considers that the reference to India in that account meant Ethiopia and that, following the third century, products from India were transported by Ethiopian traders to their own markets at Adulis or even to the ports of Clysma and Aila. Cosmas Indicopleustes (ca. 530) says that Adulis is much frequented by traders who come from Alexandria and Aila (Winstedt 1909: 72). On that issue, Warmington (1974: 139–40) states that following the fourth century " . . . the so-called trade with the 'Indians' was in reality trade with the Ethiopians, and that even under Justinian in the sixth century Byzantine subjects visited not India so much as Arabia and the Auxumite realm (particularly Adulis), and the ignorance now shown about India was prodigious."

[5]For other attempts to identify the island, see *RE* 9, cols. 2000–2. On the latter point, see my article, "Asian India and African India in the Byzantine Sources: A Confusion of Ideas" (in press, *JAOS*).

BIBLIOGRAPHY

Abel, F. M.
    1938   L'Ile de Jotabé. *Revue Biblique* 47: 510–38.
Blockley, R. C.
    1983   *The Fragmentary Classicizing Historians of the Later Roman Empire.* Liverpool: Cairns.
de Boor, C.
    1883   *Theophanis Chronographia.* Leipzig; Teubner.
Bury, J. B.
    1923   *A History of the Later Roman Empire.* London: Macmillan.
CSEL
    1898   *Corpus Scriptorum Ecclesiasticorum Latinorum (Itinera Hierosolymitana Saeculi IIII–VIII),* 39. Leipzig.
Foerster, R., and Richtsteig, E., eds.
    1929   *Choricii Gazae Opera.* Leipzig: Teubner.
RE 9
    1893   *Paulys Realencyclopädie der classischen Altertumswissenschaft* 9. Stuttgart: Druckenmuller.
Jones, A. H. P.
    1986   *The Later Roman Empire: 284–602.* Baltimore: Johns Hopkins.
Letsios, D. G.
    1989   The Case of Amorkesos and the Question of the Roman Foederati in Arabia in the Vth Century. Pp. 525–38 in *L'Arabie Pré-*

islamique et son Environnement Historique et Culturel: Actes du Colloque de Strassbourg 24–27 juin 1987, ed. T. Fahd.
Rothenberg, B., and Aharoni, Y.
    1961   *God's Wilderness: Discoveries in Sinai.* Toronto: Nelson.
Sartre, M.
    1982   *Inscriptions grecques et latines de la Syria,* 13, fasc. 1. Paris: Geuthner.
Schick, A. P.
    1958   Tiran: The Straits, the Island, and its Terraces. *Israel Exploration Journal* 8: 120–30; 189–96.
Vasiliev, A. A.
    1950   *Justin the First.* Cambridge, MA: Harvard.
Warmington, E. H.
    1974   *The Commerce Between the Roman Empire and India.* 2nd ed. London: Curzon.
Wellstead, J. R.
    1832   *Travels in Arabia.* Reprinted 1978. Graz: Akademische Druck.
Wilkinson, J.
    1971   *Egeria's Travels.* London: Society for the Promotion of Christian Knowledge.
Windstedt, E. O.
    1909   *The Christian Topography of Cosmas Indicopleustes.* Cambridge: Cambridge University.

PHILIP MAYERSON

THE MEANING AND ETYMOLOGY OF THE WORD
μαν(ν)ούθιον

Cyril of Scythopolis (fl. 540), in celebrating the deeds and miracles of the monks of the Judean desert, has provided us with an unusual word in Greek: μαννούθιον or μανούθιον. G.W. Lampe's *Patristic Greek Lexicon* gives two citations from E. Schwartz's critical edition of *Kyrillus von Scythopolis* with the meaning of 'faggot.'[1] Two works published in the *Analecta Bollandiana* have produced seven other citations of the word: six in Anthony of Choziba's life of St. George of Choziba and one in his account of the miracles of the blessed virgin Mary of Choziba.[2] The editor of the *vita* cites yet another instance of the word in the *Acta Sanctorum* of 22 March from the pen of a certain Stephen, a Sabaite, who relates the martyrdom (ca. 797) of a number of monks of the monastery of Mar Saba at the hands of raiding Bedouins.[3]

What is noteworthy about the appearance of this word is that all citations come from the monasteries of the Judaean desert — Eythymius, Sabas, and Choziba — all of which are fairly close to one another. Cyril himself had spent part of his life at the monasteries of Euthymius and Sabas so that the word was a familiar part of his vocabulary.

The meaning of μαν(ν)ούθιον offers no difficulty since the context in which the word appears makes it quite clear that in the singular form it is a branch or a twig that the monks cut or gathered and stored within the monastery as kindling and firewood, most likely for the baking of bread. With one exception, in which a monk's leg is pricked by a μανούθιον that causes bleeding,[4] all are cited in the plural. The form is given as μαννουθία, or μανουθία in the manuscript tradition of Cyril, but is uniformly cited as μανουθία in the two accounts of Anthony the Sabaite and that of Stephen the Sabaite.

The following is an analysis of the contexts in which the word (M.) appears.

Gathering of M.	Cyril 72.19
	Cyril 103.30

---

1 Pp. 92.8; 130.30. Another citation appears on p. 72.19.
2 VII (1888), pp. 110.2; 111.4; 119.3; 121.19; 123.9, 14; 363.16.
3 Ibid., p. 110; *AS* III, p. 169.
4 *AB*, p. 111.4

Cutting of M.	Cyril 110.2
	Anthony 110.2
	Anthony 111.4
	Anthony 121.19
Carrying a load of M.	Anthony 363.16
	Cyril 92.8
Varia	Anthony 119.3 (went out to the M.)
	Anthony 123.9 (M. caught fire)
	Stephen 169 (M. set alight by Bedouins).

Stephen the Sabaite, the late writer of the Bedouin raid on the monastery of Mar Saba, felt it necessary to define the world *manuthia* and calls them 'bushes (θάμνους) which the fathers were accustomed to bring in and store away.'[5] However, to gain an even clearer picture of what the monks cut, gathered and stored, I sought the assistance of the Society for the Protection of Nature in Israel (SPNI). O. Cohen, the director of ROTEM, a joint project of SPNI and the Department of Botany of the Hebrew University, provided a list of a dozen or so plants that Bedouins used for kindling and firewood. The species most frequently found in the northern Judaean desert that is easily gathered and burns well is the White Broom (*Retama raetam*). Other well-known desert plants include Christ's Thorn (*Ziziphus spina-Christi*), White Wormwood (*Artemesia herba-alba*), and Wild Almond.[6]

Although the meaning of μαν(ν)ούθιον offered no difficulty in the past, its etymology presented a problem. The editor of the text appearing in the *Acta Sanctorum* sought but could find no satisfactory origin for the word. He states: *Etymon ab Hebraica lingua frustra peti apparet ex conjecturis loco citato allatis. Athanasius Kircherus noster monuit* Manuthi *Arabibus significare munitionem: quid si semi-barbaris Graecis Latinum* Minutiae *in* Manuthias *transierit? Vel a manu ducta sit in ea significatione, qua nos manipulos dicimus?*[7]

The lexicographer Du Cange, who gives the meaning of the word as '*frutex, seu potius fruticum fascis*' could only suggest a possible derivation from the Latin *manua* with a reference to the word in his *Glossarium.... latinitatis.*[8] E. Schwartz, the editor of *Kyrillus von Scythopolis*, makes no comment either on the meaning or the etymology of the word.

---

5   In the Latin translation provided in the *Acta Sanctorum* (p. 169): '...*virgultorum facibus, quos a Manuthis dicimus, collectos and repositos de more a patribus in unaquaque reperiunt, inflammandis domicilii opportunos...*'

6   The monastery of St. George or Choziba is perched high above Wadi Quelt, the only perennial stream in the region which provides an ample supply of moisture for shrubs along its banks. The monastery of Mar Saba is situated above Wadi Kidron, a major drainage system which likewise makes possible moisture for plant life along its banks. On the other hand, the monastery of Euthymius near Wadi Mukellik had far less vegetation in its neighborhood, leaving its monks to scour the hillsides and wadis far and wide for their supply of kindling and firewood.

7   P. 170.

8   *Glossarium ad scriptores media et infimae graecitatis*, cols. 873-874.

This writer detected in *-outh-* the Greek equivalent of the Semitic plural form *-ô ṭ-*. With the assistance of a knowledgeable Semitist, it became apparent that the Greek word is derived from a Semitic root with the basic meaning of 'part' or 'portion.' In biblical Hebrew it is found in a cultic or ritual context with the meaning of 'portions': in I Sam. 1:4 as *mânôṭ*, and in Neh. 12:44 and 12:47 as *menā'oṭ* and *menāôṭ*. The word is also found in Aramaic and in Syriac.[9] In the latter, its plural form of *měnoṭo*, and *menāyôt* are found with the meanings of 'parts,' 'portions,' 'fragments,' and 'relics.' Since there was a tradition at Choziba that the monastery was founded by Syrians,[10] it is likely that the word originated there and circulated among the other monasteries of the Judaean desert. Hence, with the addition of Greek endings in *-ion* and *-ia*, it acquired the meaning of 'part(s)' or 'piece(s)' with the ellipsis of 'bush(es).'

9   M. Sokaloff, *A Dictionary of Jewish Palestinian Aramaic* (1990), s.v. *mānāh*; M. Jastrow, *A Dictionary of Targumim* (repr. 1985), p. 797; R. Payne Smith, *A Compendious Syriac Dictionary* (repr. 1976), p. 283. I am indebted to Professor Baruch Levine for providing the above citations.

10 Anthony of Choziba, *AB*, p. 366.

Pl. 18. The Monastery of St. George (Choziba) in the Wadi Qelt.

Pl. 19. The Monastery of Mar Saba in the Wadi Kidron.

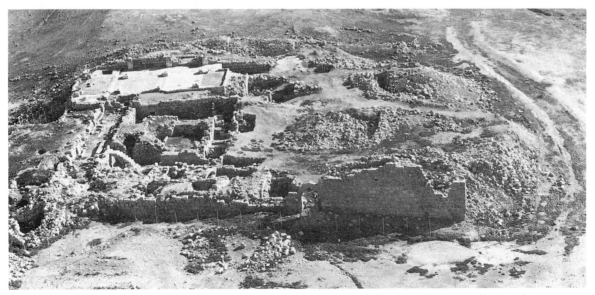

Pl. 20. The excavated Monastery of Euthymius (Khan el-Ahmar) in the plain of Adumim.

A CONFUSION OF INDIAS: ASIAN INDIA AND AFRICAN INDIA IN THE BYZANTINE SOURCES

PHILIP MAYERSON

NEW YORK UNIVERSITY

IT IS KNOWN, BUT UNFORTUNATELY not well known, that after the fourth century the perception of what region and what people were meant by the terms ’Ινδία and ’Ινδοί varied considerably in the Byzantine documents.[1] Was it subcontinental India, or Ethiopia/Axum, or was it south Arabia? There is no hint of the existence of more than one India in articles subsumed under that name in the *Oxford Classical Dictionary*, in the Greek lexica of Liddell and Scott and Lampe, and in the new *Oxford Dictionary of Byzantium*; and barely more than a hint in Pauly-Wissowa’s *Realencyclopädie*.[2] Historians, dealing with commerce between Rome and the East, however, are aware of several Indias. Warmington, speaking of the so-called trade with “Indians” following the fourth century, states that it “was in reality trade with the Ethiopians and even under Justinian in the sixth century Byzantine subjects visited not India so much as Arabia and Axumite realms (particularly Adulis) and the ignorance now shown about India was truly prodigious.”[3] As a general statement, Warmington is on the mark, but there remains a confusion in determining specifically what India is meant—Ethiopian, Arabian, or subcontinental India. Not all sources or all scholars agree. Take for example the article “India” in the new *Oxford Dictionary of Byzantium*, where it is stated that “according to Philostorgios, Constantine (*sic*) dispatched a certain Theophilos to India, where he found some Christian followers of the apostle Bartholomew.”[4] As will be shown below, Theophilus the Indian was sent by Constantius to perform his missionary work among the Homerites in Arabia Felix.

The perception of a geographical India in South Asia was preserved by several writers, notably by Ammianus Marcellinus (c. 330–395) and by Procopius of Caesarea (c. 500–post 565). Both writers, engaging in geographical digressions popular among classicizing historians, show a fairly sound knowledge of the location of subcontinental India: Ammianus especially in bk. 23, Procopius in *Wars* 1.19. Procopius, however, in *Buildings* 6.1.6 reverts to the conventional association of his age in connecting India with Ethiopia when he states that “the Nile River, flowing out of India into Egypt, divides that land into two parts as far as the sea” (Loeb trans.).

Subcontinental India receives more than a digression in *A Christian Topography*, the work of an anonymous Alexandrian merchant and aspiring theologian who, centuries later, was given the name of Cosmas and the soubriquet of Indicopleustes.[5] Although there is agreement that Cosmas knew the Red Sea trading region at first-hand, the present consensus is that he never visited India.[6] From whatever source Cosmas received his information, and to whatever extent his geography is interlarded with theological and cosmological speculation, the India he describes is a large region that includes

---

[1] Abbreviations for the standard editions used in this paper are as follows: *CSEL = Corpus Scriptorum Ecclesiasticorum Latinorum Saeculi IIII–VIII* (Leipzig, 1898). *GCS = Die griechischen christlichen Schriftsteller der ersten drei Jahrhunderte* (Leipzig, J. C. Hinrichs). *PG = Patrologia Graeca*, ed. J. P. Migne, (Paris, 1857–1904). *PL = Patrologia Latina*, ed. J. P. Migne (Paris, 1844–1904). *SC = Sources Chrétiennes* (Paris, Les Éditions du Cerf).

[2] *Paulys Realencylopädie der classischen Altertumswissenschaft*, 10:1268 (Stuttgart, 1916).

[3] E. H. Warmington, *The Commerce Between the Roman Empire and India*, 2nd ed. (London: Curzon, 1974), 139–40.

[4] (New York: Oxford Univ. Press), 2:992–93.

[5] *Cosmas Indicopleustès, Topographie Chrétienne*, ed. W. Wolska-Conus, *SC* 141 (1968): 15–16; 59–61.

[6] Idem, 17. Citations from this critical edition, 3 vols. (*SC* 141, 159, 197), are by the editor’s designation of book and paragraph. In opposition to the consensus, see H. Comes, “Did Cosmas Come to India?” *Indica* 3.1 (1966): 7–23.

India proper, Ceylon, and parts of China. He relates (2.30) that after having sailed several gulfs, he came to "Inner India (ἐπὶ ἐσωτέραν Ἰνδίαν)."[7] The phrase "Inner India" recurs several times in association with specific Far Eastern regions and products. The silk country, he states (2.45), is in "Inner(most) India (ἐν τῇ ἐσωτέρᾳ πάντων Ἰνδίᾳ)," it is called Tzinitza (= China), and is far beyond the island called by the Indians Serendiva and by the Greeks Taprobane (= Ceylon). Other citations of Inner India appear in connection with a church on Taprobane (3.65), "an island of Inner India where one finds the Indian Sea"; and with products from Barbaria (East Africa), which Cosmas says (2.49) are shipped by sea to Adulis, to the Homerites (south Arabia), to Inner India, and to Persia. Cosmas also knows of two well-known sites on the west coast of India (3.65): Male (Malabar) and Kalliana (Kalyan); and he considers (11.16) that Sindou is on "the frontier of India (ἀρχὴ τῆς Ἰνδικῆς)," where the river Indus forms the boundary between Persia and India.

As one goes back in time to the fourth century, the perception of India proper becomes dimmer and dimmer. An account, attributed to Palladius (c. 360–c. 430), of the voyage of an anonymous Theban *scholasticus* to India, dated variously between 360 and 500,

has had a long and complex textual history, since appended to it was a version of Arrian's second-century work on India. In the form of a letter from the Theban, the account records a voyage from Axum and Adulis in eastern Africa with the intention of reaching Ceylon. Precisely where the Theban made landfall is uncertain, but it is generally agreed that he reached western or southern India, either Malabar or the Bay of Bengal.[8] Before setting out for Ceylon, he stopped at Axum where he found "a princeling of India residing there (βασιλίσκος μίκρος τῶν Ἰνδῶν)." Derrett, an editor of a critical text of Palladius, apparently believing that the writer used the word India uniformly to denote India proper, interprets the remark to mean that there was a small community of Indian exporters at Axum that was ruled over by a petty Indian princeling.[9] In this instance, it is far more likely that the writer was using the word Indian in the common usage of the time to mean an Axumite (i.e., Ethiopian) ruler.[10]

There remain two mid-fourth-century texts, one pagan and the other Christian, both probably derived from a common source, that preserve a trace of several Indias; they represent itineraries from the land of the Blessed Ones (?) and the Garden of Eden through the mundane world. The *Expositio mundi et gentium* and the *Itinerary from the Paradise of Eden to the Country of the Romans* (Ὀδοιπορία κ.τ.λ.) outline a journey from a pagan paradise, or its Christian equivalent, to known and unknown places in the physical world. Of interest for this paper is the mention in the *Expositio* of *India maior* and *India minor*: the former clearly India proper since it is said to be a source for silk; the latter, after mentioning Axum, is thought to be Nubia.[11] As for the *Itinerary*, which lacks the detail present in the *Expositio*, there are only place names and numbers of stages and months needed to travel from one place to another. Starting from the Garden of Eden, and proceeding through some of the biblical topography of Gen. 2.10–12, Great India (Ἰνδία ἡ μεγάλη) is reached in 219 stages and 21 months (or a total of 349 stages).

---

[7] The comparative and superlative of ἔνδον and εἴσω, and their Latin equivalents, were used rather frequently by writers in late antiquity to modify place-names and regions, such as deserts and frontiers (*limites*), to express a relationship of distance within the geographical locality. The translation of the comparative with the word 'inner' and like words in other languages offers some difficulty in interpretation since it is often taken to mean 'closer' or 'nearer' as if it were the opposite of 'outer'. (The use of the word 'inner' with *limes* has been the cause of considerable misunderstanding because it was taken in its common acceptation.) In a geographical context, these comparatives mean 'further out', 'far removed', 'more remote'. Only rarely does one find 'outer', the opposite of 'inner' with the meaning of 'closer' or 'nearer'. (See P. Mayerson, "A Note on the Roman *Limes*: 'Inner' versus 'Outer'," *Israel Exploration Journal* 38 [1988]: 181–83; "The Saracens and the *Limes*," *Bulletin of the American Schools of Oriental Research* 262 [1986]: 44–45.) With respect to Cosmas' Inner India, Wanda-Conus 1:30[1] has put to rest the views of McCrindle and Winstedt who have argued that Inner India represents Ethiopia and/or south Arabia. Bury, who also opts for Ethiopia or south Arabia, believes that 'Inner' might be an error for 'Outer' (*A History of the Later Roman Empire* [London: Macmillan, 1923], 2:320, n. 5). To add to the confusion, there will be other regions, as will be noted, that have been designated Inner or Innermost India: Ethiopia/Axum and south Arabia.

[8] J. Duncan M. Derrett, "The History of 'Palladius' on the Races of India and the Brahmans," *Classica and Mediaevalia* 21 (1960): 77; J. Desanges, "D'Axoum à l'Assam, aux portes de la Chine: Le Voyage du 'Scholasticus de Thebes' (entre 360 et 500 après J.-C.)," *Historia* 18 (1969): 635–39.

[9] Derrett, op. cit., 109, par. 4. Also, "The Theban Scholasticus and Malabar in c. 355–60," *JAOS* 82 (1962): 26.

[10] See also G. C. Hansen, "Alexander und die Brahmanen," *Klio* 43–45 (1965): 377–78.

[11] *Expositio totius mundi et gentium*, ed. J. Rougé, *SC* 124 (1966): 150–52.

One needs an additional 7 months (210 stages) to reach Axum and another 7 to arrive at Little India ('Ινδία ἡ μικρά).[12] Unlike the *Expositio*, there is no added information to assist in distinguishing which India is meant; hence, we can only surmise that Great India is India proper and that Little India is south Arabia.

If the above is a representative group of Byzantine written sources, it is clear that the perception of what and where subcontinental India was in late antiquity was at best ill informed and fragmentary, certainly not to be compared with Hellenistic and Roman material that culminated in the *Periplus of the Erythrean Sea* of the first century A.D. It simply appears that the region was generally lost to sight. There is barely an indication of an historical event, of the kind that Ammianus reports (22.7.13) when east came west, but none of west going east, save, perhaps, peripatetic Christian monks. However, the fact that the sources, Cosmas excepted, mention other Indias indicates some intention to alert the reader to the distinction between them. The two Indias that were popularly known at this time and that were touched by historical events were Ethiopia and south Arabia. That there were two is a further complication.

The triumph of Christianity in the years between Constantine and Theodosius stirred the missionary zeal of individuals to convert the non-believers beyond the borders of the Empire. A tradition had sprung up that the apostles of Jesus—Thomas, Matthew, and Bartholomew—had been dispatched to distant regions to bring the word of God to the heathens, and, as reported by the ecclesiastical historians, "India" was one of the regions designated for missionary endeavors. However, there was no agreement among the historians as to who was sent where and what India was meant, although Rufinus, Gelasius, and Socrates had in mind Ethiopia or some geographical location within the large generalized region known as Ethiopia, whereas to Philostorgius, India was south Arabia.

According to Rufinus (c. 345–410), Matthew had been assigned Ethiopia, and Bartholomew, "Nearer India (*citerior India*), that was adjacent to it (i.e., Ethiopia). In the middle between Nearer India and Parthia, but at a considerable distance deeper within (*longo interior tractu*) lies Further India (*ulterior India*)."[13] Rufinus goes on to report the romantic story of Frumentius, who as a youngster accompanied a philosopher on an anthropological mission into Further India, survived a number of ordeals, spread the Christian faith, and ultimately was ordained Bishop of India by Athanasius of Alexandria.

Socrates (c. 380–c. 450), who follows Rufinus in many of the details regarding the evangelization of Ethiopia, reports that Matthew had been assigned Ethiopia, and Bartholomew "to that part of India bordering on Ethiopia . . . ." However, it was only during the reign of Constantine that "Inner India ('Ινδῶν τῶν ἐνδοτέρω)" became Christianized. He explains his reason for using ἐνδοτέρω so as to designate the more remote or interior region of Ethiopia that had no contact with Christian civilization.[14] There follows the story of Frumentius' adventures and his missionary work.

Gelasius Cyzicus (fl. 475), who also tells the story of Frumentius, starts his versions with a different view of the work of the early apostles: "Though Matthew preached to the Parthians, and Thomas to the Indians of Great India, yet to the far-off Indians or Parthia and their neighboring nations, the doctrine of Christ was not well-known to them." He then proceeds with the familiar story of Frumentius' experiences in "Innermost India (ἐνδοτάτην 'Ινδίαν)."[15] Gelasius also gives an account of those who attended the Council of Nicaea in 325. He states that Alexander of Alexandria represented all those churches in Egypt, Libya, the Pentapolis, and their neighborhoods "up to the districts of India."[16]

Athanasius (c. 295–373), bishop of Alexandria, makes clear that the remote region penetrated by Frumentius in the late fourth century—the Further India of Rufinus, the Inner India of Socrates, and the Innermost India of Gelasius—was Axum, which according to the *Periplus* was an eight-day journey from the Ethiopian port of Adulis. In Athanasius' *Apol. ad Const.*, Frumentius is twice cited as bishop of Axum (τῆς Αὐξούμεως).[17]

There is still to be considered the Nearer India of Rufinus. Earlier, Eusebius (*H.E.* 5.9) had told of the philosopher Pantaenus (d. c. 211) who had followed in the footsteps of Bartholomew and was sent to the East, "as far as India"—a statement that Rufinus, in translating Eusebius, found necessary to localize by the addition of a comparative: i.e., *ad Indiam citeriorem*.[18] Similarly, the so-called Sophronius (post-sixth century), who translated the thumbnail sketch of Pantaenus by Jerome (*De vir. ill.* 36), in which he states that Pantaenus found disciples of Bartholomew in India,

---

[12] Ibid., 59, 350–52.

[13] *H.E.* 10.9 = *GCS* 1908: 971–72.

[14] *PG* 67, col. 125.

[15] *GCS* 1918: 148, lines 8–13, 24.

[16] Ibid., 105, 135.

[17] *PG* 25, cols. 632, 636.

[18] *H.E.* 10.2 = *GCS* 1903.

elaborates on the word India by stating that the apostle "preached to the Indians who are called Fortunate ('Ινδοῖς τοῖς καλουμένοις Εὐδαίμοσιν)";[19] that is, Arabia Felix. It is therefore more than likely that Rufinus' Nearer India and the India that Pantaenus was reputed to have visited was south Arabia.

These oblique references to an India in south Arabia are brought more sharply into focus in the work of the Arian historian Philostorgius (c. 368–430/40) who describes the mission of Theophilus "the Indian" following the initial labors of the apostle Bartholomew in "Innermost India." Theophilus, we are told, was born on the island of Divus and spent many years among the Romans, when, c. 356, Constantius placed him at the head of an embassy "to those Indians formerly called Sabaeans but now called Homerites . . . to a region called by the Greeks Arabia Magna and Arabia Felix." Theophilus performed a number of miracles among the people and converted the ruler who built churches at Tapharum (Zafar), Adane (Aden), and at the Persian trading site near the mouth of the Persian Sea.[20]

A century or so after these ecclesiastical historians, John Malalas (c. 491–578) presents us with some 36 citations of the word India and Indians. They come, as it were, as a kind of climax to the geographical haziness associated with these two words. One must keep in mind, however, Momigliano's cautionary remarks to the effect that Malalas may be uncritical, confused and childish, yet, "he preserves many otherwise unknown facts and is of special importance for his own time."[21] I pass over with little comment 12 of Malalas' citations in the early books of the Dindorf (Bonn) edition[22]: 3 having to do with ethnic descendants of Noah's son Shem (14:5.11.14); 6 concerning heroes such as Tithonus who brought Indian troops, and Memnon who is consistently called emperor of the Indians (126:10.14.16; 128:14.17.18; cf. *Od.* 4.88); and 2 citations concerning Alexander the Great's conquest of India and being captivated by a certain widow Kandake who ruled over "Inner India" and whom Alexander took to Ethiopia (194:14–17; 197:11; *Realencyclopädie*, X:1858).

Malalas has no more to say about India and Indians until the reign of Justinian and his own lifetime. The remaining citations, with several important exceptions, deal exclusively with the struggle between the Axumites and the Himyarites, a struggle between African India and Asian India. From Malalas' perspective, the two groups are quite separate—Axum and the inner kingdoms associated with it being Indian, whereas the Homerites (Himyarites), prior to their defeat, are not. However, when the Axumites defeat the Homerites, the two regions become one India.

Malalas reports that Andas, a pagan who was to become a Christian, ruled over the Axumite Indians at the beginning of Justinian's reign (429:14). He then describes the geographical and commercial relationship between Axum and south Arabia (433:6–11): "The king of the Axumites is further inland (ἐνδότερος) than the Homerites, but the king of the Homerites is near Egypt. Roman traders travel through the land of the Homerites to Axum and to the inner (ἐνδότερα) kingdoms of the Indians. There are several kingdoms of Ethiopians and Indians; three of the Indians and four of the Ethiopians, the latter being near the sea toward the eastern regions."[23]

Malalas goes on to report that Dimnas, king of the Homerites, murdered Roman traders who were Christian, claiming that they had mistreated and killed Jews of his realm. The Axumite king Andas, unhappy at the subsequent loss of trade, declared war against the Homerites, and swore that if he were victorious, he would become a Christian. As a result of his victory, he converted and asked Justinian to have all the lands of India (πᾶσαν τὴν Ἰνδικὴν χώραν) Christianized and come under Roman rule (434:10). Indian ambassadors selected a bishop and clergy and brought them back to the land of India (434:14, 18).

Malalas completes his version of the Axumite struggle against the Homerites with the introduction of Eleseboas, the well-known king who waged war in south Arabia against Dhu-Nuwas, and the attempts made by Justinian to enlist his aid against Persian commercial interests in the regions under Eleseboas' control. Eleseboas is cited as the Indian king who fought with the king of the Amerite (= Homerite) Indians (457:3–4), and having defeated him, made a member of his family king of the Amerite Indians so that the Amerite kingdom would be under his control (457:6–7). Justinian's envoy approached Indian terri-

---

[19] *PL* 23, cols 683–86; 76; see also *Texte u. Untersuchungen zur Geschichte der altchristlichen Literatur*, Band 14.1:7, 14.

[20] *H.E.* 2.6; 3.4 = *GCS* 1913: 18, 32–34.

[21] See article "Malalas" in the *Oxford Classical Dictionary*, 2nd ed., 241.

[22] *Ioannis Malalae Chronographia*, ed. L. Dindorf (Leipzig: Bonn, 1831), cited in the above text by page number and line.

[23] Why did Roman traders have to travel through south Arabia in order to reach Axum? Or is this a bit of Malalas' myopic geography? The statement of the seven kingdoms is interesting, leading one to speculate whether Adulis was one of the Ethiopian four.

tory (i.e., Axum) by way of the Nile and the Indian (Red) Sea (459:9–10), where he met with Eleseboas, whom Malalas consistently calls king of the Indians (457:13–14; 458:7, 16, 22). Justinian's envoy asks Eleseboas not to conduct business with the Persians but to carry on trade through the territory of the Amerite Indians which he had subjugated (458:14–16). The king declared war on the Persians and sent out Saracen Indians to attack Persian territory on behalf of the Persians (458:18–19). The episode concludes with Eleseboas sending Justinian a letter and gifts by means of an Indian ambassador (459:3).

The mention of "Saracen Indians"—a most unusual, if not unique, characterization of Saracens—is significant in light of the remaining citations of Malalas concerning India. In 528, a serious disagreement arose between the *dux* Diomedes and the Saracen phylarch Arethas who took fright and "went to the inner frontier to Indian territory (εἰς τὸ ἐνδότερον λίμιτον ἐπὶ τὰ Ἰνδικά)" (434:20–23). Learning of this, Alamundarus (al-Mundhir), the Persian Saracen, overtook Arethas, captured and killed him (434:22–23; 435:1). When Mundhir was pursued by a large Roman force intent upon avenging the murder of Arethas, he too "fled with his forces to India (εἰς τὰ Ἰνδικὰ μέρη)" (438:8–10).

At this point an observation has to be made as to the location of this "inner frontier" and of the region to which both Arethas and Mundhir fled. Since India, as Malalas perceives it, is clearly located in the land of the Himyarites or in the regions surrounding Axum, the inner frontier cannot be, as this writer once thought, to the east of where Arethas and Mundhir operated during their service to Rome and Persia. The inner frontier to which both Saracens fled for safety must be the land of the Himyarites, the homeland of Kindite Arethas and Lakhmid Mundhir, far removed from Roman territory and Roman military forces.[24]

With this in mind, we turn to Malalas' final citation on India, which is concerned with the violent confrontation between the Romans and the Samaritans. The Romans, having quelled the rebellion with the help of their Saracen phylarch, allowed the latter to take 20,000 young men and women as booty and sell them in the lands of the Persians and the Indians (447:11–12). Once more, the direction in which the Samaritan prisoners were taken was not to the east, but to the south, to the "India" of the Saracens, to the land of the Himyarites.[25]

There are yet other citations concerning India and Indians, which fall into two categories: those which give no clue as to the geographical location of the place or person mentioned, and those which refer to Indian trade. Theophanes, apart from his statements cribbed from Malalas, provides a number of the former type[26]: for the year A.M. 6042 (227:1), a legate of India comes to Constantinople with an elephant; for the year A.M. 6055 (237:21), some Indian men are involved in a plot to murder Justinian; and for the year A.M. 6123 (235:10), the King of India sends congratulatory presents of pearls and precious stones to Heraclius because of his victory over the Persians. It is most likely that all these references are to Ethiopians.

The citations dealing with the so-called Indian trade are more troublesome. Although writers from the fourth century onward cite Clysma and Aila as ports on the arms of the Red Sea which receive ships and products from India, we do not know whether they refer to cargo vessels originating in the east or are craft transshipping merchandise off-loaded at other ports, or if the merchandise originated in Ethiopia, south Arabia, or even Somalia. We do know, however, that the Romans attempted to establish a customs office on the island of Iotabe in the Red Sea, apparently to intercept the income that Ethiopian and other middlemen derived from receiving, taxing, and transshipping foreign merchandise to Roman ports. Theophanes reports (141:11–14) that when Iotabe was recovered from Saracen occupiers (c. 498), it once more became a Roman trading colony that taxed cargoes coming from India and then transshipped the merchandise to other ports. In c. 534, according to Choricius, the island had to be recovered once again and "it served as a port for cargoes from India, the taxes on which were considerable."[27]

---

[24] For Arethas the Kindite, see G. Olinder, *The Kings of Kinda* (Lund: Haken Ohlsson, 1927), 53. The homeland of the Kindites is said in some Arab traditions to be Himyar, and in others to be east Arabia.

[25] I. Shahid in his *Byzantium and the Arabs in the Fourth Century* (Dumbarton Oaks: Washington, D.C., 1984), 91, n. 94, ventures to suggest that in this context India "could be construed as Ethiopia." Why suggest this remote possibility when there were plentiful south Arabian markets in the lands which the Ghassanid Arabs knew so well?

[26] *Theophanis Chronographia*, ed. C. de Boor (Leipzig: Teubner, 1883), cited in the above text by page number and line.

[27] *Choricii Gazae Opera*, ed. R. Foerster and E. Richtsteig (Leipzig: Teubner, 1929), 65–76, par. 66–67, 75. See also my paper, "The Island of Iotabê in the Byzantine Sources: A Reprise," *Bulletin of the American Schools of Oriental Research* 287 (1992): 1–4.

Epiphanius (c. 315–403) also provides information on how Indian goods entered Roman territory during the mid-third century. In the course of describing how Mani (215–277), the founder of Manichaeism, acquired his wealth, he takes us back to the source of it; namely, a hellenized Saracen from Arabia named Scythianus who traded in goods that came from India. The ports of Aila and Clysma are mentioned, but it is the port of Berenice in upper Egypt leading to the Thebaid, to Alexandria, to all Egypt, and the Pelusium that provided Scythianus with the means to acquire great wealth.[28] If this Arab is an historical figure, he likely was engaged in shipping local and transshipping Indian merchandise to Egyptian Berenice from south Arabia.

As for the port of Clysma and its connection with India, the most detailed report is that of Peter the Deacon (c. 1137), purportedly derived from the itinerary of Egeria (c. 382) and generally accepted as a missing portion of her memoir. Although it is atypical for Egeria to describe in detail a site having little to do with ecclesiastics, the church, and places mentioned in the Bible, the account, from whatever source, is informative on Clysma as a port receiving ships from India. "It is a port for India," the account states, "which is to say that it receives ships from India, for ships coming from India can come to no other port but this in Roman territory. And ships there are numerous and great, since the official (*agens in rebus*) known as the *logothete* has his residence there, the one who goes on an embassy each year to India by order of the Roman Emperor, and his ships lie there."[29]

Vasiliev accepts this statement at face value, although he dates Egeria's account to the sixth century.[30] Bury, however, considers that the reference to India meant Ethiopia and that, following the third century, products from India were transported by Ethiopian traders to their own markets of Adulis and even to ports of Clysma and Aila.[31] Cosmas Indicopleustes (c. 530) says that Adulis was much frequented by traders who came from Alexandria and Ela (= Aila).[32]

In light of the evidence from the fourth century onward, it is extremely doubtful that trading vessels originating in India proper sailed directly to Clysma, that

Clysma was the sole port that could receive Indian products, or that a Roman agent made annual trips to India to conclude commercial negotiations. The likelihood is—if Egeria's or Peter the Deacon's information is reliable—that commercial intercourse between Clysma and other ports on Roman territory and "India" went no further than Ethiopia or south Arabia.

A later report on Clysma comes from the Piacenza pilgrim (c. 578), who is generally known as Antoninus or Pseudo-Antoninus. On his tour of biblical and cultic sites in the Holy Land, he traveled from Sinai to Egypt via Clysma. He first mentions a hearsay report concerning Aila, which he states receives ships coming from India with a variety of spices.[33] At Clysma, which he says is a small city "where ships also come from India" and that "there we were given large green nuts (*nuces plenas virides*) which people believe come from paradise."[34] Whether these exotic nuts come from India proper, which is sometimes viewed as paradise, there is no sure way of knowing, although it would be most unusual for a product of this kind to be exported along with those items that could tolerate heavy custom duties on their way to Roman hands.

To conclude, this paper has attempted to sort out a number of significant Byzantine notices on India and Indians prior to the Arab conquest of the Near East and to justify them solely from a geographical point of view. In doing so the historical setting in which these sources are placed becomes far more intelligible. It should also be noted that the "confusion of Indias" that exists in the Greek and Latin notices also appears in Hebrew, Aramaic, and Syriac. For example, Rabbi Yehudah Hinduah (= ὁ Ἰνδός), who is cited in the *Babylonian Talmud* (Kiddushim 22b), is regarded as having come from the land of the Ethiopians.[35] A further sorting out of this material in the several Semitic languages would surely help to sharpen the details of the geographical and the historical picture.

---

[28] *Panarion* 66.1:7–12 in *GCS* 1933: 16–17.

[29] *CSEL* 39.116. J. Wilkinson, *Egeria's Travels* (London: S.P.C.K., 1971), 206.

[30] A. A. Vasiliev, *Justin the First* (Cambridge: Harvard Univ. Press, 1950), 365–66.

[31] Wanda-Conus, *History*, 2:318.

[32] Ibid., 2:54.

---

[33] *CSEL* 39.185, par. 40.

[34] Ibid., 187, par. 41. On nuts from India or its equivalent, see Philostorgius (*PG* 65, col. 500 = *GCS* 1913: 42, lines 25–26) and the eleventh-century historian Cedrenus (*Georgius Cedrenus*, ed. I. Bekker [Bonn: Weber, 1833], 1:267, lines 22–24).

[35] M. Jastrow, *A Dictionary of the Targum, the Babli and Yerushalmi and Midrashic Literature* (reprint New York: Judaica Press, 1985), 348. See also "India," in *Encyclopaedia Judaica*, 8:1350. On the confusion in Syriac, see A. Mingana, "The Early Spread of Christianity," The *Bulletin of the John Rylands Library* 10 (1926): 443–47.

The Use of Ascalon Wine in the Medical Writers of the Fourth to the Seventh Centuries

PHILIP MAYERSON
New York University

IT IS regrettable that Late Antiquity had no encyclopedist, no Pliny the Elder, to report on the varieties and virtues of local and foreign vintages. As it was, Pliny himself had not a word to say about the wines of Palestine, although the name of Ascalon was well known to him, not so much as the famous city of antiquity, but as the name of a kind of onion (*caepa*), the *ascalonia*, which eventually became the English word 'scallion'.[1]

It was not until the middle of the fourth century C.E. that the name of Ascalon as a wine surfaced along with the highly publicized one of its sister city, Gaza. The *Expositio Totius Mundi et Gentium* informs us that Ascalon and Gaza were outstanding cities, bustling with commercial activity, and exporting a wine of excellent quality (*vinum optimum*) to all Syria and Egypt.[2] This is all we hear of Ascalon wine in the literary sources until some time in the post mid-sixth century. Gregory of Tours (*c.* 539–594), in his *History of the Franks*, written *c.* 575, claimed that the hills around the city of Dijon 'are covered with fruitful vines which yield a fine Falernian wine that the inhabitants scorn Scalonum (= *Ascalonum*) wine'.[3] A slightly earlier reference appears in the laudatory poem of Fl. Cresconius Corippus on the accession of Justin II, the *In laudem Iustini Augusti minoris*. Written at Constantinople in 566/567, Corippus provides a descriptive list of Palestinian wines served at the coronation banquet for the emperor and his wife: *dulcia Bacchi / munera, quae Sarepta ferax, quae Gaza crearat, / Ascalon et laetis dederat quae grata colonis...prisca Palaestini miscentur dona Lyaei, / alba colore nivis blandoque levissima gusto* ('...sweet gifts of Bacchus, which fruitful Sarepta and Gaza had created and which beloved Ascalon had given to her prosperous colonists... The ancient gifts of Palestinian Lyaeus were mingled in, white with the color of snow, exceedingly light and with an agreeable taste.').[4]

---

1 Pliny, *Nat. Hist.*, 19.101–105, 107. See also Athenaeus (*c.* 200 C.E.), *Deipnosophistae* 2.68. In 3.78 he mentions a fig called *ascalonia*.
2 J. Rougé (ed.) in *Sources chrétiennes*, No. 124, XXIX, p. 162.
3 B. Krusch and W. Levinson (eds.): Gregorii Episcopi Turonensis Libri Historiarum Libri X, *Monumenta Germaniae Historica*, Hanover, 1951, I.1, p. 121.
4 A. Cameron (ed.): *Flavius Cresconius Corippus, In Laudem Iustini Augusti minoris, Libri IV*, 6, p. 63 (= III:88–90, 98–90). The editor translates *ferax* as 'wild'. I believe that

These three scanty literary citations, sufficient to prove the popularity of Ascalon wine as an export product, are augmented by its appearance in the medical works of physicians of the fourth to the seventh centuries C.E. The use of Ascalon wine in medicine is first mentioned in Oribasius (*c.* 320 — *c.* 400), a Greek medical writer and personal physician to Emperor Julian. He gives a recipe for the preparation of chamomile, an herb prominent in many medical prescriptions. The recipe calls for 21 cups of Ascalon wine, seven cups of honey and 200 chamomile seeds. The seeds and the wine are to be boiled for 21 days and then filtered.[5]

Ascalon wine next appears in the Latin translation, dated securely to 447 C.E., of Greek medical selections attributed to Cassius Felix, an African born in Cirta. To relieve stomach distress, his prescription calls for a pulverized mixture of parsley seeds and fennel, parched cumin, and a bit of pepper added in winter. 'After that', he states, 'you will give (the patient) a quantity of one spoonful of it in a drink of Ascalon wine that is hot and mixed.'[6]

While Cassius Felix calls for swallowing a spoonful of herbs with a draft of Ascalon wine, Aetius of Amida in Mesopotamia (sixth century C.E.), who practiced medicine in Constantinople, records another use for the wine. His prescription, taken from a medical writer and physician known by the name of Basilius, calls for a mixture of a precise number of ounces of althaea, chamomile, clover, linseed, fenugreek and cardamom, to be immersed in five pints of Ascalon wine for three days and then boiled to the consistency of honey. The prescription adds other compounds (olive oil, butter, goosefat, stag marrow and white wax), ultimately producing a kind of salve.[7]

These three seemingly incidental citations of Ascalon wine in the medical literature of the fourth and fifth/sixth centuries are brought into much sharper focus in the work of Alexander of Tralles. Born in Asia Minor in 525, the son of a physician and a contemporary of the historian Agathias (*c.* 531 — *c.* 580), who speaks highly of him, Alexander had an extensive practice and a reputation as an eminent physician; he was in demand in Spain, Gaul and Italy. He died in Rome in 603. Although cited as the most modern of Byzantine physicians, he was given to prescribing amulets and charms for a variety of ailments, such as quartan fever and gout.[8] Alexander

---

she has mistaken the word for *ferox*. Further, to consider all Palestinian wines 'white' on the basis of Corippus' poetic statement is risky. A more reasonable treatment on the colour of wines may be found in A.D.F. Brown: Black Wine, *Classical Review* 12 (1962), pp. 192–195.

5 J. Raeder (ed.): Orobasii Collectionum medicorum reliquae, *Corpus Medicorum Graecorum*, VI.1.1, p. 152, No. 433.7.

6 V. Rose (ed.): *Cassii Felicis de Medicina*, Leipzig, 1879, p. 101, par. 42.

7 G. Kostomiris (ed.): 'Αετίου λόγος δωδέκατος (Iatricorum liber xii), Paris, 1892, p. 64.

8 A summary of some of these amulets and charms, as well as a general account of Alexander of Tralles, can be found in W. Smith (ed.): *Dictionary of Greek and Roman Biography*

used Ascalon wine in his prescriptions more than any other physician, and, with the exception of Sarepta wine, far more than any other wine. An inventory of the named wines in his published medical works shows that his pharmacopeia held some 20 different wines from Italy, the Aegaean islands, Asia Minor, Phoenicia and Palestine. Sarepta is mentioned seven times, Ascalon six times and Gaza only twice. Alexander used Ascalon wine in medical preparations to quench thirst; in lieu of the juice of an herb; in a mixture with an herb; to assist in swallowing a medicine; to encourage urination; and as a heating medium.

The following is a summary of the prescriptions of Alexander of Tralles, in which Ascalon wine was used:

1.   In the case of a quartan fever, in which the excess of black bile is the cause of the fever, and in those cases in which the stomach contains viscous juices, or in which there is a severe obstruction of the spleen, a variety of very salty dishes are recommended. 'Only after a while', the prescription concludes, 'when the patient can no longer endure the thirst, can one give him wine from Ascalon or Gaza which he can mix (with water) as much as he likes.'[9]

2.   In the preparation of a moist eye-salve, effective against eyes full of pus, dirty abscesses and protrusion of the eyes (*myokephalon*), Alexander recommends a combination of a chemical, an herb, a gum and honey. He then states: 'The medication is prepared with the juice of groundsel (*senecio vulgaris*); but I know that it is also prepared with Ascalon wine.'[10]

3.   To relieve colic, Alexander prescribes a medication composed of a mixture of herbs and honey, warmed up and given to the patient to drink in the bath. The medication is also helpful for kidney diseases that result from obstruction, stones, or thick juices. He then prescribes yet another mixture of herbs that he claims is effective, adding, 'another excellent medication is organum (majoram) when one gram is used in a mixture of Ascalon wine or another light wine ἤ ἄλλου λεπτοῦ οἴνου). This remedy has proven itself and has relieved many of great pain.'[11]

4.   Concerning diseases of the liver, Alexander refers to an excellent powder which he has often administered against an obstruction of the organ. It consists of two parts each of costus and hemp-agrimony and one part pepper, and it is given for three days with half a cup of Ascalon wine. These instructions are followed with other details, particularly with the kinds of food to be avoided.[12]

---

and Mythology, Boston, 1870, I, pp. 126–127. Of special interest is Alexander's use of Hebrew holy names, יהוה צבאות אדני אלהי, to effect the cure of gout and rheumatism. For the Greek text of the Hebrew holy names, see T. Puschmann (ed.): *Alexander von Tralles*, Vienna, 1879 (Amsterdam, 1963), II.2, p. 585; for other charms and amulets, see pp. 581, 583.

9   *Ibid.*, I.2, p. 417.
10   *Ibid.*, II.2, p. 53.
11   *Ibid.*, p. 353.
12   *Ibid.*, p. 393.

5.   In treating eye infections caused by cold juices and viscous fluids, wait until there is no sign of excessive fluid, and then 'give the patient a bath and one of the heating wines, such as the Isaurian, the Ascalon Mysian, Truan (?), and Gaza wines. If one wants to give spiced or absinthe wine, one will achieve an even greater effect.'[13]

6.   Alexander has a long treatise on diet and its effect upon the liver and on the causes of dropsy (edema). Some of his interesting statements regarding diet are as follows: 'Diet is the most important part of the treatment of most diseases, especially the most dangerous one, including dropsy...meat must be eaten in limited quantity and should not be fatty...roast meat can be eaten unsparingly, if the patient likes it...shellfish, such as lobsters, snails, or scallops should be eaten rarely and only as a delicacy.' Of course, modern medicine would not approve of most of the other recommendations called for in this diet. However, in speaking of what drink can be served for desert, Alexander says, 'One can recommend the wines of Tyre and Ascalon, especially if they are old and mature (?), because they encourage urination.'[14]

The last member of this quintet of Byzantine physicians and medical writers is Paulus, born on the island of Aegina sometime in the seventh century C.E. Greatly admired by Arab authorities, and oft cited and translated, he probably practiced medicine in the latter part of the seventh century. His extant work is organized in seven books, the last of which contains an account of the preparation of medicines culled from earlier medical writers. Unlike Alexander of Tralles, the pharmacopeia of Paulus held few named wines, some seven of them. He appears to have favoured Amminian wine, having mentioned it in 10 prescriptions. Sarepta and Gaza wines are not in his store of drugs. As for Ascalon wine, it is cited twice, once in the well-known prescription of Basilius, also mentioned by Aetius. Paulus, however, not only makes some minor changes in the recipe, but also says that Cilician wine can be used in place of Ascalon.[15] The other prescription, a spiced wine to help in passing kidney stones, calls for an assortment of herbs, some of which are quite uncommon, several pints of honey and six pints of Ascalon wine.[16]

In sum, the Byzantine medical writings are far more informative about Ascalon wine than the literary sources. Although Gaza wine was very popular at the time, it was mentioned by only one physician, Alexander of Tralles, and then only as a heating wine and to relieve thirst when mixed, most probably with water. What, then, did physicians, particularly Alexander, find so medically useful in Ascalon wine? What properties made it more useful than the celebrated wine from Gaza? One of Alexander's prescriptions provides the answer. In his alternative recipe

---

13   *Ibid.*, (Nachtrage), p. 172.
14   *Ibid.*, II.2, pp. 455, 457.
15   J.L. Heiberg (ed.): *Pauli Aeginetae Epitome Medicae Libri Septem* (= *Corpus Medicorum Graecorum* XXII), Leipzig, 1925, II, p. 376.
16   *Ibid.*, p. 309:22.

for colic, he calls for a mixture of one gram of organum (majoram) to be used with Ascalon wine 'or another light (*leptos*) wine' (see above, p. 171). The word *leptos* is the key: the wine is 'light', not harsh or an irritant. It is the kind of wine that, when taken with other ingredients or medicaments, or as a constituent part of them, 'sits well on the stomach'.

With this in mind, let us return to the poem of Corippus for further support. At the coronation banquet of Justin II, the poet praises three wines, two of which are Palestinian: Gaza and Ascalon. He then says, 'The ancient gifts of Palestinian Lyaeus were mingled in, white with the color of snow, exceedingly light, and with an agreeable taste' (...*blandoque levissima gusto*). It is these two qualities — 'exceedingly light/agreeable taste' — that would make a wine suitable for medical use, and the wine of Ascalon fits that description.

Does Gaza wine fit the same description, since Corippus has combined the two under the term 'Palestinian'? For an answer, we must turn again to Gregory of Tours. In his *Liber in gloria Confessorum*, he recounts the story of a woman who provided the church with an ample supply of Gaza wine on behalf of her deceased husband. The wine was to be used at the Eucharist in the *sacrarium* where he was buried. The subdeacon, however, appropriated the wine and substituted the strongest kind of vinegar in its place, whereupon the ghost of the deceased husband appeared before his wife to complain. She replied that it was the strongest (*potentissimum*) Gaza wine that she had offered the church for the repose of his soul.[17] In Gregory's *History of the Franks*, in a scene of deception and violence between Claudius, a murderer, and Eberulf, a high official, Claudius calls for stronger wine. Eberulf sends his servants 'one after another to get stronger (*potentiora*) wines, those of Laodicea and those of Gaza.'[18] Gaza wine, unquestionably, was not *leptos* like Ascalon wine; it was too strong, too harsh for general medical use.

A final note. Medical writers offer surprising information that many be correlated with non-medical evidence (e.g. literary sources and archaeological material). Their work should not be overlooked.

---

17 B. Krusch (ed.): Gregorii Episcopi Turonensis Miraculata et Opera Minora, *Monumenta Germaniae Historica*, Hanover, 1959, Vol. I.2, p. 336.
18 Krusch and Levinson (above, n. 3), p. 348.